Macmillan/McGraw-Hill READING

Contributors

The Princeton Review, Time Magazine, Accelerated Reader

The Princeton Review is not
affiliated with Princeton
University or ETS.

learning through listening

Students with print disabilities may be eligible to obtain an accessible audio version of the
pupil edition of this textbook. Please call Recording for the Blind & Dyslexic at 1-800-221-4792
for complete information.

Macmillan/McGraw-Hill

*A Division of The **McGraw·Hill** Companies*

Published by Macmillan/McGraw-Hill, a division of The McGraw-Hill Companies, Inc., Two Penn Plaza, NY, NY 10121

Printed in the United States of America

6, U.5
3 4 5 6 7 8 9 073/043 05 04 03 02

Macmillan/McGraw-Hill READING

Authors

James Flood

Jan E. Hasbrouck

James V. Hoffman

Diane Lapp

Donna Lubcker

Angela Shelf Medearis

Scott Paris

Steven Stahl

Josefina Villamil Tinajero

Karen D. Wood

Macmillan
McGraw-Hill

New York   Farmington

Computer Center

Working with Words Station

Managing the

Writing Station

Word Box

Reading and Listening Station

Classroom

Social Studies Station

Teacher Directed Small Group Instruction

Sample Management Plan

Group 1	Group 2	Group 3	Group 4
With Teacher	Reading or Writing Workstation	Working with Words Station	Cross-Curricular or Computer Station
Reading or Writing Workstation	**With Teacher**	Cross-Curricular or Computer Station	Working with Words Station
Working with Words Station	Cross-Curricular or Computer Station	**With Teacher**	Reading or Writing Workstation
Cross-Curricular or Computer Station	Working with Words Station	Reading or Writing Workstation	**With Teacher**

Creating

WORKSTATIONS

Establishing independent workstations and other independent activities is the key to helping you manage the classroom as you meet with small groups.

Reading

Set up a classroom library for independent reading. Add Leveled Books as read during small-group instruction. Add other titles, also grouped by reading level. See the Theme Bibliography on pages T80–T81 for suggestions. Include titles based on discussions of students' fiction and nonfiction preferences.

- Self-Selected Reading
- Paired Reading
- Student Anthology selection from the Listening Library

Computer

Students can access the Internet to complete the Research and Inquiry activities suggested throughout the unit. Look for Internet connections in the following Research and Inquiry projects:

- Find Out More project at the end of each selection
- Cooperative Theme Project: Disaster Relief
- Cross-Curricular Activities
- Bringing Groups Together project

Writing

Focus the unit's writing projects on story writing. Weekly writing assignments are found at the end of each selection. The unit writing process project, Writing a Story, can also be the focus of the Writing Station. Equip the Writing Station with the following materials:

- Samples of published stories
- Story Writing samples, available in the **Teacher's Writing Resource Handbook**, pages 26–27

Working with Words

inquisitive *edible* *reassure*

Selection Vocabulary
Have students choose four vocabulary words and list as many words with the same base word as they can. Then they should write sentences using each vocabulary word or a related word as a noun, verb, adjective, and adverb.

High-Frequency Words
Have partners take turns holding up word cards for these high-frequency words: *different, suppose, surprise, continue, problem, finger.* When a student holds up a card, the partner must give a synonym or antonym, and then the first student must say either synonym or antonym.

Cross-Curricular
STATIONS

Set up a Cross-Curricular Station to help extend selection concepts and ideas. Suggestions for Cross-Curricular activities can be found in the Teacher's Edition.

Science

- Radios, 460
- Telescopes, 494
- Precious Metal, 508

Social Studies

- Chinese Immigrants, 450
- Ancient Greece, 474
- Map Skills, 488
- Political Cartoons, 512

Math

- Games, 458
- Weight in Space, 492
- Gold Standard, 506

Additional Independent Activities

The following independent activities are offered as a means to practice and reinforce concepts and skills taught within the unit.

PUPIL EDITION: READER RESPONSE

Story Questions to monitor student comprehension of the selection. The questions are leveled progressing from literal to critical thinking.

Story Activities related to the selection. Four activities are always provided: one writing activity, two cross-curricular activities, and a research and inquiry activity in the Find Out More project. Students are encouraged to use the Internet for research.

LEVELED PRACTICE

Each week, Reteach, Practice, and Extend pages are offered to address the individual needs of students as they learn and review skills.

McGraw-Hill Reading

Theme Chart

MULTI-AGE Classroom

Using the same global themes at each grade level facilitates the use of materials in multi-age classrooms.

GRADE LEVEL	**Experience** Experiences can tell us about ourselves and our world.	**Connections** Making connections develops new understandings.
Kindergarten	**My World** We learn a lot from all the things we see and do at home and in school.	**All Kinds of Friends** When we work and play together, we learn more about ourselves.
Subtheme 1	At Home	Working Together
Subtheme 2	School Days	Playing Together
1	**Day by Day** Each day brings new experiences.	**Together Is Better** We like to share ideas and experiences with others.
2	**What's New?** With each day, we learn something new.	**Just Between Us** Family and friends help us see the world in new ways.
3	**Great Adventures** Life is made up of big and small experiences.	**Nature Links** Nature can give us new ideas.
4	**Reflections** Stories let us share the experiences of others.	**Something in Common** Sharing ideas can lead to meaningful cooperation.
5	**Time of My Life** We sometimes find memorable experiences in unexpected places.	**Building Bridges** Knowing what we have in common helps us appreciate our differences.
6	**Pathways** Reflecting on life's experiences can lead to new understandings.	**A Common Thread** A look beneath the surface may uncover hidden connections.

Themes: Kindergarten – Grade 6

Expression	Inquiry	Problem-Solving	Making Decisions
There are many styles and forms for expressing ourselves.	**By exploring and asking questions, we make discoveries.**	**Analyzing information can help us solve problems.**	**Using what we know helps us evaluate situations.**
Time to Shine We can use our ideas and our imagination to do many wonderful things.	**I Wonder** We can make discoveries about the wonders of nature in our own backyard.	**Let's Work It Out** Working as part of a team can help me find a way to solve problems.	**Choices** We can make many good choices and decisions every day.
Great Ideas	**In My Backyard**	**Try and Try Again**	**Good Choices**
Let's Pretend	**Wonders of Nature**	**Teamwork**	**Let's Decide**
Stories to Tell Each one of us has a different story to tell.	**Let's Find Out!** Looking for answers is an adventure.	**Think About It!** It takes time to solve problems.	**Many Paths** Each decision opens the door to a new path.
Express Yourself We share our ideas in many ways.	**Look Around** There are surprises all around us.	**Figure It Out** We can solve problems by working together.	**Starting Now** Unexpected events can lead to new decisions.
Be Creative! We can all express ourselves in creative, wonderful ways.	**Tell Me More** Looking and listening closely will help us find out the facts.	**Think It Through** Solutions come in many shapes and sizes.	**Turning Points** We make new judgments based on our experiences.
Our Voices We can each use our talents to communicate ideas.	**Just Curious** We can find answers in surprising places.	**Make a Plan** Often we have to think carefully about a problem in order to solve it.	**Sorting It Out** We make decisions that can lead to new ideas and discoveries.
Imagine That The way we express our thoughts and feelings can take different forms.	**Investigate!** We never know where the search for answers might lead us.	**Bright Ideas** Some problems require unusual approaches.	**Crossroads** Decisions cause changes that can enrich our lives.
With Flying Colors Creative people help us see the world from different perspectives.	**Seek and Discover** To make new discoveries, we must observe and explore.	**Brainstorms** We can meet any challenge with determination and ingenuity.	**All Things Considered** Encountering new places and people can help us make decisions.

Brainstorms

We can meet any challenge with determination and ingenuity.

CHILD OF THE OWL **446A**

from the novel by **Laurence Yep**
illustrated by **Winson Trang**

S K I L L S			
Comprehension	**Vocabulary**	**Study Skill**	**Phonics**
• **Review** Story Elements • **Review** Make Inferences	• **Introduce** Denotation and Connotation	• Graphic Aids	• **Review** Syllable Patterns

REALISTIC FICTION

BELLEROPHON AND THE FLYING HORSE **468A**

retold by **Pamela Oldfield**

S K I L L S			
Comprehension	**Vocabulary**	**Study Skill**	**Phonics**
• **Review** Sequence of Events • **Review** Make Inferences	• **Introduce** Context Clues	• Graphic Aids	• **Review** /f/, /k/, and /s/

GREEK MYTH

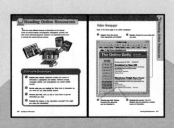

Unit Planner

Leveled Books

Easy: *A Tune for Lucy*
Independent: *Michael DeBakey: King of Hearts*
Challenge: *The Photographer*

Easy: *Hercules*
Independent: *Helen of Troy*
Challenge: *Greek Myths: Three Tales from Greek Mythology*

✓ Tested Skills

☑ **Comprehension**
Story Elements, 447A–447B, 467E–467F
Make Inferences, 467G–467H

☑ **Vocabulary**
Denotation and Connotation, 467I–467J

☑ **Study Skills**
Read a Family Tree, 466

☑ **Comprehension**
Sequence of Events, 469A–469B, 481E–481F
Make Inferences, 481G–481H

☑ **Vocabulary**
Context Clues, 481I–481J

☑ **Study Skills**
Read a Constellation Map, 480

Minilessons

Phonics and Decoding: Syllable Patterns, 451
Genre: Realistic Fiction, 449
Make Inferences, 453
Suffixes, 455
Summarize, 461

Phonics and Decoding: /f/, /k/, and /s/, 475
Genre: Myth, 471
Summarize, 473

Language Arts

Writing: Writing a Story, 467K
Grammar: Pronouns, 467M–467N
Spelling: Compound Words, 467O–467P

Writing: Writing a Story, 481K
Grammar: Subject and Object Pronouns, 481M–481N
Spelling: Homophones and Homographs, 481O–481P

Activities

Curriculum Connections

Read Aloud: "Anecdote for Fathers," 446E

Stories In Art: *Madre y Niña*, 446

Social Studies: Chinese Immigrants, 450

Math: Games, 458

Science: Radios, 460

Social Studies: Chinese Immigrants, 465

Read Aloud: "Daedalus and Icarus," 468E

Stories In Art: *Construction of a Chateau*, 468

Social Studies: Ancient Greece, 474

Art: Greek Architecture, 479

CULTURAL PERSPECTIVES

Chinese Traditions, 452

Creating Myths, 472

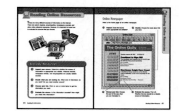

WEEK 3 Adventure In Space	**WEEK 4** Rumpelstiltskin's Daughter	**WEEK 5** The History of Money	**WEEK 6** Review, Writing, Reading Information, Assessment
Easy: *John Glenn: Space Pioneer* **Independent:** *Class Trip* **Challenge:** *City in Space: The International Space Station*	**Easy:** *Rosa Parks* **Independent:** *Eleanor Roosevelt* **Challenge:** *The Mystery of the Lost Satchel*	*Self-Selected Reading of Leveled Books*	*Self-Selected Reading*

☑ **Comprehension** Judgments and Decisions, 483A–483B, 501E–501F Sequence of Events, 501G–501H ☑ **Vocabulary** Context Clues, 501I–501J ☑ **Study Skills** Read a Flow Chart, 500	☑ **Comprehension** Story Elements, 503A–503B, 531E–531F Make Inferences, 531G–531H ☑ **Vocabulary** Denotation and Connotation, 531I–531J ☑ **Study Skills** Read a Circle Graph, 530	☑ **Comprehension** Sequence of Events, 533A–533B Judgments and Decisions, 541E–541F ☑ **Vocabulary** Context Clues, 541G–541H Denotation and Connotation, 541I–541J ☑ **Study Skills** Read a Chart, 540	☑ **Assess Skills** Story Elements Make Inferences Sequence of Events Judgments and Decisions Denotation and Connotation Context Clues Graphic Aids ☑ **Assess Grammar and Spelling** Pronouns, 543I Review Spelling Patterns, 543J ☑ **Unit Progress Assessment** ☑ **Standardized Test Preparation** Reading Online Resources , 543A
Phonics and Decoding: /îr/ and /ûr/, 491 **Genre: Informational Story,** 485 **Context Clues,** 487 **Summarize,** 493 **Make Inferences,** 495	**Phonics and Decoding:** ea words, 511 **Genre: Fairy Tale,** 505 **Summarize,** 513 **Make Inferences,** 515 **Setting,** 517 **Draw Conclusions,** 519	**Genre: Magazine Article,** 535	

Writing: Writing a Story, 501K **Grammar:** Possessive Pronouns, 501M–501N **Spelling:** Words with Suffixes, 501O–501P	**Writing:** Writing a Story, 531K **Grammar:** Indefinite Pronouns, 531M–531N **Spelling:** Words with Suffixes, 531O–531P	**Writing:** Writing a Story, 541K **Grammar:** Pronoun-Verb Agreement, 541M–541N **Spelling:** Words from Math, 541O–541P	**Unit Writing Process:** Writing a Story, 543C–543H

Read Aloud: "I Don't Want to Live on the Moon," 482E	**Read Aloud:** "The Winning of Kwelanga," 502E	**Read Aloud:** "The Story of Money," 532E	**Cooperative Theme Project Research and Inquiry:** Disaster Relief, 543
Stories In Art: *The Last Spike,* 482	**Stories In Art:** *Greasy Spoon Life,* 502	**Stories In Art:** *Otis Kaye Dollar Bill,* 432	
Social Studies: Map Skills, 488	**Math:** Gold Standard, 506	**Science:** Matter, 539	
Math: Weight in Space, 492	**Science:** Precious Metal, 508		
Science: Telescopes, 494	**Social Studies:** Political Cartoons, 512		
Math: Using Distance Formula, 499	**Art:** Fine Art, 516		
	Health: Wheat, 529		
Cosmonauts, 490	Fairy Tale Characters, 524		

Unit Resources

LITERATURE

LEVELED BOOKS

Easy
- *A Time for Lucy*
- *Hercules*
- *John Glenn: Space Pioneer*
- *Rosa Parks*

Independent
- *Michael DeBakey: King of Hearts*
- *Helen of Troy*
- *Class Trip*
- *Eleanor Roosevelt*

Challenge
- *The Photographer*
- *Greek Myths: Three Tales from Greek Mythology*
- *City in Space: The International Space Station*
- *The Mystery of the Lost Satchel*

 LISTENING LIBRARY
Recordings of the student book selections and poetry. Available on **audiocassette** or **compact disc.**

Macmillan/McGraw-Hill

Intervention

Easy Leveled Books

Skills Intervention Guide

Phonics Intervention Guide

SKILLS

LEVELED PRACTICE

Practice Book: Student practice for comprehension, vocabulary, and study skills plus practice for instructional vocabulary and story comprehension. Take-Home Story included for each lesson.

Reteach: Reteaching opportunities for students who need more help with assessed skills.

Extend: Extension activities for vocabulary, comprehension, story, and study skills.

TEACHING CHARTS
Instructional charts for modeling vocabulary and tested skills. Also available as **transparencies.**

WORD BUILDING MANIPULATIVE CARDS
Cards with words and structural elements for word building and practicing vocabulary.

LANGUAGE SUPPORT BOOK
ESL Parallel lessons and practice for students needing language support.

PHONICS/PHONEMIC AWARENESS PRACTICE BOOK Additional practice focusing on vowel sounds, phonograms, blends, digraphs, and key phonetic elements.

FLUENCY ASSESSMENT
Evaluation and practice for building reading fluency.

LANGUAGE ARTS

GRAMMAR PRACTICE BOOK
Provides practice for grammar and mechanics lessons.

SPELLING PRACTICE BOOK
Provides practice with the word list and spelling patterns. Includes home involvement activities.

DAILY LANGUAGE ACTIVITIES
Provide practice and reinforcement of grammar, mechanics, and usage skills. Available as **blackline masters** and **transparencies.**

WRITING PROCESS TRANSPARENCIES Model each stage of the writing process.

HANDWRITING HANDBOOKS
Available for instruction and practice.

McGraw-Hill School
TECHNOLOGY

interNET CONNECTION Extend lesson activities through research and inquiry ideas. Visit **www.mhschool.com/reading**

 Vocabulary PuzzleMaker provides practice with instructional vocabulary.

 Handwriting CD-ROM provides practice activities.

 MindJogger Videos Review grammar and writing skills.

Resources for
Meeting Individual Needs

	EASY	ON-LEVEL	CHALLENGE	LANGUAGE SUPPORT

UNIT 5

Child of the Owl

Leveled Book: *A Tune for Lucy*
Reteach, 149–155
Alternate Teaching Strategies, T62–T68
Writing: Description, 467L
Intervention

Leveled Book: *Michael DeBakey: King of Hearts*
Practice, 149–155
Alternate Teaching Strategies, T62–T68
Writing: Diary Entry, 467L

Leveled Book: *The Photographer*
Extend, 149–155
Writing: Prequel, 467L
Social Studies: Chinese Immigrants, 465

Teaching Strategies, 448A, 448C, 449, 455, 459, 467L
Language Support, 161–168
Alternate Teaching Strategies, T62–T68
Writing: Write a Story, 467K–467L

Bellerophon and the Flying Horse

Leveled Book: *Hercules*
Reteach, 156–162
Alternate Teaching Strategies, T62–T68
Writing: Mythological Rhymes, 481L
Intervention

Leveled Book: *Helen of Troy*
Practice, 156–162
Alternate Teaching Strategies, T62–T68
Writing: Letter to Bellerophon, 481L

Leveled Book: *Greek Myths: Three Tales from Greek Mythology*
Extend, 156–162
Writing: Athena's New Gift, 481L
Art: Greek Architecture, 479

Teaching Strategies, 470A, 470C, 471, 481I, 481L
Language Support, 169–176
Alternate Teaching Strategies, T62–T68
Writing: Write a Myth, 481K–481L

Adventure in Space

Leveled Book: *John Glenn: Space Pioneer*
Reteach, 163–169
Alternate Teaching Strategies, T62–T68
Writing: Picture Book, 501L
Intervention

Leveled Book: *Class Trip*
Practice, 163–169
Alternate Teaching Strategies, T62–T68
Writing: Documentary, 501L

Leveled Book: *City in Space: The International Space Station*
Extend, 163–169
Writing: Journal Entry, 501L
Math: Using Distance Formula, 499

Teaching Strategies, 484A, 484C, 485, 487, 491, 501E, 501L
Language Support, 177–184
Alternate Teaching Strategies, T62–T68
Writing: Write a Science Fiction Story, 501K–501L

Rumpelstiltskin's Daughter

Leveled Book: *Rosa Parks*
Reteach, 170–176
Alternate Teaching Strategies, T62–T68
Writing: Funny Poems, 531L
Intervention

Leveled Book: *Eleanor Roosevelt*
Practice, 170–176
Alternate Teaching Strategies, T62–T68
Writing: Fractured Rhymes, 531L

Leveled Book: *The Mystery of the Lost Satchel*
Extend, 170–176
Writing: Fractured History, 531L
Health: Wheat, 529

Teaching Strategies, 504A, 504C, 505, 511, 518, 525, 531I, 531L
Language Support, 185–192
Alternate Teaching Strategies, T62–T68
Writing: Write a Fractured Fairy Tale, 531K–531L

The History of Money

Review
Reteach, 177–183
Alternate Teaching Strategies, T62–T68
Writing: Time Line, 541L
Intervention

Review
Practice, 177–183
Alternate Teaching Strategies, T62–T68
Writing: Set the Scene, 541L

Review
Extend, 177–183
Writing: Letters, 541L
Science: Matter, 539

Teaching Strategies, 534A, 534C, 535, 541E, 541I, 541L
Language Support, 193–200
Alternate Teaching Strategies, T62–T68
Writing: Write a Dialogue, 541K–541L

INFORMAL

Informal Assessment

- Comprehension, 447B, 462, 463, 467F, 467H; 469B, 476, 477, 481F, 481H; 483B, 496, 497, 501F, 501H; 503B, 526, 527, 531F, 531H; 533B, 537, 541F
- Vocabulary, 467J, 481J, 501J, 531J, 541H, 541J

Performance Assessment

- Scoring Rubrics, 467L, 481L, 501L, 531L, 541L, 543H
- Research and Inquiry, 445J, 543
- Writing Process, 467K, 481K, 501K, 531K, 541K
- Listening, Speaking, Viewing, Representing Activities, 446E, 446, 448A, 448–465, 467D, 467L; 468E, 468, 470A, 470–479, 481D, 481L; 482E, 482, 484A, 484–499, 501D, 501L; 502E, 502, 504A, 504–529, 531D, 531L; 532E, 532, 534A, 534–539, 541D, 541L
- Portfolio, 467L, 481L, 501L, 531L, 541L

  Writing, 467K–L, 481K–L, 501K–L, 531K–L, 541K–L, 543C–H

  Cross Curricular Activities, 450, 458, 460; 465, 474; 479, 488, 492, 494; 499, 506, 508, 512, 516, 529, 539

- Fluency, 462, 476, 496, 526, 536

Leveled Practice

Practice, Reteach, Extend

- **Comprehension**
  Story Elements, 149, 153, 170, 174
  Make Inferences, 154, 161, 175
  Sequence of Events, 156, 160, 168, 177
  Judgments and Decisions, 163, 167, 181
- **Vocabulary Strategies**
  Denotation and Connotation, 155, 176
  Context Clues, 162, 169, 182
- **Study Skills**
  Graphic Aids, 152, 159, 166, 173, 180

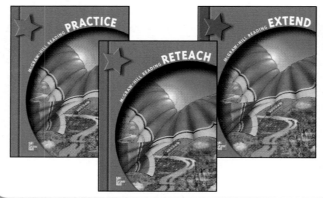

FORMAL

Selection Tests

- **Skills and Vocabulary Words**
  Child of the Owl, 41–42
  Bellerophon and the Flying Horse, 43–44
  Adventure in Space, 45–46
  Rumpelstiltskin's Daughter, 47–48
  The History of Money, 49–50

Unit 5 Assessment

- **Comprehension**
  Story Elements
  Make Inferences
  Sequence of Events
  Judgments and Decisions
- **Vocabulary Strategies**
  Denotation and Connotation
  Context Clues
- **Study Skills**
  Graphic Aids

Grammar and Spelling Assessment

- **Grammar**
  Pronouns, 159–160
- **Spelling**
  Unit 5 Assessment, 159–160

Fluency Assessment

- Fluency Passages, 70-71

Diagnostic/Placement Evaluation

- Informal Reading Inventory
- Running Record
- Placement Tests

Test Preparation

- Test Power in Teacher's Edition, 467, 481, 501, 531, 541
- Additional standardized test preparation materials available

 Reading Test Generator

- Assessment Software

Assessment Checklist

Student .... Grade ....

Teacher ....

	Child of the Owl	Bellerophon and the Flying Horse	Adventure In Space	Rumpelstiltskin's Daughter	The History of Money	Assessment Summary
LISTENING/SPEAKING						
Participates in oral language experiences						
Listens and speaks to gain knowledge of culture						
Speaks appropriately to different audiences for different purposes						
Communicates clearly						
READING						
Uses a variety of word identification strategies:						
• Syllable Patterns						
• /ou/ and /oi/						
• Denotation and Connotation						
• Context Clues, Content Area and Specialized Vocabulary						
Reads with fluency and understanding						
Reads widely for different purposes in varied sources						
Develops an extensive vocabulary						
Uses a variety of strategies to comprehend selections:						
• Make Inferences						
• Judgments and Decisions						
• Sequence of Events						
Responds to various texts						
Analyzes the characteristics of various types of texts:						
• Story Elements (Character)						
Conducts research using various sources, including:						
• Graphic Aids						
Reads to increase knowledge						
WRITING						
Writes for a variety of audiences and purposes						
Composes original texts using the conventions of written language such as capitalization and penmanship						
Spells proficiently						
Composes texts applying knowledge of grammar and usage						
Uses writing process						
Evaluates own writing and writing of others						

+ Observed   − Not Observed

Introduce the Theme

Brainstorms

We can meet any challenge with determination and ingenuity.

DISCUSS THE THEME Write the theme statement on the board and read it aloud with students. Have students think about the term *brainstorm*. Ask:

- Where do you think the term *brainstorm* comes from?

- Do you think the best solutions come from brainstorming or from careful planning? Explain your answer.

- What are other methods that we can use to solve problems?

PREVIEW UNIT SELECTIONS Have students preview the unit by reading the selection titles and looking at the illustrations. Ask:

- How might the stories, poems, and the *Time for Kids* magazine article relate to the theme Brainstorms?

- What might be some similarities and differences among these stories?

As students read the literature in this unit, encourage them to talk about how the characters, settings, and events develop the unit theme Brainstorms.

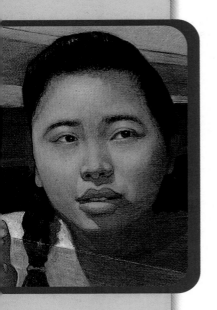

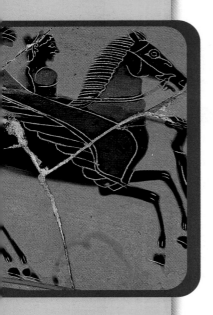

THEME CONNECTIONS

Each of the five selections relates to the unit theme Brainstorms. This thematic link will help students to make connections across texts.

Child of the Owl Casey and her grandmother realize that they can learn from each other.

Bellerophon and the Flying Horse Taming a flying horse and killing a monster, a young man becomes a hero.

Adventure in Space Astronauts work together to repair the Hubble telescope.

Rumpelstiltskin's Daughter In a twist on the classic tale, a girl solves her problems as well as everyone else's.

The History of Money This article explains how people solved the problem of paying for goods and services.

Research and Inquiry

Theme Project:
Disaster Relief

Brainstorm with the class the problems that might arise when handling a disaster. Then have groups of students choose one disaster, such as an earthquake, and create a plan to handle the problems that arise. Encourage students to include designs for evacuation routes, emergency care, and long-term relief plans.

Make a Resource Chart Have students list what they already know about solving the problems that arise from the disaster they chose. Next ask students to brainstorm some questions they would

need to answer in order to prepare their plans for disaster relief. Have students create a three-column chart. In the first column have them list their questions. In the second column have them list resources that will help them answer their questions. After they finish their research, they can write the answers in the third column. Remind students to identify and cite their sources properly.

Create a Presentation Students should include the location of the natural disaster they choose. They will need road maps of the area as well as information about local hospitals and relief organizations.

QUESTIONS	RESOURCES	ANSWERS
• What was done for similar disasters? • Who handles emergencies?	• News magazines, newspapers • Search the Internet • Government handouts	

See **Wrap Up the Theme,** page 543.

Research Strategies

Students can use the Internet to find news stories about natural disasters. Share these tips:

• Make a list of key words relevant to your topic.

• Type the specific key words into your search engine.

• Click on one website at a time to

determine if the site includes the information you need.

• Take good notes and print out the information from the website.

 Have students visit

www.mhschool.com/reading

Poetry

Read the Poem

READ ALOUD Read "I May, I Might, I Must" by Marianne Moore aloud to students. Afterward, ask:

- What does the title suggest?
- What is the speaker saying about facing impossible problems?

 Listening Library The poem is available on **audiocassette** and on **compact disc.**

PARTNER READING Each partner should read the poem aloud to the other. Have partners listen for the rhyme scheme and rhythm of the lines. Partners should read the poem as if it were part of a conversation, not as a formal poem.

Learn About Poetry

SYMBOLISM Explain:

- Symbolism is a literary device where something real—a place, an object, or a person—stands for, or represents, something else.
- Point out the word *fen.* Explain that a fen is a wet, marshy place that can be impossible to cross on foot.

Ask students what they think the fen represents. (an obstacle; a challenge)

RHYTHM Review:

- Rhythm refers to the pattern of beats in each line of a poem.
- The beats are created by stressed and unstressed syllables in each line of a poem.

Have students read the poem and clap with you to hear the rhythm.

MEET THE POET

ABOUT MARIANNE MOORE
One of the United States' foremost poets, Marianne Moore was famous for using images from the natural world, especially animals, to express her ideas about people and experiences. As editor of the Dial Press in the 1920s, she encouraged young writers and published their work. In 1952 she won the Pulitzer Prize for poetry.

BRAINSTORMS

I May,
I Might,
I Must

If you will tell me why the fen
appears impassable, I then
will tell you why I think that I
can get across it if I try.

by Marianne Moore

445

Poetry

INTERNAL RHYME Review with students that internal rhyme refers to rhyming words that occur within a line of poetry rather than at the end of the lines. Read aloud the poem and emphasize *why* in the first line, *I* in the second line, *why I* in the third line, and *I try* in the fourth so that students can hear the internal rhyme.

Oral Response

SMALL-GROUP DISCUSSION Have students share personal responses to the poem and discuss these questions:

- What feeling is communicated by the title of the poem?
- What is the poet saying about facing obstacles or challenges?
- Would you agree that determination is a big part of meeting a challenge? Why or why not?
- Share one example of how you or someone you know got past the "fen."

WRITE A POEM

Write a Poem Remind students of the ancient Greek riddle of the Sphinx: "What has one voice and becomes four-footed, two-footed, and three-footed?" (Man, who crawls as a baby, walks as an adult, and uses a cane in old age) Then have students write and illustrate poems based on a riddle. They should present their riddles to the class to solve.

Make a Bulletin Board Display Create a bulletin board display of the riddles.

Concept
- **Generations**

Comprehension
- **Story Elements**

Vocabulary
- **banister**
- **grudged**
- **porcelain**
- **rhythmically**
- **troublemaking**
- **truce**

Reaching All Learners

Anthology

Child of the Owl

Selection Summary *Child of the Owl* reveals how a young girl discovers her Asian heritage by living with her grandmother. As the story unfolds, students will identify the story elements that make this such an engaging work of fiction.

Stories in Art focuses on the **comprehension** skill

Reading Strategy applies the **comprehension** skill

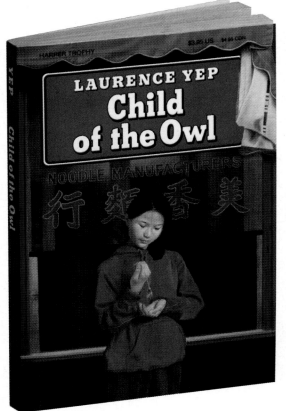

Listening Library

INSTRUCTIONAL pages 448–467

About the Author Laurence Yep, a Chinese American, writes about the history of his ancestral homeland from the point of view of a child. As Yep puts it, "A child's history ... treats its subjects with an immediateness that makes them seem to live and breathe."

Same Concept, Skills and Vocabulary!

Leveled Books

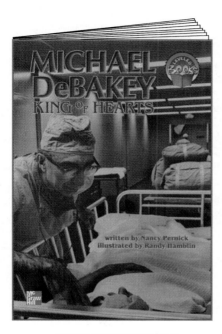

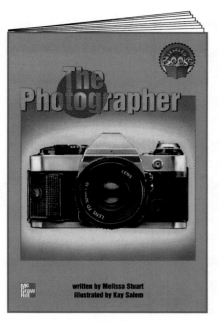

EASY
Lesson on pages 467A and 467D

INDEPENDENT
Lesson on pages 467B and 467D

🔲 *Take-Home version available*

CHALLENGE
Lesson on pages 467C and 467D

Leveled Practice

EASY
Reteach, 149–155 Blackline masters with reteaching opportunities for each assessed skill

INDEPENDENT/ON-LEVEL
Practice, 149–155 Workbook with Take-Home stories and practice opportunities for each assessed skill and story comprehension

CHALLENGE
Extend, 149–155 Blackline masters that offer challenge activities for each assessed skill

Quizzes Prepared by 📘 **Accelerated Reader®**

WORKSTATION Activities

Suggested Lesson Planner

READING AND LANGUAGE ARTS	**DAY 1** *Focus on Reading and Skills*	**DAY 2** *Read the Literature*
● **Comprehension** ● **Vocabulary** ● **Phonics/Decoding** ● **Study Skills** ● **Listening, Speaking, Viewing, Representing**	**Read Aloud: Poetry,** 446E "Anecdote for Fathers" **Develop Visual Literacy,** 446 ☑ **Review Story Elements,** 447A–447B **Teaching Chart 121** **Reteach, Practice, Extend,** 149 **Reading Strategy: Story Elements,** 447 "Grandma's Studio" **Intervention Program**	**Build Background,** 448A Develop Oral Language **Vocabulary,** 448B–448C *banister rhythmically* *grudged troublemaking* *porcelain truce* **Teaching Chart 122** Word Building Manipulative Cards **Reteach, Practice, Extend,** 150 **Read the Selection,** 448–463 ☑ **Story Elements** **Genre: Realistic Fiction,** 449 **Cultural Perspectives,** 452 **Intervention Program**
● **Curriculum Connections**	**Link** Works of Art, 446	**Link** Social Studies, 448A
● **Writing**	**Writing Prompt:** Write about a time when you visited or stayed with an older relative. Tell about what you did together and what you enjoyed most.	**Writing Prompt:** Write a telephone conversation that might have occurred between Phil and Paw-Paw about Paw-Paw having Casey come to live with her. **Journal Writing,** 463 Quick-Write
● **Grammar**	**Introduce the Concept: Pronouns,** 467M Daily Language Activity 1. Phil decided she can't take Casey. 2. The house was small, and he was crowded, too. 3. Casey smiled when it heard the joke. **Grammar Practice Book,** 129	**Teach the Concept: Pronouns,** 467M Daily Language Activity 1. The girl came, and he saw Paw-Paw. 2. Phil and Casey were in Chinatown where we ate lunch. 3. Barney is ill, and it is still in bed. **Grammar Practice Book,** 130
● **Spelling**	**Pretest: Compound Words,** 467O **Spelling Practice Book,** 129–130	**Explore the Pattern: Compound Words,** 467O **Spelling Practice Book,** 131

☑ = **Skill Assessed in Unit Test**

ⓘ **Intervention Program Available**

Read EVERY DAY

DAY 3 — Read the Literature

Rereading for Fluency, 462

Story Questions and Activities, 464–465
Reteach, Practice, Extend, 151

Study Skill, 466
☑ **Read a Family Tree**
Teaching Chart 123
Reteach, Practice, Extend, 152

Test Power, 467

Read the Leveled Books, 467A–467D
Guided Reading
Syllable Patterns
☑ Story Elements
☑ Instructional Vocabulary

ⓘ **Intervention Program**

 Social Studies, 450

✎ **Writing Prompt:** Imagine you are Casey. Write a letter to a friend explaining what has happened to you since your father became ill.

Writing Process: Writing a Story, 467K
Prewrite, Draft

Review and Practice: Pronouns, 467N
Daily Language Activity
1. Chinatown is big, and he is noisy.
2. Phil told Casey, "It will live here."
3. Paw-Paw and I—they are family.

Grammar Practice Book, 131

Practice and Extend: Compound Words, 467P
Spelling Practice Book, 132

DAY 4 — Build Skills

 Read the Leveled Books and Self-Selected Books

☑ **Review Story Elements,** 467E–467F
Teaching Chart 124
Reteach, Practice, Extend, 153
Language Support, 166

☑ **Review Make Inferences,** 467G–467H
Teaching Chart 125
Reteach, Practice, Extend, 154
Language Support, 167

Minilessons, 451, 453, 455, 461

ⓘ **Intervention Program**

  Math, 458

✎ **Writing Prompt:** Write a dialogue between Phil and his wife, talking about why Casey can't stay with them any longer.
Writing Process: Writing a Story, 467K
Revise
Meeting Individual Needs for Writing, 467L

Review and Practice: Pronouns, 467N
Daily Language Activity
1. These marks, it mean I have a temper.
2. When I looked, she saw nothing.
3. Since he lived by herself, Paw-Paw played a lot of card games.

Grammar Practice Book, 132

Proofread and Write: Compound Words, 467P
Spelling Practice Book, 133

DAY 5 — Build Skills

  Read Self-Selected Books

☑ **Introduce Denotation & Connotation,** 467I–467J
Teaching Chart 126
Reteach, Practice, Extend, 155
Language Support, 168

Listening, Speaking, Viewing, Representing, 467L

Minilessons, 453, 455, 461

Phonics Review,
Syllable Patterns, 451

Phonics/Phonemic Awareness Practice Book, 35–38

ⓘ **Intervention Program**

 Science, 460

✎ **Writing Prompt:** Write about Phil and Paw-Paw, explaining how they differ and how they are alike.

Writing Process: Writing a Story, 467K
Edit/Proofread, Publish

Assess and Reteach: Pronouns, 467N
Daily Language Activity
1. She is almost 8 o'clock.
2. When she hears the Chinese Hour, he will relax.
3. Yep sold his first story when it was 18.

Grammar Practice Book, 133–134

Assess and Reteach: Compound Words, 467P
Spelling Practice Book, 134

Read Aloud

Anecdote for Fathers
a poem by William Wordsworth

I have a boy of five years old;
His face is fair and fresh to see;
His limbs are cast in beauty's mould,
And dearly he loves me.

One morn we strolled on our dry walk,
Our quiet house all full in view,
And held such intermitted talk
As we are wont to do.

My thoughts on former pleasures ran;
I thought of Kilve's delightful shore,
Our pleasant home, when spring began,
A long, long year before.

A day it was when I could bear
Some fond regrets to entertain;
With so much happiness to spare,
I could not feel a pain.

The green earth echoed to the feet
Of lambs that bounded through the
  glade,
From shade to sunshine, and as fleet
From sunshine back to shade.

Birds warbled round me—and each
  trace
Of inward sadness had its charm;
Kilve, thought I, was a favoured place,
And so is Liswyn farm.

Continued on page T2

Oral Comprehension

LISTENING AND SPEAKING Encourage students to listen to clues about character as you read this poem. Afterward, ask:

• What do you know about the father's character?

• What do you know about the character of his son, Edward?

Ask students: How do the language and rhyme help reveal the characters?

GENRE STUDY: POETRY Discuss some of the literary devices and techniques in "Anecdote for Fathers."

• Point out that the meter of each stanza is the same. Have students count the number of syllables and the number of strong beats in each line of the first stanza. Ask: How many strong beats are in each line? Have

them scan for end rhymes.

• Discuss how the poet uses alliteration (repetition of beginning sounds) in lines such as, "His face is fair and fresh to see."

• Discuss the use and effect of dialogue within the poem. Ask: What punctuation is used? How does dialogue make the poem more personal?

Activity Break the class into groups of three. Have the groups dramatize the poem. Have one student play the father, another, the son, and a third, the speaker. Challenge students to improvise new dialogue appropriate to their characters. Remind students that such "slice of life" works need not necessarily come to a conclusive end. ▶ **Kinesthetic/Linguistic**

Visual Literacy

Artists communicate through their work. Some express ideas about their culture, their family, or their feelings. Look at this painting. What is the artist, Diego Rivera, saying to you?

~~~

Study this painting. What can you tell about the people in it? How do they feel toward each other? What might the artist be saying about the bond between mother and child? How do these people make you feel?

~~~

Look at the painting again. How does the artist control light and shadow? What mood does he create? Was he successful in showing his feelings? Explain why you think so.

Madre y Niña
by Diego Rivera

446

Objective: Analyze Character

VIEWING Draw students' attention to the composition of this painting. Ask them to discuss how the mother and daughter are posed, focusing on the spatial relationship between the two figures. Have students explore how the artist uses body language to show the characters' relationship. Discuss the effect of the background shadows.

Read the page with students, encouraging individual interpretations of the painting.

Ask students to explain their inferences about character. For example:

• The way the daughter leans her head towards her mother shows trust.

• The way that the mother links her hands together over and around her daughter shows her protectiveness.

REPRESENTING Have students pick two subjects to draw. Ask them to depict them in such a way that their relationship to one another is clear.

TESTED OBJECTIVES

Students will analyze story characters.

Skills Finder

Story Elements: Character, Setting, Plot

Introduce	65A–B
Review	369A–B, 405E–F, 447A–B, 467E–F, 503A–B, 531E–F
Test	Unit 1, Unit 4, Unit 5
Maintain	147, 179

TEACHING TIP

SETTING AND CHARACTER Remind students that the setting can affect what a character does. For example, what might Henry have done if he didn't live near a science museum or a baseball stadium?

Review Story Elements

PREPARE

Discuss Characters
Have students name a character from a book, TV show, or movie. Encourage them to describe what the character likes to do. Ask: What does this tell you about him or her?

TEACH

Define Analyze Character
Tell students: Paying close attention to a character's words, thoughts, and actions, as well as how others react to him or her, lets you make inferences about the character. The more you know about a character, the better you will understand the character's motivations, or reasons for doing things.

Uncle Henry

Henry's nephew Toby was coming for a visit. <u>Henry wanted to make sure he had a good time</u>. The last time he'd seen Toby was when Toby was two years old. <u>They had spent that visit happily playing cars for hours on the rug</u>. Henry didn't know much about kids, but <u>he knew that a twelve-year-old didn't want to play cars</u>. He decided to take Toby to the <u>new science museum and to a baseball game</u>.

Teaching Chart 121

Read the Story and Model the Skill
Display **Teaching Chart 121.** As students read, guide them to pay attention to information that helps them to understand the character better.

MODEL Henry's nephew is coming to visit. Henry wants Toby to have a good time. This tells me that Henry cares about Toby.

Analyze Character
Have students underline details that give clues about the character of Henry.

Create a Detail and Character Chart

GROUP

Have students use a Detail and Character chart to record what the details in the story tell about Henry. Help students begin the chart and then have them work in groups to finish it.

▶ Linguistic/Logical

DETAIL	CHARACTER
Henry wants Toby to have a good time.	Henry cares about Toby.
Henry realizes that a twelve-year-old is different from a two-year-old.	Henry is thoughtful.

ASSESS/CLOSE

Have students use what they know about Henry to write a short scene about something that might occur during Toby's visit. Discuss each scene and what it tells about Henry's character.

ALTERNATE TEACHING
STRATEGY

STORY ELEMENTS
For a different approach to teaching this skill, see page T62.

Intervention ▶ **Skills Intervention Guide,** for direct instruction and extra practice with story elements

Meeting Individual Needs for Comprehension

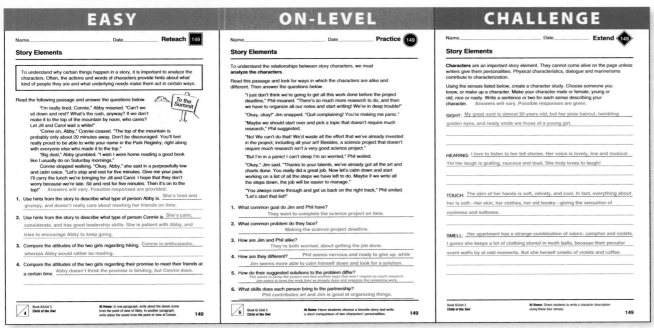

Reteach, 149   Practice, 149   Extend, 149

 **OBJECTIVES**

Students will under-
stand a story character.

Apply Story Elements

READING STRATEGY

Story Elements

Develop a strategy
for understanding
character.

1 **Find out what the
character thinks.** A
character's thoughts and
words can tell you a lot.

2 **Study the character's
actions.** What do you
learn about the character
from his actions?

3 **Use what you already
know.** How would
you feel in Andrew's
situation?

4 **Describe the character.**
What is Andrew like?
What details in the story
tell you this?

READING STRATEGY

Grandma's Studio

"But Mom, there's nothing to do here,"
Andrew said into the telephone. "Grandma
works in her studio half the day, and
Grandpa reads the paper. I can't stay here
all summer."

"Two months isn't that long," his
mother replied.

Andrew said good-bye and hung up the
phone. Two months sounded like forever.

Heading for the kitchen, Andrew saw
the open door to his grandmother's studio.
He had never been in there. Tiptoeing in,
he found an easel, giant sheets of watercolor paper, and tubes of paint. Covering
the paper with bright, wet colors suddenly
seemed tempting. He grabbed a brush and
began.

As Andrew was putting the final touches
on his painting, Grandma walked in.

She just stared at the painting on the
easel. "Impressive!" she said at last. "Have
you taken lessons?"

"Uh, no," Andrew stammered.

"Would you like to?" Grandma asked.

Before Andrew could answer, Grandma
got out more paper and dipped a brush into
the blue paint. Andrew took a new sheet,
dipped his brush in the same paint, and imi-
tated his grandmother's brushstrokes.

"Developing your painting skills takes
time," Grandma explained.

"I've got all summer," said Andrew, and
he smiled as he painted another blue line.

447

PREVIEW Have students preview "Grandma's Studio."
Remind them that writers present clues about a character by describing his or her actions, words, and
thoughts. Ask:

• Based on the title of the story and the illustrations,
what do you think Grandma does? (She is an artist.)

• Is this story fiction or nonfiction? How can you tell?
(fiction; narration and dialogue in the first paragraph)

SET PURPOSE Explain that students will apply what
they have learned about character as they read
"Grandma's Studio."

APPLY THE STRATEGY Discuss this strategy for
understanding the characters in a story.

• Pay attention to the character's words and thoughts.
How does Andrew feel at the beginning of the story?

• Note the character's actions. What does Andrew do?

• Use what you already know about people to help you
understand character. Does Andrew act like a real person? What words would you use to describe the kinds
of things Andrew does?

Activity Have each student create a Detail and
Character chart for the passage.

Build Background

cial Studies

Concept: Generations

Evaluate Prior Knowledge

CONCEPT: GENERATIONS The characters in these stories all have relationships with people of different generations. Have students discuss their own relationships with older people. What do they like best about these relationships? What things do they have in common with older people?

COMPARE INTERESTS Have students list ways in which they and older people are alike, and ways in which they are different. Discuss whether the differences are a function of age or personality. Create a Venn diagram. ▶ **Logical/Visual**

GRANDFATHER		ME
Different	**Alike**	**Different**
drinks iced tea	like to cook	drink milk
talks politics	like animals	talk about sports
walks slowly	like reading	run a lot
likes quiet	mysteries	like computer games

Graphic Organizer 14

DESCRIBE A VISIT Have students describe a visit they have had with someone from an older generation from the point of view of the older person.

Develop Oral Language

ESL Ask pairs of students to role-play meeting for the first time an older relative who lives in another country. Before they perform the role-play, have both people think about what they would like the other person to know about themselves and how they feel. Also, ask each person to try to find a way to make the other person feel comfortable.

After each role-play, discuss the feelings of both people. Ask: *Were the two people happy to meet each other? What do you think they liked about each other? What did they dislike?*

Students will use context clues to determine the meanings of vocabulary words.

banister
porcelain
truce
troublemaking
grudged
rhythmically

banister (p. 454) a railing along a staircase

porcelain (p. 457) a type of ceramic material that is hard and white

truce (p. 462) a short stop in fighting, agreed to by both sides

troublemaking (p. 455) causing a problem or difficulty

grudged (p. 460) unwillingly gave or allowed

rhythmically (p. 451) regularly repeating sounds or movements

Story Words

These words from the selection may be unfamiliar. Before students read, have them check the meanings and pronunciations of the words in the Glossary beginning on page 678 or in a dictionary.

- behavior, p. 449
- hospitalized, p. 449
- sentimental, p. 453

Vocabulary

Teach Vocabulary in Context

Identify Vocabulary Words
Display **Teaching Chart 122** and have a volunteer read it aloud. Ask students to circle each vocabulary word and then underline the clues to its meaning.

The Peace Offering

1. Casey walked up the stairs, holding onto the banister for support. 2. She carefully carried a beautiful dish made out of porcelain. 3. She was tired of fighting and hoped the present would be seen as part of a truce. 4. Her love of adventure had been mistaken for troublemaking and she was sorry about that. 5. She didn't agree with how others saw her, but she grudged they might have a point. 6. She could hear a loose sign outside banging rhythmically, like a marching drum, urging her on.

Teaching Chart 122

Discuss Meanings
Ask questions like the following to help clarify word meanings:

- Why would you have a banister on a staircase?
- What sort of things can be made out of porcelain?
- What is the opposite of a truce?
- Has anything you like to do been thought of as troublemaking? What? By whom?
- How are the words *grudged* and *unwillingly* similar in meaning?
- Can you tap your pencil erasers rhythmically on your desk tops? Show me.

Practice

Definitions

GROUP

Have one student draw a vocabulary card and give a definition for the word. Have other students guess the word from the definition. Whoever guesses correctly gets the next turn. ▶ **Linguistic**

truce **grudged** **banister**

Word Building Manipulative Cards

Create a Cartoon Strip

WRITING PARTNERS

Have students work together to create a cartoon strip that uses at least four of the vocabulary words. The words can be used in thought or speech bubbles, or in captions. ▶ **Linguistic/Spatial**

Assess Vocabulary

Use Words in Context

PARTNERS

Ask each pair of students to work together to write five journal entries that Casey or some other character might have written. Ask students to make sure that they use all of the vocabulary words. Have pairs share their journal entries with the class.

SPELLING/VOCABULARY CONNECTIONS

See Spelling Challenge Words, pages 467O–467P.

LANGUAGE SUPPORT

See the **Language Support Book**, pages 161–164, for teaching suggestions for Vocabulary.

Vocabulary PuzzleMaker

Provides vocabulary activities.

Meeting Individual Needs for Vocabulary

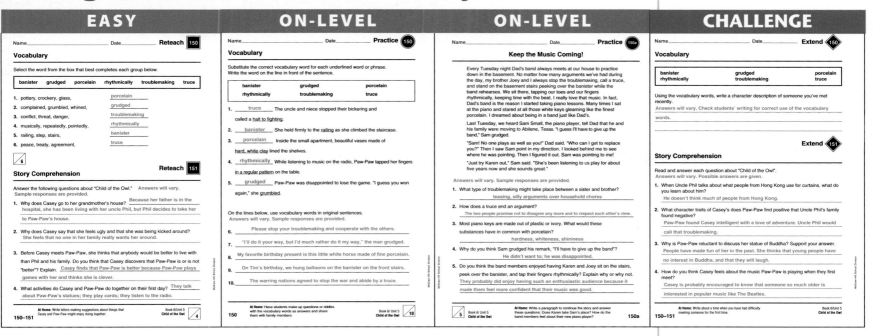

EASY — Reteach, 150

ON-LEVEL — Practice, 150

ON-LEVEL — Practice, 150a / Take-Home Story

CHALLENGE — Extend, 150

448C

Comprehension

Prereading Strategies

PREVIEW AND PREDICT Have students read the title and preview the story, looking for clues about the characters.

- Who do you think the main characters in this story are? Why?
- What do you think this story will be about?
- Do you think this story will be realistic or a fantasy? Why? (Realistic. The illustrations show real people and settings.) *Genre*

Have students record their predictions.

PREDICTIONS	WHAT HAPPENED
This story is about a girl and an older woman.	
The girl goes to visit the woman.	

SET PURPOSES What do students want to find out by reading this story? For example:

- Why does the girl look worried?
- Who is the older woman?

Child
of the
OWL

BY LAURENCE YEP

Meeting Individual Needs • Grouping Suggestions for Strategic Reading

EASY	ON-LEVEL	CHALLENGE
Read Together Read the story with students or have them use the **Listening Library**. Have students use the Detail and Character chart to record important information about the characters. Comprehension and Intervention prompts offer additional help with vocabulary and comprehension.	**Guided Instruction** You can use the Comprehension questions as you read with students. Encourage them to use the Detail and Character chart. You may want to have the students read the selection first on their own.	**Read Independently** Remind independent readers to look for clues that will help them to understand the characters better. Have them set up Detail and Character charts as on page 449. After reading, they can use their charts to help them summarize the story.

 asey was just
a small child when her
mother, Jeanie, died.
Since then, Casey has
been brought up by her
father, Barney. When
Barney is hospitalized,
Casey goes to stay with
her uncle Phil and his
family. Used to a free-
spirited life with her
father, Casey is uncom-
fortable in Phil's strict
household. In turn,
Phil's family is unwill-
ing to accept Casey's at-
titudes, ideas, and
behavior. The situation
is tense for everyone,
so Phil decides to take
Casey to San Francisco's
Chinatown to live with
Paw-Paw, her grand-
mother. On the way,
Casey is nervous. She
has never met Paw-Paw,
and she feels alone and
out of place in the unfa-
miliar setting.

ILLUSTRATED BY
WINSON TRANG

(449)

Comprehension

☑ Apply Story Elements

STRATEGIC READING Before we begin
reading, let's set up Detail and Character
charts so we can record story notes about the
characters.

DETAIL	CHARACTER

(1) Do you think Casey and her grandmother will like each other? Why or
why not? *Make Predictions*

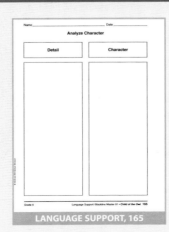
Genre

Realistic Fiction

Explain that realistic fiction:

* features events, characters, and settings
  that are like ones in the real world.

* includes a variety of well-developed characters who represent many different types
  of people found in everyday life.

* is easy to identify with on a personal level.

Activity After students read *Child of
the Owl*, have them describe how Paw-Paw's
feelings toward Casey change over time.
Then ask them to predict how the two will
feel toward each other after living together
for a few months.

449

Comprehension

2 Describe the setting of the story. (It is urban. On the radio is a song by the "new group" the Beatles so the story probably takes place in the 1960s.) Imagine you are Casey. Explain how you might respond to the setting. (Accept reasonable answers.) *Setting and Character*

TEACHING TIP

ACRONYMS Students may enjoy knowing that Morse code is a way of signaling that uses light or sound in a pattern of dots and dashes to represent letters. SOS is a signal sent out by a ship or plane to say that it is in need of urgent help. SOS stands for "Save Our Ship." Any time you use the initial letters of a phrase or title, you create an acronym.

Phil headed up Sacramento Street—a steep, slanting street that just zoomed on and on to the top of Nob Hill, where the rich people lived and where they had the swanky hotels. Phil turned suddenly into a little dead-end alley wide enough for only one car. On one side was a one-story Chinese school of brick so old or so dirty that the bricks were practically a purple color. On the other side as we drove by was a small parking lot with only six spaces for cars. Phil stopped the car in the middle of the alley and I could see the rest of it was filled with apartment houses. Somewhere someone had a window open and the radio was blaring out "I Want to Hold Your Hand" by that new group, the Beatles. I couldn't find the place where it was coming from but I did see someone's diapers and shirts hung in the windows and on the fire escape of one apartment.

"Why do they hang their laundry in the windows?" I asked Phil.

"That's what people from Hong Kong use for curtains," Phil grumbled.

The sidewalk in front of Paw-Paw's house was cracked like

450

Activity

Cross Curricular: Social Studies

CHINESE IMMIGRANTS Tell students that the author, Laurence Yep, is a descendent of Chinese immigrants. Invite students to say what they would like to know about Chinese immigrants.

RESEARCH AND INQUIRY Have students find out information about the Chinese who came to this country in the twentieth century. Ask them to work in groups to create a news story about some aspect of the Chinese immigrant experience and present it to the class. Students can create a class newspaper by putting the articles together.

▶ **Linguistic/Interpersonal**

someone had taken a sledgehammer to it, and there were iron grates over the lower windows. The steps up to the doorway were old, worn concrete painted red. To the left were the mailboxes, which had Chinese words for the names or had no labels at all. To the right were the doorbells to all the nine apartments. Phil picked out the last and rang. He jabbed his thumb down rhythmically. Three short. Three long. Three short.

"Why are you doing that?" I asked.

"Signaling your Paw-Paw," he grumbled. "She never answers just one buzz like any normal person, or even just three bursts. It's got to be nine buzzes in that way or she doesn't open the door. She says her friends know what she means."

So did I. It was Morse code for SOS. The buzzer on the door sounded like an angry bee. Phil the Pill opened the door, putting his back against it and fighting against the heavy spring that tried to swing it shut. "Go on. Up three flights. Number nine."

I walked into an old, dim hallway and climbed up the wooden steps. As I turned an angle on the stairs, I saw light burning fierce and bright from a window. When I came to it, I looked out at the roof of the Chinese school next door. Someone had thrown some old 45's and a pair of sneakers down there. If I were some kind of kid that felt sorry for herself, I would almost have said that was the way I felt: like some piece of old, ugly junk that was being kicked around on the discard pile while Barney was getting better.

I didn't stay by the window long, though, because Phil was coming up the stairs and I didn't want to act like his kids' stories about Paw-Paw had scared me. Anybody could be better than Phil the Pill and his family . . . I hoped. I stopped by the number-nine room,

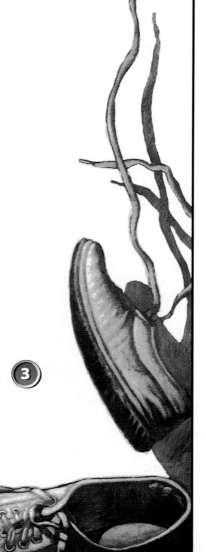

3

Comprehension

3 **CHARACTER** What can we tell about Casey so far?

MODEL I know Casey doesn't like Phil much because she doesn't tell him that the nine buzzes are Morse code. I also think that Casey might say that she doesn't feel sorry for herself, but I think she feels unwanted and is trying to act tough.

Let's write down what we know about Casey in our Detail and Character charts.

DETAIL	CHARACTER
Casey says she doesn't feel sorry for herself.	Casey wants to seem tough.

Minilesson

REVIEW/MAINTAIN

Syllable Patterns

Have students say the words *almost, escape,* and *entitled.* Ask them to snap their fingers at each syllable break.

- Ask students to identify the vowel pattern before each syllable break. Help them recognize the VC/CV in each word.
Graphophonic Cues

Activity Have partners play "Syllable Baseball" using words of two or more syllables that follow the VC/CV pattern. Each student who comes to "bat" has to name a multisyllable word, advancing the same number of bases as syllables in each correct word named. Each player gets three "outs" before the partner gets to bat.

 Phonics Intervention Guide

Comprehension

④ CHARACTER Do you see any more evidence on this page of Casey acting tough? (When her uncle calls her a *little idiot*, she just shrugs and claims it isn't her business.)

afraid to knock. It could not be the right place because I could hear "I Want to Hold Your Hand" coming through the doorway. I scratched my head and checked the numbers on the other doors on the landing. Phil the Pill was still a flight down, huffing and puffing up the steps with my duffel bag—it wasn't that heavy; Phil was just that much out of shape. "Go on. Go on. Knock, you little idiot," he called up the stairwell.

I shrugged. It wasn't any of my business. I knocked at the door. I heard about six bolts and locks being turned. Finally the door swung open and I saw a tiny, pleasant, round-faced woman smiling at me. Her cheeks were a bright red. Her gray hair was all curly and frizzy around her head and a pair of rimless, thick eyeglasses perched on her nose. She was round and plump, wearing a sweater even on a hot day like this, a pair of cotton black slacks, and a pair of open-heeled, flat slippers.

"Paw-Paw?" I asked.

"Hello. Hello." She opened up her arms and gave me a big hug, almost crushing me. It was funny,

CULTURAL PERSPECTIVES

CHINESE TRADITIONS Tell students that Paw-Paw lives in Chinatown, a section of San Francisco inhabited largely by Chinese immigrants and their descendants. Chinese holidays such as Chinese New Year are celebrated there.

RESEARCH AND INQUIRY Have students research a Chinese holiday and write about a traditional food or activity associated with it. Students can illustrate their research. ▶ **Linguistic/Spatial**

*inter***NET** **CONNECTION** Students can learn about Chinese holidays by visiting **www.mhschool.com/reading**

but even though it was like I said—Barney and me never went in much for that sentimental stuff like hugging and kissing—I suddenly found myself holding on to her. Underneath all the soft layers of clothing I could feel how hard and tough she was. She patted me on the back three times and then left me for a moment to turn down her radio. It really was her old, white, beat-up radio playing rock music.

"Hey, how about a hand?" Phil puffed as he finally got to the landing.

Paw-Paw shuffled out to the landing in her slippered feet and made shooing motions. "You can go home now. We can do all right by ourselves."

Phil heaved his shoulders up and down in a great sigh and set the bag down. "Now, Momma—"

"Go on home," she said firmly. "We need time by ourselves."

I saw that Phil must have had some fine speech all prepared, probably warning Paw-Paw about me and warning me about ingratitude. He was not about to give up such an opportunity to make a speech.

"Now, Momma—"

"Go on. You're still not too old for a swat across the backside."

Phil ran his hand back and forth along the railing. "Really, Momma. You oughtn't—"

"Go on." Paw-Paw raised her hand.

Phil gulped. The thought of having a former district president of the lawyers spanked by his own mother must have been too much for him. He turned around and started down the steps. He still had to get in the last word though. "You mind your Paw-Paw, young lady. You hear me?" he shouted over his shoulder.

Comprehension

 5 Why do you think Casey finds herself holding onto Paw-Paw? (Casey may pretend that she is tough, but she needs to feel loved.) ***Make Inferences***

6 How does Paw-Paw feel about Phil? (She doesn't seem to respect him.) Let's have two volunteers play the parts of Paw-Paw and Phil. What would Phil have said if he'd been allowed to make his speech? What would Paw-Paw's response have been? ***Role-Play***

Minilesson

REVIEW/MAINTAIN

Make Inferences

Review with students that one way to infer how a character is feeling about another character is to pay attention to how that character describes the other one. For example, is the character describing the other person in a negative or positive way?

Activity Have students reread Casey's initial description of Paw-Paw on page 452. Do they feel the description is negative or positive? Have them find details in the description that support their opinions.

Comprehension

7 Why do you think the author has both Casey and Paw-Paw understand the SOS signal, but not Phil? (Having something special in common brings people together. The author is showing that Paw-Paw and Casey might like each other.) *Author's Purpose*

ROOT WORDS Look at the word *telegraph*. There are two root words in this word. What are they? (*tele* and *graph*) What is a *telegraph*? (a device for sending messages long distances)

Fluency

PARTNER READING Have partners take turns reading the story thus far, deciding in advance who will read each page. Ask them to close their eyes while they are listening to the other person read. Remind readers to read slowly and clearly and to vary their tone to match the emotions of the characters in the story.

I waited till I heard the door slam. "Do you know what those buzzes stand for?"

"Do you?" Her eyes crinkled up.

"It stands for SOS. But where did you learn it?"

"When I worked for the American lady, her boy had a toy . . . what do you call it?" She made a tapping motion with her finger.

"Telegraph?"

"Yes. It's a good joke on such a learned man, no?" Her round red face split into a wide grin and then she began to giggle and when she put her hand over her mouth, the giggle turned into a laugh.

7 I don't think that I had laughed in all that time since Barney's accident a month ago. It was like all the laughter I hadn't been able to use came bubbling up out of some hidden well—burst out of the locks and just came up. Both of us found ourselves slumping on the landing, leaning our heads against the banister, and laughing.

Finally Paw-Paw tilted up her glasses and wiped her eyes. "Philip always did have too much dignity for one person. Ah." She leaned back against the railing on the landing before the stairwell, twisting her head to look at me. "You'll go far," she nodded. "Yes, you will. Your eyebrows are beautifully curved, like silkworms. That means you'll be clever. And your ears are small and close to your head and shaped a certain way. That means you're adventurous and win much honor."

"Really?"

She nodded solemnly. "Didn't you know? The face is the map of the soul." Then she leaned forward and raised her glasses and pointed to the corners of her

454

ROOT WORDS Write the word *telegraph* on the board. Invite a volunteer to circle the roots *tele-* and *-graph*. Explain that *tele-* is from the Greek word meaning "at a distance" and that *graph* is also from a Greek word meaning "to write." So a telegraph can send a message over long distances.

Ask students to list other words that have these roots such as *telephone, telescope, television* and *graph, photograph, autograph*.

eyes where there were two small hollows, just shadows, really. "You see those marks under my eyes?"

"Yes." I added after a moment, "Paw-Paw."

"Those marks, they mean I have a temper."

"Oh." I wondered what was to happen next.

She set her glasses back on her nose. "But I will make a deal with you. I can keep my temper under control if you can do the same with your love of adventure and intelligence. You see, people, including me, don't always understand a love of adventure and intelligence. Sometimes we mistake them for troublemaking."

"I'll try," I grinned.

I went and got my bag then and brought it inside Paw-Paw's place and looked around, trying to figure out where I'd put it. Her place wasn't more than ten by fifteen feet and it was crowded with her stuff. Her bed was pushed lengthwise against the wall next to the doorway leading out to the landing. To the right of the door was another doorway, leading to the small little cubicle of a kitchen, and next to that door was her bureau. The wall opposite the bed had her one window leading out to the fire escape and giving a view of the alley, which was so narrow that it looked like we could have shaken hands with the people in the apartment house across from us. Beneath the window was a stack of newspapers for wrapping up the garbage. Next to the window was a table with a bright red-and-orange-flower tablecloth. Paw-Paw pulled aside her chair and her three-legged stool and told me to put my bag under the table. A metal cabinet and stacks of boxes covered the rest of the wall and the next one had hooks from which coats and other stuff in plastic bags hung.

455

Comprehension

8 **CHARACTER** Let's reread what Paw-Paw says to Casey. What can you tell about Paw-Paw from her words? (She wants Casey to understand that they will both have to try hard for this living arrangement to work.)

Comprehension

9 What do the objects on Paw-Paw's bureau tell us about her? (All the photos show that family is important to her. The statues show that tradition is important, too.) *Make Inferences*

p/i **COMPOUND WORDS** Look at the words *teacup* and *cardboard* in the first paragraph. What type of words are these? (compound words) What does each word mean?

p/i **PREVENTION/INTERVENTION**

COMPOUND WORDS Write the words *teacup* and *cardboard* on the board. Explain that compound words are formed from two words that can stand on their own but can combine to create a new word. Ask students to divide each compound word into two separate words and tell the meaning of each word.

Have students brainstorm other compound words (sidewalk, blackboard, driveway, airport, brainstorm) and tell what they mean.

In the right corner of the old bureau were some statues and an old teacup with some dirt in it and a half-burnt incense stick stuck into it. The rest of the top, though, was covered with old photos in little cardboard covers. They filled the bureau top and the mirror too, being stuck into corners of the mirror or actually taped onto the surface.

Next to the photos were the statues. One was about eight inches high in white porcelain of a pretty lady holding a flower and with the most patient, peaceful expression on her face. To her left was a statue of a man with a giant-sized, bald head. And then there were eight little statues, each only about two inches high. "Who are they?" I asked.

457

Comprehension

10 **CHARACTER** How does Casey describe the objects on Paw-Paw's bureau? Do you think she likes them? Why or why not? (She seems to like them. She describes the statue of the lady as having a "patient, peaceful expression.")

ⓈELF-MONITORING STRATEGY

RELATE TO PERSONAL EXPERIENCE
Have students think of how a character's experience relates to their own experiences. This may help them better understand the character and his or her reasons for doing things.

457

Comprehension

11 **CHARACTER** How do you think Casey feels when Paw-Paw won't look at the plastic charm?

MODEL I think Casey was hoping that having the same statue would bring them closer together in the same way that knowing the SOS signal brought them closer together. When Paw-Paw won't look at the charm, Casey makes the excuse that maybe Barney has already shown it to her. I think she is trying not to let her feelings get hurt.

12 What do you think Paw-Paw will tell Casey about the statues? *Make Predictions*

tatues of some holy people," Paw-Paw said reluctantly.

There was something familiar about the last statue on Paw-Paw's bureau. It was of a fat, balding god with large ears, who had little children crawling over his lap and climbing up his shoulders. "Hey," I said. "Is that the happy god?"

Paw-Paw looked puzzled. "He's not the god of happiness."

"But they call him the happy god. See?" I pulled Barney's little plastic charm out of my pocket and pointed to the letters on the back.

11 Paw-Paw didn't even try to read the lettering. Maybe Barney had already shown it to her long ago. "He's not the god of happiness. He just looks happy. He's the Buddha—the Buddha who will come in the future. He's smiling because everyone will be saved by that time and he can take a vacation. The children are holy people who become like children again."

"What about the others, Paw-Paw?"

12 "I don't have the words to explain," Paw-Paw said curtly, like the whole thing was embarrassing her.

Activity

Cross Curricular: Math

GAMES Paw-Paw likes to play card games. In many card games, each card has a numerical value and the combinations of cards are worth a certain number of points. Players use those points to score. Have students list card games that involve getting points or keeping score.

Have students work with partners to create their own mathematical card games. For example, a game might be won by having six cards whose total value is a multiple of four. Have students write the rules of their games.

▶ **Logical/Interpersonal**

I sat down by the table on the stool, which was painted white with red flowers. "Sure you do. I think your English is better than mine."

"You don't want to know any of that stuff." With her index finger Paw-Paw rubbed hard against some spot on the tablecloth. "That stuff's only for old people. If I tell you any more, you'll laugh at it like all other young people do." There was bitter hurt and anger in her voice.

I should have left her alone, I guess; but we had been getting close to one another and suddenly I'd found this door between us—a door that wouldn't open. I wasn't so much curious now as I was desperate: I didn't want Paw-Paw shutting me out like that. "I won't laugh, Paw-Paw. Honest."

"That stuff's only for old people who are too stupid to learn American ways," she insisted stubbornly.

"Well, maybe I'm stupid too."

"No." Paw-Paw pressed her lips together tightly; and I saw that no matter how much I pestered her, I wasn't going to get her to tell me any more about the statues on her bureau. We'd been getting along so great before that I was sorry I'd ever started asking questions.

We both sat, each in our own thoughts, until almost apologetically Paw-Paw picked up a deck of cards from the table. "Do you play cards?"

"Some," I said. "Draw poker. Five-card stud. Things like that."

Paw-Paw shuffled the cards expertly. "Poker is for old men who like to sit and think too much. Now I know a game that's for the young and quick."

"What's that?"

"Slapjack." She explained that each of us took half

459

Comprehension

13 **CHARACTER** How does Paw-Paw's refusal to talk make Casey feel? (shut out, upset) What does this reaction show about Casey's feelings towards Paw-Paw? (She wants Paw-Paw to like her.)

14 Paw-Paw tells Casey, "That stuff's only for old people who are too stupid to learn American ways." Do you think Paw-Paw means what she says? Explain (No. She is hurt because young people have laughed at her in the past for her beliefs.) *Draw Conclusions*

15 From what you know about Phil, do you think he respects his mother's beliefs and traditions? Why or why not? (No; he moved away from Chinatown and he seemed critical of Paw-Paw when he dropped Casey off.) *Make Inferences*

TEACHING TIP

POINT OF VIEW Have students note that the story is written in the first person point of view. Have students identify the narrative voice, and how it affects the outcome and the telling of the story. Ask students to suppose that the story were told from a third person point of view. Encourage students to discuss how the change in point of view might alter the focus or emphasis of this story.

LANGUAGE SUPPORT

ESL Have students who are having difficulty following the story work with partners to create a Sequence of Events chart. Partners can create the chart and then illustrate each event. When students are finished have them share their charts with each other. Remind them to put the events in the order that they happened in the story.

Comprehension

(16) **CHARACTER** Why do you think Paw-Paw suggests they play the card game Slap Jack? (She probably feels bad about what just happened and wants to find a way to do something with Casey.) Let's add what we know to the Detail and Character chart.

DETAIL	CHARACTER
Casey says she doesn't feel sorry for herself.	Casey wants to seem tough.
Paw-Paw suggests that they play cards.	Paw-Paw knows Casey is hurt and wants to make it up to her.

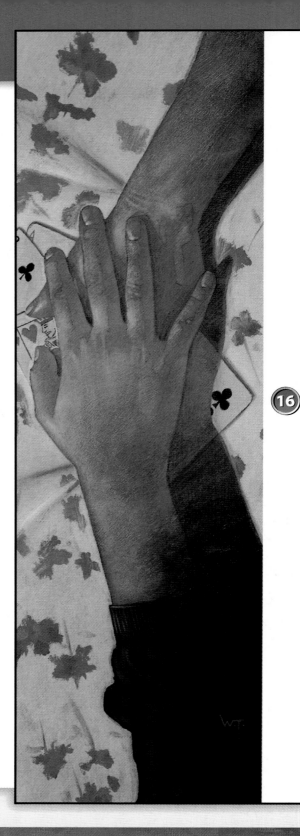

of a deck and stacked it in front without looking at it. Then we would take turns taking the top card off and putting it down in the middle. Whenever a jack appeared, the first one to put her hand over the pile of cards got it. She then mixed the new cards with all the cards she still had in front of her. The first one to get all the cards won the game. It would sound like the advantage was with the person who was putting out the card at that time, but she was supposed to turn up the card away from her so **(16)** she couldn't see it before the other player.

Paw-Paw had played a lot of card games, since she lived by herself, so she seemed to know when the jacks were going to come up. For a while all you could hear was the *slap-slap-slap*ping of cards and sometimes our hands smacking one another trying to get the pile. And sometimes I'd have more cards and sometimes Paw-Paw would. Eventually, though, she beat me. She shuffled the deck again. "You're a pretty good player," she grudged.

"Not as good as you, though."

Activity

Cross Curricular: Science

RADIOS In this story, Paw-Paw enjoys listening to her radio. Point out that the radio is a form of wireless communication. Radio waves are sent from a transmitter to a receiver.

RESEARCH AND INQUIRY Have students work in small groups to research

how a radio works. For example, how is music transmitted from a radio station to a radio? Suggest that students use their research to create an illustrated fact poster about radios.

▶ **Linguistic/Logical**

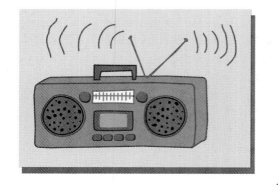

Paw-Paw shuffled the cards, tapping them against the table so the cards in the pack were all even. "We used to play all the time. Your mother, Phil, everyone. We'd hold big contests and make plenty of noise. Only when Phil got older, he only wanted to play the games fancy Americans played like—what's that word for a road that goes over water?"

"A bridge? Phil wanted to play bridge."

"Yes." Paw-Paw put the deck on the table. I wandered over to the bed.

The radio was in a little cabinet built into the headboard of the bed. I lay down on the bed and looked at the radio dial. "Do you like rock music, Paw-Paw?"

"It's fun to listen to," Paw-Paw said, "and besides, *Chinese Hour* is on that station every night."

"Chinese Hour?"

"An hour of news and songs all in Chinese." Paw-Paw slipped the cards back carefully into their box. "They used to have some better shows on that station like mystery shows."

"I bet I could find some." I started to reach for the dial.

"Don't lose that station." Paw-Paw seemed afraid suddenly.

"Don't worry, Paw-Paw, I'll be able to get your station back for you." It was playing "Monster Mash" right then. I twisted the dial to the right and the voices and snatches of song slid past and then I turned the dial back to her station, where "Monster Mash" was still playing. "See?"

"As long as you could get it back," Paw-Paw said reluctantly.

I fiddled with the dial some more until I got hold of *Gunsmoke*. It'd gone off the air three years ago but

461

Comprehension

17 How do you think Paw-Paw felt when Phil only wanted to play "fancy American games"? (Sample answer: her feelings were hurt. Perhaps she felt he was looking down at the rest of the family.) *Make Inferences*

18 Paw-Paw is afraid that Casey will not be able to find the Chinese station on her radio again. Why do you think the author chose to put this detail in? (It shows us that Paw-Paw is not that comfortable with machines. It reminds us that Paw-Paw came from a different culture.) **How might this be symbolic?** (Sample answer: It may symbolize Paw Paw's reluctance to try new things or her clinging to Chinese culture.) *Author's Purpose*

Minilesson

REVIEW/MAINTAIN

Summarize

Review with students that a summary identifies the central conflict, or basic problem, in the story and relates the main events.

Activity Ask students to think about the central conflict in the story and what has happened so far. Have each student make a list of the main events in the story. Working in groups, students should read their lists aloud, leaving out one of the events. The rest of the group should name the left-out event. Afterward, have group members work together to create a single summary of the story.

461

Comprehension

19 CHARACTER Casey says, "But you have me now, Paw-Paw." What does this tell us about her? Let's finish filling in our charts.

DETAIL	CHARACTER
Casey says she doesn't feel sorry for herself.	Casey wants to seem tough.
Paw-Paw suggests that they play cards.	Paw-Paw knows Casey is hurt and wants to make it up to her.
Casey says, "But you have me now, Paw-Paw."	Casey wants to stay with Paw-Paw. She wants to be needed.

RETELL THE STORY Invite students to retell the important events of the story, focusing on how the characters act and feel. Suggest they refer to their charts as needed. Remind students that this story is an excerpt from a novel. What do students think might happen next in the novel? Why? *Summarize*

some station was playing reruns. Paw-Paw liked that, especially the deep voice of the marshal. It was good to sit there in the darkening little room, listening to Marshal Dillon inside your head and picturing him as big and tall and striding down the dusty streets of Dodge City. And I got us some other programs too, shows that Paw-Paw had never been able to listen to before.

Don't get the idea that Paw-Paw was stupid. She just didn't understand American machines that well. She lived with them in a kind of truce where she never asked much of them if they wouldn't ask much of her.

"It's getting near eight," Paw-Paw said anxiously. It was only when I got the station back for her that she began to relax. "I was always so worried that I would not be able to get back the station, I never tried to listen to others. Look what I missed."

"But you have me now, Paw-Paw," I said.

19 "Yes," Paw-Paw smiled briefly, straightening in her chair. "I guess I do."

462

REREADING FOR *Fluency*

PARTNERS Have partners take turns reading the story aloud. Remind them that Casey is the narrator of the story so they should think about how she is feeling as they read.

READING RATE When you evaluate rate, have the student read aloud from the story for one minute. Place a stick-on note after the last word read. Count words read. To evaluate

students' performance, see the Running Record in the **Fluency Assessment** book.

i Intervention For leveled fluency lessons, passages, and norms charts, see **Skills Intervention Guide**, Part 4, Fluency.

MEET
Laurence Yep

For much of his early life, Laurence Yep knew what it was like to feel that he did not belong. He lived in a neighborhood where he was the only Chinese-American boy, and, despite his Chinese heritage, he was one of the few Chinese-American students at his school who could not speak Chinese.

Yep's feeling of being an outsider led him to read science fiction. There, he found characters and situations that seemed familiar, he says, "because in those books children were taken to other lands and other worlds where they had to learn strange customs and languages—and that was something I did every time I got on and off the bus."

Yep sold his first story when he was eighteen and was paid a penny per word. Not surprisingly, that piece was science fiction, as are many of Yep's later works. He also writes realistic novels, often drawing upon his Chinese-American background. One of these is *Dragonwings*, which was a Newbery Honor Book. Another is *Child of the Owl*, which won the Boston Globe–Horn Book Award in 1979.

Comprehension

Return to Predictions and Purposes

Review with students their story predictions and reasons for reading the story. How close were their predictions? Did they find out what they wanted to know?

PREDICTIONS	WHAT HAPPENED
This story is about a girl and an older woman.	This story is about a girl meeting her grandmother for the first time.
The girl goes to visit the woman.	As they get to know each other, the girl is happier about the idea of living with her grandmother.

INFORMAL
ASSESSMENT

STORY ELEMENTS

HOW TO ASSESS

- Ask students to pretend they are Casey and have them describe themselves.

- Have students tell how Paw-Paw feels about having Casey there.

Students should have an understanding of how both Casey and Paw-Paw feel and act. They should be able to make inferences about both characters.

FOLLOW UP If students are having trouble analyzing character, have them brainstorm adjectives to describe Casey and Paw-Paw and then give specific examples from the story.

LITERARY RESPONSE

QUICK-WRITE Suggest students record their thoughts about the story in their journals. Use the following questions to get them started:

- Do you think you would enjoy meeting Casey? What do you like best about her? Least?

- What would you like to know about Casey that the story doesn't tell you?

ORAL RESPONSE Have students share their journal writings and discuss whether or not they would recommend this story to others.

463

Story Questions

Have students discuss or write the answers to the questions on page 464.

Answers

1. Casey. *Literal/Character*

2. Through Casey's words, thoughts, and actions. *Inferential/Character*

3. Sample answer: The characters' actions and feelings seem realistic. *Inferential/Character*

4. Answers will vary. *Critical/Summarize*

5. The two in the painting are probably mother and daughter. Casey and Paw-Paw may develop a strong bond over time. *Critical/Reading Across Texts*

Write a Story For a full lesson related to this suggestion, see pages 467K–467L.

Story Questions & Activities

1. Who is the main character in the story?

2. How does the author let you know what Casey is thinking and feeling?

3. What makes this story believable? Explain.

4. What do you think is the best part of the story? Why?

5. Look carefully at the people in the painting on page 446. What do they have in common with Casey and Paw-Paw? Do you think Casey and Paw-Paw will develop such a strong bond? Why or why not?

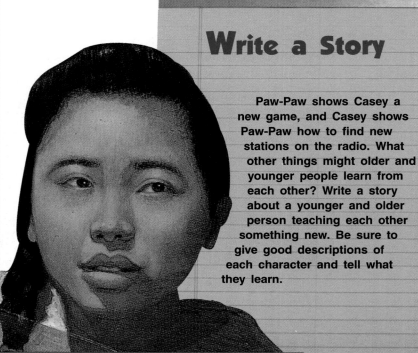

Write a Story

Paw-Paw shows Casey a new game, and Casey shows Paw-Paw how to find new stations on the radio. What other things might older and younger people learn from each other? Write a story about a younger and older person teaching each other something new. Be sure to give good descriptions of each character and tell what they learn.

Meeting Individual Needs

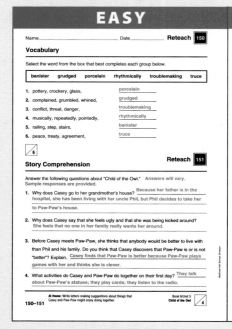

EASY

Reteach, 151

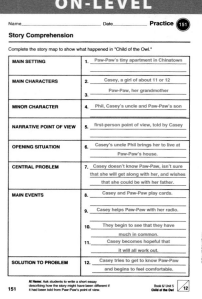

ON-LEVEL

Practice, 151

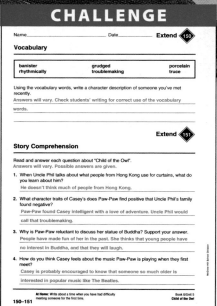

CHALLENGE

Extend, 151

Paint a Portrait

Casey's grandmother believes that the "face is a map of the soul." What do you think Casey really looks like? Scan the selection for a description of Casey. Pay special attention to what she says and what is said about her. Then use this information and the character description to paint a portrait of Casey.

Make a "Get-well" Card

How would you cheer up Barney in the hospital? Imagine that you are Casey. Make a "get-well" card for your father. Write a poem or a special message on the inside of the card. Then draw a humorous illustration on the front. Include a few words about life with Paw-Paw.

Find Out More

To get into Paw-Paw's apartment, Uncle Phil has to buzz nine times. Casey figures out that nine buzzes is Morse code for SOS. What do you know about Morse code? Who invented it, and why? Look in an encyclopedia, or use the Internet to find out about Morse code. Share your findings with your classmates.

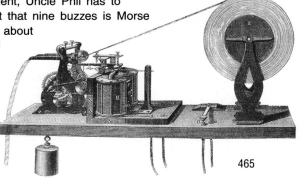

465

Story Activities

Paint a Portrait

Materials: paints, brushes, paper

ONE Suggest that students paint their own versions of Casey rather than copying images from the illustrations. Encourage students to be creative in their choice of painting styles (representational, abstract, etc.). Students can do a sketch before starting the actual painting, if they wish.

Make a Get-Well Card

Materials: construction paper, markers or crayons

PARTNERS Have students work together to design a card Casey could send to Barney. Remind them to think about what they know not only about Casey, but about Barney as well. Allow students time to view and discuss each other's cards.

Find Out More

RESEARCH AND INQUIRY Ask groups to **GROUP** discuss and list what they already know about Morse code. Then have them make a list of what they want to know. Help them use the suggested resources of information. Students may also enjoy trying to write and decipher a message in Morse code.

*inter**NET*** **CONNECTION** For more information about Morse code, students can visit **www.mhschool.com/reading**

Activity

SOCIAL STUDIES: CHINESE IMMIGRANTS Have students research in almanacs, encyclopedias, and reference books to find out about Chinese immigration to the United States in the 1800s. Then have them create reports.

What to Look For Check to see that each student:

- includes accurate statistics about the number of Chinese immigrants who arrived in the nineteenth century.
- identifies areas where Chinese immigrants settled.
- identifies occupations and major contributions of the immigrants.

CHALLENGE

Study Skills

GRAPHIC AIDS

OBJECTIVES Students will identify relationships on a family tree.

PREPARE Read the passage with students. Display **Teaching Chart 123.**

TEACH Show students the family tree and point out the relationships shown by the lines. Have a student find a brother and sister on the family tree. Have another volunteer count the number of generations shown on the family tree.

PRACTICE Have students answers questions 1–5. Review the answers with them.
1. Ethel **2.** three **3.** They are cousins. **4.** They are brothers-in-law. **5.** Answers will vary.

ASSESS/CLOSE Have students create family trees of their own. Students can exchange work and check trees for clarity.

Study Skills

Read a Family Tree

You probably know that a **family tree** is a time map of a family. It is also a diagram. A family tree shows who was married to whom, which children were born to which parents, and often, how distant relatives are related. Family trees can be short or long. If they are long, they can go back many generations.

Look at Casey's family tree. How far does it go back?

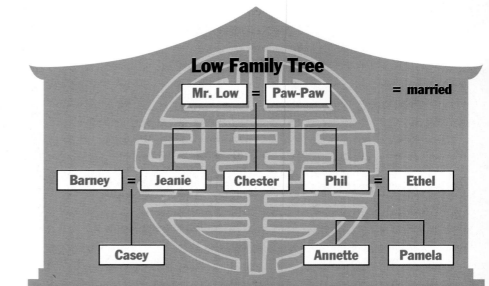

Low Family Tree

= married

Mr. Low = Paw-Paw

Barney = Jeanie   Chester   Phil = Ethel

Casey   Annette   Pamela

Use the family tree to answer these questions.

1 Who is Phil's wife?

2 How many children does Paw-Paw have?

3 How is Casey related to Annette and Pamela?

4 How is Barney related to Chester?

5 Why do you think people are interested in family trees?

Meeting Individual Needs

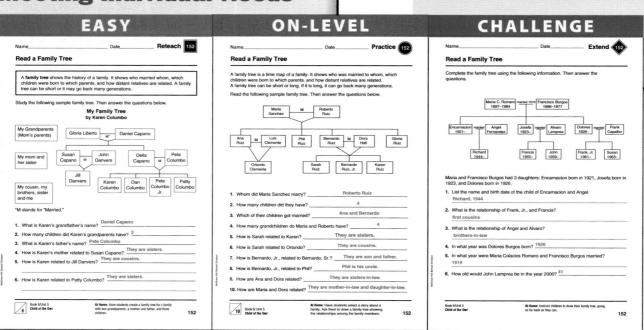

Reteach, 152   Practice, 152   Extend, 152

TEST POWER

THE PRINCETON REVIEW

Test Tip

The summary tells what the passage is mostly about.

DIRECTIONS

Read the sample story. Then read each question about the story.

SAMPLE

Harriet Beecher Stowe

In 1852, a novel was published that exposed the cruelty of slavery to a wide audience. Many people of that day already believed that enslaved people should be freed. But *Uncle Tom's Cabin*, by Harriet Beecher Stowe, broke new ground in educating people about the injustices of slavery.

Uncle Tom's Cabin was first published as a series in an antislavery newsletter. In 1852, after the Fugitive Slave Act was passed, it was published as a book. In its first week, it sold 10,000 copies. The well-received book, based on Stowe's own experiences, portrayed a kind plantation family, a brutal slaveholder, and a benevolent enslaved man, Uncle Tom.

Since then, it has been reprinted in 37 languages, and millions of copies have been sold worldwide.

1 After *Uncle Tom's Cabin* was published, what probably happened next?

  A Stowe published her second book.

  B Stowe became a teacher.

  Ⓒ Many people wanted to abolish slavery.

  D Many people visited plantations.

2 According to the passage, Harriet Beecher Stowe wrote *Uncle Tom's Cabin* to teach people about —

  F language

  Ⓖ slavery

  H plantations

  J fugitives

467

Test Power

THE PRINCETON REVIEW

Read the Page

Have students read the story and choose the *best* answers.

Discuss the Questions

Question 1: This question asks students to use their prediction skills to speculate about an outcome. Remind students to refer back to the passage to find facts that support their answer choice.

Question 2: This question asks students to evaluate what Harriet Beecher Stowe's message was in the book *Uncle Tom's Cabin*. Instruct students to read each answer choice and to eliminate answers that are about things that are not discussed in the passage. For example, the fourth answer choice says that Stowe was trying to teach about *fugitives*, but the passage never mentioned *fugitives*. Therefore, this choice should be eliminated. Have students use this process for all answer choices.

Leveled Books

written by Marina Ramos
illustrated by Charles Reid

EASY

A Tune for Lucy

Syllable Patterns

☑ Story Elements

☑ Instructional Vocabulary: *banister, grudged, porcelain, rhythmically, troublemaking, truce*

Answers to Story Questions

1. Sarah met Lucy when Lucy's cat Sebastian ran under Sarah's porch and she had to help Lucy get her cat back.
2. She brought the statue because she thought it might bring her good luck and help her make friends.
3. She was happy that she was able to teach kids again. Also, she was filled with joy that she was able to enjoy their company and listen to music, and that the girls wanted to spend time with her.
4. The story is mostly about an older woman who helps a child, and vice versa.
5. Answers will vary.

The *Story Questions and Activity* below appear in the *Easy Book*.

Story Questions

1. How did Sarah meet her neighbor and how did she help her?
2. Why did Sarah bring her statue of Mozart with her on her first day of school?
3. Why was Lucy so happy when Sarah asked her if she could bring a friend over for their piano lessons?
4. What is the story mostly about?
5. Compare and contrast Lucy and Sarah's relationship in this story with Casey and Paw-Paw in *Child of the Owl*.

We Can Learn From Everyone We Meet

Have students talk about times when someone outside of school taught them something they did not already know. Did it take them a long time to learn? Were they able to use what they had learned later on?

from A Tune for Lucy

Guided Reading

PREVIEW AND PREDICT Ask students to look at the illustrations and the title page and predict what they will be reading about. Ask volunteers to link the title, chapter headings and illustrations with specific predictions. List the predictions on the board.

SET PURPOSES What do students want to find out as they read this story? For example, students may be interested in finding out who Lucy is.

READ THE BOOK Students can read to themselves while you monitor their reading. Use the questions below to help students understand the book.

Page 5: What character traits does Sarah show by her actions on this page? (helpfulness, interest in others, affection for animals) *Character*

Page 6: What four words do you see with the /ē/ sound spelled *ea* in the third paragraph on the page? (teach, really, beneath). *Phonics and Decoding*

Page 11: You can understand the word *rhythmically* on this page by taking it apart. What word is the base word? (rhythm) What does the *ly* ending usually mean? (the word is an adverb) So, what can you tell about the meaning of *rhythmically*? (It describes *tapped*, and explains how she tapped her hand.) *Vocabulary*

Page 14: What can you infer from Sarah's talking about learning to play the piano in the summer? (She really enjoys learning to play, since she mentioned that instead of other things she had done in the summer, such as move.) *Make Inferences*

RETURN TO PREDICTIONS AND PURPOSES Look at the predictions students wrote. How many were accurate?

LITERARY RESPONSE Discuss these questions:

- Compare Lucy and Sarah. What do they have in common? How are they different?

- Imagine that this story continues. What do you think will happen next?

Also see the story questions and activity in *A Tune for Lucy*.

Leveled Books

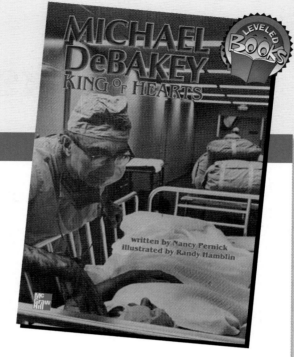

INDEPENDENT

Michael DeBakey: King of Hearts

☑ **Story Elements**

☑ **Instructional Vocabulary:** *banister, grudged, porcelain, rhythmically, troublemaking, truce*

Guided Reading

PREVIEW AND PREDICT Guide students to discuss the illustrations. Have them make predictions about Dr. DeBakey's life and accomplishments.

SET PURPOSES Ask students what they want to learn about Dr. DeBakey. They might want to know, for instance, whether he was good just in science or in other areas, too.

READ THE BOOK Have students first read the story independently. Use the questions below to help guide students' reading.

Page 4: What does the story about his cap reveal about DeBakey's values? (He learned that it is important to share things in life.) *Character*

Page 7: What does the word *truce* mean here? (an agreement) *Vocabulary*

Page 8: Why was DeBakey's first medical invention important? (The roller pump he invented would later become an important aspect of open-heart surgery). *Important and Unimportant Information*

Pages 13–16: Do you think the title of the book fits Dr. DeBakey? Why? (Encourage students to summarize the last three pages—his medical work with heart transplants and the personal "heart" he gives to educate people about the heart.) *Summarize*

RETURN TO PREDICTIONS AND PURPOSES Review students' predictions and reasons for reading. Discuss the importance of DeBakey's contributions to science.

LITERARY RESPONSE Discuss these questions:

• What did you learn in this nonfiction book?

• What else would you like to know about Dr. DeBakey? How might you find this information?

Also see the story questions and activity in *Michael DeBakey: King of Hearts.*

Answers to Story Questions

1. to care about other people, to share, honesty, pride, self-discipline, to sew, to manage money
2. DeBakey has gained a world-wide reputation as an expert on the heart. He has devoted his career to heart-related surgery, research, and teaching.
3. hard-working, concerned about others, creative, a good problem-solver, able to do many things at once, willing to share what he knows with younger people, interested in new ways of doing things
4. Dr. DeBakey's many talents and his determination have won him many honors, and his dedication to his work has led to an improved quality of life for people with heart disease.
5. Answers will vary.

The *Story Questions and Activity* below appear in the *Independent Book*.

Story Questions

1. What values and skills did Michael DeBakey learn from his parents?
2. Why has Dr. DeBakey been called "the King of Hearts"?
3. How would you describe Dr. DeBakey?
4. What is the main idea of the book?
5. Grandma in *Child of the Owl* and Dr. Michael DeBakey both have seen a great deal of change in the 20th century. What do you think they have in common? What would they talk about if they met?

Write a Play

Using facts in this book and information from your own research, write a script for a play about Michael DeBakey. Working with a partner, you may wish to role-play the script and record it on tape to share with other students.

from Michael DeBakey: King of Hearts

Leveled Books

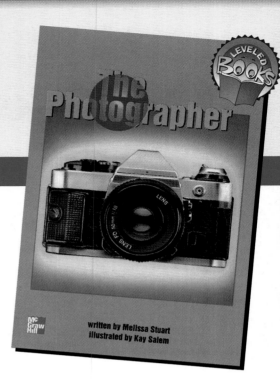

CHALLENGE

The Photographer

☑ **Story Elements**

☑ **Instructional Vocabulary:** *banister, grudged, porcelain, rhythmically, troublemaking, truce*

written by Melissa Stuart
illustrated by Kay Salem

Answers to Story Questions

1. Janna used to be a nature photographer; the photographs were all from her past career.
2. As she came to know Janna, she became more fond of her and found her to be a very interesting person.
3. She admired Janna's pictures, so she decided to use the medium of photography for her project, using her dog as her subject.
4. It is about a young girl who volunteers to spend time with an elderly person. They befriend each other, and they each enjoy and benefit from the relationship.
5. Answers will vary.

The *Story Questions and Activity* below appear in the *Challenge Book*.

Story Questions

1. Why was it that many of the pictures on Janna's wall were of animals?
2. What made Sara's feeling about the visits change as she kept going back?
3. How did Janna's pictures influence Sara's choice for a project?
4. What is this story mostly about?
5. Compare and contrast Sara and Janna's relationship to that of Casey and Paw-Paw in *Child of the Owl*.

Favorites for Photos

Pretend you have the same assignment as Sara. Make a list of images that you might want to photograph to complete the assignment. Then choose one and tell about your choice.

from The Photographer

Guided Reading

PREVIEW AND PREDICT Ask students to list the ways they can preview what they will be reading. Then ask students to use these ways to preview and make predictions about *The Photographer*.

SET PURPOSES Ask students what in their previewing made them curious. What do they want to know about this book? For example, do they wonder what role photography plays in this book?

READ THE BOOK Have students read independently. Refer to the questions below to help gauge student comprehension of the book.

Page 2: How can you tell from the context what the word *banister* means? (Sara holds it as she walks up an inclined path.) *Vocabulary*

Page 7: What can you infer about Sara from the fact that she brings along Asta to visit Janna? (She is considerate and wants to make Janna happy.) *Make Inferences*

Page 11: What do Sara and Janna have in common? (love of animals, interest in photography) *Character*

Page 13: Explain how Sara readied the photograph for her assignment. (chose the photo, cropped the photo, mounted it on matte board) *Steps in a Process*

RETURN TO PREDICTIONS AND PURPOSES Were predictions students made about the book accurate? Ask students what clues in previewing led to their accurate predictions.

LITERARY RESPONSE Discuss these questions:

- Explain the role that photography plays in this book.
- Why do you think Sara decided to put Janna in the photograph instead of Asta?

Also see the story questions and activity in *The Photographer*.

Bringing Groups Together

Anthology and Leveled Books

Connecting Texts

GENERATION CHARTS All these books feature relationships between people of different generations. Ask students to create and fill out a Generation chart that explores these relationships. Then talk about the relationships described in the books. Discuss how the relationships are alike, and how they are different.

Child of the Owl	A Tune for Lucy	Michael DeBakey: King of Hearts	The Photographer
• Casey, Paw-Paw • child, grand-mother • They find they have much in common, and teach each other.	• Lucy, Sarah • friends of different generations • They become friends, and Lucy teaches Sarah piano and becomes less lonely herself.	• Michael DeBakey, his parents • parents, child • Parents inspire him to study hard, share, and help others.	• Sara, Janna • friends of different generations • Friendship: Sara keeps Janna company; Janna teaches her to take photographs.

Viewing/Representing

GROUP PRESENTATIONS Divide the class into groups, one for each of the four books. (For *Child of the Owl,* combine students of different reading levels.) Have each group create a radio play based on the story, choose parts, and read the play to the class.

AUDIENCE RESPONSE Ask students to develop and use a set of criteria to evaluate the other groups' presentations. Students can also discuss what they learned from the other groups' presentations, and how their radio play is similar and different from the others.

Research and Inquiry

FINDING A NEW HOBBY People in each of these selections have different interests: Paw-Paw likes to play cards and listen to music, Michael DeBakey is fascinated by medicine, Sarah finds she likes piano, and Sara takes up photography. Ask students to think of a hobby or interest they have thought of exploring, and research that interest with manuals or hobby books. Students should discover:

• what materials or equipment is needed

• more details about their hobby or interest

• how to get involved in their area

 If students use the Internet, suggest they visit ***www.mhschool.com/reading***

 **OBJECTIVES**

Students will analyze story characters.

Skills Finder	
Story Elements: Character, Setting, Plot	
Introduce	65A–B
Review	369A–B, 405E–F, 447A–B, 467E–F, 503A–B, 531E–F
Test	Unit 1, Unit 4, Unit 5
Maintain	147, 179

TEACHING TIP

CHARACTER TRAITS If students are having a hard time thinking of character traits, suggest they reread the passage and then brainstorm a list of adjectives that came to mind.

Afterwards, they can choose the ones they feel best describe Casey.

SELF-SELECTED
Reading

Students may choose from the following titles.

ANTHOLOGY
• Child of the Owl

LEVELED BOOKS
• A Time for Lucy
• Michael DeBakey, King of Hearts
• The Photographer
Bibliography, pages T80–T81

467E   *Child of the Owl*

Review Story Elements

PREPARE

Discuss Analyzing Character

Review: Ask students to tell you how a reader can better understand a character and his or her behavior. Students should know to look at a character's words, thoughts, and actions.

TEACH

Read "Casey Shops" and Model the Skill

Ask students to pay close attention to information that can help them better understand the character as you read **Teaching Chart 124** with them.

Casey Shops

Casey walked alone through the unfamiliar streets of Chinatown. The stuff in the windows of the stores seemed strange to her. She didn't even know what most of it was. She tried to memorize the items so she could ask Paw-Paw about them. She would have gone in and asked the storekeepers, but she wanted to buy a new deck of cards for Paw-Paw before the stores closed. She knew how much Paw-Paw liked cards, and that old deck of hers was looking tattered.

Teaching Chart 124

Discuss story information that helps readers determine what character traits Casey has.

MODEL   Casey wants to ask Paw-Paw what the stuff in the store windows is. This tells me that Casey is interested in learning about her new neighborhood.

Analyze Character

Have students underline and discuss details that give clues to Casey's character traits.

Create a Character Trait Web

GROUP

Have students use the information from the chart to create a character trait web for Casey. Help students get started. ▶ **Linguistic**

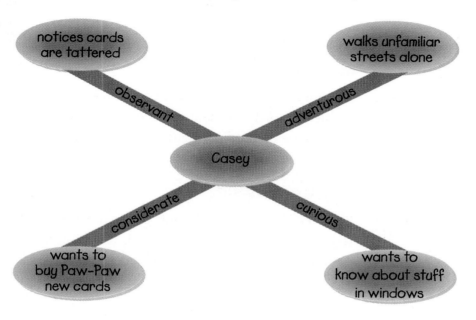

notices cards are tattered

walks unfamiliar streets alone

observant

adventurous

Casey

considerate

curious

wants to buy Paw-Paw new cards

wants to know about stuff in windows

ASSESS/CLOSE

Write a Scene for the Character

Have students work together and use what they know about Casey to write a scene about her. They can write it in either the first or third person. Invite partners to share and discuss their writing with the class.

ALTERNATE TEACHING STRATEGY

STORY ELEMENTS

For a different approach to teaching this skill, see page T62.

Intervention ▶ Skills

Intervention Guide, for direct instruction and extra practice of story elements

Meeting Individual Needs for Comprehension

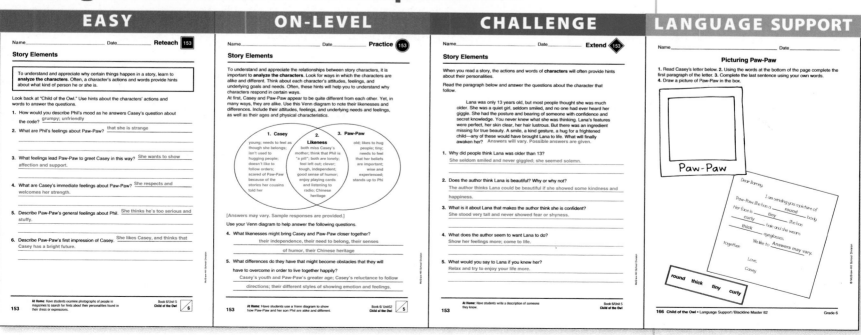

EASY
Reteach, 153

ON-LEVEL
Practice, 153

CHALLENGE
Extend, 153

LANGUAGE SUPPORT
Language Support, 166

467F

OBJECTIVES

Students will use story clues to make inferences.

Skills Finder

Make Inferences

Introduce	39G-H
Review	63G-H, 83G-H, 109E-F, 467G-H, 481G-H, 531G-H
Test	Unit 1, Unit 5
Maintain	335, 351, 515, 557, 625

TEACHING TIP

MAKE INFERENCES

- Remind students to draw on their own personal experience and knowledge to help them make inferences.

- Help students see that being able to figure out what is going on involves them in the story and makes the story more interesting to read.

Review Make Inferences

PREPARE

Discuss Inferences Remind students that authors don't always give complete information about a character, setting, or action, and it is up to the reader to use clues in the text to figure out what is going on.

TEACH

Read "Phil" and Model the Skill Read "Phil" aloud. Ask students to use the information in the passage to infer as much as possible both about Phil and about what happened with him and the other characters.

Phil

Phil's car squealed out of Chinatown, just barely keeping to the speed limit. He hated Chinatown with all its noise and crowded buildings. He'd be glad when he got home, where it was much better. He was glad he had left Casey there with Paw-Paw. He was glad to be away from the two of them. How dare they have treated him in such a way! He couldn't wait to get back to his own family, to people who respected him and listened to what he had to say.

Teaching Chart 125

Ask a volunteer to underline the first sentence that tells something about Phil.

MODEL Since the car is *Phil's car*, I can infer that he is driving it, and since he is *squealing* out of Chinatown, he is in a hurry to leave.

Create an Inference Chart

Have students create an Inference chart from the clues they found in "Phil." Help them get started. ▶ Linguistic

GROUP

CLUE	INFERENCE
Phil's car squeals out of Chinatown.	Phil is driving and is upset or in a hurry.
Phil hates the noise and crowding of Chinatown.	Phil lives in a quiet place that is not crowded.
He is glad to be going where people respect him.	Phil is upset with Casey and Paw-Paw because he feels they don't respect him.

ASSESS/CLOSE

Make and Compare Inferences

Have small groups of students choose passages from *Child of the Owl* and individually write down everything they can infer from that passage. Then have students within the groups compare and discuss their inferences.

ALTERNATE TEACHING STRATEGY

MAKE INFERENCES

For a different approach to teaching this skill, see page T64.

 **Intervention** ▶ **Skills Intervention Guide,** for direct instruction and extra practice with making inferences

Meeting Individual Needs for Comprehension

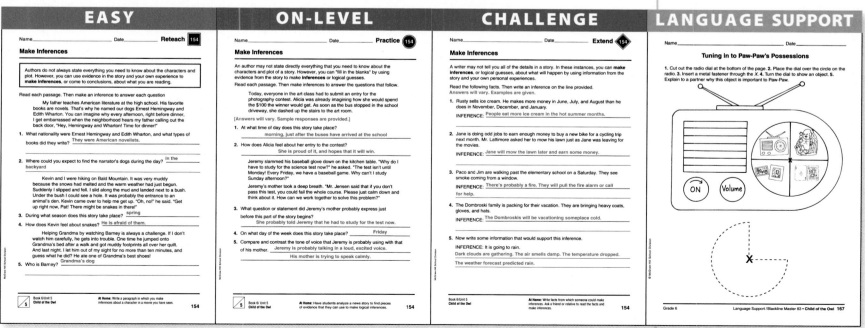

EASY — Reteach, 154

ON-LEVEL — Practice, 154

CHALLENGE — Extend, 154

LANGUAGE SUPPORT — Language Support, 167

OBJECTIVES

Students will identify the use of connotation and denotation.

Skills Finder
Denotation and Connotation

Introduce	467I-J
Review	531I-J, 541I-J
Test	Unit 5

TEACHING TIP

CONNOTATION Tell students that connotations can sometimes be personal, and that different people might have different connotations for the same word. If a writer is using a word for its connotation, it is important he or she gives clues to the connotation.

Introduce Denotation and Connotation

PREPARE

Explain Denotation and Connotation
Write the word *home* on the chalkboard. Under it write *connotation* and *denotation*. Ask students to define the word *home*. (a place where you live or belong) Write the definition under *denotation*. Then ask them what the word *home* means to them, such as *a place of safety* or *family*. Write their answers under *connotation*.

TEACH

Have students read the passage on **Teaching Chart 126,** directing them to pay attention to the usage of the word *door*.

The Door

Casey wanted to know about the statues in Paw-Paw's home. But Casey's interest seemed to make Paw-Paw angry. Paw-Paw didn't want to talk about them, even though it was obvious that the statues were important to her. This made Casey feel as if there were a door between them—a door that wouldn't open. They had been getting so close before, and Casey couldn't bear for Paw-Paw to shut her out now.

Teaching Chart 126

MODEL Casey feels that there is a closed door between herself and Paw-Paw. The denotation of *door* is a barrier that opens and closes. What is the connotation, or emotional meaning, of the word for Casey? I think for her *door*, must suggest something negative.

Discuss Connotation
Help students see that Casey views the door as something negative, a barrier that keeps her and Paw-Paw apart.

PRACTICE

Identify Connotations

GROUP

Have volunteers underline the information that helps them to understand the connotation of the word *door* as used in the passage. Ask students to discuss whether or not they like the use of the word *door* in this passage.

ASSESS/CLOSE

Write a Paragraph

Have students brainstorm a list of nouns and then discuss both the connotations and denotations of those words. Have them choose one or two words and use them in a paragraph so that their connotations are clear.

ALTERNATE TEACHING STRATEGY

·······································

CONNOTATION AND DENOTATION

For a different approach to teaching this skill, see page T65.

 **Intervention** ▶ **Skills**

Intervention Guide, for direct instruction and extra practice of denotation and connotation

---

Meeting Individual Needs for Vocabulary

EASY	ON-LEVEL	CHALLENGE	LANGUAGE SUPPORT

EASY

Name_____ Date_____ **Reteach** 155

Denotation and Connotation

A word's **denotation** is its dictionary definition. The same word might also have a **connotation**, or a more emotional definition, based on the positive or negative feelings that it creates in a reader.

Example: "I have a secret," she hissed. (negative connotation)
"I have a secret," she whispered. (positive connotation)

In the chart below, the words in each pair of sentences have the same denotation. However, one has a more positive connotation and one has a more negative connotation. Write **positive** or **negative** to show each word's connotation.

Word	Shared Denotation	Words in Sentences	Connotations
1. firm	strong	She was very firm about her rules.	positive
tough		She was very tough about her rules	negative
2. sneak	move	Did they sneak into the movie theater?	negative
stroll		Did they stroll into the movie theater?	positive
3. scorching	giving off heat	The scorching sun was above.	negative
warming		The warming sun was above.	positive
4. nibbled	ate	We nibbled on some snacks.	positive
devoured		We devoured the snacks.	negative
5. shared	told	He shared news about his friends.	positive
exposed		He exposed the news about his friends.	negative
6. exhausted	tired	I'm exhausted from walking all day.	negative
sleepy		I'm sleepy from walking all day.	positive

At Home: Decide whether the following words have positive or negative connotations: *announce, mumble, shout, ask, purr, complain, request, demand, suggest, offer, snort, contribute, whine, clarify.*

155   Book 6/Unit 5 **Child of the Owl** 12

Reteach, 155

ON-LEVEL

Name_____ Date_____ **Practice** 155

Denotation and Connotation

A word's **denotation** is its dictionary definition. The same word might also have a **connotation**, or a more emotional definition, based on the positive or negative feelings that it creates in a reader.
Read each pair of words. Write whether each word has a more positive or a more negative connotation. Then write the denotation that the words share. Finally, use each word in a sentence that shows its positive or negative connotations.
Answers will vary. Sample responses are provided.

Words	Connotations		Shared Denotation
skinny	1. negative	3.	thin
slim	2. positive		

4. Sentence: The boy was too skinny because he had been sick.
5. Sentence: The boy was slim because he ate healthy food and exercised daily.

Words	Connotation		Shared Denotation
fragrance	6. positive	8.	smell
odor	7. negative		

9. Sentence: The fragrance of the flowers was sweet.
10. Sentence: The odor of the perfume was over-powering.

Words	Connotation		Shared Denotation
alerted	11. positive	13.	to let someone know
warned	12. negative		ahead of time

14. Sentence: He alerted me about the heavy traffic.
15. Sentence: He warned me about my poor attendance.

Words	Connotation		Shared Denotation
fussy	16. negative	18.	careful,
precise	17. positive		detail oriented

19. sentence: She was fussy about how we packed the boxes.
She was precise about her career goals.

At Home: Separate synonyms for the word move into these groups: Words with Positive Connotations, Words with Negative Connotations, and Words with Neutral Connotations.

155   Book 6/ Unit 5 **Child of the Owl** 19

Practice, 155

CHALLENGE

Name_____ Date_____ **Extend** 155

Denotation and Connotation

The **denotation** of a word is its dictionary definition. But some words have a **connotation** as well. Connotations are the emotions or associations suggested by certain words.

Look at the pairs of words below. Each pair has a similar denotation, or definition. Circle the word with a negative connotation in each pair and tell what emotions or associations are suggested. Feel free to use your dictionary.
Answers will vary. Possible answers are given.

1. freedom / (license) It suggests the use of freedom to go over the line; to take advantage of freedom to do something wrong.

2. (nosy)/ curious It suggests prying, or wrongly intruding into another's affairs.

3. assertive / (aggressive) While an assertive person is applauded, an aggressive person is usually not. Aggression suggests taking assertiveness a step too far.

4. (mousy) / quiet Quiet does not suggest, or connote, a negative judgment, whereas mousy suggests that the person would not stand up for him or herself even if it were important to do so.

Write sentences for the words with a positive connotation.

_____
_____
_____
_____
_____

At Home: Have students use the words *squandered* and *lost* in sentences.

155   Book 6/Unit 5 **Child of the Owl**

Extend, 155

LANGUAGE SUPPORT

Name_____ Date_____

Creative Connotations

1. Read the sentence at the top of each set of boxes below. 2. Draw a picture for each sentence using the directions at the bottom of each box as a guide.

Phil was out of shape.	
Answers may vary.	Answers may vary.
Draw a shape.	Draw someone who is not fit.

Phil asked for a hand.	
Answers may vary.	Answers may vary.
Draw a hand.	Draw someone helping someone else.

Casey felt like a door closed between them.	
Answers may vary.	Answers may vary.
Draw a door.	Draw two people with a problem between them.

168 Child of the Owl • Language Support / Blackline Master 84   Grade 6

Language Support, 168

Writing a Story

Prewrite

WRITE A STORY Present this writing assignment: Paw-Paw shows Casey a new game, and Casey shows Paw-Paw how to find new stations on the radio. Write a story about a younger person and an older person teaching each other something new. Be sure to provide vivid descriptions of each character and to tell what they learn.

BRAINSTORM IDEAS Have the class brainstorm a list of adjectives and descriptive details for the younger and older characters. Then have students work independently to develop the two characters and to create a setting and plot for their story.

Strategy: Make a Flow Chart Once students have developed their characters and thought of a plot, have them list the main events of their story in a flow chart. Remind them that the story events should follow a progression that leads to a convincing conclusion.

Draft

USE THE FLOW CHART Students should refer to their flow charts as they write their drafts, making sure to include the thoughts and feelings of their characters as they react to each story event.

Revise

SELF-QUESTIONING Ask students to assess their drafts.

- Are my characters realistic?
- Do their words, thoughts, and feelings give a clear picture of who the characters are?
- At the conclusion of the story, did the younger and older characters learn a valuable lesson from each other?

PARTNERS Have partners share stories and give each other feedback.

Edit/Proofread

CHECK FOR ERRORS Students should reread their stories to check for spelling, grammar, and punctuation mistakes.

Publish

MAKE AN ANTHOLOGY Students can make an anthology of their stories, complete with photographs and illustrations. When the table of contents and cover are finished, photocopy the book and give each student a copy.

One Rainy Afternoon

By Tatiana Vega

"Sorry, honey," Ana's grandmother said softly, "maybe you can meet Myra tomorrow." Ana shook her head sadly as she watched the rain pounding their minivan outside. "She's going away with her family tomorrow and won't be back for two whole weeks."
Mrs. Montero smiled and said, "You remind me of your mom when she was your age."
"Really?" asked Ana, raising an eyebrow. Ten minutes later, she was sitting with her grandmother on the couch, looking through old photos of her mom and Lisa.
Then Ana said, "You know, Grandma, I could spend these two weeks organizing your photos and making a video album with you..."
"Really?" asked Mrs. Montero, raising an eyebrow.

Presentation Ideas

DESIGN A POSTER Suppose that your story was expanded into a movie. Use your story to design a movie poster for it.

▶ *Viewing/Representing*

IMPROVISATION Ask students to read their stories from the front of the room. Then have the class brainstorm a list of new situations for the characters. Finally have a group of students choose one situation and improvise the scene. ▶ *Speaking/Listening*

Consider students' creative efforts, possibly adding a plus (+) for originality, wit, and imagination.

Excellent	Good	Fair	Unsatisfactory
4: The writer • develops realistic characters with engaging dialogue and detail that reflects their thoughts and feelings. • presents a well-constructed plot in which both characters learn from each other. • creates a lively, entertaining story with a beginning, middle, and end.	**3:** The writer • focuses on distinct aspects of both characters' personalities. • constructs a plot in which both characters learn from each other. • creates a believable story with a beginning, middle, and end.	**2:** The writer • presents vague character traits. • leaves the plot unclear as to whether both characters have actually learned from each other. • creates a story with a beginning, middle, and end.	**1:** The writer • fails to adequately develop each character. • presents a plot in which only one of the characters learns from the other. • does not present a clear beginning, middle, and end.

Incomplete 0: The writer leaves the page blank or fails to respond to the writing task. The student does not address the topic or simply paraphrases the prompt. The response is illegible or incoherent.

For a 6-point or an 8-point scale, see pages T109–T110

Meeting Individual Needs for Writing

EASY	ON-LEVEL	CHALLENGE
Description Have students draw pictures of Phil, Casey, and Paw-Paw. Then have them list as many adjectives as they can to describe each of these characters.	**Diary Entry** Tell students: As Paw-Paw, write an entry in your diary describing the events and feelings you experienced the first day that Casey came to live with you. You may want to write about old memories that Casey has stirred up.	**Prequel** Based on what students know about the characters, have them write a scene that takes place when Casey is living with Phil's family.

Listening and Speaking

LISTENING STRATEGIES As improvisations are performed, have students:

• face the group performing and listen carefully.

• listen for the flow of the improvised scene to see if the ideas are connected.

SPEAKING STRATEGIES Encourage students who are performing improvisations to:

• use varied vocal tones to engage the audience.

• speak clearly.

LANGUAGE SUPPORT

ESL Suggest that English learners create their character traits webs with English-fluent partners. Have them review the phrasing and spelling of the actions, emotions, and physical descriptions in the web.

PORTFOLIO Invite students to include their essays or another writing project in their portfolios.

5 Day Grammar and Usage Plan

LANGUAGE SUPPORT

ESL Remind students that *he* and *she, him* and *her* are used exclusively for people and domesticated animals, while *it* is used for all inanimate objects.

DAILY LANGUAGE ACTIVITIES

Write each day's Activity on the board or use **Transparency 21.** Have students orally correct each sentence.

Day 1
1. Phil decided she can't take Casey.
2. The house was small, and he was crowded, too.
3. Casey smiled when it heard the joke.

Day 2
1. The girl came, and he saw Paw-Paw.
2. Phil and Casey were in Chinatown where we ate lunch.
3. Barney is ill, and it is still in bed.

Day 3
1. Chinatown is big, and he is noisy.
2. Phil told Casey, "It will live here."
3. Paw-Paw and I—they are family.

Day 4
1. These marks, it mean I have a temper.
2. When I looked, she saw nothing.
3. Since he lived by herself, Paw-Paw played a lot of card games.

Day 5
1. She is almost 8 o'clock.
2. When she hears the Chinese Hour, he will relax.
3. Yep sold his first story when it was 18.

Daily Language Transparency 21

Suggested answers on transparency

DAY 1 Introduce the Concept

Oral Warm-Up Read aloud: *Pat, Kim, Jan, and I are going to the mall.* Elicit the use of the pronoun *we* by asking the class to write a follow-up sentence.

Introduce Pronouns Discuss the following information:

Pronouns

- A **pronoun** is a word that takes the place of one or more nouns and the words that go with the nouns.

- The **antecedent,** or **referent,** of a pronoun is the word or group of words to which the pronoun refers. Pronouns and antecedents must agree.

Present the Daily Language Activity. Have students use the pronouns *he, it,* and *she* to correct the sentences. Then ask them to identify the antecedent, or referent, that each pronoun replaces.

 Assign the daily Writing Prompt on page 446C.

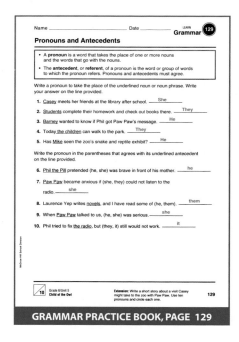

GRAMMAR PRACTICE BOOK, PAGE 129

DAY 2 Teach the Concept

Review Pronouns Ask students to explain what a pronoun and its antecedent, or referent, are and give examples of each in sentences.

Introduce Personal Pronouns There are both singular and plural pronouns; *you* may be either.

Pronouns

- Singular pronouns are *I, you, he, she, it, me, him, her.*

- Plural pronouns are *we, you, they, us, them.*

Present the Daily Language Activity and ask the students to correct the sentences orally by using the pronoun that matches its antecedent. Then have students write two sentences: in one, they should use a singular pronoun; in the other, a plural pronoun.

 Assign the daily Writing Prompt on page 446C.

GRAMMAR PRACTICE BOOK, PAGE 130

Pronouns

Learn from the Literature Review how pronouns should match their antecedents. Then read this sentence from *Child of the Owl*:

> **Phil stopped the car in the middle of the alley and I could see the rest of it was filled with apartment houses.**

After you finish reading, ask students what the antecedents are for the words *I* and *it*. (Casey, the narrator; the alley)

Identify Pronouns Present the Daily Language Activity and have students correct the sentences orally by using pronouns that match their referents.

Have partners each choose a paragraph (not dialogue, however) in the selection. As they read, have them list the pronouns and their antecedents.

 Assign the daily Writing Prompt on page 446D.

Review Pronouns Write the sentences from the Daily Language Activities for Days 1 through 3 on the board. Ask volunteers to draw an arrow from each pronoun to its antecedent. Then present the Daily Language Activity for Day 4.

Mechanics and Usage Pronouns are part of many contractions. Review contractions. Display and discuss:

> **Contractions**
> - A contraction may be formed by combining a pronoun and a verb.
> - An apostrophe shows where one or more letters have been left out.

Write on the board the pronouns *I, he, she, it, we, you, they*, and the verbs *am, is, are, have, has, had, will*. Write the contractions that can be formed, such as *I'm, we've, they'd, you'll.*

 Assign the daily Writing Prompt on page 446D.

Assess Use the Daily Language Activity and page 133 of the **Grammar Practice Book** for assessment.

Reteach Write pronouns on index cards. Ask students to take turns choosing a card and using the pronoun in an oral sentence that includes the antecedent.

Pass out long strips of colored paper and ask students to use their best handwriting to write two sentences: One will contain nouns, while the second will contain pronouns that replace the nouns. Post the sentences on the board.

Use page 134 of the **Grammar Practice Book** for additional reteaching.

 Assign the daily Writing Prompt on page 446D.

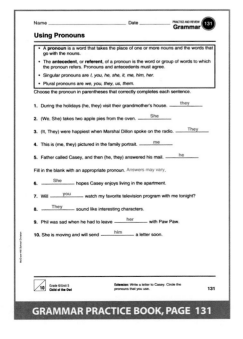

GRAMMAR PRACTICE BOOK, PAGE 131

GRAMMAR PRACTICE BOOK, PAGE 132

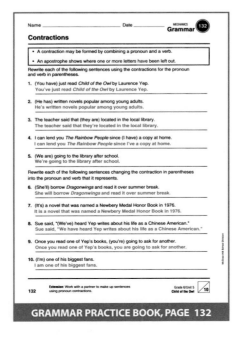

GRAMMAR PRACTICE BOOK, PAGE 133

GRAMMAR PRACTICE BOOK, PAGE 134

5Day Spelling Plan

ESL Write a list of compound words on the board and ask English learners to identify the three different forms: those that are written as two separate words, those written as a single word, and those joined by hyphens.

DICTATION SENTENCES

Spelling Words

1. The newborn needs his mother.
2. I have twenty-one minutes to finish.
3. The fool had no common sense.
4. The car was now old-fashioned.
5. When should I use a question mark?
6. He drank from a teacup.
7. We put the plates on the tablecloth.
8. We buy ready-made shirts.
9. I put on my bathrobe after my bath.
10. I like to read science fiction.
11. My friends live in apartment houses.
12. My brother-in-law is part of my family.
13. A fire escape is outside my window.
14. We cooked applesauce on the stove.
15. The self-reliant girl won't ask for help.
16. I point with my index finger.
17. We made a cross-country trip.
18. Our clever plan was foolproof.
19. The contact lens hurt my eye.
20. The silkworms made the silk.

Challenge Words

21. The banister is part of the stairway.
22. I grudged the money to pay the fine.
23. The plate was made from porcelain.
24. We dance rhythmically to the music.
25. A truce will stop the fighting.

DAY 1 Pretest

Assess Prior Knowledge Use the Dictation Sentences and **Spelling Practice Book** page 129 for the pretest.

Spelling Words		Challenge Words
1. newborn	11. **apartment houses**	21. banister
2. twenty-one	12. brother-in-law	22. **grudged**
3. common sense	13. **fire-escape**	23. **porcelain**
4. old-fashioned	14. applesauce	24. **rhythmically**
5. question mark	15. self-reliant	25. **truce**
6. **teacup**	16. **index finger**	
7. **tablecloth**	17. cross-country	
8. ready-made	18. foolproof	
9. bathrobe	19. contact lens	
10. science fiction	20. **silkworms**	

*Note: Words in **dark type** are from the story.*

Word Study On page 130 of the **Spelling Practice Book** are word study steps and an at-home activity.

DAY 2 Explore the Pattern

Sort and Spell Words Write the words *newborn, common sense*, and *twenty-one* on the chalkboard. Have students identify which compound word is written as one word, as two separate words, and as words joined by a hyphen. Have students read the Spelling Words and sort them as below.

One Word	old-fashioned	question mark
newborn	ready-made	science fiction
teacup	brother-in-law	apartment houses
tablecloth	self-reliant	fire escape
bathrobe	cross-country	index finger
applesauce	**Two Words**	contact lens
foolproof	common sense	
silkworms		
Hyphenated		
twenty-one		

Word Wall Have students create a word wall based on the word sort and add more words from their reading.

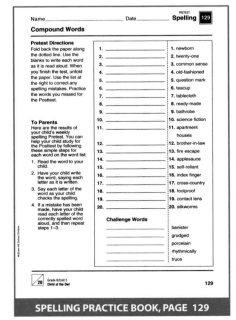

SPELLING PRACTICE BOOK, PAGE 129

WORD STUDY STEPS AND ACTIVITY, PAGE 130

SPELLING PRACTICE BOOK, PAGE 131

Compound Words

DAY 3 Practice and Extend

Word Meaning: Definitions Have students break down the Spelling Words into the individual words. Have groups of students work together to create new compounds from the base words (such as firehouses) and define them. If the compounds are not in a dictionary, have students create appropriate definitions.

If students need extra practice, have partners give each other a midweek test.

Glossary Remind students that the Glossary gives the word history of some words. Have students

- look up each Challenge Word to find the one with the word history. (*truce*)

- tell the meaning of the Middle English word from which *truce* comes.

- tell how the Middle English word and the Old English word explain the word *truce*.

DAY 4 Proofread and Write

Proofread Sentences Write these sentences on the chalkboard, including the misspelled words. Ask students to proofread, circling incorrect spellings and writing the correct spellings. There are two spelling errors in each sentence.

> My brother-in law put plates on the tabel cloth. (**brother-in-law, tablecloth**)
>
> She read sciencefiction on the fire-escape. (**science fiction, fire escape**)

Have students create additional sentences with errors for partners to correct.

 Have students use as many Spelling Words as possible in the daily Writing Prompt on page 446D. Remind students to proofread their writing for errors in spelling, grammar, and punctuation.

DAY 5 Assess and Reteach

Assess Students' Knowledge Use page 134 of the **Spelling Practice Book** or the Dictation Sentences on page 467O for the posttest.

Personal Word List If students have trouble with any words in the lesson, suggest they add them to their personal lists of troublesome words in their journals. Have students illustrate the words and write captions for their pictures.

Students should refer to their word lists during later writing activities.

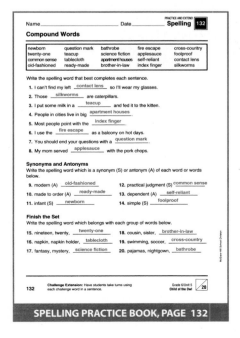

SPELLING PRACTICE BOOK, PAGE 132

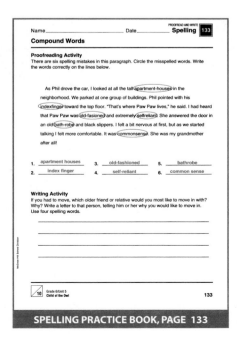

SPELLING PRACTICE BOOK, PAGE 133

SPELLING PRACTICE BOOK, PAGE 134

Concept
- **Mythology**

Comprehension
- **Sequence of Events**

Vocabulary
- **ferocious**
- **lavishly**
- **rash**
- **reassure**
- **thunderous**
- **waving**

Reaching All Learners

Anthology

Bellerophon and the Flying Horse

Selection Summary Students will find out about mythological heroes and creatures as they read the ancient Greek myth of a boy who slays a monster and becomes a hero.

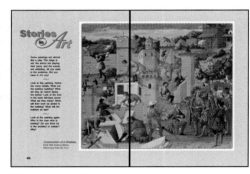

Stories in Art focuses on the **comprehension** skill

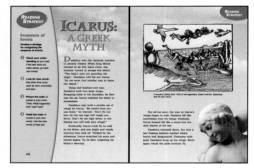

Reading Strategy applies the **comprehension** skill

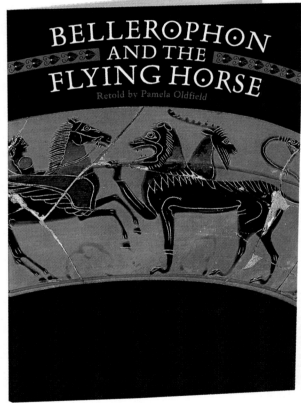

Listening Library

INSTRUCTIONAL pages 470–481

About the Author Pamela Oldfield, a native of England and a former schoolteacher, has intrigued young readers with more than 40 books. Her topics range from the supernatural to mythology, of which *Bellerophon and the Flying Horse* is a superb example.

Leveled Books

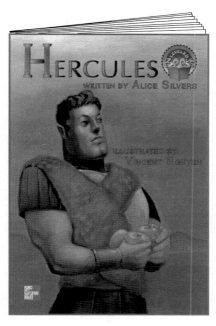

EASY
Lesson on pages 481A and 481D

INDEPENDENT
Lesson on pages 481B and 481D

CHALLENGE
Lesson on pages 481C and 481D

Leveled Practice

EASY
Reteach, 156–162 Blackline masters with reteaching opportunities for each assessed skill

INDEPENDENT/ON-LEVEL
Practice, 156–162 Workbook with Take-Home stories and practice opportunities for each assessed skill and story comprehension

CHALLENGE
Extend, 156–162 Blackline masters that offer challenge activities for each assessed skill

Quizzes Prepared by Accelerated Reader®

WORKSTATION Activities

Social Studies ...	Ancient Greece, *474*
Art	Greek Architecture, *479*
Language Arts ..	Read Aloud, *468E*
Cultural Perspectives	Creating Myths, *472*
Writing...........	Myth, *478*
Research and Inquiry	Find Out More, *479*
Internet Activities........	www.mhschool.com/reading

Suggested Lesson Planner

	DAY 1 Focus on Reading and Skills	**DAY 2** Read the Literature

- **Comprehension**
- **Vocabulary**
- **Phonics/Decoding**
- **Study Skills**
- **Listening, Speaking, Viewing, Representing**

DAY 1 — Focus on Reading and Skills

 Read Aloud: Greek Myth, 468E
"Daedalus and Icarus"

Develop Visual Literacy, 468

☑ **Review Sequence of Events,** 469A–469B
Teaching Chart 127
Reteach, Practice, Extend, 156

 Reading Strategy: Sequence of Events, 469
"Icarus: A Greek Myth"

🛈 Intervention Program

DAY 2 — Read the Literature

Build Background, 470A
Develop Oral Language

Vocabulary, 470B–470C

| *ferocious* | *rash* | *thunderous* |
| *lavishly* | *reassure* | *waving* |

Teaching Chart 128
Word Building Manipulative Cards
Reteach, Practice, Extend, 157

 Read the Selection, 470–477
☑ Sequence of Events
☑ Make Inferences

Genre: Myth, 471

Cultural Perspectives, 472

🛈 Intervention Program

- **Curriculum Connections**

Link Works of Art, 468

Link Social Studies, 470A

- **Writing**

 Writing Prompt: What is a hero? Write a description of the qualities you think a hero must have.

 Writing Prompt: Bellerophon is set to receive an award for his bravery. Write the speech the town's mayor will give explaining why Bellerophon is receiving the award.

 Journal Writing, 477
Quick-Write

- **Grammar**

Introduce the Concept: Subject and Object Pronouns, 481M
Daily Language Activity
1. He and me read about the king.
2. Argos and them were enemies.
3. She and him admired the horse.

Grammar Practice Book, 135

Teach the Concept: Subject and Object Pronouns, 481M
Daily Language Activity
1. The old farmer warned he and we about the monster.
2. The path took he and she home.
3. The boy and her like Bellerophon.

Grammar Practice Book, 136

- **Spelling**

Pretest: Homophones and Homographs, 481O
Spelling Practice Book, 135, 136

Explore the Pattern: Homophones and Homographs, 481O
Spelling Practice Book, 137

DAY 3 — *Read the Literature*

DAY 4 — *Build Skills*

DAY 5 — *Build Skills*

DAY 3 — Read the Literature	DAY 4 — Build Skills	DAY 5 — Build Skills

Rereading for Fluency, 476

Story Questions and Activities, 478–479
   Reteach, Practice, Extend, 158

Study Skill, 480
   ☑ Read a Constellation Map
   Teaching Chart 129
   Reteach, Practice, Extend, 159

Test Power, 481

 Read the Leveled Books, 481A–481D
   Guided Reading
   /f/, /k/, /s/
   ☑ Sequence of Events
   ☑ Instructional Vocabulary

ⓘ Intervention Program

 Read the Leveled Books and Self-Selected Books

   ☑ **Review Sequence of Events,** 481E–481F
   Teaching Chart 130
   Reteach, Practice, Extend, 160
   Language Support, 174

   ☑ **Review Make Inferences,** 481G–481H
   Teaching Chart 131
   Reteach, Practice, Extend, 161
   Language Support, 175

   Minilessons, 473, 475

ⓘ Intervention Program

Read Self-Selected Books

   ☑ **Introduce Context Clues,** 481I–481J
   Teaching Chart 132
   Reteach, Practice, Extend, 162
   Language Support, 176

   Listening, Speaking, Viewing, Representing, 481L

   Minilessons, 473

   Phonics Review, 475
   /f/, /k/, /s/

   Phonics/Phonemic Awareness Practice Book, 51–54

ⓘ Intervention Program

 Social Studies, 474

 Writing Prompt: You are a villager who watched as Bellerophon killed the Chimera. Expain to your neighbor exactly what happened.

Writing Process: Writing a Story, 481K
   Prewrite, Draft

 Writing Prompt: You are Bellerophon. Explain to the king who sent you on the mission to kill the Chimera why you did what you did.

Writing Process: Writing a Story, 481K
   Revise

Meeting Individual Needs for Writing, 481L

Writing Prompt: Who is your hero? Write an essay intended to convince a committee that your candidate deserves to be called a hero.

Writing Process: Writing a Story, 481K
   Edit/Proofread, Publish

Review and Practice: Subject and Object Pronouns, 481N
   Daily Language Activity
   1. You and me can kill the Chimera.
   2. There is no love between her and we.
   3. The King and me shall rule the land.

   Grammar Practice Book, 137

Review and Practice: Subject and Object Pronouns, 481N
   Daily Language Activity
   1. Her and I thanked the hero.
   2. The horse returned to they.
   3. There are no secrets between him and I.

   Grammar Practice Book, 138

Assess and Reteach: Subject and Object Pronouns, 481N
   Daily Language Activity
   1. Athena gave you and I this bridle.
   2. Him and Pegasus flew away.
   3. The Chimera looked at it and they.

   Grammar Practice Book, 139, 140

 Practice and Extend: Homophones and Homographs, 481P
   Spelling Practice Book, 138

 Proofread and Write: Homophones and Homographs, 481P
   Spelling Practice Book, 139

 Assess and Reteach: Homophones and Homographs, 481P
   Spelling Practice Book, 140

Read Aloud

Daedalus and Icarus
a myth

The island of Crete was ruled by King Minos, whose reputation for wickedness had spread to every shore. One day he summoned to his country a famous inventor named Daedalus. "Come, Daedalus, and bring your son, Icarus, too. I have a job for you, and I pay well."

King Minos wanted Daedalus to build him a palace, with soaring towers and a high, curving roof. In the cellars there was to be a maze of many corridors—so twisting and dark that any man who once ventured in there would never find his way out again.

"What is it for?" asked Daedalus. "Is it a treasure vault? Is it a prison to hold criminals?"

But Minos only replied, "Build my labyrinth as I told you. I pay you to build, not to ask questions."

So Daedalus held his tongue and set to work. When the palace was finished, he looked at it with pride, for there was nowhere in the world so fine. But when he found out the purpose of the maze in the cellar, he shuddered with horror.

Continued on pages T3–T4

Oral Comprehension

LISTENING AND SPEAKING Encourage students to pay attention to the sequence of events and to the character's method of problem solving in this retelling of a Greek myth. After reading the myth aloud, ask:

- What problem did Daedalus face after building a palace for King Minos?
- How does he try to solve it?

Discuss the problems connected with facing the consequences of one's own actions. Then ask: In what way is Icarus responsible for his own death?

GENRE STUDY: MYTH Discuss some of the literary devices and techniques in "Daedalus and Icarus."

- Explain that myths, like tall tales, may have characters perform exaggerated deeds. Ask: "What examples of

exaggerated deeds are found in this myth?"

- Have students compare and contrast the reactions of Daedalus and Icarus regarding the treatment they received from King Minos.
- Ask students to use clues in the myth to define the characters. Ask: Which character do you admire most? Least? Why?

Activity Explain that Greek myths are the source of many tales that are still told today in a variety of forms, ranging from movies and videos to comic books and cartoons. (In fact, in the Skills selection students will be reading a different version of this myth. How are the two versions alike and different?) Have students look for examples of these and prepare a class display.
▶ **Linguistic/Spatial**

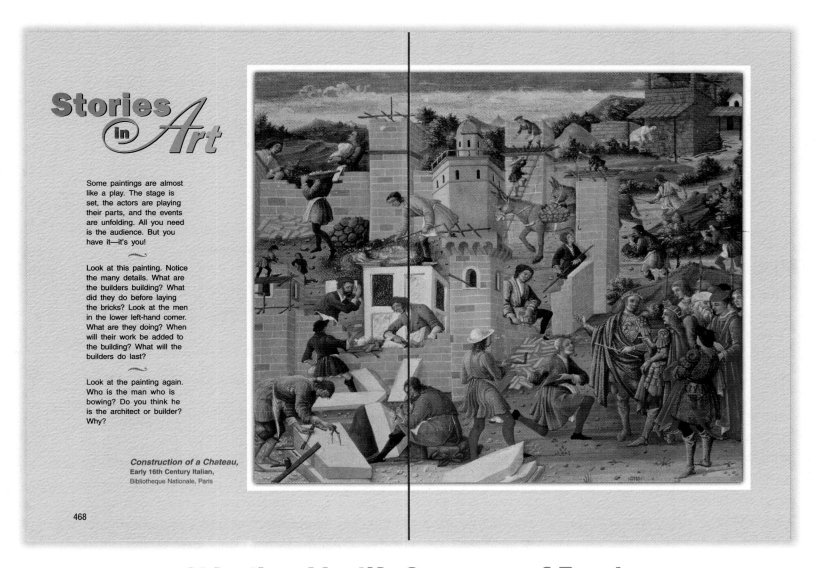

Stories in Art

Some paintings are almost like a play. The stage is set, the actors are playing their parts, and the events are unfolding. All you need is the audience. But you have it—it's you!

Look at this painting. Notice the many details. What are the builders building? What did they do before laying the bricks? Look at the men in the lower left-hand corner. What are they doing? When will their work be added to the building? What will the builders do last?

Look at the painting again. Who is the man who is bowing? Do you think he is the architect or builder? Why?

Construction of a Chateau,
Early 16th Century Italian,
Bibliotheque Nationale, Paris

468

Objective: Identify Sequence of Events

VIEWING Ask students if they notice anything odd about the perspective in this picture. Do size relationships make sense here? Explain that at the time of the painting, artists often didn't use proper perspective. Discuss how the perspective in this painting allows one to see most of the action and the sequence of events involved in building a chateau.

Read the page with students, encouraging individual interpretations of the paintings.

Ask students to discuss the sequence of events in the painting. For example:

- Builders are laying mortar before laying bricks. You can see the bricks in a pile next to them.
- The interior of the chateau will be built later.

REPRESENTING Have students draw a picture depicting a sequence of events. They should experiment with different perspectives in their drawing.

OBJECTIVES

Students will recognize how the time order of events in a story can help them understand character and plot.

Skills Finder

Sequence of Events

Introduce	41A–B
Review	101A–B, 431G–H, 469A–B, 481E–F, 501G–H, 533A–B
Test	Unit 1, Unit 5

TEACHING TIP

SEQUENCE OF EVENTS
Review with students that only the main points or most important details are included when discussing sequence of events. For example, if Bellerophon had seen juicy berries while he journeyed, this would not be an important detail. If he picked the berries and became ill from eating them, this detail would be important enough to include when discussing sequence of events.

Review Sequence of Events

PREPARE

Discuss Sequence of Events
Have a volunteer share the sequence of events of a familiar story. List the events in order on the board. Then list the events out of order. Discuss how the plot would change if the events were not given in the order in which they happened in the story.

TEACH

Read the Story and Model the Skill
Review that paying attention to the sequence of events in a story helps readers keep track of the characters and plot.

The Boy with No Home

Long ago in ancient Greece there was a homeless boy named Bellerophon who went to live in the sky with Athena, the goddess of wisdom. He stayed in the sky palace for many days, talking and laughing with all the people there. Then, one day, Athena grew jealous and sent Bellerophon away. Bellerophon was sent back to Earth, where he journeyed alone for weeks. He was tired and wished to have a place to stay. At last, he came upon a small house and was happy.

Teaching Chart 127

Display **Teaching Chart 127.** As you read the story, have students think about the sequence of events.

MODEL Sometimes when I read, I get lost and can't figure out how a character ended up where he or she did. If I go back and think about what has happened, I can list the order of events in a story. This strategy helps me remember what happened to the character.

Identify Clue Words
Have students underline words and phrases that give clues to the sequence of events.

Create a Sequence of Events Chart

ONE

Have students create a Sequence of Events chart for "The Boy with No Home." Ask them to be sure to place the events in the order in which they happened in the story. ▶ **Linguistic/Logical**

Bellerophon goes to live in the sky palace with Athena.

Athena becomes jealous and sends him away.

Bellerophon returns to Earth.

After much searching, he finds a place to stay.

Graphic Organizer 17

Explain Time Order in Sequence of Events

Have students explain how one event follows another in time order in the story "The Boy with No Home." Ask them to tell how this chronological order can help them remember sequence of events.

ALTERNATE TEACHING STRATEGY

SEQUENCE OF EVENTS

For a different approach to teaching this skill, see page T68.

i Intervention ▶ Skills Intervention Guide, for direct instruction and extra practice of sequence of events

Meeting Individual Needs for Comprehension

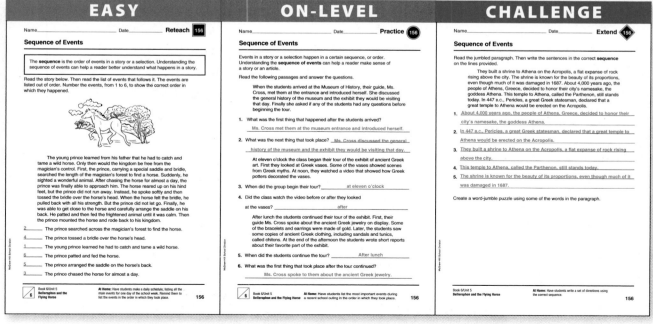

Reteach, 156   Practice, 156   Extend, 156

Apply Sequence of Events

Reading Strategy

Sequence of Events

Develop a strategy for recognizing the sequence of events.

1. **Check your understanding** as you read. If the plot does not make sense, go back and reread.

2. **Look for clue words** that show time order, such as *next, eventually,* and *later.*

3. **Picture the order** of events in your mind. Think: What happened first? next? last?

4. **Retell the order** of events in your own words. Use the clue words to help you.

ICARUS: A GREEK MYTH

READING STRATEGY

A woodcut dating from 1493 of the legendary Greek inventor, Daedalus, and his son Icarus

Daedalus was the cleverest inventor in ancient Greece. When King Minos refused to let him leave Crete, the inventor vowed to escape the island. "The king's men are guarding the ships," Daedalus told his son Icarus. "So we must find another way to leave the island."

Using bird feathers and wax, Daedalus built two large wings. Strapping them to his shoulders, he flew into the air. Icarus watched his father in amazement.

Daedalus next built a smaller set of wings for Icarus. "Be careful how you use them," he warned. "Don't fly too low, for the sea fogs will weigh you down. Don't fly too high either, or the blazing sun will melt your wings!"

Eventually, Icarus could fly as well as his father, and one bright and windy morning they took off. Thrilled by the adventure, Icarus stretched his arms and soared higher. Up he flew, forgetting his father's warning.

But all too soon, the wax on Icarus's wings began to melt. Feathers fell like snowflakes from his wings. Suddenly, Icarus himself fell like a stone into the dark depths of the sea.

Daedalus swooped down, but only a few floating feathers marked where Icarus had disappeared. Overcome with grief, Daedalus hung up his wings. Never again would the great inventor fly.

469

PREVIEW Have students preview "Icarus: A Greek Myth." Remind them that recognizing sequence of events means understanding how events happen in time order. Ask:

- What kind of story is this? (fiction or myth) What makes you think that? (the title and illustrations)

- What clues about the myth do you get from the title and illustrations? (It is about a man and a boy, possibly father and son. They fly in the sky using wings.)

SET PURPOSE Explain that students will apply what they have learned about sequence of events as they read "Icarus: A Greek Myth."

APPLY THE STRATEGY Discuss this strategy for determining sequence of events:

- Look for clue words such as *next, eventually,* and *later* that will help you understand the time order of the events.

- Picture the order of events in your mind. Focus on what happened first, second, and so on.

- Retell the order of events in your own words.

- As you read, review in your mind what has happened.

Activity Have each student create a Sequence of Events chart for the passage.

Build Background

Link

Social Studies

Concept: Mythology

Evaluate Prior Knowledge

CONCEPT: MYTHOLOGY This story and the Leveled Books are set in ancient times and describe mythological characters and events. Point out to students that mythological elements are often fantastic rather than realistic. Discuss with students why people might want to read about gods, goddesses, and mortal heroes performing fantastic deeds.

IDENTIFY MYTHOLOGICAL ELEMENTS Have students create a chart that identifies the mythological characters, settings, and events in **Teaching Chart 127,** "The Boy with No Home." Help students get started.

▶ **Logical/Spatial**

CHARACTER	SETTING	PLOT
Athena, goddess of wisdom	sky palace	Boy from ancient Greece goes to live in the sky with Athena.

Graphic Organizer 30

EXTEND THE MYTH Invite students to continue the plot of "The Boy with No Home." What will happen to Bellerophon on Earth? What acts of bravery might he perform?

ONE **WRITING**

Develop Oral Language

INTERVIEW MYTHOLOGICAL CHARACTERS Review the anthology **ESL** selection and prepare a list of information about the mythological characters of Athena, Bellerophon, Pegasus, and the Chimera, including each character's name, clothing, food, home, special role with human beings, and so forth. Ask students to take turns asking you interview questions. Write key words and phrases on the board.

Then ask students to pretend to be one of these characters and ask them similar questions about themselves. Encourage them to invent details, if they wish. Provide language support as needed.

TEACHING TIP

MANAGEMENT When you are working with language learners or another small group, sometimes the rest of the class falls off task. Arrange the group in such a way that you can still interact with the class.

LANGUAGE SUPPORT

See the **Language Support Book,** pages 169–172, for teaching suggestions for Build Background.

OBJECTIVES

Students will use context clues to determine the meanings of vocabulary words.

lavishly
thunderous
waving
ferocious
rash
reassure

Definitions

lavishly (p. 472) given in great amounts

thunderous (p. 475) extremely loud like thunder

waving (p. 477) gesturing by moving arms up and down

ferocious (p. 473) fierce, dangerous

rash (p. 473) very quick

reassure (p. 474) to soothe or calm

Vocabulary

Teach Vocabulary in Context

Identify Vocabulary Words Display **Teaching Chart 128** and read it with students. Have students circle each vocabulary word and underline other words that are clues to its meaning.

A Party for Bellerophon

1. When Bellerophon arrived at the <u>palace</u>, the king entertained him (lavishly) with <u>much food and drink</u>. **2.** Every time the musicians finished a song, the party guests would burst into <u>loud,</u> (thunderous) <u>applause</u>. **3.** Suddenly, a messenger ran in, (waving) his <u>arms madly to get the king's attention</u>. **4.** A (ferocious) monster was <u>terrorizing the kingdom</u>. **5.** Hearing this, the king <u>immediately</u> made the (rash) decision to leave the party. **6.** The queen <u>tried to</u> (reassure) the guests, <u>but everyone was very upset</u>.

Teaching Chart 128

Story Words

These words from the selection may be unfamiliar. Before students read, have them check the meanings and pronunciations of the words in the Glossary beginning on page 678 or in a dictionary.

• implore, p. 473

• vilest, p. 473

• goddess, p. 474

• bridle, p. 474

• frightful, p. 476

Discuss Meanings Ask questions like these to help clarify word meanings:

• Would it be fun to be entertained lavishly? Why?

• What noises besides thunder are thunderous?

• When have you seen a crossing guard waving?

• What characters have you seen in movies or read about in books that were ferocious? What did they do?

• Have you ever made a rash decision? Did you regret it? Why?

• How would you reassure a frightened pet?

Practice

Role-Play a Monster

ONE

Have students take turns role-playing a ferocious monster. Other students can role-play "risking their lives" to ask the monster questions that use vocabulary words. ▶ **Linguistic/Kinesthetic**

 thunderous

 rash

 waving

> Word Building Manipulative Cards

Write Scenes

WRITING

Invite students to write dialogue for a dramatic scene about a party in which someone is entertained lavishly. Have them try to use all the vocabulary words in their scene. Students may refer to the Glossary. ▶ **Linguistic**

Assess Vocabulary

Use Words in Context

GROUP

Ask groups of four students to write song lyrics based on Bellerophon or some other mythical young hero. Tell students to use all of the vocabulary words in the lyrics. Then have the groups sing their lyrics using a well-known melody to others in the class.

SPELLING/VOCABULARY CONNECTIONS

See Spelling Challenge Words, pages 481O–481P.

LANGUAGE SUPPORT

See the **Language Support Book**, pages 169–172, for teaching suggestions for Vocabulary.

Vocabulary PuzzleMaker

Provides vocabulary activities.

Meeting Individual Needs for Vocabulary

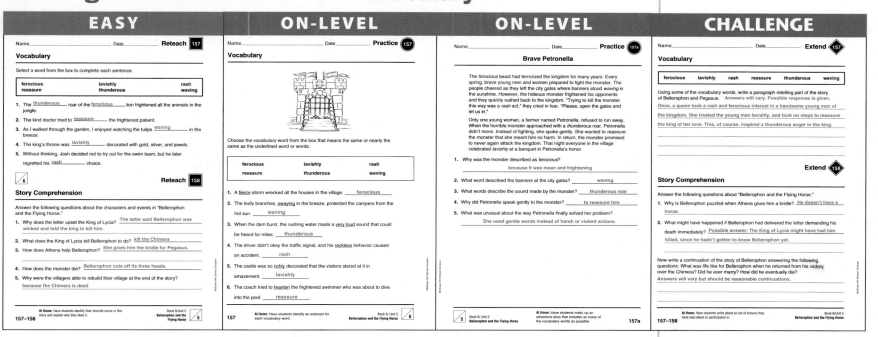

Reteach, 157

Practice, 157

Practice, 157a
Take-Home Story

Extend, 157

470C

Comprehension

Prereading Strategies

PREVIEW AND PREDICT Have students read the title and preview the illustrations, looking for clues to the sequence of events in the story.

- Where and when does this story take place?
- What is this story probably about?
- Will this story be realistic or mythic? How can you tell? (Mythic: there is no such thing as a flying horse.) *Genre*

Have students prepare a Predictions chart telling what they expect will happen.

PREDICTIONS	WHAT HAPPENED
There will be a flying horse who helps someone.	
Bellerophon does some fantastic deed.	

SET PURPOSES What do students want to find out by reading the story? For example:

- How does Bellerophon get to ride the flying horse?
- Why does Bellerophon risk his life?

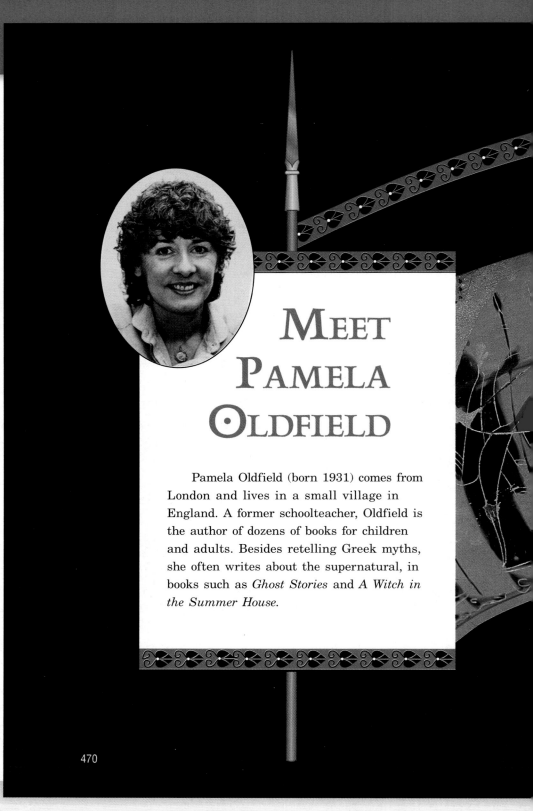

MEET PAMELA OLDFIELD

Pamela Oldfield (born 1931) comes from London and lives in a small village in England. A former schoolteacher, Oldfield is the author of dozens of books for children and adults. Besides retelling Greek myths, she often writes about the supernatural, in books such as *Ghost Stories* and *A Witch in the Summer House.*

470

Meeting Individual Needs • Grouping Suggestions for Strategic Reading

EASY	ON-LEVEL	CHALLENGE
Read Together Read the story together or invite students to use the **Listening Library**. Ask them to use the Sequence of Events chart to record the order of events in the story as they read. Comprehension and Intervention prompts offer additional help with vocabulary and comprehension.	**Guided Instruction** Choose from the Comprehension questions as students read the story with you, or after they have played the **Listening Library**. Have them use the Sequence of Events chart to record the important events as they read.	**Read Independently** Have students read independently and fill in the Sequence of Events chart as they read. After reading, they can use their charts to summarize the plot of the story.

BELLEROPHON AND THE FLYING HORSE

Retold by Pamela Oldfield

Bellerophon, riding Pegasus, fights the Chimera *6th century B.C.*
Detail from red-figured cup from Rhodes, Greece   The Louvre, Paris

ⓞNCE LONG AGO A YOUNG MAN NAMED BELLEROPHON was staying with the King of Argos. The king's wife was impressed by Bellerophon and said as much to her husband. She talked about him so much that the king grew tired of listening to her. ①

471

Comprehension

☑ **Apply Sequence of Events**

☑ **Apply Make Inferences**

STRATEGIC READING Before we begin reading, let's prepare a Sequence of Events chart so that we can keep track of the order of events.

Sequence of Events

[box]

⬇

[box]

① **SEQUENCE OF EVENTS** In the three sentences on this page, you learn a lot about what has already happened. What missing details could you include to describe the sequence of events? (Possible answer: Bellerophon told stories about his brave acts to the queen; the king begins to feel jealous.)

Genre

Myth

Explain that a myth:

• is usually set in the ancient world.

• features gods and mortals as characters that are often archetypes with recognizable human traits.

• often contains a struggle between good and evil.

Activity After students read *Bellerophon and the Flying Horse*, have them explain how the plot of this myth features a struggle of good versus evil.

Comprehension

 SEQUENCE OF EVENTS How can I keep track of how much time has passed as I read?

MODEL As I read, I look for clues that tell me how much time is passing between events. Phrases like *day after day* tell me that many days have passed. Other words or phrases that tell me about time are *at last, at once, soon, right from the start,* and *several days.* Understanding the time frame of a story will help me keep the order of events clear in my mind.

TEACHING TIP

MYTHS Have students discuss the differences between a story that is realistic fiction and a myth. Point out that Greek myths tell of gods, goddesses, and mortal heroes and heroines. Explain that a culture's myths are important because they reveal something about how that culture thinks about the world and natural phenomena. Have students compare the character of Bellerophon with heroes portrayed in our culture in books, movies, and newspapers. Point out that myths illustrate themes that are both universal and timeless. Often their characters are archetypes, or the original model on which other similar characters are based through time and diverse cultures.

"All you talk about is Bellerophon," he grumbled. "Try to think about something different for a change. The boy is far too young to be a hero."

His foolish wife took no notice. Day after day she told the king how handsome Bellerophon was, how clever and how brave. At last the king grew so jealous that he decided to get rid of Bellerophon, but without telling his wife. He handed Bellerophon a sealed letter and asked him to deliver it to the King of Lycia.

"This is a most important letter," he told Bellerophon. "Be sure you give it to him."

Bellerophon agreed to deliver the letter and set off at once. He soon reached Lycia and met the king. The two of them got on well right from the start. The king entertained him so lavishly that it was several days before Bellerophon remembered the letter.

"Forgive me, Your Majesty," he said. "I was asked to give you this." The king opened the letter. As he read it he turned quite pale.

"Whatever is the matter?" asked Bellerophon. "Is it bad news?" The king made no answer, but began to mutter to himself.

"This is treachery," he whispered. "I cannot believe it." Then he looked up at Bellerophon. "Never ask me about this letter," he commanded, and he threw it straight on the fire.

That night when Bellerophon went to bed he wondered about what was in the letter, but he was tired and soon fell asleep. The king, however, could not sleep. The letter had given him a terrible shock. It said that Bellerophon was a wicked young man and asked the king to have him killed.

"How could I do such a thing?" murmured the king. "Bellerophon seems such a pleasant young

472

CULTURAL PERSPECTIVES

CREATING MYTHS Explain that throughout history many cultures have created myths. Greek myths are among the earliest and the best known.

RESEARCH AND INQUIRY Have groups research the creation of myths in many cultures, including that of ancient Greece. Have them give an oral report that tells what they have learned and includes their personal response.
▶ **Linguistic/Interpersonal**

man, and he is a guest in my house. The King of Argos is known for his hot temper and he may soon regret this rash decision."

He paced up and down until at last he had an idea. "I shall send Bellerophon to slay the Chimera," he decided. "He may well die in the attempt, but if he succeeds even the King of Argos will have to admit that he is a true hero."

So the next day the king told Bellerophon about the ferocious monster that was causing distress to the people of his kingdom, and begged him to do something about it.

"The Chimera is ruining their lives," said the king. "I implore you to destroy it for me. You will find it over in the hills where the sun rises."

Bellerophon was rather puzzled by all this, but he agreed to go. He walked for many miles without seeing a sign of the monster and eventually stopped to ask an old farmer if he was going in the right direction. When Bellerophon mentioned what he was looking for, the old man's eyes widened in alarm.

"Stay away from the Chimera," he warned Bellerophon. "It's the vilest creature ever born. Plenty of young men have tried to kill it, but they have all died in the attempt."

"Perhaps I will have better luck," said Bellerophon hopefully. The old farmer shook his head.

"Young people today just will not listen to reason," he grumbled, "but if you are determined to get yourself killed, take that path through the woods. It will lead you to the Chimera."

Chimera second half of the 6th century B.C. Detail from Greek kylix The British Museum, London

473

Comprehension

③ MAKE INFERENCES The King of Lycia has certain reasons for not killing Bellerophon. Besides the information given about the king in the story, what inferences can you make about his character based on his decision not to kill Bellerophon?

MODEL In the story, the king asks himself, "How could I do such a thing?" If he were a person who did not question what he read or heard about other people, or if he were a person who made rash decisions, he might have just killed Bellerophon. Thinking about what a character does not do can tell me just as much as what a character does do.

WORD STRUCTURE What ending does the word *vilest* contain? What does the ending mean?

Comprehension

 SEQUENCE OF EVENTS Let's write on our charts the sequence of events that we have read so far.

> Bellerophon stays with the King and Queen of Argos, but the king becomes jealous.

⬇

> Bellerophon takes letter from the King of Argos to the King of Lycia, which tells the king to kill Bellerophon.

⬇

> The King of Lycia sends Bellerophon to slay Chimera instead.

⬇

> An old farmer tells Bellerophon where to find the monster.

4 Bellerophon thanked the farmer politely and went on his way, trying not to be alarmed by what he had been told. He was not looking forward to fighting the Chimera, but if he turned back without even trying he would be called a coward.

An hour later he sat down to rest, and to his astonishment a beautiful woman appeared before him.

"I am Athena, goddess of wisdom," she told him. "I know you plan to fight the Chimera and I will help you." She held out a bridle, and as Bellerophon took it from her she smiled at him and vanished.

5 "How odd," thought Bellerophon, staring at the bridle. "What possible use could a bridle be when I have no horse?" The bridle was of finest white leather studded with gold and decorated with precious jewels. "I shall take it with me," he said, and went on his way, puzzling over the strange gift. What Bellerophon did not notice was that far above him Pegasus, the winged horse of the gods, was wheeling and prancing among the clouds. Suddenly the snow-white horse flew down to earth to drink at a spring of pure water. Bellerophon was overjoyed when he saw the graceful creature before him. Now he knew why Athena had given him the bridle.

He approached the horse slowly, speaking softly to reassure him. "I know you are Pegasus," he said. "You are always ridden by the gods. I am not a god, but Athena has given me this bridle and I must ride you when I go to fight the

474

Cross Curricular: Social Studies

ANCIENT GREECE What was government like in an ancient Greek city like Athens? Was there a king during the Golden Age of Greece? Was it a democracy?

RESEARCH AND INQUIRY Have students research the form of government in the Greek city-state of Athens. Ask them

to compare the Athenian form of government with their own state or national government.

▶ **Linguistic/Logical/Spatial**

inter NET **CONNECTION** Students can learn more about ancient Greece by visiting **www.mhschool.com/reading**

dreadful Chimera." Pegasus nodded his head as if he understood, but just as Bellerophon reached out to touch him, the horse sprang into the air and out of reach. For a moment Bellerophon thought the horse would fly away, but then he came down again to drink. Eventually Bellerophon gave up his attempt to catch the horse. He put down the bridle and stood by, quietly observing. Pegasus was a fine animal with hoofs and wings of silver and a flowing mane and tail. Suddenly Bellerophon ran forward, jumped onto the horse's back, and clung to its mane. The horse tried every trick he knew to throw off his unwanted rider. He flew up into the air and swooped down again, but somehow Bellerophon managed to stay on its back. At last Pegasus flew down to land beside the spring once more.

Bellerophon guessed that now Pegasus would wear the bridle and he slipped it over the horse's head. Then he sprang once more onto the horse's back. "Take me to the Chimera!" he cried and Pegasus leaped upward, tossing his head with excitement.

They flew for many miles until at last they came to a valley where the grass and trees were trampled and broken. Far below them a village lay in ruins. From the dark hills beyond the valley they heard a ⎡thunderous⎤ rumbling roar.

Center:
Athena holding a shield with an image of Pegasus *c. 500–490* B.C. *Panathenaic amphora The Metropolitan Museum of Art, New York Rogers Fund, 1907 (Accession no. 07.286.79)*

475

Comprehension

5 Why do you think Athena gives him a bridle? Sometimes authors give us a hint as to what is coming next. This is a literary device called *foreshadowing*. How is Athena's gift of the bridle a hint? (It foreshadows the appearance of Pegasus.) ***Author's Purpose***

6 **SEQUENCE OF EVENTS** A lot happens between Bellerophon and Pegasus. Retell the order of events from the time that Bellerophon first gets the bridle to the time that he can actually put the bridle on the horse. (Bellerophon speaks softly to the horse, reaches out to touch him; horse jumps away, comes down to drink; Bellerophon puts bridle down and watches, then runs forward and jumps onto horse's back; horse tries to throw Bellerophon but can't.)

Minilesson

REVIEW/MAINTAIN

/f/, /k/, and /s/

Have students pronounce the names *Bellero**ph**on* and **Ch**imera*, as well as the words *telegra**ph**, cou**gh**, te**ch**nology* and **sc**ene*.

- Ask students to identify the sounds of /f/, /k/, and /s/ and their spellings. *Graphophonic Cues*

Activity Encourage small groups to brainstorm ideas to create a list of other /f/, /k/, and /s/ words with similar spellings. Have groups compare lists and cross off repeated words. Create a wall chart and list the remaining words under each spelling.

 Phonics Intervention Guide

Comprehension

7 **SEQUENCE OF EVENTS** Let's complete our charts by listing the rest of the events in sequence.

> Bellerophon stays with the King and Queen of Argos, but the king becomes jealous.

> Bellerophon takes letter from the King of Argos to the King of Lycia, which tells the king to kill Bellerophon.

> The King of Lycia sends Bellerophon to slay Chimera instead.

> An old farmer tells Bellerophon where to find the monster.

> With help of Pegasus, Bellerophon kills Chimera.

RETELL THE STORY Have volunteers retell the story. *Summarize*

STUDENT SELF-ASSESSMENT

- How did using the strategy of sequence of events help me to understand the order of events in the story?

TRANSFERRING THE STRATEGY

- When might I try using this strategy again? In what other reading could the chart help me?

Pallas Athena (bronze)
Archaeological Museum
Piraeus, Greece

476

"That must be the Chimera," whispered Bellerophon. He leaned forward and reassuringly patted the horse's neck, but his own heart beat faster at the thought of what was to come. Pegasus showed no fear, but flew on toward the rumbling sound. Soon they were confronted by a horrible sight. The Chimera rose up before them . . . this was no ordinary beast—the monster had *three heads*!

One head roared—it was the head of a lion. The second head hissed—it was the head of a giant snake. The third and last head bleated like a goat and had two sharp horns.

Bellerophon was terrified. He almost wished he could turn back, but then he remembered Athena. She had sent Pegasus to help Bellerophon and that made him feel much braver.

"Death to the cruel Chimera!" he shouted, and drew out his sword. The lion's head reached out toward him, its mouth ready to swallow him up, but the winged horse darted sideways and Bellerophon cut off the head with one mighty blow. The Chimera's rage was frightful.

REREADING FOR *Fluency*

PARTNERS Partners can take turns reading several paragraphs to each other. Encourage them to listen for pauses at commas and drops in intonation at ends of sentences.

READING RATE When you evaluate rate, have the student read aloud from the story for one minute. Place a stick-on note after the last word read. Count words read. To evaluate

students' performance, see the Running Record in the **Fluency Assessment** book.

i Intervention For leveled fluency lessons, passages, and norms charts, see **Skills Intervention Guide**, Part 4, Fluency.

The snake's head lunged at Bellerophon, hissing loudly, but down came the sword again. Chop! And away rolled the snake's head.

"Two heads gone and one to go!" shouted Bellerophon, but the Chimera was not going to be beaten quite so easily. Without warning it reared up on its hind legs and reached out with its fearsome claws. They sank into the winged horse, who whinnied with pain. Silver feathers floated down and the beautiful white mane was suddenly speckled with blood.

The sight of the horse's blood made Bellerophon forget his own fear. Without a thought for his own safety he slashed again and again at the goat's head until that too lay bleeding on the ground. Now the Chimera had lost all three of its heads, and it collapsed in a heap.

Bellerophon waited, his sword at the ready, but the Chimera would rise no more.

A great cry went up as the people ran from their hiding places in the ruined village. "The Chimera is dead!" they cried, cheering and waving as Pegasus and Bellerophon flew skyward once more. They watched the young man and the horse as they rose higher and higher and disappeared at last among the rolling clouds.

The grateful people then set about rebuilding their village and replanting their crops. The memory of the beautiful white horse and its valiant rider would live on in their hearts forever. Bellerophon had escaped death, and no one could now doubt that he was indeed a hero.

477

Comprehension

Return to Predictions and Purposes

Review with students their predictions about the myth and their reasons for reading the story. Were their predictions correct? Did they find out what they wanted to know?

PREDICTIONS	WHAT HAPPENED
There will be a flying horse who helps someone.	The flying horse helps Bellerophon slay the Chimera.
Bellerophon does some fantastic deed.	Bellerophon saves a village with help from Athena and Pegasus.

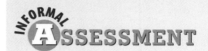

SEQUENCE OF EVENTS

HOW TO ASSESS

- Have students review the sequence of events in the selection.
- Ask students to plan a sequence of events that would comprise a sequel to the story.

Students should recognize that knowing the chronological order of events in a story will help them understand the plot.

FOLLOW UP If students have difficulty remembering the order of events in the story, have them refer back to the story and picture the main events. Remind them that visualizing the action in a story can help them better understand a selection.

LITERARY RESPONSE

QUICK-WRITE Invite students to record their thoughts about the selection. These questions may help them get started:

- How did Athena's belief in Bellerophon help him to feel brave?
- What do you think Bellerophon will do next?

ORAL RESPONSE Ask students to share their journal writings and to discuss why societies created myths and why people still need them today. What can myths inspire people to do?

477

Story Questions

Have students discuss or write the answers to the questions on page 478.

Discuss with a partner

Answers:

1. He must risk his life to slay a creature.
   Literal/Details

2. The King of Lycia does not want to follow the letter's instructions, so he sends Bellerophon to slay the Chimera.
   Inferential/Sequence of Events

3. Caring about others can inspire people to perform brave acts. *Inferential/Draw Conclusions*

4. a hero's success against all odds
   Critical/Summarize

5. Answers will vary. *Critical/Reading Across Texts*

Write a Myth For a full lesson related to this suggestion, see pages 481K–481L.

Story Questions & Activities

1. What life-or-death challenges does Bellerophon face?

2. How does the delivery of the letter trigger all the events that follow it in the story?

3. What lessons about human nature are taught in this myth?

4. What is this myth mainly about?

5. What traits does Bellerophon share with another superhuman hero you have read about or have seen in movies? What are the differences between the two heroes?

Write A Myth

Like Bellerophon, most heroes of myths face challenges that mean life or death. Now write your own myth. Invent an amazing hero and a larger-than-life challenge. Weave your myth around a strong idea or moral. Be sure to show a clear sequence of events. Explain what happens first, second, third, and so on. Give your myth a title. Then help design a class book of myths.

Meeting Individual Needs

EASY	ON-LEVEL	CHALLENGE
Reteach, 158	Practice, 158	Extend, 158

Decorate a Clay Pot

Greek potters often decorated their jars and other pottery with characters from Greek myths. Now it's your turn. Use clay that dries in the air to make a pot, a bowl, a cup, or a jar. Decorate your work with scenes from the myth you wrote. Use acrylic paints. Then display your handiwork in class.

Make a Map

Find out where Greece is. Trace a map of Europe. Label each country and shade in the area that makes up the country of Greece.

Find Out More

Like "Bellerophon and the Flying Horse," myths describe the actions of superhuman heroes. They also tell about fantastic creatures. Find another Greek myth in which a hero slays a monster, such as *Theseus and the Minotaur*. Compare Bellerophon's task with the task of this other Greek hero. Share your findings.

479

Story Activities

Decorate a Clay Pot

Materials: self-drying clay, acrylic paints

ONE Invite students to discuss the shapes and colors used in ancient Greek pottery. Have them compare the style of this ancient pottery with modern ceramics. Discuss common design elements found in ancient Greek art.

Make a Map

Materials: tracing paper, construction paper, colored pencils or crayons

PARTNERS Provide maps of Europe, such as elevation, historical, or political maps. Discuss with students how maps have different purposes and invite partners to choose a specific purpose for their maps of Greece.

Find Out More

RESEARCH AND INQUIRY Encourage **GROUP** students to list the sequence of events in the two Greek myths they compare. Ask them to focus on the similarities and differences between the myths.

interNET CONNECTION For more information about mythology students can visit **www.mhschool.com/reading**

FORMAL ASSESSMENT

After page 479, see the Selection Assessment.

ART: GREEK ARCHITECTURE Have students research the Athenian Age of Greek architecture. Ask them to create a poster that illustrates the three types of Greek columns. Have students bring in photos from magazines of current structures that make use of these columns.

What to Look For Check to see that each student:

- creates a poster that shows the three types of columns (doric, ionic, corinthian) and labels them.
- identifies the three types of columns in photos of current structures.

CHALLENGE

Study Skills

GRAPHIC AIDS

OBJECTIVES Students will

• learn how to read a constellation map.

PREPARE Read the passage with students. Display **Teaching Chart 129.**

TEACH Point out to students that the ancient Greeks thought that constellations had been put in the sky by gods. Have students discuss why myths were used to explain nature.

PRACTICE Have students answer questions 1–5. Review the answers with them. **1.** six **2.** because it is shaped like a horse **3.** Possible answer: to explain a myth of Hercules **4.** No; the map shows the constellations during the month it is visible. **5.** Possible answer: In case you are lost, you can use stars to guide you.

ASSESS/CLOSE Have students research how enslaved people in the South followed "the Drinking Gourd" (the Big Dipper) to escape to freedom.

Study Skills

Read a Constellation Map

Some planets, stars, and constellations are named for Greek gods and heroes. When astronomers in ancient Greece began to study the sky, they divided it into regions that had certain groups of stars. They named these constellations after the Greek figures the stars seemed to form. Most of our constellations were devised and named by early civilizations such as the Greeks and Romans.

Look at this constellation map. It shows the sky as it appears from the North Pole, with the North Star directly overhead. To use this map, face south and turn it so that the current month is at the bottom. The stars at the bottom are seen in most of the United States.

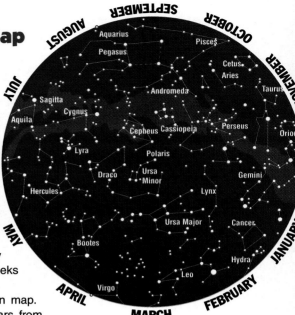

Use the constellation map to answer these questions.

1 How many stars make up Cygnus?

2 How do you think the constellation Pegasus got its name?

3 Why do you think there is a constellation called Hercules?

4 Can every star and constellation be seen during each month of the year? Use the map to explain.

5 Why do you think it is important to know how to read a constellation map?

Meeting Individual Needs

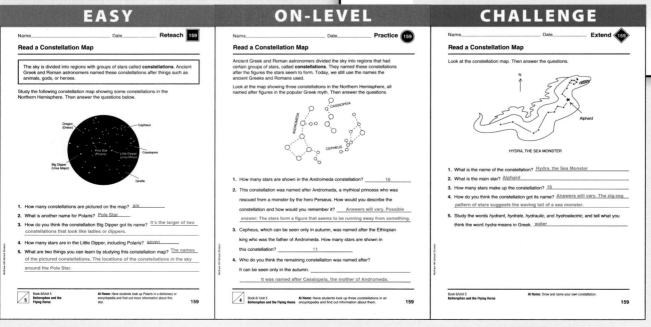

Reteach, 159   Practice, 159   Extend, 159

TEST POWER

DIRECTIONS

Read the sample story. Then read each question about the story.

SAMPLE

The Music of the Bodhran

The bodhran is an ancient frame drum. Pronounced *bow-rawn*, this Irish instrument is played with a double-headed drumstick called a *cipin*.

Although no one knows exactly how old the drum is, or where it was originally developed, it has been played for centuries. Some believe that the drum originated in Africa and was used mostly as a noisemaker in celebrations. Others believe that Celtic people carried the drum from its origins in Central Asia through Europe, and eventually to Ireland.

Today the bodhran is an <u>accompaniment</u> instrument in traditional Irish music. Players follow the rhythm of the music while a fiddle, bagpipe, or flute plays the melody. In fact, the bodhran rarely plays alone. But when the bodhran is played well, there is no sound like it!

1 The word <u>accompaniment</u> in this passage means —

(A) supporting

B melody

C quiet

D traveling

2 Which is the best summary for this passage?

F The bodhran originated in Africa.

G The bodhran is an accompaniment instrument.

(H) The bodhran is an ancient instrument that when played well has a beautiful sound.

J The bodhran is played with a double-headed drumstick.

481

Test Power

THE PRINCETON REVIEW

Read the Page

Have students read the passage. Remind them to summarize the passage in their own words.

Discuss the Questions

Question 1: This question asks students to define a word in context. Ask students to replace the underlined word with each of the answer choices until they find the answer that best fits the information from the passage. Remind students that there are clues in the text that will help them.

Question 2: This question asks students for the best summary of the passage. Explain to students that wrong answer choices might contain information that is stated in the passage but *do not say* what the passage is *mostly* about. The *best* answer will summarize the *entire* passage.

Leveled Books

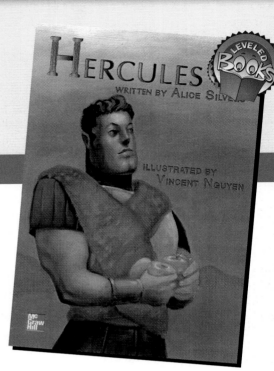

EASY

Hercules

/f/, /k/, /s/

☑ **Sequence of Events**

☑ **Instructional Vocabulary:**
ferocious, lavishly, rash, reassure, thunderous, waving

Guided Reading

PREVIEW AND PREDICT Read the title and discuss the illustrations. Have students make predictions about the obstacles Hercules will face.

SET PURPOSES Ask students what they want to learn about Hercules as they read this story. For example, they might wish to discover how he uses his strength and wisdom in his labors.

READ THE BOOK Have students first read the story themselves as you monitor their reading progress. Use the questions below to help guide their reading.

Pages 2–4: What are the major events so far in Hercules' life? (He's half-mortal, strangled snakes, worked on farm, and killed a lion.) *Sequence of Events*

Page 4: What's another word that means *ferocious* and could be used to describe the lion? (Answers may vary: fierce, brutal, savage) *Vocabulary*

Page 6: What vowel sound do you hear in *bare?* (/âr/) What letters spell this sound? (are) *Phonics and Decoding*

Page 8: Imagine you are the King of Argos. Do you think your twelfth task will really defeat Hercules and prevent him from gaining freedom? Why or why not? *Judgments and Decisions*

Pages 13–16: How does the author show that Hercules is smart? (To get the golden apples, Hercules tricks Atlas.) *Draw Conclusions*

RETURN TO PREDICTIONS AND PURPOSES Review students' predictions and reasons for reading. Discuss the importance of Hercules not only using his strength, but also his brain.

LITERARY RESPONSE Discuss these questions:

• What do Hercules' labors tell you about his character?

• Which of Hercules' labors did you find the most exciting? Why?

Also see the story questions and activity in *Hercules.*

Answers to Story Questions

1. He killed a lion who attacked the cattle he was guarding.
2. They would probably show his great strength and courage.
3. He means that because Atlas tried to trick him in the first place he tricked Atlas into taking back the weight of the sky.
4. It is mostly about how Hercules won his freedom by taking the golden apples from the garden.
5. Answers will vary.

The *Story Questions and Activity* below appear in the *Easy Book*.

Story Questions

1. What happened to the teenage Hercules after he went to live in the mountains near his home?
2. Based on what you have learned about Hercules in this myth, what do you think his later adventures would demonstrate about his character?
3. What do you think Hercules means when he says to Atlas, "One good turn deserves another"?
4. What is *Hercules* mostly about?
5. Do you think Bellerophon handled his task from the King of Argos better than Hercules or worse?

Learn About a Labor

In all, Hercules performed Twelve Labors for the King of Argos. Read about Hercules' other adventures in a book about Greek mythology in your school library. Write a one-paragraph summary of your favorite adventure. Then, using pictures from magazines and newspapers as well as your own original drawings, make a collage that illustrates this adventure.

from Hercules

Leveled Books

INDEPENDENT

Helen of Troy

☑ **Sequence of Events**

☑ **Instructional Vocabulary:**
ferocious, lavishly, rash, reassure, thunderous, waving

Guided Reading

PREVIEW AND PREDICT Invite students to look through the book and discuss the illustrations. Have them make predictions about who Helen is and what might happen in the story.

SET PURPOSES On the board, list questions students have about the story. For instance, they might want to know why the story starts in Greece or what the chapter titles are about.

READ THE BOOK Observe the students' progress as they read the story independently. Ask such questions as:

Page 4: What vocabulary word on this page describes how Zeus reacted to the goddesses' dispute? (He *reassured* the goddesses.) *Vocabulary*

Pages 8–11: What were the consequences of Paris and Helen's running away together? (Menelaus vowed revenge against Paris for stealing his wife and invaded Troy, which resulted in a bloody war.) *Cause and Effect*

Page 12: How did the Greeks finally win the war? (The Greeks left a wooden horse outside the city gates. The Trojans brought the horse into the city. That night, an army of Greek soldiers snuck out of their hiding place inside the horse and defeated the Trojans.) *Sequence of Events*

Page 16: How do you think Helen felt about being the cause of the war? (Answers will vary. Make sure students justify their responses.) *Make Inferences*

RETURN TO PREDICTIONS AND PURPOSES Review students' predictions and reasons for reading the story.

LITERARY RESPONSE Discuss:

• Who's your favorite character in this story? Explain your reason for choosing that person.

• Would you recommend this story to a friend? Why or why not?

Also see the story questions and activity in *Helen of Troy.*

Answers to Story Questions

1. Paris had to decide which of the three goddesses was the most beautiful.
2. Possible answer: Aphrodite felt bad about the trouble she had caused, and realized that Helen should not be punished for it.
3. He was expressing his fear that the Greek soldier who encouraged the Trojans to take the wooden horse was really playing a trick on them.
4. The story is mostly about the Trojan War and the part that Helen played in causing the conflict.
5. Answers will vary.

The *Story Questions and Activity* below appear in the *Independent Book*.

Story Questions

1. What important decision took place just before Helen left her husband, Menelaus, to go to Troy with Paris?
2. Why do you think Aphrodite went to help Helen escape from Troy after the Greeks had ruined it?
3. Why do you think the old Trojan wise man says that they should fear the Greeks even when they bear gifts?
4. What is this story mostly about?
5. How do the gods and goddesses in this story behave in comparison with those in *Bellerophon and the Flying Horse*?

Be a Reporter

Imagine you are a reporter living at the time of the Trojan War. Interview, then write an article about one of the major characters in the war. Remember to include a headline and a map or illustration if necessary.

from Helen of Troy

Leveled Books

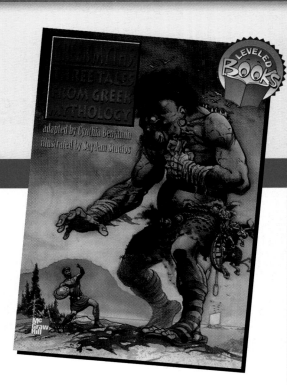

CHALLENGE

Greek Myths: Three Tales from Greek Mythology

☑ **Sequence of Events**

☑ **Instructional Vocabulary:**
ferocious, lavishly, rash, reassure, thunderous, waving

Guided Reading

PREVIEW AND PREDICT Have the readers look at the book's illustrations. Divide the students into groups of three and ask each group member to predict what one of the three stories will be about.

SET PURPOSES Students should divide a sheet of paper into three vertical columns. Have them label each with the title of one of the myths, then write down a purpose for reading that myth.

READ THE BOOK Students can read the story independently or with a partner. Use the questions below to help guide their reading.

Pages 2–4: How does helping another person make Midas an even richer man? (In return for his kindness, the gods grant Midas a wish, and he wishes for the golden touch.) *Sequence of Events*

Page 6: Look at the word *thunderous*. What words in the sentence suggest what *thunderous* means? (*Rang out* suggests that thunderous means loud.) *Vocabulary*

Pages 8–10: What actions by Odysseus show that he is very clever? (He calls himself Noman; and escapes from the Cyclops under the sheep) *Character*

Page 11: What vocabulary word could be used to describe the King's decision to leave his daughter on the mountain? (*rash*) *Vocabulary*

Page 15: Do you think Aphrodite was fair in favoring Hippomenes? (Answers will vary. Encourage students to justify their responses.) *Judgments and Decisions*

RETURN TO PREDICTIONS AND PURPOSES Have students review their predictions and purpose for reading, and share their findings with classmates.

LITERARY RESPONSE Discuss:

• Out of the three myths, which one did you like the best? Explain why.

• What image was the most vivid for you? Why?

Also see the story questions and activity in *Greek Myths: Three Tales from Greek Mythology.*

Answers to Story Questions

1. They were just returning from the Trojan War.
2. that riches don't necessarily make him happy; he should think before speaking
3. She liked being independent.
4. It is mostly about the adventures of Greek heroes and the gods who helped them.
5. Answers will vary.

The *Story Questions and Activity* below appear in the *Challenge Book.*

Story Questions

1. Why were Odysseus and his men so tired and hungry?
2. What did Midas learn by the end of his story?
3. Why didn't Atalanta want to marry anyone?
4. What is this book mostly about?
5. Compare the actions of the gods and goddesses in these stories to those in *Bellerophon and the Flying Horse.*

Write a Play

Look in your library and find other Greek myths. Then write a one-act play that is based on your favorite myth. You can use the plays in your reading book as a guide for the correct form. Include a list of the props, costumes, and sets that would be needed for a production of your play.

from Greek Myths

Bringing Groups Together

Anthology and Leveled Books

Connecting Texts

OVERCOMING OBSTACLES WEB Write the story titles on the board and discuss overcoming obstacles with the class. Then have students create a web to compare how the characters from the stories overcame difficult situations. Call on volunteers from each reading group. Use their suggestions to complete the web.

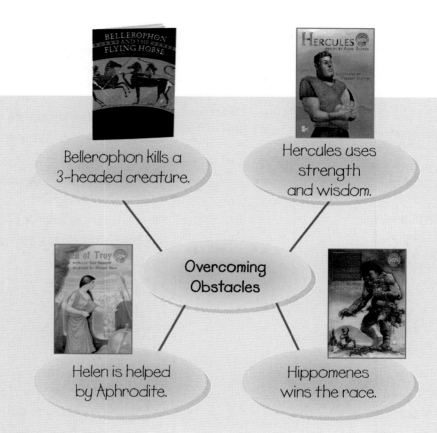

Viewing/Representing

GROUP PRESENTATIONS Help students form six groups, each assigned to one of the six myths. Students should brainstorm a list of the most important events in the stories. Then have each group plan and enact a brief sequence of events showing the hero or heroine overcoming great obstacles. For example, one group might show Hercules overcoming obstacles in his twelfth labor.

AUDIENCE/RESPONSE Have the audience give feedback on the presentation, evaluating it in terms of content, credibility, and delivery.

Research and Inquiry

MORE ABOUT OVERCOMING OBSTACLES Invite students to investigate people in history or literature who have overcome great obstacles. Students can do the following:

- Ask family members and other adults to tell about a person who has overcome great obstacles.

- Visit the school or local library to search for real stories and literary ones dealing with the theme.

- Present their findings to the class.

interNET CONNECTION Have students visit **www.mhschool.com /reading** to find out more about heroes in Greek mythology.

OBJECTIVES

Students will

- identify the chronological arrangement of events in the plot.

- recognize that time-order words or phrases signal important events in a story.

Skills Finder

Sequence of Events

Introduce	41A-B
Review	101A-B, 431G-H, 469A-B, 481E-F, 501G-H, 533A-B
Test	Unit 1, Unit 5

TEACHING TIP

SEQUENCE OF EVENTS

Have students pantomime the story to emphasize the need for a logical sequence of events. Invite another student to serve as the narrator to describe the events in the story as they are being pantomimed.

SELF-SELECTED Reading

Students may choose from the following titles.

ANTHOLOGY

- Bellerophon and the Flying Horse

LEVELED BOOKS

- Hercules
- Helen of Troy
- Greek Myths: Three Tales from Greek Mythology

Bibliography, pages T78–T79

Review Sequence of Events

PREPARE

Discuss Time Order and Sequence of Events

Ask: What if authors did not use time-order words or phrases in their stories to show sequence of events? Let's read a passage and omit the time-order words. Why isn't it easy to follow what is happening?

TEACH

Read "The Ferocious Chimera" and Model the Skill

Have students look for events that are out of time order as you read the **Teaching Chart 130** passage with them.

The Ferocious Chimera

Long ago, there was a ferocious Chimera who terrorized a village. After many weeks of this horror, the king offered a reward to anyone who could slay the monster. More time passed, and no one volunteered. ~~Bellerophon thought of Athena after chopping off the first head of the Chimera.~~ The village people were afraid to leave their homes. ~~Bravely, Bellerophon slayed the monster. Then the monster hissed at Bellerophon.~~ Then one day a young man named Bellerophon came to the village on a flying horse.

Teaching Chart 130

MODEL This story is very confusing to me. I think that something is wrong with the time order of events. The story mentions that Bellerophon chops off the first head of the monster before anyone had volunteered to do it. Also, Bellerophon slays the monster before Bellerophon has been introduced in the story.

Reread the chart and have students cross out events that are not in time order.

PRACTICE

Create a Sequence of Events Chart

PARTNERS

Ask students, working in pairs, to sequence events on a chart in order to give a summary of the story "The Ferocious Chimera." Help students get started. ▶ **Linguistic/Logical**

```
┌─────────────────────────────────────────────┐
│      The Chimera terrorizes a village.        │
└─────────────────────────────────────────────┘
                      ▼
┌─────────────────────────────────────────────┐
│   The king offers a reward to slay the Chimera.│
└─────────────────────────────────────────────┘
                      ▼
┌─────────────────────────────────────────────┐
│            No one volunteers.                 │
└─────────────────────────────────────────────┘
```

ASSESS/CLOSE

Draw a Cartoon

GROUP

Invite groups to use their charts to draw a cartoon depicting each event in "The Ferocious Chimera." Then ask students to cut out each panel of the cartoon and mix up the panels. Have another group try to put the panels in the correct order.

ALTERNATE TEACHING STRATEGY

SEQUENCE OF EVENTS

For a different approach to teaching this skill, see page T68.

ⓘ Intervention ▶ Skills Intervention Guide, for direct instruction and extra practice of sequence of events

Meeting Individual Needs for Comprehension

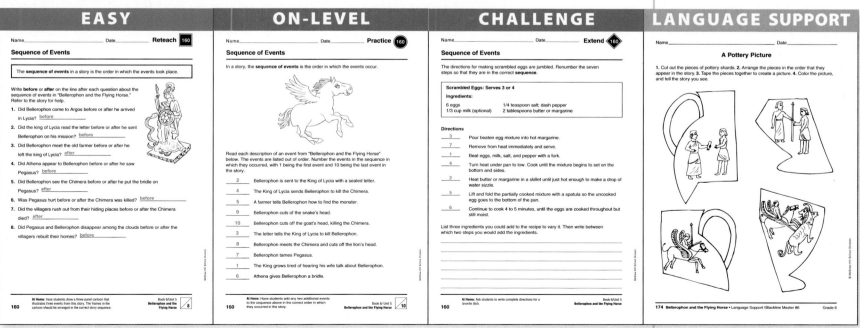

EASY	ON-LEVEL	CHALLENGE	LANGUAGE SUPPORT
Reteach, 160	Practice, 160	Extend, 160	Language Support, 174

OBJECTIVES

Students will make inferences about characters based on information in a text.

Skills Finder	
Make Inferences	
Introduce	39G-H
Review	63G-H, 83G-H, 109E-F, 467G-H, 481G-H, 531G-H
Test	Unit 1, Unit 5
Maintain	335, 351, 515, 557, 625

TEACHING TIP

ARCHETYPE Have students describe how the characters in the story are like other people or characters with whom they are familiar. Ask them to explain how knowing about these people or characters can help them understand the characters in an ancient myth. Explain that an *archetype* is the original model for a character—the prototype. Often in myths, characters are archetypal.

Review Make Inferences

PREPARE

Discuss Make Inferences

Explain: In many stories, information about a character is not directly stated. Readers have to figure out what a character will do from his or her thoughts, feelings, or hesitations.

TEACH

Read the Story and Model the Skill

Have students make inferences about character as you read **Teaching Chart 131** with them.

What Will He Do?

Everyone in the village was afraid of the Chimera. One by one, people went to the palace to ask the king for help. The king refused to speak with anyone about it. He remained locked in his safe castle. <u>Athena, the goddess of wisdom, went to speak with Bellerophon. She offered him a bridle for a magic horse. Bellerophon listened to what Athena told him. He looked at the magic horse for a long time. He thought about all the people who had been hurt by the Chimera.</u>

Teaching Chart 131

Have students underline clues that help them make inferences about what Bellerophon will do. Model using the clues to make an inference.

MODEL I think that Bellerophon will help the people of the village. He has not spoken, and the story does not tell me what he is feeling. But from his thoughts and hesitation, I think he is concerned about the people who have been hurt by the Chimera. Also, the story tells me that Athena goes to speak with him. Since she is the goddess of wisdom and has chosen to give him the magic bridle, he will probably decide to go after the Chimera.

PRACTICE

Create an Inference Chart

GROUP

Have students create an Inference chart for "What Will He Do?" Ask them to locate clues that help them make inferences about the characters in the story and to list these clues on their charts. They can then write the inference they made.

▶ **Linguistic/Logical**

CLUE	INFERENCE
The king refuses to speak with the villagers.	The king is not a caring ruler, or he may be afraid of the people.

ASSESS/CLOSE

Use the Chart for Other Selections

Ask students to create a similar Inference chart for the people in the nonfiction selection *Adventure in Space*. Have them use their charts to summarize the astronauts who took part in the mission.

ALTERNATE TEACHING STRATEGY

MAKE INFERENCES

For a different approach to teaching this skill, see page T64.

Intervention **Skills**
Intervention Guide, for direct instruction and extra practice in making inferences

Meeting Individual Needs for Comprehension

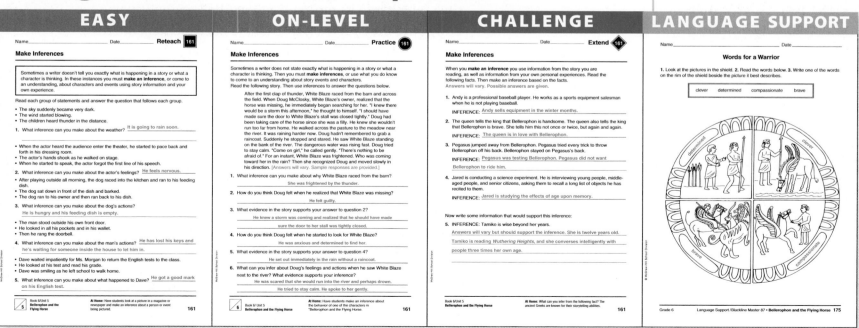

Reteach, 161   Practice, 161   Extend, 161   Language Support, 175

OBJECTIVES

Students will use context clues to define specialized vocabulary.

Skills Finder

Context Clues

▸ Introduce	63I-J
▸ Review	239I-J, 307I-J, 317I-J, 481I-J, 501I-J, 541G-H
▸ Test	Unit 1, Unit 3, Unit 5
▸ Maintain	277, 415, 487, 563, 609

LANGUAGE SUPPORT

ESL English learners may need extra support as they use context clues to define unfamiliar words in a reading. If they can tell from the passage what the word probably means in their first language, suggest that they use bilingual dictionaries or illustrate the word and ask an English-fluent student to verify whether or not it is the same.

Review Context Clues

PREPARE

Discuss Context Clues

Explain: Context clues can help you figure out the meaning of specialized vocabulary. Write this sentence on the chalkboard: *The cook put onions, potatoes, carrots into the ___ and stirred the boiling mixture with a spoon.* Have students guess the missing "cooking" word and tell you which clues they used to make their guess. *(saucepan)*

TEACH

Read the Passage and Model the Skill

Have students listen for unfamiliar words and specialized vocabulary as you read **Teaching Chart 132** with them.

A Special Horse

The (stallion) was the most beautiful <u>horse</u> Bellerophon had ever seen. Its (mane) was <u>thicker</u> and <u>longer</u> than any other horse's. When the horse (whinnied), its <u>voice sounded more like a song</u> than a <u>regular horse sound</u>. When Bellerophon put the (bridle) around the horse's head, the horse delicately took the (bit) <u>into its mouth</u>. Carefully, Bellerophon <u>swung his body onto</u> the (saddle) on the horse's back. He took the (reins) <u>in his hands</u> and <u>steered</u> the horse into the sky.

Teaching Chart 132

MODEL I can see that this passage is about horses. A lot of the words used are special words about the behavior of horses and the equipment used to ride them. I will use what I know about horses and other words and phrases in the passage to help me figure out the meaning of these special words.

Have students figure out the meaning of *bridle* in the fourth sentence. (the part of a horse's harness that fits over the head, including the bit and reins) Ask them to describe the clues they used to define the word.

PRACTICE

Identify Specialized Vocabulary and Context Clues

Ask students to circle the specialized vocabulary relating to horses in the passage. Then have them underline the context clues that helped them figure out the meaning of the specialized vocabulary.

▶ **Linguistic/Logical**

GROUP

ASSESS/CLOSE

Write a Poem Using Specialized Vocabulary

Ask partners to use the specialized vocabulary words in the passage to write a poem about a horse. Have volunteers read their poems aloud to the class. Students may wish to draw an illustration with their poem. Display poems in the Poets' Corner or on the bulletin board.

PARTNERS

ALTERNATE TEACHING STRATEGY

CONTEXT CLUES

For a different approach to teaching this skill, see page T67.

i Intervention ▶ **Skills Intervention Guide,** for direct instruction and extra practice of context clues

---

Meeting Individual Needs for Vocabulary

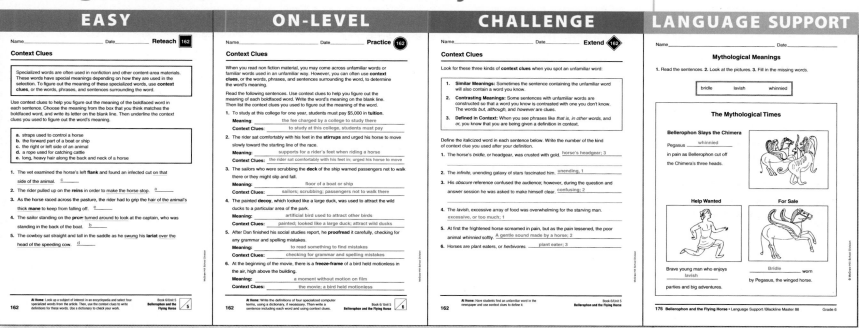

EASY

Name_____ Date_____ **Reteach** 162

Context Clues

Specialized words are often used in nonfiction and other content-area materials. These words have special meanings depending on how they are used in the selection. To figure out the meaning of these specialized words, use **context clues**, or the words, phrases, and sentences surrounding the word.

Use context clues to help you figure out the meaning of the boldfaced word in each sentence. Choose the meaning from the box that you think matches the boldfaced word, and write its letter on the blank line. Then underline the context clues you used to figure out the word's meaning.

a. straps used to control a horse
b. the forward part of a boat or ship
c. the right or left side of an animal
d. a rope used for catching cattle
e. long, heavy hair along the back and neck of a horse

1. The vet examined the horse's left **flank** and found an infected cut on that side of the animal. _c_
2. The rider pulled up on the **reins** in order to make the horse stop. _a_
3. As the horse raced across the pasture, the rider had to grip the hair of the animal's thick **mane** to keep from falling off. _e_
4. The sailor standing on the **prow** turned around to look at the captain, who was standing in the back of the boat. _b_
5. The cowboy sat straight and tall in the saddle as he swung his **lariat** over the head of the speeding cow. _d_

At Home: Look up a subject of interest in an encyclopedia and select four specialized words from the article. Then, use the context clues to write definitions for these words. Use a dictionary to check your work.
162 · Book 6/Unit 5 · Bellerophon and the Flying Horse · 5

ON-LEVEL

Name_____ Date_____ **Practice** 162

Context Clues

When you read non fiction material, you may come across unfamiliar words or familiar words used in an unfamiliar way. However, you can often use **context clues**, or the words, phrases, and sentences surrounding the word, to determine the word's meaning.

Read the following sentences. Use context clues to help you figure out the meaning of each boldfaced word. Write the word's meaning on the blank line. Then list the context clues you used to figure out the meaning of the word.

1. To study at this college for one year, students must pay $5,000 in **tuition**.
   Meaning: _the fee charged by a college to study there_
   Context Clues: _to study at this college, students must pay_
2. The rider sat comfortably with his feet in the **stirrups** and urged his horse to move slowly toward the starting line of the race.
   Meaning: _supports for a rider's feet when riding a horse_
   Context Clues: _the rider sat comfortably with his feet in; urged his horse to move_
3. The sailors who were scrubbing the **deck** of the ship warned passengers not to walk there or they might slip and fall.
   Meaning: _floor of a boat or ship_
   Context Clues: _sailors; scrubbing; passengers not to walk there_
4. The painted **decoy**, which looked like a large duck, was used to attract the wild ducks to a particular area of the park.
   Meaning: _artificial bird used to attract other birds_
   Context Clues: _painted; looked like a large duck; attract wild ducks_
5. After Dan finished his social studies report, he **proofread** it carefully, checking for any grammar and spelling mistakes.
   Meaning: _to read something to find mistakes_
   Context Clues: _checking for grammar and spelling mistakes_
6. At the beginning of the movie, there is a **freeze-frame** of a bird held motionless in the air, high above the building.
   Meaning: _a moment without motion on film_
   Context Clues: _the movie; a bird held motionless_

At Home: Write the definitions of four specialized computer terms, using a dictionary, if necessary. Then write a sentence including each word and using context clues.
162 · Book 6/ Unit 5 · Bellerophon and the Flying Horse · 6

CHALLENGE

Name_____ Date_____ **Extend** 162

Context Clues

Look for these three kinds of **context clues** when you spot an unfamiliar word:

1. **Similar Meanings:** Sometimes the sentence containing the unfamiliar word will also contain a word you know.
2. **Contrasting Meanings:** Some sentences with unfamiliar words are constructed so that a word you know is contrasted with one you don't know. The words but, although, and however are clues.
3. **Defined in Context:** When you see phrases like that is, in other words, and or, you know that you are being given a definition in context.

Define the italicized word in each sentence below. Write the number of the kind of context clue you used after your definition.

1. The horse's *bridle*, or headgear, was crusted with gold. _horse's headgear; 3_
2. The *infinite*, unending galaxy of stars fascinated him. _unending; 1_
3. His *obscure* reference confused the audience; however, during the question and answer session he was asked to make himself clear. _confusing; 2_
4. The *lavish*, excessive array of food was overwhelming for the starving man. _excessive, or too much; 1_
5. At first the frightened horse screamed in pain, but as the pain lessened, the poor animal *whinnied* softly. _A gentle sound made by a horse; 2_
6. Horses are plant eaters, or *herbivores*. _plant eater; 3_

At Home: Have students find an unfamiliar word in the newspaper and use context clues to define it.
162 · Book 6/Unit 5 · Bellerophon and the Flying Horse

LANGUAGE SUPPORT

Name_____ Date_____

Mythological Meanings

1. Read the sentences. 2. Look at the pictures. 3. Fill in the missing words.

bridle	lavish	whinnied

The Mythological Times

Bellerophon Slays the Chimera

Pegasus _whinnied_ in pain as Bellerophon cut off the Chimera's three heads.

Help Wanted

Brave young man who enjoys _lavish_ parties and big adventures.

For Sale

Bridle worn by Pegasus, the winged horse.

176 Bellerophon and the Flying Horse • Language Support/Blackline Master 88   Grade 6

Reteach, 162   **Practice, 162**   **Extend, 162**   Language Support, 176

481J

Writing a Story

TEACHING TIP

Technology
Point out to students that if you accidentally delete something, you can use the *Undo* typing command on your word-processing program.

Sequence of Events
Make sure students understand how to organize the steps in a process. Model how to use words like *first, next, after that,* and *then* to place the steps in time order.

Handwriting CD-ROM

Prewrite

WRITE A MYTH Present this writing assignment: Like Bellerophon, most heroes of myths face challenges that mean life or death. Now write your own myth. Invent an amazing hero and a larger-than-life challenge. Weave your myth around a strong idea or moral. Be sure to show a clear sequence of events. Explain what happens first, second, third, and so on. Give your myth a title. Then help design a class book of myths.

BRAINSTORM IDEAS Have students brainstorm a list of challenges other than slaying monsters. Guide them to think about real-life famous people or literary characters who have faced serious challenges.

Strategy: Create a Story Chart Have students use a story chart to define and organize the elements of their myth. Suggest that they follow these steps:

- Define the setting.
- List the characters.
- State the hero's challenge.
- Outline the sequence of events leading to the story's resolution.

Draft

USE THE STORY CHART Remind students that a chart is only a guide, and they are free to change their ideas as they write. Invite them to create unusual characters and unexpected turns of events.

Revise

SELF-QUESTIONING Have students assess their drafts.

- Have I created an interesting hero and plot?
- Is there a strong idea or moral in my myth?
- Have I presented a clear sequence of events?

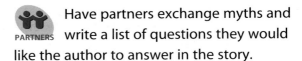 Have partners exchange myths and write a list of questions they would like the author to answer in the story.

Edit/Proofread

CHECK FOR ERRORS Students should reread their myths to check for spelling, grammar, and punctuation mistakes.

Publish

CREATE A BOOK The class can create an anthology of their myths. Encourage students to write introductions to their myths in which they describe their writing process.

> *The Return of the Sun*
>
> Long ago there was a girl named Fortunata. She lived with her family in a small house in a little country village. Every day the sun shone and the people in the village were happy.
> Then, one day, the sun went away. Darkness fell on the little village. Weeks passed without the sun and the plants began to die. People got sick. Everyone was unhappy and scared. No one knew what to do.
> One day, Fortunata met an old woman. The old woman told her she knew where the sun had gone, but that she was too frail to go there. Only a young person like Fortunata could reach the sun's hiding place.

Presentation Ideas

CREATE A POSTER Have students envision their myth as a movie and create a poster advertising it. Show samples of movie posters and discuss their successful elements of design. ▶ **Viewing/Representing**

WRITE A THEME SONG Have students consider the theme or moral of their myths and write a song based on it.
▶ **Speaking/Listening**

Consider students' creative efforts, possibly adding a plus (+) for originality, wit, and imagination.

Scoring Rubric

Excellent	Good	Fair	Unsatisfactory
4: The writer	**3:** The writer	**2:** The writer	**1:** The writer
• displays creativity in developing the myth.	• presents a solid concept for character and plot.	• presents a weak concept for character and plot.	• has not met the criteria for the hero and the challenge.
• weaves the myth around a strong idea or moral.	• uses a governing idea or moral.	• does not connect the plot to a suitable idea or moral.	• does not connect actions to a moral or an idea.
• presents a well-constructed story with a beginning, middle, and end.	• presents a clear progression of story events from conflict to solution.	• does not show a clear progression of story events.	• does not present a logical sequence of events and solution.

Incomplete 0: The writer leaves the page blank or fails to respond to the writing task. The student does not address the topic or simply paraphrases the prompt. The response is illegible or incoherent.

For a 6-point or an 8-point scale, see pages T109–T110.

Meeting Individual Needs for Writing

EASY	ON-LEVEL	CHALLENGE
Mythological Rhymes Have students write short rhymes about the characters in *Bellerophon and the Flying Horse*. They may wish to illustrate their rhymes in the style of ancient Greek art.	**Letter to Bellerophon** Ask students to write a letter to Bellerophon telling him what they think about his act of bravery. Have them include how they would have felt in his shoes. Remind them to use correct letter form.	**Athena's New Gift** Have students think of another gift that Athena could give to Bellerophon. This gift can inspire them to think of a new challenge that Bellerophon could face. They can then use this challenge as the basis for a short story.

Viewing and Speaking

VIEWING STRATEGIES
Have students:
• make sure their poster illustrates the main idea.
• decide if the poster has convinced them to see the movie advertised.

SPEAKING STRATEGIES
Encourage students to:
• describe what features of the poster they like the most.
• suggest ways to improve the poster to better advertise the movie.

LANGUAGE SUPPORT

ESL ESL students can share myths from their native culture with their classmates. Provide time for the class to ask questions about the myths.

 Invite students to include their myths or another writing project in their portfolios.

5 Day Grammar and Usage Plan

LANGUAGE SUPPORT

Compound subjects bedevil many writers and speakers of English. One trick is to separate the elements. Finding the error in the sentence "Me went there" is easier than in "He and me went there."

DAILY LANGUAGE ACTIVITIES

Write each day's Activity on the board or use **Transparency 22.** Have students correct each sentence out loud.

Day 1
1. He and me read about the king.
2. Argos and them were enemies.
3. She and him admired the horse.

Day 2
1. The old farmer warned he and we about the monster.
2. The path took he and she home.
3. The boy and her like Bellerophon.

Day 3
1. You and me can kill the Chimera.
2. There is no love between her and we.
3. The King and me shall rule the land.

Day 4
1. Her and I thanked the hero.
2. The horse returned to they.
3. There are no secrets between him and I.

Day 5
1. Athena gave you and I this bridle.
2. Him and Pegasus flew away.
3. The Chimera looked at it and they.

Daily Language Transparency 22

Suggested answers on transparency

DAY 1 — Introduce the Concept

Oral Warm-Up: Read aloud: *John and he met Susan and me.* Ask students to identify the subject and the predicate. Then point out the pronouns.

Introduce Subject Pronouns
Present:

Subject Pronouns

* A **subject pronoun** is used as the subject of a sentence.

* Use a subject pronoun when the pronoun is part of a compound subject.

* *I, you, he, she, it, we,* and *they* are subject pronouns.

Display this example: *Henry and me went to the store.* Elicit from the students that the subject pronoun *I* should replace *me.*

Present the Daily Language Activity and have students orally correct each sentence by using a subject pronoun.

 Assign the daily Writing Prompt on page 468C.

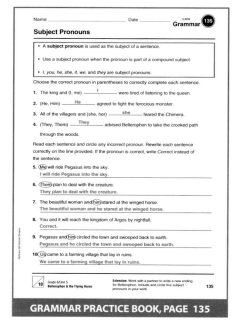

GRAMMAR PRACTICE BOOK, PAGE 135

DAY 2 — Teach the Concept

Review Subject Pronouns Have students define subject pronouns.

Introduce Object Pronouns Discuss:

Object Pronouns

* An **object pronoun** is used as the object of a verb or as the object of a preposition, such as *for, at, with,* or *to.*

* Use an object pronoun when the pronoun is part of a compound object.

* *Me, you, him, her, it, us,* and *them* are object pronouns.

Display: *That was between him and I.* Tell students that the object pronoun *me* should replace *I.*

Present the Daily Language Activity. Have students correct each sentence orally by replacing the subject and object pronouns. Then have them use object pronouns in two or three sentences.

 Assign the daily Writing Prompt on page 468C.

GRAMMAR PRACTICE BOOK, PAGE 136

Subject and Object Pronouns

DAY 3 — Review and Practice

Learn from the Literature Review the difference between a subject pronoun and an object pronoun. Then read this sentence from *Bellerophon and the Flying Horse*:

> She talked about him so much that the king grew tired of listening to her.

Ask students to identify the subject pronoun (she) and the object pronouns (him, her).

Use Subject and Object Pronouns Present the Daily Language Activity and ask students to fix each sentence orally by correcting the subject and object pronouns.

Ask students to read a page from the story and to make a chart of the subject and object pronouns they find.

 Assign the daily Writing Prompt on page 468D.

DAY 4 — Review and Practice

Review Subject and Object Pronouns Write the corrected sentences from the Daily Language Activities for Days 1 through 3 on the board. Then invite volunteers to underline the subject pronouns and circle the object pronouns. Then present the Daily Language Activity for Day 4.

Mechanics and Usage Students can review using *I* and *me* before they begin the daily Writing Prompt on page 468D.

> **Using *I* and *Me***
>
> - Always write the pronoun *I* with a capital letter.
> - Use *I* or *me* last when talking about yourself and another person.

 Assign the daily Writing Prompt on page 468D.

DAY 5 — Assess and Reteach

Assess Use the Daily Language Activity and page 139 of the **Grammar Practice Book** for assessment.

Reteach Ask volunteers to take turns making lists of subject and object pronouns on the chalkboard. Then ask other volunteers to take turns using one or two of the words in a sentence they say to the class, explaining if the pronouns are used as subjects or as objects. Check off the pronouns as they are used.

Ask a group of volunteers to create a bulletin board that explains the rules that govern using subject and object pronouns.

Use page 140 of the **Grammar Practice Book** for additional reteaching.

 Assign the daily Writing Prompt on page 468D.

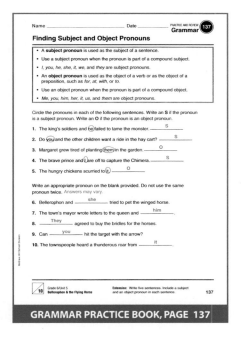

GRAMMAR PRACTICE BOOK, PAGE 137

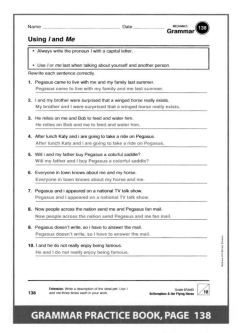

GRAMMAR PRACTICE BOOK, PAGE 138

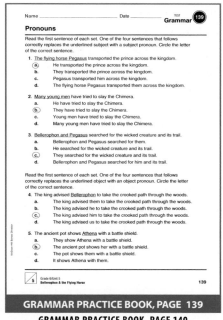

GRAMMAR PRACTICE BOOK, PAGE 139

GRAMMAR PRACTICE BOOK, PAGE 140

5 Day Spelling Plan

ESL Explain that the root word *phone* has to do with speaking and sound, and the root *graph* relates to writing. Guide students to understand that *homophones* are words that sound alike but are spelled differently, and *homographs* are written alike but have different meanings (and often different pronunciations).

DICTATION SENTENCES

Spelling Words

1. I walked straight ahead.
2. A dove is a bird.
3. We shear the wool from the sheep.
4. Let's hire a clown for the party.
5. Don't let the baby swallow that marble.
6. The loud racket kept me awake.
7. We sailed through the strait.
8. I could see through the sheer curtains.
9. We left the laundry in a hamper.
10. We flew higher than ever before.
11. Our vain efforts did not help us.
12. I eat rice cereal.
13. The principal is head of the school.
14. The song had a happy refrain.
15. I ate a kernel of corn.
16. A bass is a kind of fish.
17. A vein carries blood to the heart.
18. He made it a principle to be fair to all.
19. The colonel was in the army.
20. Every week we watched the serial.

Challenge Words

21. The ferocious lion is locked in a cage.
22. She lavishly bought all the flowers.
23. We will reassure the scared child.
24. The show got thunderous applause.
25. I saw the boy waving his hand.

Assess Prior Knowledge Use the Dictation Sentences at the left and **Spelling Practice Book** page 135 for the pretest. Allow students to correct their own papers. Students who require a modified list may be tested on the first ten words.

Spelling Words		Challenge Words
1. **straight**	11. vain	21. **ferocious**
2. dove	12. cereal	22. **lavishly**
3. shear	13. principal	23. **reassure**
4. hire	14. refrain	24. **thunder-**
5. swallow	15. kernel	**ous**
6. racket	16. bass	25. **waving**
7. strait	17. vein	
8. sheer	18. principle	
9. hamper	19. colonel	
10. **higher**	20. serial	

*Note: Words in **dark type** are from the story.*

Word Study On page 136 of the **Spelling Practice Book** are word study steps and an at-home activity.

SPELLING PRACTICE BOOK, PAGE 135

WORD STUDY STEPS AND ACTIVITY, PAGE 136

Sort and Spell Words Review that homophones are words that sound the same but have different spellings and meanings. Homographs are words that are spelled the same but have different meanings and sometimes different pronunciations. Have students read the Spelling Words, sort the homophones into pairs, and think of two different meanings for each homograph.

homophones	vein	homographs
straight	cereal	dove
strait	serial	swallow
shear	principal	racket
sheer	principle	hamper
hire	kernel	refrain
higher	colonel	bass
vain		

Word Wall Have students create a word wall based on the word sort and add more words from their reading.

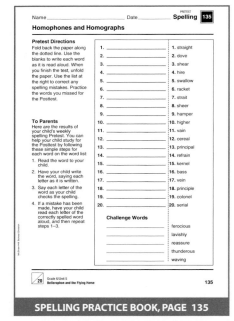

SPELLING PRACTICE BOOK, PAGE 137

Homophones and Homographs

DAY 3 — Practice and Extend

Word Meaning: Context Tell students that associating a homophone with the correct context can help them to spell the word correctly. Ask them to write context sentences in which they correctly use pairs of homophones. Example: I ate *cereal* while watching a *serial*. Then have them write sentences for the homographs and ask partners to define the word from the context.

If students need extra practice, have partners give each other a midweek test.

Glossary Review how some entries show word history. Have students

• write the Challenge Words and find the one with the word history. (*lavishly*)

• write the language and the meanings of the words from which *lavish* comes.

• discuss how the meanings of the French words relate to the meaning of *lavish*.

DAY 4 — Proofread and Write

Proofread Sentences Write these sentences on the chalkboard, including the misspelled words. Ask students to proofread, circling incorrect spellings and writing the correct spellings. There are two spelling errors in each sentence.

The (kernal) planted only one (colonel) of corn in each hole. (colonel, kernel)

They sang about a dove and a (swalow) in the (refrein). (swallow, refrain)

Have students create additional sentences with errors for partners to correct.

WRITING Have students use as many Spelling Words as possible in the daily Writing Prompt on page 468D. Remind students to proofread their writing for errors in spelling, grammar, and punctuation.

DAY 5 — Assess and Reteach

Assess Students' Knowledge Use page 140 of the **Spelling Practice Book** or the Dictation Sentences on page 481O for the posttest.

JOURNAL **Personal Word List** If students have trouble with any words in the lesson, suggest they add them to their personal lists of troublesome words in their journals. Have students make up clues or "memory helpers" that can help them remember the correct spelling of a homophone. Example: The princi*pal* is my *pal*.

Students should refer to their word lists during later writing activities.

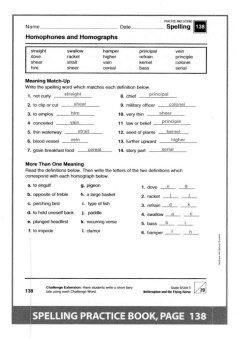

SPELLING PRACTICE BOOK, PAGE 138

SPELLING PRACTICE BOOK, PAGE 139

SPELLING PRACTICE BOOK, PAGE 140

Concept
- Space Exploration

Comprehension
- Judgments and Decisions

Vocabulary
- bloodstream
- compartment
- deliberately
- handshake
- maneuvering
- void

Anthology

Adventure in Space

Selection Summary *Adventure in Space* tells the true story of a team of astronauts sent into space to repair the orbiting Hubble Telescope, and the inventiveness, keen judgments, and decisions that produced success.

Stories in Art focuses on the **comprehension** skill

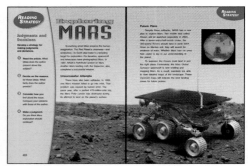

Reading Strategy applies the **comprehension** skill

Listening Library

INSTRUCTIONAL pages 484–501

About the Author Born in Philadelphia but now a Texan, Elaine Scott writes about real objects, real people, and real events. She says that "Often boys and girls will ask me if everything in my books is true, and I ... answer, 'Yes, everything happened just as I said.'"

About the Author A resident of New York City, Margaret Miller has collaborated with Elaine Scott on several nonfiction books. Miller comes to each project with her experience both as a writer and an award-winning photographer.

Leveled Books

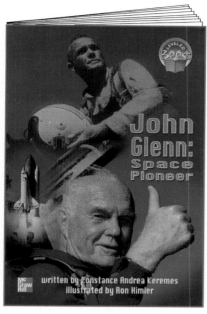

EASY
Lesson on pages 501A and 501D

INDEPENDENT
Lesson on pages 501B and 501D
🏠 *Take-Home version available*

CHALLENGE
Lesson on pages 501C and 501D

Leveled Practice

EASY
Reteach, **163–169** Blackline masters with reteaching opportunities for each assessed skill

INDEPENDENT/ON-LEVEL
Practice, **163–169** Workbook with Take-Home stories and practice opportunities for each assessed skill and story comprehension

CHALLENGE
Extend, **163–169** Blackline masters that offer challenge activities for each assessed skill

Quizzes Prepared by **Accelerated Reader**

WORKSTATION Activities

Social Studies ... Map Skills, *488*

Science .... Telescopes, *494*

Math .... Weight in Space, *492*
Distance Formula, *499*

Language Arts .. Read Aloud, *482E*

Cultural Perspectives ..... Cosmonauts, *490*

Writing .... Science Fiction Story, *498*

Research and Inquiry .... Find Out More, *499*

Internet Activities .... www.mhschool.com/reading

Suggested Lesson Planner

READING AND LANGUAGE ARTS

- Comprehension
- Vocabulary
- Phonics/Decoding
- Study Skills
- Listening, Speaking, Viewing, Representing

- Curriculum Connections
- Writing
- Grammar
- Spelling

DAY 1 — Focus on Reading and Skills

 Read Aloud: Poetry, 482E
"I Don't Want to Live on the Moon"

Develop Visual Literacy, 482

☑ **Introduce Judgments and Decisions,** 483A–483B
   Teaching Chart 133
   Reteach, Practice, Extend, 163

 Reading Strategy: Make Judgments and Decisions, 483
"Exploring Mars"

Intervention Program

 Works of Art, 482

 Writing Prompt: What qualities do you think an astronaut should have? Explain why you think these are important.

Introduce the Concept: Possessive Pronouns, 501M
Daily Language Activity
1. Our's telescope is now in orbit.
2. Her's skills are the best.
3. Their's problem was solved in space.

Grammar Practice Book, 141

Pretest: Words with Suffixes, 501O
Spelling Practice Book, 141, 142

DAY 2 — Read the Literature

Build Background, 484A
Develop Oral Language

Vocabulary, 484B–484C

bloodstream	*handshake*
compartment	*maneuvering*
deliberately	*void*

Teaching Chart 134
Word Building Manipulative Cards
Reteach, Practice, Extend, 164

 Read the Selection, 484–497
☑ **Judgments and Decisions**
☑ **Make Inferences**

Genre: Informational Story, 485

Cultural Perspectives, 490

Intervention Program

 Science, 484A

 Writing Prompt: You are a mission control engineer. Write a first-person account that explains how the astronauts worked together to make the mission successful.

Journal Writing, 497
Quick-Write

Teach the Concept: Possessive Pronouns, 501M
Daily Language Activity
1. The astronauts were ready to take they're best shot.
2. This new spacesuit is mine's.
3. Yours telescope needs a new lens.

Grammar Practice Book, 142

Explore the Pattern: Words with Suffixes, 501O
Spelling Practice Book, 143

DAY 3 — Read the Literature

Rereading for Fluency, 496

Story Questions and Activities, 498–499
Reteach, Practice, Extend, 165

Study Skill, 500
✓ Read a Flow Chart
Teaching Chart 135
Reteach, Practice, Extend, 166

Test Power, 501

 **Read the Leveled Books,** 501A–501D
Guided Reading
/îr/, /ûr/
✓ Judgments and Decisions
✓ Instructional Vocabulary

ⓘ **Intervention Program**

 Activity Social Studies, 488

 Writing Prompt: Write an extended caption for the photograph on page 494. Explain in more detail what the astronauts inside and outside the shuttle are doing.

Writing Process: Writing a Story, 501K
Prewrite, Draft

Review and Practice: Possessive Pronouns, 501N
Daily Language Activity
1. You're flight is about to begin.
2. This new telescope is their's.
3. It's eyes are made of ten tiny mirrors.

Grammar Practice Book, 143

Practice and Extend: Words with Suffixes, 501P
Spelling Practice Book, 144

DAY 4 — Build Skills

 **Read the Leveled Books and Self-Selected Books**

✓ **Review Judgments and Decisions,** 501E–501F
Teaching Chart 136
Reteach, Practice, Extend, 167
Language Support, 182

✓ **Review Sequence of Events,** 501G–501H
Teaching Chart 137
Reteach, Practice, Extend, 168
Language Support, 183

Minilessons, 487, 491, 493, 495

ⓘ **Intervention Program**

 Activity Math, 492

 Writing Prompt: Imagine you are Kathy Thornton. Explain to a friend what your job was on the mission.

Writing Process: Writing a Story, 501K
Revise

Meeting Individual Needs for Writing, 501L

Review and Practice: Possessive Pronouns, 501N
Daily Language Activity
1. Mine fondest dreams have come true.
2. The best telescope in space is our.
3. His's plans will work.

Grammar Practice Book, 144

Proofread and Write: Words with Suffixes, 501P
Spelling Practice Book, 145

DAY 5 — Build Skills

Read Self-Selected Books

✓ **Review Context Clues,** 501I–501J
Teaching Chart 138
Reteach, Practice, Extend, 169
Language Support, 184

Listening, Speaking, Viewing, Representing, 501L

Minilessons, 487, 493, 495

Phonics Review, 491
/îr/ and /ûr/

Phonics/Phonemic Awareness Practice Book, 45–48

ⓘ **Intervention Program**

Activity Science, 494

Writing Prompt: Write a letter to the editor explaining why the Hubble repair mission proves that the manned space program should or should not be continued.

Writing Process: Writing a Story, 501K
Edit/Proofread, Publish

Assess and Reteach: Possessive Pronouns, 501N
Daily Language Activity
1. Their are the right tools.
2. Yours tools and my are over there.
3. His' telescope has it's problems.

Grammar Practice Book, 145, 146

Assess and Reteach: Words with Suffixes, 501P
Spelling Practice Book, 146

Read Aloud

I Don't Want to Live on the Moon
a poem by Jeff Moss

I'd like to visit the moon
On a rocket ship high in the air.
Yes, I'd like to visit the moon,
But I don't think I'd like to live there.
Though I'd like to look down at the earth from above,
I would miss all the places and people I love.
So although I might like it for one afternoon
I don't want to live on the moon.

I'd like to travel under the sea,
I could meet all the fish everywhere.
Yes, I'd travel under the sea,
But I don't think I'd like to live there.
I might stay for a day if I had my wish,
But there's not much to do when your friends are all fish,
And an oyster and clam aren't real family,
So I don't want to live in the sea.

Continued on page T4

Oral Comprehension

LISTENING AND SPEAKING Encourage students to think about the problems and decisions the poet faces as you read the poem aloud. Afterward, ask:

• What problems does the poet foresee in living on the moon or under the sea?

• What has the poet decided about where and how he prefers to live?

Discuss students' vacation preferences. Ask: Why do you think some people go to faraway places while others like to stay close to home?

GENRE STUDY: POETRY Discuss some of the literary devices and techniques in "I Don't Want to Live on the Moon."

• Have students write down the last word of each line. Ask them to note the variation in rhyme scheme between the first four lines *(abab)* and the last four lines (ccaa) in the first and second stanzas. Ask: Which rhyme scheme does the third stanza follow? *(aabb)*

• Discuss the poet's repeated sentiments in the first and fourth stanzas. Ask: What would the poet miss most of all if he lived on the moon?

• Ask students to identify an unrealistic trip that the poet describes in the poem.

Activity Help students create and display storyboards that depict places described in the poem. Remind students that the illustrations should convey why these places appeal to them. ▶ **Spatial**

Develop Visual Literacy

Stories in Art

Songs, poems, stories, news articles, and history books have been written about the event in this picture. Yet none is more famous than this painting showing the moment when the last spikes were hammered into the tracks of the transcontinental railroad.

Look at this painting. What can you tell about the setting? Who are the people in the picture? What can you tell about them? Who are the men by the tracks? What are they doing? Why do you think this painting is so famous? Do you like it? Explain your reasons.

Imagine that you are one of the eyewitnesses in the painting. Do you think that this railroad will change the country? In what ways? How will it affect travel in the future?

482

The Last Spike, May 10, 1869, Union Pacific Railroad, Promontory Point, Utah by Thomas Hill

Objective: Make Judgments and Decisions

VIEWING In this painting, Thomas Hill has captured an important historic moment. Have students study the painting and comment on what they see. Discuss how the artist draws the viewer's attention to the central event, the driving of the last spike. Ask them why the artist chose such a literal title for the painting.

Read the page with students, encouraging individual interpretations of the painting.

Have students give reasons for their judgments and decisions about the painting. For example:

- The artist chose to paint the scene so that viewers feel as though they are part of the crowd. I think this was a good decision.

- The title of the painting immediately tells the viewer the exact moment in history depicted in the painting.

REPRESENTING Invite students to dramatize the moment in the painting. Suggest that in their skits, the actors express judgments about the success of the railroad.

OBJECTIVES

Students will analyze and make judgments and decisions.

Skills Finder

Judgments and Decisions

Introduce	483A–B
Review	501E-F, 541E-F
Test	Unit 5

LANGUAGE SUPPORT

ESL Discuss the difference between a judgment and a decision. Lead students to understand that a judgment takes place in the mind, but that a decision involves taking action. Explain that you can keep a judgment secret, but a decision will be obvious to other people.

TEACHING TIP

REASONED JUDGMENTS Review: people make reasoned judgments based upon facts, which can be proven true by evidence. Opinions cannot be proven. Ask students to identify examples and facts behind some reasoned judgements in "Adventure in Space." Remember: although based upon evidence, reasoned judgments do involve some subjectivity.

Introduce Judgments and Decisions

PREPARE

Discuss Making Judgments and Decisions

Invite students to think of times when they have had to make an important decision. Ask: What are some reasons you had for making that decision? What did you decide to do?

TEACH

Define Judgments and Decisions

Tell students: Everyone makes judgments about whether or not they like or agree with something—or think it is right or wrong. Everyone also makes decisions. Some decisions are more difficult to make than others. However, all decisions involve taking a course of action.

Crunch Time

There were only five seconds to go! The basketball game was tied. The coach called a time out. She designed a play for Maria to take the last shot. Maria was the team's leading scorer.

Maria was being guarded closely by two players. She wasn't open for a good shot. Maria passed the ball to wide-open Katy, who was a great shooter. Swish. Game over. Victory!

Teaching Chart 133

Read the Passage and Model the Skill

Display **Teaching Chart 133.** As the story is read, encourage students to pay attention to the reasons Maria had to pass the ball to Katy for the last shot.

MODEL Maria had a tough decision to make. She had to think quickly about what she had to do. I think that even if Katy had missed the shot, it was still a good decision.

Draw Conclusions

Suggest that students underline the reasons for Maria's decision and circle the decision that she made.

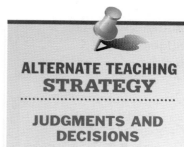

ALTERNATE TEACHING STRATEGY

JUDGMENTS AND DECISIONS

For a different approach to teaching this skill, see page T66.

PRACTICE

Create a Judgments and Decisions Chart

ONE

By using a Judgments and Decisions chart, invite students to identify and discuss the reasons for Maria's decision. Help them begin filling in the chart and have students complete it. ▶ **Linguistic/Logical**

MARIA'S DECISION	MARIA'S REASONS
pass the ball to Katy	Maria is closely guarded.
	Katy is wide-open.
	Katy is a great shooter.

ASSESS/CLOSE

Make Judgments and Decisions

Ask students what words they would use to describe Maria's decision. (thoughtful, reasonable under the circumstances) In what other situations would Maria need to make decisions? (in school, at home)

ℹ️ **Intervention** ▶ **Skills Intervention Guide,** for direct instruction and extra practice of judgments and decisions

Meeting Individual Needs for Comprehension

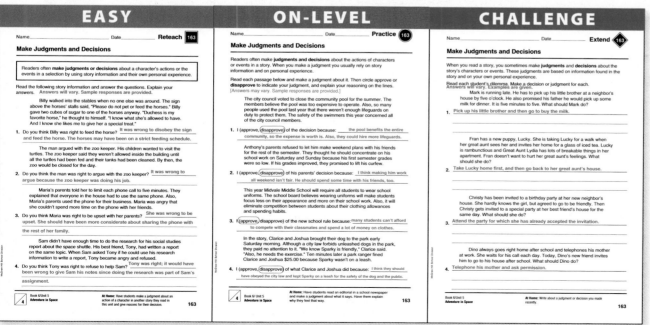

Reteach, 163   Practice, 163   Extend, 163

OBJECTIVES

Students will make judgments and decisions.

Apply Judgments and Decisions

READING STRATEGY

READING STRATEGY

Judgments and Decisions

Develop a strategy for making judgments and decisions.

1 **Read the article.** What ideas does the author present about the subject?

2 **Decide on the reasons** for those ideas. What facts does the author provide?

3 **Consider how you feel** about the issue. Compare your opinions with those of the author.

4 **Make a judgment.** Do you think Mars exploration should continue?

Exploring MARS

Something about Mars inspires the human imagination. The Red Planet's closeness—and similarities—to Earth also make it a tempting target for exploration. For decades, spacecraft and telescopes have photographed Mars. In 1997, NASA's *Pathfinder* landed on Mars. Another Mars landing craft, the *Sojourner*, also completed a successful mission.

Unsuccessful Attempts

There have also been setbacks. In 1999, one Mars mission failed to go into orbit. That problem was caused by human error. The same year, after a perfect 470-million-mile trip, the Mars *Polar Lander* was destroyed during its attempt to land on the planet's surface.

Future Plans

Despite those setbacks, NASA has a new plan to explore Mars. Two mobile labs called *Rovers* will be launched separately in 2003. After a seven-and-a-half-month cruise, the 300-pound *Rovers* should land in early 2004. Once on Martian soil, they will search for evidence of water. Whether Mars has—or once had—water is key to our understanding of the planet.

To succeed, the *Rovers* must land in just the right place. Fortunately, the *Mars Global Surveyor* spacecraft is now orbiting and mapping Mars. As a result, scientists are able to view detailed maps of the landscape. These improved maps will indicate the best landing zones for future probes.

483

PREVIEW Have students preview "Exploring Mars." Remind them that making a judgment means to form an opinion based on what you know and what you have learned from reading. Ask:

• What kind of ideas do you expect the author to present? (information about when and how Mars was explored)

SET PURPOSE Explain that students will apply what they have learned about making judgments and decisions as they read "Exploring Mars."

APPLY THE STRATEGY Discuss this strategy for making judgments and decisions:

• Identify the main points of the article. What does it say about why we are exploring Mars?

• Identify evidence that supports the main ideas.

• Consider your own thoughts and ideas about the topic.

• Make a judgment based on evidence from the article and your own opinion. Would you agree or disagree that it is a good idea to continue exploring Mars? Why?

Activity Have each student create a Judgments and Decisions Chart for the passage.

Build Background

Science

Concept: Space Exploration

Evaluate Prior Knowledge

CONCEPT: SPACE EXPLORATION These stories describe adventures in space. Help students understand that many daring exploits astronauts have taken place in space.

CHART JOURNEYS INTO SPACE Have students record what they know about space flight and space exploration by using a chart like the following. ▶ **Logical/Visual**

Who explores in space and why?	Countries send astronauts and robots to gather samples and other information, and to perform experiments in space.
What do they explore?	Astronauts and robots explore the surface of the moon and other planets.
Where and **when** do they explore?	Since the Soviet launch of *Sputnik* in 1957, the U.S. has explored the moon, the planet Mars, and other areas in space.

Graphic Organizer 31

PLAN A SPACE JOURNEY Have students

GROUP **WRITING** work in small groups to plan a voyage into space. It might be a trip to explore the moons of Jupiter or a landing on Mars. What supplies would they need? What would they do? What would they see? What would be the reason for their mission?

Develop Oral Language

DISCUSS SPACE TRAVEL Invite students

ESL to discuss their "space exploration" charts and their plans for a journey into space. Ask them to brainstorm ideas to create two lists, one of what they might see during their voyage, the other of their experiences during their journey. If possible, bring in illustrated books about space travel and ask students to describe what they see.

After students become comfortable with talking about space travel, invite them to role-play an experience they might have in space. It could be a space walk, as described in *Adventure in Space*, an experiment, or an emergency, such as a close call in landing a space shuttle. Afterward, discuss students' scenes and compile a list of "space words" on the board.

TEACHING TIP

MANAGEMENT After you begin the "space exploration" chart with students, explain the Plan a Space Journey writing activity. Have small groups continue working on these activities.

While groups are working, present the Develop Oral Language activity to students who need help with oral language skills.

LANGUAGE SUPPORT

See the **Language Support Book**, pages 177–180, for teaching suggestions for Build Background.

 **OBJECTIVES**

Students will use context clues to determine the meanings of vocabulary words.

 **efinitions**

void (p. 489) an empty space

maneuvering (p. 487) a skillful or clever move or action

deliberately (p. 492) done or said with careful thought; slowly, as though allowing time for decision

compartment (p. 489) a separate section

handshake (p. 487) an act in which two people grip and shake each other's hands

bloodstream (p. 489) the blood flowing through the body

Story Words

These words from the selection may be unfamiliar. Before students read, have them check the meanings and pronunciations of the words in the Glossary beginning on page 678 or in a dictionary.

- astronauts, p. 486
- mission, p. 487
- shuttle, p. 487
- handrails, p. 489
- universe, p. 489

void
maneuvering
deliberately
compartment
handshake
bloodstream

Vocabulary

Teach Vocabulary in Context

Identify Vocabulary Words   Display **Teaching Chart 134** and read the passage with students. Ask them to circle each vocabulary word and underline other words that suggest clues to its meaning.

Mission in Space

1. On the monitor, Mission Control watched as the shuttle entered the empty (void) of outer space. **2.** Watching the skillful (maneuvering) of the astronauts, the team on the ground hoped that the astronauts had a workable plan to recover the space telescope. **3.** Slowly and (deliberately), the shuttle approached the telescope. **4.** With only one chance to grab the telescope, the astronaut reached into a separate (compartment) at the control panel and ejected the robot arm. **5.** Instantly, the mechanical arm reached out to the telescope in a movement that resembled a (handshake). **6.** Now the astronauts were ready for their space walk, but first they had to breathe pure oxygen in order to get rid of the nitrogen that flowed in their (bloodstream).

Teaching Chart 134

Discuss Meanings   Use the following questions to help clarify the word meanings:

- Does oxygen flow through the bloodstream?
- Should a toolbox have a compartment for nails?
- Do some people deliberately not tell the whole truth?
- When is a firm handshake too firm?
- What is the most graceful maneuvering you have ever seen a skater do on ice?
- What does it mean that space is a void?

Practice

Demonstrate Word Meaning

PARTNERS

Have students work in pairs to choose a vocabulary card from a pile and act out its meaning for other students to guess.
▶ **Kinesthetic/Linguistic**

Word Building Manipulative Cards

Write Context Sentences

WRITING

Invite students to use the vocabulary words to write riddles. Tell them to use as many vocabulary words as they can in their riddles. Have students refer to their Glossary if needed. ▶ **Linguistic**

SPELLING/VOCABULARY CONNECTIONS

See Spelling Challenge Words, pages 5010–501P

LANGUAGE SUPPORT

See the **Language Support Book**, pages 177–180, for teaching suggestions for Vocabulary.

 **Vocabulary PuzzleMaker**

Provides vocabulary activities.

Assess Vocabulary

Use Words in Context

GROUP

Have students work in small groups to create a five-panel cartoon strip about the astronauts who repaired the Hubble Space Telescope. Tell students to use all of the vocabulary words in speech balloons as part of the comic strip. Display the finished cartoon strips on a bulletin board.

Meeting Individual Needs for Vocabulary

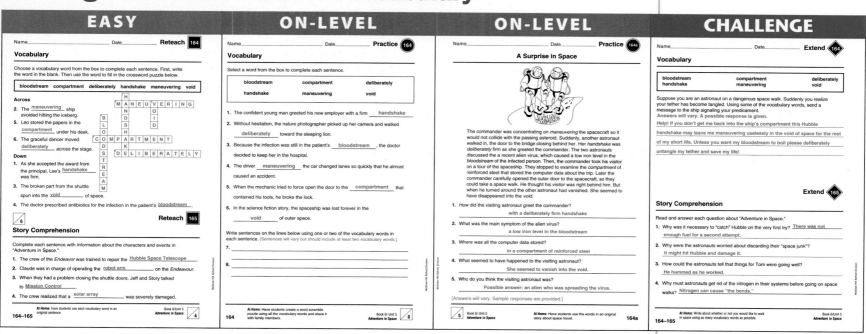

Reteach, 164   Practice, 164   Practice, 164a
Take-Home Story   Extend, 164

484C

Comprehension

Prereading Strategies

PREVIEW AND PREDICT Have students preview the selection by reading the title and the introduction, and by looking at the photographs.

- What do you think this selection will be about?

- Which do you think will be more important in this selection—facts or imagination? (facts) *Genre*

- What do you think the main idea of this selection will be?

Have students prepare a Predictions chart.

PREDICTIONS	WHAT HAPPENED
I will learn about a team of astronauts working together.	
I will learn about decisions the astronauts had to make.	

SET PURPOSES What do students want to find out by reading? For example:

- What was life like for these astronauts?

- What decisions did the astronauts make?

Adventure

Meet Elaine Scott

"'Curious' is a word that describes me well," says Elaine Scott. Her curiosity has led her to write books on a wide range of topics. Scott has written about what goes on behind the scenes in television shows and movies. She has written about the making of comic strips, the making of oil, and what it is like to be a twin. Besides her nonfiction work, Scott has also written a novel, *Choices.*

Scott's follow-up book to *Adventure in Space* is called *Close Encounters: Exploring the Universe with the Hubble Space Telescope.* It was awarded the 1999 American Institute of Physics Award. Today, Scott makes her home in Houston, Texas.

Meet Margaret Miller

Margaret Miller has worked with Elaine Scott on several successful nonfiction books for young people. Besides her work as a writer, Miller is also a talented photographer. She has created numerous books of photographs, and was awarded a 1992 *New York Times* Best Illustrated Children's Book for her photographs in *Where Does It Go?* Currently, Miller lives in New York City.

484

Meeting Individual Needs • Grouping Suggestions for Stategic Reading

EASY	ON-LEVEL	CHALLENGE
Read Together Read the selection with students or have them use the **Listening Library**. Have students use the Judgments and Decisions chart on page 485 as they read. Comprehension and Intervention prompts offer additional help with vocabulary and comprehension.	**Guided Instruction** Choose from the Comprehension questions as you read the story with students or after they have played the **Listening Library**. Help students use the Judgments and Decisions chart to record important judgments and decisions as they read.	**Read Independently** Set up a chart with students, as on page 485, and have them fill it in as they read. After reading, they can use their Judgments and Decisions charts to summarize the selection and to make a final judgment based on any new information they discover.

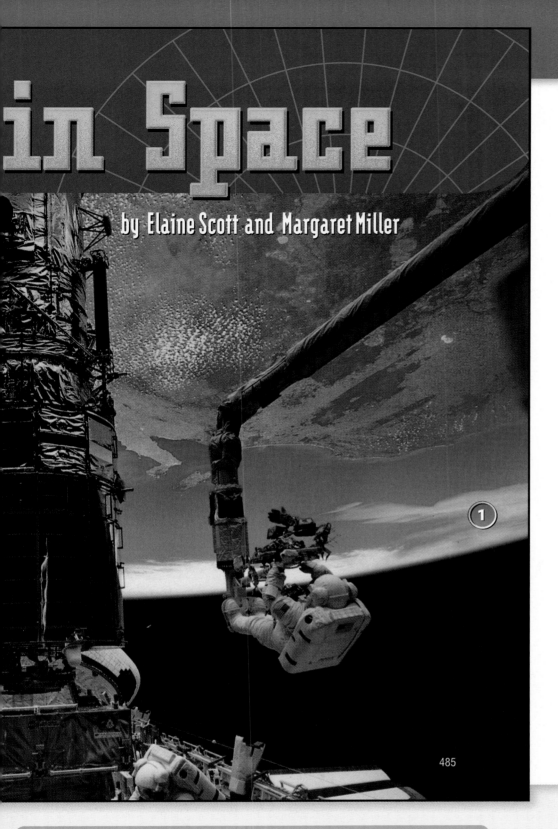

in Space

by Elaine Scott and Margaret Miller

485

Comprehension

☑ **Apply Judgments and Decisions**

☑ **Apply Make Inferences**

STRATEGIC READING Before we begin reading, let's prepare a Judgments and Decisions chart so that we can keep track of the judgments and decisions as we read.

JUDGMENTS AND DECISIONS	REASONS

① JUDGMENTS AND DECISIONS
Look at this photograph. The astronaut appears to be undertaking a dangerous job. Why do you think astronauts would want to take such a risk? (Risks are part of an astronaut's job; they do the job for the adventure and scientific discoveries that might better humankind.)

Genre

Informational Story

Explain that an informational story:

- presents nonfiction information in the context of a real-life story.
- gives facts about a topic, usually in time order.
- may include photographs, captions, and illustrations.

Activity After students read *Adventures in Space*, have them explain why a floating screw could be dangerous for the Hubble telescope.

LANGUAGE SUPPORT

A blackline master of the Judgments and Decisions chart is available in the **Language Support Book.**

Comprehension

(2) **JUDGMENTS AND DECISIONS**
Why do you think NASA decided to fix the Hubble Space Telescope? Do you agree with NASA's decision? Why or why not?

MODEL I don't really know why NASA decided to fix the Hubble Space Telescope. I think maybe they made the decision after thinking about the money they had already spent on it. Their decision probably was the right one considering the fact that the telescope could give them important information about the universe.

Introduction

For centuries scientists have dreamed of putting a telescope in orbit. With the success of the first space flights, this dream took a giant step closer to becoming a reality. In 1990 NASA, the United States space agency, launched the Hubble Space Telescope. Free from the blur of Earth's atmosphere, this instrument could see farther and more clearly than any telescope on Earth.

Yet two months after the telescope was launched, it ran into problems. Someone had made a mistake. The Hubble's mirror was a little too flat, and the telescope needed new "glasses" to help focus light correctly. The winglike solar arrays, which power the Hubble's cameras and instruments, seemed to be having trouble, too. Their shaking had to be stopped. The gyroscopes were also a problem. Three had already failed. If another one failed, the telescope could not be pointed in the direction that the scientists wanted. The Hubble would be useless.

(2) After much thought, NASA decided to fix the space telescope. By building COSTAR, an instrument with ten tiny mirrors, it would give the Hubble new "glasses." It also decided to give it a new camera, WF/PC II, to study objects at the farthest ends of the universe. Now it just needed to find the right astronauts to do the job.

It found seven. Richard Covey would fly the space shuttle *Endeavour*. His backup would be Kenneth Bowersox, nicknamed "Sox." Story Musgrave, Jeffrey Hoffman, Kathryn Thornton, and Thomas Akers would make the space walks needed to repair the telescope. Claude Nicollier would operate the robot arm that carried the space-walking astronauts. All in all, NASA seemed to have a plan. All the astronauts had to do was make the plan work. That would be the hard part. It would also be one of the greatest adventures in space.

486

Fluency

READ WITH INTONATION Have small groups of four students read the Introduction together. Challenge groups to read page 486 as though they were newscasters introducing a special report.

Have each student practice reading the first sentence aloud with an appropriate tone of voice. Have group members choose certain words or phrases to read with emphasis, such as the phrase "giant steps" in the second sentence.

Each student should read one paragraph. Have group members offer encouragement and constructive feedback.

Early on the third day, *Endeavour* was rapidly catching up with the telescope. The crew was excited. Just before sunset, they spotted the Hubble. It was a beautiful sight, glowing blue and silver in the fading light. "Now it's all eyeballs and hands," Sox said, **③** as he and Commander Dick Covey took over from Mission Control and fired small burns from the maneuvering rockets. Slowly and gently, the shuttle approached the forty-three-foot-long telescope looming outside its windows. The rocket burns used fuel, and Ken Bowersox was worried. He knew that there was only one chance to capture the Hubble. If they weren't in the right position, there wouldn't be enough fuel for a second attempt. If they didn't grab the Hubble on their first and only try, the mission would have failed before **④** it began.

Claude was ready at the controls of the robot arm, waiting for the right moment. *Endeavour* glided into place below the telescope. Claude reached out with the mechanical arm and snared it! The telescope was safe, snugly tucked into the payload bay. With relief, Dick Covey radioed Mission Control. "Houston, *Endeavour* has a firm handshake with Mr. Hubble's telescope. It's quite a sight." The first crucial step of the repair mission was over. It was time for the space walks to begin.

The shuttle's robot arm (left) is poised, waiting for the right momentum to capture the Hubble Space Telescope and anchor it in the orbiter's payload bay.

487

Comprehension

③ **MAKE INFERENCES** From what you have read in the introduction and seen in the pictures, what do you think the phrase "eyeballs and hands" refers to? (It refers to the telescope, which is like an eyeball because it views things, and the robot arm that Claude operates.)

④ **JUDGMENTS AND DECISIONS** Why do you think Ken Bowersox and the team decide to be very careful when capturing the Hubble Space Telescope? (They know that there is only enough fuel for one try.) Let's add this to our charts.

JUDGMENTS AND DECISIONS	REASONS
take special precautions to capture the Hubble	not enough fuel for second try

Minilesson
REVIEW/MAINTAIN
Context Clues

Remind students that nearby words often give clues to the meaning of unfamiliar words.

- Ask students to read the third sentence in the second paragraph, in which the word *snared* appears.
- Have them identify nearby words that give clues to the meaning of *snared*. (reached out with the mechanical arm)

Activity Challenge students to say in their own words what *snared* means. (grabbed, grasped) Encourage them to write and illustrate a context sentence for *snared*.

ESL Write on the chalkboard technical words such as *telescope, gyroscope, payload bay,* and *Mission Control*. Help students define each term and explain its importance in the story. You may wish to use simple diagrams on the board to clarify the meaning of some of these terms.

The meaning of some unusual verbs on this page, such as *grab, snared,* and *tucked* can be partially understood through context clues. Help clarify the meanings further by acting them out. Use a rubber ball or other similar object as you demonstrate, and then have students demonstrate, what each action looks like.

Comprehension

⑤ **MAKE INFERENCES** Imagine that you are the astronaut in the picture. In your own words, as an astronaut, tell why the handrails are going to help you repair the Hubble Space Telescope.

MODEL I'm not used to walking around in space, and these handrails will help me walk and keep my balance while I'm trying to repair this big telescope. Imagine that you're going down an escalator. You need handrails to hold on to, don't you? Well it's the same thing in space—except you won't fall down, you'll float away!

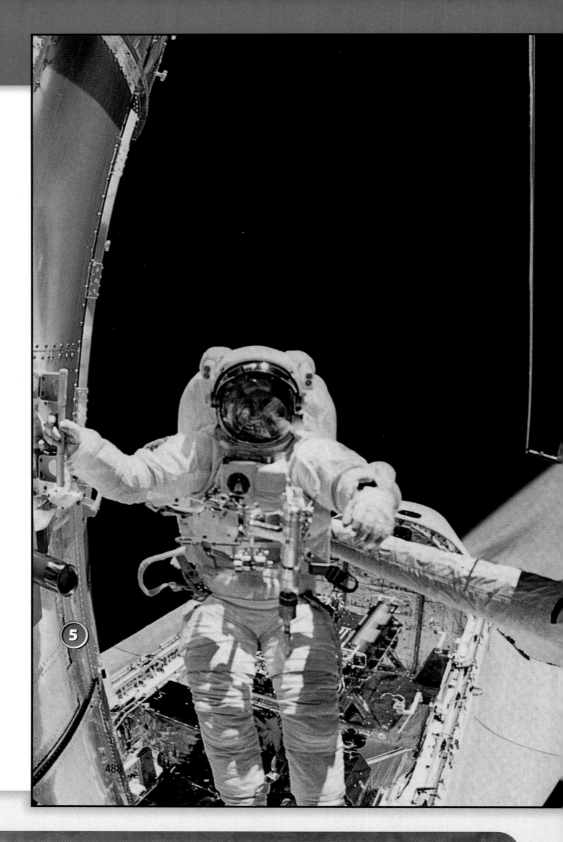

488

Cross Curricular: Social Studies

MAP SKILLS Display a map of the United States. Have students

- locate NASA Headquarters in Houston, Texas, and the Kennedy Space Center in Cape Canaveral, Florida.

- estimate the distance between Houston, Texas, and Cape Canaveral,

Florida. (about 1,000 miles)

- give reasons that the Kennedy Space Center at Cape Canaveral was chosen as a launching site. (good climate and clear skies; water for possible rescues)

▶ **Mathematical/Spatial**

TEXAS AND FLORIDA

Cape
Canaveral

Now the first surprise took its "bite." One of the solar arrays was badly twisted. Would it roll up as planned? Story and Jeff would look more closely the next day, when the "house calls" on Hubble would begin. Commander Dick Covey summed up the spirit of the crew when he said, "We are ready. We are inspired. Let's go fix this thing."

The next day, Kathy and Tom helped Story and Jeff put on their space suits. Their very lives would depend on them. Outer space is just that—space. It is a void. There is nothing in it—no oxygen, no hydrogen, no carbon dioxide—nothing. Human beings without protection would die in that environment in a matter of seconds. The air would rush out of our lungs. Our blood would boil, our skin expand. And as if that weren't a terrible enough picture, we would roast or freeze, depending on whether it was day or night.

While the Hubble Space Telescope was being designed, Story Musgrave suggested that it be fitted with handrails to make it easier for space-walking astronauts to service it. Story uses those handrails on his first space walk.

Going out into space is not like going out your front door. Story and Jeff entered and left the shuttle through its air lock, a small chamber with two hatches, or doors. Before leaving the shuttle, they had to breathe pure oxygen for about forty minutes in order to get rid of the nitrogen in their bloodstream. In outer space, nitrogen can cause a painful and dangerous condition known as the bends. After their "pre-breathe" was over, all of the air was pumped out of the air lock. Now it was a vacuum, just like space. The astronauts could safely open the outer door and float into the payload bay. "It's an exciting moment when you open the air lock and see the entire universe staring you in the face," Jeff said, as he and Story started the first space walk.

For safety, Story and Jeff each attached themselves to the shuttle with a tether, a long metal cable. Moving deliberately and cautiously, Story pulled himself hand over hand along the sixty-foot length of the payload bay to the waiting telescope. His feet secured in foot restraints, Jeff got a ride on Claude's robot arm. All went well as they replaced the faulty gyroscopes—until they tried to close the doors to the instrument compartment. A second surprise took a "bite."

489

Comprehension

6 What do the astronauts do to prepare for their first space walk? (They put on their space suits, breathe pure oxygen for about 40 minutes in order to get rid of the nitrogen in their bloodstreams, and pump all the air out of the airlock.) *Sequence of Events*

COMPOUND WORDS Find the words *bloodstream* and *handrails* on this page. What kinds of words are these. What do they mean?

PREVENTION/INTERVENTION

COMPOUND WORDS Remind students that compound words are formed from two words that can stand on their own but combine to make a word with a new meaning.

- Ask a volunteer to write the words *bloodstream* and *handrails* on the board, to divide them into two separate words, and to tell the meaning of each smaller word.

- Have another volunteer tell the meaning of the compound words.

- Challenge students to find other compound words in the selection and to add them to a list in their notebooks. Have them check the meaning of these compound words and to compare lists and definitions with a partner.

Comprehension

7 **JUDGMENTS AND DECISIONS**
What quick decision did Story Musgrave make about closing the compartment doors of the telescope? (He used a special tool called a come-along to hold the doors together so that he was free to push the doors closed.) **Was it a good decision? Explain.** (Yes; it enabled him to bolt the door.)

8 **JUDGMENTS AND DECISIONS**
Why did the astronauts decide to work on the solar array at "night"? (The solar array was still producing electricity from the sun, so they had to work during the "night.")

One door sagged slightly below the other, and they would not close. Jeff and Story struggled with the balky doors. Because they no longer matched, the closing bolt would not slide home. The astronauts used their power tools with no results. They talked to Mission Control and even considered leaving the doors slightly ajar. But Story was determined. In a move that was not rehearsed ahead of time, he went to the toolbox and removed a tool called a come-along. The come-along held the two doors together, leaving Story's hands free to push on them and force the closing bolt home. The operation was a success, and Story and Jeff earned a new **7** nickname from NASA—Mr. Goodwrench.

Next, the crew turned their attention to the twisted solar array. The solar arrays were designed to roll up like window shades. The undamaged array rolled up smoothly for storage, but the other would not roll up because it was warped. The Even Couple—Kathy and Tom—would have to throw it overboard the next day, before installing the new arrays.

Story and Jeff put Kathy and Tom in their space suits for the second space walk and sent them off to work. Kathy rode the robot arm while Tom floated. The damaged solar array was still producing electricity from the sun, so Kathy and Tom had to work during the orbiting **8** "night." They had lights on their space helmets, like miners, and from inside the shuttle, Story helped by shining a spotlight on the work area. Still, it was hard for them to see exactly what they were doing. Kathy steadied the large floppy array while Tom unfastened it.

The solar arrays were attached to the telescope with electrical connectors similar to the plugs on the back of a computer. Each connector had many small pins that could be easily bent—especially by someone trying to plug or unplug them wearing bulky space gloves! The connectors and bolts were essential to the telescope's life. If they were damaged during this repair, the new arrays could not be installed. Without solar energy, the Hubble would have no electricity. Without electricity, the Hubble would have no life.

On the fifth space walk, Story Musgrave and Jeff Hoffman performed final repairs. Here they prepare to put new covers on the telescope's magnetometers.

490

CULTURAL PERSPECTIVES

COSMONAUTS Explain that the space race between the United States and the Soviet Union began with the Soviet launch of *Sputnik* in 1957. Point out that the first person in space was a cosmonaut—Yuri Gagarin—in 1961.

RESEARCH AND INQUIRY Have students research the contributions that cosmonauts have made to space exploration. Suggest that they also mention recent joint space missions, such as *Mir*, made by the United States, the former Soviet Union, and other countries.

491

Comprehension

9 **JUDGMENTS AND DECISIONS**
Look at the photograph of the Hubble Space Telescope. Why is solar energy so important to it? (The Hubble gets its electricity from solar energy, which is captured by the solar arrays. Without solar energy, the Hubble would have no electricity. Without electricity, the Hubble would have no life.)

9

LANGUAGE SUPPORT

ESL To clarify the meanings of some of the complex explanations on page 490, use simple diagrams on the chalkboard as you paraphrase the words in the book. For example, you can draw the doors described in the first paragraph, and then add the closing bolt and the come-along, and show how Story used it to make the doors stay closed.

Minilesson

REVIEW/MAINTAIN

/îr/ and /ûr/

Have students say the words *reindeer* and *pierce*. Point out /îr/ can be spelled *eer, ier,* or *ere*. Then have students say the words *turned* and *earn*. Point out /ûr/ can be spelled *ur, ear, our,* or *er*.

• Give examples of homophones with /îr/ and /ûr/ spelled differently, such as *peer/pier* and *heard/herd*. Ask students to name other homophones with /îr/ and /ûr/. *(deer/dear, tier/tear; earn/urn, turn/tern)* **Graphophonic Cues**

Activity Have partners write riddles with /îr/ and /ûr/ homophones.

 Phonics Intervention Guide

491

Comprehension

(10) **MAKE INFERENCES** How do you think Kathy feels riding on the end of the robot arm? (She probably feels nervous because she knows that she alone will hold the array and must keep it steady so as not to damage the telescope.)

SELF-MONITORING STRATEGY

REREADING Because the selection is filled with important scientific and technological information, students may wish to reread a part of the selection to understand the terminology or events taking place.

The team worked slowly and deliberately as *Endeavour* fell around the Earth. At last, Kathy, riding on the end of the robot arm, was ready for the crucial and dangerous moment when she alone would hold the array. She had to keep it steady and still. If it flopped around it could hit and damage the telescope. The Hubble had enough trouble; Kathy did not want to "break what isn't broken," as Jeff would say. She waited for Tom's instructions.

"Coming out real smooth," Tom said. "Four inches . . . six inches . . . eight inches out." His voice was calm, a gentle coach.

Kathy said, "OK, Claude, real easy." She truly had her hands full, as the robotic arm pulled her slowly away from the telescope.

"OK, K.T. I'm letting go," said Tom.

"I have it," Kathy answered. The array was perfectly steady and Kathy exclaimed with delight, "Holy moley, a piece of cake!"

But tension mounted again. Everyone was worried about the moment when Kathy would toss the array overboard. It had to be done in daylight, when the entire crew could see clearly. No one wanted the array to hit the top of the Hubble on its **(10)** way to becoming space junk. Poised on the end of the robot arm, Kathy held it over her head and waited for the sun to rise over Africa.

"I think I see sunrise coming, K.T.," Tom said.

At last, the word came from Story, inside the shuttle. "OK, Tom. Tell K.T. to go for release."

Tom had one request. "Can you just hang on one second, so I can get to where I can watch?" He moved to get a better view, then said, "OK, K.T. You ready?"

"Ready."

"Got a go for release," Tom said. The moment had come. "OK. No hands!" Kathy said as she let go of the 350 pounds of useless metal and fabric.

"There it goes," said Tom. The panel revolved and drifted away. Sox fired a few small burns from the shuttle's rockets to move *Endeavour* and the telescope out of danger. In the void of space, the maneuver caused an artificial wind.

Kathy's voice came over the radio again. "Wonder what it's going to do when it starts flapping in the breeze?"

Suddenly, as she saw the great orange array flexing over the desert, she exclaimed, "It's almost like a bird, Tom. Look at it!" They stared at the incredible sight of a giant "bird" soaring over the African desert below.

492

Cross Curricular: Math

WEIGHT IN SPACE The weightlessness of space changes the way people relate to objects. Discuss with students what they think it would be like to be able to lift hundreds of pounds and hurl it long distances. Ask them to use their experience in water as a reference point.

RESEARCH AND INQUIRY Encourage students to research their weight on the moon and on other planets. Then have them use graph paper to chart the various weights. ▶ **Mathematical/Spatial**

Perched on the end of the robot arm, Kathy Thornton steadies the damaged solar array while she waits for dawn and the right moment to release it.

493

Comprehension

(11) JUDGMENTS AND DECISIONS
Look at the picture of Kathy holding the damaged solar array. Let's write on our charts the important decisions the astronauts have made so far and the reasons for their decisions.

JUDGMENTS AND DECISIONS	REASONS
take special precautions to capture the Hubble	not enough fuel for second try
use special tool to close doors	need to secure instruments
work on the solar array at "night"	because array is still producing electricity from sun, making it dangerous to install new arrays

493

Comprehension

(12) JUDGMENTS AND DECISIONS
Why is it important for Tom to give Kathy exact instructions for guiding COSTAR into place? (Kathy is holding COSTAR in front of her face, and she can't see what she is doing. He needs to tell her how to slide it into place.) Let's add this to our charts.

JUDGMENTS AND DECISIONS	REASONS
take special precautions to capture the Hubble	not enough fuel for second try
use special tool to close doors	need to secure instruments
work on the solar array at "night"	because array is still producing electricity from sun, making it dangerous to install new arrays
astronauts move cautiously and give exact instructions	to prevent ruining mirror and crippling telescope

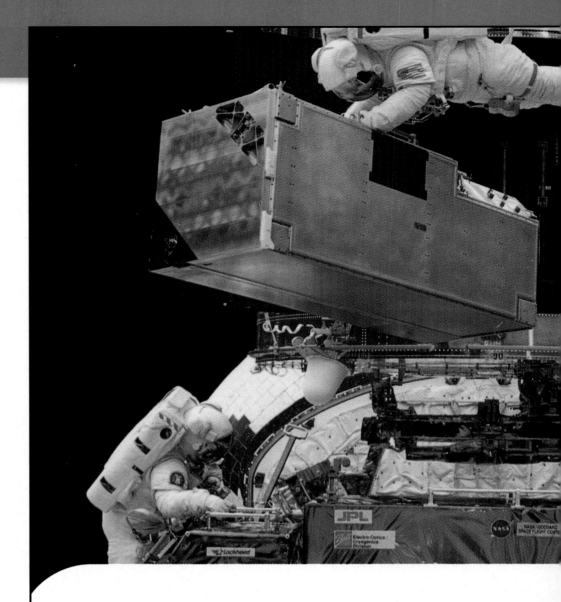

(12) Because COSTAR had to be held directly in front of her face, Kathy Thornton relies on Tom Akers's instructions while guiding it into place.

494

Cross Curricular: Science

TELESCOPES Explain that throughout history telescopes have played a major role in exploring the planets and stars.

RESEARCH AND INQUIRY Have students research the history of the telescope and investigate different kinds of

telescopes in use today. Suggest that they give an oral presentation of their findings.
▶ **Linguistic/Interpersonal**

interNET CONNECTION Students can learn about telescopes by visiting
www.mhschool.com/reading

steady and Story removed the protective cover on the mirror. One slight touch or bump, and the mirror could have been contaminated or knocked out of alignment, a catastrophe that would have crippled the telescope. The astronauts' movements were slow, precise, and delicate. Everyone relaxed a bit when that job was finished, and Jeff said excitedly, "I hope we have a lot of eager astronomers ready to use this beautiful thing."

On the fourth walk, Kathy and Tom became orbiting eye doctors and slid the refrigerator-sized COSTAR into the telescope. Kathy moved the six-hundred-pound instrument with ease, but COSTAR was in front of her face. She knew she had only millimeters of clearance, but she couldn't see what she was doing. Once again, her partner became her eyes, and COSTAR slid into place without a hitch. Tom hummed while he worked. Later, Claude recalled that sound and said, "It was good to hear Tom humming, because we knew when Tom was humming things were going well. And Tom was humming most of the time!"

When the Hubble's "glasses" were in place, Kathy said, "I think everyone can breathe a sigh of relief." Jeff added, "It should be exciting to see what the Hubble can do with a new set of eyeballs." **(13)**

The results of all the planning and practice were becoming more and more obvious as each team of astronauts completed their space walks successfully. On the third space walk, Story and Jeff installed the new camera, WF/PC II. The critical moment came when Jeff held the camera

495

Comprehension

(13) Kathy and Tom seem to make a great team. Why have the authors emphasized the importance of teamwork to the mission? (Possible answer: Without teamwork, such a delicate, dangerous mission would not succeed.) *Critical Thinking: Authors' Craft*

P/i MULTIPLE-MEANING WORDS
Reread the caption on page 494. What does the word *place* mean in this sentence? What is a synonym of the word *place* as it is used here? (position)

Minilesson

REVIEW/MAINTAIN
Make Inferences

Remind students that in order to make inferences, they need to understand information or ideas that the authors do not directly state in the selection.

- Have students reread page 495.
- Ask them what inferences they can make about the COSTAR installation. Was it going well? How do they know? (Tom was humming, and Claude inferred from the humming that things were going well.)

Activity Have students write a short paragraph that explains or supports their answers. They should use evidence from the text as well as their own experiences.

P/i PREVENTION/INTERVENTION

MULTIPLE-MEANING WORDS
Have students reread the caption that contains the words *into place* on page 494 and write the phrase on the board. Explain that the word *place* has many meanings and that as it is used here, *into place* is an idiom, meaning *into position*.

Have students provide other idioms that include the word *place*, such as *in place*, as in *running in place*; *in the first place*; to *put in one's place*; and so on. Challenge students to define each idiom before looking it up under *place* in the dictionary.

Comprehension

(14) **JUDGMENTS AND DECISIONS**
Why do the astronauts decide to chase after the dropped screw? (It could contaminate the Hubble.) Let's complete our charts to show how the astronauts' judgments and decisions help make the mission successful.

JUDGMENTS AND DECISIONS	REASONS
take extra precautions to capture the Hubble	not enough fuel for second try
use special tool to close doors	need to secure instruments
work on the solar array at "night"	because array is still producing electricity from sun, making it dangerous to install new arrays
astronauts move cautiously and give exact instructions	to prevent ruining mirror and crippling telescope
capture the dropped screw	could contaminate the Hubble Space Telescope

RETELL THE STORY Have partners write a paragraph summarizing the astronauts' decisions. *Summarize*

STUDENT SELF-ASSESSMENT

• How did the strategy of making judgments and decisions help me understand the selection?

TRANSFERRING THE STRATEGY

• When might I try using this strategy again? In what other reading could the chart help me?

On the fifth EVA, when Story and Jeff were winding up the repairs, a tiny screw came loose and floated away. On Earth, a dropped screw is not a disaster. In space, it could (14) be. It could contaminate the Hubble.

Jeff and Claude spotted it at the same time; Claude noticed it even from his position inside the shuttle. The "famous screw chase," as Story called it, was on. Jeff rode the arm while Claude steered him toward the floating screw, in hot pursuit. Later Jeff said, "When we were chasing it, I actually felt like a kid riding on a merry-go-round, going after the brass ring, holding on with one hand and reaching out." Jeff got the "brass ring," and he and Story finished up their work. They did a final cleanup of the payload bay and reentered the shuttle, knowing that the Hubble was now ready to go. The time had come to send it on its way.

Claude raised the towering observatory from its workbench and released it into orbit once again. As it moved into the blackness of space, its orange solar arrays glowed in the sunset. "It will look far into the cosmos and far into the past," he said. "It is a time machine as well as a space exploration machine."

Looking out the shuttle's window, Tom was wistful. "The payload bay really looks empty."

In a record-breaking five space walks—no mission to space had ever had that many—the heroes of STS-61 had accomplished what many said could not be done. It was time for these space mechanics to return to Earth.

496

REREADING FOR *Fluency*

PARTNERS Encourage students to choose an exciting part of the selection to read to a partner, using expression and feeling.

READING RATE When you evaluate rate, have the student read aloud from the story for one minute. Place a stick-on note after the last word read. Count words read. To evaluate

students' performance, see the Running Record in the **Fluency Assessment** book.

(i) **Intervention** For leveled fluency lessons, passages, and norms charts, see **Skills Intervention Guide**, Part 4, Fluency.

Repaired and ready to observe the universe, the Hubble Space Telescope floats away from *Endeavour's* cargo bay.

(Left) Kathy Thornton works on COSTAR. A checklist containing vital information was attached to the sleeve of each astronaut's space suit.

497

Comprehension

Return to Predictions and Purposes

Review with students their predictions and reasons for reading the selection. Were their predictions correct? Did they find out what they wanted to know?

PREDICTIONS	WHAT HAPPENED
I will learn about a team of astronauts working together.	The astronauts worked closely together to repair the Hubble Space Telescope.
I will learn about decisions the astronauts had to make.	The decisions and maneuvers they made in space were accurate and careful, making the mission a success.

INFORMAL **ASSESSMENT**

JUDGMENTS AND DECISIONS

HOW TO ASSESS

- Can students see how the decisions made in space helped to complete the mission?

- Can students see that space explorers base their decisions on reasons and solid evidence?

Students should recognize that the astronauts' judgments and decisions, as well as their own about the selection, need to be based on reasons.

FOLLOW UP If students have difficulty making judgments and decisions about the text, choose a few details or incidents and model the kinds of judgments and decisions that readers can form from them.

LITERARY RESPONSE

QUICK-WRITE Have students record their thoughts about the selection. Use the following

JOURNAL questions to help them get started:

- What parts of the story did you find the most interesting or exciting?

- What did you learn about the job of an astronaut? Would you like to be an astronaut someday? Why or why not?

- How did making the right decisions affect the outcome of the mission?

ORAL RESPONSE Have students share their journal writings and discuss how they better appreciate the decision-making process involved in space exploration. Which decision did they think was the hardest to make?

Story Questions

Have students discuss or write answers to the questions on page 498.

Answers

1. The shuttle didn't have enough fuel for a second attempt.
   Literal/Judgments and Decisions

2. Possible answer: by making decisions and working as a team. *Inferential/Inferences*

3. Possible answer: NASA's decision probably was based on the money already spent and on the scientific benefits of the project. *Inferential/Judgments and Decisions*

4. Astronauts must work together to repair equipment in space. *Critical/Summarize*

5. Answers will vary. *Critical/Reading Across Texts*

Write a Science Fiction Story For a full lesson, see pages 501K–501L.

Story Questions & Activities

1. Why did the *Endeavour* have only one chance to capture the Hubble?

2. How does the crew overcome the obstacles they encounter in space?

3. Why do you think NASA decided to fix the Hubble Space Telescope? Explain.

4. What is the main idea of this selection?

5. In a record-breaking five spacewalks, the space heroes had accomplished what many people thought could not be done. First, decide what makes these astronauts modern heroes. Then compare their mission with the task Bellerophon performs.

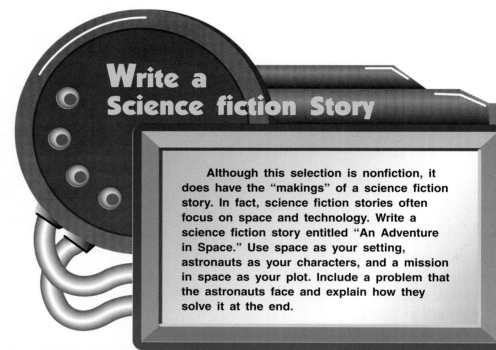

Write a Science fiction Story

Although this selection is nonfiction, it does have the "makings" of a science fiction story. In fact, science fiction stories often focus on space and technology. Write a science fiction story entitled "An Adventure in Space." Use space as your setting, astronauts as your characters, and a mission in space as your plot. Include a problem that the astronauts face and explain how they solve it at the end.

Meeting Individual Needs

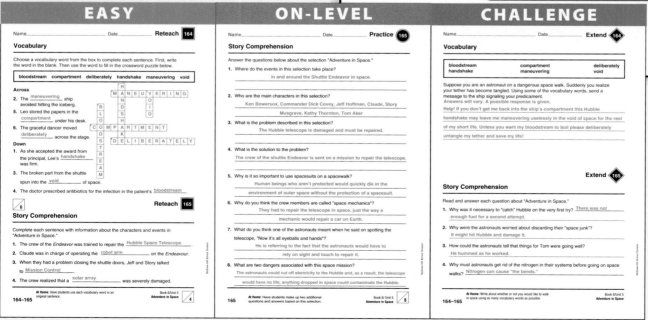

Reteach, 165   Practice, 165   Extend, 165

Create a Mobile

Make a space mobile of planets, stars, constellations, astronauts, and a spacecraft or space station. Cut out pictures from old books or magazines, or use your own colored drawings. Paste them on cardboard and then cut them out. Make a frame for your mobile from one or two metal coat hangers. Then use dental floss, clear fishing line, or yarn to hang the objects from the frame so that they move like real objects in space.

Give a Talk

What would it be like to be part of the crew of the *Endeavour*? Imagine that you are one of the astronauts. Give a talk to a group about something that happened to you during the mission. Explain a decision that you had to make. Then tell how it felt to be in space. How do you now feel about Earth?

Find Out More

NASA, the United States Space Agency, worked with 16 other countries to create the Hubble Space Telescope. Find out about some of NASA's other projects. Use an encyclopedia, a book about NASA, or the NASA website on the Internet. Write a short report about one of the projects, stressing its goals and achievements.

499

Story Activities

Create a Mobile

Materials: pictures from magazines, construction paper, cardboard, 2 or 3 coat hangers, yarn, paste, magic markers

 GROUP Have students work in small groups to sketch a design for their mobile. Encourage them to make the individual pieces and help them hang their mobiles in the classroom.

Give a Talk

ONE Have students list some of the decisions made by the crew of the *Endeavour*. Suggest that they choose one decision and prepare a talk about why it was important. Encourage students to tell the outcome of the decision and its effect on the mission.

Find Out More

GROUP **RESEARCH AND INQUIRY** Have students work in small groups to brainstorm questions they would like answered about the Hubble Space Telescope and other NASA projects.

interNET **CONNECTION** For more information about the Hubble Space Telescope, students can visit *www.mhschool.com/reading*

FORMAL **ASSESSMENT**

After page 499, see the Selection Assessment.

MATH: DISTANCE FORMULA

Planet	Velocity Around Sun
Mercury	29.75 miles per sec.
Jupiter	8.12 miles per sec.

Ask students to find the number of miles that:

- Mercury travels in orbit around the Sun in 5 seconds. *(148.75 miles)*

- Jupiter travels in orbit around the Sun in 5 minutes. *(2,436 miles)*

What to Look For Check to see that each student:

- multiplies orbital speed of Mercury by 5.
- multiplies speed of Jupiter by 60, then multiplies 487.2 by 5.

Study Skills

GRAPHIC AIDS

TESTED ✓ **OBJECTIVES** Students will:

- trace the flow of information in a flow chart
- use the flow chart to describe alternative outcomes to the same event

PREPARE Preview the flow chart, explaining that most events have two possible outcomes. Display **Teaching Chart 135.**

TEACH Have students follow the flow of the arrows throughout the chart, describing each outcome as they go.

PRACTICE Review answers 1–5 with students. **1.** The launch will be rescheduled. **2.** to reach coordinates and lock missiles on the giant asteroid **3.** No, the press conference takes place only if the astronauts destroy the asteroid. **4.** The top box would be the final step of a failed mission. The bottom box would be the final step if the asteroid is destroyed. **5.** Sample answers: It can help you plan out the steps you will need to take.

ASSESS/CLOSE Have students describe events of one possible path through the flow chart.

STUDY SKILLS

Read a Flow Chart

Instead of making lists, NASA might have organized the instructions attached to the astronauts' sleeves into a flow chart. A **flow chart** is a diagram that shows the steps in a process. Some flow charts show different possible steps, depending on outcomes along the way. This flow chart is for a space mission described in a science fiction novel.

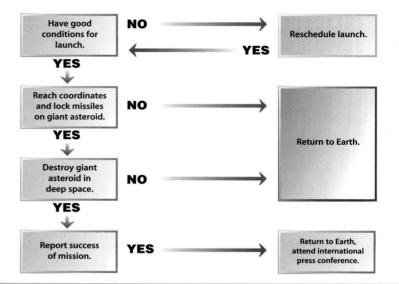

Use the flow chart to answer these questions.

1. What will happen if conditions are not good for the launch?

2. What is the next goal to be achieved after a successul launch?

3. Will there be a press conference if the astronauts fail to destroy the giant asteroid? Why or why not?

4. There are two boxes marked "Return to Earth." How do they reflect the mission's success or failure?

5. How might creating a flow chart help you when you are starting your next big research assignment?

Meeting Individual Needs

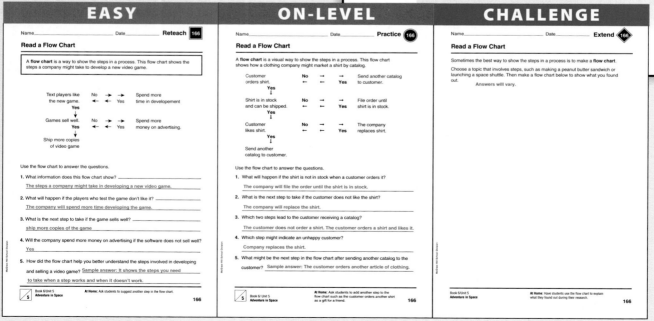

Reteach, 166   **Practice, 166**   **Extend, 166**

TEST POWER

DIRECTIONS

Read the sample story. Then read each question about the story.

SAMPLE

Ancient Mayan Civilization

The Mayan people were perhaps the most advanced of all ancient cultures. Despite that, this culture remains a mystery.

The Mayans developed a complex writing system and had a keen understanding of natural science. They charted the movements of the sun, the stars, and the planets before the first telescope was ever invented. They were talented artists; they created wonderful pottery, weavings, and paintings. The Mayans were agriculturally advanced. They could harvest crops in even the most difficult conditions.

But as mysteriously as their culture appeared, the Mayan culture disappeared. Some historians think that the Mayans died from <u>famine</u>. They believe that the population had grown so large that it could not support itself. The land could not produce enough food to feed the people.

1 The word <u>famine</u> in this passage means —

A eating bad meat

B poisoning themselves

C a severe food shortage

D growing population

2 The Mayan culture remains a mystery to historians because —

F the Mayan people probably wanted it that way

G the Mayan culture disappeared

H the Mayan leaders were unlike other leaders of the time

J the Mayan artistry was so advanced

501

Test Power

THE PRINCETON REVIEW

Read the Page

Have students read the passage and answer *all* of the questions.

Discuss the Questions

Question 1: This question asks students to define a word in context. Remind students to look for clues in the sentences near the underlined word. The sentences following *famine* say that the "population had grown so large that it could not support itself" and that "the land could not produce enough food . . . . " Students should be able to infer that *famine* means *a severe food shortage*.

Question 2: This question asks students to understand a cause-and-effect relationship. Ask, "Why does the Mayan culture remain a mystery to historians?" Have students support the answers they give with facts from the passage. Then have them compare their answers against the actual answer choices.

Leveled Books

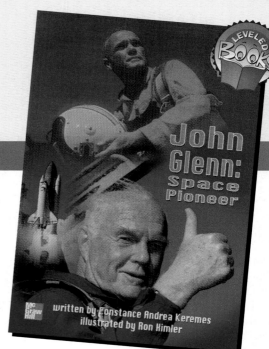

EASY

John Glenn: Space Pioneer

/îr/, /ûr/

☑ **Judgments and Decisions**

☑ **Instructional Vocabulary:** *bloodstream, compartment, deliberately, handshake, maneuvering, void*

written by Constance Andrea Keremes illustrated by Ron Himler

Guided Reading

PREVIEW AND PREDICT After discussing the illustrations with students, have them make predictions about what they think will happen during John Glenn's journey into space.

SET PURPOSES Ask students what they think they will learn about space and space exploration from this selection.

READ THE BOOK Encourage students to read the story by themselves. Then ask them to interact with text by answering the following questions:

Pages 2–3: Do you feel Glenn's children made a good decision naming the capsule *Friendship*? (Students should support their answers.) *Judgments and Decisions*

Page 5: How did Glenn differ from other astronauts who had preceded him into space? (He didn't get dizzy or suffer from stomach sickness) *Compare and Contrast*

Page 7: What part of speech is *maneuvering* on this page—noun, adjective, or verb? (verb) *Vocabulary*

Page 9: What vowel sound do you hear in the beginning of the word *turned*? (/ûr/) *Phonics and Decoding*

Page 12: Would you say Glenn had more or less support than he had on his first journey in space? (He had seven additional crew members, and many more pounds of thrust.) *Draw Conclusions*

Page 16: Reread the last sentence. How do you think the author feels about elderly people participating in space exploration? (She feels people of all ages can participate.) *Author's Point of View*

RETURN TO PREDICTIONS AND PURPOSES Review students' predictions and their purpose for reading.

LITERARY RESPONSE Discuss:

- What do you think of Glenn's two space voyages?

- What are your feelings about space exploration? Would you participate?

Also see the story questions and activity in *John Glenn: Space Pioneer.*

---

i Intervention ▶ **Skills**

Intervention Guide, for direct instruction and extra practice in vocabulary and comprehension

Answers to Story Questions

1. Project Mercury's goal was to send Americans into space.
2. They did not want to alarm him; they hoped they could solve it themselves.
3. It provided data for research on aging; it showed that elderly people are capable of performing in zero G.
4. Answers will vary.
5. John Glenn is a hero whose space journeys sparked our imagination and provided us with useful information on space travel and aging.

The *Story Questions and Activity* **below appear in the** *Easy Book.*

Story Questions

1. What was the purpose of Project Mercury?
2. Why didn't Mission Control tell Glenn about the problem with the heat shield?
3. How was Glenn's 1998 space trip beneficial?
4. Why is John Glenn considered a hero?
5. What is the main idea of the book?

Cosmos Commentary

Space flights provide valuable information, but do you think they are worth the danger and expense? Prepare a news show commentary to present to your classmates. In it, express your viewpoint. Use facts from the books to support your opinion. You may also use information from other books or magazines.

from *John Glenn: Space Pioneer*

Leveled Books

INDEPENDENT

Class Trip

☑ **Judgments and Decisions**

☑ **Instructional Vocabulary:** *bloodstream, compartment, deliberately, handshake, maneuvering, void*

Guided Reading

PREVIEW AND PREDICT Students can preview the book by looking at the title and illustrations. Ask: Can you predict what type of book this is from the illustrations?

SET PURPOSES Talk with students about what they want to learn from reading this book. Ask students: Why do people like to read science fiction?

READ THE BOOK Ask students to read independently. Use these questions to gauge student understanding:

Page 5: Do you think these students are right to be uninterested in the idea of a trip to XL3? (Answers will vary, but should be based on reason. Possible response: They are used to space travel, and although this planet is new, it doesn't sound very unusual or interesting to them, so they are right to be uninterested.) *Judgments and Decisions*

Page 6: Sometimes you can understand a compound word by studying the smaller words that make it up. What two words

make up *handshake*? (hand, shake) Based on what you know about these words, what does this compound word mean? (*Handshake* means to clasp hands.) *Vocabulary*

Pages 14–16: Why do you think Rie decides to keep the glittering cave a secret? (She is afraid the beauty of the cave will be destroyed if it becomes a tourist attraction.) *Draw Conclusions*

RETURN TO PREDICTIONS AND PURPOSES Were students accurate in their guesses about what might happen in the story?

LITERARY RESPONSE Ask students:

- How do you think this class is like one on Earth? How is it different?

- What do you think the best thing would be about living on a space station? The worst thing?

Also see the story questions and activity in *Class Trip*.

Answers to Story Questions

1. They thought XL3 sounded like a boring planet.
2. Answers will vary. She will probably keep the secret because she wants to protect the planet.
3. Answers should support statement.
4. A space-age trip to a distant planet that reveals a lost world to a young girl.
5. Answers will vary.

The *Story Questions and Activity* below appear in the *Independent Book*.

Story Questions

1. Why were most students not very interested in the field trip?
2. Will Rie keep her secret of the lost world on XL3, or tell people about it? Why do you think so?
3. Do you think Rie behaved responsibly? Why or why not?
4. What is this story mostly about?
5. Do you think Rie would be interested in the Hubble spacecraft and its work?

Take the Shuttle

Find information about the most recent space shuttle mission, including how many miles it traveled, how many astronauts were aboard, what its purpose was, and any other interesting facts. Using this information, make a poster that tells the story of the shuttle mission, including any photos or drawings you can find.

from Class Trip

Leveled Books

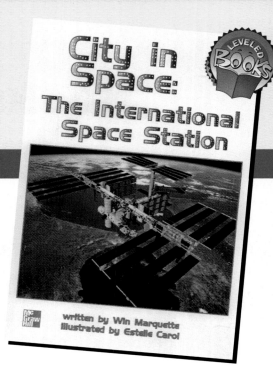

City in Space: The International Space Station

written by Win Marquette
Illustrated by Estelle Carol

CHALLENGE

City in Space: The International Space Station

☑ **Judgments and Decisions**

☑ **Instructional Vocabulary:** *bloodstream, compartment, deliberately, handshake, maneuvering, void*

Guided Reading

PREVIEW AND PREDICT Ask students to preview the title, chapters, illustrations, and captions in the book and make predictions about the story.

SET PURPOSES Ask students to list three topics they think they will learn more about in this book.

READ THE BOOK Ask students to read the book independently. As they read, ask them to take note of subjects about which they are interested. One of these may serve as a research project topic later. Use these questions to gauge their understanding.

Page 3: Summarize the resources necessary to make the space station a reality. (Sixteen countries are involved, more than 100,000 people, and many types of talents and skills.) *Summarize*

Page 10: Astronauts on the space station will be conducting research. Based on what you know, do you think the money involved would be better spent on Earth or in space? (Answers will vary, but should be based on reason.) *Judgments and Decisions*

Page 13: What words and phrases around the word *void* help explain its meaning? ("outside the station," "outer space") *Vocabulary*

Page 15: What do you think the requirements for astronauts working on the space station will be? (scientific knowledge, manual dexterity, physical fitness, good mental health) *Draw Conclusions*

RETURN TO PREDICTIONS AND PURPOSES Discuss students' predictions. Did the topics on their lists appear in the book?

LITERARY RESPONSE Ask students:

- What do you think is the most useful knowledge that astronauts on the space station are likely to gain?

- Is the enormous expense of the space station justified? Why or why not?

Also see the story questions and activity in *City in Space: The International Space Station.*

Answers to Story Questions

1. They want to discover medicines that target proteins that cause disease.
2. As students are invited to participate in space experiments, they will become more interested in exploring outer space.
3. Experiments can be conducted in space on such things as recycling and purification systems, as well as waste disposal.
4. An international space station can bring together people from all around the world in a common mission to discover ways to make life better on Earth.
5. Answers will vary.

The *Story Questions and Activity* below appear in the *Challenge Book.*

Story Questions

1. What do scientists hope to discover by studying protein crystals in space?
2. How can the international space station inspire young people?
3. How might a station in outer space benefit the environment on Earth?
4. What is the main idea of the book?
5. Which would you rather do, repair spacecraft like the astronauts in *Adventure in Space,* or live and work on the International Space Station?

Keep a Space Log

Suppose you are the first student to live and work on the ISS. What are your responsibilities on the craft? With what sort of crew are you serving? Where do you sleep? How do you eat? Write a diary of your first week on the ISS.

from *City in Space: The International Space Station*

Bringing Groups Together

Anthology and Leveled Books

Connecting Texts

SPACE WEB Discuss space exploration with the entire class. Have students make a web that helps show the different ways in which these stories deal with the topic of space. Call on volunteers from each of the reading levels and use their responses to complete the web.

Adventure in Space
Crew goes to space to fix Hubble telescope.

John Glenn
John Glenn is first man to orbit Earth in a spacecraft.

Space

Class Trip
Class on a space station takes a trip to a newly opened planet.

City in Space
International space station is set to open.

Viewing/Representing

GROUP PRESENTATIONS Divide the class into four groups, one for each story. (For *Adventure in Space* combine students of different reading levels.) Have each group design, write and illustrate their stories in picture book form. Remind students to use colorful, explanatory illustrations and keep the language simple enough for younger students to understand.

AUDIENCE RESPONSE Ask students to present their picture books to the class. Their classmates should then ask questions.

Research and Inquiry

MORE ABOUT SPACE Ask students to choose an area of interest (ancient astronomy, planets, stars, etc.), and find out more. They should present a brief oral or video report to the rest of the class. As they research, students should consider:

- How can I present this information so everyone will understand it?

- How can I make this information interesting to my classmates?

interNET CONNECTION If students use the Internet, suggest they visit *www.mhschool.com/reading* to learn more about space exploration.

OBJECTIVES

Students will

- understand that judgments and decisions are supported by evidence and reasons.

- identify and make judgments and decisions.

Skills Finder

Judgments and Decisions

Introduce	483A–B
Review	501E–F, 541E–F
Test	Unit 5

LANGUAGE SUPPORT

ESL Pair English-language learners with proficient readers for the Assess/Close activity. Encourage partners to work together to choose a movie or fairy tale to retell, decide how to make it different, and write the new ending.

SELF-SELECTED Reading

Students may choose from the following titles.

ANTHOLOGY

- Adventure in Space

LEVELED BOOKS

- John Glenn: Space Pioneer
- Class Trip
- City in Space: The International Space Station

Bibliography, pages T80–T81

Review Judgments and Decisions

PREPARE

Discuss Judgments and Decisions

Review: Everyone has to make decisions in life. Some decisions are easy; others are difficult. However, all decisions involve making a judgment or having a reason for taking a particular action.

TEACH

Read the Passage and Model the Skill

Ask students to pay close attention to the reason that the team decided to capture the Hubble as you read **Teaching Chart 136** with them.

Capturing the Hubble

The team slowly approached the floating telescope. <u>Even under the best of circumstances, capturing the telescope was no easy task.</u> But all the <u>maneuvering had used up a lot of *Endeavour's* fuel</u>. A quick look at *Endeavour's* fuel gauge told the team the worrisome truth. <u>There was only enough fuel for a single attempt. There was not enough fuel for a second try.</u> They would have to capture the Hubble on their first attempt or not at all.

Teaching Chart 136

Discuss clues in the passage that can help readers determine the team's reasons for making the decision to try to capture the telescope on the first attempt.

MODEL The passage tells me that capturing an object in space is difficult under normal circumstances. It also tells me that since *Endeavour* had already used up a lot of fuel, the team must get everything right the first time.

PRACTICE

Identify Reasons for Making Judgments and Decisions

GROUP

Have students underline reasons and circle the team's decision in "Capturing the Hubble." Then ask them to discuss in small groups how knowing the reasons for important decisions can make a story clearer and more interesting.

▶ **Logical/Linguistic**

ASSESS/CLOSE

Rewrite a Familiar Fairy Tale with New Judgments and Decisions

Encourage students to create a new ending for a well-known movie or fairy tale. Have them base the ending on a decision made by one of the characters that is different from the original story. For example, in *Cinderella*, Cinderella could decide not to try on the glass slipper because she feels that a marriage to the prince will not work.

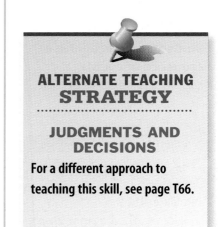

ALTERNATE TEACHING STRATEGY

JUDGMENTS AND DECISIONS

For a different approach to teaching this skill, see page T66.

Intervention ▶ **Skills**

Intervention Guide, for direct instruction and extra practice of judgments and decisions

Meeting Individual Needs for Comprehension

EASY	ON-LEVEL	CHALLENGE	LANGUAGE SUPPORT

Reteach, 167   Practice, 167   Extend, 167   Language Support, 182

Review **Sequence of Events**

OBJECTIVES

Students will recognize a sequence of events.

Skills Finder

Sequence of Events

Introduce	41A-B
Review	101A-B, 431G-H, 469A-B, 481E-F, 501G-H, 533A-B
Test	Unit 1, Unit 5

TEACHING TIP

SEQUENCE OF EVENTS

Point out that many works do not use time-order words and may describe events out of order. If students have trouble, suggest they

• sum up each event on an index card.

• try to arrange the cards in time-order.

• add a time-order word, such as *first* or *finally*, at the beginning of each card.

• read the cards aloud to check the sequence.

PREPARE

Discuss Sequence of Events

Point out that many events may happen in a story and that knowing the sequence in which these events take place can help make the selection clearer.

TEACH

Read the Passage and Model the Skill

Read "Successful Steps in Space." Ask students to notice the sequence of events.

Successful Steps in Space

The team hired to repair the Hubble Space telescope had to take a number of important "steps" in space. First, they had to fix a damaged solar array. Next, they had to install a new camera. Then, they had to put in COSTAR, the Hubble's new "glasses." Finally, they had to chase and capture a loose screw that could have been dangerous to the Hubble Space Telescope. All in all, accomplishing these tasks led to a successful mission of repairing the Hubble Space telescope.

Teaching Chart 137

Ask a volunteer to circle the time-order words that help make the sequence of events clear. Then have another volunteer underline the sentences that show the sequence of events. Offer modeling.

MODEL Looking back at the story, I see that the team was well prepared. They took care of things in order, even when they had to deal with surprises like the screw coming loose.

PRACTICE

Create a Sequence of Events Chart

PARTNERS

Have partners create a Sequence of Events chart. Help them get started. ▶ **Visual/Logical**

Sequence of Events

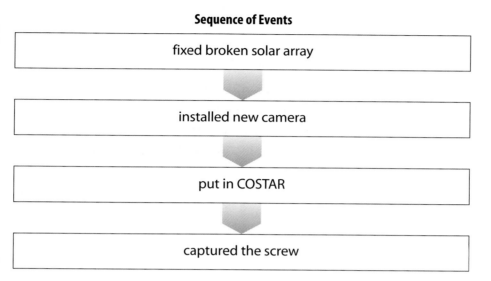

fixed broken solar array
installed new camera
put in COSTAR
captured the screw

ASSESS/CLOSE

Use the Chart to Summarize

Encourage students to use the Sequence of Events chart to give an oral summary of the tasks performed by the astronauts to complete a successful mission.

Meeting Individual Needs for Comprehension

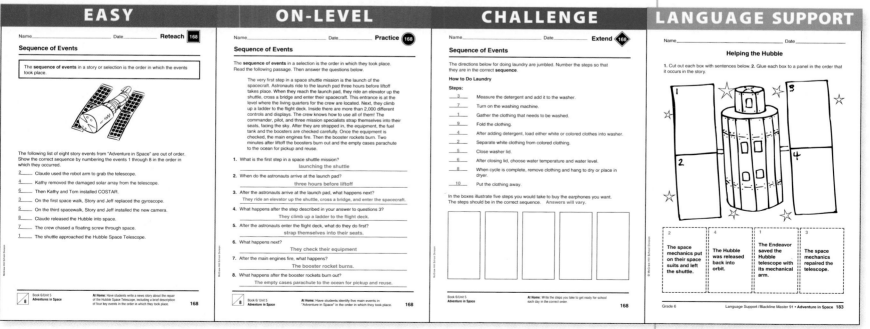

EASY	ON-LEVEL	CHALLENGE	LANGUAGE SUPPORT
Reteach, 168	Practice, 168	Extend, 168	Language Support, 183

Review **Context Clues**

OBJECTIVES

Students will

- identify context clues.
- use context clues to figure out the meaning of an unfamiliar word.

Skills Finder

Context Clues

Introduce	63I-J
Review	239I-J, 307I-J, 317I-J, 481I-J, 501I-J, 541G-H
Test	Unit 1, Unit 3, Unit 5
Maintain	277, 415, 487, 563, 609

TEACHING TIP

CONTEXT Remind students that they can come to understand the meaning of an unfamiliar word by looking at the words around it or at the passage as a whole. Often context clues for a word appear in a different paragraph.

PREPARE

Discuss Context Clues

Explain: You can often understand the meaning of a word by looking at the words around it, at the paragraph or passage as a whole, or sometimes, at any illustrations near it. For example, think about this sentence: "Winning or losing depended on her answer to one crucial question." Even if you don't know the meaning of the word *crucial*, you can figure out from the other words in the sentence that it means "important."

TEACH

Read the Passage and Model the Skill

Have students read the passage on **Teaching Chart 138.**

A Tricky Situation

No one said "do or die," but they all knew it was a critical decision. This tactic would be the trickiest action of the voyage. If the crew did not do it correctly, their future would be the dark, empty abyss of space. Nothing could be left to chance. There could be no miscalculations in their figures or plans, no doors left open or ajar, not even slight errors induced by stress, no matter how nervous the situation made them.

Teaching Chart 138

Discuss clues in the passage that help students figure out the meaning of unfamiliar words.

MODEL As I read this, I come across a word I don't really know—*critical*. I don't see much in the word itself that helps me figure it out. But when I look at the words around it—"*do or die*" and *decision*—I get the idea that something that is critical is something that is extremely important.

PRACTICE

Identify Context Clues in a Paragraph

PARTNERS

Circle the words *critical, tactic, abyss, miscalculations, ajar,* and *induced.* Have students underline the context clues that help them figure out the meaning of these words. Then have partners discuss the words' meanings. ▶ **Linguistic**

ASSESS/CLOSE

Write a Paragraph with Context Clues

PARTNERS

Read the following words aloud and have one partner write them down: *critical, tactic, abyss, miscalculations, ajar,* and *induced.* Then have pairs write a paragraph that uses all the words. Partners should include context clues in their paragraph so that their readers will be able to figure out the meaning of these words.

ALTERNATE TEACHING STRATEGY

CONTEXT CLUES

For a different approach to teaching this skill, see page T67.

Intervention ▶ **Skills**

Intervention Guide, for direct instruction and extra practice of context clues

Meeting Individual Needs for Vocabulary

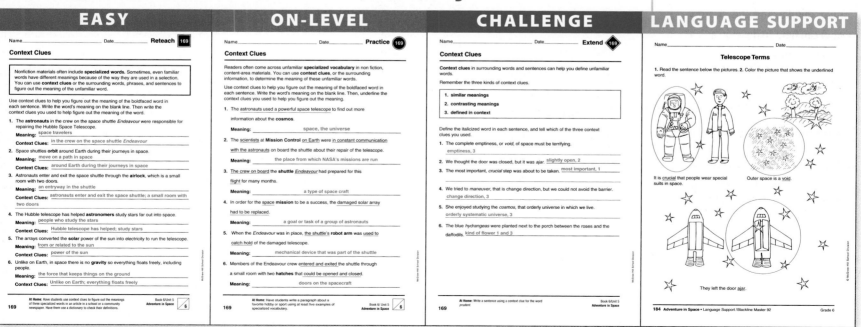

Reteach, 169   Practice, 169   Extend, 169   Language Support, 184

Writing a Story

GRAMMAR/SPELLING CONNECTIONS

See the 5-day Grammar and Usage Plan on possessive pronouns, pages 501M–501N.

See the 5-Day Spelling Plan on words with suffixes, pages 501O–501P.

TEACHING TIP

Technology As they go through the drafting process, students should save their work every ten minutes. Most software programs have an 'autosave' function you can activate for this purpose.

Story Plan Remind students that a good story has a clear beginning, middle, and end. A story plan can help to develop a cohesive story line.

Handwriting CD-ROM

Prewrite

WRITE A SCIENCE-FICTION STORY Present this writing assignment: Although this selection is nonfiction, it does have the "makings" of a science-fiction story. In fact, science-fiction stories often focus on space and technology. Write a science-fiction story entitled "An Adventure in Space." Use space as your setting, astronauts as your characters, and a mission in space as your plot. Include a problem that the astronauts face and explain how they solve it at the end.

BRAINSTORM IDEAS Have students brainstorm about the kinds of details that would be important in a science-fiction story set in space. What is the purpose of this information?

Strategy: Make a Web Have students make a story web, with the major circles being the main events of their stories. From these events can come spokes and other circles that contain details and less important events.

Draft

USE THE WEB To draft their stories, students should develop the ideas in their webs using details and dialogue where appropriate. Remind them to check that the story develops logically.

Revise

SELF-QUESTIONING Ask students to assess their drafts.

- Do my characters face an interesting problem?
- Does the solution make the story effective?
- Have I included information appropriate for a science-fiction story?

Have students share their stories with a partner to get feedback.

Edit/Proofread

CHECK FOR ERRORS Students should reread their stories to check for spelling, grammar, and punctuation mistakes.

Publish

MAKE A BOOK Students can make a class anthology of stories, complete with author biographies and a table of contents.

> An Adventure in Space
>
> "Stop the creatures from outer space," demanded an informer.
>
> NASA got word that space creatures from Garzon Galaxy were planning an attack on Earth. NASA's mission was to stop them.
>
> In space, the astronauts launched their high-powered telescope to monitor the space creatures' advances. Just as the space creatures started their attack, the telescope located their position.
>
> The astronauts, using the telescope, were able to defeat the space creatures and send them back to Garzon!

Presentation Ideas

USE DRAWINGS Ask students to illustrate their stories. Include these illustrations in the class anthology. ▶ **Viewing/Representing**

RADIO PLAYS Have students turn their stories into radio plays. Working in groups, they can perform the plays for the rest of the class. ▶ **Speaking/Listening**

Consider students' creative efforts, possibly adding a plus (+) for originality, wit, and imagination.

Scoring Rubric

Excellent	Good	Fair	Unsatisfactory
4: The writer	**3:** The writer	**2:** The writer	**1:** The writer
• presents an inventive story idea.	• presents a strong story idea.	• does not present clearly conceived characters or actions.	• presents a confused story idea.
• creates a well-constructed story.	• creates a coherent story.	• constructs a story with gaps in coherence.	• does not order events.
• displays a firm understanding of the genre.	• includes details suited to the genre.	• does not display an awareness of the genre.	• merely outlines actions, presenting no details.

Incomplete 0: The writer leaves the page blank or fails to respond to the writing task. The student does not address the topic or simply paraphrases the prompt. The response is illegible or incoherent.

For a 6-point or an 8-point scale see pages T109–T110.

Meeting Individual Needs for Writing

EASY	ON-LEVEL	CHALLENGE
Picture Book Have students write and illustrate a picture book about space for kindergarten children.	**Documentary** Ask students to think about how *Adventure in Space* could be made into a documentary film. Have them write outlines of the events they would include and explain how they would present them in the film.	**Journal Entry** Tell students to imagine they are astronauts writing a space log. Ask them to jot down some of their most memorable moments in space, including the major events that occurred during their mission and any conclusions they drew about their experiences.

Listening and Speaking

LISTENING STRATEGIES
As radio plays are presented, have students:

• face the speaker and listen attentively.

• listen for keys facts on how to prepare for the impending storm.

SPEAKING STRATEGIES
Encourage students to:

• vary volume and tone of voice for emphasis.

• use dramatic intonations to create suspense.

LANGUAGE SUPPORT

ESL ESL students can review the dialogue in their stories with a fluent partner. They should discuss whether the dialogue suits the characters and whether the writer has used proper punctuation.

PORTFOLIO Invite students to include their stories or another writing project in their portfolios.

5 Day Grammar and Usage Plan

ESL Ownership is conveyed in different ways in different languages. Pair English learners with English-fluent students and have them make a chart comparing English possessive formation with possessive formation in the English learner's first language.

DAILY LANGUAGE ACTIVITIES

Write each day's activity on the board or use **Transparency 23.** Students can correct the sentences orally.

Day 1
1. Our's telescope is now in orbit.
2. Her's skills are the best.
3. Their's problem was solved in space.

Day 2
1. The astronauts were ready to take they're best shot.
2. This new spacesuit is mine's.
3. Yours telescope needs a new lens.

Day 3
1. You're flight is about to begin.
2. This new telescope is their's.
3. It's eyes are made of ten tiny mirrors.

Day 4
1. Mine fondest dreams have come true.
2. The best telescope in space is our.
3. His's plans will work.

Day 5
1. Their are the right tools.
2. Yours tools and my are over there.
3. His' telescope has it's problems.

Daily Language Transparency 23

Suggested answers on transparency

DAY 1 — Introduce the Concept

Oral Warm-Up: Write *its* and *it's* on the board. Point out that these are the most commonly mixed-up words in English. Ask volunteers to use them in sentences.

Introduce Possessive Pronouns To possess something means to own it. Present the following:

Possessive Pronouns

- A **possessive pronoun** takes the place of a possessive noun. It shows who or what owns something.

- Some possessive pronouns are used before nouns (*my, your, his, her, its, our, your, their*).

Present the Daily Language Activity and have students correct the sentences orally. Then ask them to write sentences using the possessive pronouns *our, her,* and *their*.

 Assign the daily Writing Prompt on page 482C.

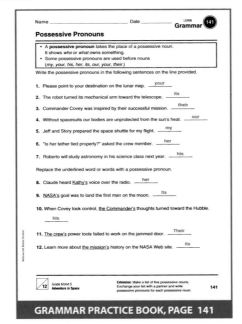

GRAMMAR PRACTICE BOOK, PAGE 141

DAY 2 — Teach the Concept

Review Possessive Pronouns Ask students to explain what a possessive pronoun is, and offer an example.

Learn More about Possessive Pronouns Some of the most common errors in English occur with misused possessive pronouns. Present:

Possessive Pronouns

- Some possessive pronouns can stand alone (*mine, yours, its, ours, yours, theirs*).

- Do not confuse the pronouns *its, your, their,* and *theirs* with the contractions *it's, you're, they're,* and *there's.*

Present the Daily Language Activity, and have students orally correct the sentences. Then have them use the pronouns *their, mine,* and *your* in their own sentences.

 Assign the daily Writing Prompt on page 482C.

GRAMMAR PRACTICE BOOK, PAGE 142

Possessive Pronouns

DAY 3 — Review and Practice

Learn from the Literature Ask students to define and list possessive pronouns. Then read this sentence from *Adventure in Space*:

> **Next, the crew turned their attention to the twisted solar array.**

After you finish reading, ask students what the possessive pronoun in the sentence is. Invite volunteers to identify who owns what in this sentence.

Form Possessive Pronouns Present the Daily Language Activity, and have students correct each sentence orally. Then have them write their own sentences using the pronouns *your, theirs,* and *its*.

Have partners find possessive pronouns in the selection and copy the sentences in which they appear.

 WRITING Assign the Daily Writing Prompt on page 482D.

DAY 4 — Review and Practice

Review Subject and Object Pronouns Ask students to create sentences using these pairs of words: *your, you're; they're, their; there's, theirs*. Ask students to exchange papers and check each other's work. Then present the Daily Language Activity for Day 4.

Ask students to review these rules for distinguishing between contractions and possessives before beginning the daily Writing Prompt on page 482D.

Contractions and Possessives

- An apostrophe takes the place of letters left out of a contraction.

- Possessive pronouns do not have apostrophes. Do not confuse possessive pronouns with contractions.

 WRITING Assign the daily Writing Prompt on page 482D.

DAY 5 — Assess and Reteach

Assess Use the Daily Language Activity and page 145 of the **Grammar Practice Book** for assessment.

Reteach Make a list on the board of all the possessives, as well as the contractions with which they are confused. Ask students to form small groups and take turns using each of the words in sentences, having group members check each other's work for accuracy.

Point out that mistakes in using possessives are common in advertisements and signs. Set aside part of a bulletin board and ask students to post examples of misuse that they see in ads or signs.

Use page 146 of the **Grammar Practice Book** for additional reteaching.

 WRITING Assign the daily Writing Prompt on page 482D.

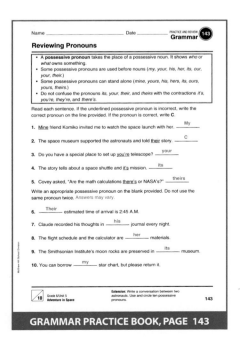

GRAMMAR PRACTICE BOOK, PAGE 143

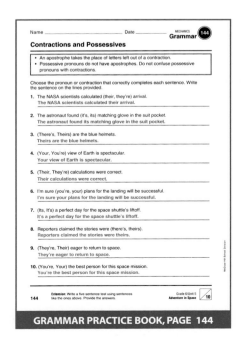

GRAMMAR PRACTICE BOOK, PAGE 144

GRAMMAR PRACTICE BOOK, PAGE 145

GRAMMAR PRACTICE BOOK, PAGE 146

5 Day Spelling Plan

LANGUAGE SUPPORT

ESL Review with students that suffixes can help them tell what part of speech a word is. For example: *-able* and *-ible usually* indicate an adjective; *-ity, -ation, -ion* indicate a noun.

DICTATION SENTENCES

Spelling Words

1. Some cars run on electricity.
2. The operation saved his life.
3. We can learn through exploration.
4. Rubber is flexible.
5. The ice caused considerable trouble.
6. Is that a combination lock?
7. Gravity is a natural force.
8. The baby is sweet and lovable.
9. We may do what's permissible.
10. The interruption made me late.
11. I don't doubt the reality of this story.
12. Conservation efforts saved the trees.
13. The doll was a collectible item.
14. An abbreviation is a short form.
15. Perspiration makes your skin wet.
16. The good work was admirable.
17. In anticipation of rain, we wore hats.
18. We enjoyed the festivity of the party.
19. You can think of the imaginable.
20. The convertible top can be put down.

Challenge Words

21. The bloodstream carries nutrients.
22. The desk has a secret compartment.
23. We deliberately took the short path.
24. He greets me with a handshake.
25. Maneuvering in a tiny space is hard.

DAY 1 — Pretest

Assess Prior Knowledge Use the Dictation Sentences and **Spelling Practice Book** page 141 for the pretest. Allow students to correct their own papers.

Spelling Words		Challenge Words
1. **electricity**	11. **reality**	21. **blood-stream**
2. operation	12. conserva-tion	22. **compart-ment**
3. **explo-ration**	13. collectible	23. **deliber-ately**
4. flexible	14. abbrevia-tion	24. **hand-shake**
5. consider-able	15. perspira-tion	25. **maneu-vering**
6. combina-tion	16. admirable	
7. gravity	17. anticipation	
8. lovable	18. festivity	
9. permissible	19. imaginable	
10. interrup-tion	20. convertible	

*Note: Words in **dark type** are from the story.*

Word Study On page 142 of the **Spelling Practice Book** are word study steps and an at-home activity.

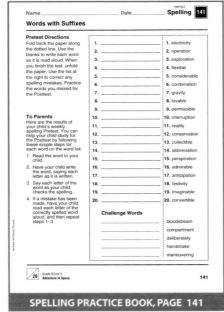

SPELLING PRACTICE BOOK, PAGE 141

WORD STUDY STEPS AND ACTIVITY, PAGE 142

DAY 2 — Explore the Pattern

Sort and Spell Words Write *operation* on the board and underline the suffix *-ion*. Have students identify the base word. (*operate*) Do the same for *explo-ration*, underlining *-ation*. Then have students sort the words as below.

Words with

-ion	*-ity*	*-ible*
operation	electricity	flexible
interruption	gravity	permissible
abbreviation	reality	collectible
anticipation	festivity	convertible

-ation	*-able*	
exploration	considerable	
combination	lovable	
conservation	admirable	
perspiration	imaginable	

Spelling Patterns Ask which base words change their spellings when the suffix is added. (*operate, explore, combine, grave, love, permit, conserve, abbreviate, perspire, admire, anticipate, festive, imagine*)

SPELLING PRACTICE BOOK, PAGE 143

Words with Suffixes

DAY 3 Practice and Extend

Word Meaning: Suffixes Remind students that knowing the meaning of a word's suffix will help them define the word. Give students the following definitions: *-ion* and *-ation* mean "the act of" or "the state of being;" *-ity* means "the state of being;" *-able* and *-ible* mean "able to be" or "worthy of being." Ask students to define each word based on the meaning of its suffix.

If students need extra practice, have partners give each other a midweek test.

Glossary Review how glossary entries show parts of speech. Have students

- write each Challenge Word.

- write which part of speech they think each word is.

- use the Glossary to check and correct their work.

DAY 4 Proofread and Write

Proofread Sentences Write these sentences on the chalkboard, including the misspelled words. Ask students to proofread, circling incorrect spellings and writing the correct spellings. There are two spelling errors in each sentence.

> The whole (oparation) took (considerible) time. (operation, considerable)
>
> The festivity was in (anticapation) of the (expluration) of Mars. (anticipation, exploration)

Have students create additional sentences with errors for partners to correct.

 WRITING Have students use as many Spelling Words as possible in the daily Writing Prompt on page 482D. Remind students to proofread their writing for errors in spelling, grammar, and punctuation.

DAY 5 Assess and Reteach

Assess Students' Knowledge Use page 146 of the **Spelling Practice Book** or the Dictation Sentences on page 501O for the posttest.

Personal Word List If students have trouble with any lesson words, suggest they add them to their personal lists of troublesome words in their journals. Encourage them to write the base word next to each word with a suffix.

Students should refer to their word lists during later writing activities.

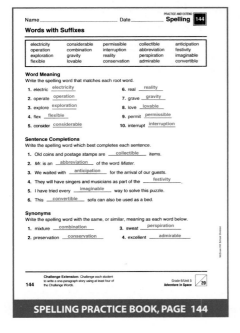

SPELLING PRACTICE BOOK, PAGE 144

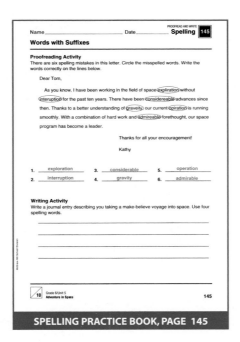

SPELLING PRACTICE BOOK, PAGE 145

SPELLING PRACTICE BOOK, PAGE 146

501P

Concept
- Taking Responsibility/ Taking a Stand

Comprehension
- Story Elements

Vocabulary
- barley
- coincidences
- knickers
- mufflers
- sheepishly
- sweeten

Anthology

Rumpelstiltskin's Daughter

Selection Summary In this spin-off of a favorite fairy tale, students will find out how a young girl takes a stand against a miserly king and teaches him the true meaning of riches.

Stories in Art focuses on the **comprehension** skill

Reading Strategy applies the **comprehension** skill

Listening Library

INSTRUCTIONAL pages 504–531

About the Author and Illustrator As an award-winning creator of children's books, Diane Stanley writes and illustrates her own work. Stanley began learning her trade as a child by drawing pictures for stories produced by her writer-mother, Fay Stanley. Later, she became a medical illustrator but found this lacked the freedom and creativity she could have working on children's books. Stanley illustrated her first children's book in 1977. In 1983, she broke further ground with a book she both illustrated and wrote.

Same Concept, Skills and Vocabulary!

Leveled Books

EASY
Lesson on pages 531A and 531D

INDEPENDENT
Lesson on pages 531B and 531D

CHALLENGE
Lesson on pages 531C and 531D

Leveled Practice

EASY

Reteach, 170–176 Blackline masters with reteaching opportunities for each assessed skill

INDEPENDENT/ON-LEVEL

Practice, 170–176 Workbook with Take-Home stories and practice opportunities for each assessed skill and story comprehension

CHALLENGE

Extend, 170–176 Blackline masters that offer challenge activities for each assessed skill

Quizzes Prepared by Accelerated Reader®

WORKSTATION Activities

Social Studies . . .	Political Cartoons, *512*
Science	Precious Metal, *508*
Math	Gold Standard, *506*
Art	Fine Art, *516*
Health	Wheat, *529*
Language Arts . .	Read Aloud, *502E*
Cultural Perspectives	Fairy Tale Characters, *524*
Writing	Fractured Fairy Tale, *528*
Research and Inquiry	Find Out More, *529*
Internet Activities	www.mhschool.com/reading

READING AND LANGUAGE ARTS	**DAY 1** Focus on Reading and Skills	 **DAY 2** Read the Literature

READING AND LANGUAGE ARTS

- **Comprehension**
- **Vocabulary**
- **Phonics/Decoding**
- **Study Skills**
- **Listening, Speaking, Viewing, Representing**

DAY 1 — Focus on Reading and Skills

 Read Aloud: Folk Tale, 502E
"The Winning of Kwelanga"

Develop Visual Literacy, 502

☑ **Review Story Elements,** 503A–503B
Teaching Chart 139
Reteach, Practice, Extend, 170

 Reading Strategy: Story Elements, 503
"The Cougar"

ⓘ Intervention Program

DAY 2 — Read the Literature

Build Background, 504A
Develop Oral Language

Vocabulary, 504B–504C

barley	knickers	sheepishly
coincidences	mufflers	sweeten

Teaching Chart 140
Word Building Manipulative Cards
Reteach, Practice, Extend, 171

 Read the Selection, 504–527
☑ Story Elements
☑ Sequence of Events

Genre: Fairy Tale, 505

Cultural Perspectives, 524

ⓘ Intervention Program

- **Curriculum Connections**

 Link Works of Art, 502 | **Link** Social Studies, 504A

- **Writing**

Writing Prompt: Choose a fairy tale that you like. Write what you think happened after the story ended.

Writing Prompt: Write, from the king's point of view, an explanation of how he became a hero.

Journal Writing, 527
Quick-Write

- **Grammar**

Introduce the Concept: Indefinite Pronouns, 531M
Daily Language Activity
1. Everyone know about Rumpelstiltskin.
2. Many listens to his fantastic stories.
3. Someone turn straw into gold.

Grammar Practice Book, 147

Teach the Concept: Indefinite Pronouns, 531M
Daily Language Activity
1. Several also tries to do it.
2. Very few comes close.
3. Anything spin better than nothing.

Grammar Practice Book, 148

- **Spelling**

Pretest: Words with Suffixes, 531O
Spelling Practice Book, 147, 148

Explore the Pattern: Words with Suffixes, 531O
Spelling Practice Book, 149

Meeting Individual Needs

 = **Skill Assessed in Unit Test**

 Intervention Program Available

 **Read EVERY DAY**

DAY 3 Read the Literature	**DAY 4** Build Skills	**DAY 5** Build Skills
Rereading for Fluency, 526	**Read the Leveled Books and Self-Selected Books**	**Read Self-Selected Books**
Story Questions and Activities, 528–529 Reteach, Practice, Extend, 172	☑ **Review Story Elements,** 531E–531F **Teaching Chart 142** Reteach, Practice, Extend, 174 Language Support, 190	☑ **Review Denotation and Connotation,** 531I–531J **Teaching Chart 144** Reteach, Practice, Extend, 176 Language Support, 192
Study Skill, 530 ☑ Read a Circle Graph **Teaching Chart 141** Reteach, Practice, Extend, 173	☑ **Review Make Inferences,** 531G–531H **Teaching Chart 143** Reteach, Practice, Extend, 175 Language Support, 191	**Listening, Speaking, Viewing, Representing,** 531L
Test Power, 531	**Minilessons,** 511, 513, 515, 517, 519	**Minilessons,** 513, 515, 517, 519
Read the Leveled Books, 531A–531D Guided Reading *ea* Words ☑ Story Elements ☑ Instructional Vocabulary	**Writer's Craft,** 518	**Phonics Review,** 511 *ea* Words **Phonics/Phonemic Awareness Practice Book,** 9–12
Intervention Program	**Intervention Program**	**Intervention Program**

Activity Math, 506	**Activity** Science, 508	**Activity** Social Studies, 512; Art, 516
✏ **Writing Prompt:** Summarize this story to a friend, making sure to mention the main points in the plot. **Writing Process: Writing a Story,** 531K Prewrite, Draft	✏ **Writing Prompt:** Imagine you are taking down the conversation as Rumpelstiltskin's wife explains the story to her granddaughter. **Writing Process: Writing a Story,** 531K Revise **Meeting Individual Needs for Writing,** 531L	✏ **Writing Prompt:** Compare and contrast the kingdom before and after Rumpelstiltskin's daughter gets involved. **Writing Process: Writing a Story,** 531K Edit/Proofread, Publish
Review and Practice: Indefinite Pronouns, 531N Daily Language Activity 1. Somebody fetch Meredith and Rumpelstiltskin from the farm. 2. Both fears the worst. 3. Someone save them. **Grammar Practice Book,** 149	**Review and Practice: Indefinite Pronouns,** 531N Daily Language Activity 1. Nobody like a greedy king. 2. Few wants to do anything for him. 3. No one die by failing to do a job. **Grammar Practice Book,** 150	**Assess and Reteach: Indefinite Pronouns,** 531N Daily Language Activity 1. Everyone in the kingdom now love the king. 2. Many gives the king gifts. 3. Everything work out in the end. **Grammar Practice Book,** 151, 152
Practice and Extend: Words with Suffixes, 531P **Spelling Practice Book,** 150	**Proofread and Write: Words with Suffixes,** 531P **Spelling Practice Book,** 151	**Assess and Reteach: Words with Suffixes,** 531P **Spelling Practice Book,** 152

Read Aloud

The Winning of Kwelanga
a Zulu folk tale

Near the Mountains of the Dragon, there once lived a great chief named Ngazulu. He had a daughter who was so beautiful and gentle that she was called Kwelanga, which means sunrise.

It was the chief's desire that Kwelanga be married to a man worthy of her. So all suitors were put to impossible tests. Naturally all failed to win her.

One day a young man named Zamo heard about this. At once he decided to try his luck. His father tried to dissuade him. He said, "We are poor people. How dare you think of marrying the daughter of the chief?"

His mother said, "Oh, Zamo! Every man who has tried has lost his life. Do you think you would fare any better?"

But Zamo said, "I can't whistle with another man's mouth. I must try it myself."

So one day Zamo went to Chief Ngazulu and said, "Greetings, Nkosi." Then he waited for the chief to speak.

Continued on pages T5–T6

Oral Comprehension

LISTENING AND SPEAKING Read this Zulu folk tale aloud. Encourage a discussion of story elements and characters. Afterward, ask:

• What is the hero of the story like?

• What problems must be solved first, second and third? How?

Then reread the folktale. Ask students to think about the ending. Ask: Why do you think the chief's daughter helped Zamo?

GENRE STUDY: FOLK TALE Discuss some of the literary devices and techniques in "The Winning of Kwelanga."

• Remind students that folk tales generally feature a simple plot with events that repeat. Ask: What event in this folk tale repeats?

• Discuss with students that characters in folk tales are stereotypes, usually extremely good or bad. Ask: Which characters in this tale would you consider good? Why?

• Have students identify the theme or message of the folk tale.

Activity In this folk tale, Zamo is on a quest in which he must pass several tests in order to achieve his goal. In groups, have students create maps that trace the course of his quest. ▶ **Spatial**

Stories in Art

Look at this painting quickly. What do you see? You probably see a still life of an American breakfast. If you look again, you might just see someone vacuuming under the egg!

What can you tell about this painting? Does it make you laugh? Why? What kind of setting is this? How does the title give you a clue? Notice the tablecloth and other details. How do they help you to figure out who the woman might be?

Look at the painting again. Why is the breakfast larger than the woman? What could the artist be saying about her life? How does he make his point by showing something usual in an unusual way?

Greasy Spoon Life by John Holcroft, 1996

502

Objective: Analyze Story Elements

VIEWING Have students study *Greasy Spoon Life* and discuss what is realistic and unrealistic about the painting. Ask them what effect is created by using a realistic painting style to show something that is not realistic. Have students examine the use of colors, particularly how the woman's dress matches the tablecloth.

Read the page with students, encouraging individual interpretations of the painting.

Ask students to make inferences about character and setting. For example:

- The woman looks as though she is a hard worker. She is even cleaning under the fried egg.

- Greasy Spoon is a nickname for a diner, so the setting is probably a diner.

REPRESENTING Have students pick an ordinary scene to draw. They should add a twist to their illustrations by using an unusual scale.

OBJECTIVES

Students will make inferences about character.

Skills Finder

Story Elements:
Character, Setting, Plot

Introduce	65A–B
Review	369A–B, 405E–F, 447A–B, 467E–F, 503A–B, 531E–F
Test	Unit 1, Unit 4, Unit 5
Maintain	147, 179

TEACHING TIP

CHARACTER If students are having difficulty analyzing the character of the miller's daughter, have them say how she is like or unlike people they know in their real lives. Discuss the fact that the miller, a braggart, and his modest daughter are character types that appear throughout world literature, both ancient and modern. These universal types are called *archetypes*.

Review Story Elements

PREPARE

Discuss Character Invite students to talk about their favorite characters from books or movies. Have them list the character traits that contributed to their choices. Write students' responses on the board and discuss similarities.

TEACH

Define Character Explain: When readers make inferences about a character, they look at the words, thoughts, and actions of that character.

The Miller's Daughter

Once there was a miller who had a daughter. She worked at her father's mill and always had a kind word for everyone. People often came and asked her advice. The miller liked to brag to everyone that his daughter could solve any problem. The girl asked her father to stop bragging about her as it embarrassed her. She had to ask him several times before he finally stopped.

Teaching Chart 139

Read the Story and Model the Skill Display **Teaching Chart 139.** Have students think about the characters as you read the story aloud.

MODEL The main character in this story is the miller's daughter. I can tell she is a nice person because she always has a kind word for everyone. And since people ask her for advice, she's probably wise, too.

Analyze Character Have students underline words or phrases in the passage that suggest character traits of the miller's daughter.

PRACTICE

Create a Character Analysis Chart

GROUP

Have students create a Character Analysis chart for the characters in "The Miller's Daughter." Ask students to infer character traits based on what they read. ▶ **Linguistic/Logical**

CHARACTER	TRAITS
daughter	kind, wise, modest
miller	brags

ASSESS/CLOSE

Explain Character Inferences

Have students explain why they made the inferences they did about the characters in the story. Then ask them how the miller might react if a king came to ask the miller's daughter for advice.

ALTERNATE TEACHING STRATEGY

STORY ELEMENTS

For a different approach to teaching this skill, see page T62.

ℹ️ **Intervention** ▶ **Skills Intervention Guide**, for direct instruction and extra practice in story elements

---

Meeting Individual Needs for Comprehension

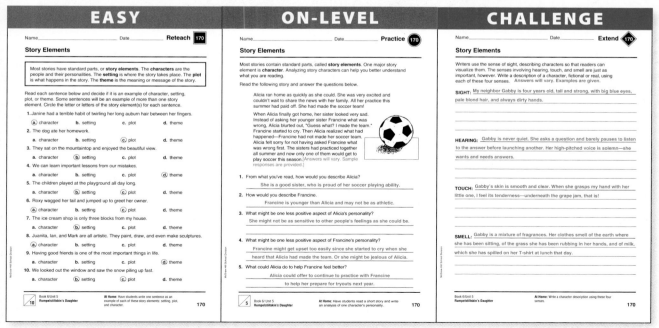

Reteach, 170   **Practice, 170**   **Extend, 170**

TESTED **OBJECTIVES**

Students will under-
stand a story character.

Apply <u>Story Elements</u>

READING STRATEGY

Character

Develop a strategy for understanding a story character.

1 **Look for details** that describe the way a character acts.

2 **Note what the** character thinks and says.

3 **Think about what** the character's words and actions reveal.

4 **Use what you know** to help you understand the character.

5 **Ask yourself:** What is this character like? How would I describe the character?

The Cougar

Out on the hillside, Tika's sheep were grazing peacefully. Suddenly, the flock scattered to reveal a cougar in the field.

"Ba-a-a-ad ca-a-a-at!" Tika called out, hoping to distract it from the flock.

"Who said that?" the cougar asked.

"Ba-a-a-ad ca-a-a-at!" Tika called again. The cougar looked in Tika's direction.

"Ba-a-a-ad Ca-a-a-at!" Tika repeated, moving slowly toward a nearby tree. The cougar followed her. It prepared to attack. As it did, Tika ducked behind the tree.

The cougar slammed into the tree and fell backward. It stood up, shook its head, and looked around for Tika.

"There you are, my delicious snack!" the cougar said. It crouched and crept toward Tika once more. The cougar pounced. As it did, Tika ducked behind a rock.

The cougar slammed against the boulder and slid back down to the ground.

"I am so hungry I can hardly see," the cougar sobbed.

Tika slowly stepped closer. "Poor cougar," she said. "I will share half the food in my pack with you if you will leave my sheep alone."

"It's a deal!" the cougar said.

"Cougar, you may be old, but you're still wise," Tika said, as the two of them sat down to a fine lunch together.

READING STRATEGY

503

PREVIEW Have students preview "The Cougar." Remind them that a character's thoughts, actions, and words give clues to his or her character. Ask:

- What is the setting of this story? *(a country hillside)*

- What do you think this story will be about? *(a cat on the prowl for food)*

SET PURPOSE Explain that students will apply what they have learned about character as they read "The Cougar."

APPLY THE STRATEGY Discuss this strategy for understanding character in a story:

- Look for details about the main character's actions.

- Think of what the character's words and actions reveal about her. Does she run away? What does she say?

- Describe the character in terms of character traits that real people have.

Activity Have each student create a Character Chart for the passage.

Build Background

Social Studies

Concept: Taking Responsibility/ Taking a Stand

Evaluate Prior Knowledge

CONCEPT: TAKING RESPONSIBILITY/ TAKING A STAND One of the characters in this story risks her safety to help others. What might you infer about a character like this? Do you know any people in real life who have risked their own safety to help others? What do you think about these people?

RELATE ACTION TO CHARACTER Have students create a chart that shows how action and character are linked. Ask them to list at least four actions and the type of characters who might perform these actions.

▶ **Logical/Spatial**

ACTION	CHARACTER TRAITS
save people from a burning building	brave, considerate of others

Graphic Organizer 31

WRITE A SCENE Invite students to
  choose an action from their charts and write a short scene about a character who performs this action. Ask them to include dialogue and other details that portray character.

Develop Oral Language

DISCUSS RESPONSIBLE ACTIONS

ESL Tell a brief story about someone who decides to risk his or her own safety to help others. For example, a woman is driving home from work and sees a car on fire just ahead on the road. She stops and helps the people get out of the car. Then give students a chance to discuss this person's actions and the reasons why some people are willing to put the welfare of others first in situations like this.

Write key words and phrases on the chalkboard. Then ask students to take turns making statements about the woman or the situation. Invite them to use the words or phrases on the board, or to make original statements.

LANGUAGE SUPPORT

See the **Language Support Book**, pages 185–188, for teaching suggestions for **Build Background**.

504A

Students will use context and structural clues to determine the meanings of vocabulary words.

mufflers
knickers
barley
sweeten
coincidences
sheepishly

Vocabulary

Teach Vocabulary in Context

Identify Vocabulary Words
Read **Teaching Chart 140** and have students circle vocabulary words and underline the context clues that help define them.

 **Definitions**

mufflers (p. 524) warm scarves that are wrapped around the neck and face in cold weather

knickers (p. 524) short pants that come to just below the knee

barley (p. 521) a type of grain

sweeten (p. 508) to make sweet by adding sugar or honey

coincidences (p. 508) happenings of two events at the same time

sheepishly (p. 521) meekly or with embarrassment for having done something wrong

Naughty, Naughty

1. One cold winter, a thief in the king's village stole all the mufflers from around the people's necks. **2.** The thief stole the knickers off their bony legs. **3.** The thief stole the barley they had harvested from the fields. **4.** The thief stole the honey they used to sweeten their cereal. **5.** Then, in one of those unlikely coincidences, the thief's mother caught him stealing a muffler. **6.** She scolded him in front of the entire village, and he sheepishly returned everything he had stolen.

Teaching Chart 140

Story Words

These words from the selection may be unfamiliar. Before students read, have them check the meanings and pronunciations of the words in the Glossary beginning on page 678 or in a dictionary.

• whopper, p. 506
• goldsmith, p. 512
• carriage, p. 512
• portcullis, p. 514
• iota, p. 514

Discuss Meanings
Ask questions like these to help clarify word meanings:

• When would you need a muffler, during a blizzard or during a heat wave?

• Do knickers end above or below the knee?

• Can you make bread or cakes from barley?

• Why would you want to sweeten food? What foods do you sweeten?

• Would it be a coincidence if your brother offered to take you to get ice cream when you had some extra money?

• Would you act sheepishly if you got caught taking more than your share of dessert?

Practice

Question and Answer

ONE

Have students choose a vocabulary card and give clues for the word on the card. The student who guesses correctly takes the next turn.

▶ **Linguistic/Kinesthetic**

barley   sweeten   mufflers

Word Building Manipulative Cards

Cartoons

WRITING

Have students draw cartoons about a medieval village and a king. Encourage students to use as many vocabulary words as possible in their speech balloons. Display the results around the class.

▶ **Linguistic/Spatial**

Assess Vocabulary

Use Words in Context

GROUP

Ask groups of students to create five nursery rhymes, each using one of the vocabulary words. Ask students to illustrate each rhyme. When the rhymes and illustrations are completed, have students make a class book of all the nursery rhymes.

SPELLING/VOCABULARY CONNECTIONS

See Spelling Challenge Words, pages 531O–531P.

LANGUAGE SUPPORT

See the **Language Support Book**, pages 185–188, for teaching suggestions for Vocabulary.

Vocabulary PuzzleMaker

Provides vocabulary activities.

Meeting Individual Needs for Vocabulary

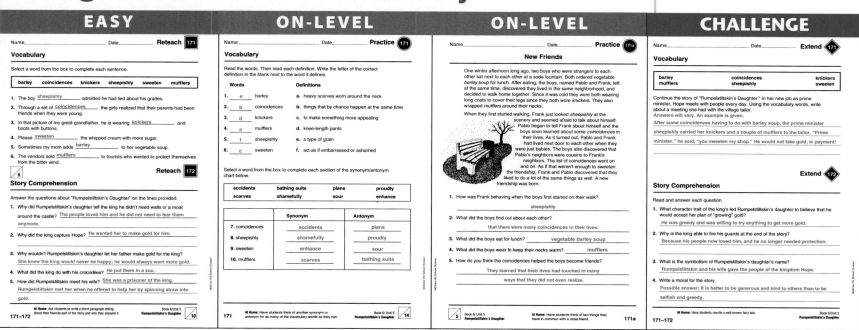

Reteach, 171   **Practice, 171**   **Practice, 171a**
                                                    Take-Home Story   **Extend, 171**

Comprehension

Prereading Strategies

PREVIEW AND PREDICT Have students read the title and preview the illustrations, looking for clues to character.

- Where and when does this story take place?
- Who is Rumpelstiltskin?
- What is this story probably about?
- Will this story be realistic or fantasy? How can you tell? (Fantasy. The people and settings in the illustrations look fanciful.) *Genre*

Have students record their predictions about the story.

PREDICTIONS	WHAT HAPPENED
There will be a greedy king in the story.	
Rumpelstiltskin's daughter outwits the king.	

SET PURPOSES What do students want to find out by reading the story? For example:

- What happens between the king and Rumpelstiltskin's daughter?
- How does Rumplestiltkin's daughter help people?

Meet Diane Stanley

Diane Stanley never thought she would become a writer and an illustrator of children's books until her own children were born. When she was growing up, she and her mother would create books together. However, her mother would write the stories, and she would draw the pictures to go with them. As an adult, Stanley continued her career as an artist by illustrating medical books.

Today, Stanley has published more than 20 books. Some of these books, like *Rumpelstiltskin's Daughter*, are funny and have a little twist. Stanley has also written illustrated biographies. In fact, her subjects include such famous people from history as Peter the Great, William Shakespeare, and Queen Elizabeth I. In keeping with a family tradition, Stanley wrote several of these books with a family member. This time it was with her husband.

504

Meeting Individual Needs • Grouping Suggestions for Strategic Reading

EASY

Read Together Students can read the story with you or use the **Listening Library**. Have them use the Character chart to record their inferences. Comprehension and Intervention prompts offer additional help with vocabulary and comprehension.

ON-LEVEL

Guided Instruction You may want to have students read the selection first on their own. Encourage them to fill out the Character chart. Then read the story with the class using the Comprehension questions or have them use the **Listening Library**.

CHALLENGE

Read Independently Have students read independently and fill out the Character chart. Remind them to look for links between a character's behavior and their own experiences as they make their inferences. After reading, they can use their charts to compare and contrast characters in the story.

Comprehension

☑ **Apply Story Elements**

☑ **Apply Sequence of Events**

STRATEGIC READING Understanding why characters behave as they do will help you understand the story better. Before we begin reading, let's prepare a Character chart to help us make notes about characters.

ACTION	CHARACTER TRAIT

① **CHARACTER** Look at the illustration of the king and Rumpelstiltskin's daughter. Describe what you think each character is like based on the picture and your personal experience.

LANGUAGE SUPPORT

This chart is available as a blackline master in the **Language Support Book.**

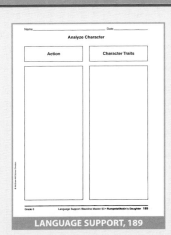

Fairy Tale

Explain that a fairy tale:

- features characters that have never existed in the real world.
- has a plot with a conflict between good and evil.
- may exist in many versions from diverse cultures.

Activity After students read *Rumpelstiltskin's Daughter,* have them explain what modern elements have been introduced to this old fairy tale.

Comprehension

② CHARACTER What can you tell about the character of the miller from his actions? Do you think he realizes what problems he's causing his daughter?

MODEL The story tells me the miller is a liar. Since his lies get his daughter into trouble, I can infer he is not a thoughtful person. I know that many liars do not like to admit they lie, so I can also infer that the miller does not realize the problems he is causing his daughter.

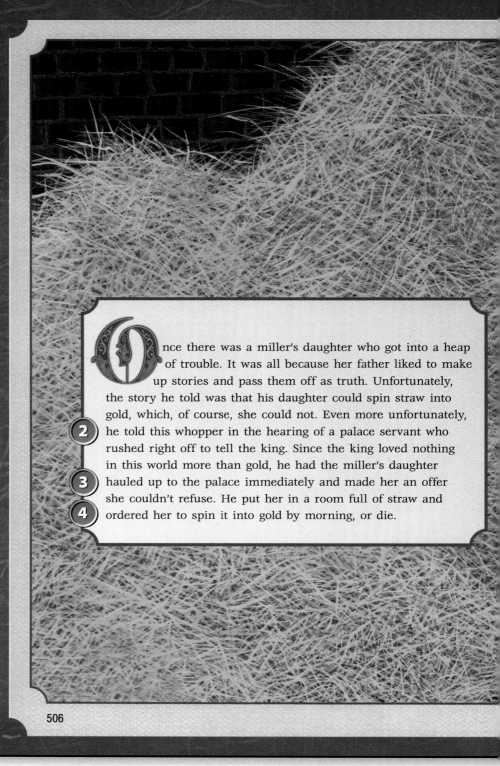

Once there was a miller's daughter who got into a heap of trouble. It was all because her father liked to make up stories and pass them off as truth. Unfortunately, the story he told was that his daughter could spin straw into gold, which, of course, she could not. Even more unfortunately, **②** he told this whopper in the hearing of a palace servant who rushed right off to tell the king. Since the king loved nothing in this world more than gold, he had the miller's daughter **③** hauled up to the palace immediately and made her an offer she couldn't refuse. He put her in a room full of straw and **④** ordered her to spin it into gold by morning, or die.

506

Cross Curricular: Math

GOLD STANDARD How much is an ounce of gold worth? The price of gold changes daily. Governments store their gold in brick-like bars called ingots.

RESEARCH AND INQUIRY Have students research the price of gold over the course of a month. Ask them to make a line graph charting the changes in price.

▶ **Mathematical/Spatial**

 Students can learn more about gold by visiting **www.mhschool.com/reading**

507

Comprehension

③ **SEQUENCE OF EVENTS** Quite a lot happens in the first paragraph of the story. What has happened so far?

MODEL The miller brags that his daughter can spin straw into gold. The king hears of this and has the miller's daughter taken to the palace. He tells her that she has to spin a room full of straw into gold by morning or she will die. By reviewing what has happened in the story so far, I can be sure that I understand the plot.

④ The author says that the king made the miller's daughter "an offer that she couldn't refuse." Using clues from the text, describe the author's attitude towards the king. (The author seems to be making fun of the king. He comes across as greedy and mean.) *Tone*

507

Comprehension

5 **CHARACTER** What can you infer about the character of Rumpelstiltskin? Do you think that he is as greedy as the king? Why or why not? (No, he asks for a cheap necklace as payment.)

6 Whom does the heroine of a traditional fairy tale usually end up marrying? (the prince) What has happened in the plot of this story that lets you know this will not be a traditional fairy tale? (Meredith says that she would rather marry Rumpelstiltskin than the king.) *Plot*

TEACHING TIP

IRONY Explain that irony is a literary device that can relate to plot, character, or tone. Most often it sets up a disparity between the reader's expectations and what actually occurs in the text. It adds a humorous or irreverent twist to a narrative. Point out the last line on page 508: "'You've got to be kidding,' Meredith said. 'I'd rather marry *you* than that jerk!'" Ask: What is ironic about this statement? (Meredith changes our expectations of a conventional fairy tale female.) Discuss how irony contributes to the language and plot of this tale.

By one of those unlikely coincidences so common in fairy tales, no sooner had the king closed and bolted the door than a very small gentleman showed up and revealed that he really *could* spin straw into gold. Furthermore, he offered to do it in exchange for her necklace, which was made of gold-tone metal and wasn't worth ten cents. **5** Naturally, she agreed.

The next morning, the king was so overjoyed with his room full of gold that he rewarded the miller's daughter by doubling the amount of straw and repeating his threat. Once again, Rumpelstiltskin (for that was his name) arrived to help her out. This time she gave him her cigar-band pinkie ring.

After this second success, the king was practically apoplectic with greed. He proceeded to empty every barn in the neighborhood of straw and to fill the room with it. This time, he added a little sugar to sweeten the pot: If she turned it all into gold, he would make her his queen. You can just imagine how the miller's daughter was feeling when Rumpelstiltskin popped in for the third time.

"That's quite a pile," he said. "I suppose you want me to spin it into gold."

"Well, the situation has changed just a bit," said the miller's daughter (who also had a name—it was Meredith). "If you *don't*, I will die. If you *do*, I marry the king."

Now *that*, thought Rumpelstiltskin, has possibilities. After all, getting to be the queen was a big step up for a miller's daughter. She would surely pay him anything. And there was only one thing in the world he really wanted—a little child to love and care for.

"Okay, here's the deal," he said. "I will spin the straw into gold, just like before. In return, once you become queen, you must let me adopt your firstborn child. I promise I'll be an excellent father. I know all the lullabies. I'll read to the child every day. I'll even coach Little League."

6 "You've got to be kidding," Meredith said. "I'd rather marry *you* than that jerk!"

508

Cross Curricular: Science

PRECIOUS METAL Gold is a precious metal that is so soft it can be made into many different shapes. Gold also conducts electricity better than most other metals, except silver and copper. The purity of gold is measured in karats with 24 karats representing pure gold.

RESEARCH AND INQUIRY Invite students to research the properties and uses of gold. Ask them to create an illustrated poster showing their findings.
▶ Spatial/Logical

509

Comprehension

7 **SEQUENCE OF EVENTS** Who can offer a summary of the fairy tale *Rumpelstiltskin?* How is the sequence of events in that story different from the sequence of events so far in *Rumpelstiltskin's Daughter?* (In the original story, the miller's daughter marries the king and Rumpelstiltskin is the villain.)

p/i **CONTEXT CLUES** What does *apoplectic* mean? (feeling an emotion so intensely that a blood vessel could burst) *Semantic Cues*

TEACHING TIP

CULTURAL HISTORY Have students compare and contrast the modern retelling of this fairy tale to the original fairy tale. Ask students to note the differences and then explain what these differences reveal about the society that originally created this tale and our present-day society.

---

p/i **PREVENTION/INTERVENTION**

CONTEXT CLUES Write the word *apoplectic* on the board. Have volunteers point to words and phrases in the story that give clues to its meaning. *(greed; he proceeded to empty every barn in the neighborhood of straw)* Discuss with students how it might feel to be overcome with greed. Have them describe the physical sensations one might experience. Guide them to see that they can use context clues and their own personal experiences to determine the meaning of unfamiliar words. *Semantic Cues*

509

Comprehension

8 **CHARACTER** What do you learn about Meredith's character? (She sees that Rumpelstiltskin is a good man. She is perceptive and decisive.) Let's begin our chart.

ACTION	CHARACTER TRAIT
Meredith marries Rumpelstiltskin instead of the king.	Meredith is perceptive and decisive.

Visual Literacy

VIEWING AND REPRESENTING

Have students look at the illustration of the castle on pages 510–511. From what point of view is it illustrated? (from above) How does this make the castle look? (elongated, forbidding) Why might an artist choose to draw something from this perspective?

Suggest that students lie on the floor and look up at something such as a desk or chair. If possible, have them make a quick sketch of the object.

Really?" said Rumpelstiltskin, and he blushed all the way from the top of his head to the tip of his toes (which admittedly wasn't very far, because he was so short).

"Sure," she said. "I like your ideas on parenting, you'd make a good provider, and I have a weakness for short men."

So Rumpelstiltskin spun a golden ladder, and they escaped out the window. They were married the very next day and lived happily together far, far away from the palace.

510

511

Comprehension

9 How do you think the king will react when he comes to unlock the door and discovers that the room is empty? What makes you think he will react this way? *Make Predictions*

Minilesson

REVIEW/MAINTAIN

ea Words

Have students pronounce the words *weakness, pleasure,* and *greatly.* Point out that the first vowel sound in each word is spelled *ea.*

- Ask students what vowel sounds they hear in the first syllable of each word. (/ē/, /e/, /ā/)
- Write the three words on the board and have a volunteer identify the letters that stand for the /ē/, /e/, /ā/ sounds. *Graphophonic Cues*

Activity Have students write words with /ē/, /e/, /ā/ spelled *ea* on index cards. Divide students into teams. Have a member of a team pick a card and pantomime the word on the card. Both teams try to guess the word. The team that guesses the word correctly takes the next turn.

 Phonics Intervention Guide

LANGUAGE SUPPORT

ESL Students who are having trouble following the sequence of events may benefit from role-playing what has happened in the story so far. Encourage them to improvise dialogue and use appropriate body language to portray character. After the role-play, invite volunteers to list the sequence of events that were re-enacted on the board.

511

Comprehension

10 **SEQUENCE OF EVENTS** A lot of time passes during the first two paragraphs on page 512. What might be a possible sequence of events that could occur between the time Meredith and Rumpelstiltskin got married and when their daughter turned sixteen? (Answers will vary.)

SELF-MONITORING STRATEGY

VISUALIZE When readers visualize the action in a story, it helps reinforce story elements. By forming mental pictures of characters and events, readers are more likely to remember the sequence of events.

eredith and Rumpelstiltskin lived a quiet country life, raising chickens and growing vegetables. Every now and then, when they needed something they couldn't make or grow, Rumpelstiltskin would spin up a little gold to buy it with.

Now, they had a daughter, and she was just as sunny and clever as you would expect her to be, having such devoted parents. When she was sixteen, they decided she ought to see **10** more of the world, so every now and then they allowed her to take the gold into town to exchange it for coins and to do a little shopping.

The goldsmith grew curious about the pretty country girl who came in with those odd coils of gold. He mentioned it to his friend the baker, who mentioned it to the blacksmith, who **11** mentioned it to the tax collector, who hurried to the palace and told the king.

It may not surprise you to learn that the king hadn't changed a bit. If anything, he was greedier than before. As he listened, his eyes glittered. "I once knew a miller's daughter who could make gold like that," he said. "Unfortunately, she got away. Let's make sure *this* one doesn't."

So the next time Rumpelstiltskin's daughter went to see the goldsmith, two of the king's guards were waiting for her. In a red-hot minute, she was in a carriage and speeding toward the palace. And what she saw on the way broke her heart. Everywhere the fields lay barren. Sickly children stood begging beside the road. Nobody in the kingdom had anything anymore, because the king had it all.

512

Cross Curricular: Social Studies

POLITICAL CARTOONS Most newspapers publish satirical cartoons about political leaders or events. Humor is a good way for people to express their opinions about the government.

RESEARCH AND INQUIRY Have students research political cartoons found in their local newspapers. Discuss the elements of a political cartoon. (timely topic, humor, known characters) Invite students to create political cartoons about the king. ▶ **Linguistic/Spatial**

513

Comprehension

 11 What inference can you make about the characters who live in the village? (They like to gossip.) **What if the characters in the village did not like to gossip? Would the story change? How?** (The king would not hear about Rumpelstiltskin's daughter.) **Make Inferences**

IDIOMS What does a *red-hot minute* mean? (very fast)

PREVENTION/INTERVENTION

IDIOMS Write the phrases *red-hot minute* and *broke her heart* on the board. Invite volunteers to define the phrases. Guide students to understand that these phrases are idioms, language in which the actual meaning of words cannot be predicted by their literal meanings. Help students see that idioms can be a more imaginative way of using words. Have students brainstorm other idioms to substitute for the idioms on page 512, such as *lightning quick* and *tore her apart*.

Comprehension

12 **How do the guards act?** (They gnash their teeth and clutch their swords.) **Why do you think the author has all the guards act the same way?** (To show that they lack any individuality. They are like a machine.) *Author's Purpose*

TEACHING TIP

STORY STRUCTURE Discuss the structure of this story, which divides neatly into two parts. As students read on, have volunteers explain how the events in the first part of the story—with Meredith, Rumpelstiltskin, and the king—foreshadow the events in the second part—with Rumpelstiltskin's daughter and the king. Students should notice how Hope is able to persuade the king to treat her more leniently than he treated her mother.

Fluency

PARTNER READING This story provides an opportunity for students to practice fluent reading of a humorous story.

- Have partners discuss the humor in the story, pointing to specific sentences and language they find funny.

- Have them determine the best tone to use when narrating.

- Have partners alternate reading pages and listening critically to each other.

514 *Rumpelstiltskin's Daughter*

---

12 inally they reached the palace. There were high walls around it and a moat full of crocodiles. Armed guards were everywhere, gnashing their teeth, clutching their swords, and peering about with shifty eyes. As the carriage went over the bridge and under the portcullis, the hungry people shook their fists at them. It was not a pretty sight.

Rumpelstiltskin's daughter was taken at once to the grand chamber where the king sat on his golden throne. He didn't waste time on idle pleasantries.

"Where did you get *this*?" he asked, showing her the gold.

"Uh . . . ," said Rumpelstiltskin's daughter.

"I thought so," said the king. "Guards, take her to the tower and see what she can do with all that straw."

Rumpelstiltskin's daughter looked around. She saw a pile of straw the size of a bus. She saw a locked door and high windows. She gave a big sigh and began to think. She knew her father could get her out of this pickle. But she had heard stories about the king all her life. One room full of gold would never satisfy him. Her father would be stuck here, spinning, until there was not an iota of straw left in the kingdom.

After a while she climbed the pile of straw and thought **13** some more. She thought about the poor farmers and about the hungry children with their thin faces and sad eyes. She put the two thoughts together and cooked up a plan. Then **14** Rumpelstiltskin's daughter curled up and went to sleep.

514

515

Comprehension

13 **CHARACTER** Rumpelstiltskin's daughter is in a bad situation, and yet she thinks of the poor farmers and the hungry children. What can you infer about her character? (She is kind, unselfish, and brave.)

14 What plan do you think Rumpelstiltskin's daughter has thought up? *Make Predictions*

Minilesson
REVIEW/MAINTAIN
Make Inferences

Review: Inferences about characters are based on information presented in the story and readers' personal experiences.

Guide students to make inferences about the way Rumpelstiltskin and Meredith raised their daughter.

• Do you think Rumpelstiltskin's daughter's upbringing had anything to do with her concern for poor people? What stories about the king might she have heard during her life?

Activity Ask students to make inferences about the way Rumpelstiltskin's daughter might live her life in the future.

Comprehension

15 **CHARACTER** From what we have
read so far, what can you tell about
Meredith and Rumpelstiltskin's daughter?
Let's add the information to our charts.

ACTION	CHARACTER TRAIT
Meredith marries Rumpelstiltskin instead of the king.	Meredith is perceptive and decisive.
Rumpelstiltskin's daughter thinks up a plan and goes to sleep.	Rumpelstiltskin's daughter is resourceful and brave.

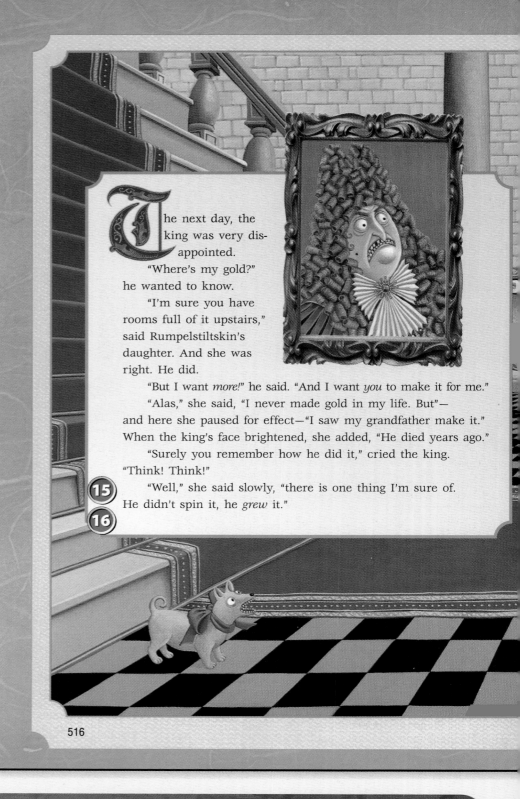

The next day, the king was very disappointed.

"Where's my gold?" he wanted to know.

"I'm sure you have rooms full of it upstairs," said Rumpelstiltskin's daughter. And she was right. He did.

"But I want *more!*" he said. "And I want *you* to make it for me."

"Alas," she said, "I never made gold in my life. But"— and here she paused for effect—"I saw my grandfather make it." When the king's face brightened, she added, "He died years ago."

"Surely you remember how he did it," cried the king. "Think! Think!"

15
16
"Well," she said slowly, "there is one thing I'm sure of. He didn't spin it, he *grew* it."

516

Cross Curricular: Art

FINE ART The paintings in the picture
on page 517 may look familiar. They are
copies of famous paintings, but with a
twist. Point to the picture of the Mona
Lisa and ask students if anyone recognizes it. Have students look for other
paintings in the illustrations. Who is the
subject in all of them? (the king) Have students work with a partner and research a
famous painting or artist of their choice.
Have each group present their findings to
the class. ▶ **Linguistic/Interpersonal**

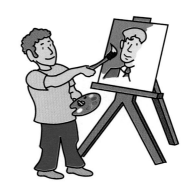

517

Comprehension

16 Rumpelstiltskin's daughter says that she cannot make straw into gold, but that she saw her grandfather do it. What effect does this statement have on the king? (He desperately wants her to remember how her grandfather made gold.) Do you think this was the effect that she wanted? (Yes, it seems to be part of her plan.) *Cause and Effect*

Comprehension

17 **CHARACTER** What can we tell about the king by his actions? Let's add this information to our charts.

ACTION	CHARACTER TRAIT
Meredith marries Rumpelstiltskin instead of the king.	Meredith is perceptive and decisive.
Rumpelstiltskin's daughter thinks up a plan and goes to sleep.	Rumpelstiltskin's daughter is resourceful and brave.
The king whines about giving gold to the farmer.	The king is greedy, selfish, and childish.

Writer's Craft

PARALLEL STRUCTURE

Explain: A sentence has correct parallel structure when it consistently repeats a word, phrase, or part of speech in the same form.

Example: Read the following sentence from page 518: "They drove under the portcullis, over the bridge, and out into the countryside." Emphasizing the preposition that begins each phrase—*under, over,* and *out.* Ask: What part of speech is each word? Discuss how the writer's use of prepositions to begin each phrase makes the phrases parallel.

GROUP Ask students to identify other examples of parallel structure as they read. Have them discuss the effect of parallel structure on the quality of the writing.

The next morning the king and Rumpelstiltskin's daughter got into his glittering coach, with two guards up front and two guards behind and a huge bag of gold inside. They drove under the portcullis, over the bridge, and out into the countryside. At the first farm they came to, they stopped and sent for the farmer. He was thin and ragged and barefoot. So were his wife and children.

"Now tell the farmer he must plant this gold coin in his field, and you will come back in the fall to collect everything it has grown. Tell him you will give him another gold coin for his pains," she whispered.

17 "Do I *have* to?" the king whined.

"Well, I don't know," she said. "That's how my grandfather always did it."

18 "Okay," said the king. "But this better work." He gave the farmer two gold coins, and they hurried on to the next farm.

19 By the end of the week they had covered the entire kingdom.

518

LANGUAGE SUPPORT

ESL Because of their accuracy and detail, you can use the pictures in this story to review key events, character descriptions, and even the attitudes of characters. On pages 518 and 519, for example, students can point out all the characters (including the four guards). They can see the physical characteristics of all the people, and they can even see the dubious expression on the king's face as he hands over the gold coins, and the hopeful one on the farmer's face as he holds out his hand for the money.

519

Comprehension

18 **SEQUENCE OF EVENTS** What time-order words or phrases help you to follow the sequence of events on page 518? (the next morning; at the first farm; now; come back in the fall; to the next farm; by the end of the week)

19 What has Rumpelstiltskin's daughter succeeded in doing? (She has tricked the king into giving gold to the hungry farmers.) *Draw Conclusions*

Minilesson
REVIEW/MAINTAIN
Draw Conclusions

Explain to students that an author will often give clues about a character without directly stating what they are like. By using two or more ideas or pieces of information, readers can draw conclusions about the character.

• Ask students to reread page 518. What conclusions can they draw about the king? (He is so greedy that he does not even notice his people are starving.)

Activity Ask students to draw a conclusion about what Rumpelstiltskin's daughter has made the king do.

519

Comprehension

20 If you could ask Rumpelstiltskin and Meredith how they feel about their daughter being with the king, what do you think they would say? Pantomime their facial expressions and body language as they first find out their daughter has been taken. What might they say to each other? *Role-Play*

SUFFIXES Sometimes a suffix added to a base word completely changes the meaning of the word. What is the suffix in *restless*? (*-less*) How does *-less* change the meaning?

All through the summer the king was restless. "Is it time yet?" he would ask. "Is the gold ripe?"

"Wait," said Rumpelstiltskin's daughter.

Finally August came and went.

"Now," she said. "Now you can go and see what has grown in the fields."

So once again they piled into the glittering coach (with two guards up front and two guards behind) and brought along wagons to carry the gold and a lot more guards to protect it.

As they neared the first farm, the king gasped with joy. The field shone golden in the morning sun.

20 "Gold!" he cried.

"No," said Rumpelstiltskin's daughter, "something better than gold."

520

PREVENTION/INTERVENTION

SUFFIXES Write the sentence on the board: *All through the summer the king was restless.* Have a volunteer underline the suffix in *restless*. Elicit from students that the suffix *-less* means *without*. Brainstorm other words to which the suffix *-less* can be added, such as *hope, grace,* and *hair.* Have students use both forms of the words in sentences.

"How can anything be better than gold?" said the king.

"It's wheat," she said. "You can eat it. You can't eat gold."

Before the king could start turning purple, the farmer and his family came running toward the carriage. In their arms they carried baskets of wheat and barley and apples and green beans and pumpkins and corn and I don't know what all. They piled it into the wagon and kissed the king's hand, grinning ear to ear. I can promise you that nothing like that had ever happened to the king before.

"Well," he said sheepishly, "maybe there will be gold at the next place."

521

Comprehension

21 Why are the farmer and his family running toward the king with food and smiling? (They think the king is a hero because he gave them gold to grow food.) *Cause and Effect*

22 **CHARACTER** Does the king's behavior surprise you? Why or why not? Do you think he is changing? In what ways?

MODEL I think the king didn't lose his temper because the farmer and his family brought him gifts. The text said that nothing like that had ever happened to him before. I think the king liked all the attention. However, he still seems just as greedy, because he is hoping there will be gold at the next place.

TEACHING TIP

POINT OF VIEW Have students note that the story is written from a third-person point of view. Ask students to think how the story might be different if it were told in the first person, by Rumpelstiltskin's daughter. Have them give examples of how this would change aspects of the story.

521

Comprehension

23 Do you think the king is really a hero? Who is the real hero? Explain your answer. (No; Rumpelstiltskin's daughter is the real hero. She got food to the people.) *Draw Conclusions*

24 Why does the author have the guards gnashing their teeth, clutching their swords, and peering about with shifty eyes? (It shows that the guards have not changed at all. They are still threatening.) *Author's Purpose*

P/i **CONTEXT CLUES** What does the word *sumptuous* mean in the second paragraph? (lavish, magnificent) *Semantic Cues*

TEACHING TIP

IRONY Remind students that irony works to subvert the reader's expectations of a text—through its tone, plot, characterization, or language. This retelling of a familiar fairy tale is ironic in part because the young girl is the heroine and ends up saving the people—rather than the king—the expected, conventional hero. Ask: How are the plot and language ironic?

23 ut everywhere it was the same. The land prospered, the children looked healthy, and the king was a hero. At the end of the week they returned to the palace with all the food the wagons could carry.

The cook was so overjoyed, he put on a sumptuous feast to celebrate. Unfortunately, there was no one to invite except Rumpelstiltskin's daughter and the guards, who spent the whole meal gnashing their teeth, clutching their swords, and peering **24** about with shifty eyes.

"I wish they'd quit that," said Rumpelstiltskin's daughter.

522

P/i **PREVENTION/INTERVENTION**

CONTEXT CLUES Have students reread the sentence on page 522 that contains the word *sumptuous*. Ask students what words are clues to the meaning of the word *sumptuous*. *(food, feast, celebrate)* Help students to understand that sumptuous means lavish or magnificent.

Invite students to read the last paragraph containing the word *shifty*. Ask them to identify context clues to help them figure out the meaning of *shifty*. *(peering about, eyes)* Then have them tell what they think *shifty* means. *Semantic Cues*

After dinner, the king spoke. "That was all very nice, my dear," he said, "but you must have been mistaken. That was how your grandfather grew *food*, not how he made gold." **25**

"Right," she said as she pulled her shawl tightly around her shoulders and gazed longingly at the fire. Even in the palace she could feel the chill of autumn. *Time for phase two*, she thought. **26**

"Of course you're right," she said. "I told you it was long ago. But I think I remember now. He didn't grow gold. He *knitted* it with golden knitting needles." **27**

523

Comprehension

25 **CHARACTER** The king does not seem to understand that he was tricked. What can you tell about him from this? (He is so vain and conceited that he cannot imagine anyone trying to trick him.)

26 Rumpelstiltskin's daughter seems to have another plan. Do you think her plan will be to help herself or to help the other people in the kingdom? How did you reach this conclusion? (Based on her past actions, her plan will help other people.) *Draw Conclusions*

27 What do you think her plan will be? (Answers will vary. Students may predict that Rumpelstiltskin's daughter will find a way to help the people of the kingdom.) *Make Predictions*

Comprehension

28 **CHARACTER** Based on what has happened before, do you think the king will go along with Rumpelstiltskin's daughter's new plan? Why? (Yes; he is greedy and wants more gold.)

29 How is Rumpelstiltskin's daughter like her father? (They both have unusual abilities. Her unusual ability is understanding the king's character and solving problems in a clever, logical way, while Rumpelstiltskin has magical powers.) *Compare and Contrast*

So the next day they loaded the coach with knitting needles, a bag of gold, and lots and lots of yellow wool. Then they headed off under the portcullis, over the bridge (with two guards up front and two guards behind), and out into the countryside.

At the first cottage they came to, they asked to see the granny. She hobbled to the door in her rags and curtsied to the king.

"Now," whispered Rumpelstiltskin's daughter, "give her a bag of wool and a pair of needles. Tell her to knit it all up and you will come back in a month to collect your riches. Give **28** her a gold coin for her pains."

"Do I *have* to?" the king whined.

"My grandfather always did," she said. "I would, if I were you."

And so they went all over the kingdom, hiring every granny they **29** could find.

At the end of the month, the king ordered his coach and wagons, rounded up his guards, and went to see the grannies. As he neared the first cottage, he heard the sound of singing. Looking out the window, the king saw the happy villagers waiting there to greet him, cheering wildly as he passed. And every one of them was warm as toast in yellow woolly clothes.

"Gold!" cried the king.

"Something better than gold," said Rumpelstiltskin's daughter. "Your people will be warm all winter."

Everyone brought presents for the king. By the time he got back to his palace, he had seventeen sweaters, forty-two mufflers, eight vests, one pair of knickers, one hundred and thirty-five pairs of socks, twelve nightcaps, and a tam-o'-shanter. All the color of gold.

524

524 *Rumpelstiltskin's Daughter*

CULTURAL PERSPECTIVES

FAIRY TALE CHARACTERS Every culture has its own fairy tales. Although the settings may be different, the kinds of characters that appear in these tales usually have similarities. Often there are characters with magical powers like Rumpelstiltskin. There are also cruel kings and clever women.

Activity Have students work in groups to read fairy tales from other lands. Have each group investigate one country and act out a fairy tale from that country for the class.

▶ **Kinesthetic/Interpersonal**

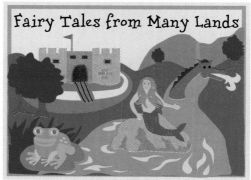

Fairy Tales from Many Lands

Comprehension

30 Why do the villagers give presents to the king? (They think that he is kind and generous for giving them the knitting needles and the wool.) **Do you think he deserves the presents?** *Judgments and Decisions*

TEACHING TIP

PARODY Help students recognize that *Rumpelstiltskin's Daughter* is a parody, or work that imitates a literary form for comic effect. Explain to students that Diane Stanley creates a parody of a fairy tale by mixing traditional plot devices and dialogue with modern ones. Then ask students to compare and contrast *Rumpelstiltskin's Daughter* with the traditional fairy tale *Rumpelstiltskin*. Also ask students to explain how the author's style and the humorous mood help make *Rumpelstiltskin's Daughter* enjoyable to read.

LANGUAGE SUPPORT

ESL Students who have difficulty understanding the causes and effects in the story may benefit from role-play. List key events from the story on the board, such as the king handing out knitting needles and wool and the villagers giving him presents.

Have partners role-play an event. The audience should be able to identify the cause and effect in each event.

525

Comprehension

③¹ CHARACTER Hope was able to make the king change his behavior. What does this tell us about her? Let's finish our charts.

ACTION	CHARACTER TRAIT
Meredith marries Rumpelstiltskin instead of the king.	Meredith is perceptive and decisive.
Rumpelstiltskin's daughter thinks up a plan and goes to sleep.	Rumpelstiltskin's daughter is resourceful and brave.
The king whines about giving gold to the farmer.	The king is greedy, selfish, and childish.
Rumpelstiltskin's daughter causes the king to change his behavior.	She is clever and creative.

RETELL THE STORY Have students retell the main events in the story. Encourage them to use their Character charts to include important information about the main characters. Ask a volunteer to tell why the name *Hope* is symbolically appropriate for Rumpelstiltskin's daughter and to suggest a fitting name for the king. *Summarize*

STUDENT SELF-ASSESSMENT

- How did the strategy of analyzing character help me to understand the story?

TRANSFERRING THE STRATEGY

- How can this strategy help me understand other things I read?

o they suit me?" asked the king as he tried them on.
"Absolutely," said Rumpelstiltskin's daughter.
The guards just stood there, gnashing their teeth, clutching their swords, and peering about with shifty eyes.
"Don't you think it's time you got rid of them?" she suggested. "And the walls and the moat and the crocodiles, too. You don't need them anymore—your people love you now."
She was right, as always, so the king set the guards to work tearing down the walls. And with the stones, they built a zoo for the crocodiles and houses for the poor.
"Are you sure you don't remember how your grandfather made gold?" asked the king one day.
"I'm afraid not," she said.
"It's a terrible pity," he sighed. "But you did try. And as a reward, I have decided to make you my queen."

526

REREADING FOR *Fluency*

GROUP Small groups can choose roles and reread the story. Encourage them to keep in mind the humorous tone as they read.

READING RATE When you evaluate rate, have the student read aloud from the story for one minute. Place a stick-on note after the last word read. Count words read. To evaluate

students' performance, see the Running Record in the **Fluency Assessment** book.

ⓘ Intervention For leveled fluency lessons, passages, and norms charts, see **Skills Intervention Guide**, Part 4, Fluency.

"Why don't you make me prime minister instead," suggested Rumpelstiltskin's daughter.

And so the king did just that. He built her a nice house near the palace, and once a month she took time off to visit her parents. The people of the kingdom never went cold or hungry again. And whenever the king started worrying about gold, she sent him on a goodwill tour throughout the countryside, which cheered him right up.

Oh, and I forgot to tell you— Rumpelstiltskin's daughter had a name, too. It was Hope.

527

Comprehension

Return to Predictions and Purposes

Review with students their story predictions and reasons for reading the story. Were their predictions correct? Did they find out what they wanted to know?

PREDICTIONS	WHAT HAPPENED
There will be a greedy king in the story.	There was a greedy king who changed his ways.
Rumpelstiltskin's daughter outwits the king.	Rumpelstiltskin's daughter tricked the king into changing his ways.

INFORMAL ASSESSMENT

STORY ELEMENTS

HOW TO ASSESS

- Have students refer to their Character charts to tell you which information about the character was implied and which was stated in the text.

Students should realize that not all information about a character is stated in a story.

FOLLOW UP If students have trouble understanding how to analyze character, have them refer back to their Character charts. Read each action with students and give absurd character traits for each action. Have students decide whether or not they would believe these traits based on the characters' actions.

LITERARY RESPONSE

QUICK-WRITE Invite students to record their thoughts about the story. These questions may help them get started:

- Is this a traditional fairy tale?
- What do you think Hope will do as prime minister?

ORAL RESPONSE Have students share their journal writings and discuss the lesson or moral of this fairy tale.

COMPARING DIFFERENCES Have students read the original fairy tale *Rumpelstiltskin*. Then lead students in a discussion to compare and contrast the two stories. Have students identify elements from the original that were included, in some form, in the variant. Elicit why students feel these changes might have been made. Urge students to read other fractured fairy tales.

527

Story Questions

Have students discuss or write the answers to the questions on page 528.

Answers:

1. The king, who goes from being cruel and greedy to being kind. *Literal/Character*

2. The title of the story; much of the story is about how she solves the main problem of the story. *Inferential/Draw Conclusions*

3. She cares about people and is very clever. *Inferential/Character*

4. It is about fanciful characters with unusual abilities. *Critical/Summarize*

5. Answers will vary. *Critical/Reading Across Texts*

Write a Fractured Fairy Tale For a full writing process lesson related to this writing suggestion, see the Writing a Story lesson on pages 531K–531L.

Story Questions & Activities

1. Which character changes the most in the story? How?

2. How do you know that Rumpelstiltskin's daughter is the main character in this version of the fairy tale?

3. Why would Rumpelstiltskin's daughter make a good prime minister? Explain.

4. How would you complete this sentence? This story is a fairy tale because _____.

5. Compare Rumpelstiltskin's daughter with Cinderella or another female character from a fairy tale you know. How are the characters alike? How do they differ?

Write a Fractured Fairy Tale

You may not have expected some of the things that happened in this fairy tale, especially if you knew the original story of Rumpelstiltskin. Such twists in character and plot make this selection a fractured fairy tale. Choose one of your favorite fairy tales and write a funny version of it. For example, the three little pigs might be weightlifters who are not afraid of anyone. Besides differences in character, your story might have a different setting, plot, or ending.

Meeting Individual Needs

EASY	ON-LEVEL	CHALLENGE
Reteach, 172	Practice, 172	Extend, 172

Build a Castle

Even today, most kings and queens live in castles and palaces. Suppose that a royal family asked you to build a castle for them. What would you make the castle look like? Would it be modern? Make a sketch of your castle. Then use your sketch to build a model from cardboard sheets, cardboard tubes from paper towels, construction paper, craft sticks, and other art materials.

Meet the King

Draw a Poster

Suppose you were Hope. How much would you charge to meet the king? Why would people want to meet him, anyway? Draw a poster that will make people want to see and hear the king. Illustrate your poster, and give the subject of his "talk." Include the date, time, and place so that people will know when and where to meet the king.

Find Out More

In the story, Rumpelstiltskin's daughter chooses the job of prime minister over that of becoming the queen. What is a prime minister? How is it different from a president? Start by looking in an encyclopedia or a social studies textbook. Gather facts and take notes. Then draw a chart or a Venn diagram to show how the important duties of a prime minister and a president are similar, yet different.

Story Activities

Build a Castle

Materials: various art supplies such as cardboard tubes, construction paper, craft sticks

PARTNERS Discuss with students how castles are different from other dwellings. Ask why many castles have high walls, ramparts, moats, and drawbridges. Provide photographs and illustrations of various castles for reference.

Draw a Poster

Materials: posterboard, markers

ONE Provide examples of eye-catching posters and discuss the elements of design with students. Guide them to see that successful posters are usually simple, informative, and bold. Have students discuss which elements they find particularly powerful in each poster.

Find Out More

RESEARCH AND INQUIRY Discuss the various types of government with students. Ask them to tell which government they prefer and why.

interNET CONNECTION For more information about governments, students can visit **www.mhschool.com/reading**

HEALTH: WHEAT
Have students research and produce a group chart on the importance of wheat to worldwide nutrition.

What to Look For Check responses to see that students:

- have reported on a variety of nations

- show their annual amount of imported/exported wheat

- compile statistics on wheat's contributions to a healthy diet

- feature geographical and economic factors in wheat production and consumption.

CHALLENGE

FORMAL ASSESSMENT

After page 529, see the Selection Assessment.

Study Skills

GRAPHIC AIDS

TESTED ✓ OBJECTIVES Students will:

• interpret a circle graph and use it to compare and contrast data.

PREPARE Preview the circle graph, pointing out that it shows how a whole (United States Wheat Production in 1999) is divided into parts (wheat production by state). Display **Teaching Chart 141.**

TEACH Ask students how the Wheat Production graph is divided. Make sure students note that the greater the state's wheat production, the greater their portion of the graph is.

PRACTICE Have students answer questions 1–5. Review the answers with them. **1.** 5% **2.** North Dakota **3.** Kansas **4.** North Dakota; 6% **5.** As the 34% would need to be divided by 41 (the remaining number of states), the answer would be less than 1%.

ASSESS/CLOSE Show a different circle graph and ask students about the data shown.

Study SKILLS

Read a Circle Graph

Rumpelstiltskin's daughter taught the king that wheat is better than gold. The United States is one of the largest wheat-growing countries in the world. Some states grow more wheat than others. A **circle graph** can show how the parts of a whole are related. This circle graph shows how much wheat is produced by different states in the United States.

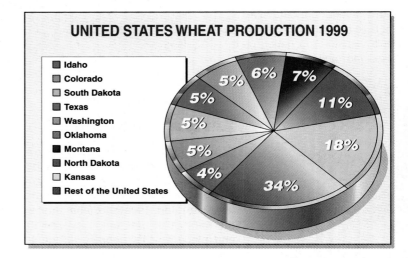

UNITED STATES WHEAT PRODUCTION 1999

☐ Idaho
☐ Colorado
☐ South Dakota
☐ Texas
☐ Washington
☐ Oklahoma
☐ Montana
☐ North Dakota
☐ Kansas
☐ Rest of the United States

Use the circle graph to answer these questions.

❶ What percentage of the wheat is grown in Texas?

❷ Which state grows 11% of the wheat?

❸ Which state is the largest wheat producer?

❹ Which state grows more wheat, North Dakota or South Dakota? How much more?

❺ Is the average wheat production of the states not named greater or less than 1%? Explain.

Meeting Individual Needs

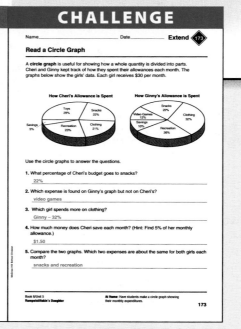

EASY	ON-LEVEL	CHALLENGE
Reteach, 173	Practice, 173	Extend, 173

TEST POWER

Test Tip

Always read the directions carefully.

DIRECTIONS

Read the sample story. Then read each question about the story.

SAMPLE

The Great White Shark

One of the scariest and most misunderstood creatures of the ocean is the Great White Shark. Its large triangular dorsal fin and rows of 3-inch, razor-sharp teeth distinguish the Great White. When a shark loses a tooth, another one is ready to replace it.

Great Whites usually live in the warmer waters off the coast of Australia or in the Caribbean. The Great White feeds on the remains of dead animals. Its reputation as a "man-eater" comes from the occasional encounter between a swimmer and a wandering, hungry shark. Even though the bite of a Great White can prove fatal, it should be noted that this shark is not inclined to attack humans. Shark attacks are very rare, although the excitement they cause tends to outweigh their infrequency.

1 The Great White Shark can be best described as —

  (A) powerful

  B angry

  C lonely

  D impatient

2 According to the passage, which of these is probably one of the biggest reasons a Great White Shark might attack a human?

  F The shark's determination

  G The shark's size

  (H) The shark's hunger

  J The shark's fear

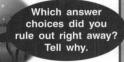

Which answer choices did you rule out right away? Tell why.

531

Test Power

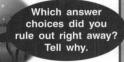

Read the Page

Have students read the passage. Remind students to summarize the passage in their own words and to read *all* of the answer choices before choosing one.

Discuss the Questions

Question 1: This question requires students to determine how the Great White Shark should be best described based on the information in the passage. Students will need to infer the answer to this question based on facts presented in the passage. Remind students to refer back to the passage *before* choosing an answer.

Question 2: This question requires students to recall a supporting fact. Have students review the passage. Explain that students should eliminate answer choices that discuss things that are *not* mentioned in the passage.

Leveled Books

Answers to Story Questions

1. Blacks had to attend segregated, inferior schools; they had to give up their bus seats to white people; they could not use the same restaurants, water fountains, elevators, and movie theaters as whites.

2. She saw an urgent need for black people to improve their lives, and she was tired of the gross injustices they faced. She felt she could help fellow blacks by sharing her skills with them.

3. She risked the danger of being beaten by the bus driver or the police; she risked being jailed and fined; she lost her job and received death threats, yet she never backed down from her protest.

4. Rosa Parks, an individual willing to stand up and challenge an unfair law, was able to help achieve justice for her people.

5. Answers will vary.

The *Story Questions and Activity* below appear in the *Easy Book.*

Story Questions

1. What injustices did Southern African Americans face at the time of Rosa's childhood?

2. Why was Rosa determined to be an active part of the civil rights movement?

3. How did Rosa's bus protest and lawsuit demonstrate her extraordinary courage?

4. What is the main idea of the book?

5. Do you think Hope in *Rumpelstiltskin's Daughter* would be able to face the same challenges that Rosa Parks faced?

Learn About a Leader

Research another important leader in the American civil rights movement, such as Sojourner Truth, Frederick Douglass, Harriet Tubman, Dr. Martin Luther King, Jr., Malcolm X, or Jesse Jackson. Find out about the challenges that the person faced, and how he or she struggled to overcome them. Then create a time line that shows the important events and achievements in the person's life.

from *Rosa Parks*

EASY

Rosa Parks

ea Words

☑ **Character**

☑ **Instructional Vocabulary:**
barley, coincidences, knickers, mufflers, sheepishly, sweeten

Guided Reading

PREVIEW AND PREDICT Have students look at the book's illustrations and then write down some predictions about this book.

SET PURPOSES Invite students to list in their notebooks some questions they may have about Rosa Parks and her determination to take a stand against segregation.

READ THE BOOK Have students read the story independently. When they have finished, review the text with these questions:

Pages 2–4: How do you think that growing up poor affected Rosa Parks? (She learned to not take anything for granted; she learned to face challenges.) *Character*

Page 3: Have students pause at the word *each* and pronounce it correctly. Then ask them to think of other words that have the /ē/ sound writen as *ea* (reach, peach). *Phonics and Decoding*

Page 7: What does *sheepishly* mean? How does the text help you figure out its meaning? (acting bashful or meek—as having done something wrong) *Vocabulary*

Pages 10–11: How did the bus boycott affect the civil rights movement? (It hurt the bus company financially; it drew national attention to Rosa's case; it showed that the community could work together.) *Cause and Effect*

Pages 12–13: How did Rosa and other African Americans deal with Rosa's arrest? (Her lawyers won an appeal on her case. The boycott continued.) Ask students why Montgomery was called a "walking city." (African Americans did not ride buses and walked to work.) *Problem and Solution*

RETURN TO PREDICTIONS AND PURPOSES Invite students to review their predictions and purpose for reading.

LITERARY RESPONSE Ask students:

• Did you learn anything new about the civil rights movement? Explain.

• What can you learn from Rosa Parks's story?

Leveled Books

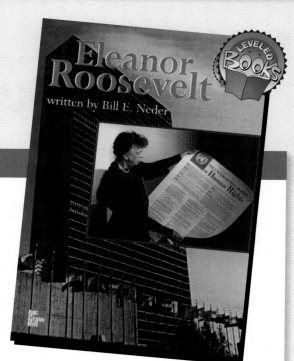

INDEPENDENT

Eleanor Roosevelt

☑ **Story Elements**

☑ **Instructional Vocabulary:**
barley, coincidences, knickers, mufflers, sheepishly, sweeten

Guided Reading

PREVIEW AND PREDICT Ask students to page through the book, paying attention to the illustrations. What can they tell about the book by previewing it?

SET PURPOSES Have students write down what they think they can learn by reading this book.

READ THE BOOK Ask students to read the book independently. When they have finished, ask the following questions:

Page 4: What does this page tell you about Eleanor? What does it tell you about Franklin? (She was concerned about others and showed him how poor people lived; he was interested in learning from Eleanor and wanted to help the poor.) *Character*

Page 13: How does the word *bitterly* on this page help you understand the meaning of *sweeten*? (You can see that the two words are being used in opposition to one another.) *Vocabulary*

Page 15: What can you tell about Eleanor Roosevelt from her willingness to take a stand even when it could have harmed her husband's career? (She had integrity and was wholly committed to her beliefs.) *Make Inferences*

Page 16: Why did Truman call Eleanor the "First Lady of the World"? (She was continuing the work she had done as First Lady of the United States, but now doing it for the world.) *Draw Conclusions*

RETURN TO PREDICTIONS AND PURPOSES Ask students to think about the predictions they made. Did they learn what they wanted to learn from this book?

LITERARY RESPONSE Ask students to answer these questions:

• Why, do you think, Eleanor Roosevelt was loved by so many?

• What would you ask Eleanor Roosevelt if you could speak to her today?

Also see the story questions and activity in *Eleanor Roosevelt*.

Answers to Story Questions

1. She had low self-esteem and saw herself as an ugly and awkward girl.
2. She knew from her own childhood how it felt to suffer. Her school experience in England had also taught her how much a single individual can do to improve someone else's life.
3. He knew that she was a well-beloved figure around the world, and therefore people at the U.N. would be likely to heed her words and messages. Also, she had shown great competence in her past political endeavors.
4. The main idea is that Eleanor Roosevelt, as a teacher, mother, and First Lady, led an effective struggle for human rights by helping the poor and needy and by urging cooperation among different peoples and nations.
5. Answers will vary.

The *Story Questions and Activity* below appear in the *Independent Book.*

Story Questions

1. What difficulties did Eleanor face as a child?
2. Which of Eleanor's early experiences made her devote her life to the struggle for human rights?
3. Why, do you think, did President Truman choose Eleanor to represent the United States at the United Nations?
4. What is the main idea of the book?
5. How are the heroines of *Rumplestiltskin's Daughter* like Eleanor Roosevelt?

Local Help

Research an organization in your own community that helps the poor and needy, such as the Red Cross or a local soup kitchen. Find out exactly what services the organization provides. Write a report that details the organization's activities and how you think you could help them.

from Eleanor Roosevelt

Leveled Books

CHALLENGE

The Mystery of the Lost Satchel

☑ **Story Elements**

☑ **Instructional Vocabulary:**
barley, coincidences, knickers, mufflers, sheepishly, sweeten

Guided Reading

PREVIEW AND PREDICT Ask students to look at the title of the book and the chapters as well as at the illustrations. What do they predict this story will be about?

SET PURPOSES Have students write down what they think they will learn from reading this selection.

READ THE BOOK Students can read the book independently. Ask them to take notes about the clues that help Elaine solve the mystery. Then have students answer these questions:

Page 5: What word is a synonym for *mufflers*? (scarves) *Vocabulary*

Pages 8–12: List the places that Elaine visits to solve the mystery. (First, the bicycle shop; then the clothing store; the boarding house; the china store; Mrs. Foley's; finally, the lumber mill) *Sequence of Events*

Page 16: What characteristics does Elaine have that enable her to find the owner of the satchel? (She is smart, conscientious, resourceful, and curious.) *Character*

RETURN TO PREDICTIONS AND PURPOSES Did the predictions the students made turn out to be correct?

LITERARY RESPONSE Discuss these questions:

- What makes a good mystery story?

- Do you enjoy reading mysteries? Why or why not?

Also see the story questions and activity in *The Mystery of the Lost Satchel.*

Answers to Story Questions

1. She is afraid someone else might come along and steal it.

2. She wants to prove she is an able detective; she is intrigued by the pairs of items and the single bell.

3. She is responsible because she makes sure that the lost bag gets back to its owner. She is smart because she is able to use clues from the items to trace the owner.

4. The story is mostly about how a thirteen-year-old girl takes responsibility for a lost bag she finds and uses clues to trace its owner.

5. Answers will vary.

The *Story Questions and Activity* below appear in the *Challenge Book.*

Story Questions

1. Why does Elaine take the bag instead of leaving it on the park bench?

2. Why do you think Elaine is so determined to find the owner of the bag?

3. How can you tell that Elaine is both responsible and smart?

4. What is the story mostly about?

5. What does Elaine have in common with the heroines of *Rumpelstiltskin's Daughter*?

Show the Time

This story takes place in the year 1900. Suppose someone found a bag at the turn of the 20th century. List 10 items that might show the finder that it was the year 2000.

from The Mystery of the Lost Satchel

Activities

Bringing Groups Together

Anthology and Leveled Books

Connecting Texts

RESPONSIBILITY CHART In these selections, people take responsibility and make things happen. Ask students to fill in the part of this chart that refers to the book or books they read. Then discuss the entire chart with the class. Compare both the ways people decide to take responsibility and the results of their actions.

Rumpelstiltskin's Daughter	Rosa Parks	Eleanor Roosevelt	The Mystery of the Lost Satchel
• Hope takes responsibility for changing the king's greedy behavior.	• Rosa Parks refused to move to the back of the bus, beginning the Montgomery bus boycott that changed the laws.	• Eleanor Roosevelt spent much of her adult life drawing attention to the situation of the poor and those who were discriminated against.	• Elaine decides to take responsibility for the satchel and find its owner.

Viewing/Representing

GROUP PRESENTATIONS Divide the class into groups, one for each of the four books read in the lesson. (For *Rumpelstiltskin's Daughter*, combine students of different reading levels.) Ask students to create an awards ceremony in honor of the key person in the book. They should design the actual award and conduct the ceremony, which might include speeches and songs, in front of the rest of the class.

AUDIENCE RESPONSE Ask students in the audience to imagine that they are reporters. Have them ask questions after the ceremony.

Research and Inquiry

TAKE A STAND Ask students to take a position on an issue that they feel strongly about. Students should research the issue and then write an essay in which they declare their position. The essays should include:

- facts to support the stand

- the student's informed opinions

- quotations from experts supporting the student's position

 Students can learn more by visiting **www.mhschool.com/reading**

Review Story Elements

OBJECTIVES

Students will make inferences about and analyze characters.

Skills Finder

Story Elements:
Character, Setting, Plot

Introduce	65A-B
Review	369A-B, 405E-F, 447A-B, 467E-F, 503A-B, 531E-F
Test	Unit 1, Unit 4, Unit 5
Maintain	147, 179

TEACHING TIP

ROLE-PLAY Have students role-play the story to further emphasize the difference between a developed and an undeveloped character. Discuss the role-plays with students and ask them which character was more interesting to watch.

SELF-SELECTED
Reading

Students may choose from the following titles.

ANTHOLOGY

- Rumpelstiltskin's Daughter

LEVELED BOOKS

- Rosa Parks
- Eleanor Roosevelt
- The Mystery of the Lost Satchel

Bibliography, pages T80–T81

PREPARE

Discuss Character Traits
Ask: What if the author presented characters without any description? What if a main character had no dialogue or action in a story? Would you understand that character? Would you want to read the story?

TEACH

Analyze Character
Review with students that believable, interesting characters contribute to a well-developed plot.

No Hope

Rumpelstiltskin's daughter was named Hope. The greedy king wanted her to spin straw into gold. Hope didn't know how to do this. "You must spin gold or else you will die," yelled the king in his high voice. He pulled on his wild, black hair, then threw his crown across the room and would not speak to anyone else for the rest of the night.

Later, he went to check on Hope. She still had not spun the straw into gold. The king's face turned purple and he screamed for his guards.

Teaching Chart 142

Read "No Hope" and Model the Skill
Have students look for character traits as you read the **Teaching Chart 142** passage with them.

MODEL The title of the story is "No Hope" and that is exactly what I think when I analyze the character Hope in the story—she is not there! There is no physical description of her, no way to know what she thinks or feels. The author never tells us here what she does, only what she cannot do.

Find Character Traits
Have students underline the clues that help show the king's character in the story.

Create a Character Chart

GROUP

Ask students to create possible character traits for Hope in the story "No Hope." Have them write examples of dialogue and action that would suggest these traits. Small groups can collaborate on a chart like the one below. ▶ **Linguistic/Logical**

CHARACTER TRAIT	EXAMPLES
brave	Hope laughed when she saw the king.

ASSESS/CLOSE

Extend the Story

Invite students to use their charts to create a third character for the story "No Hope." Have them list traits and examples of these traits and then rewrite the story to include the new character.

ALTERNATE TEACHING STRATEGY

STORY ELEMENTS

For a different approach to teaching this skill, see page T62.

Intervention ▶ **Skills**

Intervention Guide, for direct instruction and extra practice with story elements

Meeting Individual Needs for Comprehension

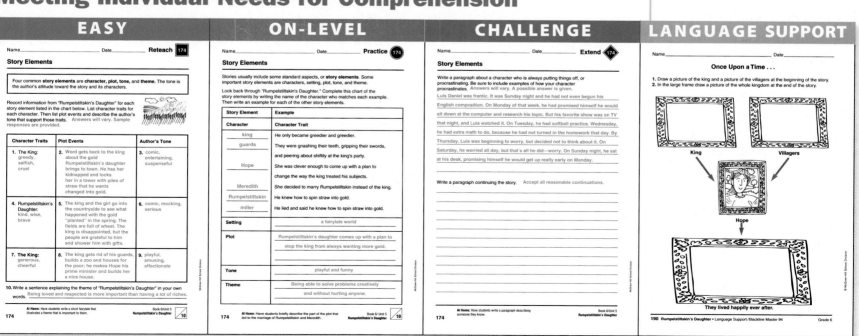

Reteach, 174   Practice, 174   Extend, 174   Language Support, 190

OBJECTIVES

Students will identify information that is implied rather than stated in a text and make inferences about characters.

Skills Finder

Make Inferences

Introduce	39G–H
Review	63G–H, 83G–H, 109E–F, 467G–H, 481G–H, 531G–H
Test	Unit 1, Unit 5
Maintain	335, 351, 515, 557, 625

TEACHING TIP

IMPLICIT

INFORMATION Have students restate the implied information in more direct terms. For example, they could say: *The king likes living in a dirty castle. The king is rude.* Write students' responses on the board along with the corresponding implied information from the story.

Review Make Inferences

PREPARE

Discuss Making Inferences

Ask: How do you get to know a new person? If you are deciding whether or not to be friends with a person, do you pay attention to what he or she says and does? Describe some things people could say that would make you decide not to be friends with them.

TEACH

Understand Making Inferences

Review: Information about characters in a story is often implied rather than directly stated. Sometimes you must read between the lines.

Shall We Be Friends?

When Hope arrived at the castle, she noticed how dirty everything was. When she was introduced to the king, he did not shake her hand. Instead, he pointed at her with one long, grimy finger and demanded that she bow to him.

"I don't like your dress," said the king in a nasty tone of voice. His guards stood around him, clutching their swords and glaring right at Hope.

Teaching Chart 143

Read "Shall We Be Friends?" and Model the Skill

Have students make inferences about the characters as you read the **Teaching Chart 143** passage with them.

MODEL As I read, I look for clues about the characters to help understand the story. From the title I infer Hope and the king will decide whether or not to be friends. Since the king is disagreeable and dirty, I guess Hope will not like him.

Identify Clues

Have students underline clues that help them make inferences about the character of the king.

PRACTICE

Create an Inference Chart

GROUP

Have groups make Inference charts. Have students list the clues that help them make inferences about the character of the king in *Rumpelstiltskin's Daughter* on their charts. They can then rewrite the inference as a direct statement that could be found in the story.

▶ **Linguistic/Logical**

INFERENCE	DIRECT STATEMENT
"Do I have to?" the king whined.	The king is greedy and childish.

ASSESS/CLOSE

Use the Chart

Ask students to use the same chart to analyze a story they have written. After completing the charts, have them discuss any new ideas they have for their stories.

ALTERNATE TEACHING STRATEGY

MAKE INFERENCES

For a different approach to teaching this skill, see page T64.

Intervention ▶ **Skills Intervention Guide**, for direct instruction and extra practice with making inferences

Meeting Individual Needs for Comprehension

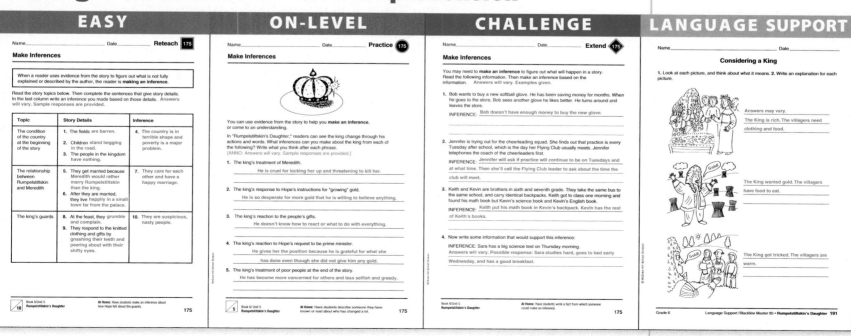

Reteach, 175   Practice, 175   Extend, 175   Language Support, 191

531H

**OBJECTIVES**

Students will distinguish denotative and connotative meanings of words and phrases.

Review **Denotation** and **Connotation**

Skills Finder

Denotation and Connotation	
Introduce	467I-J
Review	531I-J, 541I-J
Test	Unit 5

LANGUAGE SUPPORT

ESL Students who have difficulty understanding the difference between denotative and connotative meaning may benefit from drawing connotative pictures of the words and phrases in "The Ladder of Gold." Ask them to think how each word or phrase makes them feel and to use color and other visual techniques to portray that emotion.

PREPARE

Discuss Literal and Emotional Meanings

Discuss how authors often choose words for both their literal and emotional meanings. For example, the literal meaning of an empty plate is that there is nothing on the plate. The emotional meaning might be sadness because there is nothing to eat.

TEACH

Understand Denotation and Connotation

Review with students that *denotation* is the literal dictionary meaning of a word, and *connotation* is the emotional meaning that is associated with a word and enhances its literal meaning.

The Ladder of Gold

Meredith sat in the cold, locked tower room and tried not to cry. If she did not spin the roomful of straw into gold by morning, she would be put to death by the king. Suddenly, a funny little man appeared. "I will spin the straw into gold for you," he said. "Then you can marry the king."

"But I don't want to marry the king! He looks like a rat," cried Meredith.

"Marry me instead," said the little man, and he spun a golden ladder so they could make their escape from the dark, cold castle.

Teaching Chart 144

Read "The Ladder of Gold" and Model the Skill

Have students listen for denotative and connotative meanings as you read **Teaching Chart 144** with them.

MODEL In this story, Meredith sits in a cold, locked tower room. That is the literal, denotative meaning of where Meredith is sitting. The word *cold* not only suggests that the temperature is low but also that the room is lonely and isolated.

Find Literal Meanings

Have students underline denotative words and phrases that also have connotative meaning.

Create a
Denotation and
Connotation
Chart

GROUP

Have students write denotative words and phrases from "The Ladder of Gold" and the connotative meanings of those words on a chart.

▶ Linguistic/Logical

DENOTATION	CONNOTATION
cold, locked tower room	lonely, isolated
roomful of straw	worthless

ASSESS/CLOSE

Find Connotative
Meaning

Ask students to look back through *Rumpelstiltskin's Daughter* to find connotative meanings for the literal meanings of denotative words and phrases.

ALTERNATE TEACHING
STRATEGY
....
DENOTATION AND
CONNOTATION
For a different approach to teaching this skill, see page T65.

Intervention ▶ Skills
Intervention Guide, for direct instruction and extra practice with denotation and connotation

Meeting Individual Needs for Vocabulary

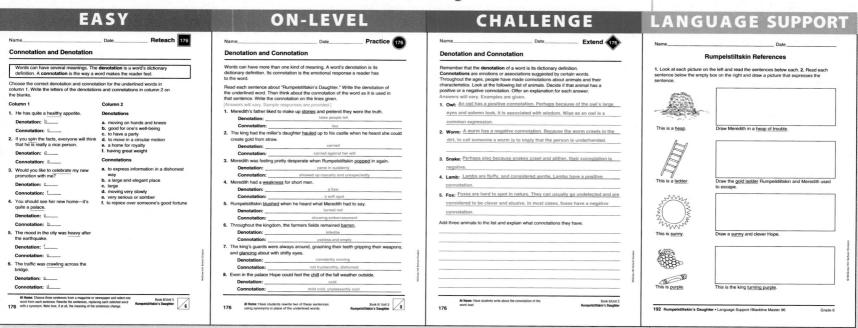

Reteach, 176   Practice, 176   Extend, 176   Language Support, 192

Writing a Story

TEACHING TIP

Technology
Point out that many times the spell-checker on a computer will not recognize all the words in a story. Tell students to use the dictionary to check the spelling of unusual words.

Handwriting
Remind students to leave space between the title and the rest of the story when making their final copy. They may want to print the title in all capital letters, especially on the cover page. For specific instruction on handwriting, see pages T70–T75.

Handwriting CD-ROM

Prewrite

WRITE A FRACTURED FAIRY TALE
Present this writing assignment: You may not have expected some of the things that happened in this fairy tale, especially if you knew the original story of Rumpelstiltskin. Such twists in character and plot make this selection a fractured fairy tale. Choose one of your favorite fairy tales and write a funny version of it. For example, the three little pigs might be weightlifters who are not afraid of anyone. Besides differences in character, your story might have a different setting, plot, or ending.

BRAINSTORM IDEAS Have students think of funny stories they have enjoyed in the past. Ask them to tell what makes them laugh in a story. Write their responses on the board.

Strategy: Create a Chart Explain to students that charts can help them organize the information in the original fairy tale and provide a sequential order for the material they change. Suggest the following:

- Summarize the major problem and solution in the original fairy tale on the left side of the chart.

- List major characters and events in the original fairy tale on the left side of the chart.

- List the corresponding information for their fractured fairy tale on the right side of the chart.

Draft

USE THE CHART Remind students that they are free to change the ideas on their charts as they draft their stories. Invite them to embellish the new version with unexpected plot twists and funny characters.

Revise

SELF-QUESTIONING Ask students to assess their drafts.

- Will a reader recognize that I have based my fractured fairy tale on an original story?

- Have I created funny twists in the story?

- Does my story have a beginning, middle, and end?

PARTNERS Have partners exchange work and discuss how the new tale differs from the original story.

Edit/Proofread

CHECK FOR ERRORS Students should reread their tales to check for spelling, grammar, and punctuation mistakes.

Publish

READ THE STORY Ask students to read their fractured fairy tales aloud. Encourage students to tell the writers which twists in the story were most entertaining.

> ...Orangella told herself that she wasn't sorry she had left the ball late and, trapped inside her coach, was turned into a pumpkin along with it. Life was so much easier now that she wasn't being ordered around by her wicked stepmother. She got to spend her days sunning herself in the pumpkin patch instead.
>
> But the truth was that she had fallen in love with the prince. She overheard the other pumpkins in the patch saying that the prince was going around to all the houses looking for the girl who had lost the glass slipper. How could she prove to him that the slipper was hers if she didn't have any feet?

Presentation Ideas

DRAW A CARTOON Have students create a cartoon with a caption based on one scene in their fractured fairy tale. Compile a class cartoon book. ▶ **Viewing/Representing**

ACT IT OUT Have groups of students act out each other's fractured fairy tales. Allow time for students to gather or make props and costumes. ▶ **Speaking/Listening**

Thumbalina's Lost Brother

Consider students' creative efforts, possibly adding a plus (+) for originality, wit, and imagination.

Scoring Rubric

Excellent	Good	Fair	Unsatisfactory
4: The writer • twists the old story to create an entertaining, original fractured fairy tale. • presents a well-developed story. • uses a mature writing style.	**3:** The writer • presents some humorous plot and character twists. • creates a complete tale. • has a clear style but makes some technical errors.	**2:** The writer • recreates too much of the original tale. • presents a thin or unfinished story. • makes frequent technical errors.	**1:** The writer • summarizes the original tale or writes a story not based on an old tale. • presents disconnected events. • exhibits extensive technical difficulty.

Incomplete 0: The writer leaves the page blank or fails to respond to the writing task. The student does not address the topic or simply paraphrases the prompt. The response is illegible or incoherent.

For a 6-point or an 8-point scale, see pages T109–T110.

Meeting Individual Needs for Writing

EASY	ON-LEVEL	CHALLENGE
Funny Poems Have students write short, funny poems about the characters in *Rumpelstiltskin's Daughter*. Remind them that their poems do not have to rhyme. They may wish to illustrate their poems.	**Fractured Rhymes** Ask students to write couplets about the characters and events in *Rumpelstiltskin's Daughter*. The couplet should express a point in a concise, witty manner.	**Fractured History** Have students choose a historical event and write a fractured tale about it. For example, they may choose the signing of the *Declaration of Independence* and have the signers use invisible ink by mistake.

Listening and Viewing

LISTENING STRATEGIES
As the captioned cartoons are read aloud, encourage students to:

• face the reader and listen attentively.

• summarize the cartoons in their own words.

VIEWING STRATEGIES
Have students:

• explain how the cartoon illustrations support the main idea of the scenes from the fairy tales.

• describe the traits of the illustrated characters.

LANGUAGE SUPPORT

ESL ESL students may want to base their fractured fairy tale on a familiar story from their own culture. They can create a storyboard instead of writing a full tale.

 Invite students to include their fractured fairy tales or another writing project in their portfolios.

Write some indefinite pronouns such as *everybody, nothing, something, both, few,* and *others.* Ask students to identify the singular and plural pronouns.

DAILY LANGUAGE ACTIVITIES

Write the activity on the board or use **Transparency 24.** Have students orally correct the sentences by making the verbs match the indefinite pronouns.

Day 1

1. Everyone know about Rumpelstiltskin.
2. Many listens to his fantastic stories.
3. Someone turn straw into gold.

Day 2

1. Several also tries to do it.
2. Very few comes close.
3. Anything spin better than nothing.

Day 3

1. Somebody fetch Meredith and Rumpelstiltskin from the farm.
2. Both fears the worst.
3. Someone save them.

Day 4

1. Nobody like a greedy king.
2. Few wants to do anything for him.
3. No one die by failing to do a job.

Day 5

1. Everyone in the kingdom now love the king.
2. Many gives the king gifts.
3. Everything work out in the end.

Daily Language Transparency 24

Suggested answers on transparency

Oral Warm-Up Ask volunteers to use *everyone, someone, anyone* sentences. Elicit from students that these pronouns do not refer to specific persons or things.

Introduce Indefinite Pronouns Present:

Indefinite Pronouns

- An **indefinite pronoun** does not refer to a particular person, place, or thing.

- Use a singular verb with a singular indefinite pronoun, such as *anybody, anyone, anything, each, everybody, everyone, everything, nobody, nothing, somebody, someone, something.*

Present the Daily Language Activity, and have students orally correct the sentences by using these verbs: *knows, listen, turns.* Then ask them to write sentences in the present tense, using *everyone, many,* and *someone.*

 Assign the daily Writing Prompt on page 502C.

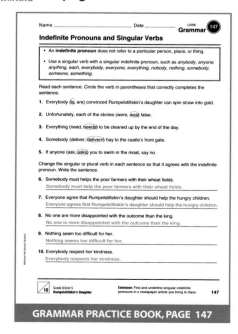

GRAMMAR PRACTICE BOOK, PAGE 147

Review Indefinite Pronouns Have students orally give examples of indefinite pronouns in sentences.

Expand on Indefinite Pronouns Present the following:

Indefinite Pronouns

- Use a plural verb with a plural indefinite pronoun, such as *both, few, many, others, several.*

Present the Daily Language Activity, and have students orally correct the sentences by using these verbs: *try, come, spins.* Then have them write three present-tense sentences, using *several, few,* and *anything.*

 Assign the daily Writing Prompt on page 502C.

GRAMMAR PRACTICE BOOK, PAGE 148

Indefinite Pronouns

DAY 3 — Review and Practice

Learn from the Literature Review indefinite pronouns. Read this sentence from *Rumpelstiltskin's Daughter*:

> **Nobody in the kingdom had anything anymore, because the king had it all.**

Have students identify the indefinite pronouns. (*Anymore* is an indefinite adverb.)

Use Indefinite Pronouns Present the Daily Language Activity, and have students orally correct the sentences by using these verbs: (*fetches, fear, saves.*)

Have students rewrite a paragraph from *Rumpelstiltskin's Daughter*, using indefinite pronouns in place of all nouns. Have them explain what they discover.

 WRITING Assign the daily Writing Prompt on page 502D.

DAY 4 — Review and Practice

Review Indefinite Pronouns Write the sentences from the Daily Language Activities for Days 1 through 3 on the board. Ask students to replace each indefinite pronoun and the verb that matches it. Then present the Daily Language Activity for Day 4.

Mechanics and Usage Before students begin the daily Writing Prompt on page 502D, review quotation marks. Discuss:

Quotations

- Use **quotation marks** before and after the words of a direct quotation.
- Begin a quotation with a capital letter.
- Begin a new paragraph and use a separate set of quotation marks when the speaker changes in dialogue.

 WRITING Assign the daily Writing Prompt on page 502D.

DAY 5 — Assess and Reteach

Assess Use the Daily Language Activity and page 151 of the **Grammar Practice Book** for assessment.

Reteach Have students write a sentence using each of the indefinite pronouns listed on Day 1 and Day 2.

Orally review the rules for agreement between indefinite pronouns and verbs.

Have students create a word wall that lists all the singular and plural indefinite pronouns. Divide them into groups and label the groups.

Use page 152 of the **Grammar Practice Book** for additional reteaching.

WRITING Assign the daily Writing Prompt on page 502D.

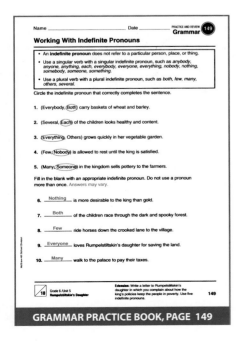

GRAMMAR PRACTICE BOOK, PAGE 149

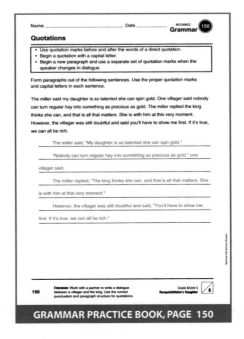

GRAMMAR PRACTICE BOOK, PAGE 150

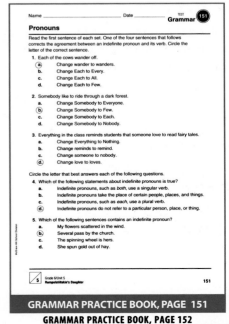

GRAMMAR PRACTICE BOOK, PAGE 151

GRAMMAR PRACTICE BOOK, PAGE 152

5Day Spelling Plan

ESL Help students to identify known base words in the Spelling Words and to use them in sentences. Point out that since *-ance* and *-ence* are pronounced exactly the same way, students will have to memorize the spellings.

DICTATION SENTENCES

Spelling Words

1. We praise her <u>excellent</u> work.
2. Her <u>attendant</u> helped her get dressed.
3. The <u>restless</u> boy couldn't sit quietly.
4. The noise caused a <u>disturbance</u>.
5. Teachers will speak at the <u>conference</u>.
6. I am a <u>resident</u> of this town.
7. The bugs were an <u>annoyance</u>.
8. I know the <u>occupant</u> of that house.
9. Her invention showed her <u>cleverness</u>.
10. Libraries have <u>reference</u> books.
11. That lady is an <u>acquaintance</u> of mine.
12. The stubborn girl was <u>persistent</u>.
13. If you are blind, you are <u>sightless</u>.
14. He was a <u>descendant</u> of an old tribe.
15. Fast falls can cause <u>dizziness</u>.
16. The <u>occurrence</u> of snow is rare here.
17. The baby gives us <u>boundless</u> joy.
18. <u>Emptiness</u> filled the hollow tree.
19. The <u>correspondent</u> wrote letters.
20. Let's stay, <u>regardless</u> of the time.

Challenge Words

21. We ate <u>barley</u> and rice.
22. <u>Coincidences</u> are not planned.
23. <u>Mufflers</u> are scarves.
24. Act <u>sheepishly</u> if you get caught.
25. Sugar will <u>sweeten</u> this tea.

DAY 1 Pretest

Assess Prior Knowledge Use the Dictation Sentences and **Spelling Practice Book** page 147 for the pretest. Allow students to correct their own papers. Students who require a modified list may be tested on the first ten words.

Spelling Words		Challenge Words
1. **excellent**	11. acquain-	21. **barley**
2. attendant	tance	22. **coinci-**
3. **restless**	12. persistent	**dences**
4. distur-	13. sightless	23. **mufflers**
bance	14. descen-	24. **sheep-**
5. confer-	dant	**ishly**
ence	15. dizziness	25. **sweeten**
6. resident	16. occurrence	
7. annoy-	17. boundless	
ance	18. emptiness	
8. occupant	19. correspondent	
9. cleverness	20. regardless	
10. reference		

*Note: Words in **dark type** are from the story.*

Word Study On page 148 of the **Spelling Practice Book** are word study steps and an at-home activity.

DAY 2 Explore the Pattern

Sort and Spell Words Write *dizziness* on the board. Have students identify the base word and the suffix. (*dizzy, -ness*) Ask how the spelling of the base word changes. (*y changes to i*) Have students sort the words as below.

Words with		
-ness	*-ant*	*-ance*
cleverness	attendant	disturbance
dizziness	occupant	annoyance
emptiness	descendant	acquaintance
-less	*-ent*	*-ence*
restless	excellent	conference
sightless	resident	reference
boundless	persistent	occurrence
regardless	correspon-	
	dent	

Spelling Patterns Have students identify which base words change their spelling when the suffix is added and identify the changes. (*excel, reside, occupy, dizzy, occur, empty*)

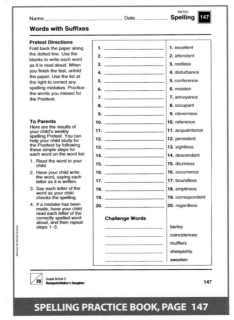

Words with Suffixes

DAY 3 — Practice and Extend

Word Meaning: Suffixes Review with students how knowing the meaning of a word's suffix helps to define the word. Give students the following definitions: -*ness* means "the state of being"; -*less* means "without"; -*ant* and -*ent* mean "doing or being" or "one who does"; -*ance* and -*ence* mean "the process of" or "the state of." Ask students to define each word based on the meaning of its suffix.

If students need extra practice, have partners give each other a midweek test.

Glossary Review how a Glossary entry shows multiple meanings. Have students

- predict which Challenge Word will be listed with multiple meanings. (*mufflers*)

- check the Glossary to see if they are correct.

- use both meanings of the word to write context sentences.

DAY 4 — Proofread and Write

Proofread Sentences Write these sentences on the chalkboard, including the misspelled words. Ask students to proofread, circle incorrect spellings, and write the correct spellings. There are two spelling errors in each sentence.

The restless occupent caused a disturbence. (occupant, disturbance)

The persistant dizzyness was an annoyance. (persistent, dizziness)

Have students create additional sentences with errors for partners to correct.

 Have students use as many Spelling Words as possible in the daily Writing Prompt on page 502D. Remind students to proofread their writing for errors in spelling, grammar, and punctuation.

DAY 5 — Assess and Reteach

Assess Students' Knowledge Use page 152 of the **Spelling Practice Book** or the Dictation Sentences on page 531O for the posttest.

 Personal Word List If students have trouble with any words in the lesson, suggest they add them to their personal lists of troublesome words in their journals. Have students write a context sentence for each word.

Students should refer to their word lists during later writing activities.

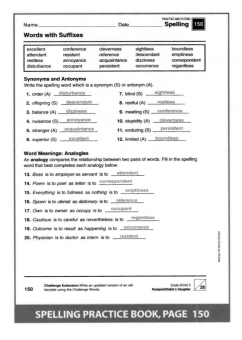

SPELLING PRACTICE BOOK, PAGE 150

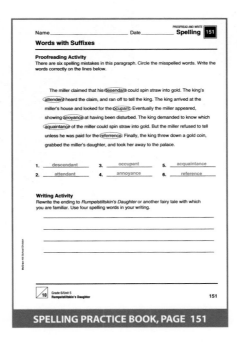

SPELLING PRACTICE BOOK, PAGE 151

SPELLING PRACTICE BOOK, PAGE 152

531P

Cumulative Review

with **Expository Text**

Time to Review

Anthology

The History of Money

Selection Summary Salt, shells, tea leaves, seeds, camels, and dried fish have all been used as money. Students will learn how these early forms of money gave way to precious metals as well as paper currency.

Stories in Art focuses on the **comprehension** skill

Reading Strategy applies the **comprehension** skill

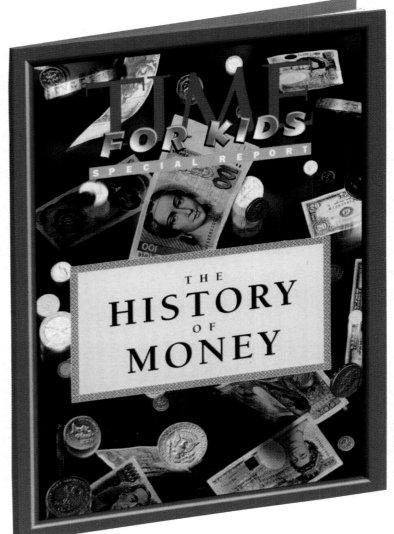

Listening Library

INSTRUCTIONAL pages 534–541

Time to Reread

Reread Leveled Books

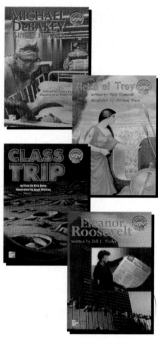

EASY
Lesson on pages 541A and 541D

INDEPENDENT
Lesson on pages 541B and 541D

CHALLENGE
Lesson on pages 541C and 541D

🏠 *Take-Home version available*

Leveled Practice

EASY
Reteach, 177–183 Blackline masters with reteaching opportunities for each assessed skill

INDEPENDENT/ON-LEVEL
Practice, 177–183 Workbook with Take-Home stories and practice opportunities for each assessed skill and story comprehension

CHALLENGE
Extend, 177–183 Blackline masters that offer challenge activities for each assessed skill

Quizzes Prepared by 📖 **Accelerated Reader**

WORKSTATION Activities

Science . . . . Matter, *539*

Math . . . . Compare Currencies, *539*

Art . . . . Design a Coin, *539*

Language Arts . . Read Aloud, *532E*

Writing . . . . Dialogue, *538*

Research and Inquiry . . . . . . Find Out More, *539*

Internet Activities . . . . www.mhschool.com/reading

Suggested
Lesson Planner

READING AND LANGUAGE ARTS	DAY 1 — Focus on Reading and Skills	DAY 2 — Read the Literature

READING AND LANGUAGE ARTS

- ● Comprehension
- ● Vocabulary
- ● Phonics/Decoding
- ● Study Skills
- ● Listening, Speaking, Viewing, Representing

DAY 1 — Focus on Reading and Skills

 Read Aloud: Social Studies Nonfiction, 532E
"The Story of Money"

Develop Visual Literacy, 532

☑ **Review Sequence of Events,** 533A–533B
   Teaching Chart 145
   Reteach, Practice, Extend, 177

 Reading Strategy: Sequence of Events, 533
"Quarters for the States"

 Intervention Program

DAY 2 — Read the Literature

Build Background, 534A
Develop Oral Language

Vocabulary, 534B–534C

automated	currency	loans
bartering	fee	teller

Teaching Chart 146
Word Building Manipulative Cards
Reteach, Practice, Extend, 178

 Read the Selection, 534–537
   ☑ Sequence of Events
   ☑ Make Inferences

Genre: Magazine Article, 535

 Intervention Program

● Curriculum Connections

 Works of Art, 532

 Social Studies, 534A

● Writing

Writing Prompt: What would you do if you won a thousand dollars to give to a charity? Explain to which organization you would give it, and why.

Writing Prompt: Write a funny dialogue between two people who are trying to barter different things to get what they want.

Journal Writing, 537
Quick-Write

● Grammar

Introduce the Concept: Pronoun-Verb Agreement, 541M
Daily Language Activity
1. We is learning about money.
2. They uses silver money, not paper.
3. It have ridges on it.

Grammar Practice Book, 153

Teach the Concept: Pronoun-Verb Agreement, 541M
Daily Language Activity
1. Not everybody are in need of money.
2. He says he never use money.
3. Few has enough money these days.

Grammar Practice Book, 154

● Spelling

Pretest: Words from Math, 541O
Spelling Practice Book, 153, 154

Explore the Pattern: Words from Math, 541O
Spelling Practice Book, 155

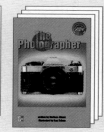

Meeting Individual Needs

 = Skill Assessed in Unit Test

 Intervention Program Available

Read EVERY DAY

DAY 3

Rereading for Fluency, 536

Story Questions and Activities, 538–539
Reteach, Practice, Extend, 179

Study Skill, 540
☑ **Read a Chart**
Teaching Chart 147
Reteach, Practice, Extend, 180

Test Power, 541

 Read the Leveled Books, 541A–541D
Guided Reading
Phonics
☑ **Comprehension**

ⓘ Intervention Program

  **Social Studies,** 539

 Writing Prompt: Which do you think is better, a barter system or a monetary one? Explain your choice.

Writing Process: Writing a Story, 541K
Prewrite, Draft

Review and Practice: Pronoun-Verb Agreement, 541N
Daily Language Activity
1. He spend money in that store.
2. It are in the mall near the bank.
3. Everyone have an account there.

Grammar Practice Book, 155

Practice and Extend: Words from Math, 541P
Spelling Practice Book, 156

DAY 4

 Read the Leveled Books and Self-Selected Books

☑ **Review Judgments and Decisions,** 541E–541F
Teaching Chart 148
Reteach, Practice, Extend, 181
Language Support, 198

☑ **Review Context Clues,** 541G–541H
Teaching Chart 149
Reteach, Practice, Extend, 182
Language Support, 199

ⓘ Intervention Program

 Writing Prompt: You are thinking of making this article into a movie, a play, or a TV special. Write a different title for each, and a catchy description to interest a production company.
Writing Process: Writing a Story, 541K
Revise
Meeting Individual Needs for Writing, 541L

Review and Practice: Pronoun-Verb Agreement, 541N
Daily Language Activity
1. Do you provides banking services?
2. They is going to the ATM.
3. We has time to count the money.

Grammar Practice Book, 156

Proofread and Write: Words from Math, 541P
Spelling Practice Book, 157

DAY 5

 Read Self-Selected Books

☑ **Review Denotation and Connotation,** 541I–541J
Teaching Chart 150
Reteach, Practice, Extend, 183
Language Support, 200

Listening, Speaking, Viewing, Representing, 541L

ⓘ Intervention Program

 Writing Prompt: Write an explanation of how a credit card works for a brochure a bank wants to create.

Writing Process: Writing a Story, 541K
Edit/Proofread, Publish

Assess and Reteach: Pronoun-Verb Agreement, 541N
Daily Language Activity
1. If they sprints, they'll be there on time.
2. Nothing here be as old as that coin.
3. I has learned a lot about money.

Grammar Practice Book, 157–158

Assess and Reteach: Words from Math, 541P
Spelling Practice Book, 158

Social Studies

Read Aloud

The Story of Money

a nonfiction article by Carolyn Kain

Exchange of Goods

Long ago, people had to wander from place to place searching for food. But about 10,000 years ago, people found that if they collected seeds and planted them, a crop would grow. They also learned to tame wild animals. Now they had a permanent food supply and there was no need to wander. Gradually small villages grew up.

These people made baskets, sacks, and pots for storing their food. They also made tools to dig the land, harvest their crops, and build their homes. Over the years, they discovered that some people were better at making pots, while others were better at making baskets or hoes. The pot-maker might exchange a pot for some food, or a tool. Someone who made an ax might feel it was worth four pots, because the ax took longer to make. The people must have agreed upon a fair way of exchanging items.

Continued on pages T6–T7

Oral Comprehension

LISTENING AND SPEAKING Ask students to listen for the sequence of events as you read this nonfiction article. Afterward, ask:

• How did people first exchange goods and services?

• Why did people first start using forms of money?

Continue the discussion by displaying several dollar bills. Ask: Why are these bills valuable?

GENRE STUDY: SOCIAL STUDIES ARTICLE

Discuss some of the literary devices and techniques in "The Story of Money."

• Point out that headings are often used in nonfiction articles. Ask: How do the headings in this essay help you find information?

• Discuss with students that a nonfiction article usually gives short descriptions of events, discoveries, and ideas. Ask: Why did the barter system not always work well?

• Remind students that nonfiction pieces present facts in logical order. Ask: Why were banks set up?

Activity Have groups of students design their own currency. They will need colored pencils, paper, and scissors. Tell students to think about the factors described in the nonfiction essay—the symbols and markings on the bills, as well as the value and size of each bill. Groups can share their currencies.

▶ **Spatial/Mathematical**

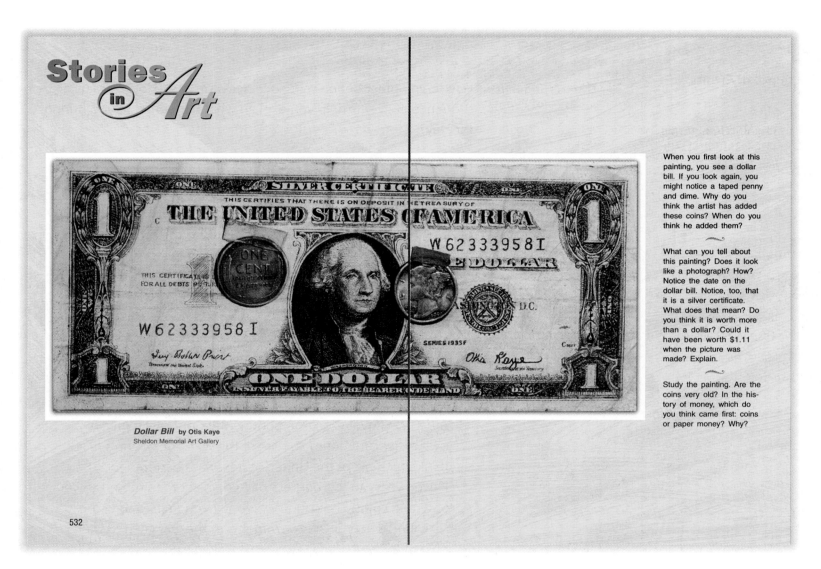

Stories in Art

When you first look at this painting, you see a dollar bill. If you look again, you might notice a taped penny and dime. Why do you think the artist has added these coins? When do you think he added them?

What can you tell about this painting? Does it look like a photograph? How? Notice the date on the dollar bill. Notice, too, that it is a silver certificate. What does that mean? Do you think it is worth more than a dollar? Could it have been worth $1.11 when the picture was made? Explain.

Study the painting. Are the coins very old? In the history of money, which do you think came first: coins or paper money? Why?

Dollar Bill by Otis Kaye
Sheldon Memorial Art Gallery

532

Objective: Identify Sequence of Events

VIEWING This painting is so realistic that it looks like a photograph. Have students study the painting carefully and then describe it in their own words. Ask them if their own familiarity with the elements in the painting makes it easy to recall the details. Have students comment on some differences between this money and the money they see every day.

Read the page with students, encouraging individual interpretations of the painting.

Students can make observations about sequence of events. For example:

- The artist probably painted the dollar bill first and then added the coins later.

- He probably made a detailed drawing of the bill before painting it.

REPRESENTING Have students make a series of drawings showing an everyday object. They should change the object somehow in each drawing.

Review Sequence of Events

OBJECTIVES

Students will determine the sequence of events in a selection.

Skills Finder

Sequence of Events

Introduce	41A-B
Review	101A-B, 431G-H, 469A-B, 481E-F, 501G-H, 533A-B
Test	Unit 1, Unit 5

LANGUAGE SUPPORT

ESL Write time-order words such as *first, next,* and *last* on separate cards. Have volunteers hold the cards and position themselves in sequential order.

PREPARE

Discuss Sequence of Events Have a volunteer define sequence of events. Ask: How does using sequence of events help you explain what happened to you during the day?

TEACH

Define Time-Order Words Remind students that time-order words such as *first, next,* and *last* signal the sequence of events. Other clues to the sequence of events may be given in dates and times in an article or story.

Early Money in the United States

In the beginning, people in the American colonies used money from many European countries. At the time of the American Revolution, the Continental Congress issued its own American money to pay for the war. The nation's first bank, the Bank of the United States, was chartered in 1781. Eleven years later, Congress passed an act to mint both silver and gold coins. The country's money was unified until the Civil War, when both governments in the war created their own money.

Teaching Chart 145

Read the Passage and Model the Skill Display **Teaching Chart 145.** Ask students to pay attention to words and dates that signal the sequence of events.

MODEL When I read the words *In the beginning* and then *At the time of the American Revolution,* I know that the writer is telling things in the order in which they happened.

Identify Time-Order Words Ask students to underline the time-order words that show the sequence of events.

Create a Sequence of Events Chart

GROUP

Have students use a Sequence of Events chart to record the events in the **Teaching Chart** passage in the order in which they occurred.

▶ Visual

Sequence of Events

American money came into existence during the American Revolution.

In 1781, the first U.S. bank was established.

In 1792, gold and silver coins were minted.

During the Civil War, both sides created their own money.

Put Events in Sequence

Have students think of an event such as going to a concert. Ask them to create a sequence of events chart of the event. Next have them scramble the events on their charts. Then have partners exchange scrambled events and put them in the correct order.

ALTERNATE TEACHING STRATEGY

SEQUENCE OF EVENTS

For a different approach to teaching this skill, see page T68.

 **Intervention** ▶ **Skills Intervention Guide**, for direct instruction and extra practice with sequence of events

Meeting Individual Needs for Comprehension

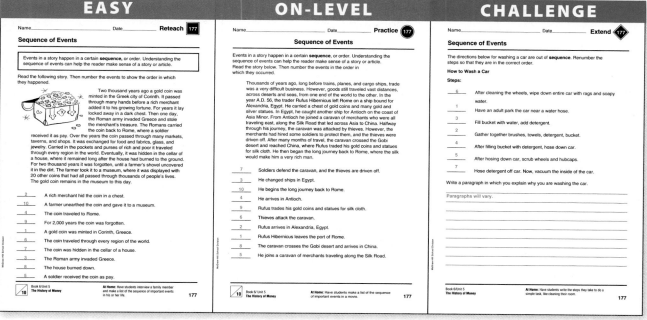

Reteach, 177   Practice, 177   Extend, 177

OBJECTIVES

Students will recognize sequence of events.

Apply Sequence of Events

READING STRATEGY

Sequence of Events

Develop a strategy for recognizing the sequence of events.

1. **Picture the order** of events in your mind. What happens first? next? last?

2. **Look for clue words,** such as *first, then, next,* and *in the end.* Dates are also clues to time order.

3. **As you read,** check your understanding. Ask yourself: What happened first? What might happen next?

4. **Go back and reread** if the order of events does not make sense.

5. **Retell the order of events** in your own words.

533

Quarters for the States

For a long time, coin collectors had complained that American coins lacked variety. The 50 State Quarters Program has changed all that. Under the program, the United States Mint is redesigning the quarter. In all, there will be 50 new designs that will honor the 50 states.

Who Goes First?

Each year between 1999 and 2008, five new quarters will be released. The mint is issuing the coins in the order in which the states joined the Union. As the first state to join, Delaware was honored with the first quarter. Coins for Pennsylvania, New Jersey, Georgia, and Connecticut also appeared in 1999. The year 2000 gave us quarters honoring Massachusetts, Maryland, South Carolina, New Hampshire, and Virginia.

Design Decisions

How does the Mint decide on the designs? First, each state presents several suggestions for its coin. (Most states suggest historical sites or state symbols.) The Mint then produces designs for these ideas. Next, the United States Fine Arts Commission and the Secretary of the Treasury review the designs and make a recommendation. In the end, the governor of the state makes the final choice.

The new design appears only on the back of the quarter. George Washington remains on the front. When all the state quarters have been produced, however, the Mint will stop making them. After 2008, a totally new quarter design will be introduced.

THE QUARTER

WEIGHT:	5.679 grams
DIAMETER:	24.26 mm
THICKNESS:	1.75 mm
COMPOSITION:	91.67% copper
	8.33% nickel
EDGE:	Reeded

PREVIEW Have students preview "Quarters for the States." Remind them that the sequence of events tells what happens first, next, and last. Ask:

- Is this passage fiction or nonfiction? How can you tell? (nonfiction; straightforward information, no narration or dialogue)

- What is the passage about? (quarters that have been redesigned to honor the 50 states of the United States)

SET PURPOSE Explain that students will apply what they have learned about sequence of events as they read "Quarters for the States."

APPLY THE STRATEGY Discuss this strategy for determining sequence of events:

- Look for dates and for clue words such as *first, then, next,* and *in the end* to help you know the time order.

- Picture the order of events in your mind. What happened first? Next?

- Retell the order of events to a partner.

- If you are not sure of the order of events, reread.

Activity Have each student create a Sequence of Events chart for the passage.

Build Background

Social Studies

Concept: Money

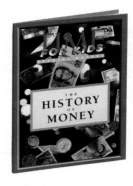

Evaluate Prior Knowledge

CONCEPT: MONEY Money helps people get the goods and services they need. Ask students to share what they know about money and why it's needed.

PUT EVENTS IN ORDER Have students list what they know about how money was created. Ask: What did money replace? Create a flow chart. ▶ **Logical/Visual**

> Family members shared things they grew and made.

▼

> People exchanged goods within villages.

▼

> Villages traded with other villages.

▼

> Groups of people developed their own money to make trading easier.

Graphic Organizer 17

FIRST TRADE Ask students to imagine that they are ancient people traveling to trade in a country never before visited by outsiders. How will they try to establish contact and trade? Have them write what they would do to make this first trading trip a success.

ONE **WRITING**

Develop Oral Language

DISCUSS MONEY Display or share **ESL** pictures of different kinds of money. Have students describe what they see. Then discuss how money is used. Ask students to brainstorm what they can buy with money. Write the words on the board. Discuss the meaning of each word and have students use it in a sentence.

Have students imagine that they live in a time when there is no money. Ask: How do you get what you need? Have small groups create skits that try to answer this question. Encourage students to use the words listed on the chalkboard.

Invite the groups to perform their skits for the class. Then have the class discuss the solutions the different groups found.

TEACHING TIP

MANAGEMENT To make sure that every student has the chance to practice performing before a group, tell groups that every student must have a speaking part in the skit.

LANGUAGE SUPPORT

See the **Language Support Book**, pages 193–196, for teaching suggestions for Build Background.

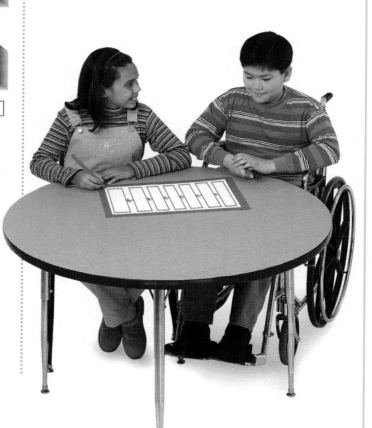

OBJECTIVES

Students will use context clues to determine the meanings of vocabulary words.

Definitions

teller (p. 536) a bank clerk who gives out or receives money

automated (p. 536) controlled by machines

fee (p. 537) a charge for a service

currency (p. 536) money used in a country

loans (p. 537) money given that must be repaid

bartering (p. 535) trading goods and services without using money

Story Words

These words from the selection may be unfamiliar. Before students read, have them check the meanings and pronunciations of the words in the Glossary beginning on page 678 or in a dictionary.

- cowrie, p. 535
- depositors, p. 537

teller
automated
fee
currency
loans
bartering

Vocabulary

Teach Vocabulary in Context

Identify Vocabulary Words Display **Teaching Chart 146** and read it with students. Ask volunteers to circle the vocabulary word in each sentence and underline the words that give clues to the word's meaning.

A Long Way

1. Today, many of the duties that used to be done by a bank teller, a real person, are done by machines. **2.** You see these replacements for people, such as automated teller machines, every day. **3.** For a fee that is often a dollar, these machines give you money. **4.** Suddenly, you have real currency to buy what you need. **5.** Sometimes you can even get a loan from these machines, but don't forget you have to repay it. **6.** We've come a long way from the days of bartering, when you traded something to get what you wanted.

Teaching Chart 146

Discuss Meanings Ask questions like these to help clarify word meanings:

- What does the teller do with the money you deposit?
- If a person's job is now automated, how does the work get done?
- Are you charged a fee for your locker?
- Where can you spend U.S. currency?
- How is a loan different from a gift?
- If you are bartering your glove for a friend's bat, will you need money?

Activities

Practice

Use Verbal Clues Have partners take turns choosing a vocabulary card and giving one clue to its meaning. The other student wins the card by guessing the word. ▶ **Linguistic/Interpersonal**

  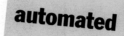

Word Building Manipulative Cards

Write Captions   Have students find or draw pictures that illustrate at least three of the vocabulary words. Ask them to write captions for the pictures, using as many vocabulary words as possible. ▶ **Visual/ Linguistic**

Assess Vocabulary

Use Words in Context Ask students to write a business letter to the president of a local bank. Tell students that the letter should request information about borrowing money to open a new business. Tell students use as many of the vocabulary words as possible. Have students share letters.

Meeting Individual Needs for Vocabulary

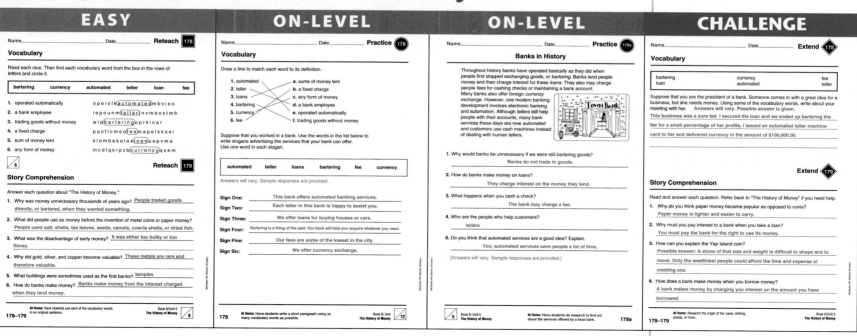

EASY	ON-LEVEL	ON-LEVEL	CHALLENGE
Reteach, 178	Practice, 178 Take-Home Story	Practice, 178a	Extend, 178

Comprehension

Prereading Strategies

PREVIEW AND PREDICT Have students read the title and preview the article by looking at the headings, illustrations, and captions.

- What information does the title give you about the article?
- What information in the captions suggests that events will be presented in sequential order?
- What will this article be about?
- What tells you this article is nonfiction? (the word *history* in the title, photographs of real-life objects, factual captions) *Genre*

SET PURPOSES What do students hope to learn by reading this article? For example:

- What was the first form of money?
- How and why did money change?

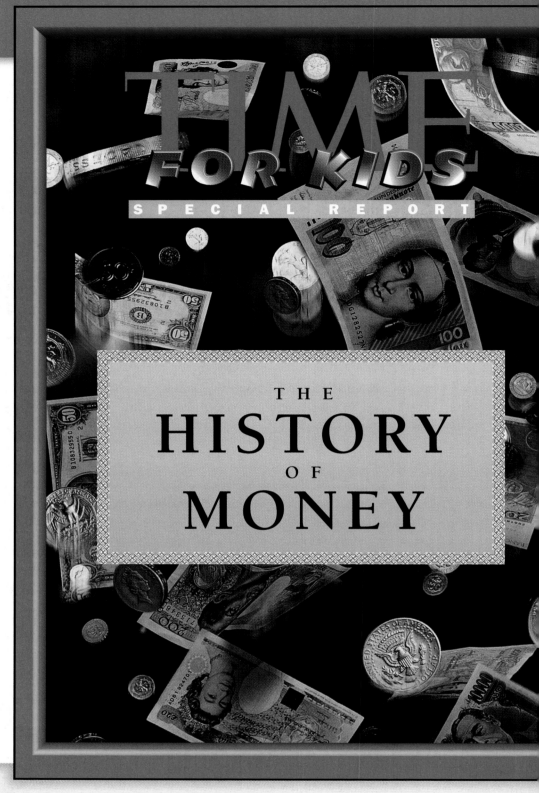

TIME FOR KIDS
SPECIAL REPORT

THE
HISTORY
OF
MONEY

Meeting Individual Needs · Grouping Suggestions for Strategic Reading

EASY	ON-LEVEL	CHALLENGE
Read Together Read the article with students or suggest they listen to the **Listening Library** while they read. Have students use the Sequence of Events chart to record information. Comprehension and Intervention prompts offer additional help with decoding, vocabulary, and comprehension.	**Guided Instruction** Choose from the Comprehension questions as you read the story with students or after they have played the **Listening Library**. Have them fill in information on the Sequence of Events chart as they read.	**Read Independently** Ask students to read on their own. Remind them that paying attention to the order of events can give them a clearer understanding of the article. Have them create a Sequence of Events chart to fill in as they read. After reading, they can use it to help summarize the article.

COVER: FPG; WAMPUM: MANSELL/TIME INC; CHINESE PAPER MONEY/TIME LIFE PICTURE COLLECTION; COWRIE SHELLS: BERNHEIM-RAPHO/LIAISON

From Camels to Coins

Thousands of years ago, no one needed money. People traded what they had in order to get what they wanted from others. A person might trade an animal skin for grain, or pottery for food. This is called *bartering.* For bartering to work, each trader must have something the other wants. That didn't always work out. Soon communities invented money—tokens that had the same value to everyone in the marketplace. **1**

Early "money" varied from culture to culture. People traded salt, shells, tea leaves, seeds, camels, or dried fish for the things they needed. The ancient Chinese used cowrie shells. Some Native Americans used *wampum,* small polished shells or beads strung together. But seeds and tea leaves often blew away. And can you imagine taking a couple of camels as cash when you go shopping? To make buying easier, people began using precious metals as money. Gold, silver, and copper were hard to find and therefore valuable. **2**

This paper money from China was issued in the 9th century.

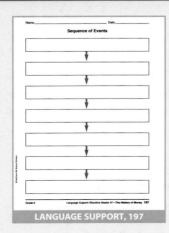

Cowrie shells have been used as money in many cultures. These are from Africa.

This beaded belt from the 1600s is an example of *wampum.*

535

Comprehension

☑ **Apply Sequence of Events**

☑ **Apply Make Inferences**

STRATEGIC READING Before we begin reading, let's prepare a Sequence of Events chart so we can keep track of the events described in the article.

1 **SEQUENCE OF EVENTS** What are some time-order words on this page, including dates and times, that help show the sequence of events? *(thousands of years ago, soon)* Let's list the events on the chart.

2 **MAKE INFERENCES** Using the information given on this page and your own knowledge, what can you infer about why gold, silver, and copper coins made buying easier? (These metals were valuable, so people wanted them; they were easy to carry and tough enough to pass through many hands.)

Genre

Magazine Article

Explain that a social studies article in a magazine:

• gives a short description of events, discoveries, or ideas.

• presents facts in logical order.

• includes special text features, such as headings, sidebars, captions, charts, and diagrams.

Activity After students read *The History of Money,* have them identify who the article states were the first bankers.

LANGUAGE SUPPORT

This chart is available as a blackline master in the **Language Support Book.**

Name_____ Date_____
Sequence of Events

Comprehension

 MAKE INFERENCES What inferences can you make about why people use credit cards and checks instead of cash? (more convenient, safer than carrying cash)

 SEQUENCE OF EVENTS How can you tell the order of events described on this page? (by the time-order words and dates: *years ago, in 2500* B.C., *later, now, today*) Let's complete the chart.

Thousands of years ago, people got things from others by bartering.

⬇

Soon communities invented "money," such as shells, seeds, and camels.

⬇

In 2500 B.C., precious metals were used as money in Egypt and Asia.

⬇

Later metal money was used widely in Europe and the Middle East.

⬇

1,800 years ago, the Chinese invented paper money.

⬇

Now there are about 140 different kinds of currencies in the world.

⬇

Today checks and credit cards are often used instead of cash.

ORGANIZE INFORMATION Ask volunteers to tell the most important information they have learned from the article. Then have partners write sentences that summarize the article. *Summarize*

About 4,500 years ago, in 2500 B.C., precious metals were used to pay for goods and services in Egypt and Asia. Later, metal money began to be used in Europe and the Middle East. When the Chinese invented paper and printing 1,800 years ago, they began using paper money.

Now there are about 140 different kinds of money, or currencies, in use in the world. When you travel in another country and want to buy things, you usually have to exchange your money for the currency of the country you are in.

Today we can also pay for things with credit cards or checks. ATM (automated teller machine) cards allow us to get cash whenever we need it. Money has come a long way. We'll never have to carry change for a camel again!

◄ A Hebrew coin called a shekel dates from around A.D. 80.

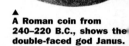
◄ This is one of the first coins made in Persia, from about 400 B.C.

▲ A Roman coin from 240–220 B.C., shows the double-faced god Janus.

◄ This Egyptian gold coin dates from 170–117 B.C.

DID YOU KNOW? MONEY FACTS

◆ The Bank of North America, the first U.S. bank, opened in Philadelphia, Pennsylvania, in 1781.

◆ About 63 billion checks are written and cashed in the U.S. each year.

◆ The piggy bank got its name from a kind of clay called *pygg*. Long ago, people stored their money in pygg-clay jars. Later, these jars were made in the shape of a pig and were called piggy banks.

◆ On Yap Island in the Pacific, money is a stone with a hole in the middle so the stone can be rolled with a long pole. Yap money stones can weigh more than 500 pounds and be 12 feet across.

536

REREADING FOR *Fluency*

 Have students form small groups and take turns reading paragraphs aloud.

READING RATE When you evaluate rate, have the student read aloud from the story for one minute. Place a stick-on note after the last word read. Count words read. To evaluate students' performance, see the

Running Record in the **Fluency Assessment** book.

ⓘ **Intervention** ▶ For leveled fluency lessons, passages, and norms charts, see **Skills Intervention Guide**, Part 4, Fluency.

HOW BANKS MAKE MONEY

Ancient temples were the first banks. Temples were a safe place to store precious metals. Some temples exchanged foreign coins and made loans to people.

As trade between different cities and countries increased, traveling merchants paid money changers to exchange coins from different cities. Money changers also exchanged coins for gold or silver. They were the first bankers.

Modern banks provide many money-related services. Your money can earn more money in a bank. The bank pays you a fee, called interest, for allowing it to use your money.

Banks make money by lending money. The bank uses your money and other depositors' money to make loans. If you borrow money from a bank, you must pay back the amount you borrowed plus an extra fee. That fee is also called interest. The interest that borrowers pay the bank is more than the interest the bank pays you for letting it use your money. The difference between what borrowers pay in interest and the interest the bank pays out to its depositors is the bank's profit.

FIND OUT MORE
Visit our website:
www.mhschool.com/reading

TOP RIGHT: JOHN MEYER FOR TIME FOR KIDS; BOTTOM RIGHT: CORBIS; OPPOSITE PAGE: DAVID ARKY

Based on an article in *TIME FOR KIDS*.

Money Matters

◆ Arrange 10 pennies in a triangle, as shown above.

◆ Can you move only three pennies in such a way that the triangle points down instead of up?

A Yap Island rock coin.

Comprehension

Return to Predictions and Purposes

Ask students to review the predictions they made about the article. Were their predictions accurate? Did the article answer their questions?

INFORMAL ASSESSMENT

SEQUENCE OF EVENTS

HOW TO ASSESS

• Have students give a quick oral summary of the history of money.

• Ask students to identify words that signal sequence of events.

Students should be able to tell the important events, from bartering to using ATM cards, in the correct sequence and to identify time-order words and phrases that show sequence of events.

FOLLOW UP

Students who cannot give a time-order summary of the sequence of events in this article should go over their Sequence of Events charts with you to see if they listed the important events in order.

LITERARY RESPONSE

QUICK-WRITE Have students record their thoughts about the article. Ask: Do you agree that using money is better than bartering? How does money make your life easier?

ORAL RESPONSE Have volunteers share their writings and discuss the information they found the most interesting.

RESEARCH AND INQUIRY Have groups of students use the library or Internet to research an aspect of money that interests them. Possible topics include: how coins are minted; how gold bullion is stored and protected; rare coins and paper money; the new European currency.

inter NET CONNECTION For more information or activities on this topic go to *www.mhschool.com/reading*

Story Questions

Have students discuss or write answers to the questions on page 538.

Answers:

1. They bartered something they had for something they wanted from others.
   Literal/Sequence of Events

2. Different cultures valued different items.
   Inferential/Make Inferences

3. Possible answer: People want money to buy what they can't produce themselves.
   Critical/Make Inferences

4. Bartering; the use of money of all types; coins made of precious metals; paper money; credit cards and checks.
   Critical/Summarize

5. The illustration makes you think about what currency looks like and how it's used.
   Critical/Reading Across Texts

Write a Dialogue For a lesson related to this writing activity, see pages 541K–541L.

Story Questions & Activities

1. How did people "buy" things before there was money?

2. Why did early forms of money vary from culture to culture?

3. Why do you think paper money and coins have become so important throughout the years?

4. What different types of payment does this selection describe?

5. What does the picture on page 532 add to this selection? Explain.

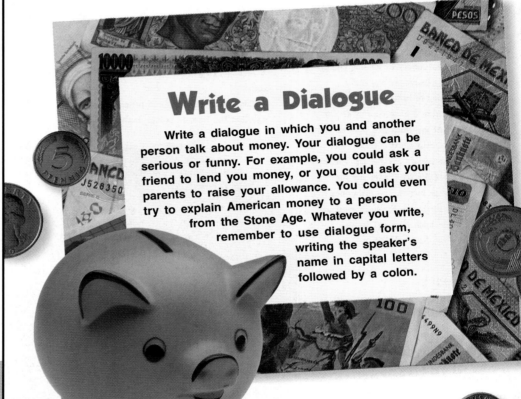

Write a Dialogue

Write a dialogue in which you and another person talk about money. Your dialogue can be serious or funny. For example, you could ask a friend to lend you money, or you could ask your parents to raise your allowance. You could even try to explain American money to a person from the Stone Age. Whatever you write, remember to use dialogue form, writing the speaker's name in capital letters followed by a colon.

Meeting Individual Needs

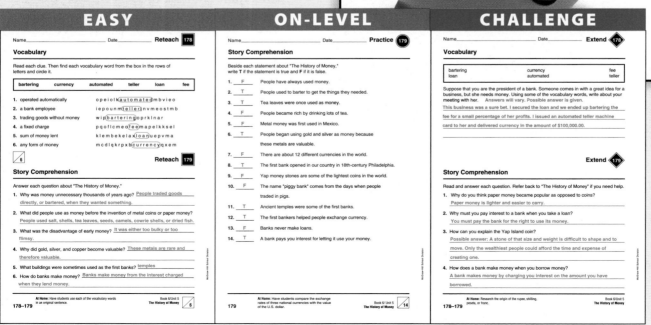

Reteach, 179   Practice, 179   Extend, 179

Design a Coin

One of the first coins was made in Persia, in about 400 B.C. Use modeling clay that dries in the air to make a coin that could be used in a country today. To make your coin interesting, you could use seashells, colored beads, toothpicks, and other small objects. Be sure to include a motto as well as a label that states your coin's value and its country of origin.

Compare Currencies

How many Mexican pesos are there in one U.S. dollar? How many Kenyan shillings? How many Turkish lira? Make a chart to show the exchange rate for five or six countries. Then figure out how much a $100 bicycle would cost in each of these currencies.

| Mexico | Kenya | Turkey |

Find Out More

Find out more information about one of these topics:
- the history of paper money
- Benjamin Franklin's role in establishing the first U.S. bank
- An unusual type of money used today.

Take notes on the information you find. Use your notes to give an oral report to your group or the class.

Story Activities

Design a Coin

Materials: pencil, paper, air-drying modeling clay, as well as small objects such as beads

ONE Have students brainstorm ideas on paper before they design their coins. For inspiration, bring in books on money that show coins. Students can explain to the class why they chose their particular designs.

Compare Currencies

Materials: pencil, paper, colored pencils

GROUP Have students research exchange rates in the newspaper or on the Internet. They can also call money exchange firms to get the most recent rates for German marks, French francs, and Dutch guilders. Each group member can choose a different currency to research, and then students can help each other calculate the cost of a $100 bicycle in each currency.

Find Out More

RESEARCH AND INQUIRY Have each group choose one of the three topics to research. Encourage students to use different sources to research their topics. Group members can put their information together and decide which to include in their oral report.

interNET CONNECTION For more information about money, students can visit
www.mhschool.com/reading

SCIENCE: MATTER Gold, silver, and copper are metals used in making coins. They are also examples of elements. Have students research these elements and chart them comparing the following properties: density, melting point, boiling point, and practical uses.

What to Look For Check responses to see that each student:
- creates a three-column, four-row chart
- accurately compares the three elements

CHALLENGE

539

Study Skills

GRAPHIC AIDS

OBJECTIVES (TESTED) Students will understand how to read a chart.

PREPARE Display **Teaching Chart 147.** Read the first paragraph with students.

TEACH Have students look at the chart. What is the purpose of this chart? (to show the differences among coins)

PRACTICE Have students answer questions 1–5. **1.** the coin from Persia **2.** They are all made of metal **3.** to facilitate moving it by placing a pole through the middle and rolling it **4.** Possible answer: to facilitate transport without tearing clothes, purses, or skin. Square coins can cause such problems. **5.** It helps show the difference among the various coins.

ASSESS/CLOSE Ask students to make their own charts comparing U.S. coins. Charts should show an understanding of the differences and similarities among the coins.

Study SKILLS

Read a Chart

From the Yap money stone to the Italian lira and the U.S. dollar, coins and paper money differ from country to country. Some money has unusual designs, mottoes, or symbols. Other money is plain looking. Some countries change the look of their money every few decades. Others have never redesigned their currency.

Look at the chart below. Notice the style of the ancient and modern coins. What are the similarities and differences?

COINS – PAST AND PRESENT

A Hebrew coin called a shekel dates from around A.D. 80.

A Roman coin from 240–220 B.C. shows the double-faced god Janus.

An Egyptian gold coin dates from 170–117 B.C.

One of the first coins, made in Persia, from about 400 B.C.

The copper penny is the U.S. coin of the smallest denomination.

The Yap Island coin can weigh more than 500 pounds and can be as big as 12 feet across.

Use the chart to answer these questions.

1. Is the coin from Rome or Persia older?

2. How are the Persian, Roman, Egyptian, and Hebrew coins alike?

3. Why is there a hole in the Yap Island coin?

4. Why do you think most coins are round?

5. How does this chart help you to understand the history of money?

Meeting Individual Needs

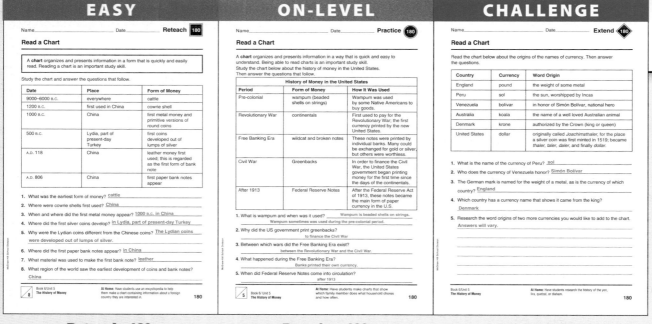

Reteach, 180   Practice, 180   Extend, 180

TEST POWER

DIRECTIONS

Read the sample story. Then read each question about the story.

SAMPLE

A Saturday at the Community Center

Mark really liked living close to the County Community Center. He enjoyed taking the classes offered at the center on Saturdays. During the last three years, Mark has taken several of the classes at the center, and he is very excited about the watercolor class this coming Saturday.

The new schedule for Saturday classes looks like this:

Time	Room 1	Room 2
3:00	Buying a house	Guitar
3:30		Painting with watercolor
4:00	Movie: Boomtown	
4:30		Piano
5:00		Pottery
5:30		
6:00	Karate	Ballet
6:30	Yoga	

1 According to the schedule, which of these classes will be held first?

  A Pottery

  B Karate

  C Yoga

  (D) Piano

2 According to the schedule, what time will the watercolor class begin?

  (F) 3:30

  G 4:00

  H 4:30

  J 5:00

Test Power

THE PRINCETON REVIEW

Read the Page

Have students read the text above the schedule, the schedule itself, both questions, and *all* of the answer choices.

Discuss the Questions

Question 1: This question refers specifically to the information on the schedule. Direct students back to the schedule. They will have to find what time each of the four classes is being held and then choose the one that is held first. Ensure that students read the question and each of the answer choices carefully and eliminate wrong answers.

Question 2: This question also requires students to interpret the information on the schedule. Direct students to review the schedule to determine when the watercolor class is held. Remind students to be careful that they choose the *beginning* time of the class.

Self-Selected Reading
Leveled Books

Intervention ▸ **Skills**

Intervention Guide, for direct instruction and extra practice in vocabulary and comprehension

Phonics

- syllable patterns
- /f/, /k/, /s/
- /îr/ and /ûr/
- *ea* words

☑ Comprehension

- Story Elements
- Sequence of Events
- Judgments and Decisions

Answers to Story Questions

Answers will vary and should include examples and details from the stories students have read.

EASY

Story Questions for Selected Reading

1. Which illustrations best helped you understand the book?
2. What changes took place in the person's life as described in the book?
3. What did you learn about a particular time or place from this book?
4. What would you write about in a continuation of this book?
5. What did you like best about the book? Least?

Make a Portrait

Paint a portrait of a person in the book you read.

EASY

UNIT SKILLS REVIEW

Phonics

☑ **Comprehension**

Help students select an Easy Book to read and apply phonics and comprehension skills for this unit.

Guided Reading

PREVIEW AND PREDICT Ask students to thumb through the book, looking at the illustrations and the title of the book. What do they think the subject of this book will be?

SET PURPOSES Have students write down what they expect to find out from this book.

READ THE BOOK Students can read the book independently. Then ask the following questions:

- Choose one page in the book. What words can you find with the /f/, /k/, /s/, or /ûr/ sound? *Phonics and Decoding*

- How would you describe the main person in this book? What qualities does he or she have? *Character*

- What is the order of the main events in the book? *Sequence of Events*

- What major decision did a person in this book have to make? Did you agree with that decision? Why or why not? *Judgments and Decisions*

RETURN TO PREDICTIONS AND PURPOSES Ask students to look back at the predictions they made. Were they correct? Did they learn what they thought they would learn?

LITERARY RESPONSE Ask students the following questions:

- Which quality of a person in the book you read would you most like to have yourself? Why?

- Would you recommend this book to a friend? Why or why not?

Self-Selected Reading
Leveled Books

UNIT SKILLS REVIEW

☑ **Comprehension**

Help students select an Independent book to read and apply comprehension skills from this unit.

Guided Reading

PREVIEW AND PREDICT Ask students to make predictions about this book, based on the title and illustrations. Have them write down their predictions to check later.

SET PURPOSES What do students want to learn as they read this book?

READ THE BOOK Students can read the book independently. After students have finished, ask:

- What are the important events in this book? In what order did they occur? *Sequence of Events*

- How would you describe the key person in the book? How did the person display these qualities? *Character*

- What was the best part of this book? The worst? Explain your answers with supporting evidence. *Judgments and Decisions*

RETURN TO PREDICTIONS AND PURPOSES Ask students to look at their list of predictions, noting which were right and which were not. Did students learn what they expected to learn?

LITERARY RESPONSE Students can respond to the selections by answering these questions:

- Which person in this book did you like best? Why?

- What book have you read that most reminds you of this book? Why?

☑ **Comprehension**

- **Story Elements**

- **Sequence of Events**

- **Judgments and Decisions**

Answers to Story Questions

Answers will vary and should include examples and details from the stories students have read.

Story Questions for Selected Reading

1. How did a person or an event influence the main figure in the book?

2. What are some other ways in which this book could have ended?

3. What effect did a person in the book have on other people?

4. Imagine very different characteristics for the key person in the book. How would these different characteristics affect events in the book?

5. If you could ask the author a question, what question would you ask?

Make an Ad

Create a magazine ad for the book you read.

Self-Selected Reading
Leveled Books

☑ Comprehension

- Story Elements
- Sequence of Events
- Judgments and Decisions

Answers to Story Questions

Answers will vary and should include examples and details from the stories students have read.

CHALLENGE

Story Questions for Selected Reading

1. What event in this book was the most important? Why do you think so?

2. How would this book have been different if a character had made a different decision? Explain what might have happened.

3. What discoveries do people make in the book? What realizations do they have?

4. How would this book be different if it were written from another point of view?

5. How would different illustrations have changed this book?

Design a Book Jacket

Create a book jacket for the selection that you read. Include a cover illustration and reviews to be printed on the back cover.

CHALLENGE

UNIT SKILLS REVIEW

☑ **Comprehension**

Help students select a Challenge Book to read and apply comprehension skills from this unit.

Guided Reading

PREVIEW AND PREDICT Have students make predictions about this book, based on the illustrations, title, and title page.

SET PURPOSES Ask students to list the reasons why they want to read this book and what they hope to learn from their reading.

READ THE BOOK Students can read the book independently. Then review the text, using the following questions as a guide.

- What are the main events in this book? In what order do they occur? *Sequence of Events*

- How would you describe a main character in the book? Which actions or descriptive details reveal these qualities? *Character*

- Do you think this book is successful? Why? Does it achieve the purposes you think the author had when writing the book? Support your answer with evidence. *Judgments and Decisions*

RETURN TO PREDICTIONS AND PURPOSES Were the students' predictions correct? Did they learn what they thought they would?

LITERARY RESPONSE Ask students to respond to the selections by answering these questions:

- If you were to meet a main character from this book, what would you ask him or her?

- Would you recommend this book to a friend? Why or why not?

Bringing Groups Together

Anthology and Leveled Books

Connecting Texts

SOLUTIONS CHART Divide the class into groups of students who have read the same book in the unit. On a chart, each group should list a problem discussed in the book and the solution to the problem. Then have students compare how the problems were solved in the books. What enabled people to solve the problem? Can students come up with alternative solutions?

A Tune for Lucy	Michael DeBakey: King of Hearts	The Photographer	John Glenn: Space Pioneer
• Lucy, Sarah • friends of different generations • They become friends, and Lucy teaches Sarah piano and becomes less lonely herself.	• Michael DeBakey, his parents • parents, child • Parents inspire him to study hard, share, and help others.	• Sara, Janna • friends of different generations • Friendship: Sara keeps Janna company; Janna teaches her to take photographs.	• The automatic control system that corrected the drifting of the capsule used up a great deal of fuel. • Glenn maneuvered the capsule himself.

Viewing/Representing

GROUP PRESENTATIONS Ask groups of students who have read the same book to interview the people in the book who created a problem, faced a problem, or solved a problem. Ask each group to conduct the interviews in front of the rest of the class.

AUDIENCE RESPONSE Encourage the interviewers to take questions from the audience. Students may want to know more about the feelings, thoughts, and reactions of the people being interviewed.

Research and Inquiry

INVESTIGATING DEEPER Ask students what has piqued their interest about the problems and solutions in the book they read. Ask them to find out more by these methods:

- Use the Internet and library books for research.

- Read newspaper and magazine articles.

- Interview someone who knows about the topic.

Students can present their research in a report.

 interNET CONNECTION Students can learn more by visiting **www.mhschool.com/reading**

 Students can write and draw what they learned in their journals.

JOURNAL

Students will practice how to make judgments when they read.

Skills Finder

Judgments and Decisions

Introduce	483A-B
Review	501E-F, 541E-F
Test	Unit 5

LANGUAGE SUPPORT

ESL Review the ideas expressed in "Who Needs Money?" Ask students to list the judgments made by the author of that paragraph. Then ask them what decisions they think the author would make and what actions he or she would take, based on those judgments.

SELF-SELECTED Reading

Students may choose from the following titles.

ANTHOLOGY

• The History of Money

LEVELED BOOKS

• All titles for the unit

Bibliography, pages T80–T81

Instruct students to select books at an appropriate level of difficulty—books in which they can read most of the words and can use context and language-structure clues and letter-sound correspondences to decode the rest.

541E   *The History of Money*

Review Judgments and Decisions

PREPARE

Discuss Making Judgments and Decisions

Review: When you make a judgment about something you've read, you use your personal knowledge as well as reason to evaluate the information.

TEACH

Read the Passage and Model the Skill

Have a volunteer read **Teaching Chart 148.** Ask students to think about whether they agree or disagree with what the author is saying.

Who Needs Money?

I think we should throw out money. It just leads to anger and bitterness. No one ever has enough, and money causes nothing but unhappiness between friends and family members. Instead, I think we should go back to bartering. Then, no one would need to earn so much money. Instead, people would have just what they needed. Life would be much better.

Teaching Chart 148

Discuss Author's Viewpoint

Have students discuss the author's viewpoint in the passage.

MODEL Based on what I know about money and people, I do not agree that money always leads to anger and bitterness. Sometimes money can help improve someone's life.

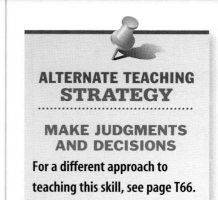

ALTERNATE TEACHING
STRATEGY

MAKE JUDGMENTS AND DECISIONS

For a different approach to teaching this skill, see page T66.

PRACTICE

Evaluate Judgments and Decisions

GROUP

Have students underline the author's reasons for viewing money as a negative influence. Ask them to circle the author's reasons for replacing money with bartering. Using reason and their own knowledge, students should then explain whether they find the author's arguments persuasive.

ASSESS/CLOSE

Make Judgments

Ask students to choose an article they've read recently and evaluate the reasoning in it. They should present their judgments in a paragraph.

 **Skills**

Intervention Guide, for direct instruction and extra practice with judgments and decisions

Meeting Individual Needs for Comprehension

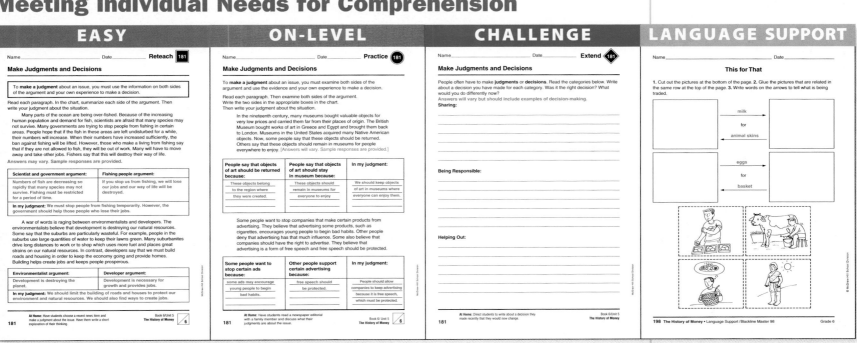

EASY	ON-LEVEL	CHALLENGE	LANGUAGE SUPPORT

Reteach, 181 · Practice, 181 · Extend, 181 · Language Support, 198

OBJECTIVES

Students will identify context clues that help them understand the meaning of specialized vocabulary.

Skills Finder

Context Clues

Introduce	63I-J
Review	239I-J, 307I-J, 317I-J, 481I-J, 501I-J, 541G-H
Test	Unit 1, Unit 3, Unit 5
Maintain	277, 415, 487, 563, 609

TEACHING TIP

CONTEXT CLUES Point out that sometimes specialized words appear more than once in a passage. If students are unsure of the meaning after seeing the first reference, they should keep an eye out for other references that might help them understand the definition of the word.

Review Context Clues

PREPARE

Discuss Context Clues and Specialized Vocabulary   Explain that some subject areas have their own special vocabulary. Sailors, for example, use a *compass* to navigate. Students can usually figure out the meaning of these words from the context in which they appear.

TEACH

Read the Passage and Model the Skill   Have students read the passage on **Teaching Chart 149.**

The Future of Money

No longer do people have to ⟨barter⟩ goods to get what they need in exchange. People now use money. Around the world, many ⟨currencies⟩ exist. Though their names might sound strange—the pound, the lira, the peso, the baht, the euro—there are ways today for someone in the United States to know exactly how much a foreign currency is worth in U.S. dollars on any day. You can find out in newspapers and even on the Internet what the ⟨rate of exchange⟩ is.

Teaching Chart 149

Identify Context Clues   Help students to define *barter* in the first sentence. Ask a volunteer to underline the nearby words that give clues to its meaning.

MODEL   I don't know the word *barter*, but I can guess the meaning from the words that come right after it. When a person barters, he or she exchanges goods with someone else.

PRACTICE

Identify Context Clues

GROUP

Ask a volunteer to circle the word *currencies* and the phrase *rate of exchange* on **Teaching Chart 149.** Then have volunteers underline the words that help show the meaning of the specialized vocabulary in context. ▶ **Linguistic**

ASSESS/CLOSE

Use Context Clues

Have students choose a word from a story or article they've read recently and write a context paragraph for it. Have partners exchange paragraphs and identify the context clues that help them understand the meaning of the word.

ALTERNATE TEACHING STRATEGY

CONTEXT CLUES

For a different approach to teaching this skill, see page T67.

i **Intervention** ▶ **Skills Intervention Guide,** for direct instruction and extra practice in context clues

Meeting Individual Needs for Vocabulary

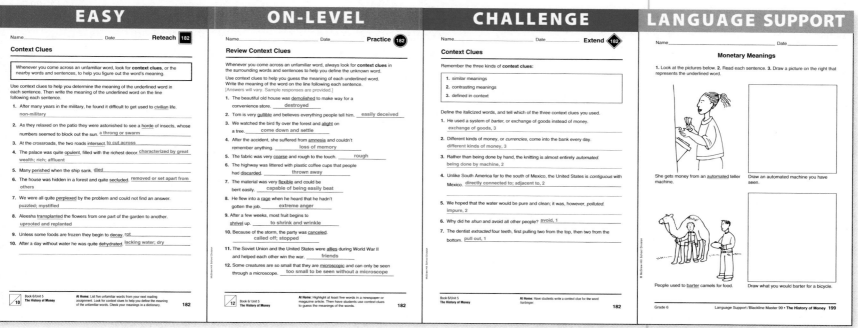

EASY	ON-LEVEL	CHALLENGE	LANGUAGE SUPPORT
Reteach, 182	Practice, 182	Extend, 182	Language Support, 199

OBJECTIVES

Students will review the denotations and connotations of words.

Skills Finder

Denotation and Connotation	
Introduce	467I-J
Review	531I-J, 541I-J
Test	Unit 5

LANGUAGE SUPPORT

Ask students to draw pictures of situations involving the two types of wealthy people in the passage. Then ask them to think of words that describe what the characters are like. Divide the words they give into two lists: Positive and Negative Connotations. For example, the words *save* and *thrifty* have positive connotations, while *hoard* and *stingy* have negative connotations.

Review Denotation and Connotation

PREPARE

Discuss Denotation and Connotation

Review: The denotation of a word is its dictionary meaning; the connotation of a word is the feeling or ideas associated with it.

TEACH

Read the Passage and Model the Skill

Review with students that an idea or emotion suggested by a word is called *connotation*. The *denotation* is the literal dictionary meaning of a word. Have students listen for denotative and connotative meanings as you read the passage on **Teaching Chart 150** with them.

Money Matters

Wealthy people have very different ideas about what to do with their money. Some are stingy; they do not help those less fortunate than they are, but instead hoard their money so that they can spend it on themselves. Often they build great houses, monuments to their wealth, to impress their friends. Other rich people are thrifty; they save their money so that they can help others by giving to charity. These people are committed to building warm homes for their families as well as communities that care about their members. These people are truly wealthy.

Teaching Chart 150

Ask students to discuss the connotation of the word *stingy*.

MODEL The word *stingy* has a negative connotation. It conveys to me that these rich people are selfish.

PRACTICE

Differentiate Between Denotations and Connotations

GROUP

Ask students to reread "Money Matters." Have them underline the words that have positive connotations and circle the words that have negative connotations. Students should then explain the connotation of each word. ▶ **Linguistic**

ASSESS/CLOSE

Use Denotation and Connotation

Ask students to rewrite a sentence in the passage to make a sentence with positive connotations take on negative connotations or to make a sentence with negative connotations take on positive connotations.

ALTERNATE TEACHING STRATEGY

DENOTATION AND CONNOTATION

For a different approach to teaching this skill, see page T65.

Intervention ▶ **Skills Intervention Guide**, for direct instruction and extra practice with denotation and connotation

Meeting Individual Needs for Vocabulary

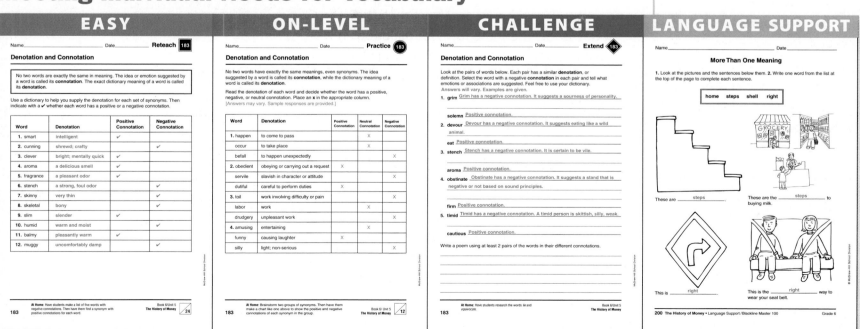

Reteach, 183   Practice, 183   Extend, 183   Language Support, 200

Writing a Story

GRAMMAR/SPELLING CONNECTIONS

See the 5-Day Grammar and Usage Plan on pronoun-verb agreement, pages 541M–541N.

See the 5-Day Spelling Plan on words with words from math, pages 5410–541P.

TEACHING TIP

Technology Point out to students that you can use the Format commands on your word processor to make your dialogue look as if it's from a printed book. A hanging indent, for example, lets you indent every line after the first one.

Written Dialogue Remind students that well-written dialogue should sound like real conversation and reflect the personalities of the characters who are speaking.

Handwriting CD-ROM

Prewrite

WRITE A DIALOGUE Present this writing assignment: Write a dialogue in which you and another person talk about money. Your dialogue can be serious or funny. For example, you could ask a friend to lend you money, or you could ask your parents to raise your allowance. You could even try to explain American money to a person from the Stone Age. Whatever you write, remember to use dialogue form, writing the speaker's name in capital letters followed by a colon.

BRAINSTORM IDEAS Have students brainstorm specific topics related to money. They can narrow their choices later.

Strategy: Make Webs Having chosen their topics, students can make a web for each character in their dialogue. The webs should include the characters' thoughts and feelings about the subject.

Draft

USE THE WEBS Using their webs to guide them, students should construct their dialogues. Show them the form for dialogue and encourage them to think of individual ways that people express themselves in everyday conversation.

Revise

SELF-QUESTIONING Ask students to assess their drafts.

- Did I make my point in the dialogue?
- Does the dialogue sound like real conversation?
- What can a reader learn about the characters by reading my dialogue?

PARTNERS Ask students to read each dialogue and discuss possible improvements.

Edit/Proofread

CHECK FOR ERRORS Ask students to check their work for spelling, grammar, and usage mistakes.

Publish

MAKE A BOOK Create a class book of the dialogues. Place a copy of the anthology in the school library so that students in other classes who want to perform short scenes can use it as a reference.

An Easy Choice

BOB: Hey, Vince. Can I borrow some money?
VINCE: Again?
BOB: Yeah, again. I need five bucks.
VINCE: You need five bucks, or you _want_ five bucks?
BOB: I need it. I really need it this time.
VINCE: Like last time, when you really needed to go to that movie?
BOB (He sounds hurt.): That was a really good movie. I really enjoyed it.
VINCE: But you didn't really need to see it.
BOB: Come on, Vince. Can I have the money?
VINCE: No.
BOB: No? You're kidding.
VINCE: Not until you repay me the five you owe me.
BOB: I thought we were friends.
VINCE: We are! And if you want to keep it that way, do the right thing.
BOB: Okay, you're right. I'll pay you back on Monday, when Mr. Dean pays me for mowing the lawn.

Presentation Ideas

SET THE STAGE Students can draw the scene presented in their dialogues to show the setting and the appearance of the characters. ▶ **Viewing/Representing**

PERFORM THE DIALOGUE Students can perform their dialogues in pairs. Have them practice one student's work and then the other's, before presenting the dialogues to the class. ▶ **Speaking/Listening**

Consider students' creative efforts, possibly adding a plus (+) for originality, wit, and imagination.

Scoring Rubric

Excellent	Good	Fair	Unsatisfactory
4: The writer	**3:** The writer	**2:** The writer	**1:** The writer
• constructs a dialogue that makes a point or tells a story and holds the audience's attention.	• constructs a coherent conversation.	• loses track of the purpose of the dialogue.	• does not use dialogue to tell a story or make a point.
• creates two original characters.	• creates two distinct characters.	• does not create fully distinct characters.	• creates indistinguishable characters.
• presents believable dialogue.	• uses language to convey personalities.	• uses stilted or generic language.	• includes extensive errors in language use.

Incomplete 0: The writer leaves the page blank or fails to respond to the writing task. The student does not address the topic or simply paraphrases the prompt. The response is illegible or incoherent.

For a 6-point or an 8-point scale, see pages T109–T110.

Meeting Individual Needs for Writing

EASY

Time Line Have students create time lines of the history of money. They should write labels explaining key facts.

ON-LEVEL

Set the Scene Have students write a description of a market where people have come to barter goods. Remind them to use telling details to bring the scene to life.

CHALLENGE

Letters Have students imagine they are writing a letter to their boss asking for a raise. They should list all the reasons why they need a raise, using business letter style. Then students should write a letter back from the boss, explaining why the raise will or will not be granted.

Listening and Speaking

LISTENING STRATEGIES
As dialogues are performed, encourage students to:
• listen attentively.
• jot down questions to ask later if any of the dialogue is unclear.

SPEAKING STRATEGIES
Encourage students to:
• speak fluently.
• vary volume and tone of voice for emphasis.

LANGUAGE SUPPORT

ESL ESL students can role-play with a partner before writing their dialogues. A fluent partner can help them use English idioms.

PORTFOLIO Invite students to include their dialogues or another writing project in their portfolios.

5 Day Grammar and Usage Plan

LANGUAGE SUPPORT

ESL Pair English learners with native speakers and have partners work on the Daily Language Activities together.

DAILY LANGUAGE ACTIVITIES

Write each day's activity on the board or use **Transparency 25.** Have students correct the sentences orally.

Day 1
1. We is learning about money.
2. They uses silver money, not paper.
3. It have ridges on it.

Day 2
1. Not everybody are in need of money.
2. He says he never use money.
3. Few has enough money these days.

Day 3
1. He spend money in that store.
2. It are in the mall near the bank.
3. Everyone have an account there.

Day 4
1. Do you provides banking services?
2. They is going to the ATM.
3. We has time to count the money.

Day 5
1. If they sprints, they'll be there on time.
2. Nothing here be as old as that coin.
3. I has learned a lot about money.

Daily Language Transparency 25

Suggested answers on transparency

541M *History of Money*

DAY 1 Introduce the Concept

Oral Warm-Up Read aloud: *I have no doubt that he is my brother.* Ask students to identify the pronouns. Then elicit why the verb forms *have* and *is* are used.

Review Agreement A verb must agree with its subject pronoun.

Pronoun Verb Agreement

Pronouns	Verb
he, she, it	walks, is, was, has
we, you, they, I	walk, am, was, have

Present the Daily Language Activity, and have students correct the sentences orally by using these verb forms: *are, use, has.* Then ask them to write two sentences in which the verbs *have* and *be* agree with subject pronouns.

 Assign the daily Writing Prompt on page 532C.

DAY 2 Teach the Concept

Review Agreement Ask students to offer a definition of pronoun-verb agreement and an example. Then ask them to say the pronoun and its correct verb in the Daily Language Activity for Day 1.

Review Indefinite Pronouns Verbs must also agree with indefinite pronouns.

Indefinite Pronouns

- Use a singular verb with a singular indefinite pronoun.
- Use a plural verb with a plural indefinite pronoun.

Present the Daily Language Activity, and have students correct the sentence orally using these verb forms: *is, uses, have.* Then have them write a sentence containing an indefinite pronoun that agrees with its verb.

 Assign the daily Writing Prompt on page 532C.

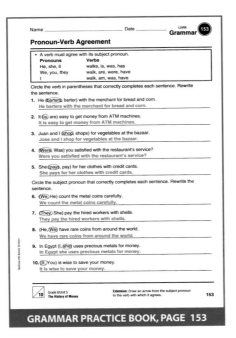

GRAMMAR PRACTICE BOOK, PAGE 153

GRAMMAR PRACTICE BOOK, PAGE 154

Pronoun-Verb Agreement

Learn from the Literature Review pronoun-verb agreement by reading this sentence from *The History of Money*:

> **Today we can also pay for things with credit cards or checks.**

Ask students to identify the pronoun and its verb. (we can pay)

Pronoun-Verb Agreement Present the Daily Language Activity, and have students correct the sentence orally by using these verb forms: *spend, is, has*.

Have students choose a sentence from the selection and change a noun to a pronoun, making sure the verb agrees. (Example: *Early "money" varied from culture to culture. It varied from culture to culture.*)

 Assign the daily Writing Prompt on page 532D.

Review Pronoun-Verb Agreement Write the sentences from the Daily Language Activities for Days 1 through 3 on the board. Ask volunteers to explain why a particular verb form was used in each sentence. Then present the Daily Language Activity for Day 4.

Mechanics and Usage Before students complete the daily Writing Prompt on page 532D, review these rules for titles:

Titles of Works

- Underline or use italics for titles of books, plays, newspapers, magazines, movies, and TV series.

- Put quotation marks around titles of poems, short stories, essays, songs, articles, and book chapters.

 Assign the daily Writing Prompt on page 532D.

Assess Use the Daily Language Activity and page 157 of the **Grammar Practice Book** for assessment.

Reteach Ask each small group of students to create a matching game with verbs and pronouns. They can list verbs on one side of a piece of paper and, on the other side, pronouns (out of order) that agree with them. Have groups exchange games and solve them by drawing lines from the correct verb to the correct pronoun.

The class might want to create a larger version of the matching game to put on the bulletin board.

Use page 158 of the **Grammar Practice Book** for additional reteaching.

 Assign the daily Writing Prompt on page 532D.

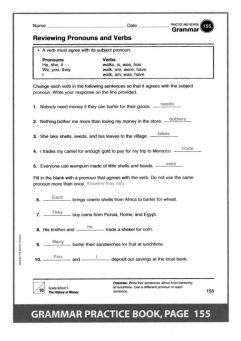

GRAMMAR PRACTICE BOOK, PAGE 155

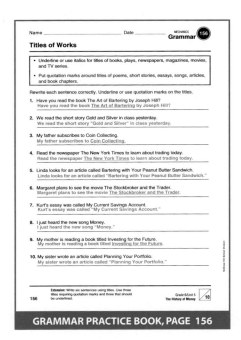

GRAMMAR PRACTICE BOOK, PAGE 156

GRAMMAR PRACTICE BOOK, PAGE 157

GRAMMAR PRACTICE BOOK, PAGE 158

5 Day Spelling Plan

LANGUAGE SUPPORT

 ESL Review how to identify stressed and unstressed syllables. Present several Spelling Words and have students read them aloud and underline the stressed syllables. If students are unsure, suggest they check a dictionary.

DICTATION SENTENCES

Spelling Words

1. I mailed the bank my <u>interest</u> payment.
2. Can I <u>borrow</u> money to buy a hat?
3. <u>Division</u> broke the group into parts.
4. A <u>percent</u> is an amount.
5. The <u>addition</u> of tax increased her bill.
6. One slice is a <u>fraction</u> of the pear.
7. It was a <u>metric</u> measurement.
8. A <u>positive</u> number is more than zero.
9. Let's <u>calculate</u> the answer to the sum.
10. It is <u>customary</u> to help a friend.
11. I <u>predict</u> we will soon win.
12. <u>Deposit</u> your money in a bank.
13. The <u>discount</u> made the price cheap.
14. A <u>negative</u> number is less than zero.
15. The cloudy sky makes rain <u>probable</u>.
16. A <u>decimal</u> uses the number ten.
17. Let's <u>tally</u> the amount.
18. A <u>dividend</u> is a number to be divided.
19. In <u>subtraction</u>, things are taken away.
20. <u>Statistics</u> are a collection of data.

Challenge Words

21. <u>Bartering</u> is a way to trade for things.
22. We use <u>currency</u> for payment.
23. He charged a <u>fee</u> to help us.
24. She gave me a <u>loan</u> to buy a car.
25. The <u>automated</u> bank gives me cash.

DAY 1 Pretest

Assess Prior Knowledge Use the Dictation Sentences at the left and **Spelling Practice Book** page 153 for the pretest. Allow students to correct their own papers. Students who require a modified list may be tested on the first ten words.

Spelling Words		Challenge Words
1. **interest**	11. predict	21. **bartering**
2. **borrow**	12. deposit	22. **currency**
3. division	13. discount	23. **fee**
4. percent	14. negative	24. **loan**
5. addition	15. probable	25. **automated**
6. fraction	16. decimal	
7. metric	17. tally	
8. positive	18. dividend	
9. calculate	19. subtraction	
10. customary	20. statistics	

*Note: Words in **dark type** are from the story.*

Word Study On page 154 of the **Spelling Practice Book** are word study steps and an at-home activity.

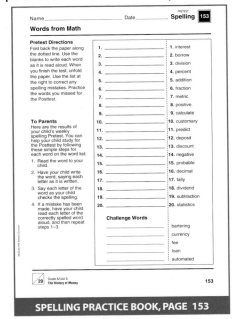

SPELLING PRACTICE BOOK, PAGE 153

WORD STUDY STEPS AND ACTIVITY, PAGE 154

DAY 2 Explore the Pattern

Sort and Spell Words Review that the part of a word said with more stress is called the stressed syllable. Present *fraction, percent, interest, deposit*. Have students tell which syllables are stressed. Point out that the stressed syllable has a short vowel sound. Have students sort the Spelling Words according to the type of vowel sound in the stressed syllable.

Words with short vowel sounds		
a	*i*	*o*
fraction	interest	borrow
calculate	division	positive
tally	addition	deposit
subtraction	predict	probable
	discount	
e	dividend	*u*
percent	statistics	customary
metric		
negative		
decimal		

Word Wall Have students create a word wall based on the word sort and add more words from their reading.

SPELLING PRACTICE BOOK, PAGE 155

Words from Math

DAY 3 — Practice and Extend

Word Meaning: Definitions Remind students that words can have more than one meaning. Have students identify the Spelling Words with multiple meanings and write a definition for each one that does not relate to math. Ask them to check their definitions in a dictionary. Have partners exchange definitions and guess the words.

If students need extra practice, have partners give each other a midweek test.

Glossary Review how accent marks in an entry show if a syllable is stressed or unstressed. Because a one-syllable word is always accented, no accent mark is shown for it. Have students

- write each Challenge Word that is more than one syllable.

- say each word, divide it into syllables, and mark the accented syllables.

- use the Glossary to check their work.

DAY 4 — Proofread and Write

Proofread Sentences Write these sentences on the chalkboard, including the misspelled words. Ask students to proofread, circling incorrect spellings and writing the correct spellings. There are two spelling errors in each sentence.

It is customary to pay intrest when you borow money. **(interest, borrow)**

I pradict you will owe a fraction of that persent. **(predict, percent)**

Have students create additional sentences with errors for partners to correct.

 Have students use as many Spelling Words as possible in the daily Writing Prompt on page 532D. Remind students to proofread their writing for errors in spelling, grammar, and punctuation.

DAY 5 — Assess and Reteach

Assess Students' Knowledge Use page 158 of the **Spelling Practice Book** or the Dictation Sentences on page 541O for the posttest.

Personal Word List If students have trouble with any words in the lesson, suggest they add them to their personal lists of troublesome words in their journals. Have students write definitions for the words.

Students should refer to their word lists during later writing activities.

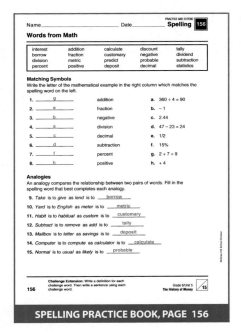

SPELLING PRACTICE BOOK, PAGE 156

SPELLING PRACTICE BOOK, PAGE 157

SPELLING PRACTICE BOOK, PAGE 158

Wrap Up the Theme

Brainstorms

We can meet any challenge with determination and ingenuity.

REVIEW THE THEME Read the theme statement to students. Ask: How did the stories and articles read in this unit fulfill the theme Brainstorms? Which selection presented the most difficult problem? Why? Which had the most interesting solution? Can you think of a solution that is better than any of the ones presented in this unit? If so, explain.

READ THE POEM Before reading the poem "My Uncle Dan" by Ted Hughes, have students look at the illustration. Ask: What do you think the tone of this poem will be? Read the poem aloud. Does this poem fit the theme Brainstorms? How? What types of problems does Uncle Dan solve? Which invention do you think is the most ridiculous? Have students brainstorm a list of other "perfectly useless inventions."

 Listening Library The poem is available on **audiocassette** or on **compact disc.**

MAKE CONNECTIONS Have students work in small groups to brainstorm a list of ways that the stories, poems, and the *Time for Kids* magazine article relate to the theme Brainstorms. Groups can then compare their lists as they share them with the class.

Have students tell which selections they liked best. Discuss the types of selections they most enjoy listening to or reading.

LOOKING AT GENRE

Have students review *Child of the Owl* and *Bellerophon and the Flying Horse.* How is *Child of the Owl* part of a novel? What makes *Bellerophon and the Flying Horse* a myth?

Help students list the key characteristics of each literary form or genre. Can they name other novels (or parts of novels) or myths that have these same characteristics?

NOVEL *Child of the Owl*	MYTH *Bellerophon and the Flying Horse*
• A long fictional story. • Detailed settings and plot. • Three-dimensional characters.	• Set in ancient times. • Sometimes explains important natural events. • Often includes gods, goddesses, and larger-than-life heroes.

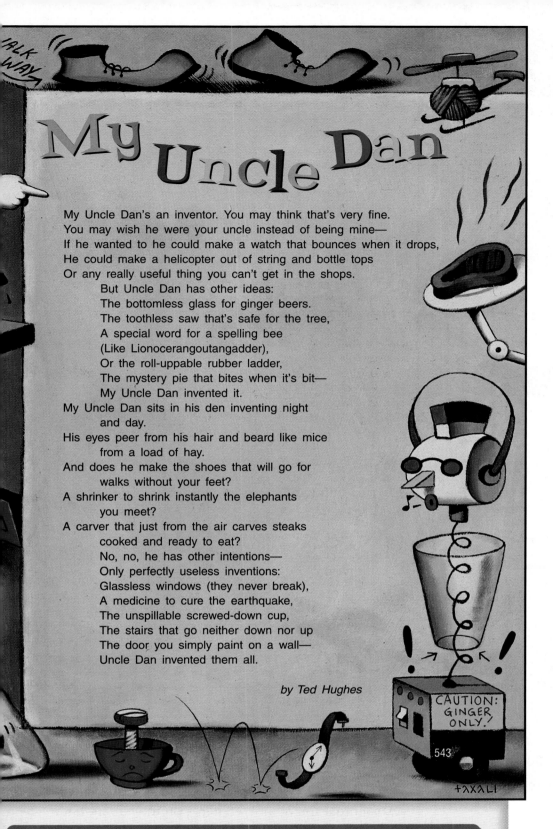

My Uncle Dan

My Uncle Dan's an inventor. You may think that's very fine.
You may wish he were your uncle instead of being mine—
If he wanted to he could make a watch that bounces when it drops,
He could make a helicopter out of string and bottle tops
Or any really useful thing you can't get in the shops.
But Uncle Dan has other ideas:
The bottomless glass for ginger beers.
The toothless saw that's safe for the tree,
A special word for a spelling bee
(Like Lionocerangoutangadder),
Or the roll-uppable rubber ladder,
The mystery pie that bites when it's bit—
My Uncle Dan invented it.
My Uncle Dan sits in his den inventing night
and day.
His eyes peer from his hair and beard like mice
from a load of hay.
And does he make the shoes that will go for
walks without your feet?
A shrinker to shrink instantly the elephants
you meet?
A carver that just from the air carves steaks
cooked and ready to eat?
No, no, he has other intentions—
Only perfectly useless inventions:
Glassless windows (they never break),
A medicine to cure the earthquake,
The unspillable screwed-down cup,
The stairs that go neither down nor up
The door you simply paint on a wall—
Uncle Dan invented them all.

by Ted Hughes

LEARNING ABOUT POETRY

Literary Devices: Rhyme Read the poem aloud; then ask students to point out the words that rhyme at the end of lines. (fine, mine, drops, stops, shops, etc.) Tell students that rhyme adds to the sound of a poem and, in this case, to its humorous tone. Ask students if they prefer poems that rhyme to those that don't. Have them discuss how the rhyming lines in this poem make the poem fun to read aloud.

Response Activity
Humorous rhyming poetry gives students a chance to see just how hard it is to write humor or comedy. Have students write short, humorous, rhyming poems about small problems they face every day, like getting up on time, avoiding cavities, getting homework done, or sharing a room at home. Have students read the poems aloud.

Research *and Inquiry*

Complete the Theme Project: Disaster Relief Review with each group the extent of their research so far. Ask if they need any material that they couldn't find. Arrange for a trip to the library, if necessary, to supplement students' findings. Remind students that their plans must include evacuation routes, emergency care, and long-term relief and that every member of the group must help in both the writing and presentation of the plan.

Make a Classroom Presentation
Allow adequate time for students to practice their presentations. Students should speak responsibly to present ethical messages. Be sure to leave time for a question-and-answer period.

Draw Conclusions Have students draw conclusions about what they have learned from researching their natural disaster. Was the resource chart they made helpful? What other resources did they use? What did students discover about solving the problems that arise from an emergency? How does what they discovered relate to the theme of Brainstorms and problem-solving?

Ask More Questions/Revise Questions What additional questions do students now have about the disaster they researched? Encourage students to form and revise questions such as: What would I do if that type of disaster struck my home, school, or community? In what ways could I help?

Reading Online Resources

There are many different sources of information on the Internet. There are search engines, encyclopedias, newspapers, journals, and other online reference resources. However, it is important to know how to evaluate the sources that you choose.

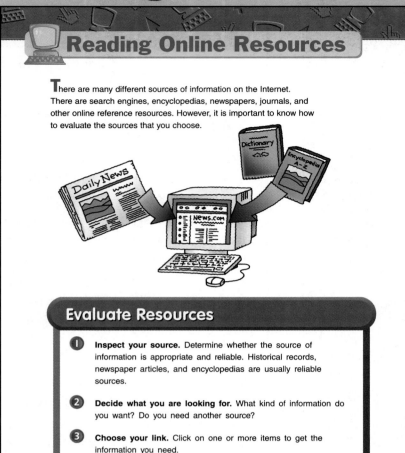

Evaluate Resources

1. **Inspect your source.** Determine whether the source of information is appropriate and reliable. Historical records, newspaper articles, and encyclopedias are usually reliable sources.

2. **Decide what you are looking for.** What kind of information do you want? Do you need another source?

3. **Choose your link.** Click on one or more items to get the information you need.

4. **Evaluate the source.** Is the information accurate? How might you check this information?

Online Newspaper

Here is the home page of an online newspaper.

1. **Inspect.** Does the source seem appropriate and reliable?

2. **Decide.** Choose the news story that you want.

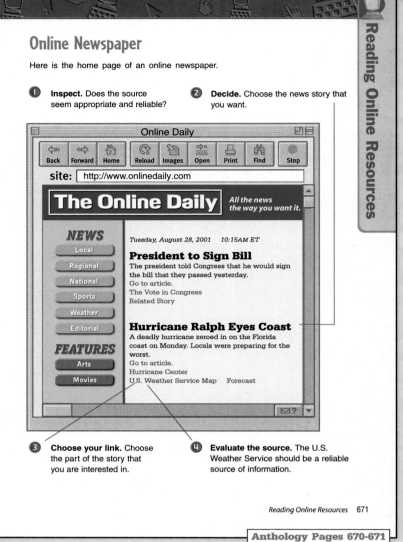

3. **Choose your link.** Choose the part of the story that you are interested in.

4. **Evaluate the source.** The U.S. Weather Service should be a reliable source of information.

Anthology Pages 670-671

Reading Online Resources

OBJECTIVES Students will:

- use electronic technology as a source of information
- evaluate online sources for appropriateness and reliability

INTRODUCE Have volunteers share their experiences of researching information online and why they find some web sites more helpful than others. Then ask students to read the opening paragraph on page 670. Then read aloud and discuss the points under **Evaluate Sources.**

MODEL It isn't always easy to tell whether a web site is reliable. I find that sites run by museums, schools, and official organizations and agencies tend to provide accurate information. I also look for sites that have a lot of links. In my experience, those sites provide the greatest coverage of related topics and therefore are most useful.

PRACTICE/APPLY Ask students to read page 671. Explain that the numbered items on the left are one student's suggestions for how to make the most of a web site. Ask:

- What other main news stories could you click on this page?
- Why would an online newspaper probably be a reliable source?
- In what ways are links on a web page useful?

As students **preview** pages 672–673, ask: How is this online newspaper page laid out? *(Set Purposes)*

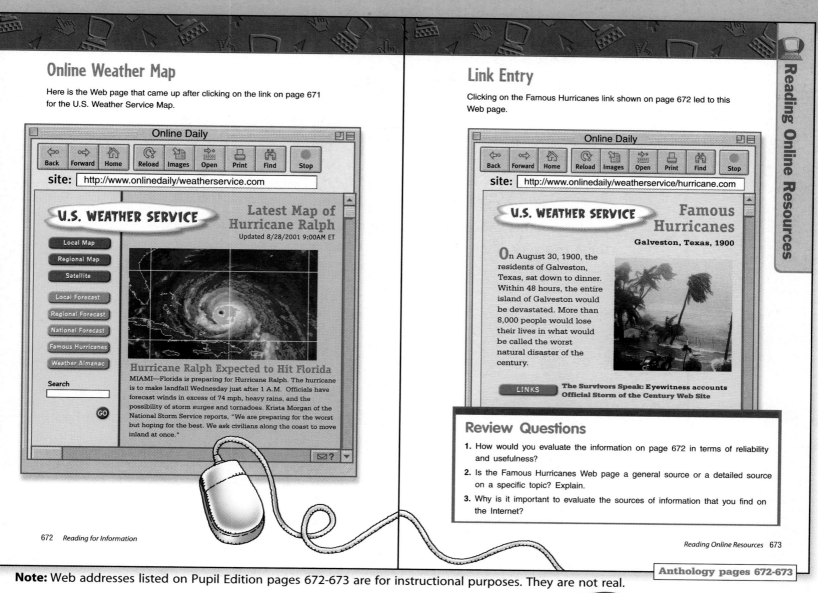

Online Weather Map

Here is the Web page that came up after clicking on the link on page 671 for the U.S. Weather Service Map.

Online Daily

Back | Forward | Home | Reload | Images | Open | Print | Find | Stop

site: http://www.onlinedaily/weatherservice.com

U.S. WEATHER SERVICE

Local Map
Regional Map
Satellite
Local Forecast
Regional Forecast
National Forecast
Famous Hurricanes
Weather Almanac

Search

GO

Latest Map of Hurricane Ralph
Updated 8/28/2001 9:00AM ET

Hurricane Ralph Expected to Hit Florida

MIAMI—Florida is preparing for Hurricane Ralph. The hurricane is to make landfall Wednesday just after 1 A.M. Officials have forecast winds in excess of 74 mph, heavy rains, and the possibility of storm surges and tornadoes. Krista Morgan of the National Storm Service reports, "We are preparing for the worst but hoping for the best. We ask civilians along the coast to move inland at once."

Link Entry

Clicking on the Famous Hurricanes link shown on page 672 led to this Web page.

Online Daily

Back | Forward | Home | Reload | Images | Open | Print | Find | Stop

site: http://www.onlinedaily/weatherservice/hurricane.com

U.S. WEATHER SERVICE   **Famous Hurricanes**

Galveston, Texas, 1900

On August 30, 1900, the residents of Galveston, Texas, sat down to dinner. Within 48 hours, the entire island of Galveston would be devastated. More than 8,000 people would lose their lives in what would be called the worst natural disaster of the century.

The Survivors Speak: Eyewitness accounts
Official Storm of the Century Web Site

Review Questions

1. How would you evaluate the information on page 672 in terms of reliability and usefulness?

2. Is the Famous Hurricanes Web page a general source or a detailed source on a specific topic? Explain.

3. Why is it important to evaluate the sources of information that you find on the Internet?

Anthology pages 672-673

Note: Web addresses listed on Pupil Edition pages 672-673 are for instructional purposes. They are not real.

ANSWERS TO REVIEW QUESTIONS

1. The account of Hurricane Ralph seems reliable since it quotes the National Storm Service. Details about the hurricane's location and time would be useful for residents in the area.

2. The Famous Hurricanes web page offers a detailed source on a specific topic.

3. Since anyone can place information on the Internet, it is up to the reader to decide whether or not it is appropriate and reliable.

TRANSFER THE STRATEGY

Ask: How might this lesson on using and evaluating Internet sources change the way you do research?

Explain: How might online resources help you complete assignments in social studies or science?

Discuss: Brainstorm different ways that finding reliable information on the Internet can help you in everyday life.

Activity

Historical Hurricanes

What to do:

1. Each group of classmates can decide on a different hurricane to research online.

2. Use newspapers, weather maps, and links to other reliable web sites related to your hurricane.

3. Take notes on the facts about the hurricane as well as any eyewitness reports, or print out the page(s) of information. If possible, print out photographs of the damage.

4. Set up a large chart on the bulletin board, using the following headings: Hurricane, When, Where, Damage, Eyewitness Reports.

5. Each group should contribute its research and photographs to the chart.

Writing a Story

CONNECT TO LITERATURE In *Child of the Owl* the author tells a story about a Chinese-American girl who goes to live with her grand-mother, whom she does not know. Have students review how these two very different people learn to get along with each other.

GROUP

Patty had never been in a play before. But when the school play auditions were announced, she found herself walking to the auditorium.

Once there, the music director asked her to sing. He sat at the piano to accompany her. For some reason, she wasn't nervous. "Maybe I figure I haven't got a chance," she thought.

To Patty's surprise, she got a big role in the production. That was when she got nervous! More than anything else, Patty wondered what it would be like on opening night.

Now Patty is in every play at school. If you ask what she wants to be, she giggles, "A veterinarian," just to see if she can fool you.

Prewrite

PURPOSE & AUDIENCE Students will write stories for their class-mates about a fictional character who has to deal with something unfamiliar, such as meeting a new person or moving to a new place. Remind students to keep their purpose and audience in mind as they write.

STRATEGY: MAKE A STORY CHART Help students explore ideas for characters and storylines. Ask them to jot down traits that they want to create for their main character. Have them discuss ideas for what kind of problems the main character might encounter in an unfamiliar situation. Then show them how to use a story chart to sketch out the plot.

Use **Writing Process Transparency 5A** to model a story chart.

FEATURES OF STORY WRITING

- tells a sequence of original narrative events
- has a beginning, a middle, and an end
- can explore setting, character, plot, and dialogue

TEACHING TIP

ORGANIZATION Help students use their story charts effectively. Have them create lists under each heading for details of setting, character, and plot. Suggest that they summarize events at the end. Encourage them to consider the specific ways that the main character can adapt to an unfamiliar situation.

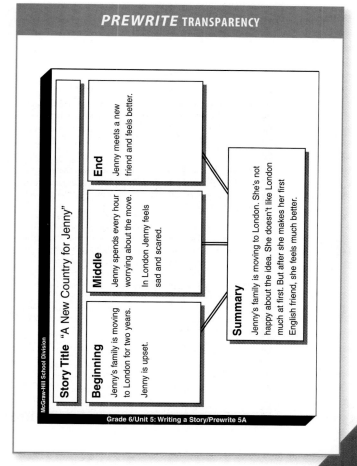

PREWRITE TRANSPARENCY

McGraw-Hill School Division

Story Title "A New Country for Jenny"

Beginning
Jenny's family is moving to London for two years.
Jenny is upset.

Middle
Jenny spends every hour worrying about the move.
In London Jenny feels sad and scared.

End
Jenny meets a new friend and feels better.

Summary
Jenny's family is moving to London. She's not happy about the idea. She doesn't like London much at first. But after she makes her first English friend, she feels much better.

Grade 6/Unit 5: Writing a Story/Prewrite 5A

Writing a Story

Draft

STRATEGY: FREEWRITING Invite students to write freely from imagination. Guide them to create interesting personalities for their main characters and to explore humor and emotions in their writing. Suggest that they have fun experimenting with unexpected plot twists. They can refer to their charts for theme ideas and plot structure, but invite them to add imaginative events and sensory details.

WORD CHOICE Remind students that in a story, transition words are important in moving the story along. Point out that writers use time-order words to help readers and listeners follow the sequence of events in the story. Suggest that students keep a list of time-order words handy as they draft their stories. Time-order words include *first, next, now, then, later, before, not long after, at last, meanwhile, during*, and *finally*.

Use **Writing Process Transparency 5B** as a model.

LANGUAGE SUPPORT

Some students may need help developing an original main character. Suggest that they use someone they know as a jumping-off point. Guide them to write a list of new physical and personality traits to change the character in an appropriate way.

DRAFT TRANSPARENCY

A New Country for Jenny

One Summer evening, Jenny's Father gathared the family into the livingroom and told them they were moving to London for two years.

"London?" Jimmy gasped. "Dad, I'm on the football team. First string!"

There mom said, "Take it easy, Jimmy. Your a good soccer player and people play alot of soccer in London.

Jenny was to surprised to say anything. She spent every hour worrying about the move. It probably would be more bad than the move before.

In London every one spoke English. And it was almost as if they were speaking a diffrent language. Jenny felt sad and scared. As it opened the door to their new apartment and dragged in their bags, a door opened across the hall.

"Are you moving in" a girl asked. Jenny nodded.

I'm Heather" the girl said and smiled. "I'm almost twelve."

"I'll be twelve in January," Jenny said. "My name is Jenny."

"Would you like to come in and have tea with my mother and I? I'd also like you to meet my cat. His name is Dolby." Heather said.

"Please, Mom?" Jenny asked. Her mother smiled and said, "Sure, honey."

When Jenny came back two hours later she was tired so that she just had toast and a glass of milk. Then she climbed in to bed to dream about her new home.

McGraw-Hill School Division

Grade 6/Unit 5: Writing a Story/Draft 5B

Revise

Have students work in teams to share revision ideas. Coach them in offering concrete suggestions for character and plot possibilities. Each team can make comment sheets noting their suggested revisions as well as what they liked best about the other teams' work.

Use **Writing Process Transparency 5C** for classroom discussion of the revision process. Ask students to comment on how revisions may have improved this writing example.

STRATEGY: ELABORATION Discuss with students ways to elaborate on their drafts. Encourage them to look at their stories with a fresh eye. Write these questions on the board for students to think about as they revise:

- What do my characters learn in the story?

- If I've used dialogue, does it help tell the story and sound realistic?

- Are my events clear and in a logical order?

- Did I show how the main character adapts to something unfamiliar?

REVISE TRANSPARENCY

A New Country for Jenny

One Summer evening, Jenny's Father gathared the family into the livingroom and told them they were moving to London for two years.

"London?" Jimmy gasped. "Dad, I'm on the football team. First string!"

There mom said, "Take it easy, Jimmy. Your a good soccer player and people play alot of soccer in London.

Jenny was to ~~surprised~~ shocked to say anything. She spent every hour worrying about the move. It probably would be more bad than the move before.

In London every one spoke English. And it was almost as if they were speaking a diffrent language. Jenny felt sad and scared. As it opened the door to their new apartment and dragged in their ~~bags~~ luggage, a door opened across the hall.

"Are you moving in" a slender girl asked. Jenny nodded.

I'm Heather" the girl said and smiled. "I'm almost twelve."

"I'll be twelve in January," Jenny ~~said~~ answered. "My name is Jenny."

"Would you like to come in and have tea with my mother and I? I'd also like you to meet my cat. His name is Dolby." Heather ~~said~~ added.

"Please, Mom?" Jenny asked. Her mother smiled and said, "Sure, honey."

When Jenny came back two hours later she was tired so that she just had toast and a glass of milk. Then she climbed in to bed to dream about her new home.

Grade 6/Unit 5: Writing a Story/Revise 5C

McGraw-Hill School Division

Writing a Story

Edit/Proofread

After students finish revising their texts, have them proofread for final corrections and additions.

GRAMMAR/SPELLING CONNECTIONS

See the 5-day Grammar and Usage Plans on pronouns, pp. 467M–467N, 481M–481N, 501M–501N, 531M–531N, and 541M–541N.

See the 5-day Spelling Plans, 467O–467P, 481O–481P, 501O–501P, 531O–531P, and 541O–541P.

GRAMMAR, MECHANICS, USAGE

- Use comparative adjectives (*-er*) to compare two and superlative adjectives (*-est*) to compare three or more.

- Use *better and best* to compare two things.
- Use subject and object pronouns correctly.

MAKE A BOOK Invite students to bind their stories into a class anthology. Have them read their stories to a younger class.

Use **Writing Process Transparency 5D** as a proofreading model and **Writing Process Transparency 5E** to discuss presentation ideas for their writing.

PROOFREAD TRANSPARENCY

A New Country for Jenny

One Summer evening, Jenny's Father gathered the family into the livingroom and told them they were moving to London for two years.

"London?" Jimmy gasped. "Dad, I'm on the football team. First string!"

Their There mom said, "Take it easy, Jimmy. You're a good soccer player, and people play a lot of soccer in London."

Jenny was to surprised to say anything. She spent every hour worrying about the move. It probably would be more bad worse than the move before.

In London every one spoke English. And but it was almost as if they were speaking a diffrent language. Jenny felt sad and scared. As it they opened the door to their new apartment and dragged in their bags, luggage a door opened across the hall.

"Are you moving in?" a slender girl asked. Jenny nodded.

"I'm Heather," the girl said and smiled. "I'm almost twelve."

"I'll be twelve in January," Jenny said. answered "My name is Jenny."

"Would you like to come in and have tea with my mother and I? me I'd also like you to meet my cat. His name is Dolby," added Heather said.

"Please, Mom?" Jenny asked. Her mother smiled and said, "Sure, honey."

When Jenny came back two hours later, she was tired so that she just had toast and a glass of milk. Then she climbed in to bed to dream about her new home.

McGraw-Hill School Division

Grade 6/Unit 5: Writing a Story/Proofread 5D

PUBLISH TRANSPARENCY

A New Country for Jenny

One summer evening, Jenny's father gathered the family into the living room and told them they were moving to London for two years.

"London?" Jimmy gasped. "Dad, I'm on the football team. First string!"

Their mom said, "Take it easy, Jimmy. You're a good soccer player, and people play a lot of soccer in London."

Jenny was too shocked to say anything. She spent every hour worrying about the move. It probably would be worse than the move before.

In London everyone spoke English, but it was almost as if they were speaking a different language. Jenny felt sad and scared. As they opened the door to their new apartment and dragged in their luggage, a door opened across the hall.

"Are you moving in?" a slender girl asked. Jenny nodded.

"I'm Heather," the girl said and smiled. "I'm almost twelve."

"I'll be twelve in January," Jenny answered. "My name is Jenny."

"Would you like to come in and have tea with my mother and me? I'd also like you to meet my cat. His name is Dolby," Heather added.

"Please, Mom?" Jenny asked. Her mother smiled and said, "Sure, honey."

When Jenny came back two hours later, she was so tired that she just had toast and a glass of milk. Then she climbed into bed to dream about her new home.

McGraw-Hill School Division

Grade 6/Unit 5: Writing a Story/Publish 5E

Presentation Ideas

GUESS THE ENDING Volunteers can give clues about their stories. Classmates can guess how the story will end. ▶ **Listening**

MAKE AN AUDIOTAPE Students can work with a partner to dramatize their stories on cassette tape. ▶ **Speaking**

Assessment

- Ask students to self assess their writing. Present the writing features, page 543D, in question form on chart.

- For a 6-point or an 8-point scale, see the writing rubrics on T109–T110.

Listening and Speaking

LISTENING STRATEGIES
- Be alert as you listen.
- Consider what the speaker is saying.
- Ask questions during discussions.

SPEAKING STRATEGIES
- Speak loud enough.
- Support your opinions.
- Use gestures to engage your audience.
- Use time-order words to clarify the sequence of events.

Scoring Rubric; 6-Trait Writing

Excellent	Good	Fair	Unsatisfactory
4: The writer	**3:** The writer	**2:** The writer	**1:** The writer
• **Ideas & Content** creates an entertaining, richly-detailed story about dealing with something unfamiliar; characters, setting, and events are skillfully developed.	• **Ideas & Content** presents a focused, original interesting story with distinct characters, setting, and events.	• **Ideas & Content** attempts to write a story; may not elaborate adequately; may lose control of the narrative after a good beginning.	• **Ideas & Content** may not understand how to tell a story; writing may go off in several directions, without a sense of purpose.
• **Organization** unfolds an elaborately-planned narrative; sequence moves the reader smoothly through events; inviting beginning and satisfying ending.	• **Organization** has a carefully-planned narrative strategy; story is easy to follow, through beginning, middle, and end; ideas, details, and events are connected.	• **Organization** may not craft a finished narrative; may have trouble tying ideas and events together; story line may be vague or incomplete.	• **Organization** shows extreme lack of organization that interferes with understanding the text; sequence of events may be disorganized or incomplete.
• **Voice** shows originality, liveliness, and a strong personal message that speaks directly to the reader; explores a wide range of emotions.	• **Voice** makes a strong effort to share an authentic personal message; reaches out to an audience with feelings and original style.	• **Voice** may get the basic story across, without a sense of involvement or reaching out to an audience; writing is flat and lifeless.	• **Voice** does not attempt to make sense, share ideas, or connect with a reader.
• **Word Choice** imaginative use of figurative and familiar words; sophisticated vocabulary creates a striking picture of a character who faces something new.	• **Word Choice** has effective control of both new and everyday words; vocabulary is used to enliven characters and describe events.	• **Word Choice** does not explore words that express clear ideas or feelings; may not choose words that create memorable pictures for the reader.	• **Word Choice** does not choose words that convey clear feelings or images; some word choices may detract from the meaning or impact of the story.
• **Sentence Fluency** crafts creative, effective sentences that flow in a smooth rhythm; dialogue, if used, sounds natural.	• **Sentence Fluency** crafts careful, easy-to-follow sentences; may effectively use fragments and/or dialogue to strengthen and enhance the story.	• **Sentence Fluency** may have trouble with complex sentences; sentences are understandable, but may be choppy, rambling, or awkward.	• **Sentence Fluency** constructs incomplete or confusing sentences; may have trouble understanding how words, ideas, and sentences fit together.
• **Conventions** shows strong skills in a wide range of writing conventions; proper use of the rules of English enhances clarity and narrative style.	• **Conventions** makes some errors in spelling, capitalization, punctuation or usage, but these do not interfere with understanding the story; some editing may be needed.	• **Conventions** makes enough noticeable mistakes which may interfere with a smooth reading of the story.	• **Conventions** makes repeated errors in spelling, word choice, punctuation and usage; errors prevent an even reading of the text.

Incomplete 0: This piece is either blank, or fails to respond to the writing task. The topic is not addressed, or the student simply paraphrases the prompt. The response may be illegible or incoherent.

VOCABULARY

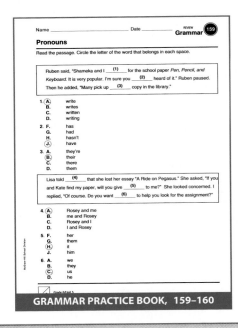

GROUP Use a variation on Twenty Questions to review the vocabulary. Say: "I'm thinking of a word. It is what you feel when you are glad that someone did something for you." Keep offering clues and taking student suggestions until the class gets the right answer. (appreciation) Continue with other words and clues.

Unit Review

Child of the Owl

banister   porcelain   troublemaking
grudged   rhythmically   truce

Bellerophon and the Flying Horse

ferocious   rash   thunderous
lavishly   reassure   waving

Adventure in Space

bloodstream   deliberately   maneuvering
compartment   handshake   void

Rumpelstiltskin's Daughter

barley   knickers   sheepishly
coincidences   mufflers   sweeten

The History of Money

automated   currency   loans
bartering   fee   teller

Name_____ Date_____ Practice **185**

Unit 5 Vocabulary Review

A. Read each vocabulary word in the first column. Then find its antonym in the second column. Write the letter of the antonym on the blank line before each word.

Column 1

1. f   sheepishly
2. e   lavishly
3. a   reassure
4. h   thunderous
5. b   sweeten
6. g   loans
7. c   maneuvering
8. d   troublemaking

Column 2

a. threaten
b. sour
c. still
d. obedience
e. simply
f. forcefully
g. repayments
h. quiet

B. Select a word from the box to complete each sentence.

| bartering | automated | bloodstream | mufflers |
| porcelain | rhythmically | handshake | barley |

1. The museum guide told us that the ___porcelain___ figurine of the dog was 100 years old.
2. Before money was used, ___bartering___ was the way that people acquired goods.
3. The cook added ___barley___, carrots, and potatoes to the stew.
4. Because of the infection in her ___bloodstream___, Marla will have to stay in bed for a few more days.
5. The jazz musician tapped her feet ___rhythmically___ as she played the piano.
6. We sealed the agreement with a ___handshake___ we didn't need a written contract.
7. By using the new ___automated___ banking system, customers can save time.

At Home: Have students identify a synonym for each   Book 6/ Unit 5

PRACTICE BOOK, 184–185

GRAMMAR

GROUP To review the skills covered in the grammar lessons, have students write a brief news account of an interesting event in school or their community. When they have finished, have students exchange papers and check for correct pronoun use.

Unit Review

Child of the Owl
Pronouns

Bellerophon and the Flying Horse
Subject and Object Pronouns

Adventure in Space
Possessive Pronouns

Rumpelstiltskin's Daughter
Indefinite Pronouns

The History of Money
Pronoun-Verb Agreement

Name _____ Date _____ REVIEW Grammar **159**

Pronouns

Read the passage. Circle the letter of the word that belongs in each space.

Ruben said, "Shameka and I ___(1)___ for the school paper *Pen, Pencil, and Keyboard.* It is very popular. I'm sure you ___(2)___ heard of it." Ruben paused. Then he added, "Many pick up ___(3)___ copy in the library."

1. (A) write
   B. writes
   C. written
   D. writing

2. F. has
   G. had
   H. hasn't
   (J.) have

3. A. they're
   (B.) their
   C. there
   D. them

Lisa told ___(4)___ that she lost her essay "A Ride on Pegasus." She asked, "If you and Kate find my paper, will you give ___(5)___ to me?" She looked concerned. I replied, "Of course. Do you want ___(6)___ to help you look for the assignment?"

4. (A) Rosey and me
   B. me and Rosey
   C. Rosey and I
   D. I and Rosey

5. F. her
   G. them
   (H.) it
   J. him

6. A. we
   B. they
   (C.) us
   D. he

Grade 6/Unit 5

GRAMMAR PRACTICE BOOK, 159–160

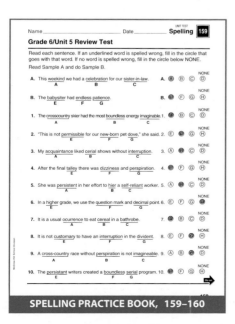

Play "Sentence Maker" to review this unit's spelling words. Distribute paper and pencils and then read the spelling words, one by one. Have students write a sentence using each of the spelling words. When they have finished, have them exchange papers to check for errors.

Unit Review

Compound Words
newborn
bathrobe
question mark
self-reliant
cross-country

Suffixes
dizziness
boundless
persistent
acquaintance
occurrence

Homophones and Homographs
hire
higher
cereal
serial
dove

Math Words
tally
decimal
dividend
deposit
customary

Suffixes
interruption   imaginable
perspiration   permissible
festivity

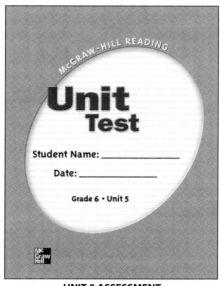

Name_____ Date_____ **Spelling** 159

Grade 6/Unit 5 Review Test

Read each sentence. If an underlined word is spelled wrong, fill in the circle that goes with that word. If no word is spelled wrong, fill in the circle below NONE. Read Sample A and do Sample B.

A. This weekend we had a celebration for our sister-in-law.   A. Ⓐ Ⓑ Ⓒ Ⓓ

B. The babysitter had endless patience.   B. Ⓔ Ⓕ Ⓖ Ⓗ

1. The crosscountry skier had the most boundless energy imaginable.   1. Ⓐ Ⓑ Ⓒ Ⓓ

2. "This is not permissible for our new-born pet dove," she said.   2. Ⓔ Ⓕ Ⓖ Ⓗ

3. My acquaintance liked cerial shows without interruption.   3. Ⓐ Ⓑ Ⓒ Ⓓ

4. After the final talley there was dizziness and perspiration.   4. Ⓔ Ⓕ Ⓖ Ⓗ

5. She was persistent in her effort to hier a self-reliant worker.   5. Ⓐ Ⓑ Ⓒ Ⓓ

6. In a higher grade, we use the question mark and decimal point.   6. Ⓔ Ⓕ Ⓖ Ⓗ

7. It is a usual ocurrence to eat cereal in a bathrobe.   7. Ⓐ Ⓑ Ⓒ Ⓓ

8. It is not customary to have an interruption in the dividend.   8. Ⓔ Ⓕ Ⓖ Ⓗ

9. A cross-country race without perspiration is not imaginable.   9. Ⓐ Ⓑ Ⓒ Ⓓ

10. The persistant writers created a boundless serial program.   10. Ⓔ Ⓕ Ⓖ Ⓗ

SPELLING PRACTICE BOOK, 159–160

Comprehension
☑ Story Elements
☑ Make Inferences
☑ Sequence of Events
☑ Judgments and Decisions

Vocabulary Strategies
☑ Denotation and Connotation
☑ Context Clues

Study Skills
☑ Graphic Aids

Writing
☑ Writing a Story

McGRAW-HILL READING

Unit Test

Student Name: _____

Date: _____

Grade 6 • Unit 5

UNIT 5 ASSESSMENT

Assessment
Follow-Up

Use the results of the formal and informal assessment opportunities in the unit to help you make decisions about future instruction.

SKILLS AND STRATEGIES	Reteach Blackline Masters	Alternate Teaching Strategies	Skills Intervention Guide
Comprehension			ℹ️
Story Elements	149, 153, 170, 174	T62	✓
Make Inferences	154, 161, 175	T64	✓
Sequence of Events	156, 160, 168, 177	T68	✓
Judgments and Decisions	163, 167, 181	T66	✓
Vocabulary Strategy			
Denotation and Connotation	140, 176	T65	✓
Context Clues	162,169	T67	✓
Study Skills			
Graphic Aids	152, 159, 166, 173, 180	T63	✓

	Alternate Writing Project—Easy	Unit Writing Process Lesson
Writing		
Writing a Story	467K–L, 481K–L, 501K–L, 531K–L, 541K–L	543C–H

McGraw-Hill School
TECHNOLOGY

*inter*NET CONNECTION Research & Inquiry Ideas. Visit
www.mhschool.com/reading

Glossary

Introduce students to the Glossary by reading through the introduction and looking over the pages with them. Encourage the class to talk about what they see.

Words in a glossary, like words in a dictionary, are listed in **alphabetical order.** Point out the **guide words** at the top of each page that tell the first and last words appearing on that page.

Point out examples of **entries** and **main entries.** Read through a simple entry with the class, identifying each part. Have students note the order in which information is given: entry word(s), definition(s), example sentence, syllable division, pronunciation respelling, part of speech, plural/verb/adjective forms.

Note that if more than one definition is given for a word, the definitions are numbered. Note also the format used for a word that is more than one part of speech.

Review the parts of speech by identifying each in a sentence:

inter.	*adj.*	*n.*	*conj.*	*adj.*	*n.*
Wow!	A	dictionary	and	a	glossary

v.	*adv.*	*pron.*	*prep.*	*n.*
tell	almost	everything	about	words!

Explain the use of the **pronunciation key** (either the **short key,** at the bottom of every other page, or the **long key,** at the beginning of the glossary). Demonstrate the difference between **primary** stress and **secondary** stress by pronouncing a word with both.

Point out an example of the small triangle signaling a homophone. **Homophones** are words with different spellings and meanings but with the same pronunciation. Explain that a pair of words with the superscripts **1** and **2** are **homographs**—words that have the same spelling, but different origins and meanings, and in some cases, different pronunciations.

The **Word History** feature tells what language a word comes from and what changes have occurred in its spelling and/or meaning. Many everyday words have interesting and surprising stories behind them. Note that word histories can help us remember the meanings of difficult words.

Allow time for students to further explore the Glossary and make their own discoveries.

Glossary

This Glossary can help you find the **meanings** of words in this book that you may not know. It will also help you pronounce these words. The words in the Glossary are listed in **alphabetical order**. **Guide words** at the top of each page tell you the first and last words on the page.

Each word is divided into syllables. The way to pronounce the word is given next. You can understand the pronunciation respelling by using the **Pronunciation Key** at the right. A shorter key appears at the bottom of every other page. When a word has more than one syllable, a dark accent mark (′) shows which syllable is stressed. In some words, a light accent mark (′) shows which syllable has a less heavy stress.

Glossary entries are based on entries in *The Macmillan/McGraw-Hill School Dictionary 1*.

678

Guide Words

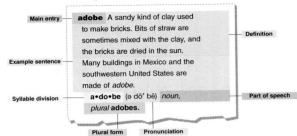

adobe/banner

First word on the page
Last word on the page

Sample Entry

Main entry — **adobe** A sandy kind of clay used to make bricks. Bits of straw are sometimes mixed with the clay, and the bricks are dried in the sun. Many buildings in Mexico and the southwestern United States are made of *adobe*. — Definition

Example sentence

Syllable division — **a•do•be** (ə dō′ bē) *noun, plural* **adobes.** — Part of speech

Plural form   Pronunciation

a	at, bad	d	dear, soda, bad
ā	ape, pain, day, break	f	five, defend, leaf, off, cough, elephant.
ä	father, car, heart	g	game, ago, fog, egg
âr	care, pair, bear, their, where	h	hat, ahead
e	end, pet, said, heaven, friend	hw	white, whether, which
ē	equal, me, feet, team, piece, key	j	joke, enjoy, gem, page, edge
i	it, big, English, hymn	k	kite, bakery, seek, tack, cat
ī	ice, fine, lie, my	l	lid, sailor, feel, ball, allow
îr	ear, deer, here, pierce	m	man, family, dream
o	odd, hot, watch	n	not, final, pan, knife
ō	old, oat, toe, low	ng	long, singer, pink
ô	coffee, all, taught, law, fought	p	pail, repair, soap, happy
ôr	order, fork, horse, story, pour	r	ride, parent, wear, more, marry
oi	oil, toy	s	sit, aside, pets, cent, pass
ou	out, now	sh	shoe, washer, fish, mission, nation
u	up, mud, love, double	t	tag, pretend, fat, button, dressed
ū	use, mule, cue, feud, few	th	thin, panther, both,
ü	rule, true, food	th	this, mother, smooth
u̇	put, wood, should	v	very, favor, wave
ûr	burn, hurry, term, bird, word, courage	w	wet, weather, reward
ə	about, taken, pencil, lemon, circus	y	yes, onion
b	bat, above, job	z	zoo, lazy, jazz, rose, dogs, houses
ch	chin, such, match	zh	vision, treasure, seizure

679

Aa

abide **1.** To put up with; bear; endure. My parents cannot *abide* a messy room. **2.** To accept and obey. A good citizen *abides* by the laws.
a•bide (ə bīd′) *verb,* **abided, abiding.**

acceptable Good enough to be accepted; satisfactory. Our plan for the bazaar was *acceptable* to everyone in the club.
▲**Synonym:** tolerable
ac•cept•a•ble (ak sep′tə bəl) *adjective.*

accompany **1.** To go together with. One of my parents always *accompanies* me to the movies. **2.** To happen at the same time as. Wind often *accompanies* rain.
ac•com•pa•ny (ə kum′pə nē) *verb,* **accompanied, accompanying.**

acculturate To acquire the culture of a particular society from infancy. Children of immigrants *acculturate* more easily than their parents because they are raised in a new environment.
ac•cul•tur•ate (ə kul′chə rāt′) *verb,* **acculturated, acculturating.**

accumulate To gather or pile up; collect. My cousin *accumulated* a number of books at college.
ac•cum•u•late (ə kü′myə lāt′) *verb,* **accumulated, accumulating.**

> **Word History**
>
> The word *accumulate* comes from the latin verb *accumulare,* meaning "to heap up." If you don't empty the trash, it will *accumulate.*

acquaint To make familiar. On the first day of school most teachers become *acquainted* with their students.
ac•quaint (ə kwānt′) *verb,* **acquainted, acquainting.**

acquire To gain as one's own. I *acquired* a taste for Mexican food after visiting Mexico.
ac•quire (ə kwīr′) *verb,* **acquired, acquiring.**

afterlife An existence after death. Some people believe that one's spirit continues to live in an *afterlife.*
af•ter•life (af′tər līf′) *noun.*

680

---

appreciation **1.** A feeling of being thankful; gratitude. I want to show my *appreciation* for your help. **2.** An understanding of the value of something. After studying carpentry, I had a better *appreciation* of fine woodworking.
ap•pre•ci•a•tion (ə prē′shē ā′shən) *noun.*

archaeologist Someone who studies the way humans lived a long time ago. *Archaeologists* dig up the remains of ancient cities and towns and then study the tools, weapons, pottery, and other things they find.
ar•chae•ol•o•gist (är′kē ol′ə jist) *noun, plural* **archaeologists.**

ashore On or to the shore or land. The children paddled the canoe *ashore.*
a•shore (ə shôr′) *adverb.*

astronaut A person trained to fly in a spacecraft. The *astronauts* landed safely on the moon.
as•tro•naut (as′trə nôt′) *noun, plural* **astronauts.**

attitude **1.** A way of thinking, acting, or feeling. Your *attitude* toward school is more enthusiastic than mine. **2.** A position of the body. The body's *attitude* often shows the feelings or thoughts of a person.
at•ti•tude (at′i tüd′ *or* at′i tūd′) *noun, plural* **attitudes.**

automate The process of making something function by itself. Bank teller machines are *automated.*
au•to•mate (ô′ tə māt′) *verb,* **automated, automating.**

Bb

badge Something worn to show that a person belongs to a certain group or has received an honor. A policeman's *badge* is his identification.
▲**Synonym:** insignia
badge (baj) *noun, plural* **badges.**

banister **1.** A railing along a staircase. When you go down stairs, you should hold onto the *banister.* **2.** The posts that support this railing. She polished the *banister* posts.
ban•is•ter (ban′ə stər) *noun, plural* **banisters.**

at; āpe; fär; câre; end; mē; it; īce; pîerce; hot; ōld; sông; fôrk; oil; out; up; üse; rüle; pu̇ll; tûrn; chin; sing; shop; thin; this; hw in white; zh in treasure. The symbol ə stands for the unstressed vowel sound in about, taken, pencil, lemon, and circus.

681

---

barley The grain of a plant that is like grass. *Barley* is used as animal feed, in cooking, and to make malt.
bar•ley (bär′lē) *noun.*

barter To trade things for other things without using money. The pioneers *bartered* grain for blankets with the natives. *Verb.* —The trading of goods or services without the use of money. Among early settlers in this country, fabrics were used as *barter*. *Noun.*
bar•ter (bär′tər) *verb,* bartered, bartering; *noun.*

bazaar 1. A market made up of rows of small shops or stalls. When we visited Cairo, we went to the *bazaar.* 2. A sale of different things for some special purpose. We baked a carrot cake for the church *bazaar.*
ba•zaar (bə zär′) *noun, plural* bazaars.

beckon To make a sign or signal by moving the hand or head. I *beckoned* to my friends to come closer.
beck•on (bek′ən) *verb,* beckoned, beckoning.

Word History

The verb **beckon** comes from the Middle English word *beknen*. Its origin, however, is the Old English word *beacen,* which means "sign."

behavior The way a person acts; manner of conducting oneself. Please be on your best *behavior* at my wedding.
be•hav•ior (bē hāv′yər) *noun, plural* behaviors.

belligerently In a quarrelsome manner.
bel•lig•er•ent•ly (bə lij′ər ənt lē) *adverb.*

blissful Full of, characterized by, or causing great happiness or joy.
▲ **Synonym:** delightful
bliss•ful (blis′ fəl) *adjective.*

bloodstream The blood flowing through the body. The *bloodstream* delivers nutrients to the body's cells.
blood•stream (blud′strēm) *noun, plural* bloodstreams.

bolt 1. To spring or move suddenly. The child *bolted* out the door. 2. To fasten with a bolt. Before the storm strikes, we will have to *bolt* the doors and windows.
bolt (bōlt) *verb,* bolted, bolting.

botanist A person who specializes in botany, the study of plants.
bot•a•nist (bot′ə nist) *noun.*

boyhood The time of being a boy. In my *boyhood* I was very shy.
boy•hood (boi′húd) *noun, plural* boyhoods.

bribe Money or gifts given to make a person do something wrong or something the person does not want to do. The court accused him of accepting a *bribe. Noun.*—To give a bribe to. I *bribed* the child to stop crying by offering her a toy. *Verb.*
bribe (brīb) *noun, plural* bribes; *verb,* bribed, bribing.

bridle The part of a horse's harness that fits over the animal's head, used to guide or control the horse. The cowboy slipped the *bridle* over the horse's head. *Noun.*—To put a bridle on. Unless you ride bareback, you will have to *bridle* the horse. *Verb.*
bri•dle (brī′dəl) *noun, plural* bridles; *verb,* bridled, bridling.

brute 1. A cruel person. I saw that *brute* kick an old dog. 2. An animal. A *brute* cannot reason or feel the way a human being does.
brute (brüt) *noun, plural* brutes.

Word History

Brute first appeared in the English language in the 15th century. It came from the Latin word *brutus,* meaning "heavy."

buffet 1. A piece of furniture having a flat top to serve food from and drawers or shelves for storing dishes, silver, and table linen. 2. A meal laid out on a buffet or a table so that guests may serve themselves. We helped ourselves to the *buffet* twice because the food was excellent.
buf•fet (bə fā′ *or* bù fā′) *noun, plural* buffets.

campsite A place suitable for setting up camp. There is too much litter at this *campsite.*
camp•site (kamp′ sit′) *noun, plural* campsites.

at; āpe; fär; cåre; end; mē; it; īce; pîerce; hot; ōld; sông; fôrk; oil; out; up; ūse; rüle; púll; tûrn; chin; sing; shop; thin; this; hw in white; zh in treasure. The symbol ə stands for the unstressed vowel sound in about, taken, pencil, lemon, and circus.

capable Having skill or power; able. A *capable* mechanic can fix many things.
▲ **Synonym:** competent
ca•pa•ble (kā′pə bəl) *adjective; adverb,* capably.

capsule 1. A small, thin case that encloses something tightly, especially one that contains a small amount of medicine and dissolves in the stomach after it is swallowed. She swallowed the *capsule* and hoped it would cure her cold. 2. A compartment of a spacecraft that carries astronauts or instruments. The space *capsule* plunged into the Pacific Ocean.
cap•sule (kap′səl) *noun, plural* capsules.

carriage 1. A vehicle that moves on wheels. Some *carriages* are pulled by horses and carry people. 2. A movable part of a machine that carries or holds up some other part. The *carriage* of the baggage car was damaged when the train derailed.
car•riage (kar′ij) *noun, plural* carriages.

cavalry A group of soldiers fighting on horseback or from tanks. When the bugle sounded, the *cavalry* charged down the hill.
cav•al•ry (kav′əl rē) *noun, plural* cavalries.

cellophane A thin, clear material made from cellulose, used to wrap food and to make clear tape. You can use *cellophane* as wrapping paper.
cel•lo•phane (sel′ə fān′) *noun.*

chariot A two-wheeled vehicle drawn by horses, used in ancient times in warfare, races, and processions. The ancient Romans entertained themselves by going to *chariot* races.
char•i•ot (char′ē ət) *noun, plural* chariots.

clockwise In the direction in which the hands of a clock move. Move the dial *clockwise* to turn on the radio.
clock•wise (klok′wiz′) *adverb; adjective.*

cobblestone A round stone, formerly used to pave streets. *Cobblestone* streets are difficult to walk on.
cob•ble•stone (kob′əl stōn′) *noun, plural* cobblestones.

coffin A box in which the body of a dead person is buried. Dracula slept in a *coffin.*
▲ **Synonym:** casket
cof•fin (kô′fin) *noun, plural* coffins.

coincidence The happening of two events at the same time or place. A coincidence seems remarkable because although it looks planned, it really is not. It was just a *coincidence* that the two couples went to the same movie.
co•in•ci•dence (kō in′si dəns) *noun, plural* coincidences.

compartment A separate division or section. My desk drawer has *compartments* for pencils, erasers, and paper clips.
com•part•ment (kəm pärt′mənt) *noun, plural* compartments.

complex Hard to understand or do. He solved a *complex* arithmetic problem. *Adjective.*—A whole made up of many connected parts. His dormitory was located in a *complex* of university buildings. *Noun.*
com•plex (kəm pleks′ *or* kom′pleks) *adjective; noun, plural* complexes.

conceal To put or keep out of sight; hide. I *concealed* my anger by smiling.
▲ **Synonym:** cover
con•ceal (kən sēl′) *verb,* concealed, concealing.

congregation 1. The people present at a religious service. The entire *congregation* left after the service. 2. A gathering or crowd of people or things. A large *congregation* assembled in the square.
con•gre•ga•tion (kong′gri gā′shən) *noun, plural* congregations.

consultation A meeting to ask advice or share ideas or opinions.
consultation (kon′səl tā′shən) *noun, plural* consultations.

contrast A difference. There's a sharp *contrast* between black and white.
con•trast (kon′trast) *noun, plural* contrasts.

controversy A disagreement; dispute. The new tax caused much *controversy.*
▲ **Synonym:** quarrel
con•tro•ver•sy (kon′trə vûr′sē) *noun, plural* controversies.

at; āpe; fär; cåre; end; mē; it; īce; pîerce; hot; ōld; sông; fôrk; oil; out; up; ūse; rüle; púll; tûrn; chin; sing; shop; thin; this; hw in white; zh in treasure. The symbol ə stands for the unstressed vowel sound in about, taken, pencil, lemon, and circus.

Glossary

G3

counselor 1. A person who helps or gives advice. She spent the summer working as a camp *counselor*. 2. A lawyer. His *counselor* was familiar with the workings of the court.
coun•se•lor (koun′sə lər) *noun*, *plural* **counselors**.

cringe To draw back in fear, surprise, or disgust; flinch; shrink. The freezing temperature of the water in the pool made me *cringe*.
cringe (krinj) *verb*, **cringed**, **cringing**.

cultivate 1. To prepare and use land for growing vegetables, flowers, or other crops. To *cultivate* land, you plow it and fertilize it before you plant seeds. 2. To plant and help to grow. That farmer *cultivates* corn.
cul•ti•vate (kul′tə vāt′) *verb*, **cultivated**, **cultivating**.

currency 1. The money used in a country. Dollars, quarters, and dimes are part of the *currency* used in the United States. 2. General use or acceptance. As more people use a new word, they give it *currency*.
cur•ren•cy (kûr′ən sē) *noun*, *plural* **currencies**.

cut-out Something cut out of or off something else. The cereal box came with a free *cut-out* prize.
cut•out (kut′ out′) *noun*, *plural* **cut-outs**.

Dd

darn To mend by making stitches back and forth across a hole. You should *darn* that hole in your sock.
darn (därn) *verb*, **darned**, **darning**.

deep-sea Of, relating to, or occurring in the deeper parts of the sea. *Deep-sea* fishing is a popular sport.
deep•sea (dēp′ sē′) *adjective*.

defect A flaw or weakness. That glass bowl has a chip, a crack, and other *defects*.
▲**Synonym:** fault
de•fect (dē′fekt *or* di fekt′) *noun*, *plural* **defects**.

deliberately 1. Carefully and slowly; not hastily or rashly. 2. Intentionally; on purpose.
de•lib•er•ate•ly (di lib′ər it lē) *adverb*.

dent To make a dent or hollow in. I *dented* the soft clay with my thumb. *Verb.*—A small hollow made in the surface of something by a blow or pressure. The accident put a *dent* in the front fender of my bike. *Noun.*
dent (dent) *verb*, **dented**, **denting**; *noun*, *plural* **dents**.

depositor One who puts money in the bank or makes a deposit. *Depositors* trust that their money will be safe in the bank.
de•pos•i•tor (di poz′ə tər) *noun*, *plural* **depositors**.

desolate 1. Without people; deserted. In the winter, that beach is desolate. 2. Miserable; cheerless. The lost child was *desolate*.
des•o•late (des′ə lit) *adjective*.

destination A place to which a person is going or a thing is being sent. My *destination* is New York.
des•tin•a•tion (des′tə nā′shən) *noun*, *plural* **destinations**.

detergent A chemical substance that is used for washing things. It may be a liquid or powder. We use *detergent* to wash the dishes.
de•ter•gent (di tûr′jənt) *noun*, *plural* **detergents**.

> **Word History**
>
> *Detergent* comes from the Latin verb *tergere*, meaning "to wipe."

devise To think out; invent; plan. We *devised* a secret code that no one could decipher.
de•vise (di vīz′) *verb*, **devised**, **devising**.

diagonal Having a slant. The dress had a pattern of *diagonal* stripes. *Adjective.*—A straight line that connects the opposite corners of a square or rectangle. He drew a *diagonal* from one corner to the other. *Noun.*
di•ag•o•nal (dī ag′ ə nəl) *adjective*; *noun*, *plural* **diagonals**.

diminish To make or become smaller. The campers' supply of food *diminished* as the days wore on.
di•min•ish (di min′ish) *verb*, **diminished**, **diminishing**.

at; āpe; fär; câre; end; mē; it; īce; pîerce; hot; ōld; sông; fôrk; oil; out; up; ūse; rüle; pùll; tûrn; chin; sing; shop; thin; this; hw in white; zh in treasure. The symbol ə stands for the unstressed vowel sound in about, taken, pencil, lemon, and circus.

dispense To give out. The town *dispensed* food and clothing to the homeless people.
dis•pense (di spens′) *verb*, **dispensed**, **dispensing**.

disrupt To break up or apart. By talking together, the two pupils were *disrupting* the whole class.
dis•rupt (dis rupt′) *verb*, **disrupted**, **disrupting**.

doff To remove an article of clothing from the body; also, to take off a hat in greeting or as a sign of respect. The man *doffed* his hat as he passed the mayor.
doff (dof *or* dôf) *verb*, **doffed**, **doffing**.

dramatically 1. In a manner having to do with plays or acting. My cousin is *dramatically* talented. 2. In a manner as exciting and interesting as a good play or story. Our team won *dramatically* by scoring the winning point in the last minute of the game.
dra•mat•ic•al•ly (drə mat′ic lē) *adverb*.

dramatics 1. The art or activity of producing or performing plays. ▲Used with a singular verb. 2. Exaggerated or theatrical behavior. ▲ Used with a plural verb.
dra•mat•ics (drə mat′iks) *noun*.

dreamer 1. One who dreams. When she went to bed, she became a *dreamer*. 2. One who lives in a world of fancy and imagination. Artists and writers are often said to be *dreamers*.
dream•er (drē′mər) *noun*, *plural* **dreamers**.

drone A low, steady humming sound. The *drone* of the car's engine made me sleepy. *Noun.*—To talk in a dull, boring way. The speaker *droned* on and on. *Verb.*
drone (drōn) *noun*, *plural* **drones**; *verb*, **droned**, **droning**.

duet A piece of music written for two singers or two musical instruments. The soprano and the pianist finished their *duet* to loud applause.
du•et (dü et *or* dū et) *noun*, *plural* **duets**.

Ee

eavesdrop To listen to other people talking without letting them know you are listening. I learned about my own surprise party by *eavesdropping* as my friends planned the party.
▲**Synonym:** overhear
eaves•drop (ēvz′drop′) *verb*, **eavesdropped**, **eavesdropping**.

> **Word History**
>
> The word *eavesdrop* once meant the area at the side of a house where rainwater on the roof would drop from the eaves to the ground. A person who stood in this place to listen in secret to people talking inside the house was said to be eavesdropping.

ecological Of or relating to ecology, the science that deals with how plants, animals, and other living things live in relation to each other and to their environment.
ecological (ek′ə loj′i kəl *or* ē′kə loj′i kəl) *adjective*.

edible Fit or safe to eat. Not all kinds of berries are *edible*.
ed•i•ble (ed′ə bəl) *adjective*.

encounter To meet in battle. The soldiers *encountered* and defeated the enemy. *Verb.*—A usually unexpected meeting. Your *encounter* with her is the talk of the school. *Noun.*
en•coun•ter (en koun′tər) *verb*, **encountered**, **encountering**; *noun*, *plural* **encounters**.

engrave 1. To cut or carve into a surface. The jeweler *engraved* my name on the back of my watch. 2. To print from a plate that has been cut with letters, figures, or designs. The printer *engraved* the invitations.
en•grave (en grāv′) *verb*, **engraved**, **engraving**.

enthusiastically In an excited, eager manner. We *enthusiastically* accepted the invitation to the picnic.
en•thu•si•as•ti•cal•ly (en thü′zē as′tik lē) *adverb*.

at; āpe; fär; câre; end; mē; it; īce; pîerce; hot; ōld; sông; fôrk; oil; out; up; ūse; rüle; pùll; tûrn; chin; sing; shop; thin; this; hw in white; zh in treasure. The symbol ə stands for the unstressed vowel sound in about, taken, pencil, lemon, and circus.

environment 1. The air, the water, the soil, and all the other things that surround a person, animal, or plant. The *environment* can affect the growth and health of living things. Zoos try to make each animal's enclosure like its natural *environment*. **2.** Surroundings; atmosphere. I loved summer camp because of the friendly *environment*.
en•vi•ron•ment (en vī′rən mənt *or* en vī′ərn mənt) *noun, plural* **environments.**

environmental Concerning or related to the environment. Recently politicians have become more responsive to *environmental* issues.
en•vi•ron•men•tal (en vī′rən mən′ təl) *adjective.*

equator An imaginary line around the earth. It is halfway between the North and South Poles. The United States and Canada are north of the *equator*.
e•qua•tor (i kwā′tər) *noun, plural* **equators.**

Word History
The word *equator* is based on the Medieval Latin word *aequator*, which means "equalizer." The equator divides Earth into northern and southern hemispheres.

equip To provide with whatever is needed. The ship was *equipped* with hoses to be used in case of fire.
▲ **Synonym:** outfit
e•quip (i kwip′) *verb,* **equipped, equipping.**

essay A short written composition on a subject. I wrote an *essay* about the need for world peace.
es•say (es′ā) *noun, plural* **essays.**

Word History
The word *essay* comes from a French word meaning "to try." The first essays modestly claimed to be only attempts to set down the writer's thoughts.

evoke To bring to mind. Seeing those pictures *evoked* childhood memories.
e•voke (i vōk′) *verb,* **evoked, evoking.**

exaggerate To make something seem larger, greater, or more important than it is. The camper *exaggerated* the size of the fish that had gotten away.
ex•ag•ger•ate (eg zaj′ə rāt′) *verb,* **exaggerated, exaggerating.**

690

---

exasperate To annoy greatly; make angry. The constant barking of our neighbor's dog has *exasperated* our family.
ex•as•per•ate (eg zas′pə rāt′) *verb,* **exasperated, exasperating.**

existence 1. The fact of being alive or real. The *existence* of some wild animals is in danger because of pollution. **2.** A way of living; life. The early colonists in America led a dangerous *existence*.
ex•is•tence (eg zis′təns) *noun, plural* **existences.**

expel To drive or force out. They *expelled* the child from school for disobeying everyone.
ex•pel (ek spel′) *verb,* **expelled, expelling.**

explosion 1. The act of bursting or expanding suddenly and noisily. The *explosion* of the bomb broke windows in the buildings nearby. **2.** A sudden outburst. The funny joke caused an *explosion* of laughter.
ex•plo•sion (ek splō′zhən) *noun, plural* **explosions.**

 Ff

famine A great lack of food in an area or country. Many people died of starvation during the *famine* in Ireland in the 1840s.
fam•ine (fam′in) *noun, plural* **famines.**

fee Money requested or paid for some service or right. The city charges a *fee* of ten dollars for a dog license.
fee (fē) *noun, plural* **fees.**

ferocious Savage; fierce. A lion can be *ferocious*.
fe•ro•cious (fə rō′shəs) *adjective; adverb,* **ferociously.**

fidget To move or act restlessly or nervously. I was so nervous about the performance that I couldn't stop *fidgeting*. *Verb.*—A nervous or restless movement. I could not control the *fidget* in my leg. *Noun.*
fidg•et (fi′ jət) *verb,* **fidgeted, fidgeting;** *noun, plural* **fidgets.**

at; āpe; fär; cãre; end; mē; it; īce; pîerce; hot; ōld; sông; fôrk; oil; out; up; ūse; rūle; pùll; tûrn; chin; sing; shop; thin; **this**; hw in white; zh in treasure. The symbol ə stands for the unstressed vowel sound in about, taken, pencil, lemon, and circus.

691

---

fleck A spot or mark. I have a *fleck* of juice on my shirt. *Noun.*—To color as if by sprinkling with dots. Impressionist paintings are often *flecked* with color. *Verb.*
fleck (flek) *noun, plural* **flecks;** *verb,* **flecked, flecking.**

flurry 1. A brief, light fall of snow. The weatherman predicted a snow *flurry* for tomorrow. **2.** A sudden outburst. There was a *flurry* of excitement when the movie star got out of the limousine.
flur•ry (flûr′ē) *noun, plural* **flurries.**

foremost First in position or importance. She was considered the *foremost* citizen of the town.
fore•most (fôr′ mōst) *adjective.*

formation 1. Something formed or made. The placement of the rocks in the garden made an interesting *formation*. **2.** The process of forming or making. The *formation* of ice from water requires a temperature below 32 degrees Fahrenheit.
for•ma•tion (fôr mā′shən) *noun, plural* **formations.**

foyer A lobby or entranceway. She opened the door and walked into the *foyer*.
foy•er (foi′ ər) *noun, plural* **foyers.**

frightful 1. Causing sudden fear; alarming. The man's mask was *frightful*. **2.** Disgusting or shocking. There was a *frightful* mess on the sidewalk.
fright•ful (frit′fəl) *adjective.*

froth A mass of bubbles formed in or on a liquid; foam. A *froth* appeared on the milk as it boiled. *Noun.*—To give out or form froth. The mixture *frothed* as it boiled. *Verb.*
froth (frôth) *noun, plural* **froths;** *verb,* **frothed, frothing;** *adjective,* **frothy.**

 Gg

generator A machine that produces electricity, steam, or other energy. The hospital had an emergency *generator* in case of a power failure.
gen•er•a•tor (jen′ə rā′tər) *noun, plural* **generators.**

goddess A female god. Gods and *goddesses* ruled the world in ancient Greece.
god•dess (god′is) *noun, plural* **goddesses.**

692

---

goldsmith One who makes and deals in articles of gold. The *goldsmith* put the new rings in the showcase.
gold•smith (gōld′smith′) *noun, plural* **goldsmiths.**

gravity The force that pulls things toward the core of the earth, the moon, or other planets. *Gravity* is the force that causes objects to fall when they are dropped.
grav•i•ty (grav′i tē) *noun, plural* **gravities.**

grimace To make a grimace. His mother *grimaced* when she saw his bad grades. *Verb.*—A twisting of the face. People often make a *grimace* when they are uncomfortable. *Noun.*
gri•mace (grim′əs *or* gri mās′) *verb,* **grimaced, grimacing;** *noun, plural* **grimaces.**

Word History
The verb *grimace* appeared in the English language in 1651. It comes from the Middle French *grimache* and the Old English *grima*, meaning "mask."

grudge To be unwilling to give or allow. Although they don't like you, they won't *grudge* you first prize if you deserve it. *Verb.*—Dislike or anger that has been felt for a long time. Those two have held a *grudge* against each other ever since kindergarten. *Noun.*
grudge (gruj) *verb,* **grudged, grudging;** *noun, plural* **grudges.**

Hh

habitat The place where an animal or plant naturally lives and grows. The natural *habitat* of fish is water.
hab•i•tat (hab′i tat) *noun, plural* **habitats.**

hamlet A very small village. New York City is much larger than a *hamlet*.
ham•let (ham′lit) *noun, plural* **hamlets.**

handrail A railing that can be gripped by the hand, used on stairways and balconies to support and protect people. The elderly woman gripped the *handrail* as she went down the stairs.
hand•rail (hand′ rāl′) *noun, plural* **handrails.**

at; āpe; fär; cãre; end; mē; it; īce; pîerce; hot; ōld; sông; fôrk; oil; out; up; ūse; rūle; pùll; tûrn; chin; sing; shop; thin; **this**; hw in white; zh in treasure. The symbol ə stands for the unstressed vowel sound in about, taken, pencil, lemon, and circus.

693

handshake An act in which two people grip and shake each other's hands. A handshake can be a way of greeting someone, a way of saying good-bye, or a way of marking an agreement. They sealed their bargain with a *handshake*.
hand•shake (hand′shāk′) *noun, plural* **handshakes.**

hard-boiled 1. Boiled until hard. A *hard-boiled* egg is boiled until its yolk and white are solid. 2. Tough and not sympathetic. The inspector was a *hard-boiled* police detective.
hard•boiled (härd′boild′) *adjective.*

hesitantly In a manner showing hesitation; unwillingly. I was *hesitant* about jumping into the lake.
▲**Synonym:** uncertainly
hes•i•tant•ly (hez′i tənt lē) *adverb.*

hibernate To spend the winter sleeping. Some bears, woodchucks, frogs, and snakes hibernate. The bear went into the cave to *hibernate*.
hi•ber•nate (hi′bər nāt′) *verb,* **hibernated, hibernating;** *noun,* **hibernation.**

honeycomb To make full of tunnels or cells like a bee's honeycomb. Secret passages *honeycombed* the castle. *Verb.*—A wax structure made by bees to store their eggs and honey. A honeycomb is made up of layers of cells that have six sides. Beekeepers often sell honey that is still in the *honeycomb. Noun.*
hon•ey•comb (hun′ē kōm′) *verb,* **honeycombed, honeycombing;** *noun, plural* **honeycombs.**

honor To show or feel great respect for a person or thing. The city *honored* the astronauts with a parade. *Verb.* — Something given or done to show great respect or appreciation. The hero received a medal and other *honors. Noun.*
hon•or (on′ər) *verb,* **honored, honoring;** *noun, plural* **honors.**

hospitalize To put a person in a hospital. I was *hospitalized* when I had my tonsils removed.
hos•pi•tal•ize (hos′pi tə liz′) *verb,* **hospitalized, hospitalizing.**

694

husky 1. Big and strong. Clint is a *husky* football player. 2. Rough and deep in sound. The bass has a *husky* voice.
hus•ky (hus′kē) *adjective,* **huskier, huskiest.**

hydroelectric Relating to electricity created by generators run by rapidly flowing water. There is a *hydroelectric* power station at the waterfall.
hy•dro•e•lec•tric (hi′drō i lek′trik) *adjective.*

hydrogen A gas that has no color, taste, or odor and that burns very easily. Hydrogen is a chemical element. It is the lightest and most abundant element in the universe. *Hydrogen* is one of the elements of which water is composed.
hy•dro•gen (hi′drə jən) *noun.*

Ii

illegible Very hard or impossible to read. The handwriting on the envelope was *illegible*.
il•leg•i•ble (i lej′ə bəl) *adjective.*

implore To ask earnestly or beg for something. I *implore* you to clear the table, even though it's my turn.
▲**Synonym:** plead
im•plore (im plôr′) *verb,* **implored, imploring;** *adverb,* **imploringly.**

improvement 1. The act of getting better. 2. A change or addition that makes something better.
im•prove•ment (im prüv′mənt) *noun, plural* **improvements.**

impudence 1. The quality of being impudent; rudeness; insolence. 2. Bold and rude speech or behavior.
im•pu•dence (im′pyə dəns) *noun.*

industrial 1. Having to do with or produced by industry. Iron smelting, coal mining, and the production of plastics are *industrial* processes. 2. Having highly developed industries. Canada is an *industrial* country.
in•dus•tri•al (in dus′trē əl) *adjective.*

inevitable Not able to be avoided; bound to happen. An *inevitable* result of closing your eyes is not being able to see.
▲**Synonym:** unavoidable
in•ev•i•ta•ble (i nev′i tə bəl) *adjective; adverb,* **inevitably.**

infantry Soldiers trained and equipped to fight on foot. The *infantry* used to be very important in winning wars.
in•fan•try (in′fən trē) *noun, plural* **infantries.**

at; āpe; fär; câre; end; mē; it; īce; pîerce; hot; ōld; sông; fôrk; oil; out; up; ūse; rüle; püll; tûrn; chin; sing; shop; thin; this; hw in white; zh in treasure. The symbol ə stands for the unstressed vowel sound in about, taken, pencil, lemon, and circus.

695

inflection 1. A change in pitch or loudness of the voice. There was a strange *inflection* in his voice. 2. The change of form that words undergo to show case, number, tense and the like. In English class we studied the *inflection* of nouns.
in•flec•tion (in flek′ shən) *noun, plural* **inflections.**

initiate 1. To be the first to do; begin; start. The new librarian *initiated* the practice of lending books for a month. 2. To make a person a member of an organization or club. The new members were *initiated* into the club.
in•i•ti•ate (i nish′ē āt′) *verb,* **initiated, initiating.**

inquisitive Eager to know; curious. An *inquisitive* student asks a lot of questions.
in•qui•si•tive (in kwiz′i tiv) *adjective.*

instinctively In a manner having to do with a way of acting or behaving that a person or animal is born with and does not have to learn. Birds build nests *instinctively*.
in•stinc•tive•ly (in stingk′tiv lē) *adverb.*

interior 1. The inner side, surface, or part. The *interior* of the cave was dark. 2. The part of a country or region that is away from the coast or border. The *interior* of Australia is mostly desert.
in•te•ri•or (in tîr′ē ər) *noun, plural* **interiors.**

interview A meeting in which people talk face to face. I had an *interview* with the store manager for a summer job. *Noun.*—To have an interview with. The mayor was *interviewed* about the growing traffic problem. *Verb.*
in•ter•view (in′tər vū′) *noun, plural* **interviews;** *verb,* **interviewed, interviewing.**

inventory 1. A detailed list of articles on hand. The *inventory* showed all the goods the clothing store had on its shelves. 2. The articles that are on such a list. The store has a large *inventory* of sports equipment.
in•ven•tor•y (in′vən tôr′ ē) *noun, plural* **inventories.**

iota 1. A very small amount. You don't have an *iota* of evidence against me. 2. The ninth letter of the Greek alphabet. He learned how to write an *iota*.
i•o•ta (i ō′ tə) *noun.*

696

Jj

jalopy An old, run-down car. This *jalopy* won't make it all the way to Florida from New York.
ja•lo•py (jə lop′ē) *noun, plural* **jalopies.**

jubilantly In a joyous manner. They celebrated their victory *jubilantly*.
ju•bi•lant•ly (jü′bə lənt lē) *adverb.*

Kk

knickers Loose-fitting short pants gathered at the knee. My father wore *knickers* to school.
knick•ers (nik′ərz) *plural noun.*

Ll

landmark 1. An object that is familiar and serves as a guide. The church steeple is a well-known *landmark* in our town. 2. An important building, structure, or place. This Civil War battlefield is a national *landmark*.
land•mark (land′märk′) *noun, plural* **landmarks.**

laughable Causing or likely to cause a person to laugh. It was *laughable* to think that all those clowns could fit in one tiny car.
▲**Synonym:** absurd
laugh•a•ble (laf′ə bəl) *adjective.*

lavishly In an extravagant or wasteful manner. We ate *lavishly* at the expensive restaurant.
lav•ish•ly (lav′ish lē) *adverb.*

Word History

The word *lavish* comes from two related words in Middle French. *Lavasse* means "downpour of rain" and *laver* means "to wash."

liberation The act or state of being or becoming free.
lib•er•a•tion (lib′ə rā′ shən) *noun.*

lifeboat A boat used for saving lives at sea or along the shore. *Lifeboats* are often carried on larger ships.
life•boat (lif′bōt′) *noun, plural* **lifeboats.**

at; āpe; fär; câre; end; mē; it; īce; pîerce; hot; ōld; sông; fôrk; oil; out; up; ūse; rüle; püll; tûrn; chin; sing; shop; thin; this; hw in white; zh in treasure. The symbol ə stands for the unstressed vowel sound in about, taken, pencil, lemon, and circus.

697

loan To lend something to someone. Thank you for *loaning* me your pencil. *Verb.*—Something lent. We received a *loan* of five thousand dollars from the bank. *Noun.*
> **loan** (lōn) *verb*, **loaned, loaning**; *noun, plural* **loans**.

loot To steal valuable things from; plunder. The enemy soldiers *looted* the town. *Verb.*—Things that have been stolen. The thieves hid their *loot* in the barn. *Noun.*
▲ Another word that sounds like this is *lute*.
> **loot** (lüt) *verb*, **looted, looting**; *noun*.

lunar Of or having to do with the moon. The astronauts brought back *lunar* rocks for study.
> **lu·nar** (lü′nər) *adjective*.

Mm

magnetic 1. Acting like a magnet; having to do with magnets or magnetism. The needle of a compass points to the earth's *magnetic* poles. 2. Able to attract or fascinate people. The actor had a *magnetic* personality.
> **mag·net·ic** (mag net′ik) *adjective*; *adverb*, **magnetically**.

maiden A girl or young unmarried woman. *Noun.*— First or earliest. The ship's *maiden* voyage was from England to New York. *Adjective.*
> **maid·en** (mā′dən) *noun, plural* **maidens**; *adjective*.

majestic Grand and noble; dignified. The *majestic* mountains rose high above the valley.
> **ma·jes·tic** (mə jes′tik) *adjective*; *adverb*, **majestically**.

makeshift Used for a time in place of the correct or usual thing. We sometimes use our sofa as a *makeshift* bed. *Adjective.*— Something used for a time in place of the correct or usual thing. When the Venetian blinds broke, we used a sheet as a *makeshift*. *Noun.*
> **make·shift** (māk′shift′) *adjective*; *noun, plural* **makeshifts**.

698

maneuver To move or manage skillfully or cleverly. We *maneuvered* our way to the front of the crowd so we could see the parade. *Verb.*— An organized movement of soldiers or ships. The captain planned the troops' next *maneuver*. *Noun.*
> **ma·neu·ver** (mə nü′vər) *verb*, **maneuvered, maneuvering**; *noun, plural* **maneuvers**.

manhood 1. The condition or the time of being an adult male person. The adolescent boy will soon enter *manhood*. 2. Men as a group. The *manhood* and womanhood of our country always respond well in a national crisis.
> **man·hood** (man′hùd) *noun*.

marina A small harbor where boats and yachts can be docked and serviced. The *marina* suffered a lot of damage during the hurricane.
> **ma·ri·na** (mə rē′nə) *noun, plural* **marinas**.

melodrama A movie or play that emphasizes plot and action over characterization. The theater group decided to revive an old *melodrama*.
> **me·lo·dra·ma** (me′ lə drä′ mə) *noun, plural* **melodramas**.

mission 1. A group of people sent somewhere to do a special job. Four rangers formed a rescue *mission* to search for the lost child. 2. A special job or task. The space agency scheduled another *mission* to the moon.
> **mis·sion** (mish′ən) *noun, plural* **missions**.

mongrel A plant or an animal, especially a dog, that is a mixture of breeds. The dog had a noble face even though he was a *mongrel*.
> **mon·grel** (mung′grəl *or* mong′grəl) *noun, plural* **mongrels**.

monitor To watch over or observe something. Our teacher *monitored* the fire drill. *Verb.*—A student who is given a special duty to do, such as taking attendance. Last year I was the hallway *monitor*. *Noun.*
> **mon·i·tor** (mon′i tər) *verb*, **monitored, monitoring**; *noun, plural* **monitors**.

at; āpe; fär; câre; end; mē; it; īce; pîerce; hot; ōld; sōng; fôrk; oil; out; up; ūse; rūle; pùll; tûrn; chin; sing; shop; thin; this; hw in white; zh in treasure. The symbol ə stands for the unstressed vowel sound in about, taken, pencil, lemon, and circus.

699

monotonous Tiring or uninteresting because it does not change in any way. That job is *monotonous* because you have to do the same thing over and over.
▲ Synonym: tedious
> **mo·not·o·nous** (mə not′ə nəs) *adjective*; *adverb*, **monotonously**.

mortar 1. A building material made of sand, water, and lime. The workers mixed *mortar* to build the brick fireplace. 2. A thick, heavy bowl in which things are crushed or ground by using a pestle. She ground the herbs in a *mortar*.
> **mor·tar** (môr′tər) *noun, plural* **mortars**.

mortify To subject to severe embarrassment. He was *mortified* when she kissed him in front of the other students.
> **mor·ti·fy** (môr′tə fī′) *verb*, **mortified, mortifying**.

mourner A person who is feeling or showing sorrow or grief. The *mourners* walked slowly through the cemetery.
▲ Synonym: griever
> **mourn·er** (môr′nər) *noun, plural* **mourners**.

muffler 1. A warm scarf for wrapping around the neck in cold weather. 2. A device that reduces the noise made by an engine. The noisy car had a damaged *muffler*.
> **muf·fler** (muf′lər) *noun, plural* **mufflers**.

mummy A dead body that has been wrapped in cloth and specially treated to preserve it. Some ancient Egyptian *mummies* are over 3,000 years old.
> **mum·my** (mum′ē) *noun, plural* **mummies**.

murmur A low, soft sound. We heard the *murmur* of the brook. *Noun.*—To make or say with a low, soft sound. I heard you *murmur* in your sleep. *Verb.*
> **mur·mur** (mûr′mər) *noun, plural* **murmurs**; *verb*, **murmured, murmuring**.

mythology A group or collection of myths and legends. All the myths that were told and written in ancient Greece are known as Greek *mythology*.
> **my·thol·o·gy** (mi thol′ə jē) *noun, plural* **mythologies**.

700

Nn

narrative A story or report on something that happened. The writer gave a long *narrative* of her travels. *Noun.* —Telling a story. Her favorite poem was a *narrative* poem. *Adjective.*
> **nar·ra·tive** (nar′ə tiv) *noun, plural* **narratives**; *adjective*.

nimbly In a light, quick manner. The cat jumped *nimbly* onto the fence.
> **nim·bly** (nim′blē) *adverb*.

novelty 1. Something new or unusual. 2. The quality of being new.
> **nov·el·ty** (nov′əl tē) *noun, plural* **novelties**.

Oo

obstacle Something that stands in the way of progress. The roadblock was an *obstacle* to traffic.
▲ Synonym: obstruction
> **ob·sta·cle** (ob′stə kəl) *noun, plural* **obstacles**.

occupation 1. The work that a person does in order to earn a living; profession. Her *occupation* is teaching. 2. The act of occupying or the condition of being occupied. The enemy soldiers began their *occupation* of the town.
> **oc·cu·pa·tion** (ok′yə pā′shən) *noun, plural* **occupations**.

ordeal A very hard or painful experience or test. Living through the earthquake was quite an *ordeal*.
> **or·deal** (ôr dēl′ *or* ôr′dēl) *noun, plural* **ordeals**.

Pp

painstakingly In a careful manner. She wrote the report *painstakingly*, fretting over every word.
> **pains·tak·ing·ly** (pānz′tāk′ ing lē) *adverb*.

participate To join with others; take part. Everyone *participated* in the rally.
> **par·tic·i·pate** (pär tis′ə pāt′) *verb*, **participated, participating**.

at; āpe; fär; câre; end; mē; it; īce; pîerce; hot; ōld; sōng; fôrk; oil; out; up; ūse; rūle; pùll; tûrn; chin; sing; shop; thin; this; hw in white; zh in treasure. The symbol ə stands for the unstressed vowel sound in about, taken, pencil, lemon, and circus.

701

Glossary

G7

pedestal 1. A base on which a column or statue stands. The sculptor built a *pedestal* for the bronze figure. **2.** The base or other part of something that supports it. The *pedestal* of the lamp was cracked.
ped•es•tal (ped'ə stəl) *noun, plural* **pedestals.**

pep A lively, vital quality; activity; spirit. After the brisk walk outside, I was full of *pep. Noun.*—To make lively or energetic. Whenever I need to be *pepped* up, I do some exercises. *Verb.*
pep (pep) *noun; verb,* **pepped, pepping.**

perception 1. The understanding, comprehension, or knowledge that is the result of perceiving. The astronauts' *perception* of the problems that arose during their flight saved their lives. **2.** The act or power of perceiving. A cat's *perception* of colors is poor.
per•cep•tion (pər sep'shən) *noun, plural* **perceptions.**

pharaoh The title of the kings of ancient Egypt. King Tutankhamen was a *pharaoh.*
phar•aoh (fâr'ō) *noun, plural* **pharaohs.**

pillar A column that supports a building or stands alone as a monument. The roof of the porch is supported by *pillars.*
pil•lar (pil'ər) *noun, plural* **pillars.**

plunder To steal from; rob. Soldiers *plundered* the town. *Verb.*—Something stolen. The outlaws hid their *plunder* in an old shed. *Noun.*
plun•der (plun'dər) *verb,* **plundered, plundering;** *noun.*

populate 1. To live in, inhabit. Nomads *populate* the desert. **2.** To provide with members. The government wants to *populate* the new industrial complex.
pop•u•late (pop'yə lāt) *verb,* **populated, populating.**

porcelain A kind of hard, fine pottery. It is thin enough to see through when held to the light. Cups, plates, and other dishes are sometimes made of *porcelain.* Antique Chinese *porcelain* objects are very valuable.
por•ce•lain (pôr'sə lin) *noun.*

---

pore To read or study carefully. I *pored* over my notes the night before the test. *Verb.*—A very small opening in the skin or other surface. Perspiration passes through the *pores* in our skin. *Noun.*
pore (pôr) *verb,* **pored, poring;** *noun, plural* **pores.**

portcullis A grating of iron hung over the gateway of a fortified place and lowered between grooves to prevent passage. Knights in armor stormed the *portcullis.*
port•cul•lis (pôrt kul' is) *noun.*

porthole A small round window in the side of a boat or ship. It lets in both air and light. She could see the tropical island through the *porthole.*
port•hole (pôrt'hōl') *noun, plural* **portholes.**

pout To thrust out the lips to show displeasure. The children *pouted* when they were scolded.
▲**Synonym:** scowl
pout (pout) *verb,* **pouted, pouting.**

precise 1. Definite; exact. Your arrival time must be *precise.* **2.** Strict or careful. The teacher speaks in a clear and *precise* way.
pre•cise (pri sis') *adjective; adverb,* **precisely.**

prehistoric Belonging to a time before people started writing history. Mammoths and dinosaurs were *prehistoric* animals.
pre•his•tor•ic (prē'his tôr'ik) *adjective.*

prospective Likely to come about in the future. He introduced his *prospective* wife to his parents.
▲**Synonym:** expected
pro•spec•tive (prə spek'tiv) *adjective.*

prosperous Having success, wealth, or good fortune. The *prosperous* family tried to help other less fortunate families.
pros•per•ous (pros'pər əs) *adjective.*

protrude To stick out. Only the tip of an iceberg *protrudes* from the surface of the ocean.
pro•trude (prō trüd') *verb,* **protruded, protruding.**

at; āpe; fär; câre; end; mē; it; īce; pîerce; hot; ōld; sông; fôrk; oil; out; up; ūse; rūle; pûll; tûrn; chin; sing; shop; thin; this; hw in white; zh in treasure. The symbol ə stands for the unstressed vowel sound in about, taken, pencil, lemon, and circus.

---

psychology The study of the mind and of the way people or animals behave. She wants to study *psychology* when she goes to college.
psy•chol•o•gy (si kol'ə jē) *noun.*

puncture To make a hole in something with a sharp object. I *punctured* the balloon with a pin. *Verb.*— A hole made by a sharp object. They fixed a *puncture* in the tire. *Noun.*
punc•ture (pungk'chər) *verb,* **punctured, puncturing;** *noun, plural* **punctures.**

Qq

quantity 1. A number or amount. The recipe calls for a small *quantity* of milk. **2.** A large number or amount. Restaurants buy food in *quantity.*
quan•ti•ty (kwon'ti tē) *noun, plural* **quantities.**

questioningly In an inquiring manner. The judge looked *questioningly* at the witness.
ques•tion•ing•ly (kwes'chən ing lē) *adverb.*

Rr

rash Too hasty; not careful. Unfortunately, he made a *rash* decision. *Adjective.*—A condition in which red spots appear on the skin. Poison ivy causes a *rash. Noun.*
rash (rash) *adjective,* **rasher, rashest;** *noun, plural* **rashes;** *adverb,* **rashly;** *noun,* **rashness.**

ration To limit to fixed portions. The government *rationed* meat during the war. *Verb.*—A fixed portion or share, especially of food. The mountain climbers carried *rations* in their backpacks. *Noun.*
ra•tion (rash'ən *or* rā'shən) *verb,* **rationed, rationing;** *noun, plural* **rations.**

reassure To restore confidence or courage in. Before the curtain rose, the director *reassured* the actors.
▲**Synonym:** comfort
re•as•sure (rē' ə shûr') *verb,* **reassured, reassuring;** *noun,* **reassurance.**

rebellious Resisting or refusing to obey authority. The *rebellious* sailors ignored the captain's orders.
re•bel•lious (ri bel'yəs) *adjective.*

---

recite 1. To repeat something from memory. Can you *recite* the names of all the fifty states? **2.** To tell the story of. I *recited* my adventures at camp to the class.
re•cite (ri sit') *verb,* **recited, reciting.**

rectangle A figure with four sides and four right angles. A square is a *rectangle* whose four sides are of equal length.
rec•tan•gle (rek'tang'gəl) *noun, plural* **rectangles;** *adjective,* **rectangular.**

relish 1. A mixture of spices, pickles, olives, and chopped vegetables, used as a side dish and to flavor food. The *relish* tray was passed around the table after the curry was served. **2.** Interest or pleasure; enjoyment. The child opened the presents with *relish.*
rel•ish (rel'ish) *noun, plural* **relishes.**

remote 1. Not near; far away. The explorer traveled to *remote* regions. **2.** Far from cities or towns. The children grew up in a *remote* mountain village.
re•mote (ri mōt') *adjective,* **remoter, remotest;** *adverb,* **remotely;** *noun,* **remoteness.**

researcher A person who performs investigations to find facts in a particular field of study. The *researcher* observed fifteen different kinds of fish.
re•search•er (ri sûrch'ər *or* rē'sûrch'ər) *noun, plural* **researchers.**

reservoir A place where water is stored. Although there are fish in the *reservoir,* it is prohibited to go fishing there.
res•er•voir (rez'ər vwär') *noun, plural* **reservoirs.**

residence 1. A place where a person lives. You enter his *residence* from a side door. **2.** A period of time spent living in a place. After ten years' *residence* in the city, my family moved.
res•i•dence (rez'i dəns) *noun, plural* **residences.**

retrieve 1. To get back; recover. The golfer *retrieved* the ball from the pond. **2.** To find and bring back dead or wounded game. Our dog is trained to *retrieve.*
re•trieve (ri trēv') *verb,* **retrieved, retrieving;** *noun,* **retrieval.**

at; āpe; fär; câre; end; mē; it; īce; pîerce; hot; ōld; sông; fôrk; oil; out; up; ūse; rūle; pûll; tûrn; chin; sing; shop; thin; this; hw in white; zh in treasure. The symbol ə stands for the unstressed vowel sound in about, taken, pencil, lemon, and circus.

G8 *Glossary*

Glossary

rhythmically In a manner having a steady or consistent beat.
rhyth•mi•cal•ly (rĭth′mĭk lē) *adverb*.

riverbank The bank of a river. He sat on the *riverbank* and watched for boats coming downstream.
riv•er•bank (rĭv′ər bangk′) *noun, plural* **riverbanks**.

romance 1. A love affair. *Sleeping Beauty* is about the *romance* between a prince and a sleeping princess. **2.** A quality of love, excitement, mystery, or adventure. The dim lights gave a sense of *romance* to the room.
ro•mance (rō mans′ *or* rō′mans) *noun, plural* **romances**.

Word History

The word *romance* comes from an old French word that meant "something written in a Romance language." In the Middle Ages, stories of love and adventure were usually written in one of these Romance languages instead of in Latin, which was used in more serious writings.

rudder 1. A broad, flat, movable piece of wood or metal attached to the rear of a boat or ship. It is used in steering. Without a *rudder* the captain could not guide his ship. **2.** A similar piece at the tail of an aircraft. The pilot adjusted the *rudder* as he circled the airport.
rud•der (rŭd′ər) *noun, plural* **rudders**.

rummage To search completely by moving things around. I *rummaged* in the closet for my missing shoe.
▲ **Synonym:** ransack
rum•mage (rŭm′ĭj) *verb*, **rummaged, rummaging**.

Ss

saunter To walk around in a leisurely manner; stroll. The young girl *sauntered* to the candy store.
saun•ter (sôn′tər) *verb*, **sauntered, sauntering**.

savings Money that is saved. It will take all of your *savings* to buy that camera.
sav•ings (sā′vĭngz) *plural noun*.

scaffold A platform that workers stand on as they work on a building. The construction workers stood on a *scaffold*.
scaf•fold (skaf′əld) *noun, plural* **scaffolds**.

scrawl To write or draw quickly and carelessly. Somebody *scrawled* on my test paper and covered up my grade.
▲ **Synonym:** scribble
scrawl (skrôl) *verb*, **scrawled, scrawling**.

scrumptious Delicious; delightful. The chocolate cake we ate for dessert was *scrumptious*.
scrump•tious (skrump′ shəs) *adjective*.

706

---

sculpt To shape or give form to. She *sculpted* a bust of Mozart in marble.
sculpt (skulpt) *verb*, **sculpted, sculpting**.

sensor A device that detects changes in heat, sound, or pressure and sends the information to another instrument that controls it. My friend has a motion *sensor* in his car.
sen•sor (sen′sər) *noun, plural* **sensors**.

sentimental Having or showing tender feeling. The couple in the movie sang a *sentimental* song.
sen•ti•men•tal (sen′tə men′təl) *adjective*.

sever To cut or break apart. Our friendship was *severed* when she told everyone my secret.
sev•er (sev′ər) *verb*, **severed, severing**.

sharecropper A farmer, especially in the southern United States, who works the land and receives an agreed share of the crop. The *sharecroppers* had a good harvest.
share•crop•per (shâr′ krop′ər) *noun, plural* **sharecroppers**.

sheepishly In an embarrassed manner.
sheep•ish•ly (shē′ pish lē) *adverb*.

shuttle *See* space shuttle.

silhouette To show as a dark outline against a lighter background. The horse standing on the hill was *silhouetted* against the sky. *Verb.*—The outline of a figure or object filled in with black or another solid color. *Noun.*
sil•hou•ette (sil′ū et′) *verb*, **silhouetted, silhouetting**; *noun, plural* **silhouettes**.

Word History

Silhouette comes from the last name of Etienne de Silhouette, who was the French Controller of Finances for a brief time in 1767. The meaning of *silhouette* is based on his very short, almost "invisible" time on the job.

at; āpe; fär; câre; end; mē; ĭt; īce; pîerce; hot; ōld; sông; fôrk; oil; out; up; ūse; rūle; pull; tûrn; chin; sing; shop; thin; this; hw in white; zh in treasure. The symbol ə stands for the unstressed vowel sound in about, taken, pencil, lemon, and circus.

707

---

site The position or location of something. Our house is on a mountain *site* with a beautiful view.
▲ Other words that sound like this are **cite** and **sight**.
site (sĭt) *noun, plural* **sites**.

smirk To smile in a self-satisfied or silly manner. My brother *smirked* at me because he got two cookies and I only got one.
smirk (smûrk) *verb*, **smirked, smirking**.

sneer A facial expression or a remark that shows hatred or scorn. The rude child answered with a *sneer*. *Noun.* —To show or say with a sneer. The thief *sneered* at the police. *Verb.*
sneer (snîr) *noun, plural* **sneers**; *verb*, **sneered, sneering**.

somber Dark or gloomy. The sky became gray and *somber* before the thunderstorm.
som•ber (som′bər) *adjective; adverb*, **somberly**; *noun*, **somberness**.

sophisticated Having or showing much knowledge and experience of the world. I hope to be as *sophisticated* as my mother someday.
so•phis•ti•cat•ed (sə fĭs′tĭ kā′tid) *adjective; noun*, **sophistication**.

spacecraft A vehicle used for flight in outer space. Also, **spaceship**. I always wanted to see the inside of a *spacecraft*.
space•craft (spās′kraft′) *noun, plural* **spacecraft**.

space shuttle A spacecraft that carries a crew into space and returns to land on Earth. The same space shuttle can be used again. I would like to fly in a *space shuttle*.
space shut•tle (spās′ shut′əl) *noun, plural* **space shuttles**.

spacious Having a lot of space or room; large. The apartment was very *spacious*.
▲ **Synonym:** extensive
spa•cious (spā′shəs) *adjective; noun*, **spaciousness**.

spat The past tense and past participle of **spit**. He quickly *spat* out the words of the speech. *Verb.* —A short, unimportant argument or disagreement. The sisters had a *spat* about what to watch on TV. *Noun.*
spat (spat) *verb; noun, plural* **spats**.

708

---

sphinx 1. A mythical creature having a human head and a lion's body. In Greek mythology the *sphinx* had a woman's head and killed anyone who couldn't answer its riddle. **2.** The Sphinx; a large statue of this creature in Egypt. The *sphinx* was erected to honor a pharaoh.
sphinx (sfingks) *noun, plural* **sphinxes**.

splendor Magnificence; brilliance. In all its *splendor*, the mansion sits high on a hill.
splen•dor (splen′dər) *noun; adjective*, **splendorous**.

starboard The right side of a boat, ship, or aircraft when a person standing on deck faces forward. We stood on the *starboard* while sailing to sea. *Noun.*— On, of, or relating to the right side of a boat, ship, or aircraft. The tugboat moved toward the *starboard* side of the ship. *Adjective.*
star•board (stär′bərd) *noun; adjective*.

storage 1. The act of storing things or the condition of being stored. The furniture was picked up for *storage* today. **2.** A place for storing things. The chest is used as a *storage* for our toys.
stor•age (stôr′ij) *noun*.

stubbornness Obstinacy; refusal to yield or give up. The horse's *stubbornness* caused the race to be postponed.
stub•born•ness (stub′ərn nəs) *noun*.

subdue 1. To defeat; conquer. The soldiers *subdued* the enemy. **2.** To control or overcome. I *subdued* my anger.
sub•due (səb dü′ *or* səb dū′) *verb*, **subdued, subduing**.

submerge To place under or cover with some liquid, especially water. Add water until the potatoes are completely *submerged*.
sub•merge (səb mûrj′) *verb*, **submerged, submerging**.

at; āpe; fär; câre; end; mē; ĭt; īce; pîerce; hot; ōld; sông; fôrk; oil; out; up; ūse; rūle; pull; tûrn; chin; sing; shop; thin; this; hw in white; zh in treasure. The symbol ə stands for the unstressed vowel sound in about, taken, pencil, lemon, and circus.

709

Glossary

G9

suds Soapy water with foam or bubbles. When you wash the car, spread the *suds* on it first.
suds (sudz) *plural noun.*

support 1. To give strength or comfort to. The family *supported* each other during a difficult time. **2.** To hold up. The columns *support* the roof.
sup•port (sə pôrt′) *verb,* **supported, supporting;** *adjective,* **supportive.**

surprise 1. To cause to feel sudden wonder or amazement. You *surprised* me with all the gifts you brought. **2.** To come upon suddenly and unexpectedly. One morning we *surprised* two deer in our backyard.
sur•prise (sər priz′) *verb,* **surprised, surprising.**

surprisingly In a manner causing wonder or amazement. I did *surprisingly* well on the pop quiz.
sur•pris•ing•ly (sər priz′ing lē) *adverb.*

survey 1. A measuring of land. That family had a *survey* made of their property. **2.** A detailed study. The company did a *survey* to find out who used its products. *Noun.*—To view, examine, or measure as a whole. *Verb.*
sur•vey (sər vā′ *for verb;* sûr′vā *or* sər vā′ *for noun*) *noun, plural* **surveys;** *verb,* **surveyed, surveying.**

surveyor A person who takes measurements to determine the shape, area, and boundaries of a piece of land.
sur•vey•or (sər vā′ər) *noun, plural* **surveyors.**

sweeten To make or become sweet or sweeter. The cook *sweetened* the lemonade with sugar.
sweet•en (swē′tən) *verb,* **sweetened, sweetening;** *noun,* **sweetener.**

synagogue A building used by Jews for worship and religious instruction. My friend went to *synagogue* for Yom Kippur.
syn•a•gogue (sin′ə gog′) *noun, plural* **synagogues.**

710

Tt

tattoo A colored figure or design made on the skin with needles that have been dipped in colors. The sailor had *tattoos* of ships on each arm. *Noun.*—To mark with tattoos. I *tattooed* a butterfly on my arm. *Verb.*
tat•too (ta tü′) *noun, plural* **tattoos;** *verb,* **tattooed, tattooing.**

technology 1. The use of science for practical purposes, especially in engineering and industry. Space exploration contributed important changes in *technology.* **2.** Methods, machines, and devices that are used in doing things in a science or profession. X rays were an important advance in medical *technology.*
tech•nol•o•gy (tek nol′ə jē) *noun, plural* **technologies.**

teller 1. A person who works in a bank giving out and receiving money. The bank *teller* counted the deposits for the day. **2.** A person who tells or relates. He is a *teller* of tall tales.
tell•er (tel′ər) *noun, plural* **tellers.**

temporary Lasting or used for a short time only. Some students try to find *temporary* jobs for the summer.
▲ **Synonym:** makeshift
tem•po•rar•y (tem′pə rer′ē) *adjective.*

terminal 1. A station at either end of a railroad, bus, air, or other transportation line. We waited at the bus *terminal* for my sister to arrive. **2.** A keyboard and a monitor that can be connected to a computer. Before we could work, we had to connect the *terminal* to a CPU and a printer.
ter•mi•nal (tûr′mə nəl) *noun, plural* **terminals.**

thunderous Making or accompanied by a noise like thunder. The audience gave the solo violinist *thunderous* applause.
thun•der•ous (thun′dər əs) *adjective; adverb,* **thunderously.**

token 1. A piece of metal that looks like a coin and is used in place of money. **2.** A sign of something else; symbol. Please accept this gift as a *token* of our appreciation.
to•ken (tō′kən) *noun, plural* **tokens.**

at; āpe; fär; câre; end; mē; it; īce; pîerce; hot; ōld; sông; fôrk; oil; out; up; ūse; rūle; pùll; tûrn; chin; sing; shop; thin; this; hw in white; zh in treasure. The symbol ə stands for the unstressed vowel sound in about, taken, pencil, lemon, and circus.

711

---

tollbooth A stall where fees are paid, usually found at the entrance to a bridge or highway. The traffic at the *tollbooth* moved very slowly.
toll•booth (tōl′ büth′) *noun, plural* **tollbooths.**

tomb A grave or building in which a dead body is placed. The king's body was placed in an elaborate *tomb.*
tomb (tüm) *noun, plural* **tombs.**

transmitter A device that sends out radio or television signals. The *transmitter* had to be upgraded to send digital signals.
trans•mit•ter (trans mit′ər) *noun, plural* **transmitters.**

treason The betraying of one's country by helping an enemy. Giving the army's battle plans to the enemy was an act of *treason.*
trea•son (trē′zən) *noun.*

Word History

The word **treason** comes from the Latin word *traditio,* which means "the act of handing over," as in handing over information or secrets. *Treason* first appeared in the English language in the 13th century.

tremor A shaking or trembling. Earthquakes cause *tremors* in the earth.
tre•mor (trem′ər) *noun, plural* **tremors.**

triangle 1. A figure or object with three sides and three angles. The architect designed a building that was shaped like a *triangle.* **2.** A musical instrument made of a metal bar bent in the shape of a triangle. A *triangle* sounds like a bell when it is struck.
tri•an•gle (trī′ang′gəl) *noun, plural* **triangles.**

triangle *(def. 2)*

trill The rapid vibration of a musical tone. There were many *trills* in the Beethoven sonata. *Noun.*—To vibrate a musical note on an instrument or with the voice. The singer *trilled* the note with great ease. *Verb.*
trill (tril) *noun, plural* **trills;** *verb,* **trilled, trilling.**

troublemaking Willful disruption. Her *troublemaking* always upsets the teacher.
trou•ble•mak•ing (trub′ əl māk′ ing) *noun.*

712

---

truce A short stop in fighting. A *truce* is agreed to by both sides, who then try to reach a peace agreement. The enemies agreed to a *truce.*
truce (trüs) *noun, plural* **truces.**

Word History

Truce comes from a Middle English word meaning "agreement."

tutor A teacher who gives private lessons to a pupil. When I was sick for three months, I had a *tutor* at home. *Noun.*—To teach privately; act as a tutor. The college student made money by *tutoring* French. *Verb.*
tu•tor (tü′tər *or* tū′tər) *noun, plural* **tutors;** *verb,* **tutored, tutoring.**

Word History

Tutor comes from a Latin word meaning "defender" or "guardian." In some English universities, the word *tutor* was used for a graduate responsible for a younger student. From this meaning came the sense of "private teacher."

Uu

unconsciously Not intentionally; not on purpose.
un•con•scious•ly (un kon′shəs lē) *adverb.*

undersea Lying, done, or used below the surface of the sea. There have been several *undersea* explorations to photograph the remains of the *Titanic.*
un•der•sea (un′dər sē′ *or* un′dər sē′) *adjective.*

unison The making of the same sounds or movements at the same time. We recited the poem in *unison.*
u•ni•son (ū′nə sən) *noun.*

universe Everything that exists, including the Earth and all of space. It is difficult to imagine the size of the *universe.*
u•ni•verse (ū′nə vûrs′) *noun, plural* **universes.**

Word History

Universe comes from a Latin word that means "the whole world."

at; āpe; fär; câre; end; mē; it; īce; pîerce; hot; ōld; sông; fôrk; oil; out; up; ūse; rūle; pùll; tûrn; chin; sing; shop; thin; this; hw in white; zh in treasure. The symbol ə stands for the unstressed vowel sound in about, taken, pencil, lemon, and circus.

713

Glossary

Vv

valiant Brave; courageous; heroic. The *valiant* knight saved the princess from danger.
▲ **Synonym:** stouthearted
val•iant (val′ yənt) *adjective.*

victorious Having won a victory. The *victorious* army was welcomed home.
vic•to•ri•ous (vik tôr′ē əs) *adjective.*

vilest Most repulsive; most foul. It was the *vilest* smell I had ever encountered.
▲ **Synonym:** nastiest
vilest (vīl′ əst) *adjective.*

visual 1. Relating to or used in seeing. Eyeglasses are used to correct *visual* defects. **2.** Able to be seen; visible. The teacher used charts, slides, and other *visual* aids to help explain how the heart works.
vis•u•al (vizh′ü əl) *adjective.*

void An empty space. The whole group fell silent, leaving an awkward *void. Noun.* —Having no legal force; not valid. After the investigation, the election results were declared *void. Adjective.*
void (void) *noun, plural* **voids;** *adjective.*

voyage 1. A journey by water or through space. Christopher Columbus made *voyages* to the New World in 1492 and 1493. **2.** A long journey. A *voyage* around the Earth in a sailing ship takes many months.
voy•age (voi′ij) *noun, plural* **voyages.**

Ww

ware 1. Things for sale. The street vendors put their *wares* on display in the public square. **2.** Dishes, pots, and other things used for cooking or eating. We bought a new piece of ceramic *ware* at the fair.
▲ Another word that sounds like this is **wear.**
ware (wâr) *noun, plural* **wares.**

wave To move freely back and forth or up and down; move with a swaying motion. The stalks of wheat *waved* in the wind. *Verb.* —A long, moving ridge of water on the surface of a body of water. The ship rode gently over the *waves. Noun.*
wave (wāv) *verb,* **waved, waving;** *noun, plural* **waves.**

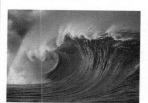

whopper 1. A monstrous lie. I told my teacher a *whopper* because I hadn't done my homework. **2.** Something unusually large. The fish I caught this weekend was a *whopper!*
whop•per (hwop′ər *or* wop′ər) *noun, plural* **whoppers.**

whopper *(def. 2)*

wide-open Having no limits or restrictions. We take our dog to the field because he needs a *wide-open* space in which to run.
wide•o•pen (wid′ ō′ pən) *adjective.*

worthwhile Good enough or important enough to spend time, effort, or money on. Doing volunteer work at the hospital is a *worthwhile* activity.
worth•while (wûrth′hwil′ *or* wûrth′wil′) *adjective.*

at; āpe; fär; câre; end; mē; it; īce; pîerce; hot; ōld; sông; fôrk; oil; out; up; ūse; rüle; pùll; tûrn; chin; sing; shop; thin; this; hw in white; zh in treasure. The symbol ə stands for the unstressed vowel sound in about, taken, pencil, lemon, and circus.

714

Glossary

Cover Illustration: Kinuko Y. Craft

The publisher gratefully acknowledges permission to reprint the following copyrighted material:

From "Alice in Wonderland" by Lewis Carroll. Copyright © 1962 Macmillan Publishing Company. Used by permission.

"Anansi and His Visitor, Turtle" from AFRICAN VILLAGE FOLK TALES by Edna Mason Kaula. Copyright © 1968 by Edna Mason Kaula. Used by permission of Philomel Books.

"Anecdote For Fathers" from POETICAL WORKS by William Wordsworth edited by Thomas Hutchinson. Copyright © 1904 Oxford Press. Used by Permission.

"Cleopatra Grows Up" from CLEOPATRA by Polly Schoyer Brooks. Copyright © 1995 by Polly Schoyer Brooks. Used by permission of HarperCollins Publishers.

"The Climb" from TO RIDE A BUTTERFLY by Patricia C. McKissack. Text copyright © 1991 by Patricia C. McKissack. Used by permission of Bantam Doubleday Dell Publishing Group, Inc.

"Daedalus and Icarus" from GREEK MYTHS by Geraldine McCaughrean. Text copyright © 1992 by Geraldine McCaughrean. Reprinted with the permission of Margaret K. McElderry Books, an imprint of Simon & Schuster Children's Publishing Division.

"The First Musician" from THE BUTTERFLY JAR by Jeff Moss. Text copyright © 1989 by Jeff Moss. Used by permission of Bantam Books, a division of Random House, Inc.

"Gong Gong" from THE RIVER THAT WENT TO THE SKY by Amoafi Kwapong. © Amoafi Kwapong 1995. Used by permission of Larousse Kingfisher Chambers.

"I Close My Book and Open a Window" by Chung On from SUNSET IN A SPIDER WEB, adapted by Virginia Olsen Baron from translations by Chung Seuk Park, Text © 1974 by Virginia Olsen Baron. Reprinted by permission of Henry Holt and Company, LLC.

"I Don't Want to Live on the Moon" from THE BUTTERFLY JAR by Jeff Moss. Text copyright © 1989 by Jeff Moss. Used by permission of Bantam Books, a division of Bantam Doubleday Dell Publishing Group, Inc.

"The Lightwell" from HOME by Laurence Yep. Copyright © 1992 by Laurence Yep. Published by HarperCollins Publishers, Inc. Reprinted by permission of the Author and Curtis Brown, Ltd.

"Long Trip" from COLLECTED POEMS by Langston Hughes. Copyright © 1994 by the Estate of Langston Hughes. Reprinted by permission of Alfred A. Knopf, Inc.

"Long Walk to Freedom" from LONG WALK TO FREEDOM by Nelson Mandela. Copyright © 1994 by Nelson Rolihlahla Mandela. Used by permission of Little, Brown and Company.

ACKNOWLEDGMENTS

The publisher gratefully acknowledges permission to reprint the following copyrighted material.

ADVENTURE IN SPACE: THE FLIGHT TO FIX THE HUBBLE by Elaine Scott, photographs by Margaret Miller. Text copyright © 1995 by Elaine Scott. Photographs copyright © 1995 by Margaret Miller. Used by permission of Hyperion Books for Children.

"Alexander the Great" Reprinted by the permission of Russell & Volkening as agents for the author. Copyright © 1968 by Olivia Coolidge, copyright renewal 1996 by the author.

"The All-American Slurp" by Lensey Namioka from VISIONS, edited by Donald R. Gallo. Copyright © 1987 by Lensey Namioka. Reprinted by permission of Lensey Namioka. All rights reserved by the Author.

"Bellerophon and the Flying Horse" from TALES FROM ANCIENT GREECE by Pamela Oldfield. Copyright © 1988 by Grisewood and Dempsey, Ltd. Used by permission of Doubleday, a division of Random House, Inc.

"A Boy of Unusual Vision" by Alice Steinbach. Article courtesy of The Baltimore Sun. Used by permission.

"Child of the Owl" from CHILD OF THE OWL by Laurence Yep. Copyright © 1977 by Laurence Yep. Published by HarperCollins Publishers, Inc. Reprinted by permission of the Author and Curtis Brown, Ltd.

"The Circuit" by Francisco Jiménez first published in the Arizona Quarterly Autumn, 1973. Copyright © 1973 by Francisco Jiménez. Reprinted by permission of the author.

"Daydreamers" by Eloise Greenfield. Text copyright © 1981 by Eloise Greenfield. Reprinted by permission of the publisher, Dial Books for Young Readers, a division of Penguin Putnam, Inc.

From EXPLORING THE TITANIC by Robert D. Ballard, cover illustration by Ken Marshall. Text copyright © Odyssey Corporation 1998. Illustration copyright © 1988 Madison Publishing Inc. Used by permission of Scholastic Inc.

"I Go Forth to Move About the Earth" by Alonzo Lopez from WHISPERING WIND by Terry Allen. Copyright © 1972 by the Institute of American Indian Arts. Used by permission of Doubleday, a division of Random House, Inc.

"I May, I Might, I Must" copyright © 1959 by Marianne Moore, © renewed 1987 by Lawrence E. Brinn and Louise Crane, Executors of the Estate of Marianne Moore from THE COMPLETE POEMS OF MARIANNE MOORE by Marianne Moore. Used by permission of Viking Penguin, a division of Penguin Putnam, Inc.

"Last Summer with Maizon" excerpts from LAST SUMMER WITH MAIZON by Jacqueline Woodson. Copyright © 1990 by Jacqueline Woodson. Used by permission of Random House, Inc.

MANDELA written and illustrated by Floyd Cooper. Copyright © 1996 by Floyd Cooper. Used by permission of Philomel Books, a division of Penguin Putnam, Inc.

Maxine W. Kumin, "The Microscope." Copyright © 1968 by Maxine W. Kumin. Reprinted by permission of the author.

Excerpt from MUMMIES, TOMBS, AND TREASURE by Lila Perl. Text copyright © 1987 by Lila Perl. Illustrations copyright © 1987 by Erika Weihs. Reprinted by permission of Clarion Books/Houghton Mifflin Company. All rights reserved.

"My Friend Flicka" as it appeared in Story Magazine from MY FRIEND FLICKA by Mary O'Hara. Text copyright © 1941 by the author. Text copyright renewed 1969 by the author. Reprinted by permission of HarperCollins Publishers, Inc.

"My Uncle Dan" from POETRY IS by Ted Hughes. Copyright © 1967 by Ted Hughes. Used by permission of Doubleday, a division of Random House, Inc.

Excerpt from NUMBER THE STARS, Copyright © 1989 by Lois Lowry. Reprinted by permission of Houghton Mifflin Company. All rights reserved.

"Opera, Karate and Bandits" from THE LAND I LOST: ADVENTURES OF A BOY IN VIETNAM by Huynh Quang Nhuong. Copyright © 1982 by Huynh Quang Nhuong. Reprinted by permission of HarperCollins Publishers.

OVER THE TOP OF THE WORLD by Will Stegner and Jon Bowermaster. Published by Scholastic Press, a division of Scholastic, Inc. Copyright © 1997 by Expeditions Unlimited, Inc. Used by permission of Scholastic, Inc.

PAINTERS OF THE CAVES by Patricia Lauber. Copyright © 1998 by Patricia Lauber. Used by permission of National Geographic Society.

"People" from ALL THAT SUNLIGHT by Charlotte Zolotow. Text copyright © 1967, renewed copyright © 1995 by Charlotte Zolotow. Reprinted by permission of Scott Treimel New York.

"The Phantom Tollbooth" by Susan Nanus, based on the book by Norton Juster. Copyright ©1977 by Susan Nanus and Norton Juster. Reprinted by permission of Samuel French, Inc.

"Purple Snake" text copyright © 1996 by Pat Mora. From the book CONFETTI: POEMS FOR CHILDREN by Pat Mora. Permission granted by Lee and Low Books, Inc., 95 Madison Avenue, New York, NY 10016.

"Rain, Rain, Go Away," from BUY JUPITER AND OTHER STORIES by Isaac Asimov. Copyright © 1975 by the author. Used by permission of Doubleday, a division of Random House, Inc.

RUMPLESTILTSKIN'S DAUGHTER by Diane Stanley. Copyright © 1997 by Diane Stanley. Used by permission of Morrow Junior Books, a division of William Morrow & Company, Inc.

"The School Play" from LOCAL NEWS by Gary Soto. Copyright © 1993 by Gary Soto. Used by permission of Harcourt, Inc.

THE SINGING MAN. Text copyright © 1994 by Angela Shelf Medearis. Illustrations copyright © 1994 by Terea Shaffer. All rights reserved. Reprinted from THE SINGING MAN by permission of Holiday House, Inc.

"A Song of Greatness" from THE CHILDREN SING IN THE FAR WEST by Mary Austin. Copyright 1928 by Mary Austin. Copyright © renewed 1956 by Kenneth M. Chapman and Mary C. Wheelwright. Reprinted by permission of Houghton Mifflin Co. All rights reserved.

S.O.R. LOSERS reprinted with the permission of Simon & Schuster Books for Young Readers, an imprint of Simon & Schuster Children's Publishing Division from S.O.R. LOSERS by Avi. Copyright © 1984 by Avi Wortis.

"Stopping by Woods on a Snowy Evening" from THE POETRY OF ROBERT FROST, edited by Edward Connery Lathem. Copyright © 1951 by Robert Frost. Copyright ©1923, 1969 by Henry Holt and Co., Inc. Reprinted by permission of Henry Holt and Co., Inc.

TA-NA-E-KA by Mary Whitebird, published in SCHOLASTIC VOICE, December 13, 1973. Copyright © 1973 by Scholastic, Inc. Used by permission.

"To Look at Any Thing" from THE LIVING SEED by John Moffitt. Copyright © 1962 by John Moffitt and renewed 1989 by Henry Moffit. Reprinted by permission of Harcourt Brace & Company.

"To You" from COLLECTED POEMS by Langston Hughes. Copyright © 1994 by the Estate of Langston Hughes. Reprinted by permission of Alfred A. Knopf, Inc.

"Travellers" by Arthur St. John Adcock from THE BOOK OF A THOUSAND POEMS. Reprinted by permission.

"Viva New Jersey" by Gloria Gonzalez. Copyright © 1993 by Gloria Gonzalez. From JOIN IN: MULTIETHNIC SHORT STORIES edited by Donald R. Gallo. Used by permission of Delacorte Press, a division of Random House, Inc.

"Mummy" from THE WAY THINGS ARE AND OTHER POEMS by Myra Cohn Livingston. Copyright © 1974 by Myra Cohn Livingston. Used by permission of Marian Reiner.

"One Time" copyright 1982, 1998 by the Estate of William Stafford. Reprinted from The Way It Is: New & Selected Poems by William Stafford with the permission of Graywolf Press, Saint Paul, Minnesota.

"Rabbit Goes Fishing" from BIG TROUBLE FOR TRICKY RABBIT! by Gretchen Will Mayo. Copyright © 1994 by Gretchen Will Mayo. Reprinted with permission of Walker and Company.

Cover Illustration

Kinuko Y. Craft

Illustration

Larry McEntire, 16; Annie Bissett, 38; Tuko Fujisaki, 39; Carl Mazer, 43; Yoshi Miyake, 42-59; Rose Zgodzinski, 62; Annie Bissett, 82; Annie Bissett, 83; David Bamundo, 83; Joe LeMonnier, 98; Stanford Kay, 108; Tom Feelings, 110-111; Linda Frichtel, 112; Annie Bissett, 136; David Bamundo, 137; Shonto Begay, 140-154; Rose Zgodzinski, 158; Stanford Kay, 186; Annie Bissett, 206; Annie Bissett, 216; Chuck Gonzales, 217; Shane Warren Evans, 220; Stanford Kay, 238; Tom Feelings, 242-255; Rose Zgodzinski, 258; David Bamundo, 259; Stanford Kay, 286; Chris Lensch, 287; Joe LeMonnier, 293; Annie Bissett, 306; Stanford Kay, 316; David Bamundo, 317; Phillip Dvorak, 318-319; Linda Montgomery, 320; Annie Bissett, 340; Annie Bissett, 341; Chuck Gonzales, 341; 344-345: Corel; insets:Gordon Wiltsie/International Arctic Project 346-347, t. & b.: Corel; inset: Gordon Wiltsie/International Arctic Project 346, t.l.: Corel 348-49 t. & b.: Corel; inset: Gordon Wiltsie/International Arctic Project 348 b.l.: Corel 350-351 t. & b.: Corel 350 t.: Gordon Wiltsie/International Arctic Project 351 b.: Gordon Wiltsie/International Arctic Project 352: Gordon Wiltsie/International Arctic Project 354: Corel; inset: Gordon Wiltsie/International Arctic Project 355 t. & b.: Corel 356: Corel 357 t. & b.: Gordon Wiltsie/International Arctic Project 358-359 t. & b.: Corel 358 inset: Gordon Wiltsie/International Arctic Project 360: Corel 361: Corel; t.l.: Gordon Wiltsie/International Arctic Project; b.r.: Corel 362: Corel; inset: Gordon Wiltsie/International Arctic Project 363: Corel; b.: Corel Peter Neumann, 353; Rose Zgodzinski, 366; Matt McElligott, 370-401; Annie Bissett, 404; Chuck Gonzales, 405; Rose Zgodzinski, 430; Chuck Gonzales, 431; Stanford Kay, 440; Bob Dombrowski, 444; Stanford Kay, 466; Joe LeMonnier, 480; Rose Zgodzinski, 530; Chris Lensch, 531; Annie Bissett, 540; Rose Zgodzinski, 541; David Bamundo, 541; Gary Taxali, 542-543; Stefano Vitale, 544; Joe LeMonnier, 548; Rose Zgodzinski, 572; Chris Lensch, 573; Stanford Kay, 598; Rose Zgodzinski, 618; Rose Zgodzinski, 634; David Bamundo, 635; Stanford Kay, 644; Tuko Fujisaki, 645; Chuck Gonzales, 686, 710, 715; John Carrozza, 690, 705; Katie Lee, 694, 701

Photography

5: b.: Russell Kaye. 5: t.: Artist, Ralph Fasanella; Courtesy The Ralph Fasanella Estate. 7: b.: Corbis-Bettmann. 8: t.: Photo by David Harp, © The Baltimore Sun. 9: t.: De Sazo/Photo Researchers. 9: b.: Ivan Turk/Slovenian Academy of Sciences. 10: Gordon Wiltsie/International Arctic Project. 11: NASA. 12: The Louvre, Paris. 13: m: NASA. 13: m: David Arky. 15: b: Robert Wallis/SABA. 15: t: Archaeological Museum, Istanbul/ Erich Lessing/Art Resource, NY. 18: Dale Kennington/Superstock. 37: t.: PhotoDisc. 37: t.: PhotoDisc. 37: t.: PhotoDisc. 37: t.: PhotoDisc. 37: t.: PhotoDisc. 37: t.: PhotoDisc. 37: t.: PhotoDisc. 37: b.: PhotoDisc. 40: Jane Wooster Scott/Superstock. 42: b.: Courtesy, Yoshi Miyake. 61: t.r.: PhotoDisc. 61: b.: Dave Bartruff. 64: Christian Pierre/Private Collection/Superstock. 66: tl: Courtesy, Gloria Gonzalez. 66-67: Estate of Ralph Fasanella. 68: Artist, Ralph Fasanella; Courtesy The Ralph Fasanella Estate. 70: Artist, Ralph Fasanella; Courtesy The Ralph Fasanella Estate. 75: Artist, Ralph Fasanella; Courtesy The Ralph Fasanella Estate. 76: Artist, Ralph Fasanella; Courtesy The Ralph Fasanella Estate. 80-81: bi: Artist, Ralph Fasanella; Courtesy The Ralph Fasanella Estate. 80-81: b: PhotoDisc. 81: t.: PhotoDisc 84: Menil Foundation, Houston, TX/Lauros-Giraudon, Paris/Superstock. 100: David David Gallery, Philadelphia/Superstock. 106: David Lomax/Robert Harding Picture Library. 107: t.: Russell Kaye. 107: m.: David Lomax/Robert Harding Picture Library. 107: b.: Werner Forman Archive/Statens Historiska Museum Stockholm/Art Resource, NY. 114: National Museum of American Art, Washington, DC/Art Resource, NY. 135: t.: Corel. 135: b.: Corel. 138: Buffalo Bill Historical Center, Cody, WY. 140: Courtesy, Shonto Begay. 157: b.: Artville. 157: t.: B. Seitz/Photo Researchers, Inc. 160: Georges Merillon/Liaison Agency, Inc. 185: t.: Vanessa Vick/Photo Researchers, Inc. 188: Romare Bearden Foundation/Licensed by VAGA, New York, NY/National Museum of American Art/ Art Resource, Inc. 205: Keren Su/Pacific Stock. 208: The Morgan Wesson Memorial Collection, Museum of Fine Arts, Springfield, MA. 214: Corbis-Bettmann. 215: Archaeological Museum, Jerash, Jordan/Erich Lessing/Art Resource, NY. 215: t.: Corel. 215: Kenneth Garrett/ National Geographic Society Image Collection. 218-219: Peter Van Rhijn/Superstock. 222: Tate Gallery, London/Art Resource, NY. 236: T.: Photo by David Harp, © The Baltimore Sun. 236: b.: Photo by David Harp, © The Baltimore Sun. 237: t.: PhotoDisc. 237: b.: Will and Deni McIntyre/Photo Researchers, Inc. 240: The Whitney Museum of American Art, NY. 242: l.: Courtesy, Gary Soto. 242: r.: Courtesy, Jack E. Davis. 256-257: b.: David Frazier/The Image Works. 257: m.: Corel. 257: t.: Corel. 257: b.r.: Corel. 260: Private Collection/Manya Igel Fine Arts Ltd., London/Bridgeman Art Library. 262: t.: Courtesy, Angela Shelf Medearis. 262: b.: Courtesy, Holiday House, Inc. 284: W. Robert Moore/National Geographic Society Image Collection. 285: tl: PhotoDisc. 285: mr: Corel. 288: Courtesy of the The Freer Gallery of Art, Smithsonian Institution, Washington, DC, acc. no. F1968.62. 290: i.: Courtesy, Patricia Lauber. 290-291: Sisse Brimberg. 292: t.: Maher Attar/Sygma. 292: b.: De Zazo/Photo Researchers. 294: Jean-Marie Chauvet/Sygma. 295: Jean-Marie Chauvet/Le Seuil/Sygma. 296: Jean-Marie Chauvet/Sygma. 298: b.l.: Sisse Brimberg. 298: b.r.: David L. Brill. 298-299: t.: Jean Vertut. 300-301: Alexander Marshak. 302-303: Sisse Brimberg. 304: b.l.: Sisse Brimberg. 304: b.: PhotoDisc. 304: b.: PhotoDisc. 304-305: c: Jean-Marie Chauvet/Sygma. 305: b.: De Sazo/Photo Researchers. 306: Erwin and Peggy Bauer. 308: Private Collection/Bridgeman Art Library. 314: r.: Ivan Turk/Slovenian Academy of Sciences. 315: t.: Artville. 315: bl: American Museum of Natural History. 322: William Allard/National Geographic Society Image Collection. 338: Michael Holford. 339: b.r.: Charles and Josette Lenars/Corbis. 339: t.: Corel. 342: National Museum of American Art, Washington, DC/Art Resource, NY. 344: i.: Gordon Wiltsie/International Arctic Project. 344-345: i: Gordon Wiltsie/International Arctic Project. 344-345: bkgd: Corel. 346-347: t.&b.: Corel; inset: Gordon Wiltsie/International Arctic Project. 346: t.l: Corel. 348-349 t.&b.: Corel; inset: Gordon Wiltsie/International Arctic Project. 348 b.l.: Corel. 348: b. l. WorldSat International Inc., Mississauga, Ontario, Canada. 350-351: t.&b.: Corel. 350: t.: Gordon Wiltsie/International Arctic Project. 351 b.: Gordon Wiltsie/International Arctic Project. 352: Gordon Wiltsie/ International Arctic Project. 354: Corel; inset: Gordon Wiltsie/ International Arctic Project. 355 t.&b.: Corel. 356: Corel. 356: b&t: Gordon Wiltsie/International Arctic Project. 358-359 t.&b.: Corel. 358 inset: Gordon Wiltsie/International Arctic Project. 360: Corel. 361: Corel; t.l.: Gordon Wiltsie/International Arctic Project; b.r.: Corel 362: Corel; inset: Gordon Wiltsie/International Arctic Project. 363: Corel; b.: Corel. 364: Gordon Wiltsie/International Arctic Project. 365: t.: Gordon Wiltsie/International Arctic Project. 365: b.: PhotoDisc. 365: b.: PhotoDisc. 365: b.i.: Corel. 368: Christie's Images. 370: r.: Courtesy, Norton Juster. 370: l.: Courtesy, Matt McElligott. 402: b.l.: PhotoDisc. 403: t.: PhotoDisc. 406: Motion Picture and Television Photo Archive. 427: Courtesy, Robert D. Ballard. 428: i.: Emory Kristof/National Geographic Image Collection. 428-429: b.: D. Boroughs/ The Image Works. 432: Motion Picture and Television Photo Archive. 438: l.: NASA. 438-439: c: Corel. 439: i.: Fred Espenak/ Science Photo Library/Photo Researchers, Inc. 442: t.r. Biophoto Associates/Science Source. 442-443: c. Science VU/Visuals Unlimited. 446: Christie's Images. 463: Courtesy, Lawrence Yep. 465: b: Science Photo Library, London/Photo Researchers, Inc. 465: t.: Artville. 468: Bibliotheque Nationale Paris/E.T. Archive. 470: Courtesy, Pamela Oldfield. 478: The British Museum, London. 479: t.: The Metropolitan Museum of Art, New York; Rogers Fund, 1907 (acc. no. 07.286.79). 482: Superstock. 484: t.: Parker Scott. 484: b.: Courtesy, Margaret Miller. 484-485: NASA. 486: NASA. 488: NASA. 490-491: NASA. 493: NASA. 496: i: NASA. 496-497: NASA. 499: t.: Mehau Kulyk/Science Photo Library, London/Photo Researchers, Inc. 499: Mehau Kulyk/Science Photo Library, London/Photo Researchers, Inc. 499: b.: NASA. 499: c.: NASA. 502: John Holcroft/Superstock. 504: Courtesy, William Morrow Publishers. 532: Sheldon Memorial Art Gallery, Nebraska Art Association, Gift of Carl Rohman. 539: t.l.: Bernheim-Rapho/Liaison Agency Inc. 539: t.r.: David Arky. 540: t.: David Arky. 540: b.: Corbis. 546: Schomburg Center, The New York Public Library/Art Resource, NY. 548: Courtesy, Floyd Cooper. 571: t.: Jose L. Pelaez Inc./The Stock Market. 571: b.: Corbis Images. 574: David Coleman/Stock Boston. 596-597: Buddy Mays Travel Stock. 600: Bibliotheque Nationale Paris/E.T. Archive. 611: Archaeological Museum, Istanbul/Erich Lessing/Art Resource, NY. 620: Sotheby's Picture Library. 633: Corbis Images. 636: National Museum of American Art, Washington, DC/Art Resource, NY. 642: b.r.: Robert Wallis/SABA. 643: m.: Tom Brakefield/DRK Photo. 643: t.: Christie's Images. 643: b.: David Parker/Science Photo Library, London/Photo Researchers, Inc. 646-647: c. Jack Jeffers/Superstock. 653: br: UPI/Corbis-Bettman. 653: tl: Corbis-Bettman. 654: c: Ken Vinocur/The Picture Cube. 655: mr: Authentic Old Ad. 658-659: bkgd: Berenholtz/The Stock Market. 667: br: Charles Lenars/Corbis. 668-669: Charles Lenars/Corbis. 676: mr: Charles E. Rotkin/Corbis. 678: l: PhotoDisc. 682:

From SEEING EARTH FROM SPACE by Patricia Lauber. Text copyright © 1990 Patricia Lauber. All rights reserved. Reprinted by permission of Orchard Books, New York.

"Soccer" First appeared in OPENING DAYS: Sports Poems, published by Harcourt Brace & Company. Reprinted by permission of Curtis Brown, Ltd.

"Stars" from REMEMBERING AND OTHER POEMS by Myra Cohn Livingston. Copyright © 1988 by Myra Cohn Livingston. The poem originally appeared in CRICKET (A Margaret K. McElderry Book). Used by permission of Marian Reiner. Simon & Schuster Children's Publishing Division.

"The Stone Dog" from ONCE IN PUERTO RICO by Pura Belpré. Copyright © 1973 by Pura Belpré. Used by permission of Frederick Warne and Co., Inc.

"Stories on Stone: Rock Art—Images from the Ancient Ones" by Jennifer Owings Dewey. Copyright © 1996 by Jennifer Owings Dewey. Used by permission of Little, Brown and Company.

"The Story of Money" by Carolyn Kain. Copyright © 1994 by Eagle Books. Used by permission of Troll Communications.

"The Story of Washing Horse Pond" from THE SPRING OF BUTTERFLIES AND OTHER FOLKTALES OF CHINA'S MINORITY PEOPLES, translated into English by He Liyi. Copyright © 1985 by William Collins Sons & Co., Ltd. Used by permission of Lothrop, Lee & Shepard Books, a division of William Morrow & Company, Inc.

"Tell Me Again!" from TO RIDE A BUTTERFLY by Else Holmelund Minarik. Text copyright © 1991 by Else Holmelund Minarik. Used by permission of Bantam Doubleday Dell Publishing Group, Inc.

"Under the Back Porch" Used by permission of Virginia Hamilton. © 1999, 2000, by Virginia Hamilton Adofk.

"The Wall of China" from A GREEN PLACE by Padraic Colum. Used by permission of Delacorte Press and the estate of Padraic Colum.

"When the Rain Came Up from China" from TALL TIMBER TALES by Dell J. McCormick. Copyright © 1986 by The Caxton Printers, Ltd. Reprinted by permission of the publisher.

"The Winning of Kwelanga" copyright © 1973 by Verna Aardema. Fist appeared in BEHIND THE BACK OF THE MOUNTAIN, published by Dial Press. Reprinted by permission of Curtis Brown, Ltd.

"Writers" from INNER CHIMES: POEMS ON POETRY selected by Bobbye S. Goldstein. Text copyright © 1992 by Bobbye S. Goldstein. Published by Wordsong/Boyds Mills Press, Inc. Reprinted by permission.

"The Young Rooster" from FABLES by Arnold Lobel. Copyright © 1980 by Arnold Lobel. Used by permission of HarperCollins Publishers.

ZB Font Method Copyright © 1996 Zaner-Bloser. Handwriting Models, Manuscript and Cursive. Used by permission.

Photography

All photographs by Macmillan/McGraw-Hill except as noted below.
111A left: Daniel Pangbourne Media/FPG. 111A right: M. Burns/Picture Perfect. 219A left: Jeff LePore/Natural Selection. 219A right: Stockbyte

Inga/Spence/The Picture Cube, Inc./Index Stock Photography. 683: Superstock. 684: Spencer Grant/Stock Boston, Inc. 685: Jeff Greenberg/Photo Researchers, Inc. 688: Tom McCarthey/The Picture Cube, Inc./Index Stock Photography. 689: Richard Wood/The Picture Cube, Inc./Index Stock Photography. 691: DiMaggio/Kalish/The Stock Market. 692: Bruno/The Stock Market. 693: John Lei/Stock Boston, Inc. 694: Superstock. 696: Myrleen Cate/PhotoEdit. 697: David Shopper/Stock Boston, Inc. 699: Robert W. Ginn/The Picture Cube, Inc./Index Stock Photography. 700: Superstock. 702: Bachmann/PhotoEdit. 704: David Young-Wolfe/PhotoEdit. 707: l.: Tony Stone Images. 707: r.: Greg Nikas/The Picture Cube, Inc./Index Stock Photography. 708: Frank P. Rossotto/ The Stock Market. 709: Camerique/ The Picture Cube, Inc./Index Stock Photography. 711: Vanessa Vick/Photo Researchers, Inc. 712: Jim Powell Advertising Photorgraphy for MHSD. 713: Jeff Rotman/The Picture Cube, Inc./Index Stock Photography. 714: Index Stock Photography.

READING STRATEGY
All illustrations and photographs are provided by the Kirchoff/Wohlberg Company for Macmillan/McGraw-Hill except as noted below:
Illustration
Diane Blasius, 19–19A; Sandra Speidel, 85–85A; Gail Piazza, 139–139A; Mike DiGiorgio, 209A, 323A, 343; Mou-Sien Tseng, 261–261A; T.L. Ary, 369–369A; Jacqui Morgan, 447–447A; Alexi Natchev, 503–503A.
Photography
41-41a, Pete Saloutos/The Stock Market; 65, Michael Lewis/Corbis; 65-65a, Will & Deni McIntyre/Photo Researchers; 65a (inset), Boccaccio/The Image Bank; 101-101a, Ted Spiegel/Corbis; 101 (top), Werner Forman Archive/Art Resource; 161-161a, Corbis/Bettmann; 161a (top), Corbis/Bettmann; 161a (bottom), AP/Wide World Photos; 189, Keren Su/Corbis; 189a, Lawrence Migdale/Stock Boston/PictureQuest; 209-209a, Sylvain Grandadam/Stone; 223, Oscar White/Corbis; 223a (left), Corbis; 223a (right), AP/Wide World Photos; 241-241a, PhotoDisc; 241a (top), Tony Freeman/PhotoEdit/PictureQuest; 241a (bottom), Robert Brenner/PhotoEdit/PictureQuest; 289-289a, David Hiser/Stone; 289a, Richard Hamilton Smith/Corbis; 309-309a, Donald C. Johnson/The Stock Market; 309a (top), Corbis; 323-323a, Superstock; 343 (top), Corbis; 343-343a, Superstock; 343a (left), Corbis; 343a (right), Corbis/Bettmann; 407, Howard Sochurek/Timepix; 407-407a, The Mariners Museum/Corbis; 433, Corbis/Bettmann; 433-433a (bottom), Corbis/Bettmann; 433a (background), Corbis; 433a (inset), Corbis/Bettmann; 469a (top), Christel Gerstenberg/Corbis; 469a (bottom), Mimmo Jodice/Corbis; 483-483a, Roger Ressmeyer/Corbis; 483a (top), Reuters NewMedia/Corbis; 483a (bottom), NASA/Photo Researchers; 533-533a, Superstock; 547, Corbis/Bettmann; 547a, Hulton-Deutsch Collection/Corbis; 575-575a, Don Smetzer/Stone; 601, Corbis; 601-601a, Superstock; 601a (top), Corbis; 621a, Larry Williams/The Stock Market; 637 (inset), Joseph Sohm/Corbis; 637-637a, Jay Syverson/Corbis; 637a, Joseph Sohm/Corbis.

READING FOR INFORMATION
All photographs are by Macmillan/McGraw-Hill (MMH); Ken Karp for MMH; and Scott Harvey for MMH, except as noted below.
Photography
Table of Contents pp. 648–649
Chess pieces, tl, Wides + Hall/FPG: Earth, mcl, M. Burns/Picture Perfect: CD's, mcl, Michael Simpson/FPG: Newspapers, bl, Craig Orsini/Index Stock/PictureQuest: Clock, tc, Steve McAlister/The Image Bank: Kids' circle, bc, Daniel Pangbourne Media/FPG: Pencils, tr, W. Cody/Corbis: Starfish, tc, Darryl Torckler/Stone: Keys, cr, Randy Faris/Corbis: Cells, br, Spike Walker/Stone: Stamps, tr, Michael W. Thomas/Focus Group/PictureQuest: Books, cr, Siede Preis/PhotoDisc: Sunflower, cr, Jeff LePore/Natural Selection: Mouse, br, Andrew Hall/Stone: Apples, tr, Siede Preis/PhotoDisc: Watermelons, br, Neil Beer/PhotoDisc: Butterfly, br, Stockbyte

664-5: bkgd, Jake Rajs/Stone, 664: bl, C Squared Studios/PhotoDisc, 674: tr, Don Farrall/PhotoDisc, 674: bl, PhotoDisc, 675: br, Michael Krasowitz/FPG, 675: bkgd, Ken Biggs/Stone, 675: tl, David Toase/PhotoDisc, 676: tr, CMCD/PhotoDisc, 672: c, Reuters New Media Inc./Corbis, 673: c, Gary Williams/Liaison,

Acknowledgments

Contents

Anecdote for Fathers
by William Wordsworth

I have a boy of five years old;
His face is fair and fresh to see;
His limbs are cast in beauty's mould,
And dearly he loves me.

One morn we stroll'd on our dry walk,
Our quiet house all full in view,
And held such intermitted talk
As we are wont to do.

My thoughts on former pleasures ran;
I thought of Kilve's delightful shore,
Our pleasant home, when spring began,
A long, long year before.

A day it was when I could bear
Some fond regrets to entertain;
With so much happiness to spare,
I could not feel a pain.

The green earth echoed to the feet
Of lambs that bounded through the glade,
From shade to sunshine, and as fleet
From sunshine back to shade.

Birds warbled round me—and each trace
Of inward sadness had its charm;
Kilve, thought I, was a favoured place,
And so is Liswyn farm.

▶My boy beside me tripped, so slim
And graceful in his rustic dress!
And, as we talked, I questioned him,
In very idleness.

"Now tell me, had you rather be,"
I said, and took him by the arm,
"On Kilve's smooth shore, by the green sea,
Or here at Liswyn's farm?"

In careless mood he looked at me,
While still I held him by the arm,
And said, "At Kilve I'd rather be
Than here at Liswyn farm."

"Now, little Edward, say why so:
My little Edward, tell me why."—
"I cannot tell, I do not know."—
"Why, this is strange," said I;

"For here are woods, and hills smooth and warm:
There surely must some reason be
Why you would change sweet Liswyn farm
For Kilve by the green sea."

At this, my boy hung down his head,
He blushed with shame, nor made reply;
And three times to the child I said,
"Why, Edward, tell me why?"

His head he raised—there was in sight,
It caught his eye, he saw it plain—
Upon the house-top, glittering bright,
A broad and gilded vane.

Then did the boy his tongue unlock,
And eased his mind with this reply:
"At Kilve there was no weather-cock;
And that's the reason why."

O dearest, dearest boy! my heart
For better lore would seldom yearn,
Could I but teach the hundredth part
Of what from thee I learn.

Daedalus and Icarus
retold by Geraldine McCaughrean

The island of Crete was ruled by King Minos, whose reputation for wickedness had spread to every shore. One day he summoned to his country a famous inventor named Daedalus. "Come, Daedalus, and bring your son, Icarus, too. I have a job for you, and I pay well."

King Minos wanted Daedalus to build him a palace with soaring towers and a high, curving roof. In the cellars there was to be a maze of many corridors—so twisting and dark that any man who once ventured in there would never find his way out again.

"What is it for?" asked Daedalus. "Is it a treasure vault? Is it a prison to hold criminals?"

But Minos only replied, "Build my labyrinth as I told you. I pay you to build, not to ask questions."

So Daedalus held his tongue and set to work. When the palace was finished, he looked at it with pride, for there was nowhere in the world so fine. But when he found out the purpose of the maze in the cellar, he shuddered with horror.

For at the heart of that maze, King Minos put a creature that was half man, half beast—a thing almost too horrible to describe. He called it the Minotaur, and he fed it on men and women!

Then Daedalus wanted to leave Crete at once, and forget both maze and Minotaur. So he went to King Minos to ask for his money.

"I regret," said King Minos, "I cannot let you leave Crete, Daedalus. You are the only man who knows the secret of the maze and how to escape from it. The secret must never leave this island. So I'm afraid I must keep you and Icarus here a while longer."

"How much longer?" gasped Daedalus.

"Oh—just until you die," replied Minos cheerfully. "But never mind. I have plenty of work for a man as clever as you."

Daedalus and Icarus lived in great comfort in King Minos's palace. But they lived the life of prisoners. Their rooms were in the tallest palace tower, with beautiful views across the island. They ate delectable food and wore expensive clothes. But at night the door of their fine apartment was locked, and a guard stood outside. It was a comfortable prison, but it was a prison, even so. Daedalus was deeply unhappy.

Every day he put seed out on the windowsill, for the birds. He liked to study their brilliant colors, the clever overlapping of their feathers, the way they soared on the sea wind. It comforted him to think that they at least were free to come and go. The birds had only to spread their wings and they could leave Crete behind them, whereas Daedalus and Icarus must stay forever in their luxurious cage.

Young Icarus could not understand his father's unhappiness. "But I like it here," he said. "The king gives us gold and this tall tower to live in."

Daedalus groaned. "But to work for such a wicked man, Icarus! And to be prisoners all our days!… We shan't stay. We shan't!"

"But we can't get away, can we?" said Icarus. "How can anybody escape from an island? Fly?" He snorted with laughter.

Daedalus did not answer. He scratched his head and stared out of the window at the birds pecking seed on the sill.

From that day onward, he got up early each morning and stood at the open window. When a bird came for the seed, Daedalus begged it to spare him one feather. Then each night, when everyone else had gone to bed, Daedalus worked by candlelight on his greatest invention of all.

Early mornings. Late nights. A whole year went by. Then one morning Icarus was awakened by his father shaking his shoulder. "Get up, Icarus, and don't make a sound. We are leaving Crete."

"But how? It's impossible!"

Daedalus pulled out a bundle from under his bed. "I've been making something, Icarus." Inside were four great folded fans of feathers. He stretched them out on the bed. They were wings! "I sewed the feathers together with strands of wool from my blanket. Now hold still."

Daedalus melted down a candle and daubed his son's shoulders with sticky wax. "Yes, I know it's hot, but it will soon cool." While the wax was still soft, he stuck two of the wings to Icarus's shoulder blades.

"Now you must help me put on my wings, Son. When the wax sets hard, you and I will fly away from here, as free as birds!"

"I'm scared!" whispered Icarus as he stood on the narrow window ledge, his knees knocking and his huge wings drooping down behind. The lawns and courtyards of the palace lay far below. The royal guards looked as small as ants. "This won't work!"

"Courage, Son!" said Daedalus. "Keep your arms out wide and fly close to me. Above all—are you listening, Icarus?"

"Y-y-yes, Father."

"Above all, don't fly too high! Don't fly too close to the sun!"

"Don't fly too close to the sun," Icarus repeated, with his eyes tight shut. Then he gave a cry as his father nudged him off the windowsill.

He plunged downward. With a crack, the feathers behind him filled with wind, and Icarus found himself flying. Flying!

"I'm flying!" he crowed.

▶ Continue reading here.

The guards looked up in astonishment, and wagged their swords, and pointed and shouted, "Tell the king! Daedalus and Icarus are…are…flying away!"

By dipping first one wing, then the other, Icarus found that he could turn to the left and the right. The wind tugged at his hair. His legs trailed out behind him. He saw the fields and streams as he had never seen them before!

Then they were out over the sea. The sea gulls pecked at him angrily, so Icarus flew higher, where they could not reach him.

He copied their shrill cry and taunted them: "You can't catch me!"

"Now remember, don't fly too high!" called Daedalus, but his words were drowned by the screaming of the gulls.

I'm the first boy ever to fly! I'm making history! I shall be famous! thought Icarus, as he flew up and up, higher and higher.

At last Icarus was looking the sun itself in the face. "Think you're the highest thing in the sky, do you?" he jeered. "I can fly just as high as you! Higher, even!" He did not notice the drops of sweat on his forehead: He was so determined to outfly the sun.

Soon its vast heat beat on his face and on his back and on the great wings stuck on with wax. The wax softened. The wax trickled. The wax dripped. One feather came unstuck. Then a plume of feathers fluttered slowly down.

Icarus stopped flapping his wings. His father's words came back to him clearly now: *"Don't fly too close to the sun!"*

With a great sucking noise, the wax on his shoulders came unstuck. Icarus tried to catch hold of the wings, but they just folded up in his hands. He plunged down, his two fists full of feathers—down and down and down.

The clouds did not stop his fall.

The sea gulls did not catch him in their beaks.

His own father could only watch as Icarus hurtled head first into the glittering sea and sank deep down among the sharks and eels and squid. And all that was left of proud Icarus was a litter of waxy feathers floating on the sea.

I Don't Want to Live on the Moon
by Jeff Moss

I'd like to visit the moon
On a rocket ship high in the air.
Yes, I'd like to visit the moon,
But I don't think I'd like to live there.
Though I'd like to look down at the earth from above,
I would miss all the places and people I love.
So although I might like it for one afternoon
I don't want to live on the moon.

I'd like to travel under the sea,
I could meet all the fish everywhere.
Yes, I'd travel under the sea,
But I don't think I'd like to live there.
I might stay for a day if I had my wish,
But there's not much to do when your friends are all fish,
And an oyster and clam aren't real family,
So I don't want to live in the sea.

▶ I'd like to visit the jungle, hear the lion roar,
Go back in time and meet a dinosaur.
There are so many strange places I'd like to be,
But none of them permanently.

So if I should visit the moon,
I will dance on a moonbeam and then
I will make a wish on a star,
And I'll wish I was home once again.
Though I'd like to look down at the earth from above,
I would miss all the places and people I love.
So although I may go, I'll be coming home soon,
'Cause I don't want to live on the moon.

The Winning of Kwelanga

A Zulu tale from southern Africa
retold by Verna Aardema

Near the Mountains of the Dragon, there once lived a great chief named Ngazulu. He had a daughter who was so beautiful and gentle that she was called Kwelanga, which means sunrise.

It was the chief's desire that Kwelanga be married to a man worthy of her. So all suitors were put to impossible tests. Naturally all failed to win her.

One day a young man named Zamo heard about this. At once he decided to try his luck. His father tried to dissuade him. He said, "We are poor people. How dare you think of marrying the daughter of the chief?"

His mother said, "Oh, Zamo! Every man who has tried has lost his life. Do you think you would fare any better?"

But Zamo said, "I can't whistle with another man's mouth. I must try it myself."

So one day Zamo went to Chief Ngazulu and said, "Greetings, *Nkosi.*" Then he waited for the chief to speak.

▶ The chief said, "Young man, what are you doing here? Have you lost your way?"

"No, *Nkosi,*" said Zamo. "This is the end of my journey. I have come to propose marriage with your daughter."

"*You* come, with no attendants, to propose marriage?" cried the chief.

"*Nkosi,*" said Zamo humbly, "it is the custom of my people to act alone."

"Proposer-of-marriage," said the chief, "are you prepared to do the tasks we will set for you?"

"I am here to try," said Zamo.

Ngazulu said, "Well, then, look yonder. Do you see that cultivated field? Kaffir corn has been sown there. Before sundown you must gather all the grain that has been scattered. Then you may speak to me of marriage."

At that moment Kwelanga passed by on her way to the stream to draw water. She swayed gracefully beneath the earthen pot balanced on her head. When she saw the handsome suitor talking with her father, she began humming a little tune.

When the young man saw Kwelanga he thought she was as pretty as a sunbird. He said, "Let me begin at once."

Zamo went straight to the field. Finding a huge basket nearby, he took it and began picking up the kernels of kaffir corn. He worked all day without resting. When the sun was about to disappear in the west, he still hadn't finished half the field.

Just then he heard someone singing from the hillside above him:

"Red grains of kaffir corn
Scattered by our mothers,
Fly back from whence you came,
Gather with the others."

Suddenly the basket was heaped with grain. Zamo looked about and saw that the field was clean. He knew that every kernel had returned to the basket, and he carried the grain to Ngazulu.

When the chief saw the filled basket, he said, "You did well, young man. But that task was too easy. Tomorrow we shall talk again."

Zamo was given food and a hut in which to sleep. Very early the following morning he went to sit near the chief's door.

When Ngazulu came out, he said, "Young man, what do you want with me?"

Zamo said, "*Nkosi,* I have come to propose marriage at this *kraal.*"

The chief said, "See that forest in the valley? If you are able to chop down all the trees before sunset, then come to me and talk of marriage."

Zamo fetched an axe and went to the forest. He set to work with all speed. Many trees fell before his axe. But the forest was large, and though he worked all day without resting, most of the trees were still left. As the sun was slipping behind the hill, he heard a sweet voice singing:

"Trees of the forest,
In the sun's red glow,
Fall before Zamo—
Bow yourselves low."

At that, the trees crashed down on every side. Not one was left standing. Just then the sun set. Zamo went to the chief and said, "*Nkosi,* have I not finished the task you gave me?"

The chief was very much surprised. He called his counselor and said, "Think of something really hard for this man to do. The tasks I have given him have been too easy."

The counselor put his hand over his mouth, as is the way with people in deep thought. Then he said, "Let Zamo come to us in the morning. We will think of something that is not so easy."

The chief and his counselor sat up all night discussing what trial to give the young man. Just as the sun was rising they came to a decision.

▶ Continue reading here.

When Zamo appeared, the counselor said, "Young man, do you see that thorn tree growing out from the edge of the cliff—the one way up high on the mountainside? You are to climb out on it and pluck the topmost thorn."

Zamo saw the scraggly tree growing out from a crag high up on the mountain. No one could climb out on that, he thought. But he said nothing and set off up a steep mountain path.

The chief and his counselor watched him go. They were sure that Zamo would not be able to climb the tree because of the thorns. Even if he should manage to crawl out on it, the tree would bend with his weight and surely throw him off into the gorge. In any event, they thought they had seen the last of him.

When Zamo reached the edge of the cliff, he looked down to see what lay beneath the thorn tree. Far, far down he saw nothing but gray rubble—the rocks of all sizes that had rolled down the mountain. He knew that to fall would mean certain death.

The trunk of the thorn tree angled outward and upward from the edge of the cliff. Zamo began to creep out on it, picking his way between big thorns. As he neared the twisted umbrella of branches, the thorns were so close together that there was no place even for fingertips. Then the tree began to bend. Zamo stopped breathing, and with great difficulty made his way back to the foot of the tree.

Just then he heard a voice singing behind him:

"Thorn tree, thorn tree,
Wind and weather worn tree,
Your topmost thorn, please
Pluck for Zamo and me."

Suddenly a small gray thorn came twirling through the air. It landed beside Zamo. He picked it up and, turning quickly, he saw Kwelanga coming toward him with out-stretched hands. He knew at once that it was she who had sung the magic songs that had helped him every time.

Zamo took Kwelanga's hand, and together they went to her father.

"Nkosi," said Zamo, "here is the topmost thorn. I have finished the tasks. Kwelanga is willing, and I have come to propose marriage at this *kraal*."

When Ngazulu saw the look of happiness on the face of his daughter, he knew that Zamo truly was worthy of her. For he knew that the best husband for a woman is the man who can make her happy.

The Story of Money
by Carolyn Kain

Exchange of Goods

Long ago, people had to wander from place to place searching for food. But about 10,000 years ago, people found that if they collected seeds and planted them, a crop would grow. They also learned to tame wild animals. Now they had a permanent food supply and there was no need to wander. Gradually small villages grew up.

These people made baskets, sacks, and pots for storing their food. They also made tools to dig the land, harvest their crops, and build their homes. Over the years, they discovered that some people were better at making pots, while others were better at making baskets or hoes. The pot-maker might exchange a pot for some food, or a tool. Someone who made an ax might feel it was worth four pots, because the ax took longer to make. The people must have agreed upon a fair way of exchanging items.

▶ The Marketplace

People carefully chose the place where they settled. Villages often grew up where there was good soil for crops, or plenty of clay for making pots, or reeds for making baskets. As a result, some villages might have more grain than they needed or more pots than they needed. If the people could not trade goods within the village, they took them to a marketplace. Here people from several villages met to exchange their goods for items they needed. This system of trading is called barter. Often it works well, but sometimes there are problems, as in the following example.

Four people, each with something to barter, arrive at the marketplace. One has fish and wants a spear, another has a spear and needs grain, a third has grain and would like a pot, and the fourth has a pot but wants a spear. Unfortunately, no one gets anything.

Precious Objects

It became obvious that a system of exchange does not always work, so people in different parts of the world developed ways of solving this problem. Certain objects were agreed upon as being precious. If you sold something, you received a number of these objects. If you then wanted to buy something, you would pay with them. These objects were used as money.

In some Pacific Islands, people used stone wheels for buying and selling goods. Cattle, tools, weapons, packets of salt, cacao beans, glass beads, and bricks of pressed tea have all been used as money. In parts of Africa, people used cowrie shells. But when traders arrived from India, they would not sell their goods for cowrie-shell money. In India thousands of these shells washed up on the beaches, so to the Indians this kind of money was worthless.

The First Coins

As trade in different parts of the world increased, it became necessary to find something that was precious to everyone. Gold and other rare metals were already valued for their beauty. In Babylon, chips from gold and silver bars were weighed and used as money. In Egypt, gold and silver bands were weighed on scales using stone or bronze weights in the shapes of animals. These animals had formerly been used as money. The first coins were made about 2,700 years ago.

In China, the first coins were called cash. In Greece, each small coin was marked with its weight. Later, important gods and rulers were pictured on the coins. Roman bronze coins pictured a cow. This reminded people that coins were valuable in the same way as cattle.

Minting Coins

Coins were both convenient and durable. As the demand for them increased, it became necessary to set up coin factories. These factories were called mints. They had to be secure, and the people working in them had to be honest. Monasteries were often used as mints.

At first the coins were made by hand. Raw metal was heated until it melted. It was then poured out to form sheets. When the sheets were cool, they were cut into blank shapes, each of the same weight. The blank was then put between two dies, each marked with a picture. The dies were stuck together so that the picture was pressed onto each side. Making each coin was a slow process. About 300 years ago, machines were developed that could quickly produce large quantities of coins.

Countries Without Money

In Europe and Asia, trade and the use of money changed the everyday lives of most people. But there were places where money was not used.

In Peru, there was plenty of gold, but it was not used to make coins. Instead, the people made magnificent ornaments and decorations for their temples. The ruler of this land was called the Inca. His people were not paid to work. Each person did his or her fair share of work for the good of everyone.

Almost 500 years ago, Francisco Pizarro and an army of Spanish soldiers went to Peru. Pizarro did not want to trade but to conquer the Inca and his land. Pizarro imprisoned the Inca, defeated his army, and took many of the people as slaves. The people's gold, stripped from their beautiful temples, was shipped back to Spain to be melted down and made into coins.

Lawbreakers

Year after year, more gold and silver were taken by the Spanish from South America. The voyage back to Spain was never easy, because Dutch, French, and English ships often lay in wait to seize the treasure on these ships. There were many pirates at sea and highwaymen on land who were willing to take great risks to make their fortune.

Others broke the law by clipping pieces of gold and silver from the edges of coins. It was difficult to tell whether a coin had been clipped, until mints began to mill the edges of coins with tiny ridges.

Many rulers tried to save their gold and silver. They started to make their coins with a mixture of cheaper metals. This meant the coins were no longer worth their weight in gold or silver, but they were still used as tokens for buying and selling goods.

Paper Money

In London, wealthy people needed safe places to store large amounts of money. Goldsmiths, who made jewelry, had strong rooms in their shops. They often locked away other people's money and valuables for safekeeping, and gave them a written receipt in return. This receipt could then be used to buy something. Goldsmiths were like the banks of today, and their receipts were England's first paper money.

Soon banks were set up especially to provide these security services. The banks each held a supply of gold. Each bank note promised to pay the person who brought it to the bank a certain amount of gold.

Early bank notes were easy to copy. Banks soon decided to number each note and print them with intricate patterns that were hard to copy. Today, bank notes have a watermark and a metal strip to make them more difficult to forge.

Practice 149

Name_____ Date_____

Story Elements

To understand the relationships between story characters, we must **analyze the characters**.

Read this passage and look for ways in which the characters are alike and different. Then answer the questions below.

"I just don't think we're going to get all this work done before the project deadline," Phil moaned. "There's so much more research to do, and then we have to organize all our notes and start writing! We're in deep trouble!"

"Okay, okay!" Jim snapped. "Quit complaining! You're making me panic."

"Maybe we should start over and pick a topic that doesn't require much research," Phil suggested.

"No! We can't do that! We'd waste all the effort that we've already invested in the project, including all your art! Besides, a science project that doesn't require much research isn't a very good science project."

"But I'm in a panic! I can't sleep I'm so worried," Phil wailed.

"Okay," Jim said. "Thanks to your talents, we've already got all the art and charts done. You really did a great job. Now let's calm down and start working on a list of all the steps we have left to do. Maybe if we write all the steps down, the job will be easier to manage."

"You always come through and get us back on the right track," Phil smiled. "Let's start that list!"

1. What common goal do Jim and Phil have?
   They want to complete the science project on time.

2. What common problem do they face?
   Making the science project deadline.

3. How are Jim and Phil alike?
   They're both worried, about getting the job done.

4. How are they different? _Phil seems nervous and ready to give up, while_
   Jim seems more able to calm himself down and look for a solution.

5. How do their suggested solutions to the problem differ?
   Phil wants to scrap the project and find another topic that won't require as much research.
   Jim wants to keep the work they've already done and organize the remaining work.

6. What skills does each person bring to the partnership?
   Phil contributes art and Jim is good at organizing things.

Book 6/ Unit 5 / **Child of the Owl** | **At Home:** Have students choose a favorite story and write a short comparison of two characters' personalities. | **149**

Practice 150

Name_____ Date_____

Vocabulary

Substitute the correct vocabulary word for each underlined word or phrase. Write the word on the line in front of the sentence.

| banister | grudged | porcelain |
| rhythmically | troublemaking | truce |

1. ___truce___ The uncle and niece stopped their bickering and called a <u>halt to fighting</u>.

2. ___banister___ She held firmly to the <u>railing</u> as she climbed the staircase.

3. ___porcelain___ Inside the small apartment, beautiful vases made of <u>hard, white clay</u> lined the shelves.

4. ___rhythmically___ While listening to music on the radio, Paw-Paw tapped her fingers <u>in a regular pattern</u> on the table.

5. ___grudged___ Paw-Paw was disappointed to lose the game. "I guess you won again," she <u>grumbled</u>.

On the lines below, use vocabulary words in original sentences.
Answers will vary. Sample responses are provided.

6. _Please stop your troublemaking and cooperate with the others._

7. _"I'll do it your way, but I'd much rather do it my way," the man grudged._

8. _My favorite birthday present is this little white horse made of fine porcelain._

9. _On Tim's birthday, we hung balloons on the banister on the front stairs._

10. _The warring nations agreed to stop the war and abide by a truce._

150 | **At Home:** Have students make up questions or riddles with the vocabulary words as answers and share them with family members | Book 6/ Unit 5 / **Child of the Owl** / 10

Practice 150a

Name_____ Date_____

Keep the Music Coming!

Every Tuesday night Dad's band always meets at our house to practice down in the basement. No matter how many arguments we've had during the day, my brother Joey and I always stop the troublemaking, call a truce, and stand on the basement stairs peeking over the banister while the band rehearses. We sit there, tapping our toes and our fingers rhythmically, keeping time with the beat. I really love that music. In fact, Dad's band is the reason I started taking piano lessons. Many times I sat at the piano and stared at all those white keys gleaming like the finest porcelain. I dreamed about being in a band just like Dad's.

Last Tuesday, we heard Sam Small, the piano player, tell Dad that he and his family were moving to Abilene, Texas. "I guess I'll have to give up the band," Sam grudged.

"Sam! No one plays as well as you!" Dad said. "Who can I get to replace you?" Then I saw Sam point in my direction. I looked behind me to see where he was pointing. Then I figured it out. Sam was pointing to me!

"Just try Karen out," Sam said. "She's been listening to us play for about five years now and she sounds great."

Answers will vary. Sample responses are provided.

1. What type of troublemaking might take place between a sister and brother?
   teasing, silly arguments over household chores

2. How does a truce end an argument?
   The two people promise not to disagree any more and to respect each other's view.

3. Most piano keys are made out of plastic or ivory. What would these substances have in common with porcelain?
   hardness, whiteness, shininess

4. Why do you think Sam grudged his remark, "I'll have to give up the band"?
   He didn't want to; he was disappointed.

5. Do you think the band members enjoyed having Karen and Joey sit on the stairs, peek over the banister, and tap their fingers rhythmically? Explain why or why not.
   They probably did enjoy having such an enthusiastic audience because it
   made them feel more confident that their music was good.

Book 6/ Unit 5 / **Child of the Owl** | **At Home:** Write a paragraph to continue the story and answer these questions: Does Karen take Sam's place? How do the band members feel about their new piano player? | **150a**

Practice 151

Name_____ Date_____

Story Comprehension

Complete the story map to show what happened in "Child of the Owl."

MAIN SETTING	1. Paw-Paw's tiny apartment in Chinatown
MAIN CHARACTERS	2. Casey, a girl of about 11 or 12
	3. Paw-Paw, her grandmother
MINOR CHARACTER	4. Phil, Casey's uncle and Paw-Paw's son
NARRATIVE POINT OF VIEW	5. first-person point of view, told by Casey
OPENING SITUATION	6. Casey's uncle Phil brings her to live at Paw-Paw's house.
CENTRAL PROBLEM	7. Casey doesn't know Paw-Paw, isn't sure that she will get along with her, and wishes that she could be with her father.
MAIN EVENTS	8. Casey and Paw-Paw play cards.
	9. Casey helps Paw-Paw with her radio.
	10. They begin to see that they have much in common.
	11. Casey becomes hopeful that it will all work out.
SOLUTION TO PROBLEM	12. Casey tries to get to know Paw-Paw and begins to feel comfortable.

151 | **At Home:** Ask students to write a short essay describing how the story might have been different if it had been told from Paw-Paw's point of view. | Book 6/ Unit 5 / **Child of the Owl** / 12

Child of the Owl • PRACTICE

Practice 152

Name_____ Date_____ **Practice** 152

Read a Family Tree

A family tree is a time map of a family. It shows who was married to whom, which children were born to which parents, and how distant relatives are related.
A family tree can be short or long. If it is long, it can go back many generations.

Read the following sample family tree. Then answer the questions below.

1. Whom did Maria Sanchez marry? _____ Roberto Ruiz _____

2. How many children did they have? _____ 4 _____

3. Which of their children got married? _____ Ana and Bernardo _____

4. How many grandchildren do Maria and Roberto have? _____ 4 _____

5. How is Sarah related to Karen? _____ They are sisters. _____

6. How is Sarah related to Orlando? _____ They are cousins. _____

7. How is Bernardo, Jr., related to Bernardo, Sr.? _____ They are son and father. _____

8. How is Bernardo, Jr., related to Phil? _____ Phil is his uncle. _____

9. How are Ana and Dora related? _____ They are sisters-in-law. _____

10. How are Maria and Dora related? _____ They are mother-in-law and daughter-in-law. _____

Book 6/ Unit 5
Child of the Owl 10

At Home: Have students select a story about a family. Ask them to draw a family tree showing the relationships among the family members.

152

Practice 153

Name_____ Date_____ **Practice** 153

Story Elements

To understand and appreciate the relationships between story characters, it is important to **analyze the characters**. Look for ways in which the characters are alike and different. Think about each character's attitudes, feelings, and underlying goals and needs. Often, these hints will help you to understand why characters respond in certain ways.

At first, Casey and Paw-Paw appear to be quite different from each other. Yet, in many ways, they are alike. Use this Venn diagram to note their likenesses and differences. Include their attitudes, feelings, and underlying needs and feelings, as well as their ages and physical characteristics.

[Answers may vary. Sample responses are provided.]

Use your Venn diagram to help answer the following questions.

4. What likenesses might bring Casey and Paw-Paw closer together?

_____ their independence, their need to belong, their senses _____

_____ of humor, their Chinese heritage _____

5. What differences do they have that might become obstacles that they will have to overcome in order to live together happily?

_____ Casey's youth and Paw-Paw's greater age; Casey's reluctance to follow _____

_____ directions; their different styles of showing emotion and feelings. _____

153

At Home: Have students use a Venn diagram to show how Paw-Paw and her son Phil are alike and different.

Book 6/ Unit5
Child of the Owl 5

Practice 154

Name_____ Date_____ **Practice** 154

Make Inferences

An author may not state directly everything that you need to know about the characters and plot of a story. However, you can "fill in the blanks" by using evidence from the story to make **inferences** or logical guesses.

Read each passage. Then make inferences to answer the questions that follow.

Today, everyone in the art class had to submit an entry for the photography contest. Alicia was already imagining how she would spend the $100 the winner would get. As soon as the bus stopped in the school driveway, she dashed up the stairs to the art room.

[Answers will vary. Sample responses are provided.]

1. At what time of day does this story take place?

_____ morning, just after the buses have arrived at the school _____

2. How does Alicia feel about her entry to the contest?

_____ She is proud of it, and hopes that it will win. _____

Jeremy slammed his baseball glove down on the kitchen table. "Why do I have to study for the science test now?" he asked. "The test isn't until Monday! Every Friday, we have a baseball game. Why can't I study Sunday afternoon?"

Jeremy's mother took a deep breath. "Mr. Jensen said that if you don't pass this test, you could fail the whole course. Please just calm down and think about it. How can we work together to solve this problem?"

3. What question or statement did Jeremy's mother probably express just before this part of the story begins?

_____ She probably told Jeremy that he had to study for the test now. _____

4. On what day of the week does this story take place? _____ Friday _____

5. Compare and contrast the tone of voice that Jeremy is probably using with that of his mother. _____ Jeremy is probably talking in a loud, excited voice. _____

_____ His mother is trying to speak calmly. _____

Book 6/ Unit 5
Child of the Owl 5

At Home: Have students analyze a news story to find pieces of evidence that they can use to make logical inferences.

154

Practice 155

Name_____ Date_____ **Practice** 155

Denotation and Connotation

A word's **denotation** is its dictionary definition. The same word might also have a **connotation**, or a more emotional definition, based on the positive or negative feelings that it creates in a reader.

Read each pair of words. Write whether each word has a more positive or a more negative connotation. Then write the denotation that the words share. Finally, use each word in a sentence that shows its positive or negative connotations.

Answers will vary. Sample responses are provided.

Words	Connotations	Shared Denotation
skinny	1. negative	3. thin
slim	2. positive	

4. Sentence: _____ The boy was too skinny because he had been sick. _____

5. Sentence: _____ The boy was slim because he ate healthy food and exercised daily. _____

Words	Connotation	Shared Denotation
fragrance	6. positive	8. smell
odor	7. negative	

9. Sentence: _____ The fragrance of the flowers was sweet. _____

10. Sentence: _____ The odor of the perfume was over-powering. _____

Words	Connotation	Shared Denotation
alerted	11. positive	13. to let someone know
warned	12. negative	ahead of time

14. Sentence: _____ He alerted me about the heavy traffic. _____

15. Sentence: _____ He warned me about my poor attendance. _____

Words	Connotation	Shared Denotation
fussy	16. negative	18. careful,
precise	17. positive	detail oriented

19. sentence: _____ She was fussy about how we packed the boxes. _____

_____ She was precise about her career goals. _____

155

At Home: Separate synonyms for the word move into three groups: Words with Positive Connotations, Words with Negative Connotations, and Words with Neutral Connotations.

Book 6/ Unit 5
Child of the Owl 19

T9

Child of the Owl • RETEACH

Story Elements

> To understand why certain things happen in a story, it is important to analyze the characters. Often, the actions and words of characters provide hints about what kind of people they are and what underlying needs make them act in certain ways.

Read the following passage and answer the questions below.

To the Summit

"I'm really tired, Connie," Abby moaned. "Can't we sit down and rest? What's the rush, anyway? If we don't make it to the top of the mountain by noon, who cares? Let Jill and Carol wait a while!"

"Come on, Abby," Connie coaxed. "The top of the mountain is probably only about 20 minutes away. Don't be discouraged. You'll feel really proud to be able to write your name in the Park Registry, right along with everyone else who made it to the top."

"Big deal," Abby grumbled. "I wish I were home reading a good book like I usually do on Saturday mornings."

Connie stopped walking. "Okay, Abby," she said in a purposefully low and calm voice. "Let's stop and rest for five minutes. Give me your pack. I'll carry the lunch we're bringing for Jill and Carol. I hope that they don't worry because we're late. Sit and rest for five minutes. Then it's on to the top!" Answers will vary. Possible responses are provided.

1. Use hints from the story to describe what type of person Abby is. She's tired and grumpy, and doesn't really care about meeting her friends on time.

2. Use hints from the story to describe what type of person Connie is. She's calm, considerate, and has good leadership skills. She is patient with Abby, and tries to encourage Abby to keep going.

3. Compare the attitudes of the two girls regarding hiking. Connie is enthusiastic, whereas Abby would rather be reading.

4. Compare the attitudes of the two girls regarding their promise to meet their friends at a certain time. Abby doesn't think the promise is binding, but Connie does.

Book 6/Unit 5
Child of the Owl
4

At Home: In one paragraph, write about the above scene from the point of view of Abby. In another paragraph, write about the scene from the point of view of Connie.

149

Vocabulary

Select the word from the box that best completes each group below.

| banister | grudged | porcelain | rhythmically | troublemaking | truce |

1. pottery, crockery, glass, _____ porcelain
2. complained, grumbled, whined, _____ grudged
3. conflict, threat, danger, _____ troublemaking
4. musically, repeatedly, pointedly, _____ rhythmically
5. railing, step, stairs, _____ banister
6. peace, treaty, agreement, _____ truce

6

Story Comprehension

Answer the following questions about "Child of the Owl." Answers will vary. Sample responses are provided.

1. Why does Casey go to her grandmother's house? Because her father is in the hospital, she has been living with her uncle Phil, but Phil decides to take her to Paw-Paw's house.

2. Why does Casey say that she feels ugly and that she was being kicked around? She feels that no one in her family really wants her around.

3. Before Casey meets Paw-Paw, she thinks that anybody would be better to live with than Phil and his family. Do you think that Casey discovers that Paw-Paw is or is not "better"? Explain. Casey finds that Paw-Paw is better because Paw-Paw plays games with her and thinks she is clever.

4. What activities do Casey and Paw-Paw do together on their first day? They talk about Paw-Paw's statues; they play cards; they listen to the radio.

At Home: Write letters making suggestions about things that Casey and Paw-Paw might enjoy doing together.

150–151

Book 6/Unit 5
Child of the Owl
4

Read a Family Tree

> A **family tree** shows the history of a family. It shows who married whom, which children were born to which parents, and how distant relatives are related. A family tree can be short or it may go back many generations.

Study the following sample family tree. Then answer the questions below.

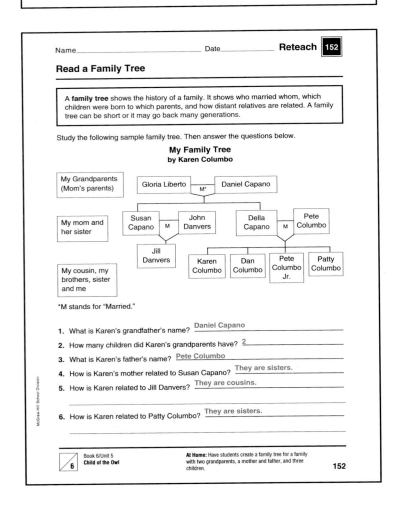

My Family Tree
by Karen Columbo

*M stands for "Married."

1. What is Karen's grandfather's name? Daniel Capano
2. How many children did Karen's grandparents have? 2
3. What is Karen's father's name? Pete Columbo
4. How is Karen's mother related to Susan Capano? They are sisters.
5. How is Karen related to Jill Danvers? They are cousins.
6. How is Karen related to Patty Columbo? They are sisters.

Book 6/Unit 5
Child of the Owl
6

At Home: Have students create a family tree for a family with two grandparents, a mother and father, and three children.

152

Story Elements

> To understand and appreciate why certain things happen in a story, learn to **analyze the characters**. Often, a character's actions and words provide hints about what kind of person he or she is.

Look back at "Child of the Owl." Use hints about the characters' actions and words to answer the questions.

1. How would you describe Phil's mood as he answers Casey's question about the code? grumpy; unfriendly

2. What are Phil's feelings about Paw-Paw? that she is strange

3. What feelings lead Paw-Paw to greet Casey in this way? She wants to show affection and support.

4. What are Casey's immediate feelings about Paw-Paw? She respects and welcomes her strength.

5. Describe Paw-Paw's general feelings about Phil. She thinks he's too serious and stuffy.

6. Describe Paw-Paw's first impression of Casey. She likes Casey, and thinks that Casey has a bright future.

153

At Home: Have students examine photographs of people in magazines to search for hints about their personalities found in their dress or expressions.

Book 6/Unit 5
Child of the Owl
6

Child of the Owl • RETEACH

Make Inferences

Authors do not always state everything you need to know about the characters and plot. However, you can use evidence in the story and your own experience to **make inferences**, or come to conclusions, about what you are reading.

Read each passage. Then make an inference to answer each question

My father teaches American literature at the high school. His favorite books are novels. That's why he named our dogs Ernest Hemingway and Edith Wharton. You can imagine why every afternoon, right before dinner, I get embarrassed when the neighborhood hears my father calling out the back door, "Hey, Hemingway and Wharton! Time for dinner!"

1. What nationality were Ernest Hemingway and Edith Wharton, and what types of books did they write? They were American novelists.

2. Where could you expect to find the narrator's dogs during the day? in the backyard

Kevin and I were hiking on Bald Mountain. It was very muddy because the snows had melted and the warm weather had just begun. Suddenly I slipped and fell. I slid along the mud and landed next to a bush. Under the bush I could see a hole. It was probably the entrance to an animal's den. Kevin came over to help me get up. "Oh, no!" he said. "Get up right now, Pat! There might be snakes in there!"

3. During what season does this story take place? spring

4. How does Kevin feel about snakes? He is afraid of them.

Helping Grandma by watching Barney is always a challenge. If I don't watch him carefully, he gets into trouble. One time he jumped onto Grandma's bed after a walk and got muddy footprints all over her quilt. And last night, I let him out of my sight for no more than ten minutes, and guess what he did? He ate one of Grandma's best shoes!

5. Who is Barney? Grandma's dog

Book 6/Unit 5 **Child of the Owl** 5

At Home: Write a paragraph in which you make inferences about a character in a movie you have seen.

154

Denotation and Connotation

A word's **denotation** is its dictionary definition. The same word might also have a **connotation**, or a more emotional definition, based on the positive or negative feelings that it creates in a reader.

Example: "I have a secret," she hissed. (negative connotation)
"I have a secret," she whispered. (positive connotation)

In the chart below, the words in each pair of sentences have the same denotation. However, one has a more positive connotation and one has a more negative connotation. Write **positive** or **negative** to show each word's connotation.

Word	Shared Denotation	Words in Sentences	Connotations
1. firm	**strong**	She was very firm about her rules.	positive
tough		She was very tough about her rules.	negative
2. sneak	**move**	Did they sneak into the movie theater?	negative
stroll		Did they stroll into the movie theater?	positive
3. scorching	**giving off heat**	The scorching sun was above.	negative
warming		The warming sun was above.	positive
4. nibbled	**ate**	We nibbled on some snacks.	positive
devoured		We devoured the snacks.	negative
5. shared	**told**	He shared news about his friends.	positive
exposed		He exposed the news about his friends.	negative
6. exhausted	**tired**	I'm exhausted from walking all day.	negative
sleepy		I'm sleepy from walking all day.	positive

155

At Home: Decide whether the following words have positive or negative connotations: announce, mumble, shout, ask, purr, complain, request, demand, suggest, offer, snarl, contribute, whine, clarify.

Book 6/Unit 5 **Child of the Owl** 12

T11

Child of the Owl • EXTEND

Story Elements

Characters are an important story element. They cannot come alive on the page unless writers give them personalities. Physical characteristics, dialogue and mannerisms contribute to characterization.

Using the senses listed below, create a character study. Choose someone you know, or make up a character. Make your character male or female, young or old, nice or nasty. Write a sentence or two for each sense describing your character. **Answers will vary. Possible responses are given.**

SIGHT: My great aunt is almost 90 years old, but her pixie haircut, twinkling
golden eyes, and ready smile are those of a young girl.

HEARING: I love to listen to her tell stories. Her voice is lovely, low and musical.
Yet her laugh is grating, raucous and loud. She truly loves to laugh!

TOUCH: The skin of her hands is soft, velvety, and cool. In fact, everything about
her is soft—her skin, her clothes, her old books—giving the sensation of
coolness and softness.

SMELL: Her apartment has a strange combination of odors: camphor and violets.
I guess she keeps a lot of clothing stored in moth balls, because their peculiar
scent wafts by at odd moments. But she herself smells of violets and coffee.

Book 6/Unit 5
Child of the Owl

At Home: Direct students to write a character description using these four senses.

149

Vocabulary

banister	grudged	porcelain
rhythmically	troublemaking	truce

Using the vocabulary words, write a character description of someone you've met recently.

Answers will vary. Check students' writing for correct use of the vocabulary
words.

Story Comprehension

Read and answer each question about "Child of the Owl".
Answers will vary. Possible answers are given.

1. When Uncle Phil talks about what people from Hong Kong use for curtains, what do you learn about him?
   He doesn't think much of people from Hong Kong.

2. What character traits of Casey's does Paw-Paw find positive that Uncle Phil's family found negative?
   Paw-Paw found Casey intelligent with a love of adventure. Uncle Phil would
   call that troublemaking.

3. Why is Paw-Paw reluctant to discuss her statue of Buddha? Support your answer.
   People have made fun of her in the past. She thinks that young people have
   no interest in Buddha, and that they will laugh.

4. How do you think Casey feels about the music Paw-Paw is playing when they first meet?
   Casey is probably encouraged to know that someone so much older is
   interested in popular music like The Beatles.

At Home: Write about a time when you have had difficulty
meeting someone for the first time.

150–151

Book 6/Unit 5
Child of the Owl

Read a Family Tree

Complete the family tree using the following information. Then answer the questions.

```
        Maria C. Romero  married 1919  Francisco Burgos
          1897–1984                      1896–1977

Encarnacion  married  Angel      Josefa   married  Alvaro    Dolores  married  Frank
  1921–              Fernandez   1923–             Lamprea    1926–            Capalbo

    Richard                  Francis    John        Frank, Jr.   Susan
    1944–                    1955–      1959–         1961–      1963–
```

Maria and Francisco Burgos had 3 daughters: Encarnacion born in 1921, Josefa born in 1923, and Dolores born in 1926.

1. List the name and birth date of the child of Encarnacion and Angel.
   Richard, 1944

2. What is the relationship of Frank, Jr., and Francis?
   first cousins

3. What is the relationship of Angel and Alvaro?
   brothers-in-law

4. In what year was Dolores Burgos born? 1926

5. In what year were Maria Colacios Romero and Francisco Burgos married?
   1919

6. How old would John Lamprea be in the year 2000? 41

Book 6/Unit 5
Child of the Owl

At Home: Instruct children to draw their family tree, going
as far back as they can.

152

Story Elements

When you read a story, the actions and words of **characters** will often provide hints about their personalities.

Read the paragraph below and answer the questions about the character that follow.

Lana was only 13 years old, but most people thought she was much older. She was a quiet girl, seldom smiled, and no one had ever heard her giggle. She had the posture and bearing of someone with confidence and secret knowledge. You never knew what she was thinking. Lana's features were perfect, her skin clear, her hair lustrous. But there was an ingredient missing for true beauty. A smile, a kind gesture, a hug for a frightened child—any of these would have brought Lana to life. What will finally awaken her? Answers will vary. Possible answers are given.

1. Why did people think Lana was older than 13?
   She seldom smiled and never giggled; she seemed solemn.

2. Does the author think Lana is beautiful? Why or why not?
   The author thinks Lana could be beautiful if she showed some kindness and
   happiness.

3. What is it about Lana that makes the author think she is confident?
   She stood very tall and never showed fear or shyness.

4. What does the author seem to want Lana to do?
   Show her feelings more; come to life.

5. What would you say to Lana if you knew her?
   Relax and try to enjoy your life more.

At Home: Have students write a description of someone
they know.

153

Book 6/Unit 5
Child of the Owl

Child of the Owl • EXTEND

Make Inferences

A writer may not tell you all of the details in a story. In these instances, you can **make inferences**, or logical guesses, about what will happen by using information from the story and your own personal experiences.

Read the following facts. Then write an inference on the line provided.
Answers will vary. Examples are given.

1. Rusty sells ice cream. He makes more money in June, July, and August than he does in November, December, and January.

   INFERENCE: People eat more ice cream in the hot summer months.

2. Jane is doing odd jobs to earn enough money to buy a new bike for a cycling trip next month. Mr. Lattimore asked her to mow his lawn just as Jane was leaving for the movies.

   INFERENCE: Jane will mow the lawn later and earn some money.

3. Paco and Jim are walking past the elementary school on a Saturday. They see smoke coming from a window.

   INFERENCE: There's probably a fire. They will pull the fire alarm or call for help.

4. The Dombroski family is packing for their vacation. They are bringing heavy coats, gloves, and hats.

   INFERENCE: The Dombroskis will be vacationing someplace cold.

5. Now write some information that would support this inference.

   INFERENCE: It is going to rain.
   Dark clouds are gathering. The air smells damp. The temperature dropped.
   The weather forecast predicted rain.

Book 6/Unit 5
Child of the Owl

At Home: Write facts from which someone could make inferences. Ask a friend or relative to read the facts and make inferences.

154

Denotation and Connotation

The **denotation** of a word is its dictionary definition. But some words have a **connotation** as well. Connotations are the emotions or associations suggested by certain words.

Look at the pairs of words below. Each pair has a similar denotation, or definition. Circle the word with a negative connotation in each pair and tell what emotions or associations are suggested. Feel free to use your dictionary.
Answers will vary. Possible answers are given.

1. freedom / (license) It suggests the use of freedom to go over the line; to take advantage of freedom to do something wrong.

2. (nosy)/ curious It suggests prying, or wrongly intruding into another's affairs.

3. assertive /(aggressive) While an assertive person is applauded, an aggressive person is usually not. Aggression suggests taking assertiveness a step too far.

4. (mousy)/ quiet Quiet does not suggest, or connote, a negative judgment, whereas mousy suggests that the person would not stand up for him or herself even if it were important to do so.

Write sentences for the words with a positive connotation.

_____

_____

_____

_____

_____

_____

_____

At Home: Have students use the words *squandered* and *lost* in sentences.

155

Book 6/Unit 5
Child of the Owl

Child of the Owl • GRAMMAR

Pronouns and Antecedents

> • A **pronoun** is a word that takes the place of one or more nouns and the words that go with the nouns.
> • The **antecedent**, or **referent**, of a pronoun is the word or group of words to which the pronoun refers. Pronouns and antecedents must agree.

Write a pronoun to take the place of the underlined noun or noun phrase. Write your answer on the line provided.

1. <u>Casey</u> meets her friends at the library after school. _____She_____

2. <u>Students</u> complete their homework and check out books there. _____They_____

3. <u>Barney</u> wanted to know if Phil got Paw Paw's message. _____He_____

4. Today <u>the children</u> can walk to the park. _____They_____

5. Has <u>Mike</u> seen the zoo's snake and reptile exhibit? _____He_____

Write the pronoun in the parentheses that agrees with its underlined antecedent on the line provided.

6. <u>Phil the Pill</u> pretended (he, she) was brave in front of his mother. _____he_____

7. <u>Paw Paw</u> became anxious if (she, they) could not listen to the radio. _____she_____

8. <u>Laurence Yep</u> writes <u>novels</u>, and I have read some of (he, them). _____them_____

9. When <u>Paw Paw</u> talked to us, (he, she) was serious. _____she_____

10. Phil tried to fix <u>the radio</u>, but (they, it) still would not work. _____it_____

Grade 6/Unit 5
Child of the Owl 10

Extension: Write a short story about a visit Casey might take to the zoo with Paw Paw. Use ten pronouns and circle each one. 129

Singular and Plural Pronouns

> • Singular pronouns are *I, you, he, she, it, me, him, her.*
> • Plural pronouns are *we, you, they, us, them.*

Circle the pronoun in each of the following sentences. Write an S if the pronoun is singular. Write a P if the pronoun is plural.

1. (I) wonder why Phil is called Phil the Pill. ___S___

2. After lunchtime (they) attend classes in Chinese. ___P___

3. The family takes plenty of picnic sandwiches with (them). ___P___

4. Will Mike and Sharon hike in the woods with (us)? ___P___

5. Chinese is an interesting language, but (it) is difficult to learn. ___S___

6. (She) is interested in Paw Paw's statue of Buddha. ___S___

Circle the pronoun in each of the following sentences. Write its antecedent.

7. Phil drove to Sacramento Street, and then (he) turned left. _____Phil_____

8. Casey was brought up by Barney, but (she) lived with Phil's family. _____Casey_____

9. The Chinese school was old, but the students loved attending (it). _____Chinese school_____

10. Phil and Casey reached Paw Paw's apartment door, and (they) rang the buzzer. _____Phil and Casey_____

11. Paw Paw looked at Phil the Pill and asked (him) to leave. _____Phil the Pill_____

12. Though Paw Paw looked hard for the glasses, the grandmother could not find (them.) _____glasses_____

Using Pronouns

> • A **pronoun** is a word that takes the place of one or more nouns and the words that go with the nouns.
> • The **antecedent**, or **referent**, of a pronoun is the word or group of words to which the pronoun refers. Pronouns and antecedents must agree.
> • Singular pronouns are *I, you, he, she, it, me, him, her.*
> • Plural pronouns are *we, you, they, us, them.*

Choose the pronoun in parentheses that correctly completes each sentence.

1. During the holidays (he, they) visit their grandmother's house. _____they_____

2. (We, She) takes two apple pies from the oven. _____She_____

3. (It, They) were happiest when Marshal Dillon spoke on the radio. _____They_____

4. This is (me, they) pictured in the family portrait. _____me_____

5. Father called Casey, and then (he, they) answered his mail. _____he_____

Fill in the blank with an appropriate pronoun. Answers may vary.

6. _____She_____ hopes Casey enjoys living in the apartment.

7. Will _____you_____ watch my favorite television program with me tonight?

8. _____They_____ sound like interesting characters.

9. Phil was sad when he had to leave _____her_____ with Paw Paw.

10. She is moving and will send _____him_____ a letter soon.

Grade 6/Unit 5
Child of the Owl 10

Extension: Write a letter to Casey. Circle the pronouns that you use. 131

Contractions

> • A contraction may be formed by combining a pronoun and a verb.
> • An apostrophe shows where one or more letters have been left out.

Rewrite each of the following sentences using the contractions for the pronoun and verb in parentheses.

1. (You have) just read *Child of the Owl* by Laurence Yep.
   You've just read *Child of the Owl* by Laurence Yep.

2. (He has) written novels popular among young adults.
   He's written novels popular among young adults.

3. The teacher said that (they are) located in the local library.
   The teacher said that they're located in the local library.

4. I can lend you *The Rainbow People* since (I have) a copy at home.
   I can lend you *The Rainbow People* since I've a copy at home.

5. (We are) going to the library after school.
   We're going to the library after school.

Rewrite each of the following sentences changing the contraction in parentheses into the pronoun and verb that it represents.

6. (She'll) borrow *Dragonwings* and read it over summer break.
   She will borrow *Dragonwings* and read it over summer break.

7. (It's) a novel that was named a Newbery Medal Honor Book in 1976.
   It is a novel that was named a Newbery Medal Honor Book in 1976.

8. Sue said, "(We've) heard Yep writes about his life as a Chinese American."
   Sue said, "We have heard Yep writes about his life as a Chinese American."

9. Once you read one of Yep's books, (you're) going to ask for another.
   Once you read one of Yep's books, you are going to ask for another.

10. (I'm) one of his biggest fans.
    I am one of his biggest fans.

Child of the Owl • GRAMMAR

Pronouns

Circle the pronoun in parentheses that correctly completes the following sentences.

1. Paw Paw hung lace curtains, and visitors could see through (them, it).

2. Casey read the novel and returned (it, him) to the library yesterday.

3. Phil the Pill tells Paw Paw (he, we) thinks she is kind.

4. Barney, will (you, her) E-mail your reply tomorrow?

5. Casey likes pie, so (she, it) asks for some.

Circle the pronoun in each of the following sentences. Write the pronoun's antecedent on the line provided.

6. Casey is going to the mall, and Barney will go with (her). _____Casey_____

7. Phil wrote a name on the letter to sign (it). _____letter_____

8. The granddaughter likes the carrots and will eat (them). _____carrots_____

9. Yep's vivid words help (us), the readers, picture Paw Paw's house.
   _____readers_____

10. Mario and Chen saw the movie, but (they) did not care for the acting.
    _____Mario and Chen_____

Pronouns and Contractions

- A **pronoun** is a word that takes the place of one or more nouns and the words that go with the nouns.
- The **antecedent**, or **referent**, of a pronoun is the word or group of words to which the pronoun refers. Pronouns and antecedents must agree.
- Singular pronouns are *I, you, he, she, it, me, him, her.*
- Plural pronouns are *we, you, they, us, them.*

Mechanics

- A contraction may be formed by combining a pronoun and a verb.
- An apostrophe shows where one or more letters have been left out.

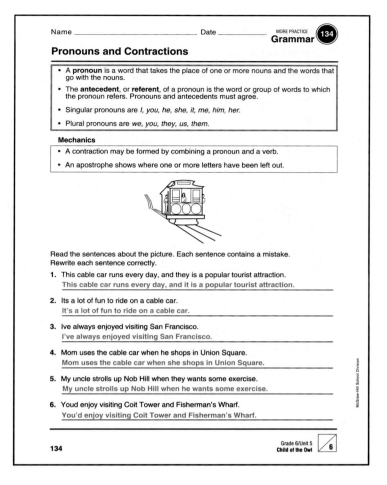

Read the sentences about the picture. Each sentence contains a mistake. Rewrite each sentence correctly.

1. This cable car runs every day, and they is a popular tourist attraction.
   This cable car runs every day, and it is a popular tourist attraction.

2. Its a lot of fun to ride on a cable car.
   It's a lot of fun to ride on a cable car.

3. Ive always enjoyed visiting San Francisco.
   I've always enjoyed visiting San Francisco.

4. Mom uses the cable car when he shops in Union Square.
   Mom uses the cable car when she shops in Union Square.

5. My uncle strolls up Nob Hill when they wants some exercise.
   My uncle strolls up Nob Hill when he wants some exercise.

6. Youd enjoy visiting Coit Tower and Fisherman's Wharf.
   You'd enjoy visiting Coit Tower and Fisherman's Wharf.

T15

Child of the Owl • SPELLING

Name_____ Date_____

Compound Words

Pretest Directions
Fold back the paper along the dotted line. Use the blanks to write each word as it is read aloud. When you finish the test, unfold the paper. Use the list at the right to correct any spelling mistakes. Practice the words you missed for the Posttest.

To Parents
Here are the results of your child's weekly spelling Pretest. You can help your child study for the Posttest by following these simple steps for each word on the word list:

1. Read the word to your child.
2. Have your child write the word, saying each letter as it is written.
3. Say each letter of the word as your child checks the spelling.
4. If a mistake has been made, have your child read each letter of the correctly spelled word aloud, and then repeat steps 1–3.

1. _____	1. newborn
2. _____	2. twenty-one
3. _____	3. common sense
4. _____	4. old-fashioned
5. _____	5. question mark
6. _____	6. teacup
7. _____	7. tablecloth
8. _____	8. ready-made
9. _____	9. bathrobe
10. _____	10. science fiction
11. _____	11. apartment houses
12. _____	12. brother-in-law
13. _____	13. fire escape
14. _____	14. applesauce
15. _____	15. self-reliant
16. _____	16. index finger
17. _____	17. cross-country
18. _____	18. foolproof
19. _____	19. contact lens
20. _____	20. silkworms

Challenge Words

_____ banister
_____ grudged
_____ porcelain
_____ rhythmically
_____ truce

Name_____ Date_____

Compound Words

Using the Word Study Steps
1. LOOK at the word.
2. SAY the word aloud.
3. STUDY the letters in the word.
4. WRITE the word.
5. CHECK the word.
   Did you spell the word right?
   If not, go back to step 1.

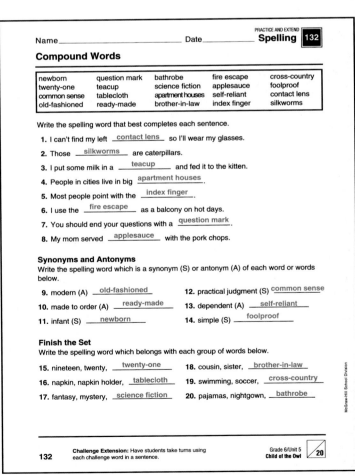

Spelling Tip
When you write out numbers between 21 and 99, remember to include the hyphen.

twenty-one   thirty-six
eighty-seven

Finish the Word
Complete each word below to form a spelling word.

1. new_____born_____
2. _____twenty_____-one
3. common _____sense_____
4. old-_____fashioned_____
5. _____question_____ mark
6. tea_____cup_____
7. _____table_____cloth
8. ready-_____made_____
9. _____bath_____robe
10. science _____fiction_____
11. _____apartment_____ houses
12. _____brother_____-in-law
13. fire _____escape_____
14. apple_____sauce_____
15. _____self_____-reliant
16. index _____finger_____
17. _____cross_____-country
18. fool_____proof_____
19. _____contact_____ lens
20. silk_____worms_____

To Parents or Helpers:
Using the Word Study Steps above as your child comes across any new words will help him or her spell words effectively. Review the steps as you both go over this week's spelling words.
Go over the Spelling Tip with your child. Take turns writing out numbers, inserting the hyphen.
Help your child complete the spelling exercise by completing each spelling word.

Name_____ Date_____

Compound Words

newborn	question mark	bathrobe	fire escape	cross-country
twenty-one	teacup	science fiction	applesauce	foolproof
common sense	tablecloth	apartment houses	self-reliant	contact lens
old-fashioned	ready-made	brother-in-law	index finger	silkworms

Sort each spelling word according to whether it is written as one word, as two words, or with a hyphen. Write each word on the appropriate line below.

One Word:
1. newborn
2. teacup
3. tablecloth
4. bathrobe
5. applesauce
6. foolproof
7. silkworms

Two Words:
8. common sense
9. question mark
10. science fiction
11. apartment houses
12. fire escape
13. index finger
14. contact lens

Hyphenated:
15. twenty-one
16. old-fashioned
17. ready-made
18. brother-in-law
19. self-reliant
20. cross-country

Name_____ Date_____

Compound Words

newborn	question mark	bathrobe	fire escape	cross-country
twenty-one	teacup	science fiction	applesauce	foolproof
common sense	tablecloth	apartment houses	self-reliant	contact lens
old-fashioned	ready-made	brother-in-law	index finger	silkworms

Write the spelling word that best completes each sentence.

1. I can't find my left _____contact lens_____ so I'll wear my glasses.
2. Those _____silkworms_____ are caterpillars.
3. I put some milk in a _____teacup_____ and fed it to the kitten.
4. People in cities live in big _____apartment houses_____
5. Most people point with the _____index finger_____
6. I use the _____fire escape_____ as a balcony on hot days.
7. You should end your questions with a _____question mark_____.
8. My mom served _____applesauce_____ with the pork chops.

Synonyms and Antonyms
Write the spelling word which is a synonym (S) or antonym (A) of each word or words below.

9. modern (A) _____old-fashioned_____
10. made to order (A) _____ready-made_____
11. infant (S) _____newborn_____
12. practical judgment (S) _____common sense_____
13. dependent (A) _____self-reliant_____
14. simple (S) _____foolproof_____

Finish the Set
Write the spelling word which belongs with each group of words below.

15. nineteen, twenty, _____twenty-one_____
16. napkin, napkin holder, _____tablecloth_____
17. fantasy, mystery, _____science fiction_____
18. cousin, sister, _____brother-in-law_____
19. swimming, soccer, _____cross-country_____
20. pajamas, nightgown, _____bathrobe_____

132   Challenge Extension: Have students take turns using each challenge word in a sentence.
Grade 6/Unit 5
Child of the Owl
20

Child of the Owl • SPELLING

Compound Words

Proofreading Activity

There are six spelling mistakes in this paragraph. Circle the misspelled words. Write the words correctly on the lines below.

As Phil drove the car, I looked at all the tall (apartment-houses) in the neighborhood. We parked at one group of buildings. Phil pointed with his (indexfinger) toward the top floor. "That's where Paw Paw lives," he said. I had heard that Paw Paw was (old-fasioned) and extremely (selfreliant). She answered the door in an old (bath-robe) and black slippers. I felt a bit nervous at first, but as we started talking I felt more comfortable. It was (commonsense). She was my grandmother after all!

1. __apartment houses__   3. __old-fashioned__   5. __bathrobe__
2. __index finger__   4. __self-reliant__   6. __common sense__

Writing Activity

If you had to move, which older friend or relative would you most like to move in with? Why? Write a letter to that person, telling him or her why you would like to move in. Use four spelling words.

_____

_____

_____

_____

Compound Words

Look at the words in each set below. One word in each set is spelled correctly. Use a pencil to fill in the circle next to the correct word. Before you begin, look at the sample sets of words. Sample A has been done for you. Do Sample B by yourself. When you are sure you know what to do, you may go on with the rest of the page.

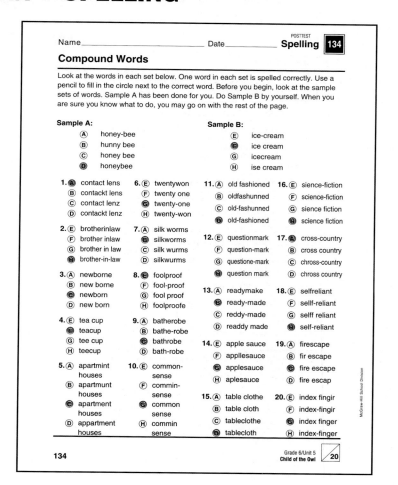

Sample A:
- (A) honey-bee
- (B) hunny bee
- (C) honey bee
- (D) honeybee

Sample B:
- (E) ice-cream
- (F) ice cream
- (G) icecream
- (H) ise cream

1.
- (A) contact lens
- (B) contackt lens
- (C) contact lenz
- (D) contackt lenz

2.
- (E) brotherinlaw
- (F) brother inlaw
- (G) brother in law
- (H) brother-in-law

3.
- (A) newborne
- (B) new borne
- (C) newborn
- (D) new born

4.
- (E) tea cup
- (F) teacup
- (G) tee cup
- (H) teecup

5.
- (A) apartmint houses
- (B) apartmunt houses
- (C) apartment houses
- (D) appartment houses

6.
- (E) twentywon
- (F) twenty one
- (G) twenty-one
- (H) twenty-won

7.
- (A) silk worms
- (B) silkworms
- (C) silk wurms
- (D) silkwurms

8.
- (E) foolproof
- (F) fool-proof
- (G) fool proof
- (H) foolproofe

9.
- (A) batherobe
- (B) bathe-robe
- (C) bathrobe
- (D) bath-robe

10.
- (E) common-sense
- (F) commin-sense
- (G) common sense
- (H) commin sense

11.
- (A) old fashioned
- (B) oldfashunned
- (C) old-fashunned
- (D) old-fashioned

12.
- (E) questionmark
- (F) question-mark
- (G) questione-mark
- (H) question mark

13.
- (A) readymake
- (B) ready-made
- (C) reddy-made
- (D) readdy made

14.
- (E) apple sauce
- (F) appllesauce
- (G) applesauce
- (H) aplesauce

15.
- (A) table clothe
- (B) table cloth
- (C) tableclothe
- (D) tablecloth

16.
- (E) sience-fiction
- (F) science-fiction
- (G) sience fiction
- (H) science fiction

17.
- (A) cross-country
- (B) cross country
- (C) chross-country
- (D) chross country

18.
- (E) selfreliant
- (F) sellf-reliant
- (G) selff reliant
- (H) self-reliant

19.
- (A) firescape
- (B) fir escape
- (C) fire escape
- (D) fire escap

20.
- (E) index fingir
- (F) index-fingir
- (G) index finger
- (H) index-finger

Bellerophon and the Flying Horse • PRACTICE

Sequence of Events

Events in a story or a selection happen in a certain sequence, or order. Understanding the **sequence of events** can help a reader make sense of a story or an article.

Read the following passages and answer the questions.

When the students arrived at the Museum of History, their guide, Ms. Cross, met them at the entrance and introduced herself. She discussed the general history of the museum and the exhibit they would be visiting that day. Finally she asked if any of the students had any questions before beginning the tour.

1. What was the first thing that happened after the students arrived?
   Ms. Cross met them at the museum entrance and introduced herself.

2. What was the next thing that took place? Ms. Cross discussed the general
   history of the museum and the exhibit they would be visiting that day.

At eleven o'clock the class began their tour of the exhibit of ancient Greek art. First they looked at Greek vases. Some of the vases showed scenes from Greek myths. At noon, they watched a video that showed how Greek potters decorated the vases.

3. When did the group begin their tour? at eleven o'clock

4. Did the class watch the video before or after they looked
   at the vases? after

After lunch the students continued their tour of the exhibit. First, their guide Ms. Cross spoke about the ancient Greek jewelry on display. Some of the bracelets and earrings were made of gold. Later, the students saw some copies of ancient Greek clothing, including sandals and tunics, called chitons. At the end of the afternoon the students wrote short reports about their favorite part of the exhibit.

5. When did the students continue the tour? After lunch

6. What was the first thing that took place after the tour continued?
   Ms. Cross spoke to them about the ancient Greek jewelry.

Vocabulary

Choose the vocabulary word from the box that means the same or nearly the same as the underlined word or words.

ferocious	lavishly	rash
reassure	thunderous	waving

1. A fierce storm wrecked all the houses in the village. ferocious

2. The leafy branches, swaying in the breeze, protected the campers from the
   hot sun. waving

3. When the dam burst, the rushing water made a very loud sound that could
   be heard for miles. thunderous

4. The driver didn't obey the traffic signal, and his reckless behavior caused
   an accident. rash

5. The castle was so richly decorated that the visitors stared at it in
   amazement. lavishly

6. The coach tried to hearten the frightened swimmer who was about to dive
   into the pool. reassure

Brave Petronella

The *ferocious* beast had terrorized the kingdom for many years. Every spring, brave young men and women prepared to fight the monster. The people cheered as they left the city gates where banners stood *waving* in the sunshine. However, the hideous monster frightened his opponents and they quickly rushed back to the kingdom. "Trying to kill the monster this way was a *rash* act," they cried in fear. "Please, open the gates and let us in."

Only one young woman, a farmer named Petronella, refused to run away. When the horrible monster approached with a *thunderous* roar, Petronella didn't move. Instead of fighting, she spoke gently. She wanted to *reassure* the monster that she meant him no harm. In return, the monster promised to never again attack the kingdom. That night everyone in the village celebrated *lavishly* at a banquet in Petronella's honor.

1. Why was the monster described as *ferocious*?
   because it was mean and frightening

2. What word described the banners at the city gates? waving

3. What words describe the sound made by the monster? thunderous roar

4. Why did Petronella speak gently to the monster? to reassure him

5. What was unusual about the way Petronella finally solved her problem?
   She used gentle words instead of harsh or violent actions.

Story Comprehension

Complete the following story chart with information about the characters and events in "Bellerophon and the Flying Horse."

Settings	1.	Argos
	2.	Lycia
Characters	3.	Bellerophon; King of Argos and his wife; King of Lycia; Chimera; Pegasus; old farmer; Athena
Point of View	4.	third person
Opening Situation	5.	Bellerophon is staying with the King of Argos and his wife. The queen talks about him so much that the King becomes tired of hearing about him and sends him away to the King of Lycia.
Central Problem	6.	Bellerophon has to kill the Chimera, a three-headed monster who is threatening the kingdom of Lycia.
Major Events	7.	Bellerophon is sent by the King of Argos to the King of Lycia with a sealed letter to deliver.
	8.	The King of Lycia reads the letter, which tells him to kill Bellerophon.
	9.	Instead, he sends Bellerophon to kill the Chimera.
	10.	The flying horse Pegasus takes Bellerophon to the Chimera.
	11.	Bellerophon kills the monster.
Situation at the End of Story	12.	Bellerophon has proved himself to be a hero.

Bellerophon and the Flying Horse • PRACTICE

Read a Constellation Map

Ancient Greek and Roman astronomers divided the sky into regions that had certain groups of stars, called **constellations**. They named these constellations after the figures the stars seem to form. Today, we still use the names the ancient Greeks and Romans used.

Look at the map showing three constellations in the Northern Hemisphere, all named after figures in the popular Greek myth. Then answer the questions.

1. How many stars are shown in the Andromeda constellation? _____16_____

2. This constellation was named after Andromeda, a mythical princess who was rescued from a monster by the hero Perseus. How would you describe the constellation and how would you remember it? _____Answers will vary. Possible answer: The stars form a figure that seems to be running away from something.

3. Cepheus, which can be seen only in autumn, was named after the Ethiopian king who was the father of Andromeda. How many stars are shown in this constellation? _____11_____

4. Who do you think the remaining constellation was named after? It can be seen only in the autumn. _____
_____It was named after Cassiopeia, the mother of Andromeda._____

At Home: Have students look up three constellations in an encyclopedia and find out information about them.

Sequence of Events

In a story, the **sequence of events** is the order in which the events occur.

Read each description of an event from "Bellerophon and the Flying Horse" below. The events are listed out of order. Number the events in the sequence in which they occurred, with 1 being the first event and 10 being the last event in the story.

____2____ Bellerophon is sent to the King of Lycia with a sealed letter.

____4____ The King of Lycia sends Bellerophon to kill the Chimera.

____5____ A farmer tells Bellerophon how to find the monster.

____9____ Bellerophon cuts of the snake's head.

____10____ Bellerophon cuts off the goat's head, killing the Chimera.

____3____ The letter tells the King of Lycia to kill Bellerophon.

____8____ Bellerophon meets the Chimera and cuts off the lion's head.

____7____ Bellerophon tames Pegasus.

____1____ The King grows tired of hearing his wife talk about Bellerophon.

____6____ Athena gives Bellerophon a bridle.

At Home: Have students add any two additional events to the sequence above in the correct order in which they occurred in the story.

Make Inferences

Sometimes a writer does not state exactly what is happening in a story or what a character is thinking. Then you must **make inferences**, or use what you do know to come to an understanding about story events and characters.
Read the following story. Then use inferences to answer the questions below.

After the first clap of thunder, White Blaze raced from the barn and across the field. When Doug McClosky, White Blaze's owner, realized that the horse was missing, he immediately began searching for her. "I knew there would be a storm this afternoon," he thought to himself. "I should have made sure the door to White Blaze's stall was closed tightly." Doug had been taking care of the horse since she was a filly. He knew she wouldn't run too far from home. He walked across the pasture to the meadow near the river. It was raining harder now. Doug hadn't remembered to grab a raincoat. Suddenly he stopped and stared. He saw White Blaze standing on the bank of the river. The dangerous water was rising fast. Doug tried to stay calm. "Come on girl," he called gently. "There's nothing to be afraid of." For an instant, White Blaze was frightened. Who was coming toward her in the rain? Then she recognized Doug and moved slowly in his direction. [Answers will vary. Sample responses are provided.]

1. What inference can you make about why White Blaze raced from the barn?
_____She was frightened by the thunder._____

2. How do you think Doug felt when he realized that White Blaze was missing?
_____He felt guilty._____

3. What evidence in the story supports your answer to question 2?
_____He knew a storm was coming and realized that he should have made sure the door to her stall was tightly closed._____

4. How do you think Doug felt when he started to look for White Blaze?
_____He was anxious and determined to find her._____

5. What evidence in the story supports your answer to question 4?
_____He set out immediately in the rain without a raincoat._____

6. What can you infer about Doug's feelings and actions when he saw White Blaze next to the river? What evidence supports your inference?
_____He was scared that she would run into the river and perhaps drown. He tried to stay calm. He spoke to her gently._____

At Home: Have students make an inference about the behavior of one of the characters in "Bellerophon and the Flying Horse."

Context Clues

When you read non fiction material, you may come across unfamiliar words or familiar words used in an unfamiliar way. However, you can often use **context clues**, or the words, phrases, and sentences surrounding the word, to determine the word's meaning.

Read the following sentences. Use context clues to help you figure out the meaning of each boldfaced word. Write the word's meaning on the blank line. Then list the context clues you used to figure out the meaning of the word.

1. To study at this college for one year, students must pay $5,000 in **tuition**.
   Meaning: _____the fee charged by a college to study there_____
   Context Clues: _____to study at this college, students must pay_____

2. The rider sat comfortably with his feet in the **stirrups** and urged his horse to move slowly toward the starting line of the race.
   Meaning: _____supports for a rider's feet when riding a horse_____
   Context Clues: _____the rider sat comfortably with his feet in; urged his horse to move_____

3. The sailors who were scrubbing the **deck** of the ship warned passengers not to walk there or they might slip and fall.
   Meaning: _____floor of a boat or ship_____
   Context Clues: _____sailors; scrubbing; passengers not to walk there_____

4. The painted **decoy**, which looked like a large duck, was used to attract the wild ducks to a particular area of the park.
   Meaning: _____artificial bird used to attract other birds_____
   Context Clues: _____painted; looked like a large duck; attract wild ducks_____

5. After Dan finished his social studies report, he **proofread** it carefully, checking for any grammar and spelling mistakes.
   Meaning: _____to read something to find mistakes_____
   Context Clues: _____checking for grammar and spelling mistakes_____

6. At the beginning of the movie, there is a **freeze-frame** of a bird held motionless in the air, high above the building.
   Meaning: _____a moment without motion on film_____
   Context Clues: _____the movie; a bird held motionless_____

At Home: Write the definitions of four specialized computer terms, using a dictionary, if necessary. Then write a sentence including each word and using context clues.

Bellerophon and the Flying Horse • RETEACH

Sequence of Events

> The **sequence** is the order of events in a story or a selection. Understanding the sequence of events can help a reader better understand what happens in a story.

Read the story below. Then read the list of events that follows it. The events are listed out of order. Number the events, from 1 to 6, to show the correct order in which they happened.

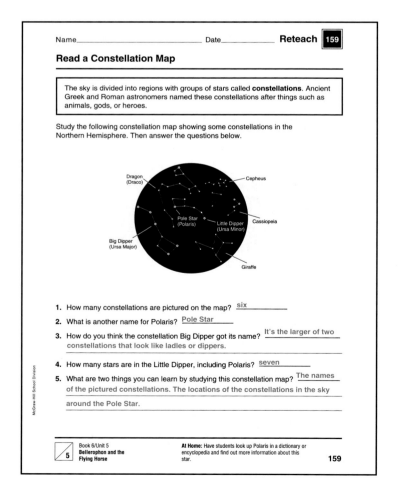

The young prince learned from his father that he had to catch and tame a wild horse. Only then would the kingdom be free from the magician's control. First, the prince, carrying a special saddle and bridle, searched the length of the magician's forest to find a horse. Suddenly, he sighted a wonderful animal. After chasing the horse for almost a day, the prince was finally able to approach him. The horse reared up on his hind feet, but the prince did not run away. Instead, he spoke softly and then tossed the bridle over the horse's head. When the horse felt the bridle, he pulled back with all his strength. But the prince did not let go. Finally, he was able to get close to the horse and carefully arrange the saddle on his back. He patted and then fed the frightened animal until it was calm. Then the prince mounted the horse and rode back to his kingdom.

2 _____ The prince searched across the magician's forest to find the horse.

4 _____ The prince tossed a bridle over the horse's head.

1 _____ The young prince learned he had to catch and tame a wild horse.

6 _____ The prince patted and fed the horse.

5 _____ The prince arranged the saddle on the horse's back.

3 _____ The prince chased the horse for almost a day.

Book 6/Unit 5
Bellerophon and the Flying Horse
6

At Home: Have students make a daily schedule, listing all the main events for one day of the school week. Remind them to list the events in the order in which they took place.

156

Vocabulary

Select a word from the box to complete each sentence.

ferocious	lavishly	rash
reassure	thunderous	waving

1. The <u>thunderous</u> roar of the <u>ferocious</u> lion frightened all the animals in the jungle.

2. The kind doctor tried to <u>reassure</u> the frightened patient.

3. As I walked through the garden, I enjoyed watching the tulips <u>waving</u> in the breeze.

4. The king's throne was <u>lavishly</u> decorated with gold, silver, and jewels.

5. Without thinking, Josh decided not to try out for the swim team, but he later regretted his <u>rash</u> choice.

Reteach 158

Story Comprehension

Answer the following questions about the characters and events in "Bellerophon and the Flying Horse."

1. Why does the letter upset the King of Lycia? <u>The letter said Bellerophon was wicked and told the king to kill him.</u>

2. What does the King of Lycia tell Bellerophon to do? <u>kill the Chimera</u>

3. How does Athena help Bellerophon? <u>She gives him the bridle for Pegasus.</u>

4. How does the monster die? <u>Bellerophon cuts off its three heads.</u>

5. Why were the villagers able to rebuild their village at the end of the story? <u>because the Chimera is dead</u>

157–158

At Home: Have students identify their favorite scene in this story and explain why they liked it.

Book 6/Unit 5
Bellerophon and the Flying Horse
5

Read a Constellation Map

> The sky is divided into regions with groups of stars called **constellations**. Ancient Greek and Roman astronomers named these constellations after things such as animals, gods, or heroes.

Study the following constellation map showing some constellations in the Northern Hemisphere. Then answer the questions below.

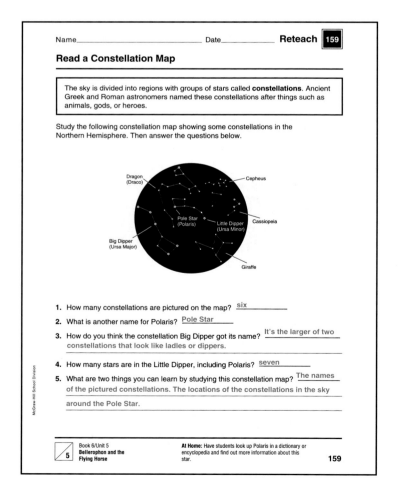

1. How many constellations are pictured on the map? <u>six</u>

2. What is another name for Polaris? <u>Pole Star</u>

3. How do you think the constellation Big Dipper got its name? <u>It's the larger of two constellations that look like ladles or dippers.</u>

4. How many stars are in the Little Dipper, including Polaris? <u>seven</u>

5. What are two things you can learn by studying this constellation map? <u>The names of the pictured constellations. The locations of the constellations in the sky around the Pole Star.</u>

5
Book 6/Unit 5
Bellerophon and the Flying Horse

At Home: Have students look up Polaris in a dictionary or encyclopedia and find out more information about this star.

159

Sequence of Events

> The **sequence of events** in a story is the order in which the events took place.

Write **before** or **after** on the line after each question about the sequence of events in "Bellerophon and the Flying Horse." Refer to the story for help.

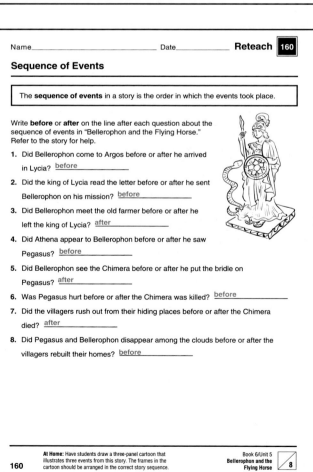

1. Did Bellerophon come to Argos before or after he arrived in Lycia? <u>before</u>

2. Did the king of Lycia read the letter before or after he sent Bellerophon on his mission? <u>before</u>

3. Did Bellerophon meet the old farmer before or after he left the king of Lycia? <u>after</u>

4. Did Athena appear to Bellerophon before or after he saw Pegasus? <u>before</u>

5. Did Bellerophon see the Chimera before or after he put the bridle on Pegasus? <u>after</u>

6. Was Pegasus hurt before or after the Chimera was killed? <u>before</u>

7. Did the villagers rush out from their hiding places before or after the Chimera died? <u>after</u>

8. Did Pegasus and Bellerophon disappear among the clouds before or after the villagers rebuilt their homes? <u>before</u>

160

At Home: Have students draw a three-panel cartoon that illustrates three events from this story. The frames in the cartoon should be arranged in the correct story sequence.

Book 6/Unit 5
Bellerophon and the Flying Horse
8

Bellerophon and the Flying Horse • RETEACH

Name_____ Date_____ **Reteach** 161

Make Inferences

Sometimes a writer doesn't tell you exactly what is happening in a story or what a character is thinking. In these instances you must **make an inference**, or come to an understanding, about characters and events using story information and your own experience.

Read each group of statements and answer the question that follows each group.

- The sky suddenly became very dark.
- The wind started blowing.
- The children heard thunder in the distance.

1. What inference can you make about the weather? _It is going to rain soon._

- When the actor heard the audience enter the theater, he started to pace back and forth in his dressing room.
- The actor's hands shook as he walked on stage.
- When he started to speak, the actor forgot the first line of his speech.

2. What inference can you make about the actor's feelings? _He feels nervous._

- After playing outside all morning, the dog raced into the kitchen and ran to his feeding dish.
- The dog sat down in front of the dish and barked.
- The dog ran to his owner and then ran back to his dish.

3. What inference can you make about the dog's actions? _He is hungry and his feeding dish is empty._

- The man stood outside his own front door.
- He looked in all his pockets and in his wallet.
- Then he rang the doorbell.

4. What inference can you make about the man's actions? _He has lost his keys and he's waiting for someone inside the house to let him in._

- Dave waited impatiently for Ms. Morgan to return the English tests to the class.
- He looked at his test and read his grade.
- Dave was smiling as he left school to walk home.

5. What inference can you make about what happened to Dave? _He got a good mark on his English test._

Name_____ Date_____ **Reteach** 162

Context Clues

Specialized words are often used in nonfiction and other content-area materials. These words have special meanings depending on how they are used in the selection. To figure out the meaning of these specialized words, use **context clues**, or the words, phrases, and sentences surrounding the word.

Use context clues to help you figure out the meaning of the boldfaced word in each sentence. Choose the meaning from the box that you think matches the boldfaced word, and write its letter on the blank line. Then underline the context clues you used to figure out the word's meaning.

a. straps used to control a horse
b. the forward part of a boat or ship
c. the right or left side of an animal
d. a rope used for catching cattle
e. long, heavy hair along the back and neck of a horse

1. The vet examined the horse's left **flank** and found an infected cut on that side of the animal. _c_

2. The rider pulled up on the **reins** in order to make the horse stop. _a_

3. As the horse raced across the pasture, the rider had to grip the hair of the animal's thick **mane** to keep from falling off. _e_

4. The sailor standing on the **prow** turned around to look at the captain, who was standing in the back of the boat. _b_

5. The cowboy sat straight and tall in the saddle as he swung his **lariat** over the head of the speeding cow. _d_

Bellerophon and the Flying Horse • EXTEND

Sequence of Events

Read the jumbled paragraph. Then write the sentences in the correct **sequence** on the lines provided.

> They built a shrine to Athena on the Acropolis, a flat expanse of rock rising above the city. The shrine is known for the beauty of its proportions, even though much of it was damaged in 1687. About 4,000 years ago, the people of Athens, Greece, decided to honor their city's namesake, the goddess Athena. This temple to Athena, called the Parthenon, still stands today. In 447 B.C., Pericles, a great Greek statesman, declared that a great temple to Athena would be erected on the Acropolis.

1. About 4,000 years ago, the people of Athens, Greece, decided to honor their city's namesake, the goddess Athena.

2. In 447 B.C., Pericles, a great Greek statesman, declared that a great temple to Athena would be erected on the Acropolis.

3. They built a shrine to Athena on the Acropolis, a flat expanse of rock rising above the city.

4. This temple to Athena, called the Parthenon, still stands today.

5. The shrine is known for the beauty of its proportions, even though much of it was damaged in 1687.

Create a word-jumble puzzle using some of the words in the paragraph.

Book 6/Unit 5
Bellerophon and the Flying Horse
At Home: Have students write a set of directions using the correct sequence.
156

Vocabulary

ferocious	lavishly	rash	reassure	thunderous	waving

Using some of the vocabulary words, write a paragraph retelling part of the story of Bellerophon and Pegasus. Answers will vary. Possible response is given.

Once, a queen took a rash and ferocious interest in a handsome young man of the kingdom. She treated the young man lavishly, and took no steps to reassure the king of her love. This, of course, inspired a thunderous anger in the king.

Story Comprehension

Answer the following questions about "Bellerophon and the Flying Horse."

1. Why is Bellerophon puzzled when Athena gives him a bridle? He doesn't have a horse.

2. What might have happened if Bellerophon had delivered the letter demanding his death immediately? Possible answer: The King of Lycia might have had him killed, since he hadn't gotten to know Bellerophon yet.

Now write a continuation of the story of Bellerophon answering the following questions: What was life like for Bellerophon when he returned from his victory over the Chimera? Did he ever marry? How did he eventually die?

Answers will vary but should be reasonable continuations.

At Home: Have students write about an act of bravery they have read about or participated in.
157–158
Book 6/Unit 5
Bellerophon and the Flying Horse

Read a Constellation Map

Look at the constellation map. Then answer the questions.

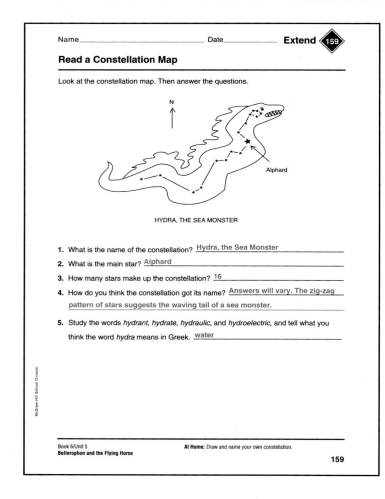

HYDRA, THE SEA MONSTER

1. What is the name of the constellation? Hydra, the Sea Monster

2. What is the main star? Alphard

3. How many stars make up the constellation? 16

4. How do you think the constellation got its name? Answers will vary. The zig-zag pattern of stars suggests the waving tail of a sea monster.

5. Study the words *hydrant*, *hydrate*, *hydraulic*, and *hydroelectric*, and tell what you think the word *hydra* means in Greek. water

Book 6/Unit 5
Bellerophon and the Flying Horse
At Home: Draw and name your own constellation.
159

Sequence of Events

The directions for making scrambled eggs are jumbled. Renumber the seven steps so that they are in the correct **sequence**.

Scrambled Eggs: Serves 3 or 4
Ingredients:
6 eggs 1/4 teaspoon salt; dash pepper
1/3 cup milk (optional) 2 tablespoons butter or margarine

Directions

3   Pour beaten egg mixture into hot margarine.

7   Remove from heat immediately and serve.

1   Beat eggs, milk, salt, and pepper with a fork.

4   Turn heat under pan to low. Cook until the mixture begins to set on the bottom and sides.

2   Heat butter or margarine in a skillet until just hot enough to make a drop of water sizzle.

5   Lift and fold the partially cooked mixture with a spatula so the uncooked egg goes to the bottom of the pan.

6   Continue to cook 4 to 5 minutes, until the eggs are cooked throughout but still moist.

List three ingredients you could add to the recipe to vary it. Then write between which two steps you would add the ingredients.

160
At Home: Ask students to write complete directions for a favorite dish.
Book 6/Unit 5
Bellerophon and the Flying Horse

Bellerophon and the Flying Horse • EXTEND

Make Inferences

When you **make an inference** you use information from the story you are reading, as well as information from your own personal experiences. Read the following facts. Then make an inference based on the facts.
Answers will vary. Possible answers are given.

1. Andy is a professional baseball player. He works as a sports equipment salesman when he is not playing baseball.

    INFERENCE: Andy sells equipment in the winter months.

2. The queen tells the king that Bellerophon is handsome. The queen also tells the king that Bellerophon is brave. She tells him this not once or twice, but again and again.

    INFERENCE: The queen is in love with Bellerophon.

3. Pegasus jumped away from Bellerophon. Pegasus tried every trick to throw Bellerophon off his back. Bellerophon stayed on Pegasus's back.

    INFERENCE: Pegasus was testing Bellerophon. Pegasus did not want Bellerophon to ride him.

4. Jared is conducting a science experiment. He is interviewing young people, middle-aged people, and senior citizens, asking them to recall a long list of objects he has recited to them.

    INFERENCE: Jared is studying the effects of age upon memory.

Now write some information that would support this inference:

5. INFERENCE: Tamiko is wise beyond her years.

    Answers will vary but should support the inference. She is twelve years old. Tamiko is reading *Wuthering Heights*, and she converses intelligently with people three times her own age.

Context Clues

Look for these three kinds of **context clues** when you spot an unfamiliar word:

1. **Similar Meanings:** Sometimes the sentence containing the unfamiliar word will also contain a word you know.
2. **Contrasting Meanings:** Some sentences with unfamiliar words are constructed so that a word you know is contrasted with one you don't know. The words *but*, *although*, and *however* are clues.
3. **Defined in Context:** When you see phrases like *that is*, *in other words*, and *or*, you know that you are being given a definition in context.

Define the italicized word in each sentence below. Write the number of the kind of context clue you used after your definition.

1. The horse's *bridle*, or headgear, was crusted with gold. horse's headgear; 3

2. The *infinite*, unending galaxy of stars fascinated him. unending, 1

3. His *obscure* reference confused the audience; however, during the question and answer session he was asked to make himself clear. confusing; 2

4. The *lavish*, excessive array of food was overwhelming for the starving man. excessive, or too much; 1

5. At first the frightened horse screamed in pain, but as the pain lessened, the poor animal *whinnied* softly. A gentle sound made by a horse; 2

6. Horses are plant eaters, or *herbivores*. plant eater; 3

T23

Bellerophon and the Flying Horse • GRAMMAR

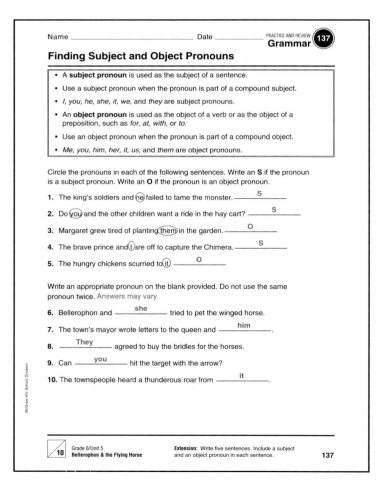

Subject Pronouns

- A **subject pronoun** is used as the subject of a sentence.
- Use a subject pronoun when the pronoun is part of a compound subject.
- *I, you, he, she, it, we,* and *they* are subject pronouns.

Choose the correct pronoun in parentheses to correctly complete each sentence.

1. The king and (I, me) _____I_____ were tired of listening to the queen.

2. (He, Him) _____He_____ agreed to fight the ferocious monster.

3. All of the villagers and (she, her) _____she_____ feared the Chimera.

4. (They, Them) _____They_____ advised Bellerophon to take the crooked path through the woods.

Read each sentence and circle any incorrect pronoun. Rewrite each sentence correctly on the line provided. If the pronoun is correct, write Correct instead of the sentence.

5. (Me) will ride Pegasus into the sky.
   I will ride Pegasus into the sky.

6. (Them) plan to deal with the creature.
   They plan to deal with the creature.

7. The beautiful woman and (him) stared at the winged horse.
   The beautiful woman and he stared at the winged horse.

8. You and it will reach the kingdom of Argos by nightfall.
   Correct.

9. Pegasus and (him) circled the town and swooped back to earth.
   Pegasus and he circled the town and swooped back to earth.

10. (Us) came to a farming village that lay in ruins.
    We came to a farming village that lay in ruins.

10 | Grade 6/Unit 5
Bellerophon & the Flying Horse

Extension: Work with a partner to write a new ending for Bellerophon. Include and circle five subject pronouns in your work.

135

Object Pronouns

- An **object pronoun** is used as the object of a verb or as the object of a preposition, such as *for, at, with,* or *to.*
- Use an object pronoun when the pronoun is part of a compound object.
- *Me, you, him, her, it, us,* and *them* are object pronouns.

Circle the incorrect pronoun, and write the correct pronoun in the blank provided.

1. The king begged (they) to destroy the Chimera. ____them____

2. Bellerophon carried the horse's bridle to (she). ____her____

3. Please take the king's message to Pegasus and (he). ____him____

4. Will the miller inspect the wheat field with the farmer and (I)? ____me____

5. The Chimera attacked the villagers and brought (they) great unhappiness.
   ____them____

Circle the object pronoun in parentheses that correctly completes each sentence.

6. The shop keeper cried out, "Stop!" to Bellerophon and (he, (him)).

7. The horses grazed idly by the pond and ignored ((it), I).

8. The soldiers exclaimed, "We will follow our king and (she, (her))!"

9. Bellerophon asked (they, (them)), "Please direct me to the nearest village."

10. Will you accompany the king and (we, (us)) to the forest?

Extension: Write a letter of complaint to the Chimera. Include five object pronouns.

136 | Grade 6/Unit 5
Bellerophon & the Flying Horse | 10

Finding Subject and Object Pronouns

- A **subject pronoun** is used as the subject of a sentence.
- Use a subject pronoun when the pronoun is part of a compound subject.
- *I, you, he, she, it, we,* and *they* are subject pronouns.
- An **object pronoun** is used as the object of a verb or as the object of a preposition, such as *for, at, with,* or *to.*
- Use an object pronoun when the pronoun is part of a compound object.
- *Me, you, him, her, it, us,* and *them* are object pronouns.

Circle the pronouns in each of the following sentences. Write an **S** if the pronoun is a subject pronoun. Write an **O** if the pronoun is an object pronoun.

1. The king's soldiers and (he) failed to tame the monster. ____S____

2. Do (you) and the other children want a ride in the hay cart? ____S____

3. Margaret grew tired of planting (them) in the garden. ____O____

4. The brave prince and (I) are off to capture the Chimera. ____S____

5. The hungry chickens scurried to (it). ____O____

Write an appropriate pronoun on the blank provided. Do not use the same pronoun twice. Answers may vary.

6. Bellerophon and ____she____ tried to pet the winged horse.

7. The town's mayor wrote letters to the queen and ____him____.

8. ____They____ agreed to buy the bridles for the horses.

9. Can ____you____ hit the target with the arrow?

10. The townspeople heard a thunderous roar from ____it____.

10 | Grade 6/Unit 5
Bellerophon & the Flying Horse

Extension: Write five sentences. Include a subject and an object pronoun in each sentence.

137

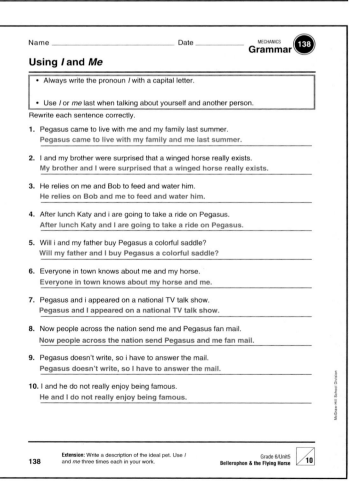

Using *I* and *Me*

- Always write the pronoun *I* with a capital letter.
- Use *I* or *me* last when talking about yourself and another person.

Rewrite each sentence correctly.

1. Pegasus came to live with me and my family last summer.
   Pegasus came to live with my family and me last summer.

2. I and my brother were surprised that a winged horse really exists.
   My brother and I were surprised that a winged horse really exists.

3. He relies on me and Bob to feed and water him.
   He relies on Bob and me to feed and water him.

4. After lunch Katy and i are going to take a ride on Pegasus.
   After lunch Katy and I are going to take a ride on Pegasus.

5. Will i and my father buy Pegasus a colorful saddle?
   Will my father and I buy Pegasus a colorful saddle?

6. Everyone in town knows about me and my horse.
   Everyone in town knows about my horse and me.

7. Pegasus and i appeared on a national TV talk show.
   Pegasus and I appeared on a national TV talk show.

8. Now people across the nation send me and Pegasus fan mail.
   Now people across the nation send Pegasus and me fan mail.

9. Pegasus doesn't write, so i have to answer the mail.
   Pegasus doesn't write, so I have to answer the mail.

10. I and he do not really enjoy being famous.
    He and I do not really enjoy being famous.

Extension: Write a description of the ideal pet. Use *I* and *me* three times each in your work.

138 | Grade 6/Unit 5
Bellerophon & the Flying Horse | 10

Bellerophon and the Flying Horse • GRAMMAR

Pronouns

Read the first sentence of each set. One of the four sentences that follows correctly replaces the underlined subject with a subject pronoun. Circle the letter of the correct sentence.

1. The flying horse Pegasus transported the prince across the kingdom.
  a. He transported the prince across the kingdom.
  b. They transported the prince across the kingdom.
  c. Pegasus transported him across the kingdom.
  d. The flying horse Pegasus transported them across the kingdom.

2. Many young men have tried to slay the Chimera.
  a. He have tried to slay the Chimera.
  b. They have tried to slay the Chimera.
  c. Young men have tried to slay the Chimera.
  d. Many young men have tried to slay the Chimera.

3. Bellerophon and Pegasus searched for the wicked creature and its trail.
  a. Bellerophon and Pegasus searched for them.
  b. He searched for the wicked creature and its trail.
  c. They searched for the wicked creature and its trail.
  d. Bellerophon and Pegasus searched for him and its trail.

Read the first sentence of each set. One of the four sentences that follows correctly replaces the underlined object with an object pronoun. Circle the letter of the correct sentence.

4. The king advised Bellerophon to take the crooked path through the woods.
  a. The king advised them to take the crooked path through the woods.
  b. The king advised he to take the crooked path through the woods.
  c. The king advised him to take the crooked path through the woods.
  d. The king advised us to take the crooked path through the woods.

5. The ancient pot shows Athena with a battle shield.
  a. They show Athena with a battle shield.
  b. The ancient pot shows her with a battle shield.
  c. The pot shows them with a battle shield.
  d. It shows Athena with them.

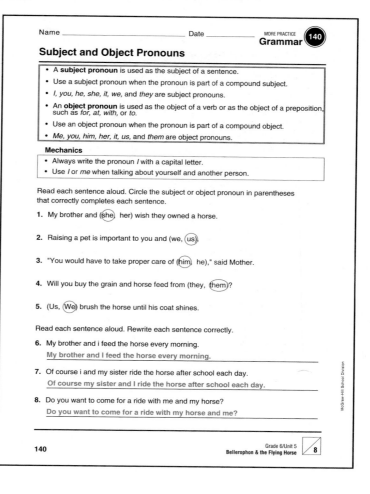

Subject and Object Pronouns

- A **subject pronoun** is used as the subject of a sentence.
- Use a subject pronoun when the pronoun is part of a compound subject.
- *I, you, he, she, it, we,* and *they* are subject pronouns.
- An **object pronoun** is used as the object of a verb or as the object of a preposition, such as *for, at, with,* or *to.*
- Use an object pronoun when the pronoun is part of a compound object.
- *Me, you, him, her, it, us,* and *them* are object pronouns.

Mechanics

- Always write the pronoun *I* with a capital letter.
- Use *I* or *me* when talking about yourself and another person.

Read each sentence aloud. Circle the subject or object pronoun in parentheses that correctly completes each sentence.

1. My brother and (she, her) wish they owned a horse.

2. Raising a pet is important to you and (we, us).

3. "You would have to take proper care of (him, he)," said Mother.

4. Will you buy the grain and horse feed from (they, them)?

5. (Us, We) brush the horse until his coat shines.

Read each sentence aloud. Rewrite each sentence correctly.

6. My brother and i feed the horse every morning.
  My brother and I feed the horse every morning.

7. Of course i and my sister ride the horse after school each day.
  Of course my sister and I ride the horse after school each day.

8. Do you want to come for a ride with me and my horse?
  Do you want to come for a ride with my horse and me?

T25

Bellerophon and the Flying Horse • SPELLING

Name_____ Date_____

Homophones and Homographs

Pretest Directions

Fold back the paper along the dotted line. Use the blanks to write each word as it is read aloud. When you finish the test, unfold the paper. Use the list at the right to correct any spelling mistakes. Practice the words you missed for the Posttest.

To Parents

Here are the results of your child's weekly spelling Pretest. You can help your child study for the Posttest by following these simple steps for each word on the word list:

1. Read the word to your child.
2. Have your child write the word, saying each letter as it is written.
3. Say each letter of the word as your child checks the spelling.
4. If a mistake has been made, have your child read each letter of the correctly spelled word aloud, and then repeat steps 1–3.

1. _____	1. straight
2. _____	2. dove
3. _____	3. shear
4. _____	4. hire
5. _____	5. swallow
6. _____	6. racket
7. _____	7. strait
8. _____	8. sheer
9. _____	9. hamper
10. _____	10. higher
11. _____	11. vain
12. _____	12. cereal
13. _____	13. principal
14. _____	14. refrain
15. _____	15. kernel
16. _____	16. bass
17. _____	17. vein
18. _____	18. principle
19. _____	19. colonel
20. _____	20. serial

Challenge Words

_____ ferocious
_____ lavishly
_____ reassure
_____ thunderous
_____ waving

Name_____ Date_____

Homophones and Homographs

Using the Word Study Steps

1. LOOK at the word.
2. SAY the word aloud.
3. STUDY the letters in the word.
4. WRITE the word.
5. CHECK the word.

Did you spell the word right? If not, go back to step 1.

Spelling Tip

Learn the meanings of common homophones to help you use the right one in your writing.

I scored **higher** than you on the math test.

The restaurant will **hire** two new waiters.

Word Scramble

Unscramble each set of letters to make a spelling word.

1.	ttasri	strait	11.	lecera	cereal
2.	rearfin	refrain	12.	ireh	hire
3.	ihhger	higher	13.	lappiinrc	principal
4.	sbsa	bass	14.	lekren	kernel
5.	lloocen	colonel	15.	triastgh	straight
6.	evod	dove	16.	siearl	serial
7.	awollws	swallow	17.	ershe	sheer
8.	hares	shear	18.	tekrac	racket
9.	nvie	vein	19.	cipprilen	principle
10.	repham	hamper	20.	ainv	vain

To Parents or Helpers:

Using the Word Study Steps above as your child comes across any new words will help him or her spell well. Review the steps as you both go over this week's spelling words.

Go over the Spelling Tip with your child. Write other sentences using homophones.

Help your child unscramble the spelling words.

Name_____ Date_____

Homophones and Homographs

straight	swallow	hamper	principal	vein
dove	racket	higher	refrain	principle
shear	strait	vain	kernel	colonel
hire	sheer	cereal	bass	serial

Sort the spelling words into homophone pairs and homographs. Write the words on the appropriate lines below.

Homophones

1.	straight	9.	cereal
2.	strait	10.	serial
3.	shear	11.	principal
4.	sheer	12.	principle
5.	hire	13.	kernel
6.	higher	14.	colonel
7.	vain		
8.	vein		

Homographs

15.	dove	18.	hamper
16.	swallow	19.	refrain
17.	racket	20.	bass

Name_____ Date_____

Homophones and Homographs

straight	swallow	hamper	principal	vein
dove	racket	higher	refrain	principle
shear	strait	vain	kernel	colonel
hire	sheer	cereal	bass	serial

Meaning Match-Up

Write the spelling word which matches each definition below.

1. not curly	straight	8. chief	principal
2. to clip or cut	shear	9. military officer	colonel
3. to employ	hire	10. very thin	sheer
4 conceited	vain	11 law or belief	principle
5. thin waterway	strait	12. seed of plants	kernel
6. blood vessel	vein	13. further upward	higher
7. grain breakfast food	cereal	14. story part	serial

More Than One Meaning

Read the definitions below. Then write the letters of the two definitions which correspond with each homograph below.

a. to engulf	g. pigeon
b. opposite of treble	h. a large basket
c. perching bird	i. type of fish
d. to hold oneself back	j. paddle
e. plunged headfirst	k. recurring verse
f. to impede	l. clamor

1. dove e g
2. racket j l
3. refrain d k
4. swallow a c
5. bass b i
6. hamper f h

T26 Annotated Workbooks

Bellerophon and the Flying Horse • SPELLING

Name_____ Date_____

Homophones and Homographs

Proofreading Activity
There are six spelling mistakes in this paragraph. Circle the misspelled words. Write the words correctly on the lines below.

The King of Lycia told Bellerophon he wanted to hiar him for a mission—to slay the Chimera. However, the king did not tell Bellerophon that his journey would be in vein. All the men that had tried to kill the Chimera had died in the attempt. Bellerophon set strait off without fear. He flew on Pegasus, the winged horse, for miles until he heard a rackit in a nearby valley. Bellerophon saw that the Chimera had three horrible heads, which tried to swalow him whole! Bellerophon rode Pegasus hire into the sky and then they dove towards the monster, killing one head with each blow.

1. _____hire_____   3. _____straight_____   5. _____swallow_____

2. _____vain_____   4. _____racket_____   6. _____higher_____

Writing Activity
What is your favorite fairy tale or myth about an evil king or a brave hero or heroine? Rewrite it, using at least four spelling words.

_____

_____

_____

_____

Name_____ Date_____

Homophones and Homographs

Look at the words in each set below. One word in each set is spelled correctly. Use a pencil to fill in the circle next to the correct word. Before you begin, look at the sample sets of words. Sample A has been done for you. Do Sample B by yourself. When you are sure you know what to do, you may go on with the rest of the page.

Sample A:
- (A) lier
- (B) lyer
- (C) liar ●
- (D) liur

Sample B:
- (E) bridel
- (F) bridall
- (G) bridell
- (H) bridal

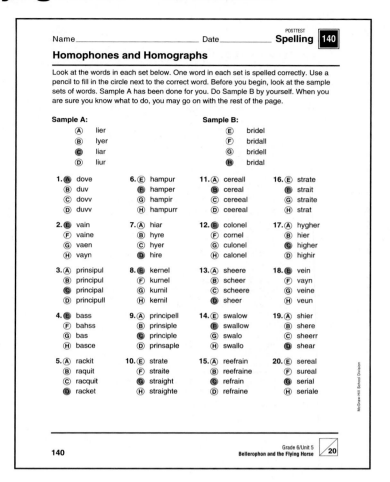

1. (A)● dove
   (B) duv
   (C) dovv
   (D) duvv

2. (E)● vain
   (F) vaine
   (G) vaen
   (H) vayn

3. (A) prinsipul
   (B) principul
   (C)● principal
   (D) principull

4. (E)● bass
   (F) bahss
   (G) bas
   (H) basce

5. (A) rackit
   (B) raquit
   (C) racquit
   (D)● racket

6. (E) hampur
   (F)● hamper
   (G) hampir
   (H) hampurr

7. (A) hiar
   (B) hyre
   (C) hyer
   (D)● hire

8. (E) kernal
   (F) kurnel
   (G) kurnil
   (H)● kernil

9. (A) principell
   (B) prinsiple
   (C)● principle
   (D) prinsaple

10. (E) strate
    (F) straite
    (G)● straight
    (H) straighte

11. (A) cereall
    (B)● cereal
    (C) cereeal
    (D) ceereal

12. (E)● colonel
    (F) cornel
    (G) culonel
    (H) calonel

13. (A) sheere
    (B) scheer
    (C) scheere
    (D)● sheer

14. (E) swalow
    (F)● swallow
    (G) swalo
    (H) swallo

15. (A) reefrain
    (B) reefraine
    (C)● refrain
    (D) refraine

16. (E) strate
    (F)● strait
    (G) straite
    (H) strat

17. (A) hygher
    (B) hier
    (C)● higher
    (D) highir

18. (E)● vein
    (F) vayn
    (G) veine
    (H) veun

19. (A) shier
    (B) shere
    (C) sheerr
    (D)● shear

20. (E) sereal
    (F) sureal
    (G)● serial
    (H) seriale

T27

Practice 163

Name_____ Date_____ Practice **163**

Make Judgments and Decisions

Readers often make **judgments and decisions** about the actions of characters or events in a story. When you make a judgment you usually rely on story information and on personal experience.

Read each passage below and make a judgment about it. Then circle approve or **disapprove** to indicate your judgment, and explain your reasoning on the lines. [Answers may vary. Sample responses are provided.]

The city council voted to close the community pool for the summer. The members believe the pool was too expensive to operate. Also, so many people used the pool last year that there weren't enough lifeguards on duty to protect them. The safety of the swimmers this year concerned all of the city council members.

1. I (approve, (disapprove)) of the decision because: ____ the pool benefits the entire community, so the expense is worth is. Also, they could hire more lifeguards.

Anthony's parents refused to let him make weekend plans with his friends for the rest of the semester. They thought he should concentrate on his school work on Saturday and Sunday because his first semester grades were so low. If his grades improved, they promised to lift his curfew.

2. I (approve, (disapprove)) of his parents' decision because: I think making him work all weekend isn't fair. He should spend some time with his friends, too.

This year Midvale Middle School will require all students to wear school uniforms. The school board believes wearing uniforms will make students focus less on their appearance and more on their school work. Also, it will eliminate competition between students about their clothing allowances and spending habits.

3. I ((approve,) disapprove) of the new school rule because: many students can't afford to compete with their classmates and spend a lot of money on clothes.

In the story, Clarice and Joshua brought their dog to the park early Saturday morning. Although a city law forbids unleashed dogs in the park, they paid no attention to it. "We know Sparky is friendly," Clarice said. "Also, he needs the exercise." Ten minutes later a park ranger fined Clarice and Joshua $25.00 because Sparky wasn't on a leash.

4. I (approve, (disapprove)) of what Clarice and Joshua did because: I think they should have obeyed the city law and kept Sparky on a leash for the safety of the dog and the public.

At Home: Have students read an editorial in a school newspaper and make a judgment about what it says. Have them explain why they feel that way.

Book 6/ Unit 5
Adventure in Space 4

163

Practice 164

Name_____ Date_____ Practice **164**

Vocabulary

Select a word from the box to complete each sentence.

bloodstream	compartment	deliberately
handshake	maneuvering	void

1. The confident young man greeted his new employer with a firm ____ **handshake**

2. Without hesitation, the nature photographer picked up her camera and walked **deliberately** ____ toward the sleeping lion.

3. Because the infection was still in the patient's ____ **bloodstream** ____, the doctor decided to keep her in the hospital.

4. The driver ____ **maneuvering** ____ the car changed lanes so quickly that he almost caused an accident.

5. When the mechanic tried to force open the door to the ____ **compartment** ____ that contained his tools, he broke the lock.

6. In the science fiction story, the spaceship was lost forever in the ____ **void** ____ of outer space.

Write sentences on the lines below using one or two of the vocabulary words in each sentence. [Sentences will vary but should include at least two vocabulary words.]

7. _____
_____

8. _____
_____

At Home: Have students create a word scramble puzzle using all the vocabulary words and share it with family members.

164

Book 6/ Unit 5
Adventure in Space 8

Practice 164a

Name_____ Date_____ Practice **164a**

A Surprise in Space

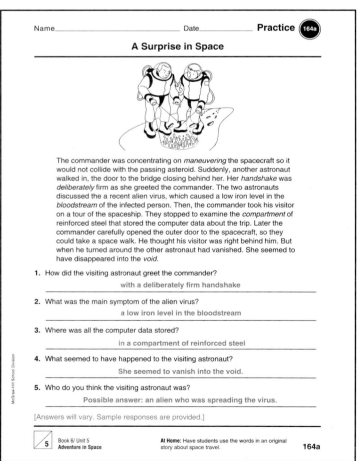

The commander was concentrating on *maneuvering* the spacecraft so it would not collide with the passing asteroid. Suddenly, another astronaut walked in, the door to the bridge closing behind her. Her *handshake* was *deliberately* firm as she greeted the commander. The two astronauts discussed a recent alien virus, which caused a low iron level in the *bloodstream* of the infected person. Then, the commander took his visitor on a tour of the spaceship. They stopped to examine the *compartment* of reinforced steel that stored the computer data about the trip. Later the commander carefully opened the outer door to the spacecraft, so they could take a space walk. He thought his visitor was right behind him. But when he turned around the other astronaut had vanished. She seemed to have disappeared into the *void*.

1. How did the visiting astronaut greet the commander?
with a deliberately firm handshake

2. What was the main symptom of the alien virus?
a low iron level in the bloodstream

3. Where was all the computer data stored?
in a compartment of reinforced steel

4. What seemed to have happened to the visiting astronaut?
She seemed to vanish into the void.

5. Who do you think the visiting astronaut was?
Possible answer: an alien who was spreading the virus.

[Answers will vary. Sample responses are provided.]

Book 6/ Unit 5
Adventure in Space 5

At Home: Have students use the words in an original story about space travel.

164a

Practice 165

Name_____ Date_____ Practice **165**

Story Comprehension

Answer the questions below about the selection "Adventure in Space."

1. Where do the events in this selection take place?
in and around the Shuttle Endeavor in space.

2. Who are the main characters in this selection?
Ken Bowersox, Commander Dick Covey, Jeff Hoffman, Claude, Story Musgrave, Kathy Thornton, Tom Aker

3. What is the problem described in this selection?
The Hubble telescope is damaged and must be repaired.

4. What is the solution to the problem?
The crew of the shuttle Endeavor is sent on a mission to repair the telescope.

5. Why is it so important to use spacesuits on a spacewalk?
Human beings who aren't protected would quickly die in the environment of outer space without the protection of a spacesuit.

6. Why do you think the crew members are called "space mechanics"?
They had to repair the telescope in space, just the way a mechanic would repair a car on Earth.

7. What do you think one of the astronauts meant when he said on spotting the telescope, "Now it's all eyeballs and hands"?
He is referring to the fact that the astronauts would have to rely on sight and touch to repair it.

8. What are two dangers associated with this space mission?
The astronauts could cut off electricity to the Hubble and, as a result, the telescope would have no life; anything dropped in space could contaminate the Hubble.

165

At Home: Have students make up two additional questions and answers based on this selection.

Book 6/ Unit 5
Adventure in Space 8

Adventure in Space • PRACTICE

Read a Flow Chart

A **flow chart** is a visual way to show the steps in a process. This flow chart shows how a clothing company might market a shirt by catalog.

Customer	**No**	→	→	Send another catalog
orders shirt.	←	←	**Yes**	to customer.

Yes
↓

Shirt is in stock	**No**	→	→	File order until
and can be shipped.	←	←	**Yes**	shirt is in stock.

Yes
↓

Customer	**No**	→	→	The company
likes shirt.	←	←	**Yes**	replaces shirt.

Yes
↓

Send another
catalog to customer.

Use the flow chart to answer the questions.

1. What will happen if the shirt is not in stock when a customer orders it?

   The company will file the order until the shirt is in stock.

2. What is the next step to take if the customer does not like the shirt?

   The company will replace the shirt.

3. Which two steps lead to the customer receiving a catalog?

   The customer does not order a shirt. The customer orders a shirt and likes it.

4. Which step might indicate an unhappy customer?

   Company replaces the shirt.

5. What might be the next step in the flow chart after sending another catalog to the

   customer? Sample answer: The customer orders another article of clothing.

Make Judgments and Decisions

When you **make a judgment** about a story character's actions or about story events, you decide what you think or feel about them. To make a judgment you should consider the reasons for and against an action using story information and your own personal experience.

Make a judgment about the following actions described in "Adventure in Space." Explain each answer. [Answers will vary. Sample responses are provided.]

1. There are always dangers involved in a space mission and a space walk. Do you think astronauts should have repaired the space telescope or should a mechanical device have been used to make the repair?

   I think it was important to repair the telescope and only human beings could have done it reliably.

2. What story information did you use to make your decision in question 1?

   When the crew first spotted the telescope an astronaut said, "Now it's all eyeballs and hands." This statement shows how important human beings were to the success of the mission, after the initial contact was made by the robot arm.

3. The damaged solar array had to be thrown overboard before a new one could be installed. Do you think it is right to dispose of these materials as "space junk" in outer space? What about the possible damage to the Hubble telescope? Explain your answer.

   I think it is okay to dispose of junk in space because the used objects won't hurt the space environment and it was important to repair the telescope.

4. What information in the story helped you make your decision in question 3?

   The astronauts performed their tasks carefully. They waited until daylight until they could see clearly before disposing of the solar array. Space is a huge, empty void.

5. Repairing the telescope was extremely difficult because one wrong move could have crippled this delicate instrument. Do you think the telescope should have been repaired? Or, should a new telescope have been made to replace it? Explain.

   I think it was better to repair it since the astronauts were well-trained. Also, it was probably less expensive to repair it than to build a new one.

Sequence of Events

The **sequence of events** in a selection is the order in which they took place. Read the following passage. Then answer the questions below.

The very first step in a space shuttle mission is the launch of the spacecraft. Astronauts ride to the launch pad three hours before liftoff takes place. When they reach the launch pad, they ride an elevator up the shuttle, cross a bridge and enter their spacecraft. This entrance is at the level where the living quarters for the crew are located. Next, they climb up a ladder to the flight deck. Inside there are more than 2,000 different controls and displays. The crew knows how to use all of them! The commander, pilot, and three mission specialists strap themselves into their seats, facing the sky. After they are strapped in, the equipment, the fuel tank and the boosters are checked carefully. Once the equipment is checked, the main engines fire. Then the booster rockets burn. Two minutes after liftoff the boosters burn out and the empty cases parachute to the ocean for pickup and reuse.

1. What is the first step in a space shuttle mission?

   launching the shuttle

2. When do the astronauts arrive at the launch pad?

   three hours before liftoff

3. After the astronauts arrive at the launch pad, what happens next?

   They ride an elevator up the shuttle, cross a bridge, and enter the spacecraft.

4. What happens after the step described in your answer to questions 3?

   They climb up a ladder to the flight deck.

5. After the astronauts enter the flight deck, what do they do first?

   strap themselves into their seats.

6. What happens next?

   They check their equipment

7. After the main engines fire, what happens?

   The booster rocket burns.

8. What happens after the booster rockets burn out?

   The empty cases parachute to the ocean for pickup and reuse.

Context Clues

Readers often come across unfamiliar **specialized vocabulary** in non fiction, content-area materials. You can use **context clues**, or the surrounding information, to determine the meaning of these unfamiliar words.

Use context clues to help you figure out the meaning of the boldfaced word in each sentence. Write the word's meaning on the blank line. Then, underline the context clues you used to help you figure out the meaning.

1. The astronauts used a powerful space telescope to find out more

   information about the **cosmos**.

   Meaning: space, the universe

2. The scientists at **Mission Control** on Earth were in constant communication with the astronauts on board the shuttle about their repair of the telescope.

   Meaning: the place from which NASA's missions are run

3. The crew on board the **shuttle** *Endeavour* had prepared for this

   flight for many months.

   Meaning: a type of space craft

4. In order for the space **mission** to be a success, the damaged solar array

   had to be replaced.

   Meaning: a goal or task of a group of astronauts

5. When the *Endeavour* was in place, the shuttle's **robot arm** was used to

   catch hold of the damaged telescope.

   Meaning: mechanical device that was part of the shuttle

6. Members of the Endeavour crew entered and exited the shuttle through

   a small room with two **hatches** that could be opened and closed.

   Meaning: doors on the spacecraft

Adventure in Space • RETEACH

Reteach 163

Name_____ Date_____ **Reteach** 163

Make Judgments and Decisions

> Readers often **make judgments or decisions** about a character's actions or the events in a selection by using story information and their own personal experience.

Read the following story information and answer the questions. Explain your answers. *Answers will vary. Sample responses are provided.*

Billy walked into the stables when no one else was around. The sign above the horses' stalls said, "Please do not pet or feed the horses." Billy gave two cubes of sugar to one of the horses anyway. "Duchess is my favorite horse," he thought to himself. "I know what she's allowed to have. And I know she likes me to give her a special treat."

1. Do you think Billy was right to feed the horse? It was wrong to disobey the sign and feed the horse. The horses may have been on a strict feeding schedule.

The man argued with the zoo keeper. His children wanted to visit the turtles. The zoo keeper said they weren't allowed inside the building until all the turtles had been fed and their tanks had been cleaned. By then, the zoo would be closed for the day.

2. Do you think the man was right to argue with the zoo keeper? It was wrong to argue because the zoo keeper was doing his job.

Maria's parents told her to limit each phone call to five minutes. They explained that everyone in the house had to use the same phone. Also, Maria's parents used the phone for their business. Maria was angry that she couldn't spend more time on the phone with her friends.

3. Do you think Maria was right to be upset with her parents? She was wrong to be upset. She should have been more considerate about sharing the phone with the rest of her family.

Sam didn't have enough time to do the research for his social studies report about the space shuttle. His best friend, Tony, had written a report on the same topic. When Sam asked Tony if he could use his research information to write a report, Tony became angry and refused.

4. Do you think Tony was right to refuse to help Sam? Tony was right; it would have been wrong to give Sam his notes since doing the research was part of Sam's assignment.

Book 6/Unit 5
Adventure in Space 4

At Home: Have students make a judgment about an action of a character in another story they read in this unit and give reasons for their decision.

163

Reteach 164

Name_____ Date_____ **Reteach** 164

Vocabulary

Choose a vocabulary word from the box to complete each sentence. First, write the word in the blank. Then use the word to fill in the crossword puzzle below.

| bloodstream | compartment | deliberately | handshake | maneuvering | void |

Across

2. The maneuvering ship avoided hitting the iceberg.

5. Leo stored the papers in the compartment under his desk.

6. The graceful dancer moved deliberately across the stage.

Down

1. As she accepted the award from the principal, Lee's handshake was firm.

3. The broken part from the shuttle spun into the void of space.

4. The doctor prescribed antibiotics for the infection in the patient's bloodstream .

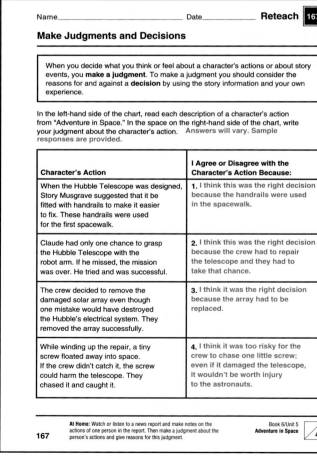

6 **Reteach** 165

Story Comprehension

Complete each sentence with information about the characters and events in "Adventure in Space."

1. The crew of the *Endeavor* was trained to repair the Hubble Space Telescope .

2. Claude was in charge of operating the robot arm on the *Endeavour*.

3. When they had a problem closing the shuttle doors, Jeff and Story talked to Mission Control .

4. The crew realized that a solar array was severely damaged.

At Home: Have students use each vocabulary word in an original sentence.

164–165 Book 6/Unit 5
Adventure in Space 4

Reteach 166

Name_____ Date_____ **Reteach** 166

Read a Flow Chart

> A **flow chart** is a way to show the steps in a process. This flow chart shows the steps a company might take to develop a new video game.

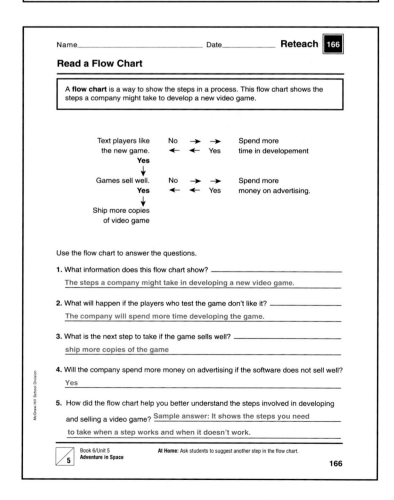

Text players like the new game.   No → →   Spend more
            ← ← Yes   time in developement
Yes ↓

Games sell well.   No → →   Spend more
Yes ← ← Yes   money on advertising.
↓

Ship more copies of video game

Use the flow chart to answer the questions.

1. What information does this flow chart show? _____
The steps a company might take in developing a new video game.

2. What will happen if the players who test the game don't like it? _____
The company will spend more time developing the game.

3. What is the next step to take if the game sells well? _____
ship more copies of the game

4. Will the company spend more money on advertising if the software does not sell well?
Yes

5. How did the flow chart help you better understand the steps involved in developing and selling a video game? Sample answer: It shows the steps you need to take when a step works and when it doesn't work.

Book 6/Unit 5
Adventure in Space 5

At Home: Ask students to suggest another step in the flow chart.

166

Reteach 167

Name_____ Date_____ **Reteach** 167

Make Judgments and Decisions

> When you decide what you think or feel about a character's actions or about story events, you **make a judgment**. To make a judgment you should consider the reasons for and against a **decision** by using the story information and your own experience.

In the left-hand side of the chart, read each description of a character's action from "Adventure in Space." In the space on the right-hand side of the chart, write your judgment about the character's action. *Answers will vary. Sample responses are provided.*

Character's Action	I Agree or Disagree with the Character's Action Because:
When the Hubble Telescope was designed, Story Musgrave suggested that it be fitted with handrails to make it easier to fix. These handrails were used for the first spacewalk.	**1.** I think this was the right decision because the handrails were used in the spacewalk.
Claude had only one chance to grasp the Hubble Telescope with the robot arm. If he missed, the mission was over. He tried and was successful.	**2.** I think this was the right decision because the crew had to repair the telescope and they had to take that chance.
The crew decided to remove the damaged solar array even though one mistake would have destroyed the Hubble's electrical system. They removed the array successfully.	**3.** I think it was the right decision because the array had to be replaced.
While winding up the repair, a tiny screw floated away into space. If the crew didn't catch it, the screw could harm the telescope. They chased it and caught it.	**4.** I think it was too risky for the crew to chase one little screw; even if it damaged the telescope, it wouldn't be worth injury to the astronauts.

167 **At Home:** Watch or listen to a news report and make notes on the actions of one person in the report. Then make a judgment about the person's actions and give reasons for this judgment.

Book 6/Unit 5
Adventure in Space 4

Adventure in Space • RETEACH

Sequence of Events

The **sequence of events** in a story or selection is the order in which the events took place.

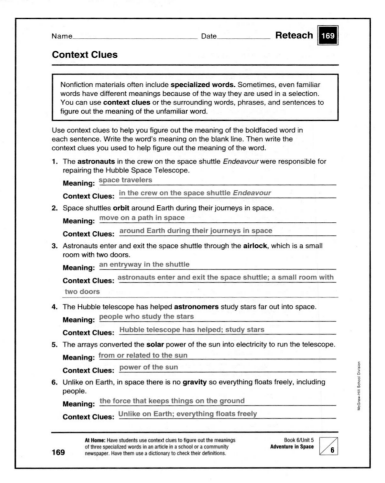

The following list of eight story events from "Adventure in Space" are out of order. Show the correct sequence by numbering the events 1 through 8 in the order in which they occurred.

2_____ Claude used the robot arm to grab the telescope.

4_____ Kathy removed the damaged solar array from the telescope.

6_____ Then Kathy and Tom installed COSTAR.

3_____ On the first space walk, Story and Jeff replaced the gyroscope.

5_____ On the third spacewalk, Story and Jeff installed the new camera.

8_____ Claude released the Hubble into space.

7_____ The crew chased a floating screw through space.

1_____ The shuttle approached the Hubble Space Telescope.

Context Clues

Nonfiction materials often include **specialized words.** Sometimes, even familiar words have different meanings because of the way they are used in a selection. You can use **context clues** or the surrounding words, phrases, and sentences to figure out the meaning of the unfamiliar word.

Use context clues to help you figure out the meaning of the boldfaced word in each sentence. Write the word's meaning on the blank line. Then write the context clues you used to help figure out the meaning of the word.

1. The **astronauts** in the crew on the space shuttle *Endeavour* were responsible for repairing the Hubble Space Telescope.

   Meaning: space travelers

   Context Clues: in the crew on the space shuttle *Endeavour*

2. Space shuttles **orbit** around Earth during their journeys in space.

   Meaning: move on a path in space

   Context Clues: around Earth during their journeys in space

3. Astronauts enter and exit the space shuttle through the **airlock**, which is a small room with two doors.

   Meaning: an entryway in the shuttle

   Context Clues: astronauts enter and exit the space shuttle; a small room with two doors

4. The Hubble telescope has helped **astronomers** study stars far out into space.

   Meaning: people who study the stars

   Context Clues: Hubble telescope has helped; study stars

5. The arrays converted the **solar** power of the sun into electricity to run the telescope.

   Meaning: from or related to the sun

   Context Clues: power of the sun

6. Unlike on Earth, in space there is no **gravity** so everything floats freely, including people.

   Meaning: the force that keeps things on the ground

   Context Clues: Unlike on Earth; everything floats freely

Adventure in Space • EXTEND

Make Judgments and Decisions

When you read a story, you sometimes make **judgments** and **decisions** about the story's characters or events. These judgments are based on information found in the story and on your own personal experience.

Read each student's dilemma. Make a decision or judgment for each.
Answers will vary. Examples are given.

Mark is running late. He has to pick up his little brother at a neighbor's house by five o'clock. He also promised his father he would pick up some milk for dinner. It is five minutes to five. What should Mark do?

1. Pick up his little brother and then go to buy the milk.
_____

Fran has a new puppy, Lucky. She is taking Lucky for a walk when her great aunt sees her and invites her home for a glass of iced tea. Lucky is rambunctious and Great Aunt Lydia has lots of breakable things in her apartment. Fran doesn't want to hurt her great aunt's feelings. What should she do?

2. Take Lucky home first, and then go back to her great aunt's house.
_____

Christy has been invited to a birthday party at her new neighbor's house. She hardly knows the girl, but agreed to go to be friendly. Then Christy gets invited to a special party at her best friend's house for the same day. What should she do?

3. Attend the party for which she has already accepted the invitation.
_____

Dino always goes right home after school and telephones his mother at work. She waits for his call each day. Today, Dino's new friend invites him to go to his house after school. What should Dino do?

4. Telephone his mother and ask permission.
_____

Book 6/Unit 5
Adventure in Space

At Home: Write about a judgment or decision you made recently.

163

Vocabulary

bloodstream	compartment	deliberately
handshake	maneuvering	void

Suppose you are an astronaut on a dangerous space walk. Suddenly you realize your tether has become tangled. Using some of the vocabulary words, send a message to the ship signaling your predicament.
Answers will vary. A possible response is given.

Help! If you don't get me back into the ship's compartment this Hubble

handshake may leave me maneuvering uselessly in the void of space for the rest

of my short life. Unless you want my bloodstream to boil please deliberately

untangle my tether and save my life!

Story Comprehension

Read and answer each question about "Adventure in Space."

1. Why was it necessary to "catch" Hubble on the very first try? There was not
enough fuel for a second attempt.

2. Why were the astronauts worried about discarding their "space junk"?
It might hit Hubble and damage it.

3. How could the astronauts tell that things for Tom were going well?
He hummed as he worked.

4. Why must astronauts get rid of the nitrogen in their systems before going on space
walks? Nitrogen can cause "the bends."

164–165

At Home: Write about whether or not you would like to walk in space using as many vocabulary words as possible.

Book 6/Unit 5
Adventure in Space

Read a Flow Chart

Sometimes the best way to show the steps in a process is to make a **flow chart**.

Choose a topic that involves steps, such as making a peanut butter sandwich or launching a space shuttle. Then make a flow chart below to show what you found out.
Answers will vary.

Book 6/Unit 5
Adventure in Space

At Home: Have students use the flow chart to explain what they found out during their research.

166

Make Judgments and Decisions

Read the categories below about which people often have to make **judgments** or **decisions**. Write about a decision you have made that involves each category. Was it the right decision? What, if anything, would you do differently now? Answers will vary, but should demonstrate knowledge of decision-making.

SCHOOL:
_____
_____
_____
_____

FRIENDS:
_____
_____
_____
_____

FAMILY:
_____
_____
_____
_____

SPORTS OR HOBBIES:
_____
_____
_____
_____

167

At Home: Write out the steps you take when making a decision.

Book 6/Unit 5
Adventure in Space

Adventure in Space • EXTEND

Sequence of Events

The directions below for doing laundry are jumbled. Number the steps so that they are in the correct **sequence**.

How to Do Laundry

Steps:

___3___ Measure the detergent and add it to the washer.

___7___ Turn on the washing machine.

___1___ Gather the clothing that needs to be washed.

___9___ Fold the clothing.

___4___ After adding detergent, load either white or colored clothes into washer.

___2___ Separate white clothing from colored clothing.

___5___ Close washer lid.

___6___ After closing lid, choose water temperature and water level.

___8___ When cycle is complete, remove clothing and hang to dry or place in dryer.

___10___ Put the clothing away.

In the boxes illustrate five steps you would take to buy the earphones you want. The steps should be in the correct sequence.   Answers will vary.

Book 6/Unit 5
Adventure in Space

At Home: Write the steps you take to get ready for school each day in the correct order.

168

Context Clues

Context clues in surrounding words and sentences can help you define unfamiliar words.

Remember the three kinds of context clues.

> 1. similar meanings
> 2. contrasting meanings
> 3. defined in context

Define the italicized word in each sentence, and tell which of the three context clues you used.

1. The complete emptiness, or *void*, of space must be terrifying.
   emptiness, 3

2. We thought the door was closed, but it was *ajar*. slightly open, 2

3. The most important, *crucial* step was about to be taken. most important, 1

4. We tried to *maneuver*, that is change direction, but we could not avoid the barrier.
   change direction, 3

5. She enjoyed studying the *cosmos*, that orderly universe in which we live.
   orderly systematic universe, 3

6. The blue *hydrangeas* were planted next to the porch between the roses and the daffodils. kind of flower 1 and 3

169

At Home: Write a sentence using a context clue for the word *prudent*.

Book 6/Unit 5
Adventure in Space

T33

Adventure in Space • GRAMMAR

Possessive Pronouns

- A **possessive pronoun** takes the place of a possessive noun. It shows *who* or *what* owns something.
- Some possessive pronouns are used before nouns (*my, your, his, her, its, our, your, their.*)

Write the possessive pronouns in the following sentences on the line provided.

1. Please point to your destination on the lunar map. ____your____

2. The robot turned its mechanical arm toward the telescope. ____its____

3. Commander Covey was inspired by their successful mission. ____their____

4. Without spacesuits our bodies are unprotected from the sun's heat. ____our____

5. Jeff and Story prepared the space shuttle for my flight. ____my____

6. "Is her tether tied properly?" asked the crew member. ____her____

7. Roberto will study astronomy in his science class next year. ____his____

Replace the underlined word or words with a possessive pronoun.

8. Claude heard <u>Kathy's</u> voice over the radio. ____her____

9. <u>NASA's</u> goal was to land the first man on the moon. ____Its____

10. When Covey took control, <u>the Commander's</u> thoughts turned toward the Hubble. ____his____

11. <u>The crew's</u> power tools failed to work on the jammed door. ____Their____

12. Learn more about <u>the mission's</u> history on the NASA Web site. ____its____

Locating Possessive Pronouns

- Some possessive pronouns can stand alone (*mine, yours, his, hers, its, ours, yours, theirs.*)
- Do not confuse the pronouns *its, your, their,* and *theirs* with the contractions *it's, you're, they're,* and *there's.*

Find the possessive pronoun in each of the following sentences.

1. The tools to install the solar arrays were ours. ____ours____

2. Jeff saw a pair of space gloves, but they were not his. ____his____

3. The job of fixing the panel was hers. ____hers____

4. The battery pack and lunar maps are theirs. ____theirs____

5. "The computer disk is mine," replied Covey. ____mine____

Circle the pronoun in parentheses that correctly completes each sentence.

6. Is the camera film (you're, (yours))?

7. Is the battery pack (you're, (yours))?

8. I believe it is ((theirs) there's).

9. (It's, (Its)) tiny screw was loose.

10. The tether is stored in ((its) it's) compartment.

11. (There's, (Theirs)) is the best view of Earth.

12. (My, (Mine)) is the space suit with the blue band.

Reviewing Pronouns

- A **possessive pronoun** takes the place of a possessive noun. It shows *who* or *what* owns something.
- Some possessive pronouns are used before nouns (*my, your, his, her, its, our, your, their.*)
- Some possessive pronouns can stand alone (*mine, yours, his, hers, its, ours, yours, theirs.*)
- Do not confuse the pronouns *its, your, their,* and *theirs* with the contractions *it's, you're, they're,* and *there's.*

Read each sentence. If the underlined possessive pronoun is incorrect, write the correct pronoun on the line provided. If the pronoun is correct, write **C**.

1. <u>Mine</u> friend Komiko invited me to watch the space launch with her. ____My____

2. The space museum supported the astronauts and told <u>their</u> story. ____C____

3. Do you have a special place to set up <u>you're</u> telescope? ____your____

4. The story tells about a space shuttle and <u>it's</u> mission. ____its____

5. Covey asked, "Are the math calculations <u>there's</u> or NASA's?" ____theirs____

Write an appropriate possessive pronoun on the blank provided. Do not use the same pronoun twice. Answers may vary.

6. ____Their____ estimated time of arrival is 2:45 A.M.

7. Claude recorded his thoughts in ____his____ journal every night.

8. The flight schedule and the calculator are ____her____ materials.

9. The Smithsonian Institute's moon rocks are preserved in ____its____ museum.

10. You can borrow ____my____ star chart, but please return it.

Contractions and Possessives

- An apostrophe takes the place of letters left out of a contraction.
- Possessive pronouns do not have apostrophes. Do not confuse possessive pronouns with contractions.

Choose the pronoun or contraction that correctly completes each sentence. Write the sentence on the lines provided.

1. The NASA scientists calculated (their, they're) arrival.
   The NASA scientists calculated their arrival.

2. The astronaut found (it's, its) matching glove in the suit pocket.
   The astronaut found its matching glove in the suit pocket.

3. (There's, Theirs) are the blue helmets.
   Theirs are the blue helmets.

4. (Your, You're) view of Earth is spectacular.
   Your view of Earth is spectacular.

5. (Their, They're) calculations were correct.
   Their calculations were correct.

6. I'm sure (you're, your) plans for the landing will be successful.
   I'm sure your plans for the landing will be successful.

7. (Its, It's) a perfect day for the space shuttle's liftoff.
   It's a perfect day for the space shuttle's liftoff.

8. Reporters claimed the stories were (there's, theirs).
   Reporters claimed the stories were theirs.

9. (They're, Their) eager to return to space.
   They're eager to return to space.

10. (You're, Your) the best person for this space mission.
    You're the best person for this space mission.

Adventure in Space • GRAMMAR

Pronouns

Circle the correct possessive pronoun or contraction in parentheses. Write the sentence correctly on the line provided.

1. "Was (your) you're) ride on the robot arm fun?" asked Tom.
   "Was your ride on the robot arm fun?" asked Tom.

2. Kathy and (her,) hers) partner worked on the spacecraft.
   Kathy and her partner worked on the spacecraft.

3. "Do you have (mine, (my)) flight helmet?" asked the cook.
   "Do you have my flight helmet?" asked the cook.

4. I don't want to eat the dessert if ((it's,) its) yours.
   I don't want to eat the dessert if it's yours.

5. The space crew reacted to (their) they're) news with enthusiasm.
   The space crew reacted to their news with enthusiasm.

6. (It's, (Its)) mechanical arm reached for the lunar rock.
   Its mechanical arm reached for the lunar rock.

7. The repair kit for the Hubble is (our, (ours)).
   The repair kit for the Hubble is ours.

8. The responsibility to repair the *Endeavour* was (my, (mine)).
   The responsibility to repair the *Endeavour* was mine.

9. Credit for the successful repair was (him, (his))
   Credit for the successful repair was his.

10. (Her) Hers) trip to space was exciting.
    Her trip to space was exciting.

Possessive Pronouns and Contractions

- A **possessive pronoun** takes the place of a possessive noun. It shows who or what owns something.
- Some possessive pronouns are used before nouns (*my, your, his, her, its, our, your, their*).
- Some possessive pronouns can stand alone (*mine, yours, his, hers, its, ours, yours, theirs*).
- Do not confuse the pronouns *its, your, their,* and *theirs* with the contractions *it's, you're, they're,* and *there's*.

Mechanics

- An apostrophe takes the place of letters left out of a contraction.
- Possessive pronouns do not have apostrophes. Do not confuse possessive pronouns with contractions.

Read the sentences about the picture. Circle the possessive pronoun in parentheses that correctly completes each sentence. Rewrite each sentence.

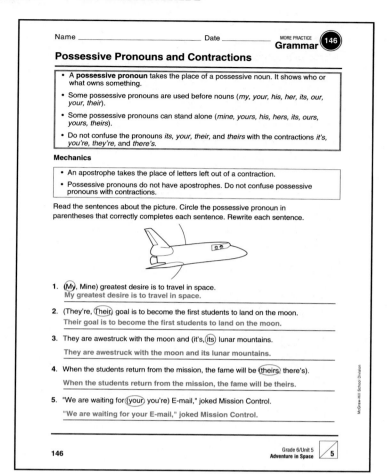

1. ((My,) Mine) greatest desire is to travel in space.
   My greatest desire is to travel in space.

2. (They're, (Their)) goal is to become the first students to land on the moon.
   Their goal is to become the first students to land on the moon.

3. They are awestruck with the moon and (it's, (its)) lunar mountains.
   They are awestruck with the moon and its lunar mountains.

4. When the students return from the mission, the fame will be (theirs) there's).
   When the students return from the mission, the fame will be theirs.

5. "We are waiting for (your) you're) E-mail," joked Mission Control.
   "We are waiting for your E-mail," joked Mission Control.

T35

Adventure in Space • SPELLING

Words with Suffixes

Pretest Directions

Fold back the paper along the dotted line. Use the blanks to write each word as it is read aloud. When you finish the test, unfold the paper. Use the list at the right to correct any spelling mistakes. Practice the words you missed for the Posttest.

To Parents

Here are the results of your child's weekly spelling Pretest. You can help your child study for the Posttest by following these simple steps for each word on the word list:

1. Read the word to your child.

2. Have your child write the word, saying each letter as it is written.

3. Say each letter of the word as your child checks the spelling.

4. If a mistake has been made, have your child read each letter of the correctly spelled word aloud, and then repeat steps 1–3.

1. _____ 1. electricity
2. _____ 2. operation
3. _____ 3. exploration
4. _____ 4. flexible
5. _____ 5. considerable
6. _____ 6. combination
7. _____ 7. gravity
8. _____ 8. lovable
9. _____ 9. permissible
10. _____ 10. interruption
11. _____ 11. reality
12. _____ 12. conservation
13. _____ 13. collectible
14. _____ 14. abbreviation
15. _____ 15. perspiration
16. _____ 16. admirable
17. _____ 17. anticipation
18. _____ 18. festivity
19. _____ 19. imaginable
20. _____ 20. convertible

Challenge Words

_____ bloodstream
_____ compartment
_____ deliberately
_____ handshake
_____ maneuvering

Words with Suffixes

Using the Word Study Steps

1. LOOK at the word.
2. SAY the word aloud.
3. STUDY the letters in the word.
4. WRITE the word.
5. CHECK the word.
   Did you spell the word right? If not, go back to step 1.

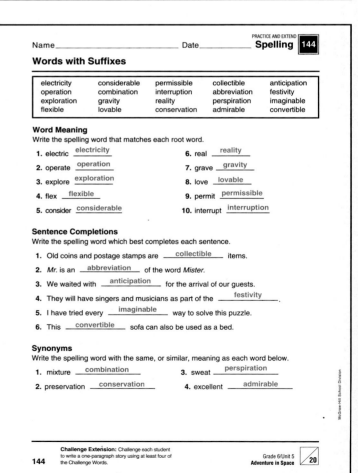

> **Spelling Tip**
>
> Remember to drop the final **e** before adding the suffix.
>
> imagine = imaginable
> admire = admirable
> combine = combination

Related Word

Write the spelling word related to each word below.

1. electric ___electricity___
2. operate ___operation___
3. explore ___exploration___
4. flex ___flexible___
5. consider ___considerable___
6. grave ___gravity___
7. love ___lovable___
8. permit ___permissible___
9. interrupt ___interruption___
10. real ___reality___
11. conserve ___conservation___
12. collect ___collectible___
13. abbreviate ___abbreviation___
14. perspire ___perspiration___
15. admire ___admirable___
16. anticipate ___anticipation___
17. festive ___festivity___
18. imagine ___imaginable___
19. convert ___convertible___
20. combine ___combination___

To Parents or Helpers:

Using the Word Study Steps above as your child comes across any new words will help him or her spell well. Review the steps as you both go over this week's spelling words.

Go over the Spelling Tip with your child. Help your child identify other words that drop the final e before adding a suffix. Help your child find the spelling words in the puzzle.

Words with Suffixes

electricity	considerable	permissible	collectible	anticipation
operation	combination	interruption	abbreviation	festivity
exploration	gravity	reality	perspiration	imaginable
flexible	lovable	conservation	admirable	convertible

Write the spelling words with the following suffixes:

-ion

1. ___operation___
2. ___interruption___
3. ___abbreviation___
4. ___anticipation___

-ation

5. ___exploration___
6. ___combination___
7. ___conservation___
8. ___perspiration___

-ity

9. ___electricity___
10. ___gravity___
11. ___reality___
12. ___festivity___

-able

13. ___considerable___
14. ___lovable___
15. ___admirable___
16. ___imaginable___

-ible

17. ___flexible___
18. ___permissible___
19. ___collectible___
20. ___convertible___

Words with Suffixes

electricity	considerable	permissible	collectible	anticipation
operation	combination	interruption	abbreviation	festivity
exploration	gravity	reality	perspiration	imaginable
flexible	lovable	conservation	admirable	convertible

Word Meaning

Write the spelling word that matches each root word.

1. electric ___electricity___
2. operate ___operation___
3. explore ___exploration___
4. flex ___flexible___
5. consider ___considerable___
6. real ___reality___
7. grave ___gravity___
8. love ___lovable___
9. permit ___permissible___
10. interrupt ___interruption___

Sentence Completions

Write the spelling word which best completes each sentence.

1. Old coins and postage stamps are ___collectible___ items.
2. Mr. is an ___abbreviation___ of the word Mister.
3. We waited with ___anticipation___ for the arrival of our guests.
4. They will have singers and musicians as part of the ___festivity___.
5. I have tried every ___imaginable___ way to solve this puzzle.
6. This ___convertible___ sofa can also be used as a bed.

Synonyms

Write the spelling word with the same, or similar, meaning as each word below.

1. mixture ___combination___
2. preservation ___conservation___
3. sweat ___perspiration___
4. excellent ___admirable___

Challenge Extension: Challenge each student to write a one-paragraph story using at least four of the Challenge Words.

Adventure in Space • SPELLING

Words with Suffixes

Proofreading Activity

There are six spelling mistakes in this letter. Circle the misspelled words. Write the words correctly on the lines below.

Dear Tom,

As you know, I have been working in the field of space (expliration) without (interuption) for the past ten years. There have been (considereable) advances since then. Thanks to a better understanding of (graveity), our current (opiration) is running smoothly. With a combination of hard work and (admireable) forethought, our space program has become a leader.

Thanks for all your encouragement!

Kathy

1. ___exploration___   3. ___considerable___   5. ___operation___
2. ___interruption___   4. ___gravity___   6. ___admirable___

Writing Activity

Write a journal entry describing you taking a make-believe voyage into space. Use four spelling words.

_____

_____

_____

_____

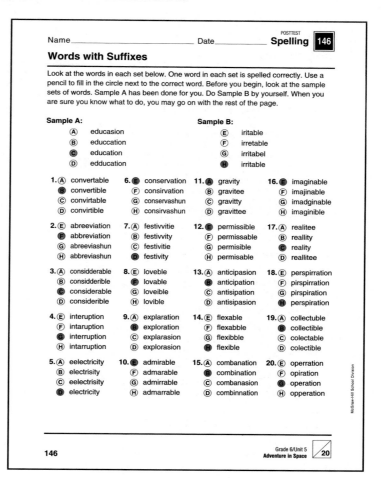

Words with Suffixes

Look at the words in each set below. One word in each set is spelled correctly. Use a pencil to fill in the circle next to the correct word. Before you begin, look at the sample sets of words. Sample A has been done for you. Do Sample B by yourself. When you are sure you know what to do, you may go on with the rest of the page.

Sample A:
(A) educasion
(B) educcation
(C) education ●
(D) edducation

Sample B:
(E) iritable
(F) irretable
(G) irritabel
(H) irritable ●

1. (A) convertable
   (B) convertible ●
   (C) convirtable
   (D) convirtible

2. (E) abreeviation
   (F) abbreviation ●
   (G) abreeviashun
   (H) abbreviashun

3. (A) considderable
   (B) considderible
   (C) considerable ●
   (D) considerible

4. (E) interuption
   (F) intaruption
   (G) interruption ●
   (H) intarruption

5. (A) eelectricity
   (B) electrisity
   (C) eelectrisity
   (D) electricity ●

6. (E) conservation ●
   (F) consirvation
   (G) conservashun
   (H) consirvashun

7. (A) festivvitie
   (B) festivvity
   (C) festivitie
   (D) festivity ●

8. (E) loveble
   (F) lovable ●
   (G) loveible
   (H) lovible

9. (A) exploration ●
   (B) exploration
   (C) explarasion
   (D) explorasion

10. (E) admirable ●
    (F) admarable
    (G) admirrable
    (H) admarrable

11. (A) gravity ●
    (B) gravitee
    (C) gravitty
    (D) gravittee

12. (E) permissible ●
    (F) permissable
    (G) permisible
    (H) permisable

13. (A) anticipasion
    (B) anticipation ●
    (C) antisipation
    (D) antisipasion

14. (E) flexable
    (F) flexable
    (G) flexibble
    (H) flexible ●

15. (A) combanation
    (B) combination ●
    (C) combanasion
    (D) combinnation

16. (E) imaginable ●
    (F) imajinable
    (G) imadginable
    (H) imaginible

17. (A) realitee
    (B) reality
    (C) reality ●
    (D) reallitee

18. (E) perspirration
    (F) pirspirration
    (G) pirspiration
    (H) perspiration ●

19. (A) collectuble
    (B) collectible ●
    (C) colectable
    (D) colectible

20. (E) operration
    (F) opiration
    (G) operation ●
    (H) opperation

T37

Rumpelstiltskin's Daughter • PRACTICE

Story Elements

Most stories contain standard parts, called **story elements**. One major story element is **character**. Analyzing story characters can help you better understand what you are reading.

Read the following story and answer the questions below.

Alicia ran home as quickly as she could. She was very excited and couldn't wait to share the news with her family. All her practice this summer had paid off. She had made the soccer team!

When Alicia finally got home, her sister looked very sad. Instead of asking her younger sister Francine what was wrong, Alicia blurted out, "Guess what? I made the team." Francine started to cry. Then Alicia realized what had happened—Francine had not made her soccer team. Alicia felt sorry for not having asked Francine what was wrong first. The sisters had practiced together all summer and now only one of them would get to play soccer this season. [Answers will vary. Sample responses are provided.]

1. From what you've read, how would you describe Alicia?

   She is a good sister, who is proud of her soccer playing ability.

2. How would you describe Francine.

   Francine is younger than Alicia and may not be as athletic.

3. What might be one less positive aspect of Alicia's personality?

   She might not be as sensitive to other people's feelings as she could be.

4. What might be one less positive aspect of Francine's personality?

   Francine might get upset too easily since she started to cry when she

   heard that Alicia had made the team. Or she might be jealous of Alicia.

5. What could Alicia do to help Francine feel better?

   Alicia could offer to continue to practice with Francine

   to help her prepare for tryouts next year.

Vocabulary

Read the words. Then read each definition. Write the letter of the correct definition in the blank next to the word it defines.

Words		Definitions
1.	e barley	a. heavy scarves worn around the neck
2.	b coincidences	b. things that by chance happen at the same time
3.	d knickers	c. to make something more appealing
4.	a mufflers	d. knee-length pants
5.	f sheepishly	e. a type of grain
6.	c sweeten	f. act as if embarrassed or ashamed

Select a word from the box to complete each section of the synonym/antonym chart below.

accidents	bathing suits	plans	proudly
scarves	shamefully	sour	enhance

	Synonym	Antonym
7. coincidences	accidents	plans
8. sheepishly	shamefully	proudly
9. sweeten	enhance	sour
10. mufflers	scarves	bathing suits

New Friends

One winter afternoon long ago, two boys who were strangers to each other sat next to each other at a soda fountain. Both ordered vegetable *barley* soup for lunch. After eating, the boys, named Pablo and Frank, left at the same time, discovered they lived in the same neighborhood, and decided to walk home together. Since it was cold they were both wearing long coats to cover their legs since they both wore *knickers*. They also wrapped *mufflers* around their necks.

When they first started walking, Frank just looked *sheepishly* at the scenery and seemed afraid to talk about himself. Pablo began to tell Frank about himself and the boys soon learned about some *coincidences* in their lives. As it turned out, Pablo and Frank had lived next door to each other when they were just babies. The boys also discovered that Pablo's neighbors were cousins to Frank's neighbors. The list of coincidences went on and on. As if that weren't enough to *sweeten* the friendship, Frank and Pablo discovered that they liked to do a lot of the same things as well. A new friendship was born.

1. How was Frank behaving when the boys first started on their walk?

   sheepishly

2. What did the boys find out about each other?

   that there were many coincidences in their lives.

3. What did the boys eat for lunch? vegetable barley soup

4. What did the boys wear to keep their necks warm? mufflers

5. How do you think the coincidences helped the boys become friends?

   They learned that their lives had touched in many

   ways that they did not even realize.

Story Comprehension

Read each sentence. Then, on the blank line, write the letter of the word or phrase that best completes the sentence.

1. Meredith is _____ b _____.

   a. Rumpelstiltskin's daughter
   b. Rumpelstiltskin's wife
   c. the Miller's wife

2. Rumpelstiltskin's daughter tells the king to give the farmers _____ a _____ to plant in their fields.

   a. gold coins
   b. golden knitting needles
   c. vegetable seeds

3. The king first offers to make Hope his _____ c _____.

   a. princess
   b. prime minister
   c. queen

4. Rumpelstiltskin wanted Meredith to give him her _____ a _____ in exchange for making the gold that would help her to become queen.

   a. first-born child
   b. knitting needles
   c. ring

5. The stone walls around the palace were used to build _____ c _____.

   a. bigger barns for the king to store his gold
   b. a bridge
   c. houses for poor people

6. Rumpelstiltskin's daughter became _____ a _____.

   a. prime minister
   b. queen
   c. president

7. The miller _____ b _____ and said his daughter could spin straw into gold.

   a. laughed
   b. lied
   c. bragged

8. Meredith, the miller's daughter, was told to make gold or _____ b _____.

   a. go to jail
   b. die
   c. be kicked out of the country

Practice 173

Name_____ Date_____ Practice 173

Read a Circle Graph

A **circle graph** shows how a whole quantity is divided into parts. The graph below shows how one family spends its monthly budget. The family takes home a total of $3,000 a month.

THE CHISHOLM FAMILY MONTHLY BUDGET

Food 18%
Housing 32%
Saving 10%
Other: Medical, Vacation, etc. 19%
Recreation 8%
Clothing 6%
Transportation 7%

Use the circle graph to answer the questions.

1. What percentage of the family's monthly budget goes to recreation? 8%

2. Which expense takes 18% of the family's budget? food

3. What is the family's single greatest expense? housing

4. How much money does the family save each month? (Hint: Find 10% of their monthly take-home pay.) $300

5. Why is a circle graph a useful way to show a monthly budget? Sample answer:

It is a visual way to show and compare how much money is spent on

on each major expense.

5 Book 6/ Unit 5
Rumpelstiltskin's Daughter

At Home: Have students find a circle graph in a newspaper or magazine and explain what information contains.

173

Practice 174

Name_____ Date_____ Practice 174

Story Elements

Stories usually include some standard aspects, or **story elements**. Some important story elements are characters, setting, plot, tone, and theme.

Look back through "Rumpelstiltskin's Daughter." Complete this chart of the story elements by writing the name of the character who matches each example. Then write an example for each of the other story elements.

Story Element	Example
Character	**Character Trait**
king	He only became greedier and greedier.
guards	They were gnashing their teeth, gripping their swords, and peering about shiftily at the king's party.
Hope	She was clever enough to come up with a plan to change the way the king treated his subjects.
Meredith	She decided to marry Rumpelstiltskin instead of the king.
Rumpelstiltskin	He knew how to spin straw into gold.
miller	He lied and said he knew how to spin straw into gold.
Setting	a fairytale world
Plot	Rumpelstiltskin's daughter comes up with a plan to stop the king from always wanting more gold.
Tone	playful and funny
Theme	Being able to solve problems creatively and without hurting anyone.

174

At Home: Have students briefly describe the part of the plot that led to the marriage of Rumpelstiltskin and Meredith.

Book 6/ Unit 5
Rumpelstiltskin's Daughter 10

Practice 175

Name_____ Date_____ Practice 175

Make Inferences

You can use evidence from the story to help you **make an inference**, or come to an understanding.

In "Rumpelstiltskin's Daughter," readers can see the king change through his actions and words. What inferences can you make about the king from each of the following? Write what you think after each phrase.
[ANNO: Answers will vary. Sample responses are provided.]

1. The king's treatment of Meredith.

He is cruel for locking her up and threatening to kill her.

2. The king's response to Hope's instructions for "growing" gold.

He is so desperate for more gold that he is willing to believe anything.

3. The king's reaction to the people's gifts.

He doesn't know how to react or what to do with everything.

4. The king's reaction to Hope's request to be prime minister.

He gives her the position because he is grateful for what she has done even though she did not give him any gold.

5. The king's treatment of poor people at the end of the story.

He has become more concerned for others and less selfish and greedy.

5 Book 6/ Unit 5
Rumpelstiltskin's Daughter

At Home: Have students describe someone they have known or read about who has changed a lot.

175

Practice 176

Name_____ Date_____ Practice 176

Denotation and Connotation

Words can have more than one kind of meaning. A word's denotation is its dictionary definition. Its connotation is the emotional response a reader has to the word.

Read each sentence about "Rumpelstiltskin's Daughter." Write the denotation of the underlined word. Then think about the connotation of the word as it is used in that sentence. Write the connotation on the lines given.
[Answers will vary. Sample responses are provided.]

1. Meredith's father liked to make up stories and pretend they were the truth.
   Denotation: tales people tell
   Connotation: lies

2. The king had the miller's daughter hauled up to his castle when he heard she could create gold from straw.
   Denotation: carried
   Connotation: carried against her will

3. Meredith was feeling pretty desperate when Rumpelstiltskin popped in again.
   Denotation: came in suddenly
   Connotation: showed up casually and unexpectedly

4. Meredith had a weakness for short men.
   Denotation: a flaw
   Connotation: a soft spot

5. Rumpelstiltskin blushed when he heard what Meredith had to say.
   Denotation: turned red
   Connotation: showing embarrassment

6. Throughout the kingdom, the farmers fields remained barren.
   Denotation: infertile
   Connotation: useless and empty

7. The king's guards were always around, gnashing their teeth gripping their weapons, and glancing about with shifty eyes.
   Denotation: constantly moving
   Connotation: not trustworthy, dishonest

8. Even in the palace Hope could feel the chill of the fall weather outside.
   Denotation: cold
   Connotation: mild cold, unpleasantly cool

176

At Home: Have students rewrite two of these sentences using synonyms in place of the underlined words.

Book 6/ Unit 5
Rumpelstiltskin's Daughter 8

Rumpelstiltskin's Daughter • RETEACH

Story Elements

> Most stories have standard parts, or **story elements**. The **characters** are the people and their personalities. The **setting** is where the story takes place. The **plot** is what happens in the story. The **theme** is the meaning or message of the story.

Read each sentence below and decide if it is an example of character, setting, plot, or theme. Some sentences will be an example of more than one story element. Circle the letter or letters of the story element(s) for each sentence.

1. Janine had a terrible habit of twirling her long auburn hair between her fingers.

   (a.) character   b. setting   c. plot   d. theme

2. The dog ate her homework.

   a. character   b. setting   (c.) plot   d. theme

3. They sat on the mountaintop and enjoyed the beautiful view.

   a. character   (b.) setting   c. plot   d. theme

4. We can learn important lessons from our mistakes.

   a. character   b. setting   c. plot   (d.) theme

5. The children played at the playground all day long.

   a. character   (b.) setting   (c.) plot   d. theme

6. Roxy wagged her tail and jumped up to greet her owner.

   (a.) character   b. setting   (c.) plot   d. theme

7. The ice cream shop is only three blocks from my house.

   a. character   (b.) setting   c. plot   d. theme

8. Juanita, Ian, and Mark are all artistic. They paint, draw, and even make sculptures.

   (a.) character   b. setting   c. plot   d. theme

9. Having good friends is one of the most important things in life.

   a. character   b. setting   c. plot   (d.) theme

10. We looked out the window and saw the snow piling up fast.

    a. character   (b.) setting   (c.) plot   d. theme

Book 6/Unit 5
Rumpelstiltskin's Daughter 10

At Home: Have students write one sentence as an example of each of these story elements: setting, plot, and character.

170

Vocabulary

Select a word from the box to complete each sentence.

barley	coincidences	knickers	sheepishly	sweeten	mufflers

1. The boy <u>sheepishly</u> admitted he had lied about his grades.

2. Through a set of <u>coincidences</u> the girls realized that their parents had been friends when they were young.

3. In that picture of my great-grandfather, he is wearing <u>knickers</u> and boots with buttons.

4. Please <u>sweeten</u> the whipped cream with more sugar.

5. Sometimes my mom adds <u>barley</u> to her vegetable soup.

6. The vendors sold <u>mufflers</u> to tourists who wanted to protect themselves from the bitter wind.

Story Comprehension

Answer the questions about "Rumpelstiltskin's Daughter" on the lines provided.

1. Why did Rumpelstiltskin's daughter tell the king he didn't need walls or a moat around the castle? <u>The people loved him and he did not need to fear them anymore.</u>

2. Why did the king capture Hope? <u>He wanted her to make gold for him.</u>

3. Why wouldn't Rumpelstiltskin's daughter let her father make gold for the king? <u>She knew the king would never be happy; he would always want more gold.</u>

4. What did the king do with his crocodiles? <u>He put them in a zoo.</u>

5. How did Rumpelstiltskin meet his wife? <u>She was a prisoner of the king.</u> <u>Rumpelstiltskin met her when he offered to help her by spinning straw into gold.</u>

At Home: Ask students to write a short paragraph telling about their favorite part of the story and why they enjoyed it.

171–172

Book 6/Unit 5
Rumpelstiltskin's Daughter 10

Use a Character Traits Map

> A **character traits map** can help you describe a character from a story and understand that character better.

Think about Rumpelstiltskin's words and actions in "Rumpelstiltskin's Daughter." Read the examples in the character traits map below. Think of a character trait that matches each example and write the character trait in the appropriate box. Answers may vary. Sample responses are provided.

CHARACTER TRAIT MAP: Rumpelstiltskin

Trait	Example
loving	The only thing Rumpelstiltskin really wanted was a child to care for.
clever; shrewd	Rumpelstiltskin asked the miller's daughter to promise him her firstborn child in exchange for helping her become queen.
bashful	Rumpelstiltskin blushed when Meredith told him she would rather marry him than the king.
clever	Rumpelstiltskin spun a golden ladder so that he and Meredith could escape.

4 Book 6/Unit 5
Rumpelstiltskin's Daughter

At Home: Ask students to choose one main character trait to describe these characters from "Rumpelstiltskin's Daughter": the King, Rumpelstiltskin, Meredith, and Hope.

173

Story Elements

> Four common **story elements** are **character, plot, tone,** and **theme.** The tone is the author's attitude toward the story and its characters.

Record information from "Rumpelstiltskin's Daughter" for each story element listed in the chart below. List character traits for each character. Then list plot events and describe the author's tone that support those traits. Answers will vary. Sample responses are provided.

Character Traits	Plot Events	Author's Tone
1. The King: greedy, selfish, cruel	2. Word gets back to the king about the gold Rumpelstiltskin's daughter brings to town. He has her kidnapped and locks her in a tower with piles of straw that he wants changed into gold.	3. comic, entertaining, suspenseful
4. Rumpelstiltskin's Daughter: kind, wise, brave	5. The king and the girl go into the countryside to see what happened with the gold "planted" in the spring. The fields are full of wheat. The king is disappointed, but the people are grateful to him and shower him with gifts.	6. comic, mocking, serious
7. The King: generous, cheerful	8. The king gets rid of his guards, builds a zoo and houses for the poor; he makes Hope his prime minister and builds her a nice house.	9. playful, amusing, affectionate

10. Write a sentence explaining the theme of "Rumpelstiltskin's Daughter" in your own words. <u>Being loved and respected is more important than having a lot of riches.</u>

At Home: Have students write a short fairytale that illustrates a theme that is important to them.

174

Book 6/Unit 5
Rumpelstiltskin's Daughter 10

Rumpelstiltskin's Daughter • RETEACH

Make Inferences

When a reader uses evidence from the story to figure out what is not fully explained or described by the author, the reader is **making an inference**.

Read the story topics below. Then complete the sentences that give story details. In the last column write an inference you made based on those details. **Answers will vary. Sample responses are provided.**

Topic	Story Details	Inference
The condition of the country at the beginning of the story	1. The fields are barren. 2. Children stand begging in the road. 3. The people in the kingdom have nothing.	4. The country is in terrible shape and poverty is a major problem.
The relationship between Rumpelstiltskin and Meredith	5. They get married because Meredith would rather marry Rumpelstiltskin than the king. 6. After they are married, they live happily in a small town far from the palace.	7. They care for each other and have a happy marriage.
The king's guards	8. At the feast, they grumble and complain. 9. They respond to the knitted clothing and gifts by gnashing their teeth and peering about with their shifty eyes.	10. They are suspicious, nasty people.

At Home: Have students make an inference about how Hope felt about the guards.

Connotation and Denotation

Words can have several meanings. The **denotation** is a word's dictionary definition. A **connotation** is the way a word makes the reader feel.

Choose the correct denotation and connotation for the underlined words in column 1. Write the letters of the denotations and connotations in column 2 on the blanks.

Column 1

1. He has quite a healthy appetite.

    Denotation: _b_

    Connotation: _c_

2. If you spin the facts, everyone will think that he is really a nice person.

    Denotation: _d_

    Connotation: _a_

3. Would you like to celebrate my new promotion with me?

    Denotation: _c_

    Connotation: _f_

4. You should see her new home—it's quite a palace.

    Denotation: _e_

    Connotation: _b_

5. The mood in the city was heavy after the earthquake.

    Denotation: _f_

    Connotation: _e_

6. The traffic was crawling across the bridge.

    Denotation: _a_

    Connotation: _d_

Column 2

Denotations

a. moving on hands and knees
b. good for one's well-being
c. to have a party
d. to move in a circular motion
e. a home for royalty
f. having great weight

Connotations

a. to express information in a dishonest way
b. a large and elegant place
c. large
d. moving very slowly
e. very serious or somber
f. to rejoice over someone's good fortune

At Home: Choose three sentences from a magazine or newspaper and select one word from each sentence. Rewrite the sentences, replacing each selected word with a synonym. Note how, if at all, the meaning of the sentences change.

Rumpelstiltskin's Daughter • EXTEND

Story Elements

Writers use the sense of sight, describing characters so that readers can visualize them. The senses involving hearing, touch, and smell are just as important, however. Write a description of a character, fictional or real, using each of these four senses.   Answers will vary. Examples are given.

SIGHT: My neighbor Gabby is four years old, tall and strong, with big blue eyes, pale blond hair, and always dirty hands.

HEARING: Gabby is never quiet. She asks a question and barely pauses to listen to the answer before launching another. Her high-pitched voice is solemn—she wants and needs answers.

TOUCH: Gabby's skin is smooth and clear. When she grasps my hand with her little one, I feel its tenderness—underneath the grape jam, that is!

SMELL: Gabby is a mixture of fragrances. Her clothes smell of the earth where she has been sitting, of the grass she has been rubbing in her hands, and of milk, which she has spilled on her T-shirt at lunch that day.

Book 6/Unit 5
Rumpelstiltskin's Daughter

At Home: Write a character description using these four senses.

170

Vocabulary

barley	coincidences	knickers
mufflers	sheepishly	sweeten

Continue the story of "Rumpelstiltskin's Daughter." In her new job as prime minister, Hope meets with people every day. Using the vocabulary words, write about a meeting she had with the village tailor.
Answers will vary. An example is given.

After some coincidences having to do with barley soup, the prime minister sheepishly carried her knickers and a couple of mufflers to the tailor. "Prime minister," he said, "you sweeten my shop." He would not take gold, in payment!

Story Comprehension

Read and answer each question.

1. What character trait of the king's led Rumpelstiltskin's daughter to believe that he would accept her plan of "growing" gold?
   He was greedy and was willing to try anything to get more gold.

2. Why is the king able to fire his guards at the end of the story?
   Because his people now loved him, and he no longer needed protection.

3. What is the symbolism of Rumpelstiltskin's daughter's name?
   Rumpelstiltskin and his wife gave the people of the kingdom Hope.

4. Write a moral for the story.
   Possible answer: It is better to be generous and kind to others than to be selfish and greedy.

Read a Circle Graph

A **circle graph** is useful for showing how a whole quantity is divided into parts. Cheri and Ginny kept track of how they spent their allowances each month. The graphs below show the girls' data. Each girl receives $30 per month.

How Cheri's Allowance is Spent

Toys 29%
Snacks 22%
Savings 5%
Recreation 23%
Clothing 21%

How Ginny's Allowance is Spent

Snacks 20%
Video Games 12%
Clothing 32%
Savings 10%
Recreation 26%

Use the circle graphs to answer the questions.

1. What percentage of Cheri's budget goes to snacks?
   22%

2. Which expense is found on Ginny's graph but not on Cheri's?
   video games

3. Which girl spends more on clothing?
   Ginny – 32%

4. How much money does Cheri save each month? (Hint: Find 5% of her monthly allowance.)
   $1.50

5. Compare the two graphs. Which two expenses are about the same for both girls each month?
   snacks and recreation

Book 6/Unit 5
Rumpelstiltskin's Daughter

At Home: Have students make a circle graph showing their monthly expenditures.

173

Story Elements

Write a paragraph about a character who is always putting things off, or procrastinating. Be sure to include examples of how your character procrastinates. Answers will vary. A possible answer is given.

Luis Daniel was frantic. It was Sunday night and he had not even begun his English composition. On Monday of that week, he had promised he would sit down at the computer and research his topic. But his favorite show was on TV that night, and Luis watched it. On Tuesday, he had softball practice. Wednesday, he had extra math to do, because he had not turned in the homework that day. By Thursday, Luis was beginning to worry, but decided not to think about it. On Saturday, he worried all day, but that's all he did—worry. On Sunday night, he sat at his desk, promising himself he would get up really early on Monday.

Write a paragraph continuing the story.   Accept all reasonable continuations.

174

At Home: Have students write a paragraph describing someone they know.

Book 6/Unit 5
Rumpelstiltskin's Daughter

Rumpelstiltskin's Daughter • EXTEND

Name_____ Date_____ Extend 175

Make Inferences

You may need to **make an inference** to figure out what will happen in a story. Read the following information. Then make an inference based on the information.   Answers will vary. Examples given.

1. Bob wants to buy a new softball glove. He has been saving money for months. When he goes to the store, Bob sees another glove he likes better. He turns around and leaves the store.

   INFERENCE: Bob doesn't have enough money to buy the new glove.

2. Jennifer is trying out for the cheerleading squad. She finds out that practice is every Tuesday after school, which is the day her Flying Club usually meets. Jennifer telephones the coach of the cheerleaders first.

   INFERENCE: Jennifer will ask if practice will continue to be on Tuesdays and at what time. Then she'll call the Flying Club leader to ask about the time the club will meet.

3. Keith and Kevin are brothers in sixth and seventh grade. They take the same bus to the same school, and carry identical backpacks. Keith got to class one morning and found his math book but Kevin's science book and Kevin's English book.

   INFERENCE: Keith put his math book in Kevin's backpack. Kevin has the rest of Keith's books.

4. Now write some information that would support this inference:

   INFERENCE: Sara has a big science test on Thursday morning.
   Answers will vary. Possible response: Sara studies hard, goes to bed early Wednesday, and has a good breakfast.

175

Name_____ Date_____ Extend 176

Denotation and Connotation

Remember that the **denotation** of a word is its dictionary definition. **Connotations** are emotions or associations suggested by certain words. Throughout the ages, people have made connotations about animals and their characteristics. Look at the following list of animals. Decide if that animal has a positive or a negative connotation. Offer an explanation for each answer.
Answers will vary. Examples are given.

1. **Owl:** An owl has a positive connotation. Perhaps because of the owl's large eyes and solemn look, it is associated with wisdom. Wise as an owl is a common expression.

2. **Worm:** A worm has a negative connotation. Because the worm crawls in the dirt, to call someone a worm is to imply that the person is underhanded.

3. **Snake:** Perhaps also because snakes crawl and slither, their connotation is negative.

4. **Lamb:** Lambs are fluffy, and considered gentle. Lambs have a positive connotation.

5. **Fox:** Foxes are hard to spot in nature. They can usually go undetected and are considered to be clever and elusive. In most cases, foxes have a negative connotation.

Add three animals to the list and explain what connotations they have.

176

T43

Rumpelstiltskin's Daughter • GRAMMAR

Name _____ Date _____
LEARN
Grammar 147

Indefinite Pronouns and Singular Verbs

- An **indefinite pronoun** does not refer to a particular person, place, or thing.
- Use a singular verb with a singular indefinite pronoun, such as *anybody, anyone, anything, each, everybody, everyone, everything, nobody, nothing, somebody, someone, something.*

Read each sentence. Circle the verb in parentheses that correctly completes the sentence.

1. Everybody (is, are) convinced Rumpelstiltskin's daughter can spin straw into gold.

2. Unfortunately, each of the stories (were, was) false.

3. Everything (need, needs) to be cleaned up by the end of the day.

4. Somebody (deliver, delivers) hay to the castle's front gate.

5. If anyone (ask, asks) you to swim in the moat, say no.

Change the singular or plural verb in each sentence so that it agrees with the indefinite pronoun. Write the sentence.

6. Somebody must helps the poor farmers with their wheat fields.
   Somebody must help the poor farmers with their wheat fields.

7. Everyone agree that Rumpelstiltskin's daughter should help the hungry children.
   Everyone agrees that Rumpelstiltskin's daughter should help the hungry children.

8. No one are more disappointed with the outcome than the king.
   No one is more disappointed with the outcome than the king.

9. Nothing seem too difficult for her.
   Nothing seems too difficult for her.

10. Everybody respect her kindness.
    Everybody respects her kindness.

Name _____ Date _____
LEARN AND PRACTICE
Grammar 148

Indefinite Pronouns and Plural Verbs

- Use a plural verb with a plural indefinite pronoun, such as *both, few, many, others, several.*

Circle the verb in parentheses that correctly completes the sentence.

1. Many of us (enjoys, enjoy) fairy tales about evil kings.

2. A few (reads, read) stories every night.

3. Both of them (wishes, wish) to marry Meredith.

4. Several (begs, beg) Rumpelstiltskin's daughter to talk to the king.

5. Others (likes, like) to eat the roasted corn.

Circle the indefinite pronoun. Write S if the indefinite pronoun is singular. Write P if it is plural.

6. A few of the coins were buried in the ground. __P__

7. Others were scattered on top of the soil. __P__

8. Somebody traveled the kingdom spreading the story of Rumpelstiltskin. __S__

9. The daughter said there was something better than gold. __S__

10. Have many seen the glittering coach with two guards? __P__

Name _____ Date _____
PRACTICE AND REVIEW
Grammar 149

Working With Indefinite Pronouns

- An **indefinite pronoun** does not refer to a particular person, place, or thing.
- Use a singular verb with a singular indefinite pronoun, such as *anybody, anyone, anything, each, everybody, everyone, everything, nobody, nothing, somebody, someone, something.*
- Use a plural verb with a plural indefinite pronoun, such as *both, few, many, others, several.*

Circle the indefinite pronoun that correctly completes the sentence.

1. (Everybody, Both) carry baskets of wheat and barley.

2. (Several, Each) of the children looks healthy and content.

3. (Everything, Others) grows quickly in her vegetable garden.

4. (Few, Nobody) is allowed to rest until the king is satisfied.

5. (Many, Someone) in the kingdom sells pottery to the farmers.

Fill in the blank with an appropriate indefinite pronoun. Do not use a pronoun more than once. Answers may vary.

6. __Nothing__ is more desirable to the king than gold.

7. __Both__ of the children race through the dark and spooky forest.

8. __Few__ ride horses down the crooked lane to the village.

9. __Everyone__ loves Rumpelstiltskin's daughter for saving the land.

10. __Many__ walk to the palace to pay their taxes.

Name _____ Date _____
MECHANICS
Grammar 150

Quotations

- Use quotation marks before and after the words of a direct quotation.
- Begin a quotation with a capital letter.
- Begin a new paragraph and use a separate set of quotation marks when the speaker changes in dialogue.

Form paragraphs out of the following sentences. Use the proper quotation marks and capital letters in each sentence.

The miller said my daughter is so talented she can spin gold. One villager said nobody can turn regular hay into something as precious as gold. The miller replied the king thinks she can, and that is all that matters. She is with him at this very moment. However, the villager was still doubtful and said you'll have to show me first. If it's true, we can all be rich.

The miller said, "My daughter is so talented she can spin gold."

"Nobody can turn regular hay into something as precious as gold," one villager said.

The miller replied, "The king thinks she can, and that is all that matters. She is with him at this very moment."

However, the villager was still doubtful and said, "You'll have to show me first. If it's true, we can all be rich."

Rumpelstiltskin's Daughter • GRAMMAR

Pronouns

Read the first sentence of each set. One of the four sentences that follows corrects the agreement between an indefinite pronoun and its verb. Circle the letter of the correct sentence.

1. Each of the cows wander off.
   - **(a)** Change wander to wanders.
   - **b.** Change Each to Every.
   - **c.** Change Each to All.
   - **d.** Change Each to Few.

2. Somebody like to ride through a dark forest.
   - **a.** Change Somebody to Everyone.
   - **(b)** Change Somebody to Few.
   - **c.** Change Somebody to Each.
   - **d.** Change Somebody to Nobody.

3. Everything in the class reminds students that someone love to read fairy tales.
   - **a.** Change Everything to Nothing.
   - **b.** Change reminds to remind.
   - **c.** Change someone to nobody.
   - **(d)** Change love to loves.

Circle the letter that best answers each of the following questions.

4. Which of the following statements about indefinite pronouns is true?
   - **a.** Indefinite pronouns, such as *both*, use a singular verb.
   - **b.** Indefinite pronouns take the place of certain people, places, and things.
   - **c.** Indefinite pronouns, such as *each*, use a plural verb.
   - **(d)** Indefinite pronouns do not refer to a particular person, place, or thing.

5. Which of the following sentences contains an indefinite pronoun?
   - **a.** My flowers scattered in the wind.
   - **(b)** Several pass by the church.
   - **c.** The spinning wheel is hers.
   - **d.** She spun gold out of hay.

Practicing With Indefinite Pronouns and Quotations

- An **indefinite pronoun** does not refer to a particular person, place, or thing.
- Use a singular verb with a singular indefinite pronoun, such as *anybody, anyone, anything, each, everybody, everyone, everything, nobody, nothing, somebody, someone, something*.
- Use a plural verb with a plural indefinite pronoun, such as *both, few, many, others, several*.

Mechanics

- Use quotation marks before and after the words of a direct quotation.
- Begin a quotation with a capital letter.
- Begin a new paragraph and use a separate set of quotation marks when the speaker changes in dialogue.

Read the following dialogue between the king and Rumpelstiltskin's daughter aloud to a partner. Then choose the verb that correctly completes each sentence. Rewrite the dialogue, using the proper quotation marks and capital letters.

Rumpelstiltskin's daughter said nobody (like, likes) a stingy king. Everyone (love, loves) me said the ruler. Many cannot (afford, affords) to feed their children when taxes are so high said the girl. The king replied times are not hard and everyone (acts, act) happy. Few (risks, risk) making their king unhappy by complaining she said.

Rumpelstiltskin's daughter said, "Nobody likes a stingy king."

"Everyone loves me," said the ruler.

"Many cannot afford to feed their children when taxes are so high," said the girl.

The king replied, "Times are not hard and everyone acts happy."

"Few risk making their king unhappy by complaining," she said.

Rumpelstiltskin's Daughter • SPELLING

Words with Suffixes

Pretest Directions
Fold back the paper along the dotted line. Use the blanks to write each word as it is read aloud. When you finish the test, unfold the paper. Use the list at the right to correct any spelling mistakes. Practice the words you missed for the Posttest.

To Parents
Here are the results of your child's weekly spelling Pretest. You can help your child study for the Posttest by following these simple steps for each word on the word list:

1. Read the word to your child.
2. Have your child write the word, saying each letter as it is written.
3. Say each letter of the word as your child checks the spelling.
4. If a mistake has been made, have your child read each letter of the correctly spelled word aloud, and then repeat steps 1–3.

1. _____ 1. excellent
2. _____ 2. attendant
3. _____ 3. restless
4. _____ 4. disturbance
5. _____ 5. conference
6. _____ 6. moisten
7. _____ 7. annoyance
8. _____ 8. occupant
9. _____ 9. cleverness
10. _____ 10. reference
11. _____ 11. acquaintance
12. _____ 12. persistent
13. _____ 13. sightless
14. _____ 14. descendant
15. _____ 15. dizziness
16. _____ 16. occurrence
17. _____ 17. boundless
18. _____ 18. emptiness
19. _____ 19. correspondent
20. _____ 20. regardless

Challenge Words
_____ barley
_____ coincidences
_____ mufflers
_____ sheepishly
_____ sweeten

Grade 6/Unit 5
Rumpelstiltskin's Daughter   20   147

Words with Suffixes

Using the Word Study Steps
1. LOOK at the word
2. SAY the word aloud.
3. STUDY the letters in the word.
4. WRITE the word.
5. CHECK the word.
   Did you spell the word right? If not, go back to step 1.

Spelling Tip
When a word ends with a silent **e**, drop the final **e** when adding a suffix that starts with a vowel.

reside + ent = resident

When a word ends with a consonant and **y**, change the **y** to **i** before adding a suffix.

dizzy + ness = dizziness

Scrambled Words
Unscramble each spelling word below.

1. selsdobun ___boundless___
2. tendendasc ___descendant___
3. selghtiss ___sightless___
4. tonpucac ___occupant___
5. caannuitcqae ___acquaintance___
6. eszinzids ___dizziness___
7. sistetnrep ___persistent___
8. lentlcexe ___excellent___
9. verlencsse ___cleverness___
10. ragesedrls ___regardless___
11. sesrlets ___restless___
12. yanancneo ___annoyance___
13. dinretse ___resident___
14. feenccoern ___conference___
15. petinsmes ___emptiness___
16. recnreuocc ___occurrence___
17. rocesdreontnp ___correspondent___
18. freenerce ___reference___
19. teandantt ___attendant___
20. streubidanc ___disturbance___

To Parents or Helpers:
Using the Word Study Steps above as your child comes across any new words will help him or her spell words effectively. Review the steps as you both go over this week's spelling words.
Go over the Spelling Tip with your child. Help your child find other examples of words which change y to i and drop the final e. Help your child complete the Spelling Activity by unscrambling each set of letters above.

148   Grade 6/Unit 5
Rumpelstiltskin's Daughter   20

Words with Suffixes

excellent	conference	cleverness	sightless	boundless
attendant	resident	reference	descendant	emptiness
restless	annoyance	acquaintance	dizziness	correspondent
disturbance	occupant	persistent	occurrence	regardless

Sort each spelling word according to the suffix which it contains. Write the words with the following suffixes:

-ness
1. ___cleverness___
2. ___dizziness___
3. ___emptiness___

-less
4. ___restless___
5. ___sightless___
6. ___boundless___
7. ___regardless___

-ant
8. ___attendant___
9. ___occupant___
10. ___descendant___

-ent
11. ___excellent___
12. ___resident___
13. ___persistent___
14. ___correspondent___

-ance
15. ___disturbance___
16. ___annoyance___
17. ___acquaintance___

-ence
18. ___conference___
19. ___reference___
20. ___occurrence___

Grade 6/Unit 5
Rumpelstiltskin's Daughter   20   149

Words with Suffixes

excellent	conference	cleverness	sightless	boundless
attendant	resident	reference	descendant	emptiness
restless	annoyance	acquaintance	dizziness	correspondent
disturbance	occupant	persistent	occurrence	regardless

Synonyms and Antonyms
Write the spelling word which is a synonym (S) or antonym (A).

1. order (A) ___disturbance___
2. offspring (S) ___descendant___
3. balance (A) ___dizziness___
4. nuisance (S) ___annoyance___
5. stranger (A) ___acquaintance___
6. superior (S) ___excellent___
7. blind (S) ___sightless___
8. restful (A) ___restless___
9. meeting (S) ___conference___
10. stupidity (A) ___cleverness___
11. enduring (S) ___persistent___
12. limited (A) ___boundless___

Word Meanings: Analogies
An **analogy** compares the relationship between two pairs of words. Fill in the spelling word that best completes each analogy below.

13. *Boss* is to *employer* as *servant* is to ___attendant___
14. *Poem* is to *poet* as *letter* is to ___correspondent___
15. *Everything* is to *fullness* as *nothing* is to ___emptiness___
16. *Spoon* is to *utensil* as *dictionary* is to ___reference___
17. *Own* is to *owner* as *occupy* is to ___occupant___
18. *Cautious* is to *careful* as *nevertheless* is to ___regardless___
19. *Outcome* is to *result* as *happening* is to ___occurrence___
20. *Physician* is to *doctor* as *intern* is to ___resident___

150   **Challenge Extension:** Write an updated version of an old fairytale using the Challenge Words.   Grade 6/Unit 5
Rumpelstiltskin's Daughter   20

Rumpelstiltskin's Daughter • SPELLING

Words with Suffixes

Proofreading Activity

There are six spelling mistakes in this paragraph. Circle the misspelled words. Write the words correctly on the lines below.

The miller claimed that his (desendant) could spin straw into gold. The king's (attendent) heard the claim, and ran off to tell the king. The king arrived at the miller's house and looked for the (ocupant) Eventually the miller appeared, showing (anoyance) at having been disturbed. The king demanded to know which (aquaintance) of the miller could spin straw into gold. But the miller refused to tell unless he was paid for the (referrence) Finally, the king threw down a gold coin, grabbed the miller's daughter, and took her away to the palace.

1. ____descendant____   3. ____occupant____   5. ____acquaintance____

2. ____attendant____   4. ____annoyance____   6. ____reference____

Writing Activity

Rewrite the ending to *Rumpelstiltskin's Daughter* or another fairy tale with which you are familiar. Use four spelling words in your writing.

_____

_____

_____

_____

Words with Suffixes

Look at the words in each set below. One word in each set is spelled correctly. Use a pencil to fill in the circle next to the correct word. Before you begin, look at the sample sets of words. Sample A has been done for you. Do Sample B by yourself. When you are sure you know what to do, you may go on with the rest of the page.

Sample A:
- (A) happeyness
- (B) happyness
- (C) happieness
- (D) **happiness**

Sample B:
- (E) depandent
- (F) **dependent**
- (G) dapendant
- (H) dapendent

1. (A) disturbence
   (B) **disturbance**
   (C) distirbence
   (D) distirbance

2. (E) **persistent**
   (F) persistant
   (G) persisstent
   (H) persisstant

3. (A) regardliss
   (B) regardles
   (C) **regardless**
   (D) ragardless

4. (E) **cleverness**
   (F) clevverness
   (G) clevirness
   (H) clevvirness

5. (A) bondless
   (B) bowndless
   (C) **boundless**
   (D) bownddless

6. (E) annoyence
   (F) **annoyance**
   (G) anoyence
   (H) anoyance

7. (A) **resident**
   (B) residant
   (C) rezident
   (D) rezidant

8. (E) exellent
   (F) exellant
   (G) excellant
   (H) **excellent**

9. (A) disiness
   (B) diziness
   (C) dissiness
   (D) **dizziness**

10. (E) ocupant
    (F) **occupant**
    (G) ocupent
    (H) occupent

11. (A) emptyness
    (B) **emptiness**
    (C) emptynes
    (D) emptines

12. (E) atendent
    (F) atendant
    (G) attendent
    (H) **attendant**

13. (A) siteliss
    (B) siteles
    (C) **sightless**
    (D) sightles

14. (E) **reference**
    (F) refference
    (G) refrence
    (H) reffrence

15. (A) **correspondent**
    (B) corrispondent
    (C) correspondant
    (D) corrispandant

16. (E) aquaintence
    (F) acquaintance
    (G) aquaintence
    (H) **acquaintance**

17. (A) resstless
    (B) **restless**
    (C) restliss
    (D) resstliss

18. (E) accurence
    (F) accurance
    (G) **occurrence**
    (H) occurance

19. (A) confrence
    (B) **conference**
    (C) confenss
    (D) conferenss

20. (E) desendant
    (F) desendent
    (G) **descendant**
    (H) descendint

T47

Practice 177

Name_____ Date_____ Practice 177

Sequence of Events

Events in a story happen in a certain **sequence**, or order. Understanding the sequence of events can help the reader make sense of a story or article. Read the story below. Then number the events in the order in which they occurred.

Thousands of years ago, long before trains, planes, and cargo ships, trade was a very difficult business. However, goods still traveled vast distances, across deserts and seas, from one end of the world to the other. In the year A.D. 56, the trader Rufus Hibernicus left Rome on a ship bound for Alexandria, Egypt. He carried a chest of gold coins and many gold and silver statues. In Egypt, he caught another ship for Antioch on the coast of Asia Minor. From Antioch he joined a caravan of merchants who were all traveling east, along the Silk Road that led across Asia to China. Halfway through his journey, the caravan was attacked by thieves. However, the merchants had hired some soldiers to protect them, and the thieves were driven off. After many months of travel, the caravan crossed the Gobi desert and reached China, where Rufus traded his gold coins and statues for silk cloth. He then began the long journey back to Rome, where the silk would make him a very rich man.

7	Soldiers defend the caravan, and the thieves are driven off.
3	He changed ships in Egypt.
10	He begins the long journey back to Rome.
4	He arrives in Antioch.
9	Rufus trades his gold coins and statues for silk cloth.
6	Thieves attack the caravan.
2	Rufus arrives in Alexandria, Egypt.
1	Rufus Hibernicus leaves the port of Rome.
8	The caravan crosses the Gobi desert and arrives in China.
5	He joins a caravan of merchants traveling along the Silk Road.

Practice 178

Name_____ Date_____ Practice 178

Vocabulary

Draw a line to match each word to its definition.

1. automated — a. sums of money lent
2. teller — b. a fixed charge
3. loans — c. any form of money
4. bartering — d. a bank employee
5. currency — e. operated automatically
6. fee — f. trading goods without money

Suppose that you worked in a bank. Use the words in the list below to write slogans advertising the services that your bank can offer. Use one word in each slogan.

automated	teller	loans	bartering	fee	currency

Answers will vary. Sample responses are provided.

Sign One: This bank offers automated banking services.

Sign Two: Each teller in this bank is happy to assist you.

Sign Three: We offer loans for buying houses or cars.

Sign Four: Bartering is a thing of the past. Our bank will help you acquire whatever you need.

Sign Five: Our fees are some of the lowest in the city.

Sign Six: We offer currency exchange.

Practice 178a

Name_____ Date_____ Practice 178a

Banks in History

Throughout history banks have operated basically as they did when people first stopped exchanging goods, or *bartering*. Banks lend people money and then charge interest for these *loans*. They also may charge people *fees* for cashing checks or maintaining a bank account. Many banks also offer foreign *currency* exchange. However, one modern banking development involves electronic banking and automation. Although *tellers* still help people with their accounts, many bank services these days are now *automated* and customers use cash machines instead of dealing with human tellers.

TOWN BANK

1. Why would banks be unnecessary if we were still bartering goods?
   Banks do not trade in goods.

2. How do banks make money on loans?
   They charge interest on the money they lend.

3. What happens when you cash a check?
   The bank may charge a fee.

4. Who are the people who help customers?
   tellers

5. Do you think that automated services are a good idea? Explain.
   Yes; automated services save people a lot of time.

[Answers will vary. Sample responses are provided.]

Practice 179

Name_____ Date_____ Practice 179

Story Comprehension

Beside each statement about "The History of Money," write **T** if the statement is true and **F** if it is false.

1. F — People have always used money.
2. T — People used to barter to get the things they needed.
3. T — Tea leaves were once used as money.
4. F — People became rich by drinking lots of tea.
5. F — Metal money was first used in Mexico.
6. T — People began using gold and silver as money because these metals are valuable.
7. F — There are about 12 different currencies in the world.
8. T — The first bank opened in our country in 18th-century Philadelphia.
9. F — Yap money stones are some of the lightest coins in the world.
10. F — The name "piggy bank" comes from the days when people traded in pigs.
11. T — Ancient temples were some of the first banks.
12. T — The first bankers helped people exchange currency.
13. F — Banks never make loans.
14. T — A bank pays you interest for letting it use your money.

The History of Money • PRACTICE

Practice 180

Read a Chart

A **chart** organizes and presents information in a way that is quick and easy to understand. Being able to read charts is an important study skill.
Study the chart below about the history of money in the United States.
Then answer the questions that follow.

History of Money in the United States		
Period	**Form of Money**	**How It Was Used**
Pre-colonial	wampum (beaded shells on strings)	Wampum was used by some Native Americans to buy goods.
Revolutionary War	continentals	First used to pay for the Revolutionary War; the first currency printed by the new United States.
Free Banking Era	wildcat and broken notes	These notes were printed by individual banks. Many could be exchanged for gold or silver, but others were worthless.
Civil War	Greenbacks	In order to finance the Civil War, the United States government began printing money for the first time since the days of the continentals.
After 1913	Federal Reserve Notes	After the Federal Reserve Act of 1913, these notes became the main form of paper currency in the U.S.

1. What is wampum and when was it used? _____ Wampum is beaded shells on strings.
   Wampum sometimes was used during the pre-colonial period.

2. Why did the US government print greenbacks?
   to finance the Civil War

3. Between which wars did the Free Banking Era exist?
   between the Revolutionary War and the Civil War.

4. What happened during the Free Banking Era?
   Banks printed their own currency.

5. When did Federal Reserve Notes come into circulation?
   after 1913

Practice 181

Make Judgments and Decisions

To **make a judgment** about an issue, you must examine both sides of the argument and use the evidence and your own experience to make a decision.

Read each paragraph. Then examine both sides of the argument.
Write the two sides in the appropriate boxes in the chart.
Then write your judgment about the situation.

In the nineteenth century, many museums bought valuable objects for very low prices and carried them far from their places of origin. The British Museum bought works of art in Greece and Egypt and brought them back to London. Museums in the United States acquired many Native American objects. Now, some people say that these objects should be returned. Others say that these objects should remain in museums for people everywhere to enjoy. [Answers will vary. Sample responses are provided.]

People say that objects of art should be returned because:	People say that objects of art should stay in museum because:	In my judgment:
These objects belong to the region where they were created.	These objects should remain in museums for everyone to enjoy	We should keep objects of art in museums where everyone can enjoy them.

Some people want to stop companies that make certain products from advertising. They believe that advertising some products, such as cigarettes, encourages young people to begin bad habits. Other people deny that advertising has that much influence. Some also believe that companies should have the right to advertise. They believe that advertising is a form of free speech and free speech should be protected.

Some people want to stop certain ads because:	Other people support certain advertising because:	In my judgment:
some ads may encourage young people to begin bad habits.	free speech should be protected.	People should allow companies to keep advertising because it is free speech, which must be protected.

Practice 182

Review Context Clues

Whenever you come across an unfamiliar word, always look for **context clues** in the surrounding words and sentences to help you define the unknown word.

Use context clues to help you guess the meaning of each underlined word.
Write the meaning of the word on the line following each sentence.
[Answers will vary. Sample responses are provided.]

1. The beautiful old house was demolished to make way for a
   convenience store. destroyed

2. Tom is very gullible and believes everything people tell him. easily deceived

3. We watched the bird fly over the forest and alight on
   a tree. come down and settle

4. After the accident, she suffered from amnesia and couldn't
   remember anything. loss of memory

5. The fabric was very coarse and rough to the touch. rough

6. The highway was littered with plastic coffee cups that people
   had discarded. thrown away

7. The material was very flexible and could be
   bent easily. capable of being easily beat

8. He flew into a rage when he heard that he hadn't
   gotten the job. extreme anger

9. After a few weeks, most fruit begins to
   shrivel up. to shrink and wrinkle

10. Because of the storm, the party was canceled.
    called off; stopped

11. The Soviet Union and the United States were allies during World War II
    and helped each other win the war. friends

12. Some creatures are so small that they are microscopic and can only be seen
    through a microscope. too small to be seen without a microscope

Practice 183

Denotation and Connotation

No two words have exactly the same meanings, even synonyms. The idea suggested by a word is called its **connotation**, while the dictionary meaning of a word is called its **denotation**.

Read the denotation of each word and decide whether the word has a positive, negative, or neutral connotation. Place an **x** in the appropriate column.
[Answers may vary. Sample responses are provided.]

Word	Denotation	Positive Connotation	Neutral Connotation	Negative Connotation
1. happen	to come to pass		X	
occur	to take place		X	
befall	to happen unexpectedly			X
2. obedient	obeying or carrying out a request	X		
servile	slavish in character or attitude			X
dutiful	careful to perform duties	X		
3. toil	work involving difficulty or pain			X
labor	work		X	
drudgery	unpleasant work			X
4. amusing	entertaining		X	
funny	causing laughter	X		
silly	light; non-serious			X

Reteach 177

Name_____ Date_____

Sequence of Events

> Events in a story happen in a certain **sequence,** or order. Understanding the sequence of events can help the reader make sense of a story or article.

Read the following story. Then number the events to show the order in which they happened.

Two thousand years ago a gold coin was minted in the Greek city of Corinth. It passed through many hands before a rich merchant added it to his growing fortune. For years it lay locked away in a dark chest. Then one day, the Roman army invaded Greece and stole the merchant's treasure. The Romans carried the coin back to Rome, where a soldier received it as pay. Over the years the coin passed through many markets, taverns, and shops. It was exchanged for food and fabrics, glass, and jewelry. Carried in the pockets and purses of rich and poor it traveled through every region in the world. Eventually, it was hidden in the cellar of a house, where it remained long after the house had burned to the ground. For two thousand years it was forgotten, until a farmer's shovel uncovered it in the dirt. The farmer took it to a museum, where it was displayed with 20 other coins that had all passed through thousands of people's lives. The gold coin remains in the museum to this day.

___2___ A rich merchant hid the coin in a chest.

___10___ A farmer unearthed the coin and gave it to a museum.

___4___ The coin traveled to Rome.

___9___ For 2,000 years the coin was forgotten.

___1___ A gold coin was minted in Corinth, Greece.

___6___ The coin traveled through every region of the world.

___7___ The coin was hidden in the cellar of a house.

___3___ The Roman army invaded Greece.

___8___ The house burned down.

___5___ A soldier received the coin as pay.

Book 6/Unit 5
The History of Money

At Home: Have students interview a family member and make a list of the sequence of important events in his or her life.

177

Reteach 178

Name_____ Date_____

Vocabulary

Read each clue. Then find each vocabulary word from the box in the rows of letters and circle it.

bartering	currency	automated	teller	loan	fee

1. operated automatically — o p e i o l k (automated) m b v i e o

2. a bank employee — i e p o u n m (teller) n v m e o s t m b

3. trading goods without money — w i p (bartering) o p r k l n a r

4. a fixed charge — p q o f l c m e o (fee) m a p e l k k s e l

5. sum of money lent — k l e m b e k e l a x (loan) u e p v m a

6. any form of money — m c d l q k r p x b (currency) q x e m

---

Reteach 179

Story Comprehension

Answer each question about "The History of Money."

1. Why was money unnecessary thousands of years ago? People traded goods directly, or bartered, when they wanted something.

2. What did people use as money before the invention of metal coins or paper money? People used salt, shells, tea leaves, seeds, camels, cowrie shells, or dried fish.

3. What was the disadvantage of early money? It was either too bulky or too flimsy.

4. Why did gold, silver, and copper become valuable? These metals are rare and therefore valuable.

5. What buildings were sometimes used as the first banks? temples

6. How do banks make money? Banks make money from the interest charged when they lend money.

At Home: Have students use each of the vocabulary words in an original sentence.

178–179

Book 6/Unit 5
The History of Money

Reteach 180

Name_____ Date_____

Read a Chart

> A **chart** organizes and presents information in a form that is quickly and easily read. Reading a chart is an important study skill.

Study the chart and answer the questions that follow.

Date	Place	Form of Money
9000–6000 B.C.	everywhere	cattle
1200 B.C.	first used in China	cowrie shell
1000 B.C.	China	first metal money and primitive versions of round coins
500 B.C.	Lydia, part of present-day Turkey	first coins developed out of lumps of silver
A.D. 118	China	leather money first used; this is regarded as the first form of bank note
A.D. 806	China	first paper bank notes appear

1. What was the earliest form of money? cattle

2. Where were cowrie shells first used? China

3. When and where did the first metal money appear? 1000 B.C. in China

4. Where did the first silver coins develop? in Lydia, part of present-day Turkey

5. Why were the Lydian coins different from the Chinese coins? The Lydian coins were developed out of lumps of silver.

6. Where did the first paper bank notes appear? in China

7. What material was used to make the first bank note? leather

8. What region of the world saw the earliest development of coins and bank notes? China

Book 6/Unit 5
The History of Money

At Home: Have students use an encyclopedia to help them make a chart containing information about a foreign country they are interested in.

180

Reteach 181

Name_____ Date_____

Make Judgments and Decisions

> To **make a judgment** about an issue, you must use the information on both sides of the argument and your own experience to make a decision.

Read each paragraph. In the chart, summarize each side of the argument. Then write your judgment about the situation.

Many parts of the ocean are being over-fished. Because of the increasing human population and demand for fish, scientists are afraid that many species may not survive. Many governments are trying to stop people from fishing in certain areas. People hope that if the fish in these areas are left undisturbed for a while, their numbers will increase. When their numbers have increased sufficiently, the ban against fishing will be lifted. However, those who make a living from fishing say that if they are not allowed to fish, they will be out of work. Many will have to move away and take other jobs. Fishers say that this will destroy their way of life.

Answers may vary. Sample responses are provided.

Scientist and government argument:	Fishing people argument:
Numbers of fish are decreasing so rapidly that many species may not survive. Fishing must be restricted for a period of time.	If you stop us from fishing, we will lose our jobs and our way of life will be destroyed.

In my judgment: We must stop people from fishing temporarily. However, the government should help those people who lose their jobs.

A war of words is raging between environmentalists and developers. The environmentalists believe that development is destroying our natural resources. Some say that the suburbs are particularly wasteful. For example, people in the suburbs use large quantities of water to keep their lawns green. Many suburbanites drive long distances to work or to shop which uses more fuel and places great strains on our natural resources. In contrast, developers say that we must build roads and housing in order to keep the economy going and provide homes. Building helps create jobs and keeps people prosperous.

Environmentalist argument:	Developer argument:
Development is destroying the planet.	Development is necessary for growth and provides jobs.

In my judgment: We should limit the building of roads and houses to protect our environment and natural resources. We should also find ways to create jobs.

181

At Home: Have students choose a recent news item and make a judgment about the issue. Have them write a short explanation of their thinking.

Book 6/Unit 5
The History of Money

The History of Money • RETEACH

Context Clues

Whenever you come across an unfamiliar word, look for **context clues**, or the nearby words and sentences, to help you figure out the word's meaning.

Use context clues to help you determine the meaning of the underlined word in each sentence. Then write the meaning of the underlined word on the line following each sentence.

1. After many years in the military, he found it difficult to get used to civilian life.
   non-military

2. As they relaxed on the patio they were astonished to see a horde of insects, whose numbers seemed to block out the sun. a throng or swarm

3. At the crossroads, the two roads intersect. to cut across

4. The palace was quite opulent, filled with the richest decor. characterized by great wealth; rich; affluent

5. Many perished when the ship sank. died

6. The house was hidden in a forest and quite secluded. removed or set apart from others

7. We were all quite perplexed by the problem and could not find an answer. puzzled; mystified

8. Aleesha transplanted the flowers from one part of the garden to another. uprooted and replanted

9. Unless some foods are frozen they begin to decay. rot

10. After a day without water he was quite dehydrated. lacking water; dry

At Home: List five unfamiliar words from your next reading assignment. Look for context clues to help you define the meaning of the unfamiliar words. Check your meanings in a dictionary.

Denotation and Connotation

No two words are exactly the same in meaning. The idea or emotion suggested by a word is called its **connotation**. The exact dictionary meaning of a word is called its **denotation**.

Use a dictionary to help you supply the denotation for each set of synonyms. Then indicate with a ✔ whether each word has a positive or a negative connotation.

Word	Denotation	Positive Connotation	Negative Connotation
1. smart	intelligent	✔	
2. cunning	shrewd; crafty		✔
3. clever	bright; mentally quick	✔	
4. aroma	a delicious smell	✔	
5. fragrance	a pleasant odor	✔	
6. stench	a strong, foul odor		✔
7. skinny	very thin		✔
8. skeletal	bony		✔
9. slim	slender	✔	
10. humid	warm and moist		✔
11. balmy	pleasantly warm	✔	
12. muggy	uncomfortably damp		✔

At Home: Have students make a list of five words with negative connotations. Then have them find a synonym with positive connotations for each word.

The History of Money • EXTEND

Sequence of Events

The directions below for washing a car are out of **sequence**. Renumber the steps so that they are in the correct order.

How to Wash a Car

Steps:

___6___ After cleaning the wheels, wipe down entire car with rags and soapy water.

___1___ Have an adult park the car near a water hose.

___3___ Fill bucket with water, add detergent.

___2___ Gather together brushes, towels, detergent, bucket.

___4___ After filling bucket with detergent, hose down car.

___5___ After hosing down car, scrub wheels and hubcaps.

___7___ Hose detergent off car. Now, vacuum the inside of the car.

Write a paragraph in which you explain why you are washing the car.

Paragraphs will vary.

At Home: Have students write the steps they take to do a simple task, like cleaning their room.

Vocabulary

bartering	currency	fee
loan	automated	teller

Suppose that you are the president of a bank. Someone comes in with a great idea for a business, but she needs money. Using some of the vocabulary words, write about your meeting with her.   _Answers will vary. Possible answer is given._

This business was a sure bet. I secured the loan and we ended up bartering the

fee for a small percentage of her profits. I issued an automated teller machine

card to her and delivered currency in the amount of $100,000.00.

Story Comprehension

Read and answer each question. Refer back to "The History of Money" if you need help.

1. Why do you think paper money became popular as opposed to coins?
   Paper money is lighter and easier to carry.

2. Why must you pay interest to a bank when you take a loan?
   You must pay the bank for the right to use its money.

3. How can you explain the Yap Island coin?
   Possible answer: A stone of that size and weight is difficult to shape and to
   move. Only the wealthiest people could afford the time and expense of
   creating one.

4. How does a bank make money when you borrow money?
   A bank makes money by charging you interest on the amount you have
   borrowed.

At Home: Research the origin of the rupee, shilling, peseta, or franc.

Read a Chart

Read the chart below about the origins of the names of currency. Then answer the questions.

Country	Currency	Word Origin
England	pound	the weight of some metal
Peru	sol	the sun, worshipped by Incas
Venezuela	bolívar	in honor of Simón Bolívar, national hero
Australia	koala	the name of a well loved Australian animal
Denmark	krone	authorized by the Crown (king or queen)
United States	dollar	originally called _Joachimsthaler_, for the place a silver coin was first minted in 1519; became _thaler, taler, daler_, and finally _dollar_.

1. What is the name of the currency of Peru? _sol_

2. Who does the currency of Venezuela honor? _Simón Bolívar_

3. The German mark is named for the weight of a metal, as is the currency of which country? _England_

4. Which country has a currency name that shows it came from the king?
   Denmark

5. Research the word origins of two more currencies you would like to add to the chart.
   Answers will vary.

At Home: Have students research the history of the yen, lira, quetzal, or diaham.

Make Judgments and Decisions

People often have to make **judgments** or **decisions**. Read the categories below. Write about a decision you have made for each category. Was it the right decision? What would you do differently now?
Answers will vary but should include examples of decision-making.

Sharing:

Being Responsible:

Helping Out:

At Home: Direct students to write about a decision they made recently that they would now change.

The History of Money • EXTEND

Context Clues

Remember the three kinds of **context clues**:

1. similar meanings
2. contrasting meanings
3. defined in context

Define the italicized words, and tell which of the three context clues you used.

1. He used a system of *barter*, or exchange of goods instead of money.
   exchange of goods, 3

2. Different kinds of money, or *currencies*, come into the bank every day.
   different kinds of money, 3

3. Rather than being done by hand, the knitting is almost entirely *automated*.
   being done by machine, 2

4. Unlike South America far to the south of Mexico, the United States is *contiguous* with
   Mexico. directly connected to; adjacent to, 2

5. We hoped that the water would be pure and clean; it was, however, *polluted*.
   impure, 2

6. Why did he *shun* and avoid all other people? avoid, 1

7. The dentist *extracted* four teeth, first pulling two from the top, then two from the
   bottom. pull out, 1

At Home: Have students write a context clue for the word *harbinger*.

Denotation and Connotation

Look at the pairs of words below. Each pair has a similar **denotation**, or definition. Select the word with a negative **connotation** in each pair and tell what emotions or associations are suggested. Feel free to use your dictionary.
Answers will vary. Examples are given.

1. **grim** Grim has a negative connotation. It suggests a sourness of personality.

   solemn Positive connotation.

2. **devour** Devour has a negative connotation. It suggests eating like a wild animal.

   eat Positive connotation.

3. **stench** Stench has a negative connotation. It is certain to be vile.

   aroma Positive connotation.

4. **obstinate** Obstinate has a negative connotation. It suggests a stand that is negative or not based on sound principles.

   firm Positive connotation.

5. **timid** Timid has a negative connotation. A timid person is skittish, silly, weak.

   cautious Positive connotation.

Write a poem using at least 2 pairs of the words in their different connotations.

_____

_____

_____

_____

_____

_____

At Home: Have students research the words *lie* and *equivocate*.

T53

The History of Money • GRAMMAR

Pronoun-Verb Agreement

- A verb must agree with its subject pronoun.

Pronouns	Verbs
He, she, it	walks, is, was, has
We, you, they	walk, are, were, have
I	walk, am, was, have

Circle the verb in parentheses that correctly completes each sentence. Rewrite the sentence.

1. He (barters, barter) with the merchant for bread and corn.
   He barters with the merchant for bread and corn.

2. It (is, are) easy to get money from ATM machines.
   It is easy to get money from ATM machines.

3. Juan and I (shop, shops) for vegetables at the bazaar.
   Jose and I shop for vegetables at the bazaar.

4. (Were, Was) you satisfied with the restaurant's service?
   Were you satisfied with the restaurant's service?

5. She (pays, pay) for her clothes with credit cards.
   She pays for her clothes with credit cards.

Circle the subject pronoun that correctly completes each sentence. Rewrite the sentence.

6. (We, He) count the metal coins carefully.
   We count the metal coins carefully.

7. (They, She) pay the hired workers with shells.
   They pay the hired workers with shells.

8. (He, We) have rare coins from around the world.
   We have rare coins from around the world.

9. In Egypt (I, she) uses precious metals for money.
   In Egypt she uses precious metals for money.

10. (It, You) is wise to save your money.
    It is wise to save your money.

10 Grade 6/Unit 5
The History of Money

Extension: Draw an arrow from the subject pronoun to the verb with which it agrees.

153

Indefinite Pronouns and Verbs

Verbs must also agree with indefinite pronouns.
- Use a singular verb with a singular indefinite pronoun.
- Use a plural verb with a plural indefinite pronoun.

Rewrite each sentence, choosing the verb in parentheses that agrees with the indefinite pronoun.

1. Everything (is, are) too expensive for the poor farmers.
   Everything is too expensive for the poor farmers.

2. No one (trade, trades) in beads at today's shopping mall.
   No one trades in beads at today's shopping mall.

3. Both of the banks (offer, offers) savings accounts.
   Both of the banks offer savings accounts.

4. A few of the dollar bills (are, is) old.
   A few of the dollar bills are old.

5. Nothing (costs, cost) over five shells in that shop.
   Nothing costs over five shells in that shop.

6. Others (require, requires) borrowers to pay interest.
   Others require borrowers to pay interest.

7. Everyone (learn, learns) that the Chinese invented paper money.
   Everyone learns that the Chinese invented paper money.

8. (Do, Does) anybody want to barter for lunch?
   Does anybody want to barter for lunch?

9. Many (have, has) piggy banks for their extra change.
   Many have piggy banks for their extra change.

10. Several (participate, participates) in the auction.
    Several participate in the auction.

154

Extension: Underline each indefinite pronoun above and label whether each is singular or plural.

Grade 6/Unit 5
The History of Money 10

Reviewing Pronouns and Verbs

- A verb must agree with its subject pronoun.

Pronouns	Verbs
He, she, it	walks, is, was, has
We, you, they	walk, are, were, have
I	walk, am, was, have

Change each verb in the following sentences so that it agrees with the subject pronoun. Write your response on the line provided.

1. Nobody need money if they can barter for their goods. __needs__

2. Nothing bother me more than losing my money in the store. __bothers__

3. She take shells, seeds, and tea leaves to the village. __takes__

4. I trades my camel for enough gold to pay for my trip to Morocco. __trade__

5. Everyone use wampum made of little shells and beads. __uses__

Fill in the blank with a pronoun that agrees with the verb. Do not use the same pronoun more than once. Answers may vary.

6. __Each__ brings cowrie shells from Africa to barter for wheat.

7. __They__ buy coins from Persia, Rome, and Egypt.

8. His brother and __he__ trade a shekel for corn.

9. __Many__ barter their sandwiches for fruit at lunchtime.

10. __You__ and __I__ deposit our savings at the local bank.

10 Grade 6/Unit 5
The History of Money

Extension: Write five sentences about food bartering at lunchtime. Use a different pronoun in each sentence.

155

Titles of Works

- Underline or use italics for titles of books, plays, newspapers, magazines, movies, and TV series.
- Put quotation marks around titles of poems, short stories, essays, songs, articles, and book chapters.

Rewrite each sentence correctly. Underline or use quotation marks on the titles.

1. Have you read the book The Art of Bartering by Joseph Hill?
   Have you read the book <u>The Art of Bartering</u> by Joseph Hill?

2. We read the short story Gold and Silver in class yesterday.
   We read the short story "Gold and Silver" in class yesterday.

3. My father subscribes to Coin Collecting.
   My father subscribes to <u>Coin Collecting</u>.

4. Read the newspaper The New York Times to learn about trading today.
   Read the newspaper <u>The New York Times</u> to learn about trading today.

5. Linda looks for an article called Bartering with Your Peanut Butter Sandwich.
   Linda looks for an article called "Bartering with Your Peanut Butter Sandwich."

6. Margaret plans to see the movie The Stockbroker and the Trader.
   Margaret plans to see the movie <u>The Stockbroker and the Trader</u>.

7. Kurt's essay was called My Current Savings Account.
   Kurt's essay was called "My Current Savings Account."

8. I just heard the new song Money.
   I just heard the new song "Money."

9. My mother is reading a book titled Investing for the Future.
   My mother is reading a book titled <u>Investing for the Future</u>.

10. My sister wrote an article called Planning Your Portfolio.
    My sister wrote an article called "Planning Your Portfolio."

156

Extension: Write six sentences using titles. Use three titles requiring quotation marks and three that should be underlined.

Grade 6/Unit 5
The History of Money 10

The History of Money • GRAMMAR

Pronouns

Write the verb in parentheses that correctly completes each sentence.

1. Everyone (wait, waits) quietly for the historian to speak. ___waits___

2. We (study, studies) interesting tales about ancient Persia. ___study___

3. Jason and she (trade, trades) coins with the shopkeeper. ___trade___

4. He (prefer, prefers) to collect stamps instead of coins. ___prefers___

5. Many (has, have) watched movies about ancient Rome. ___have___

Write the pronoun in parentheses that correctly completes each sentence.

6. (Nobody, Several) loves to study the history of money more than Maria.

   ___Nobody___

7. (You, She) know a collector who buys rare coins on the Internet. ___You___

8. (Each, Few) knows that the Bank of North America was the first U.S. bank.

   ___Each___

9. (We, He) hopes to find a rare Hebrew coin at the coin shop. ___He___

10. (Both, Nobody) use pocket calculators to balance their checkbooks. ___Both___

Pronouns, Verbs, and Titles

A verb must agree with its subject pronoun.	
Pronouns	**Verbs**
He, she, it	walks, is, was, has
We, you, they	walk, are, were, have
I	walk, am, was, have

Mechanics

- Underline or use italics for titles of books, plays, newspapers, magazines, movies, and TV series.
- Put quotation marks around titles of poems, short stories, essays, songs, articles, and book chapters.

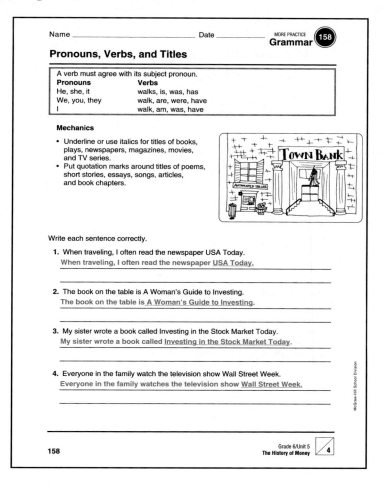

Write each sentence correctly.

1. When traveling, I often read the newspaper USA Today.

   When traveling, I often read the newspaper _USA Today._

2. The book on the table is A Woman's Guide to Investing.

   The book on the table is _A Woman's Guide to Investing._

3. My sister wrote a book called Investing in the Stock Market Today.

   My sister wrote a book called _Investing in the Stock Market Today._

4. Everyone in the family watch the television show Wall Street Week.

   Everyone in the family watches the television show _Wall Street Week._

The History of Money • SPELLING

Name _____ **Date** _____

Words from Math

Pretest Directions

Fold back the paper along the dotted line. Use the blanks to write each word as it is read aloud. When you finish the test, unfold the paper. Use the list at the right to correct any spelling mistakes. Practice the words you missed for the Posttest.

To Parents

Here are the results of your child's weekly spelling Pretest. You can help your child study for the Posttest by following these simple steps for each word on the word list:

1. Read the word to your child.
2. Have your child write the word, saying each letter as it is written.
3. Say each letter of the word as your child checks the spelling.
4. If a mistake has been made, have your child read each letter of the correctly spelled word aloud, and then repeat steps 1–3.

#		#	Word
1.	_____	1.	interest
2.	_____	2.	borrow
3.	_____	3.	division
4.	_____	4.	percent
5.	_____	5.	addition
6.	_____	6.	fraction
7.	_____	7.	metric
8.	_____	8.	positive
9.	_____	9.	calculate
10.	_____	10.	customary
11.	_____	11.	predict
12.	_____	12.	deposit
13.	_____	13.	discount
14.	_____	14.	negative
15.	_____	15.	probable
16.	_____	16.	decimal
17.	_____	17.	tally
18.	_____	18.	dividend
19.	_____	19.	subtraction
20.	_____	20.	statistics

Challenge Words

_____ bartering
_____ currency
_____ fee
_____ loan
_____ automated

Name _____ **Date** _____

Words from Math

Using the Word Study Steps

1. LOOK at the word.
2. SAY the word aloud.
3. STUDY the letters in the word.
4. WRITE the word.
5. CHECK the word.
   Did you spell the word right?
   If not, go back to step 1.

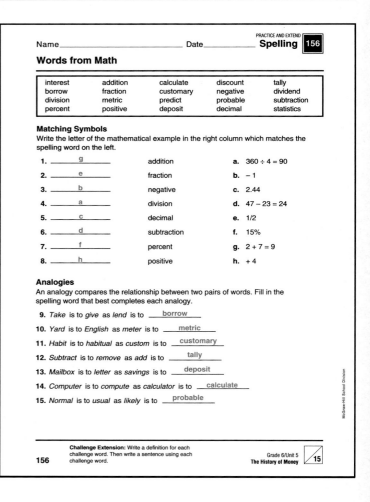

Spelling Tip

Look for word chunks that help you remember the spelling. Sometimes there may be smaller words in a longer word that will help you to spell it.

per cent   cus to mar y

dis count

Rhyme Time!

Circle the word that rhymes with each spelling word on the left.

1. division — (decision)   devotion   divide
2. discount — discuss   among   (amount)
3. fraction — picture   (traction)   react
4. calculate — combination   treatment   (demonstrate)
5. predict — prepare   (evict)   select
6. tally — (rally)   tall   trail
7. borrow — hello   (sorrow)   bore
8. percent — token   (absent)   person
9. metric — (hectic)   metal   price
10. addition — added   (admission)   adding

To Parents or Helpers:

Using the Word Study Steps above as your child comes across any new words will help him or her spell words effectively. Review the steps as you both go over this week's spelling words.

Go over the Spelling Tip with your child. Help him or her divide the longer spelling words into word chunks.

Help your child complete the Spelling Activity by circling the rhyming words.

Name _____ **Date** _____

Words from Math

interest	addition	calculate	discount	tally
borrow	fraction	customary	negative	dividend
division	metric	predict	probable	subtraction
percent	positive	deposit	decimal	statistics

Use a dictionary to find the syllable that is stressed. Then sort the spelling words by the type of short vowel sound in the stressed syllable.

Short a

1. fraction
2. calculate
3. tally
4. subtraction

Short i

5. interest
6. division
7. addition
8. predict
9. discount
10. dividend
11. statistics

Short u

12. customary

Short e

13. percent
14. metric
15. negative
16. decimal

Short o

17. borrow
18. positive
19. deposit
20. probable

Name _____ **Date** _____

Words from Math

interest	addition	calculate	discount	tally
borrow	fraction	customary	negative	dividend
division	metric	predict	probable	subtraction
percent	positive	deposit	decimal	statistics

Matching Symbols

Write the letter of the mathematical example in the right column which matches the spelling word on the left.

1. ___g___ addition **a.** $360 \div 4 = 90$
2. ___e___ fraction **b.** -1
3. ___b___ negative **c.** 2.44
4. ___a___ division **d.** $47 - 23 = 24$
5. ___c___ decimal **e.** 1/2
6. ___d___ subtraction **f.** 15%
7. ___f___ percent **g.** $2 + 7 = 9$
8. ___h___ positive **h.** $+4$

Analogies

An analogy compares the relationship between two pairs of words. Fill in the spelling word that best completes each analogy.

9. *Take* is to *give* as *lend* is to ___borrow___
10. *Yard* is to *English* as *meter* is to ___metric___
11. *Habit* is to *habitual* as *custom* is to ___customary___
12. *Subtract* is to *remove* as *add* is to ___tally___
13. *Mailbox* is to *letter* as *savings* is to ___deposit___
14. *Computer* is to *compute* as *calculator* is to ___calculate___
15. *Normal* is to *usual* as *likely* is to ___probable___

Challenge Extension: Write a definition for each challenge word. Then write a sentence using each challenge word.

The History of Money • SPELLING

Words from Math

Proofreading Activity

There are six spelling mistakes in the paragraph below. Circle the misspelled words. Write the words correctly on the lines below.

A long time ago, it was (custumary) for people to trade what they had to get what they wanted. People might (taly) their pottery bowls and trade them for some food. Depending on the harvest, a farmer might offer a (diskount) when there was an abundance of food, or perhaps (borow) from other traders when supplies were low. It is (probbable), though, that people learned how to (pradict) what supplies would be needed and in what quantity throughout the year.

1. _____customary_____   3. _____discount_____   5. _____probable_____
2. _____tally_____   4. _____borrow_____   6. _____predict_____

Writing Activity

What activities make math class more fun and interesting? Write a letter to your math teacher making some suggestions. Use four spelling words in your letter.

_____

_____

_____

_____

Words from Math

Look at the words in each set below. One word in each set is spelled correctly. Use a pencil to fill in the circle next to the correct word. Before you begin, look at the sample sets of words. Sample A has been done for you. Do Sample B by yourself. When you are sure you know what to do, you may go on with the rest of the page.

Sample A:
- (A) multiplie
- (B) multipli
- (C) multipliy
- (D) multiply

Sample B:
- (E) tryangle
- (F) triangel
- (G) triangle
- (H) tryangel

1.
(A) posative
(B) positive
(C) posativ
(D) positiv

2.
(E) dividind
(F) dividend
(G) divvidend
(H) divvidind

3.
(A) neggative
(B) negativve
(C) negative
(D) negativ

4.
(E) fraction
(F) fracion
(G) fraccion
(H) fracsion

5.
(A) probabble
(B) probable
(C) prababl
(D) prabable

6.
(E) persent
(F) pircent
(G) purcent
(H) percent

7.
(A) subtraction
(B) subractun
(C) subtracktion
(D) sibtraction

8.
(E) taly
(F) tally
(G) tallie
(H) talie

9.
(A) adition
(B) addation
(C) addition
(D) aditon

10.
(E) borrow
(F) borro
(G) borow
(H) boro

11.
(A) intrest
(B) intresst
(C) interest
(D) interesst

12.
(E) desimal
(F) decimal
(G) dessimal
(H) descima

13.
(A) depasit
(B) depossit
(C) depozit
(D) deposit

14.
(E) metric
(F) mettric
(G) metrick
(H) mettrick

15.
(A) calculate
(B) calckluate
(C) calcoolate
(D) calculat

16.
(E) divition
(F) division
(G) divicion
(H) divission

17.
(A) pridict
(B) predickt
(C) predick
(D) predict

18.
(E) discount
(F) diskount
(G) discownt
(H) diskownt

19.
(A) customary
(B) custamary
(C) custamarry
(D) customarry

20.
(E) statisstics
(F) stattistics
(G) statistics
(H) stattisstics

T57

Unit 5 Review • PRACTICE and RETEACH

Unit 5 Vocabulary Review

A. Write an answer for each question below.
[Answers will vary. Sample responses are provided.]

1. Why would a person regret a rash action?
   _____because the person didn't think before he or she acted_____

2. What is one example of a currency? _____US dollars_____

3. How might a teller help a customer? _____by accepting deposits in a bank_____

4. What are two examples of things you might store in a
   desk compartment? _____paper and pencils_____

5. How can a banister help you?
   _____You can hold on to it when walking up and down stairs_____

6. Why do people generally sign a truce? _____when they want to end a war_____

B. Select the word from the box that is a synonym for the
underlined word or words.

ferocious	fee	deliberately
void	grudged	coincidences

1. The cat, walked very <u>carefully</u> along the edge of the roof before
   jumping to a nearby tree. _____deliberately_____

2. The zoo keepers found that the new lion was too <u>fierce</u> to be kept in
   the cage with the others. _____ferocious_____

3. Maria thought seeing her sister in the crowded stores three times in
   one afternoon was one of those <u>amazing occurrences</u>. _____coincidences_____

4. The museum had a reduced entrance <u>cost</u> for students. _____fee_____

5. The astronauts looked out of their shuttle window into the <u>empty space</u> that
   surrounded them. _____void_____

6. Sheila shrugged and <u>unwillingly admitted</u> that Sarah deserved the lead
   in the school play. _____grudged_____

Unit 5 Vocabulary Review

A. Read each vocabulary word in the first column. Then find its antonym in
the second column. Write the letter of the antonym on the blank line
before each word.

Column 1		Column 2
1. __f__	sheepishly	**a.** threaten
2. __e__	lavishly	**b.** sour
3. __a__	reassure	**c.** still
4. __h__	thunderous	**d.** obedience
5. __b__	sweeten	**e.** simply
6. __g__	loans	**f.** forcefully
7. __c__	maneuvering	**g.** repayments
8. __d__	troublemaking	**h.** quiet

B. Select a word from the box to complete each sentence.

bartering	automated	bloodstream	mufflers
porcelain	rhythmically	handshake	barley

1. The museum guide told us that the _____porcelain_____ figurine of the
   dog was 100 years old.

2. Before money was used, _____bartering_____ was the way that people
   acquired goods.

3. The cook added _____barley_____, carrots, and potatoes to the stew.

4. Because of the infection in her _____bloodstream_____, Marla will have to stay
   in bed for a few more days.

5. The jazz musician tapped her feet _____rhythmically_____ as she played the piano.

6. We sealed the agreement with a _____handshake_____ we didn't need a
   written contract.

7. By using the new _____automated_____ banking system, customers can save time.

At Home: Have students identify a synonym for each
185   vocabulary word in part A.

Book 6/ Unit 5
Vocabulary Review [15]

Unit 5 Vocabulary Review

A. Complete each sentence with a vocabulary word from the box. Then use the
vocabulary word to complete the crossword puzzle.

sweeten	lavishly	handshake	bartering	thunderous	teller

Across

2. The queen's gown was
   _____lavishly_____
   decorated.

3. I was scared of the lion's
   _____thunderous_____ roar.

6. The teacher greeted each student
   with a _____handshake_____.

Down

1. By _____bartering_____, I was able to trade my old book for
   a new one.

4. Add sugar to the cake mix to _____sweeten_____ it.

5. The _____teller_____ helped Mary open a bank account.

```
        B
 L A V I S H L Y
        R
  T H U N D E R O U S
        E       W
        R       E
        I     T E
 H A N D S H A K E
        G     L T
              L E
              E N
              R
```

B. Read each vocabulary word in column 1. Then find the word in column 2 that
means the same or nearly the same thing. Write the letter of the word on the line.

Column 1		Column 2
__b__	1. void	**a.** fierce
__a__	2. ferocious	**b.** emptiness
__c__	3. automated	**c.** mechanical
__d__	4. deliberately	**d.** carefully

Unit 5 Vocabulary Review

A. Choose a vocabulary word from the box to answer each question. Write your
answer on the blank line.

currency	waving	banister	porcelain
barley	bloodstream	rash	reassure

1. If you wanted to make a sick friend feel better, what would you do? _____reassure_____

2. If you wanted to pay for a book, what would you use? _____currency_____

3. If you did something rude, without thinking, how might you describe your action?
   _____rash_____

4. Where might you find an infection in your body? _____bloodstream_____

5. What would you hold on to as you walked up the stairs? _____banister_____

6. What might a tea cup be made from? _____porcelain_____

7. What type of grain might you find in soup? _____barley_____

8. If a flag was moving in the breeze, how might you describe it? _____waving_____

B. Select a vocabulary word from the box to complete each sentence below.

grudged	rhythmically	fee	troublemaking
coincidences	maneuvering	loans	truce

1. We will have to pay an entrance _____fee_____ of $5 for the fair.

2. The _____maneuvering_____ car backed up and hit another car in the parking lot.

3. "I guess your painting was better than mine to have won first prize," Carla
   _____grudged_____.

4. The city council voted to repay all the _____loans_____ the town owed.

5. The audience clapped _____rhythmically_____ as the musicians played.

6. The _____truce_____ signed by the commanders ended the war.

At Home: Have students make up a question that can be
185   answered by one of the vocabulary words in part B.

Book 6/ Unit 5
Unit 5 Vocabulary Review [14]

Unit 5 Review • EXTEND and GRAMMAR

Unit 5 Vocabulary Review

A. Read the paragraph. Use the vocabulary words below to fill in the blanks.

loan	fee	currency	bartering
sheepishly	coincidences	handshake	

By a series of strange <u>coincidences</u> Jack finally had an opportunity to get the <u>loan</u> he needed to start his business. There was an expensive license <u>fee</u> that Jack could not afford. He spent months <u>bartering</u> his computer skills for time online at the local community college. Jack now had everything he needed to begin, except <u>currency</u> for the fee. "Who would give a loan to a young kid such as me," Jack said, grinning <u>sheepishly</u> "with nothing going for him but a great idea?" Jack now had found that person in Mrs. Colgan, a local software entrepreneur. Jack and Mrs. Colgan closed the deal with a <u>handshake</u>, a smile, and lots of paperwork.

B. On a separate piece of paper write your own story using as many vocabulary words as you can.

Answers will vary but should make correct use of the vocabulary.

At Home: Have students use *sweeten, barley, knickers, mufflers,* and *deliberately* in a paragraph.

Unit 5 Vocabulary Review

Read the paragraph. Use the vocabulary words to fill in the blanks.

grudged	rhythmically	porcelain	ferocious
lavishly	thunderous	waving	

The <u>thunderous</u> sound of water crashing on the beach woke Keesha. She knew a storm was coming, even before she checked her computer. As a meteorologist, Keesha had been trained to recognize the early signs of a <u>ferocious</u> storm. She looked out at the ocean, the water <u>rhythmically</u> rolling forward and back. Keesha put on her sun hat to shield her delicate, <u>porcelain</u> skin and began her morning walk. She saw her grouchy neighbor raising a hand and <u>waving</u> a silent hello. She was sure he felt he was greeting her <u>lavishly</u>. Keesha went up to the old man and warned him about the storm. He <u>grudged</u> a thank you, and Keesha smiled as she made her way along the windy shore.

On a separate piece of paper, create a crossword puzzle using as many vocabulary words as you can.

At Home: Use *truce, rash, reassure, bloodstream,* and *maneuvering* in a paragraph.

Pronouns

Read the passage. Circle the letter of the word that belongs in each space.

Ruben said, "Shameka and I ___(1)___ for the school paper *Pen, Pencil, and Keyboard*. It is very popular. I'm sure you ___(2)___ heard of it." Ruben paused. Then he added, "Many pick up ___(3)___ copy in the library."

1. **A.** write
   B. writes
   C. written
   D. writing

2. **F.** has
   G. had
   H. hasn't
   J. have

3. **A.** they're
   B. their
   C. there
   D. them

Lisa told ___(4)___ that she lost her essay "A Ride on Pegasus." She asked, "If you and Kate find my paper, will you give ___(5)___ to me?" She looked concerned. I replied, "Of course. Do you want ___(6)___ to help you look for the assignment?"

4. **A.** Rosey and me
   B. me and Rosey
   C. Rosey and I
   D. I and Rosey

5. **F.** her
   G. them
   H. it
   J. him

6. **A.** we
   B. they
   C. us
   D. he

Pronouns

Read the sentences below. What is the antecedent for each underlined pronoun? Circle the letter of your answer.

Casey needed to talk to Phil, so <u>she</u> called him on the phone. Paw Paw and she
___(7)___
wanted to know if he would drive <u>them</u> to the market. Phil agreed and said they
___(8)___
could ride with <u>him</u> the next day.
___(9)___

7. **A.** Casey
   B. needed
   C. so
   D. phone

8. **F.** if
   G. market
   H. wanted
   J. Paw Paw and she

9. **A.** agreed
   B. Phil
   C. with
   D. they

Read the sentences below. What form of pronoun is each underlined word?

I cannot find <u>my</u> pencil. I will ask Tom if I may borrow <u>his</u>. If not, I'll ask <u>someone</u>
(10)   (11)   (12)
else to lend me one.

10. **A.** Subject pronoun
    B. Indefinite pronoun
    C. Possessive pronoun
    D. Object pronoun

11. **F.** Indefinite pronoun
    G. Object pronoun
    H. Possessive pronoun
    J. Subject pronoun

12. **A.** Possessive pronoun
    B. Object pronoun
    C. Indefinite pronoun
    D. Subject pronoun

Unit 5 Review • SPELLING

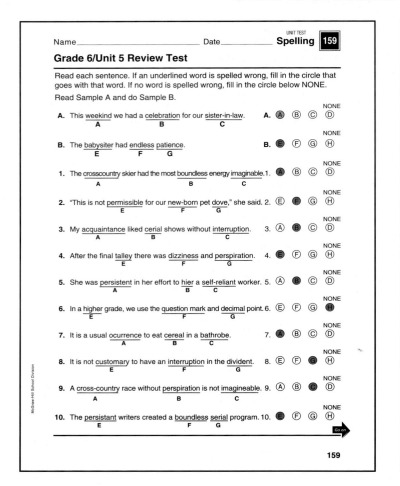

Grade 6/Unit 5 Review Test

Read each sentence. If an underlined word is spelled wrong, fill in the circle that goes with that word. If no word is spelled wrong, fill in the circle below NONE.

Read Sample A and do Sample B.

A. This <u>weekind</u> we had a <u>celebration</u> for our <u>sister-in-law</u>.   A.   Ⓐ Ⓑ Ⓒ Ⓓ NONE
     A   B   C

B. The <u>babysiter</u> had <u>endless</u> <u>patience</u>.   B.   Ⓔ Ⓕ Ⓖ Ⓗ NONE
     E   F   G

1. The <u>crosscountry</u> skier had the most <u>boundless</u> energy <u>imaginable</u>.1.   Ⓐ Ⓑ Ⓒ Ⓓ NONE
       A   B   C

2. "This is not <u>permissible</u> for our <u>new-born</u> pet <u>dove</u>," she said. 2.   Ⓔ Ⓕ Ⓖ Ⓗ NONE
          E   F   G

3. My <u>acquaintance</u> liked <u>cerial</u> shows without <u>interruption</u>.   3.   Ⓐ Ⓑ Ⓒ Ⓓ NONE
     A   B   C

4. After the final <u>talley</u> there was <u>dizziness</u> and <u>perspiration</u>.   4.   Ⓔ Ⓕ Ⓖ Ⓗ NONE
        E   F   G

5. She was <u>persistent</u> in her effort to <u>hier</u> a <u>self-reliant</u> worker. 5.   Ⓐ Ⓑ Ⓒ Ⓓ NONE
        A   B   C

6. In a <u>higher</u> grade, we use the <u>question mark</u> and <u>decimal</u> point.6.   Ⓔ Ⓕ Ⓖ Ⓗ NONE
       E   F   G

7. It is a usual <u>ocurrence</u> to eat <u>cereal</u> in a <u>bathrobe</u>.   7.   Ⓐ Ⓑ Ⓒ Ⓓ NONE
        A   B   C

8. It is not <u>customary</u> to have an <u>interruption</u> in the <u>divident</u>.   8.   Ⓔ Ⓕ Ⓖ Ⓗ NONE
       E   F   G

9. A <u>cross-country</u> race without <u>perspiration</u> is not <u>imagineable</u>. 9.   Ⓐ Ⓑ Ⓒ Ⓓ NONE
     A   B   C

10. The <u>persistant</u> writers created a <u>boundless</u> <u>serial</u> program. 10.   Ⓔ Ⓕ Ⓖ Ⓗ NONE
      E   F   G

Go on

Grade 6/Unit 5 Review Test

11. Is it <u>permisible</u> to have this <u>festivity</u> as a regular <u>occurrence</u>? 11.   Ⓐ Ⓑ Ⓒ Ⓓ NONE
      A   B   C

12. I'll <u>hire</u> someone <u>self-reliant</u> to take care of the <u>newborn</u>. 12.   Ⓔ Ⓕ Ⓖ Ⓗ NONE
      E   F   G

13. It's not <u>customery</u> nor <u>permissible</u> to omit a <u>question mark</u>.13.   Ⓐ Ⓑ Ⓒ Ⓓ NONE
        A   B   C

14. The <u>persistent</u> student learned to <u>tally</u> <u>decimel</u> numbers. 14.   Ⓔ Ⓕ Ⓖ Ⓗ NONE
       E   F   G

15. Is your <u>acquaintance</u> <u>self reliant</u> enough to go <u>cross-country</u>? 15.   Ⓐ Ⓑ Ⓒ Ⓓ NONE
        A   B   C

16. During the <u>festivity</u> we gave the <u>newborn</u> a <u>bathrob</u>.   16.   Ⓔ Ⓕ Ⓖ Ⓗ NONE
       E   F   G

17. In a state of <u>diziness</u> she <u>dove</u> off the <u>higher</u> cliff.   17.   Ⓐ Ⓑ Ⓒ Ⓓ NONE
         A   B   C

18. The <u>occurrence</u> included a <u>tally</u> of raisins in the <u>sereal</u>.   18.   Ⓔ Ⓕ Ⓖ Ⓗ NONE
       E   F   G

19. It is <u>customary</u> for the <u>festivity</u> to go without <u>interruption</u>. 19.   Ⓐ Ⓑ Ⓒ Ⓓ NONE
       A   B   C

20. My <u>aquaintance</u> will help you <u>tally</u> your <u>dividend</u> earnings. 20.   Ⓔ Ⓕ Ⓖ Ⓗ NONE
       E   F   G

21. I put a <u>deposit</u> on the fanciest <u>bathrobe</u> <u>imaginable</u>.   21.   Ⓐ Ⓑ Ⓒ Ⓓ NONE
        A   B   C

22. I was <u>persistent</u> that the <u>dividend</u> should be no <u>higher</u>.   22.   Ⓔ Ⓕ Ⓖ Ⓗ NONE
       E   F   G

23. It's <u>imaginable</u> that the <u>serial</u> will stop during the <u>festividy</u>. 23.   Ⓐ Ⓑ Ⓒ Ⓓ NONE
       A   B   C

24. It is not <u>customary</u> to have a <u>decimal</u> point in your <u>deposet</u>.24.   Ⓔ Ⓕ Ⓖ Ⓗ NONE
       E   F   G

25. The <u>dizziness</u> caused <u>persperation</u> at the <u>higher</u> peaks.   25.   Ⓐ Ⓑ Ⓒ Ⓓ NONE
       A   B   C

Grade 6/Unit 5
Unit Review Test 25

Story Elements

 OBJECTIVES Students will explore how character is exhibited in portraits, identify famous people through oral descriptions, and mime well-known characters.

Alternate Activities

Visual

A FACE FULL OF CHARACTER

 Materials: portraits of well-known individuals

Students will explore how character is expressed in portraits of famous people.

- Make available portraits or photos of famous people, past and present.

 Ask students to translate one of the portraits into a written description of the person pictured. Tell them to use every bit of visual evidence they can find to write a word picture of the person as the artist or photographer depicted him or her.

- Afterward, ask volunteers to read and discuss their work.

▶ **Intrapersonal**

Auditory

GUESS WHO?

 Materials: character-descriptive passages in biographies of famous people

Students will identify famous people by listening to character descriptions.

- Tell students that you are going to read about someone they all know. Ask them to listen carefully. After each reading, have them write down who they think is being described.

- Ask students what they heard that made them reach their conclusion.

 Invite students to think of someone well-known and to write a paragraph describing him or her. Afterward, students can read their character sketches while others try to guess the person being described.

▶ **Linguistic**

Kinesthetic

WHO AM I?

Materials: sheets of paper with the names and traits of familiar story characters

Students will explore character traits, motives, and feelings by miming a story character.

- Organize groups of 3 or 4. Give each student a piece of paper on which is written a familiar story character's name and some of the character's traits.

- Ask students to take turns portraying their character without words, while the others watch closely and try to guess who is being presented. Whoever guesses correctly should tell what actions(s) or expression(s) revealed the character.

▶ **Bodily/Kinesthetic**

See Reteach 149, 153, 174

Graphic Aids

Alternate Activities

Visual

FAMILY TREE

 Materials: example of family tree drawn on chalkboard, pencils, markers, paper

Students will construct a three-generation family tree based on a visual example.

- Draw a simple version of a three-generation family tree on the chalkboard.

- Explain the family tree to students. Then ask them to copy the pattern on a large piece of drawing paper and fill in the appropriate names for their families. Point out that grandparents' names should appear first, parents' names next, and their own and their siblings' names last.

  ▶ **Logical/Mathematical**

Kinesthetic

CAPTION FREEZE

 Students will work together to create captions for tableaus.

- Organize students into small groups. Have each group brainstorm a scene from a story they would like to act out.

- Ask one group at a time to act out its scene in front of the class. At an appropriate time during the scene, call out "Freeze."

- Tell the student audience to imagine that the tableau is a photo in a book. Invite each student to write a caption telling about the scene. Then ask volunteers to share their captions with the class.

- Continue the activity as other groups act out their scenes.

  ▶ **Bodily/Kinesthetic**

Auditory

NAME THAT CHARACTER

 Students will describe a memorable character from a favorite story.

- Organize students into pairs. Have each partner think about a character from a recently read story.

- Have partners take turns describing their characters without naming them. Encourage them to use descriptive language and details, listing as many of the character's traits as they can think of.

- Invite the other partner to record the information on a "character traits" chart.

- Have the listening partner use the information on the chart to guess the character.

  ▶ **Spatial**

See Reteach 152, 159, 166, 173, 180

Make Inferences

TESTED

✓OBJECTIVES Students will infer the punch-line of sight gags, guess which story character would say a certain thing, and infer what is happening in a pantomimed scene.

Alternate Activities

Visual

I KNOW WHAT WILL HAPPEN NEXT

ONE

Materials: a silent comedy video or a cartoon; video player and television

Students will infer the punch-line of sight gags in a silent film comedy or cartoon.

- Begin playing the video. Pause in the middle of the first sight gag. Ask students what's going to happen next. Inevitably they will be right. Ask what made them so sure. Encourage them to see that it was the combination of the evidence in front of them and their experience of similar situations in other films and cartoons.

- Go on to the next big sight gag and repeat the process.
  ▶ **Logical/Mathematical**

Auditory

WHO'D SAY THAT?

ONE

Materials: a page of 10 to 12 sentences representing well-known characters' points of view.

Students will listen to sentences that would be typical for story characters they know, and identify who would have said them.

- Compose 10 or 12 sentences representing well-known characters' points of view. These should

be invented sentences that might well be spoken by these characters. For example:

I was just going to take a quick nap. I didn't really give much thought to the fact that I was trespassing.

[Goldilocks]

- Ask the class to listen to each sentence as you read it, and to think about which story character they know would say or think such a thing. Invite students to offer their answers and explanations.
  ▶ **Logical/Mathematical**

Kinesthetic

NAME THAT SCENE

PARTNERS

Materials: slips of paper with scenarios for students to pantomime

Students will take turns pantomiming everyday situations while a partner tries to guess the activity.

- On a slip of paper, write a scenario such as:
  One person is giving directions to another.

- Pass out two situation cards to each pair. Tell students they must take turns acting out the situation without speaking.

- Partners will try to guess each other's situation.
  ▶ **Bodily/Kinesthetic**

See Reteach 154, 161, 175

Denotation and Connotation

OBJECTIVES **Students will explore the meanings of denotation and connotation through examination of photographs, art, music, and their own emotions.**

Alternate
Activities

Visual

FIGURATIVE MEANING

 Materials: abstract art pictures and clear photographs of actual objects

Students will explore the distinction between denotation and connotation by comparing and contrasting the expressive properties of representational photographs and abstract art.

- Show students a photograph of a specific object. Ask students what is being represented. Then show an abstract art picture. Point out that while no specific object is being represented, the painting may strongly suggest objects, feelings, and ideas.

- Ask students what the abstract art suggests to them, and why.

- Alternate showings and discussions of art and photos. Discuss the differences between them.

▶ **Intrapersonal**

Auditory

THE MEANING OF MUSIC

Materials: recordings of songs that tell a story, and of pieces of music that are highly suggestive of specific emotions or ideas

Students will examine songs that tell a story and other music that is evocative but non-illustrative.

- Suggest to students that one kind of music is definitely about something. For example, play a song, such as "When Johnny Comes Marching Home." Ask students what the song is about.

- Then inform students that some music isn't about anything specifically, but when people listen to it, the music makes them feel certain emotions.

- Play examples of this kind of music, such as the third movement of Chopin's second piano sonata ("The Funeral March"). Ask students what this piece suggests to them, and why.

▶ **Musical**

Kinesthetic

MEANINGFUL EXPRESSIONS

Materials: drawing materials

Students will explore the concepts of denotation and connotation by drawing their own faces in various emotional states, and by drawing abstract representations.

- Invite students to draw on separate sheets their own faces as they look when happy, angry, and unhappy. Then, on three other pieces of paper, ask them to draw abstract versions of happiness, anger, and unhappiness.

- Organize the class into groups of four. Have students take turns showing their self-portraits and their abstract representations.

- Invite other group members to identify the pictures and to discuss reasons for their answers.

▶ **Spatial**

See Reteach 155, 176, 183

Judgments and Decisions

Alternate  Activities

Visual

WHAT MAKES A GOOD PENCIL?

Materials: various types of pencils

Students will consider the characteristics of the best version of a writing tool.

- Ask students to think about the ideal pencil, one they would love to have. What does it look like? What makes it ideal? Solicit answers to these questions and write the criteria for an ideal pencil on the chalkboard.

- Then show various pencils (eyebrow, eraserless, mechanical, etc.), one by one, and ask students how well each one fits the criteria on the chalkboard. How does it make the grade? How does it fall short? Which one comes closest to the ideal?

▶ **Logical/Mathematical**

Auditory

SOUNDS GOOD TO ME

By listening to you present several versions of a short speech, students will identify good and bad elements of public speaking.

- Ask students to think about all the people they have heard giving speeches: politicians, actors, teachers, etc. Ask them to think about how a person talks when giving a speech.

- Write the following sentence on the board: *And so, my friends, if we all work together, someday the city of Townville will be the greatest city in the world.*

- Discuss rules for delivering a speech effectively (speak clearly, speak up, don't mumble, etc.). Then ask for volunteers to read the line on the board aloud.

- Encourage students to critique each delivery including their own, according to the criteria they come up with.

▶ **Linguistic**

Kinesthetic

EXERCISE JUDGMENT

 Students will work together to come up with goals for a daily exercise program.

- Organize groups of 4 or 5. Ask the groups to generate a list of three or more benefits of having the class get up once a day for a few minutes to exercise in place.

- Have groups work together to come up with a five-minute set of exercises the class can perform.

- After a reasonable length of time, invite each group to report on their criteria and perform samples of the exercises they chose. Ask each group for a description of exercises that didn't make the final cut.

▶ **Bodily/Kinesthetic**

See Reteach 163, 167, 181

Context Clues

OBJECTIVES Students will explore the strategy of using context clues by looking at, listening to, and touching the components of a particular context, and guessing what the context is.

Alternate Activities

Visual

A COMPLETE PICTURE

ONE **Materials:** several sets of pictures of components of a setting or an activity, such as: a stethoscope, a reflex hammer, and a glass of tongue depressors.

Students will look at a number of components of a particular activity or environment and draw a picture of their context.

- Show students pictures of a group of related objects. Ask them to draw a setting that would be likely to contain all of the objects.

- Invite students to show their drawings and explain their reasoning. Then repeat with other sets of pictures.
  ▶ **Intrapersonal**

Auditory

THIS SOUNDS LIKE THE PLACE

PARTNERS **Materials:** sounds of different environments, such as restaurant (or dinner-table) sounds of silverware clanking, liquid being poured into a glass, etc.

Students will listen to a number of related sounds of a particular activity or environment and draw a picture of their likely context.

- Organize students into pairs. Play (or imitate) sounds from a distinct setting. Ask students to draw a setting where they would be likely to hear the sounds you played or made.

- Have partners share their drawings and their reasoning with the class. Then repeat with other sets of sounds.
  ▶ **Logical/Mathematical**

Kinesthetic

I'VE GOT A FEELING

ONE **Materials:** paper bags containing components that go together, such as checkers and a checkerboard, or a dog bone, dog biscuit, and dog collar.

Students will examine a number of components of a particular activity or environment by touch, and name the context being represented.

- Give each student a bag of related items.

- Instruct students to feel inside their bags but not to look at any items. When they think they know what setting the items in their bags belong to, have students write it down on a piece of paper.

- Invite students to discuss what they felt in their bag and how they decided on a context for them.
  ▶ **Bodily/Kinesthetic**

See Reteach 162, 169, 182

Sequence of Events

OBJECTIVES Students will determine the proper sequence
of events in the life cycle of a metamorphosing animal, in a story
told out of order, and in a partner's favorite activity or chore.

Alternate

Visual

THE EGG COMES FIRST

 Materials: a series of pictures representing
the life cycle of a butterfly or frog

Students will draw or write the correct order of
the life cycle of a frog or butterfly to show an
understanding of sequence of events.

• Show students a mixed-up series of pictures
representing the life cycle of a butterfly or frog.

 Have students draw or write down the
life-cycle stages in correct order. Repeat
the showing as often as students request.

▶ Logical/Mathematical

Auditory

START AT THE BEGINNING

 Materials: drawing paper, pencils, pens,
crayons

Students will draw a comic strip showing the
correct order of a story they have been told out
of order.

• Distribute drawing materials to the class.

• Inform students that you are going to read
them a short story, but with its events not in
the correct order. Ask them to listen closely as
you read it.

• Before you begin a second reading of the story,
encourage students to fix it by creating a comic
strip of it in correct sequence. If asked, read the
story slowly a third time. Review students' work
in discussion. What clues led them to draw the
parts of the story in the order they chose?

▶ Logical/Mathematical

Kinesthetic

WHAT DOES YOUR PARTNER DO?

 Students will watch and imitate a partner
pretending to perform a chore or favorite
activity in correct sequence.

• Have each partner think of a favorite hobby,
chore, or sport. Encourage students to take turns
acting out the activity in 4 to 6 sequential steps.
For example, running: put on running clothes
and shoes, warm up, run, cool down, shower, get
dressed again.

• Invite the observing partner to replicate the
process in the correct sequence.

▶ Bodily/Kinesthetic

See Reteach 156, 160, 168, 177

A Communication Tool

Although typewriters and computers are readily available, many situations continue to require handwriting. Tasks such as keeping journals, completing forms, taking notes, making shopping or organizational lists, and the ability to read hand-written manuscript or cursive writing are a few examples of practical application of this skill.

BEFORE YOU BEGIN

Before children begin to write, certain fine motor skills need to be developed. Examples of activities that can be used as warm-up activities are:

- **Simon Says** Play a game of Simon Says using just finger positions.
- **Finger Plays and Songs** Sing songs that use Signed English, American Sign Language or finger spelling.
- **Mazes** Mazes are available in a wide range of difficulty. You can also create mazes that allow children to move their writing instruments from left to right.

Determining Handedness

Keys to determining handedness in a child:

- Which hand does the child eat with? This is the hand that is likely to become the dominant hand.
- Does the child start coloring with one hand and then switch to the other? This may be due to fatigue rather than lack of hand preference.
- Does the child cross midline to pick things up or use the closest hand? Place items directly in front of the child to see if one hand is preferred.
- Does the child do better with one hand or the other?

The Mechanics of Writing

DESK AND CHAIR

- Chair height should allow for the feet to rest flat on the floor.
- Desk height should be two inches above the level of the elbows when the child is sitting.
- The chair should be pulled in allowing for an inch of space between the child's abdomen and the desk.
- Children sit erect with the elbows resting on the desk.
- Children should have models of letters on the desk or at eye level, not above their heads.

PAPER POSITION

- **Right-handed children** should turn the paper so that the lower left-hand corner of the paper points to the abdomen.

- **Left-handed children** should turn the paper so that the lower right-hand corner of the paper points to the abdomen.

- The nondominant hand should anchor the paper near the top so that the paper doesn't slide.
- The paper should be moved up as the child nears the bottom of the paper. Many children won't think of this and may let their arms hang off the desk when they reach the bottom of a page.

The Writing Instrument Grasp

For handwriting to be functional, the writing instrument must be held in a way that allows for fluid dynamic movement.

FUNCTIONAL GRASP PATTERNS

- **Tripod Grasp** With open web space, the writing instrument is held with the tip of the thumb and the index finger and rests against the side of the third finger. The thumb and index finger form a circle.
- **Quadrupod Grasp** With open web space, the writing instrument is held with the tip of the thumb and index finger and rests against the fourth finger. The thumb and index finger form a circle.

INCORRECT GRASP PATTERNS

- **Fisted Grasp** The writing instrument is held in a fisted hand.

- **Pronated Grasp** The writing instrument is held diagonally within the hand with the tips of the thumb and index finger on the writing instrument but with no support from other fingers.
- **Five-Finger Grasp** The writing instrument is held with the tips of all five fingers.

TO CORRECT WRITING INSTRUMENT GRASPS

- Have children play counting games with an eye dropper and water.
- Have children pick up small objects with a tweezer.
- Do counting games with children picking up small coins using just the thumb and index finger.

FLEXED OR HOOKED WRIST

- The writing instrument can be held in a variety of grasps with the wrist flexed or bent. This is typically seen with left-handed writers but is also present in some right-handed writers. To correct wrist position, have children check their writing posture and paper placement.

Evaluation Checklist

Functional writing is made up of two elements, legibility and functional speed.

LEGIBILITY

MANUSCRIPT

Formation and Strokes

☑ Does the child begin letters at the top?

☑ Do circles close?

☑ Are the horizontal lines straight?

☑ Do circular shapes and extender and descender lines touch?

☑ Are the heights of all upper-case letters equal?

☑ Are the heights of all lower-case letters equal?

☑ Are the lengths of the extenders and descenders the same for all letters?

Directionality

☑ Are letters and words formed from left to right?

☑ Are letters and words formed from top to bottom?

Spacing

☑ Are the spaces between letters equidistant?

☑ Are the spaces between words equidistant?

☑ Do the letters rest on the line?

☑ Are the top, bottom and side margins even?

CURSIVE

Formation and Strokes

☑ Do circular shapes close?

☑ Are the downstrokes parallel?

☑ Do circular shapes and downstroke lines touch?

☑ Are the heights of all upper-case letters equal?

☑ Are the heights of all lower-case letters equal?

☑ Are the lengths of the extenders and descenders the same for all letters?

☑ Do the letters which finish at the top join the next letter?
(*l, o, v, w*)

☑ Do the letters which finish at the bottom join the next letter? (*a, c, d, h, i, k, l, m, n, r, s, t, u, x*)

☑ Do letters with descenders join the next letter? (*f, g, j, p, q, y, z*)

☑ Do all letters touch the line?

☑ Is the vertical slant of all letters consistent?

Directionality

☑ Are letters and words formed from left to right?

☑ Are letters and words formed from top to bottom?

Spacing

☑ Are the spaces between letters equidistant?

☑ Are the spaces between words equidistant?

☑ Do the letters rest on the line?

☑ Are the top, bottom and side margins even?

SPEED

The prettiest handwriting is not functional for classroom work if it takes the child three times longer than the rest of the class to complete work assignments. After the children have been introduced to writing individual letters, begin to add time limitations to the completion of copying or writing assignments. Then check the child's work for legibility.

Handwriting Models—Manuscript

A B C D E F G H
I J K L M N O P
Q R S T U V W
X Y Z

a b c d e f g h
i j k l m n o p
q r s t u v w
x y z

Handwriting Models—Cursive

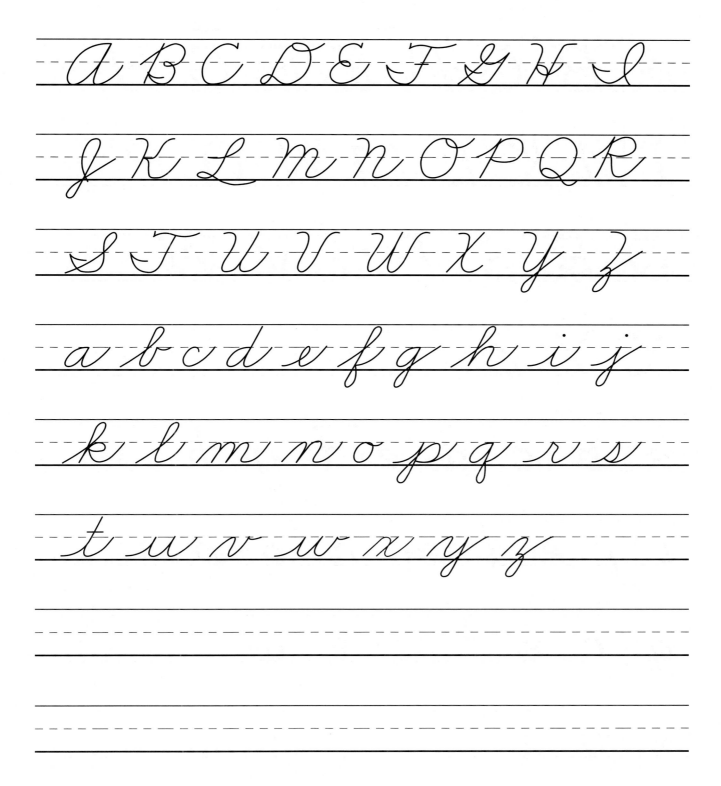

Handwriting Models—Slant

A B C D E F G H

I J K L M N O P

Q R S T U V W

X Y Z

a b c d e f g h

i j k l m n o p

q r s t u v w

x y z

Handwriting Practice

Selection Titles

Honors, Prizes, and Awards

S.O.R. LOSERS
Unit 1, p. 20
by *Avi*
Illustrated by *Randy Verougstraete*

Author: Avi, winner of Jackrabbit Award (1989) for *Romeo and Juliet Together (and alive!) at Last*; Newbery Honor Book (1991) for *True Confessions of Charlotte Doyle*; (1992) for *Nothing But the Truth*

RAIN, RAIN, GO AWAY
Unit 1, p. 86
by *Isaac Asimov*
Illustrated by *Bruno Paciulli*

Author: Isaac Asimov, winner of Hugo Award, Nebula Award (1973) for *The Gods Themselves*; Washington Post/Children's Book Guild Nonfiction Award (1985)

DAYDREAMERS
Unit 1, p. 110
by *Eloise Greenfield*

Poet: Eloise Greenfield, winner of Boston Globe-Horn Book Award (1974) for *She Come Bringing Me That Little Baby Girl*; Carter G. Woodson Award (1974) for *Rosa Parks*; ALA Notable (1975) for *Me and Neesie*; Jane Addams Book Award (1976) for *Paul Robeson*; ALA Notable (1977) for *Honey, I Love, and Other Love Poems*; Coretta Scott King Award (1978) for *African Dreams*; ALA Notable (1981) for *Daydreamers*; National Council of Teachers of English Award for Excellence in Poetry for Children (1997)

PEOPLE
Unit 2, p. 112
by *Charlotte Zolotow*

Poet: Charlotte Zolotow, winner of Caldecott Honor Medal (1953) for *The Storm Book*; (1963) for *Mr. Rabbit and the Lovely Present*; ALA Notable (1958) for *Do You Know What I'll Do?*; Christopher Award (1974) for *My Grandson Lew*; ALA Notable (1980) for *Say It!*; Carolyn W. Fried Award (1984) for *Some Things Go Together*

NUMBER THE STARS
Unit 2, p. 162
by *Lois Lowry*
Illustrated by *Larry Winborg*

ALA Notable, School Library Journal Best Books of the Year (1989), Newbery Medal, Booklist Editor's Choice, Horn Book Fanfare Selection, IRA Teacher's Choice (1990)
Author: Lois Lowry, winner of Boston Globe-Horn Book Award (1987) for *Rabble Starkey*; (1993) for *The Giver*

OPERA, KARATE, AND BANDITS
Unit 2, p. 190
by *Huynh Quang Nhuong*
Illustrated by *Robert Roth*

ALA Notable, Booklist Children's Editor's Choice, Notable Trade Book in the Field of Social Studies (1982), William Allen White Children's Book Award (1985)

Selection Titles	Honors, Prizes, and Awards
TO YOU Unit 3, p. 220 by *Langston Hughes*	**Poet: Langston Hughes,** winner of Witter Bynner Prize (1926); Harmon Foundation Literature Award (1931); Guggenheim Fellowship (1935); American Academy of Arts and Letters Grant (1946); Spingarn Medal (1960)
A BOY OF UNUSUAL VISION Unit 3, p. 224 by *Alice Steinbach* Photographs by *David Harp*	**Author: Alice Steinbach,** Pulitzer Prize in journalism in feature writing (1985)
THE SCHOOL PLAY Unit 3, p. 242 by *Gary Soto* Illustrated by *Jack E. Davis*	**Author: Gary Soto,** winner of Academy of American Poets Award (1975); American Book Award (1984) for *Living Up the Street*; Parenting's Reading Magic Award (1990); Best Books for Young Adults Award, California Library Association's John And Patricia Beatty Award, Best Books for Young Adults Award (1991) for *Baseball in April and Other Stories*; Americás Book Award, Honorable Mention (1995) for *Chato's Kitchen*; Americás Book Award, Commended List (1995) for *Canto Familiar*; (1996) for *The Old Man and His Door*; (1997) for *Buried Onions*
THE SINGING MAN Unit 3, p. 262 Adapted by *Angela Shelf Medearis* Illustrated by *Terea Shaffer*	**Coretta Scott King Honor Book for Illustration (1995)** **Author: Angela Shelf Medearis,** winner of IRA-Teacher's Choice Award, Primary Grades (1995) for *Our People*
PAINTERS OF THE CAVES Unit 3, p. 290 by *Patricia Lauber*	**New York Academy of Sciences Children's Science Book Award, honorable mention (1989)** **Author: Patricia Lauber,** winner of New York Times Notable Book, School Library Journal Best Book (1982) for *Journey to the Planets;* Newbery Honor Book Award (1987) for *Volcano*
PURPLE SNAKE Unit 3, p. 318 by *Pat Mora*	**Poet: Pat Mora,** winner of Americás Book Award, Commended List (1994) for *Pablo's Tree*; (1996) for *Confetti: Poems for Children*; (1997) for *Tomas and the Library Lady*

Selection Titles	Honors, Prizes, and Awards
MUMMIES, TOMBS, & TREASURE: SECRETS OF ANCIENT EGYPT Unit 4, p. 324 by *Lila Perl*	**Author: Lila Perl,** winner of ALA Notable (1965) for *Red-Flannel Hash and Shoofly Pie: American Regional Foods and Festivals;* Notable Trade Book in the Field of Social Studies (1989) for The *Great Ancestor Hunt*
OVER THE TOP OF THE WORLD Unit 4, p. 344 by *Will Steger and Jon Bowermaster* Photographs by *Gordon Wiltsie*	**Author: Jon Bowermaster,** winner of Lowell Thomas Award for Environmental Journalism (1995)
EXPLORING THE TITANIC Unit 4, p. 408 by *Robert D. Ballard*	**ALA Best Book for the Reluctant Young Adult Reader, School Library Journal Best Books of the Year, IRA Young Adult Choice (1989)**
THE MICROSCOPE Unit 4, p. 442 by *Maxine Kumin*	**Poet: Maxine Kumin,** winner of Pulitzer Prize in poetry (1973) for *Up Country*
I MAY, I MIGHT, I MUST Unit 5, p. 444 by *Marianne Moore*	**Poet: Marianne Moore,** winner of the Poetry Society of America's Shelley Memorial Award (1940); National Book Award (1951); Pulitzer Prize in poetry, National Book Award (1952) for *Collected Poems*; Bollinger Prize in Poetry (1952); Frost Medal for Distinguished Achievement (1967)
CHILD OF THE OWL Unit 5, p. 448 by *Laurence Yep* Illustrated by *Winson Trang*	**Boston Globe-Horn Book Award for Fiction (1977), Jane Addams Book Award (1978)** **Author: Laurence Yep,** winner of Boston Globe-Horn Book Honor in Nonfiction, Bologna Children's Book Fair Prize Non-Fiction Runner Up, Parenting's Reading Magic Award (1989) for *The Rainbow People*
ADVENTURE IN SPACE Unit 5, p. 484 by *Elaine Scott* Photographs by *Margaret Miller*	**School Library Journal Best Books of the Year, Booklist Editor's Choice, VOYA's Nonfiction Honor List (1995)**

Selection Titles	Honors, Prizes, and Awards
RUMPELSTILTSKIN'S DAUGHTER Unit 5, p. 504 retold by **Diane Stanley**	**ALA Notable (1998)**
MY UNCLE DAN Unit 5, p. 542 by **Ted Hughes**	**Poet: Ted Hughes,** winner of the Queen's Medal for *Poetry* (1974); ALA Notable (1975) for *Season Songs*; Signal Poetry Award (1979) for *Moon-Bells and Other Poems*; (1985) for *What Is the Truth?*; Guardian Award for Children's Fiction (1985) for *What Is the Truth?*
MANDELA Unit 6, p. 548 by **Floyd Cooper**	**Author/Illustrator: Floyd Cooper,** winner of Coretta Scott King Honor Book Award (1995) for *Meet Danitra Brown*
ALEXANDER THE GREAT Unit 6, p. 602 by **Olivia Coolidge**	**Author: Olivia Coolidge,** winner of Newbery Medal Honor Book (1963) for *Men of Athens*
THE CIRCUIT Unit 6, p. 622 by **Francisco Jiménez** Illustrated by **Robert Rodriguez**	**California Library Association's John and Patricia Beatty Award (1997), Americás Book Award (1997), Boston Globe-Horn Award for Fiction (1998)**
STOPPING BY WOODS ON A SNOWY EVENING Unit 6, p. 646 by **Robert Frost**	**Poet: Robert Frost,** winner of Pulitzer Prize in Poetry (1924) for *New Hampshire: A Poem with Notes and Grace Notes*; (1931) for *Collected Poems*; (1937) for *A Further Range*; (1943) for *A Witness Tree*; Poetry Society of America's Frost Medal for Distinguished Achievement (1941); Bollinger Prize in Poetry (1963)

Theme Bibliography

Trade Books

Additional fiction and nonfiction trade books related to each selection can be shared with students throughout the unit.

CHILD OF THE OWL

Journey
Patricia MacLachlan (Delacorte Press, 1991)

Journey's family is torn apart when his mother leaves. His grandfather helps him put the pieces back together. *Realistic Fiction*

The Night Journey
Kathryn Lasky (Puffin, 1986)

Rachel resents her daily visits to her great-grandmother until Nana Sasie starts to tell of her Russian childhood. *Realistic Fiction*

Sweet Whispers, Brother Rush
Virginia Hamilton (Avon, 1982)

A young girl, struggling with problems at home, develops a deeper understanding of the past. *Realistic Fiction*

BELLEROPHON AND THE FLYING HORSE

The Search for Delicious
Natalie Babbitt (Farrar, Straus and Giroux, 1969)

The King's messenger is sent searching for the meaning of "delicious." At the end of this quest, he discovers the answer. *Fiction*

Frozen Fire: A Tale of Courage
James Houston (Macmillan, 1977)

Matthew and his friend, Kayak, set out into the Arctic to search for Matthew's father, a geologist whose plane was downed in a snowstorm. *Realistic Fiction*

The Dark Is Rising
Susan Cooper (Collier, 1986)

In this Newbery Honor book, the second in The Dark Is Rising Sequence, eleven-year-old Will must defeat the forces of evil by going on a quest. *Quest/Fantasy*

Technology

Multimedia resources can be used to enhance students' understanding of the selections.

 San Francisco (Kaw Valley Films) Video, 26 min. A view of the people and geography of San Francisco.

 Lilith Summer (AIMS Multimedia) Video, 20 min. The friendship between a young girl and an elderly woman.

 Multicultural Peoples of North America, Chinese Americans (GPN) Video, 30 min. Chinese Americans share their stories.

 Mythology of Greece and Rome (Phoenix/BFA Films & Video) Video, 16 min. How myths were used to teach morals and explain nature's phenomena.

 Monsters of Greek Myths (The Chimera, Part 1) (AIMS Multimedia) 4 Filmstrips, 12 min. Video, 45 min. Bellerophon and Pegasus confront the Chimera.

 Timeless Tales: Myths of Ancient Greece (SVE) Video, 64 min. Five Greek myths are recreated through art and narration.

ADVENTURE IN SPACE

Black Stars in Orbit: NASA's African American Astronauts
Khephra Burns and William Miles (Harcourt, 1994)

The history of African Americans' contributions to NASA and space exploration, featuring astronauts as well as those who worked behind the scenes at NASA. *Nonfiction Social Studies*

To Space and Back
Sally Ride and Susan Okie (Lothrop, 1986)

The first American woman in space describes her experience aboard the space shuttle. *Nonfiction Science*

Space Exploration
Carole Scott (Knopf, 1997)

An overview of the history of space exploration that includes various missions throughout history and their findings. *Nonfiction Science*

RUMPELSTILTSKIN'S DAUGHTER

The Education of Mary
Ann Rinaldi (Hyperion, 2000)

A young racially mixed girl in 1832 New England struggles to attend school. *Realistic Fiction*

Her Stories: African American Folktales, Fairy Tales, and True Tales
Virginia Hamilton, illustrated by Leo and Diane Dillon (Blue Sky Press, 1995)

A collection of nineteen tales about African American female characters that blends legend, tall tale, and factual event. *Folk Tale*

Girls to the Rescue: Tales of Clever, Courageous Girls from around the World
Edited by Bruce Lansky (Simon and Schuster, 1995)

Ten stories that feature feisty females in settings both familiar and exotic. *Short Stories*

THE HISTORY OF MONEY

The Great Brain
John D. Fitzgerald, illustrated by Mercer Mayer (Dial, 1985)

Ten-year-old Tom Fitzgerald is brimming with ideas for raising money during the Great Depression. *Realistic Fiction*

Neale S. Godfrey's Ultimate Kids' Money Book
Neale S. Godfrey, illustrated by Randy Verougstraete (Simon & Schuster, 1998)

Playful drawings and photographs enhance this overview of the story of money, which includes a look at earning, saving, and spending. *Nonfiction*

The History of Counting
Denise Schmandt-Besserat (Morrow, 1999)

The history of one of our most important inventions. *Nonfiction Math*

 Adventures in Space: Journey to the Moon (AIMS Multimedia) Video, 27 min. Chronicle of the space race, starting with Sputnik I in 1957.

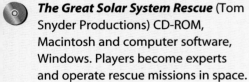 **The Great Solar System Rescue** (Tom Snyder Productions) CD-ROM, Macintosh and computer software, Windows. Players become experts and operate rescue missions in space.

Space, Earth and Atmosphere (Zenger Media) Video. Answers to some of the most difficult astronomical questions.

 Finn McCoul (AIMS/Pied Piper) Video, 30 min. Finn McCoul is a great Irish champion, but it is his wife who comes up with the plan that will keep him safe from the giant.

 From the Mixed-Up Files of Mrs. Basil E. Frankweiler (AIMS/Pied Piper) Video, 26 min. Two runaways have more than one mystery to solve before they can go home.

 Logical Journey of the Zoombinis Deluxe (ESI) CD-ROM, Macintosh, Windows. This award-winning interactive program requires players to use thinking and problem-solving skills to solve a predicament.

 Money (United Learning) Video, 14 min. Money, its history, and its defining properties are explored.

 Money, Banks, and the Role of Government (SVE Media) Video, 25 min. Learn about economic concepts and the relationships among national economies.

 The Money Story (Boston Federal Reserve Bank) Video, 33 min. An animated look at the history and functions of money.

Publishers Directory

Aladdin Paperbacks
(Imprint of Simon & Schuster Children's
Publishing)

Alaska Northwest Books
(Division of Graphic Arts Center
Publishing Co.)
3019 NW Yeon Ave.
Box 10306
Portland, OR 97296-0306
(503) 226-2402 • (800) 452-3032
Fax (503) 223-1410
www.gacpc.com

Annick Press
(Imprint of Firefly Books, Ltd.)

Atheneum
(Imprint of Simon & Schuster Children's
Publishing)

Avon Books
(Division of Hearst Corp.)
1350 Avenue of the Americas
New York, NY 10019
(212) 261-6800 • (800) 238-0658
Fax (800) 223-0239
www.avonbooks.com

**Bantam Doubleday Dell Books for
Young Readers**
(Imprint of Random House)

Peter Bedrick Books
156 Fifth Ave., Suite 817
New York, NY 10010
(800) 788-3123 • Fax (212) 206-3741

Beech Tree Books
(Imprint of William Morrow & Co.)

Blackbirch Press
260 Amity Road
Woodbridge, CT 06525
(203) 387-7525 • (800) 831-9183
www.blackbirch.com

Blue Sky Press
(Imprint of Scholastic)

Bradbury Press
(Imprint of Simon & Schuster Children's
Publishing)

BridgeWater Books
(Distributed by Penguin Putnam, Inc.)

Candlewick Press
2067 Massachusetts Avenue
Cambridge, MA 02140
(617) 661-3330 • Fax (617) 661-0565
www.candlewick.com

Carolrhoda Books
(Division of Lerner Publications Co.)

Cartwheel Books
(Imprint of Scholastic)

Children's Book Press
246 First St., Suite 101
San Francisco, CA 94105
(415) 995-2200 • Fax (415) 995-2222

Children's Press (Division of Grolier, Inc.)
P.O. Box 1795
Danbury, CT 06813-1333
(800) 621-1115 • www.grolier.com

Chronicle Books
85 Second Street, Sixth Floor
San Francisco, CA 94105
(415) 537-3730 • Fax (415) 537-4460
(800) 722-6657
www.chroniclebooks.com

Clarion Books
(Imprint of Houghton Mifflin, Inc.)
215 Park Avenue South
New York, NY 10003
(212) 420-5800 • (800) 225-3362
www.houghtonmifflinbooks.com/clarion

Crabtree Publishing Co.
350 Fifth Ave., Suite 3308
New York, NY 10118
(212) 496-5040 • (800) 387-7650
Fax (800) 355-7166
www.crabtree-pub.com

Creative Education
The Creative Co.
123 S. Broad Street
P.O. Box 227
Mankato, MN 56001
(507) 388-6273 • (800) 445-6209
Fax (507) 388-2746

Crowell (Imprint of HarperCollins)

Crown Publishing Group
(Imprint of Random House)

Delacorte
(Imprint of Random House)

Dial Books
(Imprint of Penguin Putnam, Inc.)

Discovery Enterprises, Ltd.
31 Laurelwood Dr.
Carlisle, MA 01741
(978) 287-5401 • (800) 729-1720
Fax (978) 287-5402

Disney Press
(Division of Disney Book Publishing, Inc.,
A Walt Disney Co.)
114 Fifth Ave.
New York, NY 10011
(212) 633-4400 • Fax (212) 633-4833
www.disneybooks.com

Dorling Kindersley (DK Publishing)
95 Madison Avenue
New York, NY 10016
(212) 213-4800 • Fax (212) 213-5240
(888) 342-5357 • www.dk.com

Doubleday (Imprint of Random House)

E. P. Dutton Children's Books
(Imprint of Penguin Putnam, Inc.)

Farrar Straus & Giroux
19 Union Square West
New York, NY 10003
(212) 741-6900 • Fax (212) 741-6973
(888) 330-8477

Firefly Books, Ltd.
PO Box 1338
Endicott Station
Buffalo, NY 14205
(416) 499-8412 • Fax (800) 565-6034
(800) 387-5085
www.firefly.com

Four Winds Press
(Imprint of Macmillan, see Simon &
Schuster Children's Publishing)

Fulcrum Publishing
350 Indiana Street, Suite 350
Golden, CO 80401
(303) 277-1623 • (800) 992-2908
Fax (303) 279-7111
www.fulcrum-books.com

Greenwillow Books
(Imprint of William Morrow & Co, Inc.)

Gulliver Green Books
(Imprint of Harcourt Brace & Co.)

Harcourt Brace & Co.
6277 Sea Harbor Drive
Orlando, FL 32337
(407) 345-2000 • (800) 225-3425
www.harcourtbooks.com

Harper & Row (Imprint of HarperCollins)

HarperCollins Children's Books
1350 Avenue of the Americas
New York, NY 10017
(212) 261-6500 • Fax (212) 261-6689
(800) 242-7737
www.harperchildrens.com

Harper Trophy
(Imprint of HarperCollins)

Holiday House
425 Madison Avenue
New York, NY 10017
(212) 688-0085 • Fax (212) 421-6134

Henry Holt and Company
115 West 18th Street
New York, NY 10011
(212) 886-9200 • (212) 633-0748
(888) 330-8477 • www.henryholt.com/byr/

Houghton Mifflin
222 Berkeley Street
Boston, MA 02116
(617) 351-5000 • Fax (617) 351-1125
(800) 225-3362
www.houghtonmifflinbooks.com

Hyperion Books
(Division of ABC, Inc.)
77 W. 66th St., 11th Floor
New York, NY 10023
(212) 456-0100 • www.disney.com

Just Us Books
356 Glenwood Avenue
E. Orange, NJ 07017
(973) 672-7701 • Fax (973) 677-7570
www.justusbooks.com

Kane/Miller Book Publishers
P.O. Box 310529
Brooklyn, NY 11231-0529
(718) 624-5120 • Fax (718) 858-5452
www.kanemiller.com

Alfred A. Knopf
(Imprint of Random House)

Lee & Low Books
95 Madison Avenue, Room 606
New York, NY 10016
(212) 779-4400 • Fax (212) 683-1894

Lerner Publications Co.
241 First Avenue North
Minneapolis, MN 55401
(612) 332-3344 • Fax (612) 332-7615
(800) 328-4929 • www.lernerbooks.com

Little, Brown & Co.
3 Center Plaza
Boston, MA 02108
(617) 227-0730 • Fax (617) 263-2864
(800) 759-0190 • www.littlebrown.com

Lothrop Lee & Shepard
(Imprint of William Morrow & Co.)

Macmillan
(Imprint of Simon & Schuster
Children's Publishing)

Mikaya Press
(Imprint of Firefly Books, Ltd.)

Millbrook Press, Inc.
2 Old New Milford Road
Brookfield, CT 06804
(203) 740-2220 • (800) 462-4703
Fax (203) 740-2526
www.millbrookpress.com

William Morrow Co.
(Imprint of Harper Collins)

Morrow Junior Books
(Imprint of Harper Collins)

National Geographic Society
1145 17th Street, NW
Washington, DC 20036
(800) 638-4077
www.nationalgeographic.com

Northland Publishing
(Division of Justin Industries)
Box 1389
Flagstaff, AZ 86002
(520) 774-5251 • Fax (800) 744-0592
(800) 346-3257 • www.northlandpub.com

Orchard Books (A Grolier Company)
95 Madison Avenue
New York, NY 10016
(212) 951-2600 • Fax (212) 213-6435
www.grolier.com

Oxford University Press, Inc.
198 Madison Ave.
New York, NY 10016-4314
(212) 726-6000 • (800) 451-7556
www.oup-usa.org

Penguin Putnam, Inc.
375 Hudson Street
New York, NY 10014
(212) 366-2000 • (800) 631-8571
www.penguinputnam.com

Philomel Books
(Imprint of Putnam Penguin, Inc.)

Pippin Press
Gracie Station, Box 1347
229 E. 85th Street
New York, NY 10028
(212) 288-4920 • Fax (732) 225-1562

Puffin Books
(Imprint of Penguin Putnam, Inc.)

G.P. Putnam's Sons Publishing
(Imprint of Penguin Putnam, Inc.)

Random House
1540 Broadway
New York, NY 10036
(212) 782-9000 • Fax (212) 782-9452
(800) 200-3552
www.randomhouse.com/kids

Rising Moon
(Imprint of Northland Publishing)

Scholastic
555 Broadway
New York, NY 10012
(212) 343-7500 • Fax (212) 965-7442
(800) SCHOLASTIC • www.scholastic.com

Sierra Club Books for Children
85 Second Street, Second Floor
San Francisco, CA 94105-3441
(415) 977-5500 • Fax (415) 977-5793
(800) 935-1056 • www.sierraclub.org

Silver Burdett Press
(Division of Pearson Education)
299 Jefferson Rd.
Parsippany, NJ 07054-0480
(973) 739-8000 • (800) 848-9500
www.sbgschool.com

Simon & Schuster Children's Books
1230 Avenue of the Americas
New York, NY 10020
(212) 698-7200 • (800) 223-2336
www.simonsays.com/kidzone

Gareth Stevens, Inc.
River Center Bldg.
1555 N. River Center Dr., Suite 201
Milwaukee, WI 53212
(414) 225-0333 • (800) 341-3569
Fax (414) 225-0377
www.gsinc.com

Sunburst
(Imprint of Farrar Straus & Giroux)

Tricycle Press
(Division of Ten Speed Press)
P.O. Box 7123
Berkeley, CA 94707
(510) 559-1600 • (800) 841-2665
Fax (510) 559-1637
www.tenspeed.com

Viking Children's Books
(Imprint of Penguin Putnam, Inc.)

Voyager
(Imprint of Harcourt Brace & Co.)

Walker & Co.
435 Hudson Street
New York, NY 10014
(212) 727-8300 • (212) 727-0984
(800) AT-WALKER

Warwick Publishing
162 John St.
Toronto, CAN M5V2E5
(416) 596-1555
www.warwickgp.com

Watts Publishing
(Imprint of Grolier Publishing;
see Children's Press)

Yearling Books
(Imprint of Random House)

Multimedia Resources

AIMS Multimedia
9710 DeSoto Avenue
Chatsworth, CA 91311-4409
(800) 367-2467
www.AIMS-multimedia.com

Ambrose Video and Publishing
28 West 44th Street, Suite 2100
New York, NY 10036
(800) 526-4663 • Fax (212) 768-9282
www.AmbroseVideo.com

BFA Educational Media
(see The Phoenix Learning Group)

Boston Federal Reserve Bank
Community Affairs Dept.
P.O. Box 2076
Boston, MA 02106-2076
(617) 973-3459
www.bos.frb.org

Britannica
310 South Michigan Avenue
Britannica Center
Chicago, IL 60604-4293
(800) 621-3900 • Fax (800) 344-9624

Broderbund
(Parsons Technology;
also see The Learning Company)
500 Redwood Blvd
Novato, CA 94997
(800) 395-0277 • www.broderbund.com

Carousel Film and Video
260 Fifth Avenue, Suite 705
New York, NY 10001
(212) 683-1660 • e-mail:
carousel@pipeline.com

CBS/Fox Video
1330 Avenue of the Americas
New York, NY 10019
(800) 457-0686

Cornell University Audio/Video Resource Ctr.
8 Business & Technology Park
Ithaca, NY 14850
(607) 255-2091

Coronet/MTI
(see The Phoenix Learning Group)

Direct Cinema, Ltd.
P.O. Box 10003
Santa Monica, CA 90410-1003
(310) 636-8200

Encyclopaedia Britannica Educational Corp.
310 South Michigan Avenue
Chicago, IL 60604
(800) 522-8656 • www.eb.com

ESI/Educational Software
4213 S. 94th Street
Omaha, NE 68127
(800) 955-5570 • www.edsoft.com

Films for the Humanities and Sciences
P.O. Box 2053
Princeton, NJ 08543-2053
(800) 257-5126 • Fax (609) 275-3767
www.films.com

GPN/Reading Rainbow
University of Nebraska-Lincoln
P.O. Box 80669
Lincoln, NE 68501-0669
(800) 228-4630 • www.gpn.unl.edu

Journal Films and Videos
1560 Sherman Avenue, Suite 100
Evanston, IL 60201
(800) 323-9084

Kaw Valley Films
P.O. Box 3900
Shawnee, KS 66208
(800) 332-5060

Library Video Company
P.O. Box 580
Wynnewood, PA 19096
(800) 843-3620
www.libraryvideo.com

Listening Library
One Park Avenue
Greenwich, CT 06870-1727
(800) 733-3000 • www.listeninglib.com

Macmillan/McGraw-Hill
(see SRA/McGraw-Hill)

Marshmedia
P.O. Box 8082
Shawnee Mission, KS 66208
(800) 821-3303 • Fax (816) 333-7421
marshmedia.com

MECC
(see the Learning Company)

National Geographic Society School Publishing
P.O. Box 10597
Des Moines, IA 50340-0597
(888) 225-5647
www.nationalgeographic.com

New Jersey Network
1573 Parkside Ave.
Trenton, NJ 08625-0777
(609) 530-5180

PBS Video
1320 Braddock Place
Alexandria, VA 22314
(800) 344-3337 • www.pbs.org

Phoenix Films
(see The Phoenix Learning Group)

The Phoenix Learning Group
2348 Chaffee Drive
St. Louis, MO 63146
(800) 221-1274 • e-mail:
phoenixfilms@worldnet.att.net

Pied Piper (see AIMS Multimedia)

Rainbow Educational Video
170 Keyland Court
Bohemia, NY 11716
(800) 331-4047

Social Studies School Service
10200 Jefferson Boulevard, Room 14
P.O. Box 802
Culver City, CA 90232-0802
(800) 421-4246 • Fax (310) 839-2249
socialstudies.com

SRA/McGraw-Hill
220 East Danieldale Road
De Soto, TX 75115
(888) 772-4543 • www.sra4kids.com

SVE/Churchill Media
6677 North Northwest Highway
Chicago, IL 60631
(800) 829-1900 • www.svemedia.com

Tom Snyder Productions (also see ESI)
80 Coolidge Hill Rd.
Watertown, MA 02472
(800) 342-0236 • www.teachtsp.com

Troll Associates
100 Corporate Drive
Mahwah, NJ 07430
(888) 998-7655 • Fax (800) 979-8765
www.troll.com

United Learning
6633 W. Howard St.
Niles, IL 60714-3389
(800) 424-0362
www.unitedlearning.com

Weston Woods
12 Oakwood Avenue
Norwalk, CT 06850
(800) 243-5020 • Fax (203) 845-0498

Zenger Media
10200 Jefferson Blvd., Room 94
P.O. Box 802
Culver City, CA 90232-0802
(800) 421-4246 • Fax (800) 944-5432
www.Zengermedia.com

UNIT 1

	Vocabulary	Spelling			
S.O.R. Losers	attitude bribe cringing defect pep treason	**Words with Short Vowels**			
		pressure crafty prison cleanse **rotten**	**flung** spongy **tension** abstract **brilliant**	realm **soccer** plunge hover nectar	badger missile novel summon singular
The All-American Slurp	acquainted buffet inflections relish residence rummage	**Words with long _a_ and long _e_**			
		bathe **exclaimed** complete **relief** debate	**navy** cheat keen **retreat** grief	pave obtain basin grease scheme	niece canteen **disgraced** supreme trait
Viva New Jersey	destination majestic makeshift mongrel protruding silhouetted	**Words with long _i_ and long _o_**			
		spine omit **reminded** deny soak	**private** poet boast doe tying	devote rhyme likewise quote foe	**skyline** minor strive bonus oboe
Rain, Rain, Go Away	contrast existence jubilantly pedestals psychology subdued	**Words with /ū/ and /ü/**			
		value proof rude **usually** issue	funeral mute sinew shrewd solution	troop **absolute** cue pursue universe	perfume groove **casually** curfew sewer
Time for Kids: A Viking Voyage	dreamer landmarks precise rudder site technology	**Words from Social Studies**			
		western navigate lighthouse **distant** **oars**	southern historical tropical peninsula parallel	cargo isle passage eastern **hemisphere**	foreign latitude longitude **ashore** global

Boldfaced words appear in the selection.

UNIT 2

	Vocabulary	Spelling

LAST SUMMER WITH MAIZON

Vocabulary
desolate
essay
exaggerated
fidgeted
somberly
tokens

Syllable Patterns

costume	profit	panic	**clutters**
pilot	unite	**wintry**	census
ragged	pirate	vital	suffix
hydrants	decent	recent	pronoun
tremble	factor	frustrate	minus

TA-NA-E-KA

Vocabulary
encounter
grimaced
ordeals
participate
spat
victorious

Words with /f/, /k/, and /s/

laughed	character	scent	scenery
stomach	geography	trough	chord
scientist	muscle	phrase	gopher
scissors	symphony	orchestra	crescent
enough	chemical	mechanic	phase

NUMBER THE STARS

Vocabulary
dramatics
exasperated
improvement
pouted
rationed
sophisticated

Words with /ou/ and /oi/

coward	employer	alloy	loiter
counter	browse	poise	blouse
oyster	moisture	flounder	**glowering**
embroidered	trout	**nightgowns**	**outgrown**
crouch	vowel	corduroy	boycott

OPERA, KARATE, AND BANDITS

Vocabulary
cultivate
devised
diminished
edible
mythology
retrieved

Plurals

memories	solos	scarves	halves
ashes	cuffs	concertos	sheriffs
mysteries	**buffaloes**	industries	stereos
volcanoes	earmuffs	dominoes	patios
notches	abilities	flamingos	wharves

TIME FOR KIDS: CLEOPATRA'S LOST PALACE

Vocabulary
cobblestone
deep-sea
romance
splendors
surprisingly
undersea

Words from the Arts

terrace	**temples**	mosaic	dimension
palace	**pavements**	artifact	representation
classical	structure	pyramid	**pillars**
landscape	traditional	estate	extension
fountains	exotic	primary	architecture

Boldfaced words appear in the selection.

UNIT 3

	Vocabulary	Spelling

A Boy of Unusual Vision

Vocabulary
- **diagonal**
- **inquisitive**
- **painstakingly**
- **storage**
- **unconsciously**
- **visual**

Words with and /ô/ and /ôr/

pause	ignore	**sort**	wharf
sword	ought	faucet	almanac
walrus	**fork**	foresee	resource
warp	laundry	wardrobe	thoughtless
mourn	lawyer	core	flaw

The School Play

Vocabulary
- **cut-out**
- **dented**
- **flurries**
- **frothing**
- **narrative**
- **tattoo**

Words with /är/ and /âr/

sharpen	flare	mare	despair
stared	canary	wary	starch
charm	garlic	farewell	artificial
guard	aircraft	librarian	carefree
prairie	tar	barbecue	impaired

The Singing Man

Vocabulary
- **abide**
- **acceptable**
- **boyhood**
- **famine**
- **trill**
- **wares**

Words with /îr/ and /ûr/

peer	interfere	pioneer	pier
servants	emergency	**personal**	cashmere
furnace	fierce	urgent	nourish
pearl	earnest	rehearse	sphere
pierce	journal	courtesy	burnt

Painters of the Caves

Vocabulary
- **badge**
- **engrave**
- **hibernate**
- **honeycombed**
- **scaffold**
- **sculpting**

Adding -ed and -ing

worried	**uncovered**	chiseled	recurring
preferred	**preserved**	transferred	advancing
equaled	dignified	illustrating	committed
influencing	identified	allied	anticipating
observed	permitting	reclining	implied

Time for Kids: Is This Ancient Bone the World's First Flute?

Vocabulary
- **brute**
- **complex**
- **controversy**
- **perceptions**
- **punctured**
- **researchers**

Words from Music

musical	soprano	opera	alto
major	harmony	cymbal	duration
modern	melody	accordion	dynamics
guitar	accompany	lyrics	octave
concert	percussion	crescendo	allegro

Boldfaced words appear in the selection.

UNIT 4

	Vocabulary	Spelling

MUMMIES, TOMBS & TREASURE: SECRETS OF ANCIENT EGYPT

Vocabulary
- **bazaars**
- **coffins**
- **dramatically**
- **looted**
- **pharaoh**
- **tomb**

Words with /sh/, /ch/, and /zh/

chestnut	decision	lurch	charity
shrunken	**officials**	vulture	session
treasure	tissue	partial	establish
mixture	leisure	glacier	**miniature**
foundations	vision	enclosure	**superstitious**

OVER THE TOP OF THE WORLD

Vocabulary
- accumulating
- environmental
- formation
- industrial
- remote
- submerged

Words with /ər/, /əl/, and /ən/

underwater	panel	article	fatal
samples	practical	mistaken	moral
widen	melon	**jumbles**	vapor
similar	urban	cedar	**unison**
superior	**manner**	funnel	**tremor**

THE PHANTOM TOLLBOOTH

Vocabulary
- **appreciation**
- **cellophane**
- **explosions**
- **hard-boiled**
- **tollbooth**
- **triangles**

Spelling Unstressed Syllables

suppose	album	morsel	ponder
stubborn	effort	standard	suspend
perhaps	**severe**	**applause**	collide
confess	canvas	**nuisance**	ballad
appeal	ballot	judgment	random

EXPLORING THE TITANIC

Vocabulary
- **capsule**
- **interior**
- **lifeboat**
- **maiden**
- **portholes**
- **severed**

Words with Silent Letters

headlights	moisten	bristle	salmon
rustle	drought	doughnut	nestle
calmly	resign	hasten	align
yolk	knack	acknowledge	almond
nightmare	condemn	reign	**wrought**

TIME FOR KIDS: BACK TO THE MOON!

Vocabulary
- **equipped**
- **hydrogen**
- **lunar**
- **magnetic**
- **quantities**
- **sensor**

Words from Science

rocket	**orbiting**	altitude	eclipse
crater	**comet**	constellation	thermal
telescopes	**meteors**	galaxy	asteroid
hurtle	**astronomers**	odyssey	planetarium
revolve	rotate	alien	variable

Boldfaced words appear in the selection.

UNIT 5

	Vocabulary	Spelling

CHILD OF THE OWL

Compound Words

banister	newborn	**teacup**	**apartment**	**index finger**
grudged	twenty-one	**tablecloth**	**houses**	cross-country
porcelain	common sense	ready-made	brother-in-law	foolproof
rhythmically	old-fashioned	bathrobe	**fire escape**	contact lens
troublemaking	question mark	science fiction	applesauce	**silkworms**
truce			self-reliant	

BELLEROPHON AND THE FLYING HORSE

Homophones and Homographs

ferocious	**straight**	racket	vain	bass
lavishly	dove	strait	cereal	vein
rash	shear	sheer	principal	principle
reassure	hire	hamper	refrain	colonel
thunderous	swallow	**higher**	kernel	serial
waving				

ADVENTURE IN SPACE

Words with Suffixes

bloodstream	**electricity**	combination	**reality**	admirable
compartment	operation	gravity	conservation	anticipation
deliberately	**exploration**	lovable	collectible	festivity
handshake	flexible	permissible	abbreviation	imaginable
maneuvering	considerable	interruption	perspiration	convertible
void				

RUMPELSTILTSKIN'S DAUGHTER

Words with Suffixes

barley	**excellent**	resident	acquaintance	occurrence
coincidences	attendant	annoyance	persistent	boundless
knickers	**restless**	occupant	sightless	emptiness
mufflers	disturbance	cleverness	descendant	correspondent
sheepishly	conference	reference	dizziness	regardless
sweeten				

TIME FOR KIDS: THE HISTORY OF MONEY

Words from Math

automated	**interest**	fraction	predict	decimal
bartering	**borrow**	metric	deposit	tally
currency	division	positive	discount	dividend
fee	percent	calculate	negative	subtraction
loan	addition	customary	probable	statistics
teller				

Boldfaced words appear in the selection.

UNIT 6

	Vocabulary	Spelling

MANDELA

Vocabulary
- capable
- counselor
- equator
- foremost
- nimbly
- stubbornness

Words with Prefixes

discourage	immature	impolite	decipher
unfairness	**dethroned**	unpopular	immovable
mislead	discontinue	improper	unnecessary
informal	misjudge	**inequality**	inseparable
unjustly	indirect	discontent	misbehave

MY FRIEND FLICKA

Vocabulary
- concealed
- darning
- poring
- rebellious
- sauntered
- wide-open

Words from Foreign Languages

garage	**chutes**	adobe	mirage
coyote	tempo	mustache	beret
spaghetti	macaroni	bouquet	siesta
ravine	chandelier	sierra	cello
ballet	routine	limousine	**chagrined**

ALEXANDER THE GREAT

Vocabulary
- botanists
- cavalry
- plundered
- surveyors
- tutor
- worthwhile

Words with Latin Roots

depended	suspense	graduate	postpone
position	gradual	posture	pendulum
progress	**specimens**	precede	recede
procession	porter	spectator	aggressive
transportation	inspect	portable	dispense

THE CIRCUIT

Vocabulary
- acquired
- drone
- enthusiastically
- hesitantly
- husky
- instinctively

Words with Prefixes

exchanged	export	compress	recite
project	compound	expand	composition
compete	contract	prospect	consonant
contain	**recess**	commotion	consequence
recover	proceed	respect	exhale

TIME FOR KIDS: A GREAT WALL?

Vocabulary
- ecological
- generators
- habitats
- monitor
- reservoir
- temporary

Words from Social Studies

pollution	**disaster**	procedure	evaporation
explanation	**protective**	revive	replenish
extinct	renew	**generations**	**displaced**
protest	excess	excavate	irrigation
civilization	disappearance	disprove	starvation

Boldfaced words appear in the selection.

Listening, Speaking, Viewing, Representing

☑ Tested Skill

▢ Tinted panels show skills, strategies, and other teaching opportunities

	K	1	2	3	4	5	6
LISTENING							
Learn the vocabulary of school (numbers, shapes, colors, directions, and categories)							
Identify the musical elements of literary language, such as rhymes, repetition, onomatopoeia, alliteration, assonance							
Determine purposes for listening (get information, solve problems, enjoy and appreciate)							
Understand and follow directions							
Listen critically and responsively; recognize barriers to effective listening							
Ask and answer relevant questions (for clarification; to follow up on ideas)							
Listen critically to interpret and evaluate							
Listen responsively to stories and other texts read aloud, including selections from classic and contemporary works							
Connect and compare own experiences, feelings, ideas, and traditions with those of others							
Apply comprehension strategies in listening activities							
Understand the major ideas and supporting evidence in spoken messages							
Participate in listening activities related to reading and writing (such as discussions, group activities, conferences)							
Listen to learn by taking notes, organizing, and summarizing spoken ideas							
Know personal listening preferences							
SPEAKING							
Uses repetition, rhyme, and rhythm in oral texts (such as in reciting songs, poems, and stories with repeating patterns)							
Learn the vocabulary of school (numbers, shapes, colors, directions, and categories)							
Use appropriate language, grammar, and vocabulary learned to describe ideas, feelings, and experiences							
Ask and answer relevant questions (for clarification; to follow up on ideas)							
Communicate effectively in everyday situations (such as discussions, group activities, conferences, conversations)							
Demonstrate speaking skills (audience, purpose, occasion, clarity, volume, pitch, intonation, phrasing, rate, fluency)							
Clarify and support spoken messages and ideas with objects, charts, evidence, elaboration, examples							
Use verbal communication in effective ways when, for example, making announcements, giving directions, or making introductions							
Use nonverbal communication in effective ways such as eye contact, facial expressions, gestures							
Retell a story or a spoken message by summarizing or clarifying							
Connect and compare own experiences, ideas, and traditions with those of others							
Determine purposes for speaking (inform, entertain, compare, describe, give directions, persuade, express personal feelings and opinions)							
Recognize differences between formal and informal language							
Demonstrate skills of reporting and providing information							
Demonstrate skills of interviewing, requesting and providing information							
Apply composition strategies in speaking activities							
Monitor own understanding of spoken message and seek clarification as needed							
VIEWING							
Demonstrate viewing skills (focus attention, organize information)							
Understand and use nonverbal cues							
Respond to audiovisual media in a variety of ways							
Participate in viewing activities related to reading and writing							
Apply comprehension strategies in viewing activities, including main idea and details							
Recognize artists' craft and techniques for conveying meaning							
Interpret information from various formats such as maps, charts, graphics, video segments, technology							
Knows various types of mass media (such as film, video, television, billboards, and newspapers)							
Evaluate purposes of various media, including mass media (information, appreciation, entertainment, directions, persuasion)							
Use media, including mass media, to compare ideas, information, and points of view							
REPRESENTING							
Select, organize, or produce visuals to complement or extend meanings							
Produce communication using appropriate media to develop a class paper, multimedia or video reports							
Show how language, medium, and presentation contribute to the message							

Reading: Alphabetic Principle, Sounds/Symbols

☑ Tested Skill

☐ Tinted panels show skills, strategies, and other teaching opportunities

PRINT AWARENESS	K	1	2	3	4	5	6
Know the order of the alphabet							
Recognize that print represents spoken language and conveys meaning							
Understand directionality (tracking print from left to right; return sweep)							
Understand that written words and sentences are separated by spaces							
Know the difference between individual letters and printed words							
Understand that spoken words are represented in written language by specific sequence of letters							
Recognize that there are correct spellings for words							
Know the difference between capital and lowercase letters							
Recognize how readers use capitalization and punctuation to comprehend							
Recognize the distinguishing features of a letter, word, sentence, paragraph							
Understand appropriate book handling							
Recognize that parts of a book (such as cover/title page and table of contents) offer information							

PHONOLOGICAL AWARENESS	K	1	2	3	4	5	6
Listen for environmental sounds							
Identify spoken words and sentences							
Divide spoken sentence into individual words							
Produce rhyming words and distinguish rhyming words from nonrhyming words							
Identify, segment, and combine syllables within spoken words							
Blend and segment onsets and rimes							
Identify and isolate the initial, medial, and final sound of a spoken word							
Add, delete, or substitute sounds to change words (such as *cow* to *how*, *pan* to *fan*)							
Blend sounds to make spoken words							
Segment one-syllable spoken words into individual phonemes							

PHONICS AND DECODING	K	1	2	3	4	5	6
Alphabetic principle: Letter/sound correspondence	☑	☑	☑				
Blending CVC words	☑	☑					
Segmenting CVC words	☑						
Blending CVC, CVCe, CCVC, CVCC, CVVC words	☑	☑	☑				
Segmenting CVC, CVCe, CCVC, CVCC, CVVC words and sounds	☑	☑	☑				
Initial and final consonants: /n/n, /d/d, /s/s, /m/m, /t/t, /k/c, /f/f, /r/r, /p/p, /l/l, /k/k, /g/g, /b/b, /h/h, /w/w, /v/v, /ks/x, /kw/qu, /j/j, /y/y, /z/z	☑	☑					
Initial and medial short vowels: *a, i, u, o, e*	☑	☑	☑				
Long vowels: *a-e, i-e, o-e, u-e* (vowel-consonant-e)		☑	☑				
Long vowels, including *ay, ai; e, ee, ie, ea; o, oa, oe, ow; i, y, igh*		☑	☑				
Consonant Digraphs: *sh, th, ch, wh*		☑					
Consonant Blends: continuant/continuant, including *sl, sm, sn, fl, fr, ll, ss, ff*		☑					
Consonant Blends: continuant/stop, including *st, sk, sp, ng, nt, nd, mp, ft*		☑					
Consonant Blends: stop/continuant, including *tr, pr, pl, cr, tw*		☑					
Variant vowels: including /ù/oo; /ô/a, aw, au; /ü/ue, ew		☑	☑				
Diphthongs, including /ou/ou, ow; /oi/oi, oy		☑	☑				
r-controlled vowels, including /âr/are; /ôr/or, ore; /îr/ear			☑				
Soft *c* and soft *g*			☑				
nk		☑	☑				
Consonant Digraphs: *ck*	☑	☑					
Consonant Digraphs: *ph, tch, ch*			☑				
Short *e: ea*			☑				
Long *e: y, ey*			☑				
/ü/oo		☑	☑				
/är/ar; /ûr/ir, ur, er		☑	☑				
Silent letters: including *l, b, k, w, g, h, gh*			☑				
Schwa: /ər/er; /ən/en; /əl/le;			☑				
Reading/identifying multisyllabic words		☑	☑				
Using graphophonic cues							

Reading: Vocabulary/Word Identification

☑ Tested Skill

Tinted panels show skills, strategies, and other teaching opportunities

WORD STRUCTURE	K	1	2	3	4	5	6
Common spelling patterns							
Syllable patterns							
Plurals		☑					
Possessives		☑					
Contractions		☑					
Root, or base, words and inflectional endings (-s, -es, -ed, -ing)		☑	☑	☑		☑	
Compound Words		☑	☑	☑	☑	☑	☑
Prefixes and suffixes (such as un-, re-, dis-, non-; -ly, -y, -ful, -able, -tion)			☑	☑	☑	☑	☑
Root words and derivational endings					☑	☑	☑

WORD MEANING	K	1	2	3	4	5	6
Develop vocabulary through concrete experiences, word walls, other people							
Develop vocabulary through selections read aloud							
Develop vocabulary through reading							
Cueing systems: syntactic, semantic, graphophonic							
Context clues, including semantic clues (word meaning), syntactical clues (word order), and graphophonic clues	☑	☑	☑	☑	☑	☑	☑
High-frequency words (such as the, a, and, said, was, where, is)	☑	☑					
Identify words that name persons, places, things, and actions							
Automatic reading of regular and irregular words							
Use resources and references (dictionary, glossary, thesaurus, synonym finder, technology and software, and context)							
Classify and categorize words							
Synonyms and antonyms			☑	☑	☑	☑	☑
Multiple-meaning words			☑		☑	☑	☑
Figurative language			☑	☑	☑	☑	☑
Decode derivatives (root words, such as like, pay, happy with affixes, such as dis-, pre-, un-)							
Systematic study of words across content areas and in current events							
Locate meanings, pronunciations, and derivations (including dictionaries, glossaries, and other sources)							
Denotation and connotation							☑
Word origins as aid to understanding historical influences on English word meanings							
Homophones, homographs							
Analogies							☑
Idioms							

Reading: Comprehension

PREREADING STRATEGIES	K	1	2	3	4	5	6
Preview and predict							
Use prior knowledge							
Set and adjust purposes for reading							
Build background							

MONITORING STRATEGIES	K	1	2	3	4	5	6
Adjust reading rate							
Reread, search for clues, ask questions, ask for help							
Visualize							
Read a portion aloud, use reference aids							
Use decoding and vocabulary strategies							
Paraphrase							
Create story maps, diagrams, charts, story props to help comprehend, analyze, synthesize and evaluate texts							

(continued on next page)

☑ Tested Skill

☐ Tinted panels show skills, strategies, and other teaching opportunities

SKILLS AND STRATEGIES

SKILLS AND STRATEGIES	K	1	2	3	4	5	6
Recall story details, including character and setting	☑	☑					
Use illustrations	☑	☑					
Distinguish reality and fantasy	☑	☑	☑				
Classify and categorize	☑						
Make predictions	☑	☑	☑	☑	☑	☑	☑
Recognize sequence of events (tell or act out)	☑	☑	☑	☑	☑	☑	☑
Recognize cause and effect	☑	☑	☑	☑	☑	☑	☑
Compare and contrast	☑	☑	☑	☑	☑	☑	☑
Summarize	☑	☑	☑	☑	☑	☑	☑
Make and explain inferences		☑	☑	☑	☑	☑	☑
Draw conclusions		☑	☑	☑	☑	☑	☑
Distinguish important and unimportant information				☑	☑	☑	☑
Recognize main idea and supporting details	☑	☑	☑	☑	☑	☑	☑
Form conclusions or generalizations and support with evidence from text			☑	☑	☑	☑	☑
Distinguish fact and opinion (including news stories and advertisements)				☑	☑	☑	☑
Recognize problem and solution			☑	☑	☑	☑	☑
Recognize steps in a process		☑	☑	☑	☑	☑	☑
Make judgments and decisions				☑	☑	☑	☑
Distinguish fact and nonfact				☑	☑	☑	☑
Recognize techniques of persuasion and propaganda							☑
Evaluate evidence and sources of information, including checking other sources and asking experts							☑
Identify similarities and differences across texts (including topics, characters, problems, themes, cultural influences, treatment, scope, or organization)							
Practice various questions and tasks (test-like comprehension questions)							
Paraphrase and summarize to recall, inform, and organize							
Answer various types of questions (open-ended, literal, interpretive, test-like such as true-false, multiple choice, short-answer)							
Use study strategies to learn and recall (preview, question, reread, and record)							

LITERARY RESPONSE

LITERARY RESPONSE	K	1	2	3	4	5	6
Listen to stories being read aloud							
React, speculate, join in, read along when predictable and patterned selections are read aloud							
Respond to a variety of stories and poems through talk, movement, music, art, drama, and writing							
Show understanding through writing, illustrating, developing demonstrations, and using technology							
Connect ideas and themes across texts							
Support responses by referring to relevant aspects of text and own experiences							
Offer observations, make connections, speculate, interpret, and raise questions in response to texts							
Interpret text ideas through journal writing, discussion, enactment, and media							

TEXT STRUCTURE/LITERARY CONCEPTS

TEXT STRUCTURE/LITERARY CONCEPTS	K	1	2	3	4	5	6
Distinguish forms and functions of texts (lists, newsletters, signs)							
Use text features to aid comprehension							
Understand story structure							
Identify narrative (for entertainment) and expository (for information)							
Distinguish fiction from nonfiction, including fact and fantasy							
Understand literary forms (stories, poems, plays, and informational books)							
Understand literary terms by distinguishing between roles of author and illustrator							
Understand title, author, and illustrator across a variety of texts							
Analyze character, character's motive, character's point of view, plot, setting, style, tone, mood		☑	☑	☑	☑	☑	☑
Compare communication in different forms							
Understand terms such as *title, author, illustrator, playwright, theater, stage, act, dialogue,* and *scene*							
Recognize stories, poems, songs, myths, legends, folktales, fables, tall tales, limericks, plays, biographies, autobiographies							
Judge internal logic of story text							
Recognize that authors organize information in specific ways							
Recognize author's purpose: to inform, influence, express, or entertain							
Describe how author's point of view affects text				☑	☑	☑	☑
Recognize biography, historical fiction, realistic fiction, modern fantasy, informational texts, and poetry							
Analyze ways authors present ideas (cause/effect, compare/contrast, inductively, deductively, chronologically)							
Recognize literary techniques such as imagery, repetition, flashback, foreshadowing, symbolism							

(continued on next page)

☑ Tested Skill

Tinted panels show skills, strategies, and other teaching opportunities

	K	1	2	3	4	5	6
VARIETY OF TEXT							
Read a variety of genres and understand their distinguishing features							
Use expository and other informational texts to acquire information							
Read for a variety of purposes							
Select varied sources when reading for information or pleasure							
Know preferences for reading literary and nonfiction texts							
FLUENCY							
Read regularly in independent-level and instructional-level materials							
Read orally with fluency from familiar texts							
Self-select independent-level reading							
Read silently for increasing periods of time							
Demonstrate characteristics of fluent and effective reading							
Adjust reading rate to purpose							
Read aloud in selected texts, showing understanding of text and engaging the listener							
CULTURES							
Connect own experience with culture of others							
Compare experiences of characters across cultures							
Articulate and discuss themes and connections that cross cultures							
CRITICAL THINKING							
Experiences (comprehend, apply, analyze, synthesize, evaluate)							
Make connections (comprehend, apply, analyze, synthesize, evaluate)							
Expression (comprehend, apply, analyze, synthesize, evaluate)							
Inquiry (comprehend, apply, analyze, synthesize, evaluate)							
Problem solving (comprehend, apply, analyze, synthesize, evaluate)							
Making decisions (comprehend, apply, analyze, synthesize, evaluate)							

Study Skills

INQUIRY/RESEARCH AND STUDY STRATEGIES	K	1	2	3	4	5	6
Follow and give directions							
Use alphabetical order							
Use text features and formats to help understand text (such as boldface, italic, or highlighted text; captions; headings and subheadings; numbers or symbols)							
Use study strategies to help read text and to learn and recall information from text (such as preview text, set purposes, and ask questions; use SQRRR; adjust reading rate; skim and scan; use KWL)							
Identify/frame and revise questions for research							
Obtain, organize, and summarize information: classify, take notes, outline, web, diagram							
Evaluate research and raise new questions							
Use technology for research and/or to present information in various formats							
Follow accepted formats for writing research, including documenting sources							
Use test-taking strategies							
Use text organizers (book cover; title page—title, author, illustrator; contents; headings; glossary; index)		☑	☑	☑	☑	☑	☑
Use graphic aids, such as maps, diagrams, charts, graphs, schedules, calendars		☑	☑	☑	☑	☑	☑
Read and interpret varied texts, such as environmental print, signs, lists, encyclopedia, dictionary, glossary, newspaper, advertisement, magazine, calendar, directions, floor plans, online resources		☑	☑	☑	☑	☑	☑
Use print and online reference sources, such as glossary, dictionary, encyclopedia, telephone directory, technology resources, nonfiction books		☑	☑	☑	☑	☑	☑
Recognize Library/Media center resources, such as computerized references; catalog search—subject, author, title; encyclopedia index		☑	☑	☑	☑	☑	☑

Writing

☑ Tested Skill

Tinted panels show skills, strategies, and other teaching opportunities

MODES AND FORMS	K	1	2	3	4	5	6
Interactive writing							
Descriptive writing			☑				
Personal narrative			☑	☑	☑	☑	☑
Writing that compares		☑	☑	☑	☑	☑	☑
Explanatory writing			☑	☑	☑	☑	☑
Persuasive writing				☑	☑	☑	☑
Writing a story		☑	☑	☑	☑	☑	☑
Expository writing; research report		☑	☑	☑	☑	☑	☑
Write using a variety of formats, such as advertisement, autobiography, biography, book report/report, comparison-contrast, critique/review/editorial, description, essay, how-to, interview, invitation, journal/log/notes, message/list, paragraph/multi-paragraph composition, picture book, play (scene), poem/rhyme, story, summary, note, letter							

PURPOSES/AUDIENCES	K	1	2	3	4	5	6
Dictate sentences and messages such as news and stories for others to write							
Write labels, notes, and captions for illustrations, possessions, charts, and centers							
Write to record, to discover and develop ideas, to inform, to influence, to entertain							
Exhibit an identifiable voice							
Use literary devices (suspense, dialogue, and figurative language)							
Produce written texts by organizing ideas, using effective transitions, and choosing precise wording							

PROCESSES	K	1	2	3	4	5	6
Generate ideas for self-selected and assigned topics using prewriting strategies							
Develop drafts							
Revise drafts for varied purposes, elaborate ideas							
Edit for appropriate grammar, spelling, punctuation, and features of published writings							
Proofread own writing and that of others							
Bring pieces to final form and "publish" them for audiences							
Use technology to compose, revise, and present text							
Select and use reference materials and resources for writing, revising, and editing final drafts							

SPELLING	K	1	2	3	4	5	6
Spell own name and write high-frequency words							
Words with short vowels (including CVC and one-syllable words with blends CCVC, CVCC, CCVCC)							
Words with long vowels (including CVCe)							
Words with digraphs, blends, consonant clusters, double consonants							
Words with diphthongs							
Words with variant vowels							
Words with r-controlled vowels							
Words with /ər/, /əl/, and /ən/							
Words with silent letters							
Words with soft c and soft g		˙					
Inflectional endings (including plurals and past tense and words that drop the final e and double a consonant when adding -ing, -ed)							
Compound words							
Contractions							
Homonyms							
Suffixes such as -able, -ly, -ful, or -less, and prefixes such as dis-, re-, pre-, or un-							
Spell words ending in -tion and -sion, such as station and procession							
Accurate spelling of root or base words							
Orthographic patterns and rules such as keep/can; sack/book; out/now; oil/toy; match/speech; ledge/cage; consonant doubling, dropping e, changing y to i							
Multisyllabic words using regularly spelled phonogram patterns							
Syllable patterns (including closed, open, syllable boundary patterns)							
Synonyms and antonyms							
Words from Social Studies, Science, Math, and Physical Education							
Words derived from other languages and cultures							
Use resources to find correct spellings, synonyms, and replacement words							
Use conventional spelling of familiar words in writing assignments							
Spell accurately in final drafts							

(continued on next page)

☑ Tested Skill

☐ Tinted panels show skills, strategies, and other teaching opportunities

	K	1	2	3	4	5	6
GRAMMAR AND USAGE							
Understand sentence concepts (word order, statements, questions, exclamations, commands)							
Recognize complete and incomplete sentences							
Nouns (common, proper, singular, plural, irregular plural, possessives)							
Verbs (action, helping, linking, irregular)							
Verb tense (present, past, future, perfect, and progressive)							
Pronouns (possessive, subject and object, pronoun-verb agreement)							
Use objective case pronouns accurately							
Adjectives							
Adverbs that tell how, when, where							
Subjects, predicates							
Subject-verb agreement							
Sentence combining							
Recognize sentence structure (simple, compound, complex)							
Synonyms and antonyms							
Contractions							
Conjunctions							
Prepositions and prepositional phrases							
PENMANSHIP							
Write each letter of alphabet (capital and lowercase) using correct formation, appropriate size and spacing							
Write own name and other important words							
Use phonological knowledge to map sounds to letters to write messages							
Write messages that move left to right, top to bottom							
Gain increasing control of penmanship, pencil grip, paper position, beginning stroke							
Use word and letter spacing and margins to make messages readable							
Write legibly by selecting cursive or manuscript as appropriate							
MECHANICS							
Use capitalization in sentences, proper nouns, titles, abbreviations and the pronoun *I*							
Use end marks correctly (period, question mark, exclamation point)							
Use commas (in dates, in addresses, in a series, in letters, in direct address)							
Use apostrophes in contractions and possessives							
Use quotation marks							
Use hyphens, semicolons, colons							
EVALUATION							
Identify the most effective features of a piece of writing using class/teacher-generated criteria							
Respond constructively to others' writing							
Determine how his/her own writing achieves its purpose							
Use published pieces as models for writing							
Review own written work to monitor growth as writer							

Scoring Chart

The Scoring Chart is provided for your convenience in grading your students' work.

- Find the column that shows the total number of items.
- Find the row that matches the number of items answered correctly.
- The intersection of the two rows provides the percentage score.

TOTAL NUMBER OF ITEMS

NUMBER CORRECT

	1	2	3	4	5	6	7	8	9	10	11	12	13	14	15	16	17	18	19	20	21	22	23	24	25	26	27	28	29	30
1	100	50	33	25	20	17	14	13	11	10	9	8	8	7	7	6	6	6	5	5	5	5	4	4	4	4	4	4	3	3
2		100	66	50	40	33	29	25	22	20	18	17	15	14	13	13	12	11	11	10	10	9	9	8	8	8	7	7	7	7
3			100	75	60	50	43	38	33	30	27	25	23	21	20	19	18	17	16	15	14	14	13	13	12	12	11	11	10	10
4				100	80	67	57	50	44	40	36	33	31	29	27	25	24	22	21	20	19	18	17	17	16	15	15	14	14	13
5					100	83	71	63	56	50	45	42	38	36	33	31	29	28	26	25	24	23	22	21	20	19	19	18	17	17
6						100	86	75	67	60	55	50	46	43	40	38	35	33	32	30	29	27	26	25	24	23	22	21	21	20
7							100	88	78	70	64	58	54	50	47	44	41	39	37	35	33	32	30	29	28	27	26	25	24	23
8								100	89	80	73	67	62	57	53	50	47	44	42	40	38	36	35	33	32	31	30	29	28	27
9									100	90	82	75	69	64	60	56	53	50	47	45	43	41	39	38	36	35	33	32	31	30
10										100	91	83	77	71	67	63	59	56	53	50	48	45	43	42	40	38	37	36	34	33
11											100	92	85	79	73	69	65	61	58	55	52	50	48	46	44	42	41	39	38	37
12												100	92	86	80	75	71	67	63	60	57	55	52	50	48	46	44	43	41	40
13													100	93	87	81	76	72	68	65	62	59	57	54	52	50	48	46	45	43
14														100	93	88	82	78	74	70	67	64	61	58	56	54	52	50	48	47
15															100	94	88	83	79	75	71	68	65	63	60	58	56	54	52	50
16																100	94	89	84	80	76	73	70	67	64	62	59	57	55	53
17																	100	94	89	85	81	77	74	71	68	65	63	61	59	57
18																		100	95	90	86	82	78	75	72	69	67	64	62	60
19																			100	95	90	86	83	79	76	73	70	68	66	63
20																				100	95	91	87	83	80	77	74	71	69	67
21																					100	95	91	88	84	81	78	75	72	70
22																						100	96	92	88	85	81	79	76	73
23																							100	96	92	88	85	82	79	77
24																								100	96	92	89	86	83	80
25																									100	96	93	89	86	83
26																										100	96	93	90	87
27																											100	96	93	90
28																												100	97	93
29																													100	97
30																														100

Writing a Story

6-Point Scoring Rubric

6. Exceptional

- **Ideas & Content** crafts an unusually entertaining, richly detailed original story about a character who faces a new challenge.
- **Organization** well-planned sequence moves the reader smoothly through the story; details are carefully placed to clarify events; engaging beginning and middle, and a fulfilling conclusion.
- **Voice** shows unusual originality, depth, and a wide range of emotions that speak directly to the reader; shows keen interest in the topic.
- **Word Choice** makes skillful, inventive use of figurative and everyday language; uses a variety of words to create clear images of characters and events.
- **Sentence Fluency** crafts fluid simple and complex sentences; dialogue, if used, sounds natural and strengthens the story; may experiment successfully with fragments or other devices.
- **Conventions** shows strong skills in most writing conventions; proper usage enhances clarity, meaning, and narrative style; editing is largely unnecessary.

5. Excellent

- **Ideas & Content** creates a focused, cohesive original story; extensive details show how a character deals with a new challenge.
- **Organization** unfolds a consistent, well-planned sequence that moves the reader easily through the story from beginning to end.
- **Voice** shows originality and a strong personal message that speaks directly to the reader; shows who is behind the words.
- **Word Choice** makes thoughtful, clever use of new and everyday language; uses a variety of new and everyday words.
- **Sentence Fluency** crafts careful, easy-to-follow sentences; may successfully use fragments and/or dialogue to strengthen the story; stronger control of simple sentences.
- **Conventions** may make some errors in spelling, capitalization, punctuation, or usage, which do not interfere with understanding the text; minor editing is needed.

4. Good

- **Ideas & Content** presents a solidly crafted story, with details that help to shape the events.
- **Organization** shows a capable, well-planned narrative strategy; ideas are connected; has a clear beginning and ending.
- **Voice** makes a strong effort to convey an authentic personal message to the reader; writing style is suited to the story.
- **Word Choice** shows an overall clarity of expression; correctly uses a variety of new and everyday words.
- **Sentence Fluency** crafts creative, effective sentences that flow with a smooth rhythm; dialogue, if used, sounds natural and enhances the story.
- **Conventions** shows strong skills in a wide range of conventions; correct usage and structure reinforce the story line.

3. Fair

- **Ideas & Content** has some control of crafting a story; may not give clear or elaborate details; may lose control of the story line after a good start.
- **Organization** may not have a clear structure, or may show trouble tying ideas together; reader may be confused by placement of events or details.
- **Voice** may get a basic story across, without a sense of involvement in entertaining a reader.
- **Word Choice** gets the story across; may not use words that convey clear images or feelings to the reader.
- **Sentence Fluency** may have trouble with more complicated sentences; sentences are understandable, but may be choppy or awkward; limited lengths and patterns.
- **Conventions** makes enough noticeable mistakes to interfere with a smooth reading of the story.

2. Poor

- **Ideas & Content** does not successfully tell a story; writer may present images without a narrative purpose or clear details.
- **Organization** extreme lack of structure interferes with understanding the text; no clear story line may be evident.
- **Voice** shows little involvement in sharing a story with a reader; does not bring a personal message to the writing.
- **Word Choice** does not use words that express clear feelings or images; some words may detract from understanding the text; some words are overused.
- **Sentence Fluency** constructs incomplete, rambling, or confusing sentences; may show trouble understanding how ideas, words, and sentences fit together.
- **Conventions** makes repeated errors in spelling, word choice, punctuation, and usage; few explicit connections are made between ideas.

1. Unsatisfactory

- **Ideas & Content** does not tell a story; writing may go off in several directions, without a sense of purpose.
- **Organization** disorganized, disconnected images make the story difficult to follow; there may be no evident structure at all.
- **Voice** does not address a reader or attempt to make sense; has no grasp of sharing understandable feelings and ideas.
- **Word Choice** uses words that do not relate to a story line, or are vague and confusing to the reader.
- **Sentence Fluency** constructs incomplete, rambling, or confusing sentences; text is hard to follow, and to read aloud.
- **Conventions** makes severe errors in most or all conventions, which interfere with readability; some parts of the text may be impossible to understand.

0 Incomplete: This piece is either blank, or fails to respond to the writing task. The topic is not addressed, or the student simply paraphrases the prompt. The response may be illegible or incoherent.

Writing a Story

8-Point Scoring Rubric

8	7	6	5	4	3	2	1
The writer	The writer	The writer	The writer	The writer	The writer	The writer	The writer
• has presented an entertaining story with well-developed characters, clearly described setting(s), and a well-paced plot.	• has developed an imaginative story with strong characters, setting(s), and plot.	• has developed an interesting story with believable characters, setting(s), and plot.	• has met the criteria for a story that includes clearly developed characters, setting(s), and plot.	• has written a story that includes one or two well-developed characters, a setting, and a basic plot line.	• has attempted to write a story with a setting and plot.	• has shown only some understanding of story elements, perhaps by developing one character and a simple plot, but little else.	• shows little or no understanding of story elements.
• consistently uses fluid, realistic dialogue that enhances the meaning of the story.	• often uses dialogue that adds meaning and realism to the story.	• uses expressive dialogue at various points in the story to add authenticity to the piece.	• uses some dialogue that helps to reinforce the meaning of the story.	• uses dialogue that sometimes sounds authentic.	• has created one or two characters with some important details.	• exhibits only a limited grasp of descriptive language.	• uses no descriptive language.
• maintains a tightly focused progression of story events with an inviting beginning and convincing conclusion.	• maintains a clear progression of story events with a strong beginning and conclusion.	• maintains a clear progression of story events with a good beginning and conclusion.	• maintains a logical progression of story events, with only a few minor digressions, and an adequate beginning and conclusion.	• maintains an overall structure, but may include one or two digressions that somewhat distract from understanding the story.	• does not consistently display a logical progression of events. Digressions and lack of focus may be distracting.	• often strays from the main idea, and has difficulty keeping story events in order.	• does not develop a plot or characters.
• creates vivid, well-elaborated descriptions that add clarity and authenticity to the story.	• uses engaging descriptions with meaningful elaborations throughout the story.	• uses a variety of descriptions with elaborative details throughout the story.	• uses a number of solid descriptions in the story.	• develops a good beginning, but an inadequate conclusion.	• uses descriptions that are sparse and lack elaboration.	• shows little sense of audience or narrative voice.	• shows no sense of audience.
• demonstrates an exceptionally strong narrative voice and sense of audience.	• shows a good awareness of audience and a sense of purpose throughout the piece.	• demonstrates a solid awareness of audience and purpose.	• demonstrates some sense of audience and purpose.	• does not consistently develop descriptions with elaborations.	• shows occasional awareness of audience, but a weak narrative voice.		• demonstrates problems with language, including grammar, usage, and mechanics, that seriously impair the reader's understanding.
				• displays intermittent awareness of audience.			

0 Incomplete: This piece is either blank, or fails to respond to the writing task. The topic is not addressed, or the student simply paraphrases the prompt. The response may be illegible or incoherent.